SIGNS & SYMBOLS of PRIMORDIAL MAN

THE JUDGMENT SCENE—ANI'S HEART BEING WEIGHED IN THE BALANCE.

The Company of the Gods:

SA. HU. HATHOR. HORUS. ISIS AND NEPHTHYS. NUT. SEB. TEFNUT. SHU. TEMU. RĀ-HARMACHIS.

(FROM THE PAPYRUS OF ANI (BRIT. MUS. No. 10,470, SHEET 3 AND 4).)

ANI AND HIS WIFE THUTHU ENTERING THE HALL OF JUDGMENT.

RENENET AND MESKHENET, THE GODDESSES OF BIRTH.

ANI'S SOUL. ANI'S EMBRYO. ANI'S LUCK OR DESTINY.

ANUBIS TESTING THE TONGUE OF THE BALANCE.

THOTH RECORDING THE RESULT OF THE WEIGHING.

THE DEVOURER OF THE UNJUSTIFIED.

HORUS INTRODUCING ANI INTO THE PRESENCE OF OSIRIS.

ANI JUSTIFIED KNEELING BEFORE OSIRIS.

OSIRIS THRONED WITHIN A SHRINE. BEHIND HIM ARE ISIS AND NEPHTHYS, AND BEFORE HIM, UPON A LOTUS STAND THE CHILDREN OF HORUS.

The SIGNS & SYMBOLS of PRIMORDIAL MAN

THE EVOLUTION OF RELIGIOUS DOCTRINES FROM THE ESCHATOLOGY OF THE ANCIENT EGYPTIANS

by
ALBERT CHURCHWARD
M.D., M.R.C.P., M.R.C.S., F.G.S., P.M., P.Z.

30⁰

AUTHOR OF
"ORIGIN AND ANTIQUITY OF FREEMASONRY
ETC.

A&B BOOKS PUBLISHERS
Brooklyn, New York
11201

Published by ***A&B BOOKS PUBLISHERS*** 149 Lawrence Street, Brooklyn, New York, 11201

This book purports to trace the evolution of Masonry from the eschatology of the Ancient Egyptians. A unique union of scholarship and poetry. A most interesting survey the symbolism of the race with reference to its Masonic suggestion. The illustrations throw much light on the general study of symbolism, but the author's conclusion should not be taken too seriously. Not recommended for beginners.

COVER DESIGN: *A & B BOOKS PUBLISHERS*
COVER ILLUSTRATION: *Mshindo I.*

ISBN 1-881316-73-4

97 96 95 94 5 4 3 2

published

by

A & B Books Publishers
149 Lawrence St.
Brooklyn NY 11201
(718) 596-3389

Printed in United States of America

I Dedicate

THIS WORK TO
ALL MY BROTHER MASONS
IN WHATEVER CLIME AND WHATEVER CREED
WHO BELIEVE IN AND ACKNOWLEDGE
THE ONE GREAT ARCHITECT
OF THE UNIVERSE.

INTRODUCTION

The re-publication of the book, *The Signs and Symbols of Primordial Man* at this time is more than appropriate. Dr. Albert Churchward was the best known British disciple of Gerald Massey whose six volume work, *Ancient Egypt, The Light of the World,* 2 Vols., *A Book of the Beginnings,* 2 Vols., and *Natural Genesis,* 2 Vols., set in motion a new and radical approach to the history of African Civilization and the African contribution to the social thought that went into the making of the world's three major religions, Judaism, Christianity and Islam.

It is difficult to assess the value of Dr. Churchward's great contribution to history without referring to his master teacher, Gerald Massey. Gerald Massey did not begin his career searching for Africa's place in world history. He was an agnostic whose intention was to prove that the basis of European civilization was created outside of Europe by people that some Europeans later characterized as savages without a history or a culture. His search led him to Egypt where he found proof that Western culture was, in fact, African in origin, the larger portion of it coming mainly from the Nile Valley. His disciple Albert Churchward continued his important work and in this book takes his search into another dimension.

Men like Gerald Massey and Albert Churchward were battling against a wall of European misinformation about the contributions of non-European people toward the civilization of the world and only a few radical European scholars were able to understand the full impact of Churchward's work at the time this book was written.

SIGNS AND SYMBOLS

What is the essential messages of Albert Churchward today in an era of new scholarship and new and bold challenges to old concept about the history of the world and the contribution of African people toward the origin and development of world civilization and culture? Albert Churchward begins his work with an examination of Freemasonry, its rituals, signs and symbols and their contribution to social thought. What he is saying, in essence, is that Freemasonry was a part of Nile Valley civilizations. By extension, he is also saying that higher learning, which was carefully guarded at early times in history gave birth to secret societies. In these secret societies there existed the educational approach that would lead to the establishment of the world's first universities. What he says, in fact, is that the origin of the university comes out of Nile Valley civilizations.

African people developed signs and symbols as a way of communicating and delivering messages. It is most unfortunate that most people who today are members of secret societies have no in depth knowledge of the history of the society and the unifying role it played in the early intellectual life of the Nile Valley. It is through Churchward's examination of most of the known cultures of the people of his day that the signs and symbols of primordial man is revealed.

At this juncture we need to be reminded that the Nile Valley stretches over 4,000 miles into the body of Africa and that the creations of Nile Valley civilizations cannot be attributed only to that portion of North Africa that the Greeks Called, "Egypt." The Nile river was the world's first great cultural highway, bringing people and cultures out of the body of inner Africa. This great cultural migration led to the peopling of Egypt. Making Egypt a composite civilization comprised of different African people who dwelled along the banks of the Nile river. The civilization that developed in Egypt was the culmination of civilization in Africa.

None of the components that went into the making of what we now call Egypt came from Europe or Western Asia, commonly called the Middle East. At this point in history we cannot discuss Europe, because there was no Europe - in name and as a political entity in the world, Europe did not exist. There was no mention of Europe in early ancient history because at that time Europe was very busy trying to extract herself from the impact of the last of the ice ages. Surviving and just staying alive was the most serious thing the European were engaged in at that time in early history.

In connection with this book there is also a need to examine the works of the greatest American disciple of Gerald Massey, Alvin Boyd Kuhn. Kuhn is best known for his books, *Who Is The King Of Glory?,* which, in my opinion is one of the best books on early Christianity; *Shadow of the Third Century,* deals with the conference of Nicea and its aftermath, especially the opinion of an African theologian known in history as St. Augustine. In referring to the European participation in the Conference of Nicea, St. Augustine said, in effect: "These people are trying to revamp and give back to us a concept we had for over three thousand years." St. Augustine, in identifying the early African origins of the concept that the Europeans would later call Christianity is indicating that this concept existed among African people (without the dogma and formalization) before the birth of Europe. In the Introduction to *"Who is the king of glory?"* Alvin Boyd Kuhn has this to say:

> The pick that struck the Rosetta Stone in the loamy soil of the Nile Delta in 1796 also struck a mighty blow at historical Christianity. For it released the voice of a long-voiceless past to refute nearly every one of Christianity's historical claims with a withering negative. The cryptic literature of old Egypt, sealed in silence when Christianity took its rise, but haunting it like a specter after the third century,

> now stalks forth like a living ghost out of the tomb to point its long finger of accusation at a faith that has too long thriven on falsity. For that literature now rises out of oblivion to proclaim the true source of every doctrine of Christianity as Egyptian, the product and heritage of a remote past... The books of old Egypt now unroll the sagas of wisdom which announce the inexorable truth that not a single doctrine, rite, tenet or usages in Christianity was a new contribution to world religion, but that every article and practice of that faith was a disfigured copy of ancient Egyptian systematism...

He extends his message in the following manner:

> The entire Christian Bible, creation legend, descent into and exodus from "Egypt," ark and flood allegory, Israelite 'History,' Hebrew prophecy and poetry, Gospels, Epistles and Revelation imagery, all are now proven to have been the transmission of ancient Egypt's scrolls and papyri into the hands of later generations which knew neither their true origin nor their fathomless meaning... but the sheer fact that even amid the murks of ignorance and superstition the mere ghost, shell, husk and shadow of Egypt's wisdom inspired religious piety to extremes of faith and zealotry is singular attestation of its original power and majesty.
>
> From the scrolls of papyri five thousand to ten thousand years old there comes stalking forth to view the whole story of an Egyptian Jesus raising from the dead an Egyptian Lazarus at an Egyptian Bethany, with two Egyptian Maries present, he non-historical prototype of the incident related (only) in John's Gospel.

In a collective way Gerald Massey, the master, and his disciples Albert Churchward and Alvin Boyd Kuhn have revealed the early African origins of the three major Western religions. All of these concepts were developed before the Bible was written and before the figure in history known as Jesus Christ was born. Alvin Boyd Kuhn's book, *The Lost Christianity,* also needs to be read as an extension of the views expressed in the above quoted works.

Dr. Yosef Ben Jochanan, John G. Jackson and other modern scholars have reconsidered this information and prepared it for the use and understanding of students and teachers of our time. I refer you to Dr. Jochanan's book, *The African Origins of the Major Western religions,* and John G. Jackson's book, *Man, God and Civilization.*

In conclusion, as they say in the legal profession, I rest my case.

JOHN HENRIK CLARKE
Professor Emeritus
African World History

Hunter College,
New York
August, 1993

CONTENTS

CHAPTER V

CHAPTER VI

CHAPTER VII

CHAPTER VIII

CHAPTER IX

CHAPTER X

CHAPTER XI

CHAPTER XII

CONTENTS

APPENDICES

PREFACE TO THE SECOND EDITION

THE great success of the first issue, and the numerous letters of appreciation received from many Masonic brothers, and others, has led to the issue of the second edition of "Signs and Symbols of Primordial Man." I have corrected a few printer's errors and added some fresh matter to this edition, as a further proof of my contentions set forth, and which I trust will render this volume more interesting than the former.

I have answered some of my critics of the first edition in *The Pall Mall Gazette* and *British Medical Journal*, for this country, and in *The Masonic Sun of Toronto*, for Canada and U.S.A. To others I reply with de Balzac, "fierce critics, gleaners of phrases, harpies who pervert the ideas and purposes of every one."

I fear nothing for this book from these, because it is written from decipherments of existing monuments, which are hidden mysteries to the masses owing to their having not yet learned to read the Sign Language written on the walls ; notwithstanding real gleaners of truths will know that I am correct in these translations.

ALBERT CHURCHWARD.

Royal Societies Club,
St James' Street,
December 1912.

PREFACE TO THE FIRST EDITION

In writing the explanation of the Signs and Symbols of Primordial Man, I have gone back to the foundation of the human as a beginning, and traced these signs from the first Pygmies, and their then meaning, up to the latter-day Christians, and shown the evolution and meaning of the same, back to the Primordial Signs and Symbols and Sign Language, which have never been studied or taken into account, so far as I am aware, either in Freemasonry, the Christian doctrines: or the Eschatology of the Egyptians, and without which it is impossible to form a true conception of how these later doctrines came into existence. Without these signs, only a false conception of the ancient Egyptians, their ideas as to the future life, and their belief in the immortality of the soul, could only be erroneous—as indeed we find with most writers on the subject at the present day, their studies and knowledge only going back as far as the Osirian period, which is very recent, comparatively.

I hope that it may be of some interest to my readers to know that all the materials to compile this work have been gathered from existing remnants of the past. Although my work may appear to my brother Masons not to have any connection with *Freemasonry proper*, yet, inasmuch as Freemasonry is the truest ritual we have of the past, it will prove, to those who study the subject, the correctness of my views.

In bringing forward the following, I have tried to search after the facts with a steady honesty and sincere impartiality, to find the truth after searching carefully for the evidence, the testimony of which must be a sufficient guarantee of the truth of what I state. It is an impatience of doubt and suspense, a rashness and precipitancy of judgment and hastiness to believe something that plunges people into error. In constituting oneself a searcher after truth it is necessary to judge on every point those proper and peculiar means whereby the evidence of it is to be obtained.

And here I must answer some of my critics in their criticism of my monograph. One of them stated that there are not any Masonic Signs and Symbols in use amongst the Aborigines of Australia, but they are simply gesture signs: and he further states that if these "Blacks" knew anything of Freemasonry the white man must have initiated them, a statement too absurd for any kind of argument. I have gone more particularly and explicitly into the traditional histories, and also drawn attention to the Totemic ceremonies of the Arunta and other tribes for this reason: to prove that our friend, in his criticism of the "Origin and Antiquity of Freemasonry," has shown his complete ignorance of these histories, and that there is no foundation for his making such a statement. The facts brought forward will be indisputable proof to all Masons, as well as showing that these originated from, and that these Aboriginal Australians are an exodus from, the earlier Nilotic Negroes.

Regarding the subject of Sign Language, I may here observe that one of my critics actually stated that signs and symbols were first used as *Decorative Art*, an assertion sufficiently ridiculous to prove his complete want of knowledge of the subject. There are not any facts in existence to support such an assertion on his part. Signs and Symbols were first used as a written language or ideographic marks by man to express his thoughts when he had not the articulate sounds that we now have—as will be seen later on in this work—and afterwards adopted to express secret meanings. The "Sign Language" must be studied and taken into account if one wishes to understand the natives and the Primordial.

As to the song "To the West, to the West, to the Land of the Free" being written originally by Russell, as one of my critics stated, and referring it to the United States; this cannot be so, because in Ireland there is a very old song to the same effect, dating long before *Russell*, who may have, and probably did use part of this. Maspero gives the whole Egyptian translation from the hieroglyphics, which was a "Funeral Song" or "Dead March." It was sung at the obsequies of all the dead at the burial, and its meaning will be shown later on.

The Editor of the *Ars Quatuor Coronatorum*, vol. xii., part 2, speaking of the Aborigines of Australia and the tribes of West Africa, says "that they have evolved all their ideas of science, of life, of death, and of the rebirth into a new life from their own surroundings and experience," and we suppose he also maintains they have evolved all their Totemic ceremonies from the same, because these are their ideas, acted in dramatic form.

I think it greatly to be regretted that the *haut critique* of such a magazine should be so lamentably ignorant of the whole subject as to be able to entertain those opinions against existing facts, and I think it much more to be regretted that he should have such an instrument in his hands through which to proclaim his own opinions without any foundation except his own imaginings. In the same *Transactions*, June 1899, *Brother Wynn Westcott's* statement that he does not see that much light is thrown by the "Book of the Dead" upon that "very High Church Degree, the 18th, the ritual of which has no trace of any purely Egyptian symbols, etc.," shows that he must have written the criticism in ignorance of anything pertaining to the subject, or simply to try and condemn wilfully any light that is shown which may elucidate the mysteries of the past and present.

Firstly, let me assure him that the 18th degree is not a High Church or Low Church or any Church degree at all. It is a degree founded upon the new and better Covenant, certainly, but its prototype may be found amongst the Quiché at the present day, brought on by them from the Mayas, who had it from the Egyptians. Again, I would also only ask him to look upon the symbols on his apron and collar to see if he can find them in any High Church Degree. Let him also examine the symbols in the D. R. and C., as well as the jewels and the words on it of M. W. S., the Hebrew of which has no real meaning, but the Egyptian, from which it is copied, has—see origin of the Cross. These words, let me inform him, are purely Egyptian, and cannot be found in any Church degree, high or low, but are clearly written in the *Ritual*, and if he will take the trouble to read this he will find them most clearly stated, but he will not find them elsewhere.

His observation that a little Egyptian knowledge is dangerous is true, and most applicable to critics of his *métier*, but does not concern writers who have devoted many years to the study of Egyptology and Freemasonry.

It would certainly add to the value of the *Ars Quatuor Coronatorum* if the reviewers learned something first of the subject they attempt to criticise, and did not hazard an opinion on a subject of the alphabet of whose language they are ignorant.

I contend that the information contained in the following pages is right and true, the same having been obtained from existing facts, which can be proved by any person devoting his attention to the subject. It will also be of profound interest to those studious persons, who are not Freemasons, who take an interest in the ancient signs and symbols found throughout the world, the origin and meaning of which have hitherto been unknown in most instances or an erroneous decipherment given of the various sacred signs and symbols, which are found on ancient temples, rocks and stones, papyri, etc., in many ways throughout the world.

I have not given the whole of the passages of the different degrees, as these are secrets for the initiated only, and for the brethren who belong to the higher degrees in Freemasonry, nevertheless, I have laboured to simplify the " parts " of the various degrees that they may be explicit to all who have taken them up as far as the 30th degree. At the same time the secrets are unintelligible except to those who are initiated ; for to follow them separately and accurately one must have attained the 33rd degree, *and know and understand* " The Egyptian Ritual or Book of the Dead," and *the Primordial and Sign Language.*

I have divided this work into " Chapters " and " Parts," as I think it will be more convenient for the reader to follow and trace from one point to another.

I am deeply indebted to the following for information :—especially to my friend Gerald Massey ;[1] "The Book of the Dead," with Papyri of Hunefer-Anhar, Kerasher and Netchemet ; and of Nu. Demotic Papyri of the Priests of Memphis ; Dr Le Plongeon ; Mr Holmes, Chief of the Bureau of Ethnology, Smithsonian Institute, D.C. ; Mr Marsham Adams ; Brugsch Pacha ; Messrs

[1] Since writing this book, and before I could get it published, my dear old friend for twenty years, Gerald Massey, has died, very soon after he published the greatest work of his life, " Ancient Egypt," and although there are a few passages in this work similar to his, I am indebted to him for them during his lifetime ; he was never tired of discussing the subject and assisting me. No one ever understood the mythology and *Ritual* of Ancient Egypt so well as Gerald Massey since the time of the Ancient Philosophers of Egypt. He has left a written record in " Ancient Egypt " of the facts which will be an everlasting light on the subject.

Spencer and Gillen; Professor Sergi; Dr Wallis Budge; Brother John Woolnough and Mr J. C. Hart, R.N., for the care they have devoted to the proofs; Brother Fitzgerald Marriott; Sir Harry Johnston, and others.

ALBERT CHURCHWARD.

Royal Societies Club,
63 St James' Street,
London, S.W.

ERRATA

Page 14, lines 9 and 10 from bottom *should read* "ningun Dios estan dedicados y por eso les Llamaran nemonterni, que quiere decir por démas."

Page 42, line 17 from bottom, "he" *should replace* "that."

Page 68, line 3 from bottom, "before" *should replace* "to."

Page 233, line 10 from bottom, *for* "Ainu" *read* "first exodus after the Ainu."

Page 254, line 4 from top, after "Central America" *add* "who came after and followed the totemic people."

Page 255, line 24 from bottom, *for* "Neolithic" *read* "Paleolithic."

Page 255, line 14 from bottom, *for* "they" *read* "the old Egyptians."

Page 325, line 13 from bottom, *for* "Anup" *read* "Sut."

Page 330, line 17 from bottom, insert after "Horus" the words, "at the change of the cult from South to North."

Page 408, line 10 from bottom, after "Egypt" insert "But neither the Romans or Greeks could read their hieroglyphic language," and *for* "But the Romans never understood," *read* "But the Greeks and the Romans never understood," etc.

Page 412, line 14 from bottom, *add* "See the author's work, 'Origin and Evolution of Primitive Man.'"

Page 434, line 2 from top, "he" *should be* "the."

LIST OF FULL-PAGE ILLUSTRATIONS

LIST OF TEXT ILLUSTRATIONS

INTRODUCTORY: CHAPTER I

As many have desired further information than was given in our monograph, connecting Freemasonry and the Signs and Symbols thereof, and the analogy of the same to the Eschatology of the Ancient Egyptians, we have devoted much time and study to bring forward full proofs of our contention, more especially as hitherto there have been so many contradictory opinions and theories in the attempt to supply the origin and reason, when, where and why the brotherhood of Freemasonry came into existence, and all the "different parts" and "various rituals of the different degrees." All that has been written on this has hitherto been *theories*, without any facts for their foundation, and although in the "higher degrees" of Freemasonry, Christianity, or a belief in the same is insisted upon, yet in their forms, ceremonies, P-words, Signs and Symbols, almost all are pre-Christian, and that which is not has been brought on by evolution into Christian ideas or some form of the same, but it belongs to the most ancient part of the *Ritual*,[1] as we have clearly shown and demonstrated throughout this work; time and evolution being the only factors which have made the apparent difference, and although it may give a shock to the religious susceptibilities of those who have never studied the past, but have taken as absolute facts that which has been written "according to" for history, yet, if these people will devote a little time and trouble to the study of the same, they cannot arrive at any different conclusion than we have. Facts and history are one thing; theories and "according to" are another, and it is for this reason that the present work has been written. The contents of this book will prove the very origin of all our signs and symbols, and how these have been brought on through the Stellar, Lunar and Solar Mythos to the Christian doctrines: proofs which are founded upon facts, all written on stone or papyri, that are open to all to read if they so desire. Then we have entered into a description of primary man; his thoughts, ideas and myths, and the Totemic

[1] "The Ritual of Ancient Egypt, or the Book of the Dead."

ceremonies of the various tribes throughout the world to show at a very early period they were all one and universally the same, having one home—Egypt, from whence all sprang. We have shown how the exodus spread over the world, when the Ancient Egyptians had worked out their Stellar Mythos : and how this was carried N. S. E. and W. At the present day there are various native tribes still practising these ancient rites, and where intercommunication has been limited we still find them in their primitive form. All their Totemic ceremonies and customs are the same, and although we have excellent works of *Spencer* and *Gillen*, giving many details of these at the present time, no one has hitherto traced them back to their origin in Egypt. We have therefore felt it a duty to enter into and bring forward all the proofs of this, feeling confident that in the future other workers will have less difficulty in deciphering the whole history and truth of the past, now we point out to them that the Key of the Door which discloses the archives is the Primordial and *Ritual* of Ancient Egypt, without which you cannot enter ; therefore, except one knows and understands the Primordial and *Ritual* of Ancient Egypt, it is impossible to trace back the history of this world—the history of all religions, and the history of all mankind, and that which is attached thereto. Knowing this, we venture to say that all students will, for the future, have no difficulty in treading the right path and not be wandering off into blind lanes which lead nowhere. They will trace primitive man from here in Egypt, and the exodus all over the earth. The ossified remains of these little people will prove what we have brought forward to be correct, and the actual living Paleolithic people may still be found in some parts of the world. We have shown that they have a belief in the great spirit—have the commencement of a mythos, and from this we trace the development through and up to the Stellar Mythos, which we have shown existed also all over the world, and is still found and practised by the aboriginal natives of all countries at the present time, and although the present representatives of these natives have lost the original meaning of these customs still practised amongst them, in Egypt we find the key. As this Stellar Mythos was and is, as far as native tribes are concerned, universal, it must have had one common origin, and that was Egypt. It is only by carefully studying what is still extant, and we contend that there is sufficient, that we can come to any positive conclusion upon the highest question of the primordial history and origin of our race. Following the laws of development, research has led us to bring forward such evidence, as furnished by the records and monuments of the country or nations of the world, where we find the same signs and symbols, the same myths and legends, the same sacred ceremonies and identical religious beliefs, which, when correctly interpreted, proves that only one conclusion can be definitely arrived at, which we have set forth in this work—*viz.* that the first or Paleolithic man was the Pygmy, who was evolved in Central Africa at the sources of the Nile, or Nile valley, and that from here all originated and were carried throughout the world, and that the most primitive phase of Mythology is a mode of representing certain elemental powers by means of living types which were superhuman, like the natural phenomena. The foundations of mythology were laid in the pre-anthropomorphic shape of primitive representation. Thus the typical giant, Apap, was an enormous water reptile. The typical genetrix and mother of life was a Water Cow, that represented the earth; the typical provider was a goose, etc. It was here, in the Nile valley, that the dumb mythology became articulate. Egypt alone preserved primitive gnosis and gave expression to the language of signs and symbols, and it was here that the first elemental powers were divinised—here that Totemism, Stellar, Lunar and Solar Mythology originated. In the Astro-Mythology of the Egyptians, we find the belief in the first Man-God (HORUS I.) and his death and resurrection as Amsu. In the *Ritual* of ancient Egypt we have full proof of this, and all the powers of the Great Creator of this Earth and other worlds of the Universe. We have the various stories of the great power of darkness and the great power of light, and the fight between these fully explained in their primitive and true form. We see this myth still believed in and carried on at the present day by the Aboriginal Australians and other native tribes, wherever we can gain access to their Sacred Ceremonies, and thoughts and beliefs, as *Spencer* and *Gillen* have done with these people. Then we have shown how the Stellar was evolutionised into the Lunar and Solar Mythos; how the different names of all the gods (names of the powers or attributes of the One Great God) and how even His name has been changed by the Priests, by time and evolution, up to the time when the Egyptians had worked out their perfect

Eschatology (or doctrine of final things). We have traced how the Solar Mythos was spread over some part of the world, following the Stellar, the priests merging all the latter with the former, as far as they were able, and adding more attributes in the form and names of other gods to the One Great One. We have shown when the Father was the Father of the Son and the Son was the Father of the Father, and how Mut was brought on as Isis, and HORUS I. as the child, in the Osirian doctrines at the time when their Eschatology was completed. We see how Osiris has taken the name and place of HORUS I., the first Man-God mummified: how he died and rose again in spiritual form as Ra, taking the name and place of Amsu, with all the divine titles, attributes and names which have been attached to the same. In HORUS, the child of Isis, we discover the beginning of the Christian doctrines, which will form the subject of another book. All which we have brought forward are facts, as far as the remains of the same are to be found, written on stone and papyri still extant, for all to read who are interested in these researches. Of course, in drawing the reader's attention to these signs, symbols and ceremonies, partially described, we have been obliged to safeguard the secrets of the same both "in *forms, words and descriptions of the true character, now enacted*" by our brother Freemasons; but all will be sufficiently lucid for those who are initiated, in the various degrees we have considered, to understand the proof of which, be they Egyptologists or not, cannot be denied, as the evidence is unmistakable. We have shown how primitive man first began to think and observe the laws of nature, and how from observation of these his spiritual ideas and the divination of things began to dawn upon him—how his spiritual beliefs grew, and how the first religious ideas and conceptions took place, which, from want of articulate sounds, he primarily represented by various signs and symbols, which his awakened sense of awe and wonder suggested, and out of which religion was born. All else have been built up by time and evolution.

It is only *by comparison of all* that we find in various parts of the world that we can arrive at a correct conclusion. To compare part of man's history from one or two nations alone, however great or numerous, would not lead to a right conclusion. It is only by studying the whole history of the world, and all nations from the beginning, and then comparing one with the other, that the true and definite history of man can be followed. Then we can read and understand the evolution of the human race from the Primordial. We have to study the language (sign and articulation), myths, Astro-Mythology and Eschatology; their cosmogonic ideas in all their various forms; their customs, manners and traditional history; their anatomical development; their architecture, both ancient and civilised; and the result of intimate communications that must have existed between them at some time ages ago. Having done this, we contend that the result of our labours herein set forth is correct.

CHAPTER II

> Egypt! how I have dwelt with you in dreams,
> So long, so intimately, that it seems
> As if you had borne me; though I could not know,
> It was so many thousand years ago!
> And in my gropings darkly underground,
> The long-lost memory at last is found
> Of motherhood—you mother of us all!
> And to my fellow-men I must recall
> The memory too; that common motherhood
> May help to make the common brotherhood.
>
> GERALD MASSEY.

IN writing this book, "Explanation of the Signs and Symbols of Primordial Man," we have tried to meet our critics of the monograph on the "Origin and Antiquity of Freemasonry," and perhaps to make the elucidation and connection of the past with the present more complete and plainer to our fellow brother Masons and others who may be interested in the subject.

We do this without altering the principles of that which we have already written, as there is nothing to alter or retract from what has been previously brought before our brethren and others. All we have done is to write plainly and give more details of the connecting links, so that Freemasons may be able to understand them, without exposing those secret mysteries and hidden meanings which are known to us only; and yet to keep each of the secrets of the different degrees hidden and separate from those who are not entitled to know them, whilst those who are initiated will be able to read between the lines and see that the connecting links are not wanting nor yet broken, and thus prove to them the accuracy of our beliefs.

We also have brought before our readers notices of many Totemic ceremonies and ancient signs and symbols found throughout the world, to prove that our own signs and symbols were brought down and carried on from these originals. We have shown the ancient origin of them and their signification, and how time and evolution have substituted our present interpolation.

Our object is solely to interest our brother Masons to attain to the mysteries and secrets of all the degrees of Freemasonry, and to carry out and fulfil in thought, word and deed those principles which have been inculcated with our Order, and which we believe must finally carry out the destiny of this world to its good and advancement, until the prophecies of Ezekiel and the other prophets are fulfilled, the mysteries of which are now being rapidly elucidated, and to bring before others the one true religion which has existed from time immemorial. Yet many of our brethren appear indifferent to the same.

To all earnest students the book is open, and if they will read and study its contents light will surely dawn upon them.

In the new and revised edition of the Perfect Ceremonies, according to our E. working, a theory is given that Freemasonry originated from certain guilds of workmen which are well known in history as the " Roman College of Artificers."

There is no foundation of fact for any such theory. Freemasonry is now and always was *an Eschatology*, as may be proved by the whole of our signs, symbols and words, and our rituals. More than a hundred years ago some of our brethren were of this opinion, if we may judge from the oration delivered at the opening of our Masonic Temple in 1794.

The late Brother Rev. Dr William Dodd, in delivering an oration on Masonry at the dedication of Freemasons' Hall in Great Queen Street, in February 1794, speaking of the Antiquity of Freemasonry, says : " Masons are well informed from their own private and interior records that the building of Solomon's Temple is an important era, whence they derive many mysteries of their art.

" Now be it remembered that this great event took place above 1000 years before the Christian era ; and consequently more than a century before Homer—the first of the Grecian poets—wrote : and above five centuries before Pythagoras brought from the East his sublime system of truly Masonic instruction to illuminate our Western world. But, remote as is this period, we date not from this event the commencement of our art ; for though it might owe to the wise and glorious King of Israel some of its many mystic forms and hieroglyphic ceremonies, yet certainly the art itself is cœval with Man, the great subject of it ; nay, it may well be styled cœval with Creation, when the Sovereign Architect raised on Masonic principles this beauteous globe and commanded that master science, Geometry, to lay the rule to the planetary world, and to regulate by its laws the whole stupendous system in just, unerring proportion, rolling round the central Sun.

"And as Masonry is of this remote antiquity, so is it, as may reasonably be imagined, of boundless extent. We trace its footsteps in the most distant, most remote ages and nations of the world. We find it among the first and most celebrated civilisers of the East; we deduce it regularly from the first astronomers on the plains of Chaldea; to the wise and mystic kings and priests of Egypt; the sages of Greece and the philosophers of Rome; nay, even to the rude and Gothic builders of a dark and degenerate age, whose vast temples still remain amongst us as monuments of their attachments to the Masonic arts, and as high proofs of a taste, which, however irregular, must always be esteemed—awful and venerable."

It is a pity that Freemasons of the present day do not take more interest in the legacy left them by their forefathers. Who amongst us can, even for an hour, revert to the grand and sublime tenets of our craft, and study the origin of the signs and symbols attached to them, and then suppose for one moment that all these were evolved out of a band of operative Masons at the time of the Romans?

There is neither logic nor reason in, nor are there any facts to support such a theory. No, our Grand Order has originated from the sublime teachings of Ptah, which were carried out of Egypt by Moses, and the original or first High Priests of the Druids that came to these islands, and handed down from generation to generation, and it will last to the end of the present existence of the earth.

As we pointed out in the "Origin and Antiquity of Freemasonry"—although many Masons take great interest in the past history of the craft—few, we believe, have any idea of its real origin, and it is to these, therefore, more especially, that this work is addressed. The book embodies the result of much labour on the subject, therefore we feel sure it will be of interest to all good Masons.

We say that the human race originated, or was planted, in the north-east of Africa (including the sources and the banks of the Nile), and it is a very important fact to note here that the symbology has been carried down amongst ourselves to the present day.

At the N.E.C. the newly I. is placed, and as man, by multiplication and Evolution, spread and gained knowledge, so the new brethren are taught and given knowledge and learn—or should learn—all the other sublime degrees which make up our whole.

We think this may be added to our present ritual on that particular position.

At any rate we would like to draw the attention of the Powers that be to the above remark for their consideration in any future alteration that may be made, because "from here all knowledge emanated, and unto that place shall it return."

All Masons who have attained to the R.A. & 30° must be struck by the sublime nature of the principal tenets, and although at the present time Masonry is mainly a Brotherhood of Good-fellowship, Morality and Charity, we have long since considered it a remnant of some ancient philosophy or Eschatology.

After long and careful investigation we are now able to prove the Origin and Antiquity of Freemasonry and of the many and divers Rituals—so-called—which have been in use for the past few hundred years, will show that the whole principles and tenets of the craft are the truest copy we have in existence, passed on from one generation to another, of the Eschatology of the Egyptians at the time when their mythology and belief were perfected in their Eschatology. We therefore assert that the signs, symbols, rites and ceremonies, and the principles inculcated, were identical with the Eschatology of the ancient Egyptians, carried out of Egypt by Moses and the High Priests, who came from Egypt and were afterwards known as the Druids, and that various origins, symbols and rites, practised in other parts of the world, were identical. Hence we purpose to bring forward other links in the broken chain which prove more conclusively that this was so, and that herein lies the Primordial of true Christian doctrines of the present day. We contend that the Great Pyramid of Gizeh was built in Egypt as a monument and lasting memorial of this early religion, on true scientific laws, by divine inspiration and knowledge of the laws of the Universe.

Indeed, we may look on the Great Pyramid as the first true Masonic temple in the world, surpassing all others that have ever been built, with their secrets depicted on stone, symbolically, to be read by those who have been initiated into the secret mysteries of their religion, after having passed through the various degrees, for it was only men (Theopneustics) of the greatest honour and integrity who could possibly hope to attain to the highest or most sublime degree, and then only after long and patient study and many trials had been gone through to attain that end, and here in stone is set forth the passage of the "Tuat" and Amenta. What architect of the present day would undertake to erect a Pyramid like this Great Pyramid, which could stand for so many thousands of years without repair ?

In this work we do not retraverse the works of others, giving practically all particulars of the history of the craft since the fourteenth century, as there are several well-written books of this particular part of the history of the brotherhood, more especially may we mention *Brother R. F. Gould's* exhaustive well-written volume, which represents to our brothers in a very lucid and elegant manner all details from the above date. We are going back to the origin of all, and we must ask *Brother Gould's* indulgence in differing from him as to his explanation, or attempted explanation, of his so-called "MASONS' MARKS." This will be given in full detail later on. We only wish that there were more students in Freemasonry who would take a deeper interest other than those who look upon it generally as a charity and brotherhood only, although there is no doubt that of late years greater interest has been evinced, and we have among us a few who are striving to obtain the origin and original meaning of our ceremonies, but who cannot arrive at the truth until they become students of the ancient Egyptian ritual as well.

At the same time we must express our opinion that the heads of the Craft and the Powers that be give no encouragement to the students of Masonry ; apparently their motto is : "We do not wish to know, we are content to continue as we are" ; but, however much ignorance and bigotry may oppose the evolution of the true light and truth of the secrets of the past, time and death will remove the opposition, and more enlightened men will take their places. Science will accept no bigoted dogmas as facts ; truth will be proved by research and facts found ; advancement and evolution will continue until these mysteries are solved.

Clement of Alexandria tells us that "the Egyptians neither entrusted their mysteries to everyone, nor degraded the secrets of divine matters by disclosing them to the profane, reserving them for the heir-apparent to the throne, and for such of the priests as excelled in virtue and wisdom."

Plutarch, *Pythagoras*, *Zoroaster* and others of the Greeks who visited Egypt were never initiated into the mysteries beyond the first and second degrees, and they never obtained the knowledge of all of them. This is shown by *Eusebius*.

We do not intend to enter into any religious or theological arguments: our one object is to prove that many of the forms, words, symbols, etc., which we now use, were used by our ancient brethren, possibly more than 20,000 years ago, and that then, as now, Freemasonry was scattered over the face of the globe, and that the essence of their rites and beliefs was analogous to that of our tenets, and that various passwords were given and had to be repeated before passing from one degree to another, and that these were identical with those still in use among ourselves, both as Freemasons and in the doctrines of true Christianity.

We do not wish our readers to suppose that the term "Freemasonry" was then in existence, *but that the whole ritual, signs and symbols*, etc., as we use and practise in our rites, and that the ceremonies were all identical, and many practised in the various Christian churches have their origin in these.

Proofs of Freemasonry being Universal

In 1886 *Dr Le Plongeon* published a book called "Sacred Mysteries among the Mayas and the Quiché, 11,500 Years Ago, and Freemasonry in times anterior to the Temple of Solomon," and in 1896 he supplemented this with "Queen Moo and the Egyptian Sphinx."

These books were the result of his labours and excavations of ancient cities, etc., made in Yucatan, in Mexico, where he found

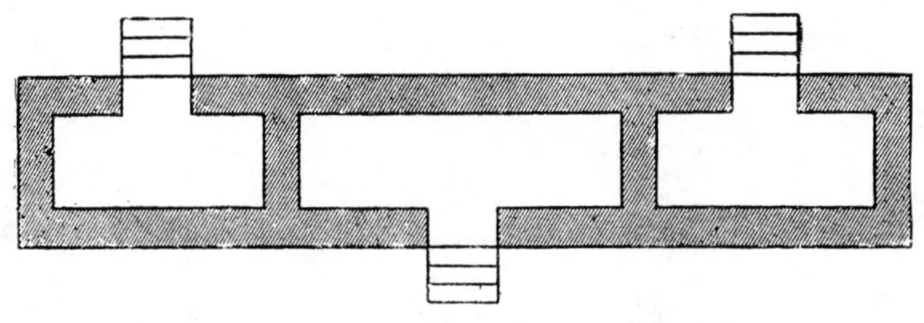

Fig. 1.—Three Temples in Uxmal, Mexico.

many of the Signs and Symbols in use amongst us. *Dr Le Plongeon* is a Freemason, and he tells us that at Uxmal he found three temples together—"oblong squares"[1]—with partitions between each, and traces of Masonic rites in the first, second and third degrees in evidence on the walls respectively.

Mr John L. Stevens, in his work "Incidents of Travel in

Fig. 2.

Central America—Chapas and Yucatan," published in 1848, has a description coinciding with *Dr Le Plongeon*, and he gives the dimensions of these, the two ends 18 ft. by 9 ft., and the

[1] Masonic Term.

central ones 34 ft. by 9 ft., he also describes another 250 ft. square, with squares or tessellated pavement, black and white. These all front the east.

Most of these temples at Uxmal were surmounted by the

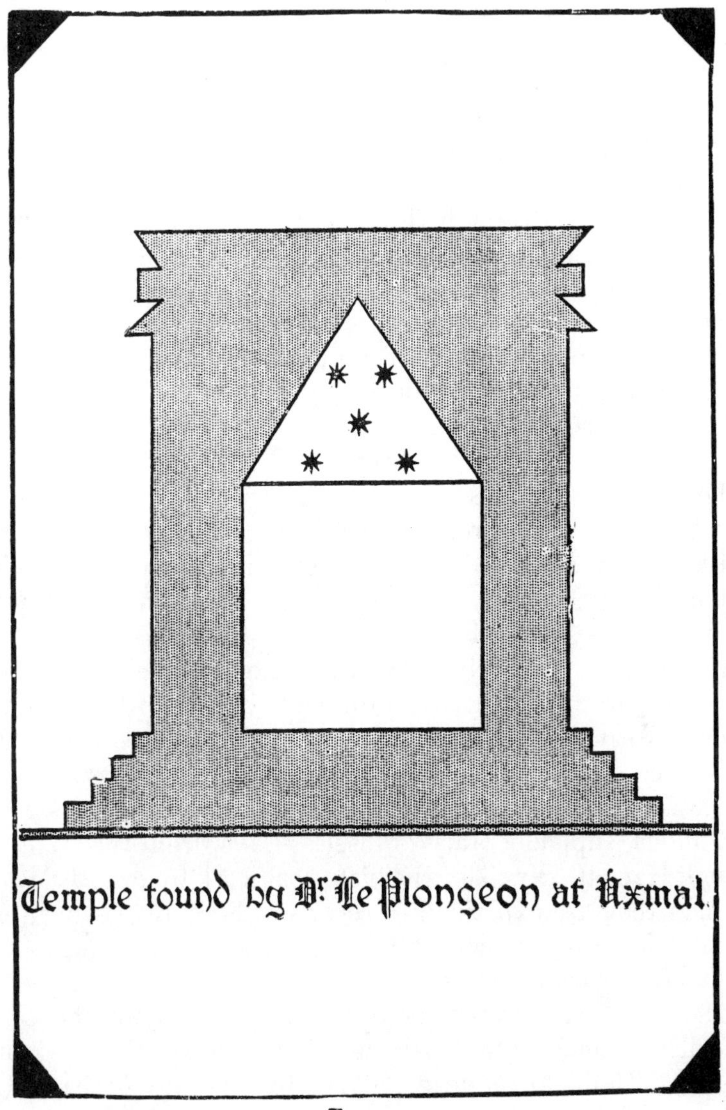

Fig. 3.

triangular arch above a square, which all R.A.M.'s will understand (the origin of which we shall have to mention hereafter).

Here we must call particular attention to the form inside the temple—a square, surmounted by a triangle, with three stars in the angles of the triangle in one temple, and five stars within the triangle in the other temple. As we shall show later on, these three stars at the corners of the triangle, with the ancient Egyptians, represented Sut, Shu and Horus, the three gods of the first or Stellar Trinity. These, with two others, represent Osiris and Isis, completing the family of Osiris, found by *Dr Le Plongeon* at Uxmal. They are also symbolical of the five mysteries and Solar Mythos.

By the family of Osiris we mean the children of Nut. These were five in number :—Osiris, Horus, Seb, Isis and Nephthys. They were not all brought forth at one place, and were not all born on the same day. They were born on the five epagomenal days of the year, according to the Solar Mythos.

On the first the birth of Osiris took place.

On the second that of Heru-ur or Horus.

On the third that of Set or Sut.

On the fourth that of Isis.

On the fifth that of Nephthys.

The first, third and fifth of the epagomenal days were considered unlucky. In Freemasonry these numbers have a peculiar significance, which all M.M.'s understand, and with the common herd of people these days are still considered as unlucky days and numbers. How many know why or the origin of it ?

The nations of ancient Mexico reckoned their time as the Egyptians, from whom they obtained their knowledge of time, seasons, festivals, etc. This may be seen and proved by their observance of the above five days as the Egyptians did. The Mexicans called them "nemonterni" or "nèn-onterni"—*i.e.* the superfluous, supplementary or useless days, from the Aztec text of Book II. chap xxxvii. of the historical work by *Father Sahagun*, in which they are explained in these words : " Estos cinco dias á ningun Dios estan dedicados y por eso les uamaran nemonterni, que quiere decir por démas."

These five days are not dedicated to any god, and hence they are called "nemonterni," which means "superfluous," "unfit," "useless," "unlucky," and in the Aztec text we are told that not anything was done on these days—no one quarrelled or got into any dispute, "because if anything adverse happened, it would continue to befall them thence for evermore." This was the same throughout Yucatan, Mexico and States of Central America at this period.

In Yucatan they were called "Xma Kaba Kin" (days without names). They were not dropped out of the reckoning, but were considered "unlucky days," and nothing was done during those days one way or the other—simply counted in silence and interpolated to make the 365 days of the year, just as the Egyptians did, and throughout the old Aztec and Maya manuscripts we find that they kept their time regularly, and those authors who have tried to prove that they "dropped time" during leap year have no authority for their statements or supposition; in fact it is a groundless theory on their part. They held their "feasts" at the same time and days of the year as did the Egyptians. All over the country they counted 365 days of the year and reckoned the one Great Year, 25,827 days in a year. This is clearly shown in the "Stella of Copan and Quirigua" and on the Altar Slabs at Palenque. All have at the top the image representation of the great day ⟜ ⊙ , followed by a date—*i.e.* the commencement and ending of the great day or great year of precession.

We cannot agree with *Dr Edward Seler* in his explanations of the foregoing. Well may he say "we have not succeeded in clearing them up." We would add that he has not succeeded in giving the true decipherment of any of his translations of the various codices of the Mayas, Mexican and Central American nations that he has attempted to, and until he recognises Egypt as the primordial and origin we are of opinion that he will not.

In the "Popul Vuh" we have a parallel story of Samson in their history of a hero named Zipanea Told, who, being captured by his enemies and placed in a pit, pulled down the building in which his captors had assembled and killed 400 of them: also, that when the ancestors of the Quiché migrated to America the Divinity parted the sea for their passage, which is parallel to the Red Sea being parted for the Israelites, and this can only be read and the meaning understood through the Astro-Mythology and *Ritual* of Ancient Egypt as an esoteric representation and not an exoteric rendering.

One of our critics asserts that all these statements are only "visionary." These temples and remains of buildings of the ancient Mayas were found and photographed by *Le Plongeon*, and we have *Admiral Boardman's, C.B.*, statement to this effect, as well as from the lips of *Le Plongeon* himself, in addition to his photographs taken on the spot. "The Popul Vuh," the sacred book of the Quiché, still exists, and herein we find the same doctrines as in Egypt and other parts of the world, which were obtained by the Quiché direct from the Mayas.

Although there may be many theories regarding the interpretation, the fact remains that the temples, with their ancient Signs and Symbols, are there, and anyone with "vision" can see them. Moreover, the hieroglyphic language of the Mayas was in many cases identical with that of the Egyptians—see later ; but we cannot agree with *Le Plongeon* in his decipherment and rendering of these ancient signs, which are of purely Egyptian origin and have a different meaning from that which he ascribes to them. These inscriptions are undoubtedly a part of the Egyptian *Ritual* written in Maya. The same story was brought from Egypt into this land at the time of the Stellar and Solar Mythos. The learned men of Mayach state that they imagined in remote ages that the vault of heaven was sustained by four pillars, placed at each of the cardinal points, and that the Creator assigned the care of them to four brothers, called in Maya, Kan-Bacab, Chac-Bacab, Zac-Bacab and Ek-Bacab. These are the four children of Horus, Amset, Hapi, Kabhsenuf and Tuamutef, representing the Man, Lion, Eagle and Ox banners of the Israelites, and Matthew, Mark, Luke and John of the Christians, to whom practically the same duty was assigned and the rendering of the name is the same. Also the duties assigned to them in chaps. cxii., cxiii. of the "Book of the Dead," were the same as we find here. Other discoveries have led to the knowledge that Stellar Mythos existed and was practised here during the Neolithic Age, because there is ample evidence of the people of the Paleolithic Age (little red or earth men) having lived in these countries, and Neolithic men are still found here practising all these Totemic ceremonies as we find in other countries. There are many tribes still living in the mountains and forests where, at present, the "white man" has not yet penetrated, and to whom even the "Solar Mythos" never reached.

The different names we find in Central America, Mexico, etc., so-called day-signs of *Dr Edward Seler* :

Mexican,	Acatl	Beeu	Kau
Zapotecs,	Tecpatl	Ezanab	Muluc
etc.	Calli	Akbal	Lx
	Tochtli	Lamat	Cauac

All correspond and are the same as the Maya "Bacabs"—*i.e.* the Red, White, Black and Yellow—the four children of Horus, situated at the N. S. E. and W., and the four supports of heaven, etc. *Dr Edward Seler's* demon, Coslahun Tox or the Cloud Spirit Moan, is Sut, and is not represented by L. and M. in his day-signs, fig. 4 (Mexican Chronology). L. is the Hawk, Horus I., with a crown of feathers—and here represents light, day—K. is Lord of the earth and heaven. M. is Sut, on whom Horus has turned his back (night). This is well shown in *Dr Budge's* book "The Gods of the Egyptians." Horus, having conquered death and darkness—*i.e.* light or the sun's rays—has pierced and driven away the clouds which shrouded the earth in darkness, when the superheated vapour had sufficiently cooled. His "dog" and "tapir" are here representatives of Anubis and, we see, have the same duties assigned them here as in Egypt. In fig. 9, D. represents Zipe, "risen"—*i.e.* Amsu or Min (holding a rope with hieroglyph on it, and signifying spiritual life)—see later on.

OTHER SIGNS FOUND BY DR LE PLONGEON AS SEEN HERE

1. The Emblem of Mortality; 2. The Skeleton in attitude of the Ka with upraised arms; 3. The Double Triangle; and 4. A Tau; these need no explanation to R.A.M.'s. Also the figure 5, Masonic Apron. This is evidently part of a carved statue of one of the priests. In "Dress," it is carved in white marble. Some signs and symbols are likewise found in Peru among the ancient Incas; also in the mural inscriptions in the Caroline Islands.

The Masonic objects found beneath the base of the obelisk known as Cleopatra's Needle, now in the Central Park, New York, likewise show that many of the symbols pertaining to the rites of modern Freemasonry were used in Egypt 3500 years ago. This obelisk was made for Hatshepsu, who lived 1600 B.C.—*i.e.* 3500 years ago. Forbes mentions that in Java is a tribe called the Karangs, supposed to be descendants of the aborigines of the island, whose old men and youths, four times a year, repair secretly in procession, by paths known only to themselves, to a sacred grove in the dense forest: the old men to worship, the youths to see and learn the mysterious litany of their fathers.

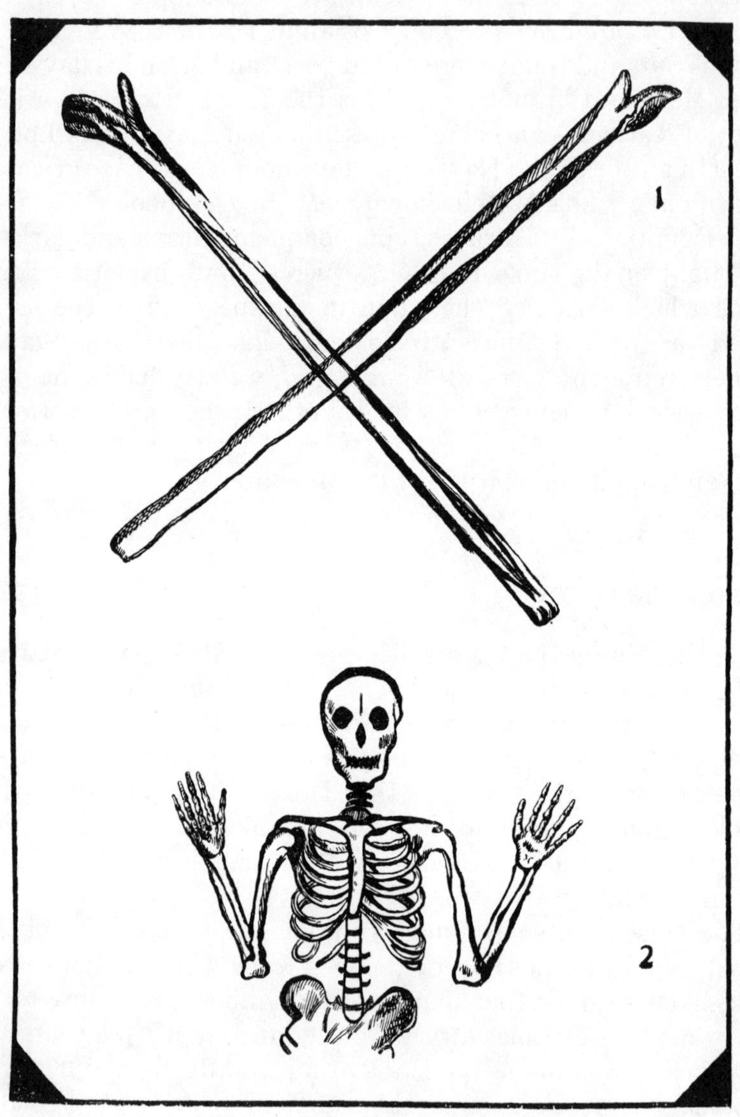

FIG. 4.—From Uxmal, Mexico.

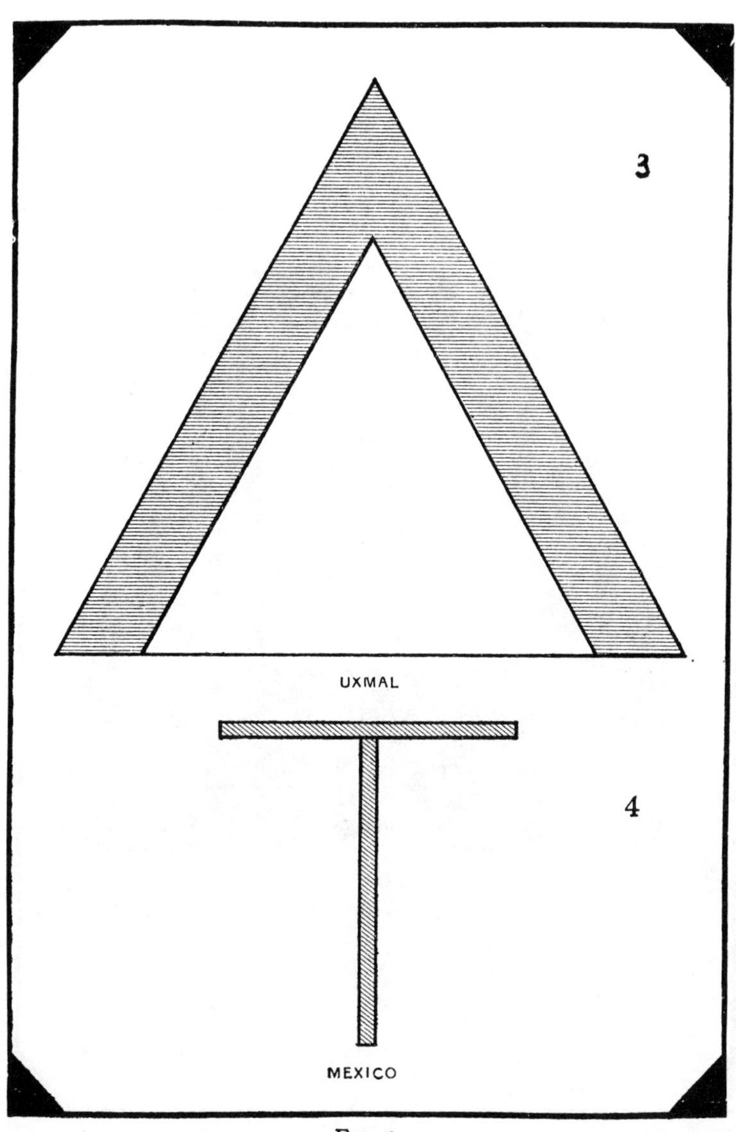

FIG. 5.

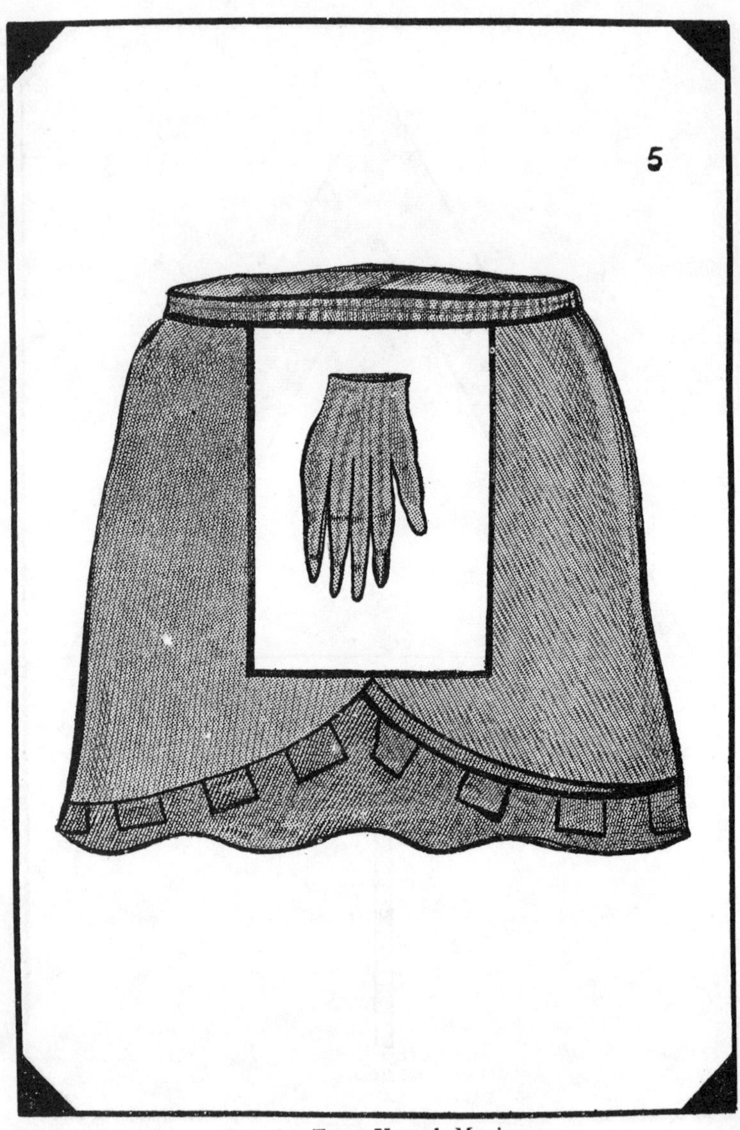

FIG. 6.—From Uxmal, Mexico.

In this grove are the ruins of terraces, laid out in quadrilateral enclosures, the boundaries of which are marked by blocks of stone laid or fixed in the ground. Here and there on the terraces are more prominent monuments, erect pillars, etc., and, especially noteworthy, a pillar erect within a square.[1] Here these despised and secluded people follow the rites and customs that have descended to them through their forefathers from vastly remote antiquity, repeating with superstitious awe a litany which they do not comprehend, the origin and purpose of which are lost in their traditions, but which may be found in the Egyptian Papyrus (Papyrus of Leyden) and the "Ritual or Book of the Dead."

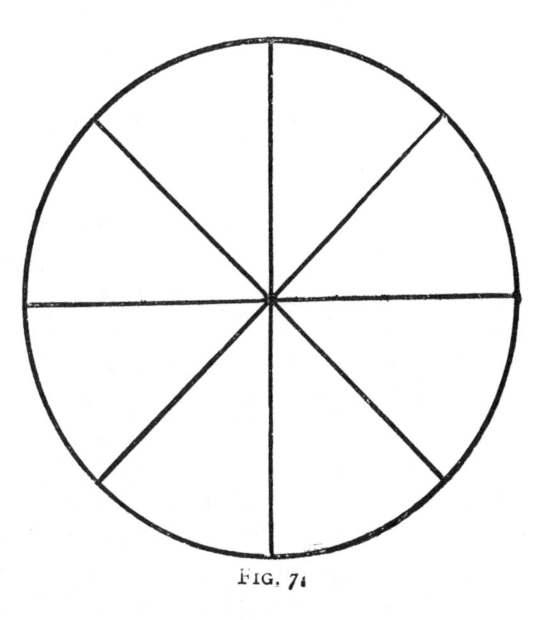

Fig. 7.

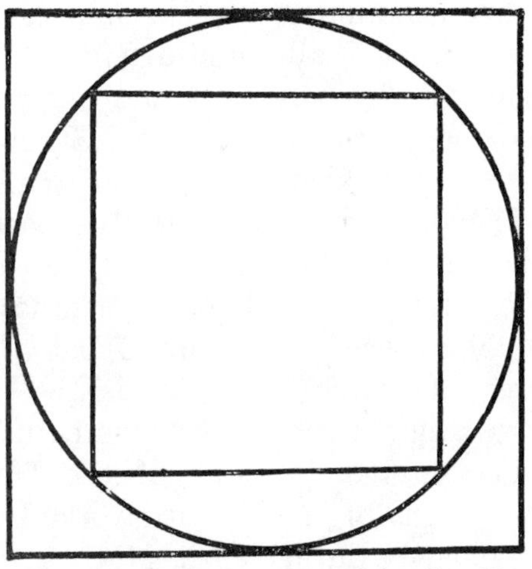

Fig. 8.—Temple mentioned by Gerald Massey, North America.

Gerald Massey mentions an ancient temple in North America, also peculiar. First a square within a circle, and both of them surmounted by another square: this may be said to correspond to our Quatuor Coronati, and with triangle added inside the inner square, and star with dot × inside the triangle, would represent the highest degree in the Eschatology—see later.

[1] See *re* N. A. Indians.

There is an octagonal heaven which may be formed of a double square. There were four gods of the four corners; four consorts were assigned to them at the second four corners or half cardinal points. Twice four points are equivalent to a double square. The square may thus be doubled like the double triangle to make an octagon, as the octonary of Taht, the Moon God. The eightfold way is equal to the square when doubled and blended in one figure.

The Japanese have an eight-forked road of heaven. A four square sign named Tesennu or Khemenu—*i.e.* No. 8 in Egyptian. Four sides of Egyptian Pyramid. Four corners Assyrian Pyramid = four sides and four corners = a double square or cube 8, = a double square and circle—*i.e.* eight half cardinal points. Quatuor Coronati subdivided = four cardinal points and eight half cardinal points. Triangle added above with three gods at the corners.

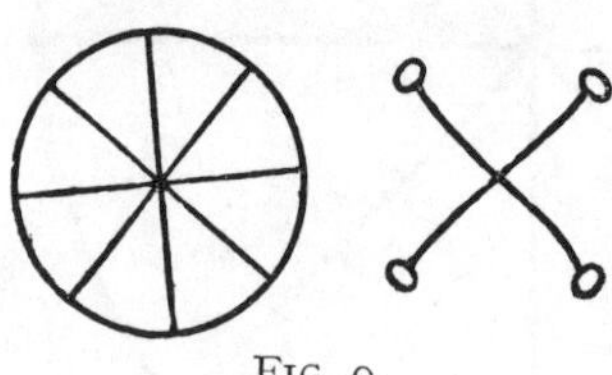

FIG. 9.

This has precisely the same meaning as the Double Triangle.

Gerald Massey is not a Mason, and we were therefore unable to learn from him if any Masonic signs existed on the walls.

We would call your attention to these photos, one from Egypt, one from Assyria and one from Mexico, identically the same and identical with our P.Z. jewels. The full explanations of these signs must be apparent to all R.A.C.'s.

The division here in twelve parts, the twelve signs of the Zodiac, twelve tribes of Israel, twelve gates of heaven mentioned in Revelation, and twelve entrances or portals to be passed through in the Great Pyramid, before finally reaching the highest degree, and twelve Apostles in the Christian doctrines, and the twelve original and perfect points in Masonry.

The twelve divisions of the Tuat, the original, were the twelve signs of the Zodiac, worked out by the Astro-Egyptian mythologists during their Mythos; then they converted their mythology into Eschatology, which must have taken many years. We find they had, so to speak, "dug out" the Underworld, and had, by divine inspiration or the study of the laws of the celestial bodies, come to the conclusion that after the death of this perishable body, the soul, which is imperishable, had to travel through many dangers and difficulties before it could join or be received again by its Divine Creator. This the Egyptians depicted most graphically, and the records are still extant in the book of "That which is in the Underworld," which they have divided into

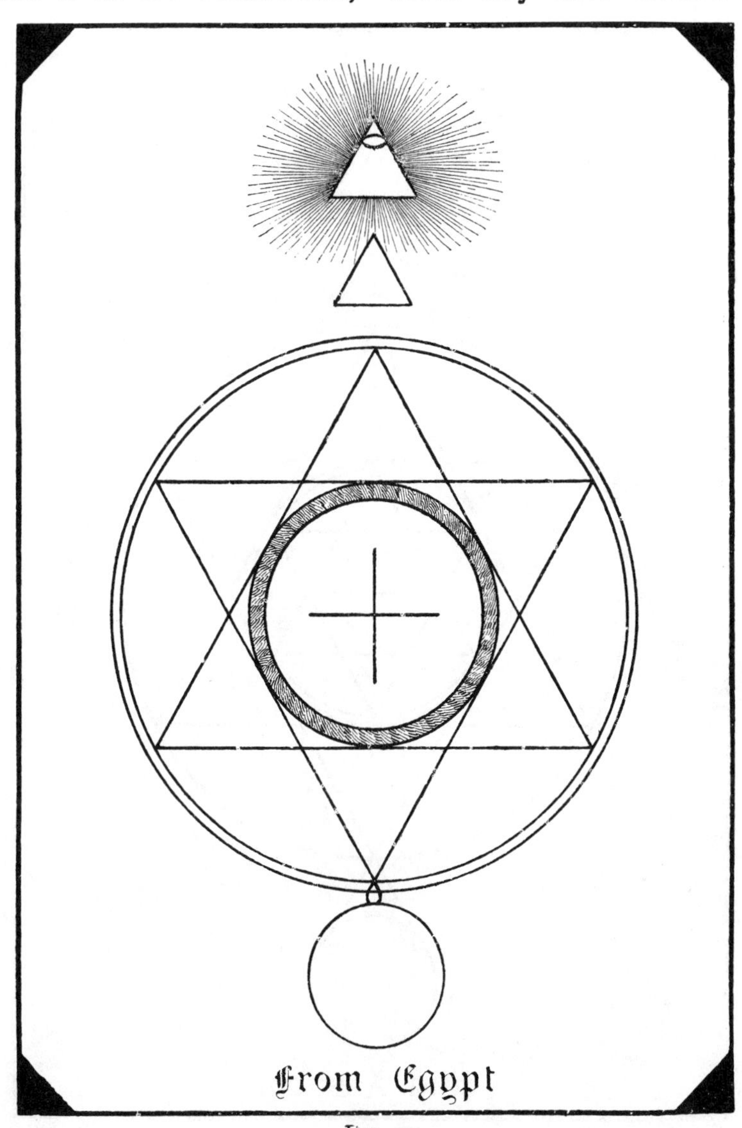

Fig. 10.

twelve divisions: "The Tuat and the Twelve Hours of the Night," which is hewn in stone in the Great Pyramid of Gizeh. In the Christian doctrine the twelve gates of heaven were taken from this. Here, in the Pyramid, the old Theopneustics taught the initiate step by step and degree after degree what the soul had to encounter and pass through before it could arrive and pass Amenta and receive the Crown of Glory in the presence of its

FIG. 12.

"each hour of the night" constituted a so-called "degree" or gate or door to pass. That all this was worked out at an early period—pre-Dynastic—we have ample proof in the fact that we find Khepera is represented as a Hawk—the Spirit—issuing from

All these ceremonies were illustrated and carried out in a dramatic form, more especially to impress upon the initiate the seriousness of the subject; and "each portion of the Tuat," and

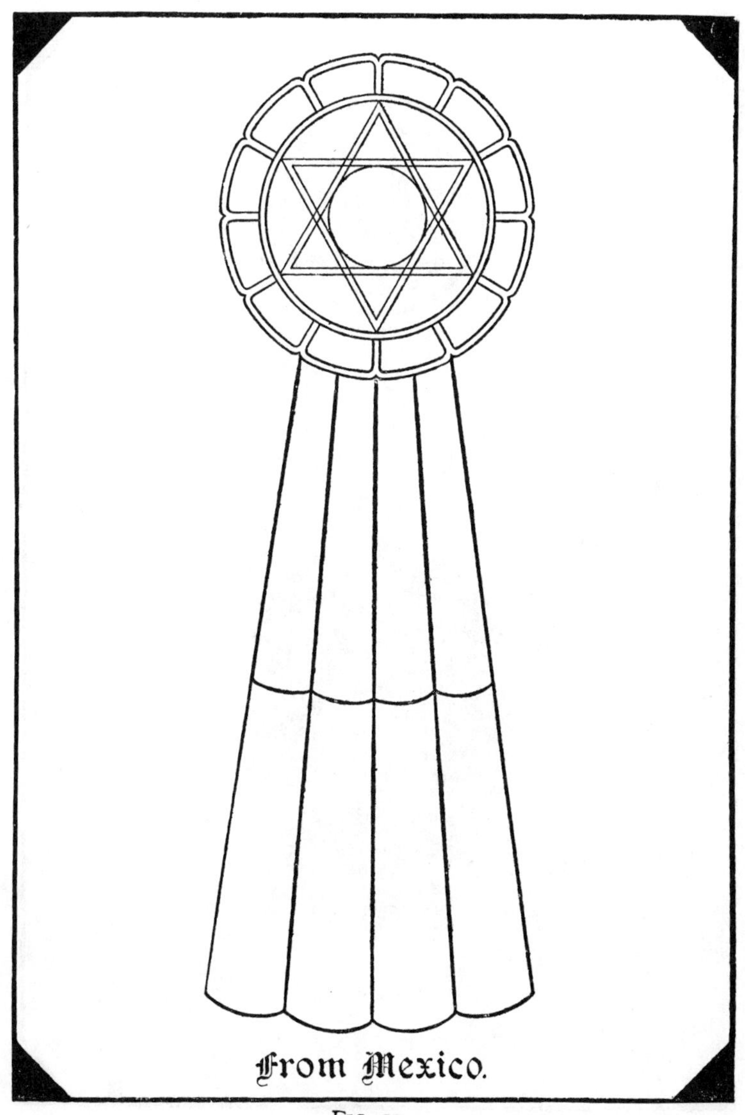

FIG. 11:

Divine Author, thus teaching him the life he must lead here on earth, and the sacrifices he must make—"to do unto others as he would they should do unto him" in his earthly corporate body that he might receive the Crown of Illumination in his spiritual.

a mummy. This would denote that they had worked out a part at least of their Eschatology. In our opinion the Great Pyramid of Gizeh was built as soon as this was completed. We know

FIG. 13.—P.Z. Jewels.

that many Egyptologists do not agree that these earlier people had any ideas or beliefs at this remote period of "life and spirit hereafter" but we must insist upon the fact, that it must have been so, because here is the proof—"The spirit issuing from the mummy." This alone is conclusive.

Amenta or the Underworld was not under the earth, as some have supposed, but a place deep down *through* the earth, and as the sun went down in the west at night and rose again in the east in the morning, so this symbolically represented the soul travelling through the Tuat and Amenta until it finally accomplished its journey and joined the Divine source again. The darkness, difficulties and dangers of the Tuat are fully set forth in the book of "That which is in the Underworld," and it is rather amusing to read *Brother Gould's* attempted ridicule "that anything we have in our Rites and Ceremonies has nothing to do with the ancients." We quote from his last work, page 5, as follows:—"Of the Mysteries, indeed, as existed in different countries, it may be said that they are distinguished by varying forms, while it is equally certain that there was a great similarity between them all. The ceremonies of initiation were invariably funereal in their character. They celebrated the death and the resurrection of some cherished being, either the object of esteem as a hero or of devotion as a god." The conformity between death and initiation is strikingly exemplified in a passage preserved by *Stobæus* from an ancient record and runs thus: "The mind is affected and agitated in death just as it is in initiation into the Grand Mysteries: the first stage is nothing but errors and uncertainties, labourings, wanderings and darkness. And now, arrived on the verge of death and initiation everything wears a dreadful aspect; it is all horrors, trembling and affrightment. But this scene, once over, a miraculous and divine light displays itself . . . perfect and initiated they are free, and, crowned and triumphant, they walk up and down in the regions of the blessed, etc., etc.—this is not Freemasonry at all." Has *Brother Gould* ever attended the I. ceremony in the West of England provinces? We think if he had ever been present at some of these in Devonshire and Cornwall it would have been instructive to him on the point. Evidently *Brother Gould* has not been initiated into the 18°. Nothing could be more strikingly conclusive than the description which he quotes of the second part of the D.R. and passing from this into the 3rd point. It is only part of the passage of the Tuat[1] which we have mentioned

[1] The Tuat was part of Amenta. (*See* next page.)

previously and is most conclusive evidence that all these mysteries were taken, copied, and brought on from the ancient Egyptian Rites, and *Brother Gould* and other Freemasons will never understand the meaning and origin of our Sublime Tenets until they have studied and unlocked the mysteries of the past. Although they have the alphabet here written as plainly as the light of day, which they ignore and ridicule, simply because they have not learned it. They express and dogmatically assert opinions which are opposed to facts, which they ignore or are ignorant of. The whole of the ceremonies of the 18° and those up to and inclusive of the 30° are simply those of the passage of the Tuat and Amenta in the Egyptian *Ritual*, brought on and much perverted, and *Brother Gould's* quotation from *Stobæus* helps to prove this rather than otherwise. On pages 5 to 12 he has given some valuable quotations from various authors regarding the rites as carried on and practised by those who obtained them originally from Egypt. The key he has missed, but let us assure him he can find it in the Egyptian and nowhere else. Here also he will find the true meaning of "Left Foot first," the origin and meaning of which will be given further on, and anyone reading what *Brother Gould* says about it, and that which we have brought forward as the true translation of the Papyri, will see where the fallacy lies, and that there is a genuine reason for so doing which has been handed down and practised by those who have preserved the true *Ritual* for ages and ages.

Added Note [1913].—The Egyptians did not believe that there was such a place as Amenta or that Ptah and his seven Pygmies really tunnelled through the earth, but expressed this "figure" in "Sign Language" to teach the Mysteries.

CHAPTER III

EVANS, in his recently published volume: "The Mycenæan Tree and Pillar Cult and its Mediterranean Relations," speaks of "The House of the Double Axe!" and gives an illustration of the three cubes, with the sign on each, of the double axe, but we take this to be the early Greek form of the Egyptian, which may be seen depicted on the Druidical stone, hereafter mentioned, lying at South Tawton Church, Devonshire, and which gives the so-called Double Axe in this form (twice repeated) followed by the syllabic sign, Mes (thrice repeated), then the syllabic sign, Seh. After this another axe then the syllabic Mes, and at the bottom, a serpent (probably Rerek). One meaning of the double axe *Netru*, is Gods, the company of Gods, and with the sign Seh, the Celestial God or Gods, or God of Heaven and Earth, the Great God.

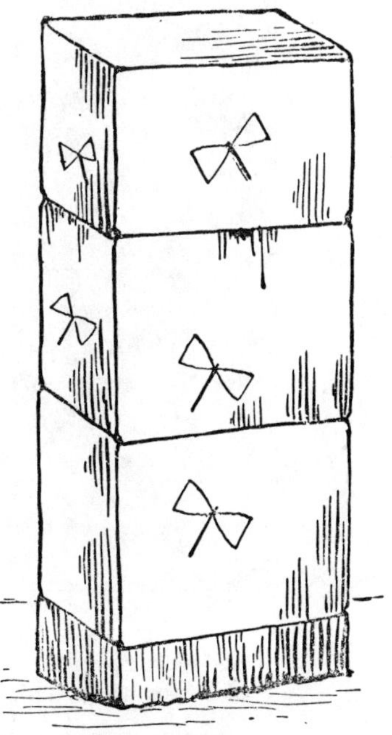

FIG. 14.

Neter may mean a God or Divine Being or Sovereignty. Mes may mean the products of the water, of the river, to bring, bearer of, to give birth to, to bring forth, to be born, produced. Mes denotes the birth or rebirth of the dead in the Mesken, and as no doubt this stone was taken from Mis-Tor or somewhere near Mis-Tor, would denote *Mes*-Tor (Egyptian). Yes-Tor is also near; this and Yes-Tor probably represents a *Kes*-Tor (Egyptian); this being a burial and embalmment, the Tor being the natural mount and type of the latter. Seh , one meaning of this is the raised Heaven, Hall, another name of Osiris ; remembering that all these syllabic signs depend upon other hieroglyphics which are obliterated, for the rendering of the true translation and meaning. Rerek was the name of a serpent fiend. These hieroglyphics are important, because

FIG. 15.—This represents the Ancient W.M.'s Chair, and part of the Lodge or Temple. In the centre of this Temple the Treble Cube of Evans was found. So-called Throne of Minos at Knossos.

of their pure Egyptian origin and of their being found cut in a granite stone, taken from Druidical remains on Dartmoor, Devonshire—as one would assume—from its present resting-place. The inscription at Otarum, on the two rectangular altars ascribed to the God of the Double Axe, is the same as the Greeks called Zeus, undoubtedly, and has the same meaning as the above, which is the same as the god Odin of the Scandinavians and the Woden, Wotan or Wuotan of the Germans.

The Axe goes back to the earliest Neolithic and probably Paleolithic age in Egypt and preceded that of the flint arrow-head or flint knife. The stone tied to the end of a stick formed the earliest club of prehistoric man, and when the stick was placed in the middle of a longish stone and fastened, and the two ends were rubbed down to sharpness, you would have two cutting edges, and in fact the first or primitive form of the Double Axe, and this is shown in many ways to have preceded the Single Axe. Considering the great importance that the axe would be to early man, not only as a weapon of defence or offence, but also to cut wood, etc., it would become first a symbol of physical force or strength and then of divinity or dominion ; it would also be used in their sacred ceremonies and would acquire therefrom a symbolic meaning as representing "power and might." Taking for granted then that the hieroglyphic [hieroglyph] represents the double axe, we are sure that it was used as a symbol of power and divinity by the pre-dynastic Egyptians long before the period when they were able to write ; but we have no means of really knowing what they called the double axe at that period. In after times, when the single axe [hieroglyph] had taken the place of the double axe, they called it, as we have already stated, "Neter." *Renouf* disagrees with many Egyptologists as regards the meaning of the word ; his opinion is that it signifies "mighty," "might," "strong" and "power."

These three cubes of *Evans*, with the double axe, show that these people must have emigrated from Egypt at a very early period indeed, because the double axe in this form was adopted first ; at the same time it shows how far they had attained in their knowledge and learning the perfections of their Stellar Mythos. Whatever the difference may be that exists as to its meaning amongst Egyptologists, there cannot be any doubt amongst Freemasons, and here in the earliest form we have the first symbolical representations of the three grand originals. Personally, our opinion of the meaning of the word "Neter," [hieroglyph] is not really God or [hieroglyph] Netru Gods. "Princes" or "Grand Masters" would be a true signification of the meaning of the word or hieroglyphic, in our opinion. The double axe first and the single axe after was of the greatest benefit and use to primitive man ; he would naturally associate it with all the highest, best and strongest qualities of his prince, chief or ruler, and so it would undoubtedly stand as the hieroglyphic (as these primitive people could not write) for the Lord or Head, a Prince, a Ruler of the people, and thus associated symbolically as the head Priest or Priests of these sacred ceremonies, and we feel that this is so, if for no other reason than that because we Freemasons have been the custodians of it for ages and ages, and still possess it in its pure form from the original as we shall show further on, as we do the 24-inch gauge and other sacred symbols, and the signification of the double axe with us is as stated above, and we therefore agree with *Renouf* that it does not mean literally God or Gods, but only "a great one," "a mighty prince" or "princes" or "rulers," and we have no means of knowing how or by what name these ancients called it. This double axe, therefore, was used as a sacred symbol at the earliest period of their Stellar Mythos in the earlier Neolithic Age and afterwards abandoned as the double axe in this form ╤ and used in this form ┐┐┐. The origin of our Gavel and double-headed Gavel is the same as the above and would further bear out *Renouf's* opinion as regards the proper translation of this hieroglyphic.

This "House of the Double Axe" here would be the representative of "The Great Chief of the Hammer" of Egypt, the same as the one we find in Mexico—see later—*i.e.* The House of Ptah.

In the Solar Mythos of the Egyptians, the double axe is likewise an emblem of the double power, and the God of the double axe is consequently a God of the double equinox—who was Har-Makhu—the Horus who passed into Atum-Ra. Another form and name was the double Harmachis, who was the "cleaver of the way" and whose double power was imaged by the two-headed weapon which has been termed the "divine double axe" of the Mycenæan cult.

The Gavel

As every Freemason knows, the "Common Gavel" used in some lodges is as a single axe ┐ and others a double ╤; in others only the W.M. has the double or its representation. Here we have it representing the force of power and might, enabling

FIG. 16.—Stone axe decorated with line ornament.

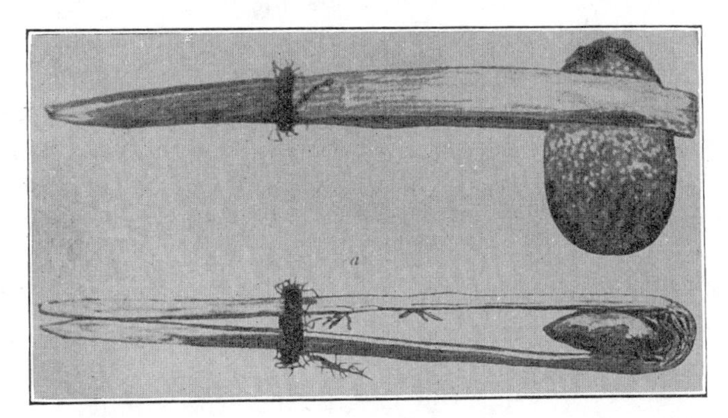

FIG. 17.—Method of hafting a ground axe. Warramunga Tribe.

FIG. 18.—Hafted ground axe. Gnanji tribe.

those principal officers, in whose hands it is placed, to keep order and symbolically suppress all unbecoming thoughts which might arise during our ceremonies. Amongst Freemasons, therefore, *Renouf's* opinion of this very ancient, if not the most ancient, symbol would be the correct one. It is interesting, also, to R.A.M.'s as the W. and P.W. from the 2nd to the 1st C——. The above is the original Egyptian word, and all P.Z.'s will recognise in this the password N—, the meaning being the same and the pronunciation being the same practically. The High Priest of each great city (or nome) in Egypt bore a special title, and at Memphis he was called "Great Chief of the Hammer." In the temple of him of the Southern wall and Setem of the "God of the Beautiful Face"—*i.e.* Ptah, and the High Priest of the Great Nome, possessed a power which was hardly inferior to that of the king himself. The High Priests of the Druids held the same power here before they were deposed, and bore the same title. That the word was very old and applied to Horus I. is undoubtedly true, as we see from the various texts: "I have risen up in the form of a hawk netri; au-a kha-kua em bak netri" shows that here netri represents Horus I. in the Stellar Mythos or was a type of the same—the Great One, the Master, the Great Spirit. In other texts it represents one self-produced—all primeval matter—powers (neter netri Kheper-Tchesef[1] paut); in another, self-production and self-begetting (hun netri aa hch utet se-mes su techersef)—*i.e.* "Boy netri heir of eternity, begetting and giving birth to himself" all representing Horus—the Great One, the Mighty One—the Master.

From the "MENDOZA CODEX," NO. 13, we find that the Mexicans when they began to spread beyond their valley of Yantepec and Cuernavaca (ancient Quauhnauac), made war on and took Tepoxtlan. They were told that this place was called "The Place of the Axe," and that Tepoxtecatl, the Pulque God, was the "God of the Axe or Great Seer of the Hammer."

We have here, in Central America, the representation of "The Great Chief of the Hammer," the same as the High Priest of Egypt at Memphis, with the same title and representative Axe — *i.e.* Ptah. Prototype of M.W.M. He wears the two crowns, representing the Earthly and Spiritual lives.

[1] We do not agree with Dr Budge in his translation of "paut" as "matter"—*i.e.* a "handful of earth." "Paut" means "a company of gods," or otherwise a *number of powers or attributes, or all the powers and attributes of* THE GOD. It is a collective noun.

The Zapotec High Priest was called Uija-tao—*i.e.* Great Seer. He possessed the power of putting himself into an ecstatic state, which distinguished between High Priests and subordinate ones, as did the Druids and Egyptians. We shall refer to this later.

The symbols on the apron are also typical, as is the collar, of which Freemasons do not need any explanation. All the different names mentioned on page 348 of *Dr Seler's* article are different names of Sut, Horus and Shu.[1]

A further proof that this is the same as the Egyptian may be found in the decipherment and explanation of the "Banner" here held in the left hand, showing that here "The Great Chief of the Hammer" was the earthly representative of Horus I. In the centre there is a square with the hieroglyphic Apt and the Tat in the centre of this. At the four corners are the ends of the four supports or pillars of heaven ○ and above the four pillars, the crown with the hieroglyphic *Ab—Heart*, and this supports a crown with the three feathers or three rods or rays of light. On the right are seven feathers, representing the seven Pole stars, or seven lights, or Seven Glorious Ones. The meaning is precisely similar to that of one of the Aats or Domains, the explanation of which we give in the chapter on the Cross. It may be read as follows :—the Cross, representing the four quarters, is here represented by the square with the four ○○

FIG. 19.—Tepoxtecatl, the so-called Pulque God, from Mexican painting in Biblioteca Nazionale, Florence.

[1] "Mexican and Central American Antiquities Calander Systems and History," published by the Smithsonian Institution, Bureau of Ethnology.

as the four supports of heaven—the four children of Horus. Apt, brow or guide of God I.U. or Lord of Tat or the Stable One—the Lord of Stability. The seven feathers, with the four supports would represent him as the Lord of Light. "*The One*" and the Seven Glorious Ones with the four children of Horus as their supports. Ab, the heart supporting a crown and the three or rods of light—the Lord of the Heart; the Light of the World, etc., would have the same meaning as the Egyptian (given further on in this work) but it is interesting to note that these Central American people nearly always preferred to use the hieroglyphic Ab (heart), whilst the Egyptians used Tep (the head). They also preserved the heart as the Egyptians did. Ab also represents "The conscience of a man and a new heart represents a new or rebirth."

Also the double axe held in his right hand signifies or is an emblem of the double power—*i.e.* the God of the double equinox, who was Har-Makhu, the Horus who passed into Atum-Ra (Ra) as the Egyptian Zeus. The single axe in front shows him as a Solar power, which cleaves its way from West to East and from horizon to horizon. He was the cleaver of the Earth (one form of Ptah) who is represented by a cleaver as an axe as a sign of the cleaver of the way. In the Egyptian the god of the double equinox who completed the course from horizon to horizon was Horus of the double force and was variously imaged by the double crown, the double Uræi, the double feathers and other dual types. He was "cleaver of the way" whose double power was likewise portrayed by the two-headed weapon which has been termed the "divine double axe" of the Mycenæan cult and is found here as in many other parts of the world variously depicted.

In all Mexican and Central American pictures where we see the opening of the body and the heart being extracted it is carefully preserved by the embalmers, and in the tomb of "Prince Cho" *Dr Le Plongeon* found the heart carefully preserved by itself in a vase in the tomb beside the body, with beautifully wrought jade knives. With the ancient Egyptians the heart was always carefully removed and separated from the other internal parts, and was enclosed in special alabaster-limestone or other kind of vases and placed with the mummy in its grave. In earliest times they regarded the heart as the seat of feelings, and spoke of the heart as rejoicing, as mourning or weeping. *Plutarch* informs us that the other parts were thrown into the river, so that the rest of the body might remain pure. But very little definite knowledge has been yet found in the texts on this subject, yet the heart must have been preserved in all cases, because of its importance in the Hall of Judgment. It was the heart that was put into the scales against the Maat, and as soon as the scales turned in his favour, then the god Thoth commanded that his heart should be restored to him and to be set again in its place. His Ba is shown hovering over, waiting for the final judgment, to be re-united. This is quite sufficient proof, we think, to show that the heart was not thrown away with the other internal parts and to account for its preservation. See Judgment Scene in Papyrus of Ani.

Amongst the Dinkas, at the present day, they have the "Great Chief of the Hammer," and the "House of the Axe" in the form of the "Sacred Spear," which their present tradition states "came down from heaven, or the clouds in a thunderstorm." They have a special hut set apart for the Great Spear, and look upon this "Great Spear" with awe and sacred feelings. Only two people are allowed to go near it, the Chief Beor or Chief of the Tribe and the "Suol" or priest, which, in the Dinka language, means "speaker." These two only can interpret the messages of the "Sacred Spear," but, as a matter of fact, it is the priest only. He places himself under self-hypnotism and then tells the Chief and others the message he has received from heaven through this sacred medium. At the present time the Spear has taken the place of the original "Stone Axe" which is the natural outcome of their knowledge of working in metals; and although these tribes have carried it down from Neolithic times, and the original meaning has become lost to them through ages of time, yet it is a most interesting and important fact that these people are the direct descendants of those who lived here in Neolithic times, and from whom colonies went out over the world, carrying the earlier Stellar Mythos and Totemic ceremonies with them. These Dinkas must be a remnant of the early Nilotic Negro, who were driven back or cut off from farther advancement to the north. The natives of New Guinea have the same peculiar way of standing and the same Totem ceremonies, etc.—see later. How soon all these native customs, traditions, myths, etc., will become obliterated now that the missionaries have begun their work amongst them, will, we think, be only a short time, and what will they find or understand of their religion, etc. ?—nothing, and so the origin of all our religions has become obliterated and erased by men, who know less than many of these poor natives of the meaning of many things, preaching an up-to-date doctrine, of which the original lies here. Let all students read through this book carefully before they form any opinion, it is written in "parts" to "keep the secrets," but in the "whole" the evidence must be conclusive to all searchers after truth, for here, in the valley of the Nile, lies the home of man and the origins of all we find throughout the world of the various Totemisms, Mythos, etc.

To summarise this sign and its meaning we must take this sign ⚹, the original sign used by the Pygmies, as the Chief —the Great One (and still recognised by them as such). Afterwards, amongst the oldest tribes, it was associated and recognised as the sign for Amsu—the risen Horus—the first man-god risen in spiritual form—see later. Amongst the Nilotic Negroes and those that followed, who went forth from Egypt at the various exodes, this sign :—one big stick with two across, was the first, then we find the double axe took its place—a stone placed in the split end of a stick and tied, and after this the single axe—a stone fixed into the end of a stick. These we find all over the world with the same meaning, and the decipherment of such must be the same. At the present day, amongst the Dinkas, who have learned the art of working in metals, the Sacred Spear has taken its place, and amongst Christian nations the Great Sword of the State.

The Three Pillars or Columns

The three Pillars as now used in our Lodges, called Wisdom, Strength and Beauty, and situated in the east, south and west, have their origin in these cubes. These prototypes were the "Three Grand Originals"—symbols of the first Trinity. In the M.M. Lodge the W.M. and J. and S.W. are the representatives. We venture to say that very few of our brethren are acquainted with the origin, which dates back to the Stellar Mythos, and then represented Horus I., Shu and Sut. The situation would be Horus I. situated at the north, Shu at the equinox or centre and Sut at the south or bottom, which may be seen in *Evans'* "Three Cubes," Horus at the top or north, Shu in the centre and Sut at the bottom or south. Wherever we find the remains of ancient

FIG. 20.—Cromlech, Louth. Drawn on stone by J. D. Harding, from a sketch by Robert O'Callaghan Newenham, Esq. Printed by C. Hullmandel.

temples of the Stellar Mythos, we find them situated in the centre temple, which is a square.

When the Stellar Mythos was evolved into the Solar, they naturally changed the positions of the "Grand Originals" or Triad, and their places then became east, south and west, because Ra took the place of Horus I., as representing the sun, which, rising in the east and setting in the west, Ra would represent the head or principal of the Trinity or Triad, the J.W. would be situated at the Meridian, and S.W. in the west to represent the setting sun, and this is what we find in all the temples of the Solar Mythos throughout the world; the great emblematical Triad of the Deity—symbolically represented.

The Hindu have these Three Pillars crowned with human heads. They are placed in the east, south and west, and are known by the same names—*viz.* Wisdom, Strength and Beauty. They represent: in the east, the Creator, who is said to have planned the great work by his infinite wisdom; executed it by his strength, and adorned it with all its beauty and usefulness for the benefit of man, and these united powers were represented in the solemn ceremony of initiation by their presiding High Priests or Hieraphants. The chief High Priest sat in the east on a high throne in all his glory, symbolising Brahma, the creator of the world; his two companions, clad in robes of equal magnificence, occupied the south and west respectively. Vishnu, the representative of the Setting Sun, in the west, and Siva, the Meridian Sun, in the south, all on raised thrones. In India, Brahma, Vishnu and Siva are considered the Triune God. Brahma as the Creator, Vishnu, the Preserver, and Siva, the Judge or Destroyer.

The Druids in their temples or Lodges had the same; that is, the Adytum was supported by three stones or pillars. The delivery of an oration after initiation was termed a "new birth." We shall mention more later on the subject of the Druids. The Mayas in Mexico and the Incas in South America had also the "Three Pillars" to represent symbolically the triune God or their Trinity. The Christians have their Trinity, as is well known. It is remarkable that every mysterious system practised in the habitable globe contained this "Triad of Deity," and until one studies the origin of all and the evolution that has taken place, and the exodes from Egypt at various times, and understands "The Ritual and primordial" also the great antiquity of these people, it is impossible to obtain the key to unlock the mystery. Theirs was the first as Stellar Trinity, which afterwards became Lunar and Solar, and they designated the attributes of this "triune God" by the names of "Wisdom," "Power" and "Goodness," which is the English for the pure translation of the Egyptian words.

These three cubes of *Evans*, with the Double Axe on each, would represent the three Grand Masters or the Three Originals, and would correspond to the representation of the Trinity and the double-edged sword of the Christians, denoting emblems of power and might. This is well depicted in our R.A.C. Every

R.A.M. must be well acquainted with the Pedestal of the Double Cubes, and the signs and symbols thereon, and the history of the recovery of the same, etc. (as also seen in 64th chapter of the Egyptian *Ritual*), and it will be quite evident to all R.A.M.'s that these three cubes of *Evans*, found situated in the centre of the temple, were practically the same as our present double cubes—with the difference only that each Grand Master had a cube for his own name or symbol—*i.e.* instead of three names being on the double cubes, a name or symbol is on each cube. Moreover, it is

THE DOUBLE SQUARE OR CUBE

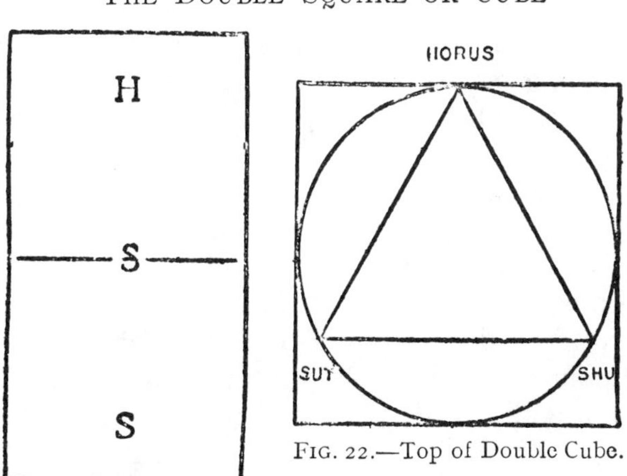

FIG. 21.—Double Cube.

FIG. 22.—Top of Double Cube.

a very important fact to Masons to know that all three "cubes" were found practically in the centre of the temples in whatever part of the ancient world we still find remains, and although we do not find all the "emblems," especially those on the top, we venture to express an opinion that very few would expect to do so after the lapse of time that has taken place since these were erected and in general use, to the present time when they have been discovered as "ruins." Nevertheless, there is quite sufficient in all and every one of these to prove that as far as the R.A. ceremonies of the present day are practised we have evidence of the same here in all these temples.

We are of an entirely different opinion from *Evans* in his decipherment of all these "early Grecian remains," but we fully acknowledge that we are very much indebted to him for his lucid description of them, his beautiful pictures of what he finds, and also the work he has put before us, but at the same time, to our minds, he has missed the whole key of decipherment, as many others of our present archæologists have done, and we hold that this is entirely due to a want of knowledge of the Egyptian *Ritual*, and the fact of not understanding the Eschatology of this and Freemasonry in the higher degrees of the present day.

The natural argument against this is that all these cubes were the same size, form, shape, etc., with the same symbol on each. Yes, quite so, but we have to take time and evolution into consideration, as well as the "lost records," and from our knowledge of the past, it will teach us that the same three cubes, one on each other, instead of side by side, is the order of the principal originals, 1st, 2nd, 3rd, and it is a very interesting fact that in all the ancient remains of temples that we find throughout the whole world, in the centre of the temples we have the cube—the double cube—or, as *Evans* has found amongst the early Greeks, the treble cube; all signifying the same as our present double cubes in R.A.M., and all the same that we find in the oldest and most ancient Egyptian, from which all these were brought forward, as may be seen from the 64th chapter of the *Ritual*. Horus, N. at the top, Shu at the middle or equinox, Sut, S. at the bottom. With two cubes only, or the double cube, Shu's is absent, it is Horus and Sut only, S. being the equinox.

Mr Evans, writing of these Cretans and Mycenæan signs that had found, states that about 20 per cent. of their Cretan hieroglyphics approach those of the Egyptian in character, and twenty out of the thirty-two linear signs are practically identical with those found in Egypt, but if we study the oldest pictorial hieroglyphics and the oldest linear signs of Egypt we find that 98 per cent. are the same; the other two signs are not definite. (From published records.) We believe it was Emanuel de Rougé who read a paper in 1859 before the Académie des Inscriptions who first drew attention and came to the conclusion that the derivation of the Phœnician, and through that all other alphabets now in use, were taken from the ancient Egyptians. They were not taken from the "hieroglyphic pictures" of the Egyptian monuments, but from the cursive characters which the Egyptians had developed out of the hieroglyphics and which were employed for literary and secular purposes; and it is proved beyond doubt that the linear signs were used and in existence in the Neolithic

Egyptian Age. Pages 295 and 298 ("The Mediterranean Races," *Sergi*) show some of these alphabetical signs found encased in clay vessels and collected by *De Morgan*, which may be compared with those discovered in the eastern Mediterranean by *Mr Evans*, as Cretan, Mycenæan or Ægean and therefore of course pre-Phœnician. These cursive characters really formed the first alphabet that ever existed, and from these the Phœnician, and hence all other, alphabets emanated. Eusebius, Plato and Tacitus all state that the Phœnicians did not claim to be themselves the inventors of the art of writing, but admitted that it was obtained by them from Egypt. Therefore the Egyptians were the inventors of the alphabet.

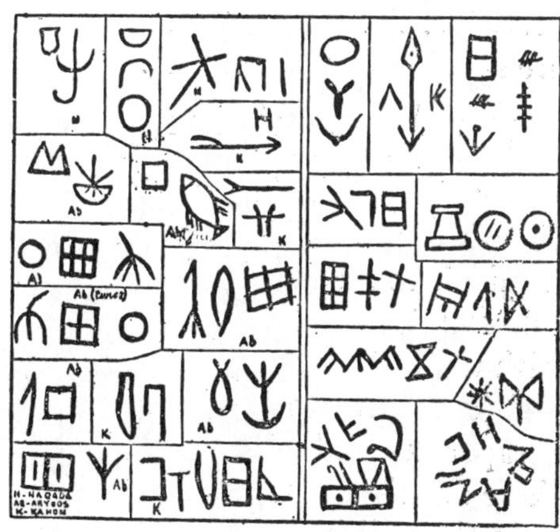

Fig. 23.—Comparison of Alphabetiform Signs (Evans).

To understand all the different Signs and writings we find throughout the world, and their apparent dissimilarity, we must go back to the various and earliest exodes from Egypt, those that went out at the time of the Stellar Mythos, Lunar and Solar. Remains of good examples of the first and last are still in existence here in England—namely, Harland Bay in Cornwall (Stellar Mythos) and the Druids, of Solar Mythos, not forgetting that in all these cases one overlapped the other.

The Sign placed above in the Egyptian and Assyrian figures is well known and used by R.A.M.'s (explanation of which will be given later on); but we notice the absence of this in the photograph from Uxmal, and we have not been able to find the sign depicted upon any of the walls or mural carvings in Mexico. These objects, found in Yucatan, are not the only objects connecting the Old with the New World. Not only in Yucatan, but throughout North and South America, we find various things common to both Europe and America, the origin of which can be traced to Egypt.

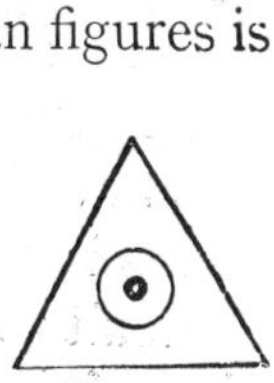

Fig. 24.

The art of weaving was practised in the two hemispheres in

prehistoric times. Woven fabrics have been found in the Swiss Lake dwellings, in Scandinavia and in nearly all parts of Europe belonging to the Neolithic Age; and in America we find the same. And it is a fact that prehistoric man of the two hemispheres had the knowledge to spin fibre and thread, to wind it on bobbins (see spindle wheels found in museums), having the same Sign on them wherever found—*viz.* the Swastika 卐 [1] and to wind it into fabrics, and whatever difference there may have been in pattern, thread or cloth, they were finally and substantially the same art, and so are likely to have been the product of the same inventor. Also, the polished stone hatchets of the two hemispheres are substantially the same. There are differences of material, of course, for in each country the workman was obliged to use such material as was obtainable. There are differences in form between the polished stone hatchets of the two hemispheres, but so also there are differences between different localities in the same hemisphere; some hatchets are long, others short, some round, others flat, some have pointed ends, others square or nearly square with unfinished ends, some are large, others small. But all these differences are to be found well preserved in each hemisphere. Scrapers have also been found in both hemispheres and in all ages; there are the same differences in material, form and appearance as in the polished stone hatchet. The art of drilling in stone was known over an extended area in prehistoric times, and we find innumerable examples which must have been prepared in both hemispheres substantially in the same manner and with the same machine. Also the art of sawing stone—also the aboriginal art of making pottery was carried on in a similar manner, their geometric decorations being common to both. Jade implements have also been found in each country, the raw material of which has never been found in sufficient quantities to justify anyone in saying that it is indigenous to all countries. It is extremely difficult to work owing to its density and hardness, yet the operation of drilling, cutting, polishing, carving, etc., must have been conducted on similar lines. The markings on all these were similar in many forms—*i.e.* there were "common markings of signs and symbols on these things in every part of the world," and,

[1] This Swastika was also the most sacred sign amongst the British Druids—see later.

as we shall prove, the Stellar Mythos was universal, and the Solar that followed, replaced or absorbed this in a greater part of the world ; but even at the present date we find that all the " aborigines " have still the remains of the earlier Stellar Mythos, where the Solar never reached them.

We fail to see the force of arguments or reasons for assuming that these various natives and prehistoric people have each and separately evolved all their ideas and Totemic ceremonies, etc., from their own surroundings and experiences, as many writers would have us believe.

We, on the contrary, say that this could not have been so, looking to the various people in different parts of the world, all having the same Totemic ceremonies, the same signs and symbols, the same works of rude arts, all point most conclusively to one common origin, and we believe that the following pages will prove that this was Egypt.

Several other Masonic signs have been met with amongst the Australian aborigines. Their form of oath is identical with that in Genesis xxiv. 9. They also name children as Leah named her child, " Gad," Genesis xxx. 2, and they adopt the —— in Deuteronomy xii., xiii., xxiii.

CHAPTER IV

Spencer and *Gillen*, speaking of the Australian tribes, say, "What we have to deal with is a great continental area, peopled most probably by men who entered from the north and brought with them certain customs. The most striking fact in regard to these customs at the present day is that, over the whole continent, so far as is known, we can detect a community of social organisations sufficient to show that all the tribes, inhabiting various parts, are the offspring of ancestors who, prior to migrating in various directions over the continent, already practised certain customs, and have the germs of an organisation which had been developed along different lines in different localities. The class and Totem systems variously modified, which are now found in different tribes, can only be adequately accounted for on the hypothesis that when their ancestors reached the country they spread about in various directions, separated into local groups and developed along various lines, without the stimulus derived from contact with outside people, each group retaining features in its customs and organisations such as can only be explained by supposing them to have had a common ancestry."

The Engwura ceremony, which forms the last of the initiatory rites of the Arunta tribe, admitting the initiate to all the most sacred secrets of the tribe, consists of a long series of ceremonies taking in all over four months to perform.[1]

The whole past history of the tribe may be said to be bound up with these Totemic ceremonies, all of which are concerned with the doings of certain Ancestors who lived in the past, back so far away that their origin has been totally forgotten, but, as we shall show later on, are identical with the Nilotic Negro of the present day, the Australian aborigines being an exodus from these early people.

[1] "The Native Tribes of Central Australia," by *Baldwin Spencer*, M.A., and *F. J. Gillen*, published by Macmillan & Co. Ltd., who have kindly allowed us to reproduce some of their plates.

The Intichiuma ceremonies of the Arunta tribe are amongst the most primitive now extant upon the earth. These are performed as sacred mysteries in various modes of Sign Language, by which the thought, the wish, the want is expressed magically in act, instead of or in addition to words.

These ceremonial rites were established as the means to memorise facts in Sign Language, when there were not any written records of the human past. In these, the knowledge was acted, the *Ritual* was exhibited and kept in ever-living memory by continual repetition, and the mysteries, Totemic or religious, were founded on the basis of action.

"The Inapertwa beings," in the Alcheringa, "who preceded men and women," were "Homo"—pre-Totemic. They were the gregarious horde of earliest man, with its general promiscuity of intercourse between the sexes—the time when all had one Sign Language, with few verbal words; and were the earliest formation of human society, distinguishable from the general body. They were divided into *two clans or moieties with a Totem for each*, and afterwards subdivided again, with a Totem to distinguish each. Each Totem or clan was recognised by its special dance—known to all. The Totem type was thus figured to Sign and Gesture Language before it could be known by name.

The Egyptian sign of Tem-tu is the Hieroglyph from whence the name is derived. It is the figure of a total, composed of two halves [hieroglyph],[1] and the whole body of natives were first divided into two halves or moieties and afterwards subdivided.

Each tribe, distinguished by its Totem, descended from the female—mother of the tribe, as the blood-motherhood which gave the blood-brotherhood, there being no fatherhood at the time, as a child did not know its own father but did its mother—the descent thus always being reckoned in the female line—mother. In Totemism the motherhood is divided between two sisters or a mother and elder daughter. The dual motherhood is followed by the twin brotherhood, which we find in Egyptian Mythology. The first thing to regulate primitive marriage was the Totem given to the girl at the time of the pubescent or marriageable state. In being Totemic she was recognised by her Zootype—*i.e.* by the reptile, beast or bird of the Totem into which she had first made her transformation at the time of puberty—all her children be-

[1] Bunsen, page 536. Tem-tu.

longed to that Totem—each clan or tribe, then, descended from "a mother" at first, who had conferred upon her, at the period of puberty, a "Totem," by which she was known and recognised throughout the world. In a state of sexual promiscuity the first thing of importance was to determine the mother-blood—thus the primary need for the Totem. The mother was first for many thousands of years—the child was known as hers from the beginning, the husband was not; her duty was that of breeder for the group—bearer for the tribe. There was no individual love allowed or, at least, not acknowledged. The human race did not descend from beasts, birds, etc., as some tales tell you (except by evolution). These were but the names of the Totemic Zootypes assigned to the mothers of the clans, when there was no individual fatherhood determinable. When the clans divided, separated, redivided and occupied different territories, each with a different name or Totem by which they were known, they had the sole right, at first at least, to live, eat and barter with other tribes that particular food which they represented by their Totem. In the social aspect Totemism was a means of regulating the supply of food. It was also a badge, crest or arms or symbol of the blood-motherhood, but it was *first of all* a sign of female pubescence and a personal means of making known the fact.

It is very often difficult to distinguish between the *human mother* in Totemism and the Great Mother in Mythology because the same types were employed. In Totemism the mother and motherhood, the sister and sisterhood, the brother and brotherhood, the girl who transformed at puberty, the two women who were ancestresses, etc., *were all human*; but when the same characters have been continued in Mythology they are not—they are super-human—they have been divinised. Totemism is not derived from Mythology—it was prior to Mythology, but it has been mixed up with it, because the same *Sign Language* was employed in both.

Totemism is the *first Sign Language in forms, symbols and ceremonies to express their ideas, thoughts and beliefs*, it is a Sign Language in all its phases, which must have taken thousands of years to work out, and to read and understand which, you must take all separately; you cannot group them together. These cannot be as a metaphysical whole; perhaps some would class them as a mathematical whole, which is best called integral, when several parts which make up the whole are really distinct from one another, and each of them may subsist apart ; of course there is a physical or essential whole which may include all the essential modes, attributes or properties which are contained in the comprehension of their ideas. These are acted symbolically and dramatically, more to impress them upon the minds of the individuals concerned, having only this "Sign Language" to enable them to transmit from one generation to another their then ideas and beliefs as regards the departed spirits—the spirit world and life hereafter, as well as what has gone before. And before Totemism, how many thousands of years did man exist "working out this Sign Language" and formulating articulate sounds ?

To answer this we must go back to the first Pygmies, probably over a million years. These began the "Sign Language" and first evolved articulate sounds. The remains of these little men have been found in the lower and upper quarternary period, 500,000 years old, and a skeleton has recently been found in a coal bed in America, the date of which would probably be more remote.

When man began to observe and think he would see different forces at work throughout all nature ; he must have noticed the changes of the moon, the movements of the stars, the sun's eclipse, seasons of the year and some of the different forces and powers in the universe, celestial as well as terrestrial. Each of these powers, these forces of nature would appeal to him, and having only a limited number of words to express his thoughts he would naturally adopt an animal, a bird, a fish or something that he could see, and by association with it would convey to his mind one of the powers or forces which would be represented by a sign or drawing of the animal or bird, etc. This would be before he had worked out "Totemism proper," but it was the beginning and origin of Totemism. We see that they represented death, night and darkness sometimes by a crocodile's tail, because the tail was the last to disappear under the water when the beast retired at night, and death, because it struck its prey with its tail to kill before eating. Its head, with eyes, for the same reason, represented light, day, etc., because it was the first part to come up out of the dark water in the morning. The serpent was often a representation of regeneration either of the soul or life because they noticed that the snake cast its skin and, so to speak, came forth a new serpent, it had regenerated itself. Dozens of other examples we could give, but these are sufficient to explain their ideas. So they defined those objects or animals or birds, etc., by a collection of such parts or properties of them as might best explain it, so far as they could observe and know and best distinguish it from other things by a collection of those properties, which, according to their observation, distinguish them from all other things into nominal essences and nominal definitions. Of course the perfect definition of any being or animal or bird always includes the definition of the name whereby it is called, for it informs us of the sense or meaning of the word and shows us what idea that word is affixed to; but the definition of the name does not by any means include a perfect definition of the thing, and therefore these definitions of things are but mere nominal descriptions, hence the reason for their so-called "compound animals," etc., which we find they pictured. It is of very little use trying to find the "Origin of Totemism" and what it originally meant by studying *only the Australian Aborigines, American Indians and other tribes in Eastern Asia, the Pacific Islands, etc.*, as *Mr Andrew Lang* appears to have done. One may certainly, after doing so, have "a guess" as he has; but it would be guess and guess again for all time. To arrive at any degree of certainty on the subject one must go to Inner Africa, amongst those tribes that have not yet been affected by the Christians and Mohammedans, and be conversant with the Stellar Mythos, the Primordial and the Ritual. In studying *only the Totemic Ceremonies of those who went out from the Nile valley thousands of years ago and carried with them the Stellar Mythos, as far as these had been evolved*, you could not arrive, from this alone, at a true and definite conclusion; you may conjecture this or that, and form various theories, but you would have no definite proof as to the origins and true meanings. But the study of these people and their Totemic Ceremonies all over the world gives you a most important and conclusive proof of one fact, and that is this: although you may find modified differences amongst various tribes in all parts of the world at this period of exodus, you still find so much that is common to all that it proves that there must have been one common centre, and they must have one common origin—and we maintain that origin was the Nile valley and sources of the Nile—old Egypt: therefore, to obtain the true meaning we shall have to make research in Central Africa amongst the Pygmies and other tribes who still practise Hypnotism and Clairvoyance: and the true meaning is as we have here shown, which is proved by what is still extant in the *Ritual*. Here only shall we find the key to the true original meaning of the "Spirit Worship."

This "Spirit Worship," so-called, arose in the mind of man when he observed the various powers and attributes of the forces of nature—water flowing, trees growing, darkness and all associated with it; the heavens as the Great Weeper, and light, which was considered as the source of life to man and all else. From these powers they would imbibe their "Spiritual Ideas," and so would commence the beginning of their "Mythos," each at first with a Sign and Symbol, and afterwards a name would be attached or connected with each power or attribute, and one greater than all would become to them "The One" Great Power or "Spirit," and then the others would be attached as attributes and powers of "The One." Thus we find Sut at first was the "Great One," because they looked upon him as the "King of Darkness"; but as soon as light and day came he was deposed, and Horus I., as god of life and light, took his place. Then was Sut put down as the "Evil One" because he was the "King of Darkness." Horus then would be symbolical of light, of life, etc.; later he says, "I am the light of the world." He represented youth, the green shoots of trees and everything that was good. But it took them ages and ages to work out this Sign Language first, and the so-called "Spirit Worship" which followed; and ages more before they had worked out "Ancestral worship," and thousands of years more must have passed before they had worked out and perfected their Eschatology.

We perfectly agree with *Spencer* and *Gillen* [1] when they state that the lack of record is no proof that certain ceremonies do not exist, when apparently all are observed, by a man who has been initiated, like *Mr Howitt*. The question would arise how far has he been initiated? Except he proved to these people that he believed in Hypnotism and Clairvoyance, we doubt if he would be admitted to their most sacred rites. *Starcke*, like ourselves, holds the opinion that Totems are relatively late, and the tribes with none are more primitive, like the Pygmies and Masaba negroes. *Mr Andrew Lang* calls this an eccentric "opinion!" but it is undoubtedly true, and few, we believe, would attempt to dispute that the Pygmies and Masaba Negroes are not of more primitive date than the Nilotic Negroes, from whom the Australian

[1] "Native Tribes of Australia"—*Spencer* and *Gillen*.

and others, possessing Totems, originated, and although the Pygmies and Masaba Negroes believe in "Spirits," they have no "Totems," and all were in common, it was only when they first divided into "moieties" that Totems were first instituted, as we have already shown. It must have taken thousands of years to evolve the Totems, because this Totemism is part or beginning of and was included in the Stellar Mythos. *Mr Lang* "believes that the Eagle Hawk and Crow were creatures in some mythos, and that in Egypt the animal gods had once, it seems all but certain, been Totems." If *Mr Andrew Lang* was conversant with the Primordial of the Egyptians, he would hardly have written "The Secret of the Totem," with the evident conviction that his "speculative opinion" is right. The Eagle Hawk is representative of Horus I., and the Crow, Sut, the same as the Eagle or Vulture, and Blackbird and Black Duck with other tribes; these are of Egyptian origin and "religious conceptions." It belongs to the Stellar Mythos, and in the origin of this Stellar Mythos lies all the secrets of Totemism. In our minds Totemism—that is, the possession by different tribes of different name-giving animals—is older than exogamy in all cases. The marital or sexual relations were at first promiscuous; then there was a division of the gregarious into two classes or communities, in which the primal promiscuity was regulated for group marriages, with the totality divided into two halves and subdivided afterwards by the Totems, which were extended more and more until they reached the "Chinese hundred families." The Arunta have traditions of a time when a man always married a sister of his own Totem, this, as tribal, followed the marriage of the brother and sister of the blood in natural endogamy—the same intermarriage that is found in African Totemism. After the tribes were subdivided and redivided, it was a case of exogamy, but the *Primary Totem* was given to the first mother of the tribe, when they first divided into clans, to distinguish or make known that the girl was pubescent, and to show or prove the motherhood, and it is proved beyond a doubt in all parts of the world that endogamy existed for a long period. The royal families of the Incas, like those of Egypt, married their sisters, which was a custom to keep the blood-motherhood pure—this was the original.

The fundamental idea, common to all nations who practise Totemic ceremonies *at the present time*, is "food." Each Totemic group is responsible for the maintenance of the supply of food which gives its name to the group, and their object is always to increase their food supply : if we are Kangaroo men we supply food for the Emu men, and in return expect them to provide Emu food for us, and so on right throughout the Totems.

Mr Lang's ideas represent to us the "most obvious and sensible appearances that he sees" ; but he should penetrate further into the "mode, nature, properties, reasons, causes and effects" of what these Totems represent. We must survey these in all their parts to obtain a complete idea of them, and consider all the modes, attributes, properties and relations of the "original" in order to obtain a comprehensive conception of the truth. When we were in Africa, living amongst many native tribes, it was only because we knew many Masonic signs and symbols, and could hypnotise clairvoyants, that we obtained their confidence to be shown and have the explanation given us of many of their most sacred ceremonies.

The belief in reincarnation must be traced back to the change of the Pole Stars in the circle of precession, mythical but not human.

One of the most interesting points, perhaps, to Mark Masons is that of the ceremony of the "Churinga" or Sacred Stone, sometimes a white stone, or, when this could not be obtained, a piece of hard wood, although originally it was supposed to be all of white stone. It is given to the initiate with his sacred name on it, which is only known to those who have been initiated to this degree, and to those of the same Totem as himself.

Perhaps the most interesting and, we might add, extraordinary proofs that this Sacred Churinga and its Sacred Mark and Name have been handed down by the brotherhood for thousands of years, lies in the fact that we still practise the same customs and observe the same solemn obligations amongst us as these poor natives of Australia, New Guinea, Solomon Islands and others, with regard to it, as may be seen by the most obtuse thinker and observer. In proof of the above, let us say, without divulging any secrets, that the Jewel given to a "Mark" is made of a white stone, of durable material, in the form of the "Northern horizon"—eight letters are engraved on one side, representing originally the SEVEN Glorious Ones with "THE ONE" added—on the other side the sacred name "which no man knows saveth he that receiveth it." It is not a mere ornamental appendage of this degree, but it is a sacred token of the rites of friendship and brotherly love, *and its presentation at any time by the owner to another "Mark"* would claim for the latter certain acts of friendship which are of solemn obligations among the fraternity. A "Mark" thus presented for the purpose of obtaining a favour is said to be pledged, though remaining in the possession of the owner: nor can it be again used by him until, either by the return of the favour or the consent of the benefactor, it has been returned: for it is a positive law of the order that no "Mark shall pledge his mark a second time until he has redeemed it from its previous pledge." This is sufficient to prove that the present custom of the "Mark Sacred Stone" is identical in every way with the Sacred Churinga, and this custom is still carried on by the aboriginal Australians and others, who brought it from Ancient Egypt.

Spencer and *Gillen* state that it is the custom amongst the various tribes to lend their Sacred Churingas to each other, and that these are always returned again to those who lent them, sacred ceremonies being performed and conducted with great solemnity, with these words: "We return your great Churinga, which have made us glad; we bring you a present of these Imituya and Uliara, and are sorry we could not bring more, but the Anthinna is scarce and hair does not grow quickly."[1] All authors hitherto have only been able to state that "the origin of the Mark is unknown," but *give a tradition* that it was founded at the building of King Solomon's Temple, seven days after the foundation stone was laid. This is on the same equivalent as these poor aborigines; they give you their version: "their fathers did it," "it has always been"; but the true meaning and decipherment has been lost to them. The mark M. D. undoubtedly is the "section" of the *Ritual* which brings on for ages past "the sacred stone, where the sacred name of him who receiveth it is marked and known only to him." Much more could be written on this part of the origin of our ceremonies, but we think we have shown enough to all students to prove our contention, and those who are interested can follow the same by reference to the *Ritual* and the Egyptian Primordial, and studying

[1] "Native Tribes of Central Australia," by *Spencer* and *Gillen*, chap. v., published by Macmillan & Co.

Spencer and *Gillen's* "Native Tribes of Central Australia," and other works which deal with this subject. "We must preserve the Secrets" from those who are not entitled to know them.

"*The Churinga was not thought to be a Spirit*," but, inasmuch as the spirit was everlasting and imperishable, *so was it symbolised by the "white stone"* or white ivory, or the most durable thing they could find.

The secret name is never uttered except on some most solemn occasion, and then only to the fully initiated or to the men of the same Totemic group, when it is spoken in a whisper; the most elaborate precautions being taken lest it should be heard by anyone who is not a member of the "group." When he dies and is buried, this name is never mentioned again by anyone, not even amongst them with whom he was initiated; this is the custom also of the natives of the Solomon Islands, New Guinea and the Hebrides Islanders. The markings on those Churingas and sacred objects differ amongst various tribes, but there are certain hieroglyphics common to all, and *Spencer* and *Gillen* state that these are associated with the oldest tradition and have existed for long ages, irrespective of their origin. These marks we see on the Churinga are found in our own islands, in India, and in fact generally all over the world. The same marks are found in Portuguese Neolithic sites and Paleolithic sites. *Mr A. Lang's* idea of the Arunta and Kaitish tribes—"*that they alone believe in the Churinga Nanga*"—is too ludicrous to discuss, and as far as reincarnation is concerned, since our own bodies must rise in spiritual form at the last day for us to receive rewards or punishments in them, there may be, perhaps, some original cells of each human body, some nuclei or some "*staminæ vitæ*" or primeval seed of life, so to speak, which may remain unchanged through all the stages of life, death, and the grave; these may become the springs and principles of resurrection, and sufficient to denominate it the same body; but if there be any such constant and vital atoms, which distinguish every human body, they are known to God only.

The natives have forgotten their origin, and they give their own interpretation. In Egypt we find the key, because the ceremonies of the Arunta and other tribes correspond in so many particulars to those in vogue in Egypt at the time of Atum, and nowhere else can we find the original.

"To him that overcometh, I will give him to eat of the hidden manna . . . and I will give to him a white stone, and in the stone a New Name written, which no man knoweth, saveth he that receiveth it" (Rev. ii. 17).

This was given to the initiate in the Totemic and religious mysteries. In the mysteries of Amenta a white stone or "Pillar of Crystal" is given to the initiate; as he comes forth in triumph from the examination, he is asked what the Judges have awarded him and he replies "a flame of fire and a Pillar of Crystal" (*Ritual*, ch. cxxv.).

Even in the earlier Christian doctrines one of the greatest gifts that could be given to the true believers of the Church of Pergamos was "a white stone," and on this stone a new name written which no man knew, save he that received it—which was the direct allusion to the older Mythos.

Collins states that in some of the Totemic ceremonies of the Australians they are equipped with long tails made of grass, representing the leopard's skin tail that hangs down behind, as seen in the Pygmy dance, and as seen in the Egyptian monuments, etc. The Sun Totem is performed by men of the Unjiamba Totem whose *maternal grandmother* was a member of the Sun Totem—one carries a small Nurtunga (a sacred pole) the other a small flat disc with a central spot of red  and lines radiating out from this to represent the rays. In the Kaitish tribe the Sun is called Okerka; it is supposed to have risen in the form of a woman in the east, and to have travelled to a place called Allumba. All this shows and proves that with these the maternal was prior to the paternal, and the oldest form amongst the Zapotecs, Mexicans and tribes of Central America is Yax Cocahmut, the Great Mother—*i.e.* the earth goddess, the earliest form of Isis, and in America is represented with the "rattling board" in her hand that representative of the Sistrum of the Egyptians. It is instructive also that an Egyptian scarabæus was found in the lake Amatitlan.

In the Stellar Mythology, the Pole and central spot of red, with lines radiating and circle around would represent the "Mount of Heaven," the North Pole Star representing Horus, Lord of the Red Crown, and the seven Pole Stars circling round. The North Pole was called "Nurtunga" and the other Pole, which was always placed south, was called "Warringa," represented Sut. Each of these, later in the Solar Mythos and Eschatology, was brought on and represented the two Tatt Pillars of the Egyptians, and is a sign of stability, establishing or founding, as is shown by its use in the ceremony of "young men making." The heaven is thus shown in two parts, north and south, as the domains of Horus and Sut, and later was followed by three divisions, which were upraised by Shu, as establisher of the equinox. This heaven in three divisions was the heaven of the Triangle, which preceded the one built on the square by Ptah. Sut and Horus had been the twin builders and the founders of north and south; Shu followed with the new foundation in the equinox—the horizons—east and west. The disc, here above shown, represents "Aten" and was an ancient form of Her-Mahu-Horus, god of the double horizon in Egypt, and was not a worship of a Solar deity: it was an emblem of the circle made by "Aten" as the god of the double horizon. We find the same disc amongst the North American Indians connected with the Swastika Totem—see later.

There are many Totemic ceremonies, which may all be traced to the time of Atum, in Egypt, all being identical with those practised there, if deciphered symbolically; such, for instance, as the subincision or Arilthа, of which no one hitherto has been able to give the reason or origin.

The traditions of the Alcheringa[1] ancestors are precisely similar to those found in "The Book of the Dead," relating how Osiris was murdered and mutilated, and how Isis and Nephthys went in search of his body and mutilated organ.—*Plutarch*.

Amongst the Warramunga, Walpari and Wulmala, the name of Alcheringa is Thuthu, which is the same as the Egyptian Tertetuu, and means the two ancestors—*i.e.* Isis and Nephthys. The two Hawks—as Isis and Nephthys may be seen depicted in the Papyrus, Trinity College, Dublin, iv., also in Berlin Museum, No. 1470 and in Plates VI. and VII. fig. 8 and fig. A in "The Book of the Dead," by Sir Le Page Renouf. These Mythical Ancestors were the pre-homo of the present race of Aborigines, when they were all a "common herd." The two Ancestors were

[1] Name given to the far past times in which the mythical ancestors of the tribe are supposed to have lived.

the first two women who were THE FIRST TWO MOTHERS, so made and distinguished by the division into two tribes, and the ceremony o f" opening" was performed, and the Totem given to each, so that the blood-motherhood might be known and kept, and these tribes have special class names for women and *count their descent on the maternal line, which is the earliest form.* Hathor or Isis—Mut—sometimes depicted by a bird, differing in various tribes and countries, but always Mut, the Great Mother. The original was "The Mother Earth" in their earliest mythology and Sign Language; and "Alpita" is Egyptian. "Aputi" is messengers—*i.e.* the two envoys. The word Kuntamara is Egyptian Kent, to slit; and many other words amongst these tribes, as well as those of New Zealand and the Solomon Islands, are purely Egyptian.

Circumcision was performed by the ancient Egyptians and also the Ariltha—see "Book of the Dead," chapter 58—"they are the drops of blood which came forth from the phallus of Ra when he went forth to perform mutilations upon himself"—*Budge*, "Book of the Dead," chapter 17. It is more than probable that the reason why circumcision and subincision were practised by the earlier Egyptians was as a preventative to disease. In all probability they found that circumcision was not sufficient in some cases to prevent disease being contracted, therefore the second ceremony and operation were insisted upon. This, with ablution after—which we find most of the Egyptians practised—would probably prove efficient. Where tribal marriages took place, it was considered important to the health and well-being of the community and to the future generations: hence the death penalty if any man was found who had not submitted to the two operations. This might have been one of their beliefs. There is also another reason why this ceremony is and was practised, and that is, to signify that the boy had now become a man and must be regarded as a begetter, an increaser, a father, a head, etc.[2] Anointing has since taken its place amongst Christian nations. *Mr Andrew Lang,* in speaking of *circumcision or subincision* (surely he does not think that these are one and the same), says

[1] On the Naopharos statuette in the Vatican there is an inscription to this effect, "that the Great Mother was born the first, in the time when as yet there had been no birth."

[2] *See* Appendix.

it is "a cruel process unknown outside Australia"; but let us assure him that it was undoubtedly the general custom at one time amongst all the nations of this period of exodus. There is a history on record that the natives of Madagascar used to practise the same rites, subincision and circumcision, but that it has died out, and very few now even practise circumcision. It was also practised amongst the Makalanges, etc., and in fact, as far as we can trace, amongst all tribes of natives at a remote period, and the meaning of it we give. Probably we shall find that it is still practised by some tribes in New Guinea, Solomon Islands and New Hebrides, and was by the Mexicans and Zapotecs, as is shown in *Seler's* "Twenty Days' Sign."

The rite is African originally. It is still practised by the Fan (or Fang) Tribes. An uncircumcised native is not considered as a man either for fighting, working or inheriting, but is regarded as a nonentity and not allowed to marry. The rite proves the reality of manhood (*Nassau*, "Fetishism of W. Africa").

We read in the history of Creation—one version—as follows :—

ȧnuk pu hat-ȧ em khefā-ȧ tataȧt-nȧ

em khaibit-ȧ kher-nȧ em re-ȧ tches-ȧ

ȧshesh-nȧ em Shu tefnet-nȧ em Ṭafnut

ȧn ȧtef-ȧ Nu (*Another Version.*)

"hat-ná em khefá-á i-ná áb-á em ṭet-á āaāa kehr em re-á áshesh-ná em Shu tāf-ná em Ṭāfnut."
Khepera-ná em neter uā netru Khemt pu re-á Kheperiut em Ta pen hāā áref Shu Tāfnut em Nu unen-sen āmi.

Here we have again, evidently in a later version, the origin and meaning—as then understood—of this act.

[1] In the Mesopotamian Creation legend we find that they copied the Egyptians and made man out of the blood of Marduk or copied this from the Assyrians, who obtained it from the Egyptians.

The meaning is clearly spiritual, and we must remember that the ancients expressed their ideas regarding spiritual life in a material and dramatic form; in fact, they had no other way of doing so, not having the language to use as we have now, and although it was expressed in a gross form the meaning was not such. The creation of man or men and women was mystical in one sense and in another Totemic, and so the history of the race may be divided into pre-Totemic and Totemic, pre-human and human. It is in Atum or Tum, the son of Ptah, that man is perfected; in him the motherhood is superseded by the fatherhood. The motherhood, which was first and primary, terminates in the mythology of Egypt, and the fatherhood takes its place at the time of Ptah, at the commencement of the Solar Mythos. The creation here is "blood and spirit," the double primitive essence first assigned to Ptah. The self-mutilation or "cutting" of the male member of Ra or Atum Ra was a mode of showing the derivation from the human father in suppression of the motherhood. The same story is found amongst the Guatemalans, their Quiché god, Tohel, is the same as the Egyptian Atum Ra—see *Bancroft*. In the section which says "that the eye of Nu was unable to make itself seen until after Shu and Tufnut hadcome into being" means: that until the thick watery vapour, which at first surrounded the earth, had sufficiently condensed to form the outer crust of the earth, the sun's rays could not penetrate through it, and so give life and birth to the cells and germs of life, which afterwards should form all those beings which have inhabited the earth, and that these first twin gods, male and female, meant to represent the first germs of life, either as water and earth, or organic cells or germs, should thus be created and nourished by them, by the divine will. A very important passage, which will enable one to understand the "History of the Creation" better, that these twin gods proceeded from Khepera in one way, as we find from one version, and from his mouth in the other version, simply expresses the action and their idea of emission of the divine words and will from the Creator.

FIG. 25.—"Mexican Antiquities," p. 616, fig. N.

We see from this figure that the Central American States had the same history of Creation. This figure depicts Atum in the act as above.

Anuk pu hat-ai em Khefà-à tataát-na em Khaibit-à Kher-ná em re-á tches-á ashesh-nà em Shu tefnet-ná em Tafnut án atef-á Nu.

We think that the words in another part of the text—Khut-ná-em ab-á—"I worked a charm upon my heart or will" *should read or be translated as*: I worked—or willed—or sent forth "a light" from my heart.

In the older version the "tears" of Khepera fell upon his organs and turned into human beings. Horus I. says to the "Chiefs of Ra": "Ye are the tears made by me, in your name of men." The tears of Horus here mean or represent the rain which waters and fructifies the earth, and this, with Ra, the sun's rays—"Chiefs of Ra" cause the germs of life to grow and "come into being." Without the rain and the sun's rays, seeds and germs could not grow or come into being. The sun was considered the greatest fecundator, and however grossly the old scribes recorded their ideas, we must remember that they had no words otherwise to record the same.

From reading the records of the past it is impossible for anyone not to comprehend the fact that they had the knowledge of evolution, and although expressed apparently in gross terms, it is quite clear that rain or "tears" and the sun's rays were the cause, in the first instance, of the germination of the primordial cells of life, and from this all others came into being. The question of the origin of the *first* cell of life on this earth, from which all the living inhabitants descended, is one that can only be answered by the Divine Creator; but, given the first cell of life, all others follow.

We cannot agree with *Dr Wallis Budge* in his assuming that Nu and Khepera were the same, quite on the contrary; Nu may be said to represent the watery vapour, and Shu, our Sun (the centre of our planetary system), Tufnut, the Moon, and Khepera was the Divine Spirit of the Great God, who made not only this Earth and our Sun and the rest of the Planets, but as we read of in another text, ten other great circles which went round him, and we know that our Sun takes 25,827 years to do this once. That this was most certainly the case may be seen further on. In this text we find that Khepera had made another eye (the first eye being our Sun), which was undoubtedly the Moon; the Moon being thrown off from our Earth as our Earth had been from the Sun; and in another version, the fact that Osiris is made to usurp the position which in the earlier versions was occupied by Khepera, shows that the Osirian doctrines were evolved out of the earlier, and that the Priests substituted one name for another. That the aborigines of Australia practise the imitation of this former rite is another good proof to those we shall bring forward, that they came out of Egypt at the time of Horus I. and before the Osirian doctrine had come into existence.

Shu, who is at a late period called the Son of Ra, is also called An-heru, the Lifter-up of the Heavens. Seb, the Earth, and Nut, the Sky, have been sleeping in each other's arms during the night, and Shu, Daylight or Sun's Rays, parts them, and then there is seen the raised sky above the earth.

The great battle between Sut and Horus primarily is spoken of in later texts as "The night of Conflict"—*i.e.* the defeat of the Children of Failure at Elephantina: "Then was conflict in the entire universe, in heaven and upon earth"—*Ritual*, chap. xvii. page 34. The "Children of Failure" are the elements of darkness, "*night*," which melt away and vanish at the approach of the sun's rays—*Day*. See "Battle of Sut and Horus," p. 8.

Nu represented the watery vapour surrounding this earth, before it had cooled down, and had Nut for his consort. Shu presented the Sun as one and the first Eye of Khepera, Tufnut, the Moon, as the other eye of Khepera. At the same time we must not forget that all these different names of gods were simply *the various attributes of the One God*. In the 17th chapter of the *Ritual* it says: "His names together compose the cycle of the gods"; an important passage if one wishes to understand the true Eschatology of these ancient people; in fact it is quite impossible to obtain any true version or idea without. The aboriginal Australians have a legend about Bymee, "The Great Father Spirit," as having a totem name for every part of his body, even to a different one for each finger and toe, which is simply the various attributes of the "Great Spirit Father." They have forgotten the original meaning but we find it in the *Ritual* in Egypt. In the 17th chapter of "The Book of the Dead" it is said: "I am the Great God—self created, that is to say, who made his names"—"the company of the gods as God." Who then is this? It is Ra, "*who created names for his members and these came into being in the form of the gods who are in the following of Ra*," and in another part of the same chapter of Khepera[1] "*that the cycle of the gods is his body*."

[1] Ra is substituted in the later texts.

This is a clear proof that all the various gods were only powers or attributes of the One God, and at the time of the Solar doctrine they had worked out and added to the original one of the Stellar; changing names, certainly, but the essence was the same.

Dr W. Budge, for instance, gives the number of gods, under the XIXth dynasty, as about 1200, and apparently believes in a distinction between the pre-dynastic element of the Egyptian doctrines and an Asiatic; the latter, he states, "was of Solar character undoubtedly, and was caused by a war, introduced into Egypt by the '*followers of Horus*,' who invaded the country and conquered the natives, settled down there and built up the great dynastic civilisation which we call Egypt." We cannot agree with this. In our opinion all the facts found up to the present time are against it, and Asia had not anything to do with bringing any civilisation or religion into Egypt; on the contrary all the proofs we have brought forward show and prove distinctly that it was otherwise. Asia and the rest of the world obtained all their knowledge originally from the Egyptians. Horus, in all his forms, was essentially Egyptian *from the first*, and was not *after* Osiris, nor did Horus bring the Solar religion into Egypt from outside, as *Dr Budge* states. Horus I. was the God of the Pole Star in the Stellar mythos and Amsu was the risen Horus, the "first man God," "risen in Spirit form," and sometimes called Min, living before the Osirian doctrines were evolved. This was followed by the Lunar and then the Solar doctrines. Then Ra came into being and Osiris: the one the God in spirit, and Osiris the god in mummified form, and "Horus the child" was brought on as the Son: therefore, to say "the followers of Horus, who brought Solar religion with them into Egypt from the East, never succeeded in dislodging Osiris from his exalted position, and his cult survived undiminished, notwithstanding the powerful influence which the Priests of Ra and the worshippers of Amen, and the votaries of Atem respectively exerc[illegible]h the country," shows that he has commenced to study the Egyptian religion much too late to obtain any true conception; that he is "much mixed up," and does not take into account the Primordial at all. Moreover, *Dr Budge*, like many other Egyptologists, evidently labours under the delusion that Horus was a historical person, whereas it was Astronomical Mythology. The wars of Horus were fought in heaven and Amenta against the Sebau, the great evil Apap, and not on earth in Egypt. He was the Lord of Life and Light, and overcame the powers of darkness and drought. These he converts into ethnical personages and glorified natural heroes, which is incorrect: Horus first fought in the Stellar Mythos, then the Solar Mythos, and finally Eschatologically, but this was not historical, it was Astronomical Mythology.

The ceremony of knocking out a front tooth in some tribes, and the throwing of the boomerang in the direction of their mother's camp, or rather their mother's Alcheringa camp, as practised by the Arunta, also the Totemic ceremony, when, after having gone through the several trials and "rites," the Initiate's hair is made white and a Totem is placed on his head, is interesting. This last ceremony is very important and instructive to the student, because if he turn to the "Papyrus of Ani," he will see it depicted that after Ani has been judged and is "justified" his hair is white and a Totem is on his head which corresponds in every particular to that spoken of by *Spencer* and *Gillen*. See in ch. cx. of *Ritual*: "My head is equipped with the white crown." We shall refer to this later on. The Arunta have a triangular stone which is only seen by the initiated men.[1]

In the ceremony of Nurtunga, the fact that the poles were placed North and South shows that the ceremonies connected with the poles must have been practised—originally—in a country where the Pole Stars, looking North and South, were known. In Australia this is impossible; therefore the inference clearly is that in Australia the ceremonies were introduced from a much earlier and older land, where all these ceremonies had been practised for many ages, some, ever since the time of Atum, 20,000 years ago or more; and it is only amongst the ancient Egyptians that we can find the true meaning and key. These divided the heavens into North and South and then Egypt into North and South, as seen by the Crown of the North and Crown of the South—hence the two poles N. and S. These are mentioned and shown in the "Pylon of the Twelfth Division of the Tuat." "In the front of this wall are two poles, each of which is surmounted by a head—one is Teru, the other Khepera—two forms of the god," etc., originally representing the two Poles of the Heavens.

[1] Some tribes in the Solomon Islands practise the same rites and ceremonies: also in the New Hebrides.

The two serpents, as shown in the photograph (page 66) are emblems probably of the two cardinal points, N. and S. In the *Ritual* serpents were often used to denote cardinal points. Four serpents are also shown on the stones found at Ollamh Fodhla in Ireland to denote 4 Quarters or 4 Powers.

It is not necessary to describe all these ceremonies. Our object is only to draw attention to them and to state that our belief is that the present explanation given by the natives is one that has been substituted for the original.

It is immaterial whether we date the exodus of the Australians before the traditional history of Osiris, which would bring us as far back as Horus I., or whether it was Osiris. Hence we contend that the proof we advance is indisputable.

Later on we shall show the connection between Totemic ceremonies and the signs and symbols found amongst the aboriginal Australians and Nilotic and Bantu negroes, as well as those in other parts of the world.

As regards traditional history, some Egyptologists might advance grave doubts as to the accuracy of the same being coincident with the history of Osiris, as mentioned by *Plutarch*, and which, as already stated, may be found in "The Book of the Dead"; but the reader could not fail to acknowledge the *identical tradition* of the history of Osiris by *Plutarch*.

The only point which occurs to the author is this, and it is one which Egyptologists may reasonably object to—namely, knowing, as we do, that the continent of Australia is one of the oldest, which is proved by the present existence of marsupial animals and geological formations, therefore the original inhabitants (Australia) might, and probably did, exist before the mythical Osiris was in Egypt. This would only prove that the whole of the inhabitants dated back still further away in the remoter ages, and came out of Egypt between the first Horus and Osiris, because Horus I. or the Blind Horus existed before Osiris, and the history of his murder, death, etc., was practically the same as that of Osiris. Horus I., or Heru-ur, or Horus the Elder, was the first man-god that we can trace; he died and rose again, and was then called. Amsu or Min, or Horus in Spirit ⚹.[1] Proof

[1] This, as far as we can trace, was the *first* Sign or Hieroglyphic for Amsu. There are various others, but evidently of a later date. Originally it meant "The Great One," "The Chief," "The Mighty One," "The Head," and is recognised as such by the Pygmies now.

of this is found in the Ritual. Osiris was only another name evolved in course of time out of the more ancient doctrines and tales, during the formation of the later Solar Mythos. Horus I. and Amsu being the first form and Stellar, and Orisis and Ra the Solar—Osiris being the man-god or "mummified" and Ra the spiritual form. This is plainly shown in the "Ritual or the Book of the Dead"; therefore the traditional history of the Australians would apply equally to either (and the only point would be the date as regards the remoter period of the past, when the exodus from Egypt took place, as we contend it did—*viz.* at the time of Horus and Stellar Mythos). Then the Mayas also have the same traditional history in Queen Moo and Prince Coh.

Some of the signs of the Churinga and Rock drawings, which *Spencer* and *Gillen* have given, are "marks" and "figures" which the Arunta tribe themselves state have been in use ever since Alcheringa—original Ancestors. They are identical with those found on the stones among the Druidical remains in the British Isles, Yucatan, Mexico and Egypt. Those found and tabulated by *Evans*—Cretan, Ægean and Proto-Egyptian—are undoubtedly Egyptian Hieroglyphics, as may be seen from photographs here shown. Two feet are also depicted on the Rock drawings in several places. These two feet would correspond with the two feet of Buddha, which we draw attention to later on, only these would be the feet of Horus I., here, and Buddha's would represent that of Osiris in the Solar mythos.

Spencer and *Gillen* give these photographs and drawings of many of the characters and signs, etc., found in various parts of the world; and many others given by different writers are not here depicted.

Several of these are parts of the fourteen Aats or domains or divisions of Sekhet-Anru, which the deceased has to reach, and in which he enjoys special privileges.

1. The brow of the waters—the God wherein is Aasekhem.
2. Ha-Sert—the God wherein is Fa-Pet, bearer of Heaven.
3. The brow of fire—the God wherein is Fa-Akk, bearer of Altars.
4. Aat of the Khus.
5. The seven Aats.
6. The serpent Rerek [hieroglyph] which may here represent the North and South poles.
7. The tank of flame.

For Inscription see over.

Churinga Ilkinia of the Ulpmerka of the Plum Tree Totem Drawn on the Rocks at Quiurnpa.

1, 2. Ilyinga or Poison Bones and Sticks made by the Arumburinga of the Ulpmerka.

3–8. Drawings for Painting on the Breasts of the Boys during the Ceremony of throwing them up in the Air.

9. Drawing for the Stomach during the same.

10. A Plum Tree, painted on the Back during the same.

11–13. Drawings for the Back and Stomach during the same.

14. Plum Tree.

15. Drawing for the Back.

16. An Unripe Plum.

17. Drawing for the Back.

18. The Head Nurtunja of Kukaitcha.

19. Ripe and Unripe Plums.

20. Nurtunja of Kukaitcha.

21. Nurtunja of Ulpmerka Men.

22. Head Nurtunja of Kukaitcha.

23. A large Nurtunja and Poison Bone of Kukaitcha.

24. Meaning not known.

25. Head Nurtunja of Kukaitcha.

26. Drawing for the Breast.

Churinga Ilkinia of the Udnirringita Totem, Drawn on the Rocks at the Emily Gorge.

4. Represents the Hand and Arm of an Alcheringa Woman leaning against the Rock.

5., 6., 7. Represent Tracks of Alcheringa Women.

For explanation of these we would refer our readers to the chapters 149-150 of "The Book of the Dead," or the chapter of the Aats, also to the papyri of Hunefer, Anhar-Kerasher and Netchemet, and the papyrus of Nu.

There is also another proof.[1] The Australians use the boomerang, which was one of the weapons of ancient Egypt, as may be seen at Deir-el-Bahari, where there is the statue of a Prince of Punt, carrying a boomerang.

And furthermore, in "The Book of the Underworld," in the region or city of the eleventh hour of the night, we see Horus I. with a disc upon his dead, surrounded by a Uræus, holding in his left hand a boomerang, one end of which terminates in the head of a serpent. The idea here suggested is either the weapon held by the god is a real serpent, which, when thrown at an enemy, will suddenly attach itself to his body, after the manner of a vicious Uræus, or will return and attach itself to its owner, after having been used. This probably is the oldest evidence we have of the boomerang having been known and used in Egypt at the time of the Stellar Mythos, because Horus I. was the principal god and situated or dwelt at the Pole Star at this time. This is a very important fact to recognise, because we find it in use among the aborigines of Australia, and in conjunction with the other signs and symbols which we have brought forward, is a proof that they emigrated from Egypt at the time of the Stellar Mythos and it is a further proof in our belief that the traditional history of their Alcheringa ancestors was derived from Horus I. and not Osiris, which would have brought their exodus thousands of years later.

It must be remembered that the boomerang is found in use amongst other nations in various parts of the world—in America it was in use amongst the Northern and Southern Indians; but this has been fully written on by other authors and it is not necessary to enlarge on the subject here. We only wish to draw attention that to Egypt we must go for the original, and that it could not have emanated from all these countries and all these different native tribes, severally and independently, without a common origin. It would not be sufficiently important, in the

[1] The boomerang is still used by certain tribes of the Nile valley from whence these Australians originated. It is also portrayed in the most ancient tombs (Lepsius Denekim, ii. 12, 60, 106, etc.).

first place, to imagine this solely as an offensive weapon or one to afford amusement, to have originated on exactly similar lines of formation which every boomerang must possess that it may be made to perform an aerial flight and return to the thrower.

It is a significant fact that on some of the boomerangs the three triangles, with apex opposite ways and concentric circles, are found together. At Springvale in the Boulia district, *Roth* says that the triangles found on the boomerangs, which are the oldest in the country, have the triangles with the apices in contact, thus:

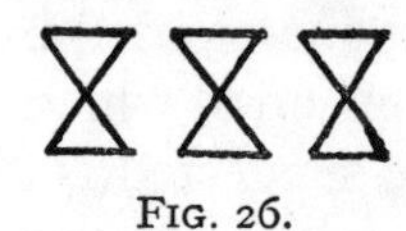

FIG. 26.

We have found the same on many of the sacred objects amongst the Indians of Mexico and Central America: we have a very old "Spear-Thrower" beautifully carved with the "ground-drawing" of the great serpent ceremony in our possession; and also with triangle, and two circles. For which we are much indebted to Mr G. Foreman.

These points should be particularly noticed as we shall draw attention to these triangles later on. Also, in a plate given in *Mr Roth's* book, we find two figures carved thus:

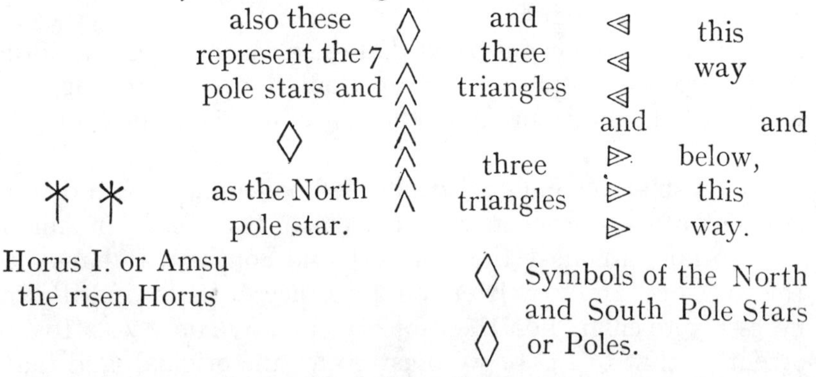

Taking into consideration that these people must have left Egypt at a very early period and that they have brought down to the present day many other signs and symbols, and Totemic ceremonies and customs, dating back to the Stellar Mythos, we should give the same meaning and explanation of the above as we have previously, and this would still more conclusively prove their common origin. Be it quite understood that these figures we bring forward are quite distinct from those writings and markings found on the "sticks" carried from one tribe to another as messengers—in one case the aborigines will give you their meaning and translation, in the other they cannot, affirming that it is "Ancestral." We note that although there are six triangles on these boomerangs, with the apices of three one way and three another, the apices are not opposite each other; at the same time we believe the proper decipherment is the same, meaning Khui Land or Land of the Spirits, and this ⚹ would represent Horus in Spirit or Amsu or the Risen Horus, or the Great One.

The ethics of these aboriginal Australians are still objective or tribal, the same as in the primitive world. The individuals are unconscious of possible interest apart from the community. The form of burial at the present time is the same as we find at Naqada, but further mention will be made of this. From the evidence we have from *Spencer* and *Gillen* we know that the Totem was first of all eaten by the members of the group as their own especial food, which is different from the belief that was previously entertained.

CHAPTER V

WE show here pure Egyptian hieroglyphics painted on the body of a man of the Worgaia tribe which are undoubtedly ideographic. These are the signs for three of the Aats, and are important and interesting as we find them in connection with the Worgaia tribe, which perform the ceremonies of the "Great Snake," and these three Aat signs have some meaning and connection with the same.

I.—This is the third Aat and is called the Aat of the Khus—the Seven Spirits. "I am the Lord of the Red Crown, which is the head of the Shining One who gives life to mankind from the heat of his mouth, and who delivers Ra from Apapi."

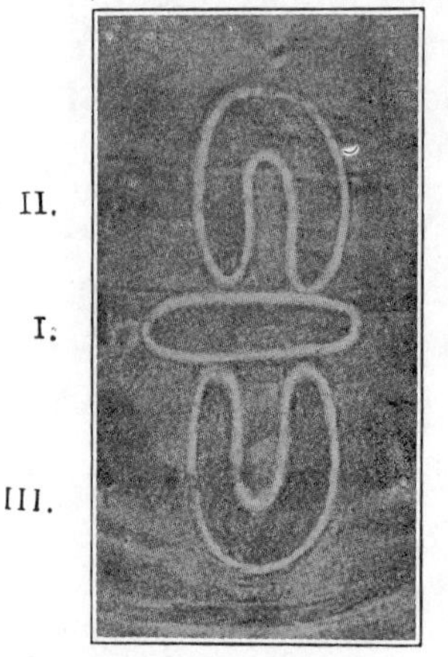

FIG. 27.—Hieroglyphic on a man of the Worgaia tribe. Reproduced by kind permission from "Native Tribes of Northern Australia," by *Prof. Baldwin Spencer* and *F. J. Gillen*, published by Macmillan & Co., London.

II.—This is the fifth Aat—the Brow of Fire—the God wherein is Fa-akh (Bearer of Altars), who is the Mighty One of the Teshert Crown, which is on the brow of the God of Light and which maintaineth in life the Two Lands and the men and women thereof by means of the flame of his mouth; he has delivered the God Ra from the fiend Apapi.

III.—This is the eighth Aat: "Hail Hahetep," Great and Mighty One of the Canal. None can obtain mastery over the water which is therein. It is mighty to be feared and the roarings which are therein are mighty. The name of the God therein is Qa-ha-hetep, and he guardeth it gladly so that none may enter, and is the Guide of the Northern Horizon.

These translated from another version may be read as follows: "Oh, this Hahotep the Very Great, the stream of which nobody takes the water for fear of its roarings. The God whose name is the Lofty One, keeps watch over it, in order that nobody may come near it. I am the Vulture which is on the stream without end. I am the Guide to the Northern Horizon."

In the ceremony of the Wollunqua they wear a representation of the White Crown of Egypt, with a Red band around ; thus representing the "Teshert Crown" or Crown of the North and South in one of its earliest forms.

The Hieroglyphics also, taken as a whole, mean the "Two Lands" – "the Northern and Southern Lands."

They divided the Celestial heavens into two divisions—North and South first—and then depicted this terrestrially in Egypt into two—the two divisions—North and South Egypt.

[hieroglyphs] The divisions of heaven—North and South.

The Aat of the Khus is the Land of the Spirits—Fa-akh, Bearer of Altars—the Mighty One of the Teshert Crown is Horus I. He maintaineth life in the "Two Lands,"—*i.e.* Celestial and Terrestrial, in the form of Amsu, the risen Horus.

Ha-hetep and Qa-ha-hetep is also Horus as Guardian in the form of a pole, surmounted by a Hawk, as guardian of "Sut" in the Hole of Water, the God whose name is the Lofty One and who keeps watch over the stream, from which nobody takes the water for fear of its roarings, and in order that nobody may come near. This water or canal is the river in the underworld, here represented by "Thapauerlu," a water hole in the Murchison range, where the Wollunqua snake is supposed by the Warramunga tribe to live. Horus is also the Guide of the Northern Horizon. The roarings which are therein are the roarings of Sut, represented here by the "Bull Roarers," which are symbolically used. *Dr W. Budge* states in his "Gods of the Egyptians," vol. i. page 156, that in the earliest times the *Egyptians divided the sky into two parts only—the East and West.* Our opinion is that it was *North and South and afterwards* East and West were added, later Ptah divided the heavens into the four quarters or square. That we are correct may be proved by reference to the "Text of Tieta" (i. 233): "and they take up his name to Horus of the two horizons, North and South," and other texts show us that Horus was "the Lord of the Northern and Southern Horizons." It was Stellar Mythos at first and not Solar, which *Dr W. Budge* assumes. Nowhere, as far as our researches go, do we find that Horus was the God mentioned as "the God of the East and Western Horizons only and primarily."

Therefore *Dr Budge* is quite wrong, the division *at first, as proved by the Ritual, was North and South.* The two poles, used in the sacred ceremonies, are the same as the Egyptian: the Northern division representing Horus by the pole Nurtunga; the Southern division represented by the pole Warringa, was the domain of Sut. The two divisions, East and West, were not formed until Shu or An-Heru came into being, and, standing on the seven steps on the mount of the equinox, lifted up the heavens and formed the two horizons, East and West, and then Horus was called "Lord of the Double Horizon," as well as "God of the Pole Star," etc. This was still Stellar Mythos, and it was not until later that Ptah came into being as the first god of the Solar Mythos that the heavens were divided in four quarters, and formed the square, with the children of Horus as the four supports for the four corners. Thus we see that these people actually are at the present day symbolically carrying out and performing part of the ceremonies of the earliest ritual of the Ancient Egyptians, and use the ancient hieroglyphics and many words of the language of this historic race to express their ideas in the remote Australian bush.

Through all these ages of years they have used and carried on these signs, symbols and ceremonies from generation to generation, the original meaning of which is now forgotten to them; yet there is sufficient left of the original to be a proof, to those who can read and know the Primordial, to unlock the "book" and read the truth, and although they have and use the signs and symbols of some of the "Gods of the Egyptians" in their earliest form, they have no knowledge of "these Gods as the latter Egyptians assumed" at the time these people left Egypt and went out into other lands. The evolution from myths into Stellar Mythos, "these types of powers were only undergoing divination," but how far they had advanced here in Australia, New Guinea, Solomon Islands and those of the New Hebrides, it is not possible to say.

From our researches all these appear to be on a par, whilst some of the Mexicans and North American Indians were further advanced in their knowledge. Whether this be so or whether these "have forgotten" and the Mexican and American Indians "have retained" the other parts of the *Ritual*, is difficult to determine; but all are "in common" and undoubtedly of the same origin—*i.e.* Egyptian Stellar Mythos. In the Mexican "Nezahualpilli," the *Fasting Prince* and the *Emerald Jewel*; the image of

Tezcatlipoca, likewise designated Talaclquani, " the Eradicator of Sins, and *the Grass Rope*," we have Horus and Min or " Amsu with the rope " of the Egyptians, which we shall refer to again later, and the prototype of the fasting of our Lord and the interceding for forgiveness of sins in the Christian doctrines.

The grass rope used in connection with the expiation of Sin will be referred to under our Cable Tow, but it is necessary to say here that this rope had existed in their first mythos, connected with Horus and Amsu, long before they brought it on in their Eschatology, and is a representation of one of the seven powers—that which leads from darkness to light.

FIG. 28.

The art of tattooing and painting the body is a Totemic mode of sign language. The Ainu of Japan, the Siberian Chukchi and Seri of Mexico only tattooed their women, which corroborates the feminine origin of the sign. The Inoil women of the Esquimaux are particularised by the figures tattooed on their face, the same as those of the Mexican, Zapotecs and Seri. The Picts, we are told by Boece, tattooed their faces and bodies with hieroglyphics (Egyptian) to distinguish one tribe from another. All these were originally Egyptian customs, as may be seen from the bas-reliefs at the temples at Philæ and Ombos.

We give the photograph here of one returning after the " Intichiuma." [1] All who are initiated must use this sign on

[1] Intichiuma—Sacred Ceremony performed by the members of a local Totemic group. Photo from " Northern Tribes of Australia," by *Baldwin Spencer* and *F. J. Gillen*," published by Macmillan & Co. Ltd., by permission, with many thanks from the author for this.

their return into camp, which may be interesting to R.A.M.'s. These traditions alone are, we think, proof that the origin and birthplace of these people was Egypt.

Amongst the Makalanga tribes of South Africa, also, we find that every tribe has its totem, and undoubtedly many customs, names, words, etc., still practised amongst them, can only be traced to the original Egyptian; however much they may have been influenced by the various and numerous people who came after, the original has never been effaced. At the present day they have the sacred triangle. In every family residence there is a place under a raised platform of poles, where three stones are set in a triangle, which are dedicated to the Ancestors of the residents. Here, at times of sickness, or at the sowing or harvesting of corn, the family collects a hoe, an axe, and, if the head of the family be a smith, a hammer is also placed by the stones, and ceremonies are gone through around this triangle which are said to be "Ancestor Customs."[1] Although this book does not give one, very many real details about the ruins, ancient customs, ancient words, etc., being evidently written more to show the present value of Ancient Gold Workings, etc., found here, still there is sufficient in it to prove that the oldest of the "*Ancients*" were Egyptian, and that those who came after, to a great extent, polluted and obliterated the originals; still there is so much of the original left as to leave no doubt in our minds.

Mafeking is an Egyptian word for copper, and copper therefore should be freely found in this neighbourhood. Although we have no knowledge at present of any copper having been found in this now well-known place, we feel no doubt about its being there and that it will be discovered in due time, as these ancient Egyptians never gave a name without having good reason for doing so.

We must here point out to *Messrs Hall* and *Neal* that no such thing as "Phallic Worship" existed, although it has been stated by several authorities who ought to know better. What occurred were "Festivals," held at stated periods, called "Phallic Festivals" if those authorities wish for that particular name. Our "May-pole Dance" and Festival is the remnant of the same, brought on and up to date, so as to correspond and fall into line

[1] See "Ancient Ruins of Rhodesia," by *Hall* and *Neal*, and "Great Zambabwe," by *R. N. Hall*.

with the "Christian doctrines." It was a Festival in honour of seed time, fructifying or increasing or generating, but was *not* a worship. *Mr Hall* tells us that these Makalanga still practise the festival of the "New Moon," the same as the ancient Egyptians. Their burial customs are either in the "sitting" position—*i.e.* "The Thrice-bent Man," or their bodies are laid lengthwise on the left side, *facing the North*; this, as we have stated elsewhere, is the same as the Aboriginal Australians, people at Harlyn Bay, Cornwall, and Mexico, and all people of the Neolithic and Stellar Mythos. These men have the same three rods or bars as the Druids, representing the three feathers, marked on their foreheads or bodies thus /|\ or \|/. As we shall point out and prove later on, these three rods or rays of light are the name of I. A. U., son of Ptah, and also the name of ancient Egypt—see "Pierrot," p. 754. "The Bird Stone Pillar,"[1] found here, in the ruins of Zambabwe, is the Horus Hawk or Vulture of Horus I. (the Vulture form was the older), and was one of the ancient miners' Mascots for "good luck." We find, in whatever part of the world these ancient miners had great workings, that they always took with them and set up this, their "Mascot," to keep away the evil one, as we have shown above. "Horus set himself over Sut in the form of a Hawk." The Golden-headed Hawk, found here, is also a type of Isis. All the tribes here are divided and have their "Totems" and marriage laws the same as in the Australian and others that we have already brought forward—thus: if a man be of the tribe, whose totem is a lion, he must not marry a woman of that tribe, but must marry a "Heart" or one of some other totem. These natives still know many of the "Star signs," but probably at the present day have forgotten most of what their "*Ancients*" knew: they, however, still know and draw Orion, the Morning and Evening stars; and the Pleiades in their rising and setting mark the sowing and reaping seasons, as did the ancient Egyptians, and the Barotse still practise a

[1] These remnants of the past are quite sufficient to prove to those gentlemen who recently explored these ruins, and came to the conclusion that they date only a few hundred years, that they are entirely wrong in their conclusions.

Brother Lt.-Col. E. L. de Cordes, 30°, who was in South Africa for three years, informed the writer that in one of the "Ruins" there is a "stone-chamber," with a vast quantity of Papyri, covered with old Egyptian hieroglyphics. A Boer hunter discovered this, and a large quantity was used to light a fire with, and yet still a larger quantity remained there now.

primitive form of embalming. Many of the natives still wear the "Horus hair-lock." In the oldest native huts we find the "pottery whorls" as used by other natives at the time of the Stellar Mythos, which we have mentioned elsewhere. *Mr Hall* states that the whorls, which are found in the ruins, and which are doubtless antique, are made of soapstone and are excellently finished. *Mr Hall*, in his work, "Great Zambabwe," draws a page of customs (100-101) of the Makalanga and the Jews, showing that they are the same, and evidently arrives at the conclusion that they derived all these from the "Jews of ancient times," and are descendants of the same. We cannot agree with *Mr Hall* and others who have come to this conclusion. No doubt many of the customs are the same, because we know that the Jews borrowed nearly all their laws and customs from the ancient Egyptians, and therefore they would be identical with them; but the undoubted proof that these "*Ancients*" came down from ancient Egypt at the time of the Stellar Mythos, as found here, is unmistakable evidence; their burial customs—the face to the North; their totemic and tribal customs and ceremonies; in marriage ceremonies—sub-incision has died out—the Horus Hawk; the /|\ or \|/ sign; these rods or rays of light; the name of I. A. U., the son of Ptah, "The Light of the World," and the name of ancient Egypt, all are sufficient to prove the origin of the "*Ancients*."

From the "find" in the recently opened tomb in Egypt—date about B.C. 2000—18th dynasty—we are of opinion that most of the gold of this district went direct to Egypt, for in this tomb were found a gold chariot and large quantities of other articles, all gold or overlaid with gold, and an inscription:—"This gold was brought from the Land of the South." We must not overlook such facts as these when trying to decipher the history of the past. *Facts* are true, *theories* very seldom are.

That others visited and inhabited these regions afterwards, there is no doubt, and that Solomon may have obtained the principal part of his gold from here we would not say "nay to"; but that the "*Ancients*" were certainly not of Jewish origin, nor obtained their customs and totemic ceremonies, etc., from them, but from the ancient Egyptians, at the time of the Stellar Mythos, the foregoing are positive proofs of. There is evidence also that although these nations still have and practise these

Stellar rites they must have changed their names at some time after, because the word " Makalanga " means " the people of the Sun," and so the Stellar doctrines, although they have never altogether been forgotten and obliterated, the origin must have been brought on by them. We should have been glad if *Mr Hall* had taken more photographs of the various " markings " he mentions, as it is quite possible that the Swastika and the sign of the " Khui Land " and " Zodiacal West " still may be found amongst them. Their skulls correspond to those of the Egyptian.

Luban worship has now, comparatively speaking, lost its hold on the people of Uganda. The ancient " Spirit Houses," which used to be found everywhere, have practically disappeared. If you come across a former " Spirit Priest," he hastens to disclaim the position, and it is very difficult to learn anything about the ancient religion of the people. Mohammedanism was the first cause of the breakdown in their ancient worship, and now Christianity, which is spreading rapidly. The Tordites practise tribal scarring, knocking out front teeth, and believe in the same legend of the Great Serpent, which they say dwells in " Crater Lake," and cast in gifts to propitiate it, sometimes human sacrifices; so also the Bakonji practise the same as the above, and circumcision and a history of sub-incision, and have a peculiar embossing, as have the Australians, on their skins, which they make by cutting the skin with some sharp instrumen , introducing a foreign substance, and then allowing the skin to heal. *They all believe in the spirit of their ancestors, and they build " Spirit Houses," about* 18 *inches high, conical in shape, and have a small opening through which they insert fruit, etc., to propitiate the spirits. Here we have an early belief of " Ancestor Worship " as well as " Spirit Worship."*

Fathers Burgo and *Juan deCordova's* descriptions of some of the ceremonies amongst the Zapotecs, Mexicans and Maya Indians in the forest, telling how they " drew blood from under the tongue " and sprinkled feathers and leaves with it, etc., etc., show by their interpretation of the same how little they understood the practice of some of the ceremonies of the Stellar Mythos, or the History of the Creation in the Egyptian Mythos, of which this and many other ceremonies they describe, prove from whence these customs were obtained.

The " Borgian Codex," " Codex Vaticanus " and " Tellerino

Romensis" show figures here of the practice of self-mutilation (not castration, as is stated by German translators), but that of *sub-incision*. These two forms or ceremonies correspond with the two Histories of Creation by the Egyptians—see pages 59-60, and the whole history of Horus and Isis is plainly set forth in the above Codices.

The "Emerald Jewel," the image of Tezcatlipoca or Tlaelquani, the eradicator of sins, and Chachilnhtololin, who bores out his eyes with a sharpened bone, are types of Horus and the Blind Horus.

One of the principal precious stones of the Mayas, Mexicans and Zapotecs was green, and represented hieroglyphically as lustrous bodies, with eyes at the four corners—*i.e.* sending rays in four directions, representing Horus — Her-uatch-f Prince of the Emerald Stone, and the four children of Horus. The *Ritual* says: "I am the Tablet of felspar," Green Stone Uat amulet that was placed in the tomb as a type of that which was for ever green, fresh, young, and represented eternal youth: also the name of the person whose death is announced, and should be read as Xilolt or Cacamatl—*i.e.* Young Ear of Corn—is Horus.

At Philæ, the god "Corn Spirit" is represented with Stalks and Ears of Corn springing from its mummy, *near running water*. It is Horus represented as a bringer forth of food in the shape of corn—a type of the eternal, manifested by renewal of food, produced from the element of water in inundation—*i.e.* "an Ear of Corn near a fall of water" is the present symbol. The ear of corn, green wheat ear of the mysteries, which was held in the hand of Neith or Isis in Virgo, and still survives in the star Spica of this constellation, represents there Horus the child as bringing food or giver of food by the water of inundation or rising of the Nile, the food of Egypt being dependent on the periodical overflow of the Nile.

The identity of the pèco-Xolo or the Lightning Dog of the Mayas with Anubis, must be apparent to all, and in the legend contained in chap. iv. Book V. of "Origen de los Indios," by *Fra Gregoria Garcia*, we have the whole tale of Horus I. and Sut so plainly set forth, that it might have been copied from the *Ri ual* direct; also the hieroglyphics and picture-signs, with a mountain

THE DUAL GOD HORUS-SET, OR
THE BLACK GOD AND THE WHITE GOD.

F

and thatched house on the top, and in the front sits a man whose name is represented by the Eagle's head above—nica qahuayohca qu toca cuitli qu toconcol—*i.e.* here is the place called yauayolica Cuitli—*i.e.* "hawk is the ancestor"—*i.e.* Horus I. This is the Egyptian Mount of Heaven—the *Ritual* says:—"A very high mountain, I hold myself in thy inclosure": also, "A divine domain hath been constructed for me, I know the name of it; the name of it is the Garden of Aarru," *Ritual*, ch. 109. The inclosure, or, as represented here, a "thatched house," was a dwelling place at the summit of the mount, which the Egyptians expanded to a city—the City of the Blessed, the Holy City, the Heavenly City, the Eternal City, the City of the Great King, here represented by Horus I. and his thatched house on the top of a mountain.

The hieroglyphic for Isis we find associated with her here also

It is not necessary in this work to bring forward further proofs than we are doing to support our contention that these people obtained all the sacred writings and forms and ceremonies and religious doctrines from the ancient Egyptians. There is everything shown plainly in these old codices, and their practices, signs and hieroglyphics, which, if you know the key, you cannot go wrong in the decipherment of, but at present all the translators, as far as we know, have not known the key—the Egyptian *Ritual*, and Primordial, and so have built up an entirely erroneous construction, and in our opinion it will be of little use for the Smithsonian Institute and their Bureau of American Ethnology to translate the German interpretation and issue it to the public *with their present ideas and interpretations and agreeing with the same. It will be diffusing incorrect interpretations, and only* in comparing it with the Egyptian mythos can one obtain a correct explanation. The people of these countries (Central America) had to express their spiritual ideas in the "same gross way" as the ancient Egyptians did, not having the words then as we have now, and "until this is recognised, they will be for ever stumbling about in the dark."

The "Bull Roarer," used by the aboriginal Australians, and the Totemic ceremonies of the Great Snake, as described in

Spencer and *Gillen's* work, "Northern Tribes of Central Australia," are more proofs to show that these people came out of Egypt at the time of the Stellar Mythos. For the explanation we must go back to the myth of the battle of Horus with Sut:—"When Sut was hard pressed by Horus he changed himself into a Serpent, which hissed loudly, and he sought a hole for himself in the ground, wherein he hid himself and lived thereafter, whereupon he was called the monster Ba [hieroglyphs] and Horus set himself above this hole in the form of a pole, on the top of which the head of Horus appears in the shape of a hawk, so that Sut may never come forth again therefrom." As the result of this the serpent was called "Hisser" or "Roarer," and the hissing or roaring would be to give notice of danger, so as to warn or frighten away the weak. Hence the use of the "Bull Roarer" as a warning of danger to women and others or that the evil one was abroad in that neighbourhood.[1] Anyone reading the totemic ceremonies and the traditional history of the great snake, "Wollunqua," that still lives in the water-hole, called "Thapauerlu," situated in the Murchison range, cannot fail to identify this totemic ceremony and traditional history with that of the battle of Horus and Sut, and the result of the same. The pole over the serpent's hole, with the hawk's head at the top, represents the North Pole, and Sut or Set, underneath the hole, the South Pole. Amongst these aborigines they make a mound and on it trace the representation of the Great Snake, with its head to the North and tail to the South.

This is what *Spencer* and *Gillen* say:—"The Wollunqua is regarded as a huge beast, so large that if it were to stand up on its tail its head would reach far away into the heavens. It lives now in a large water-hole, called Thapauerlu, hidden away in a lonely valley amongst the Murchison range, and there is always the fear that it may take it into its head to come out of its hiding-place and do some damage.

"The striking feature of the design is the tracks of a man, who is reported to have lived with the snake at Thapauerlu, and to

[1] There was another use for the "Roarer" and explanation (Egyptian) which when used by women was "to call the young men"—it is not necessary to give further explanation here—but necessary to mention it.

The name of the instrument in Egyptian is Menait, literally signifies the whirler—original instrument of magical power.

have followed him up when he started off on his wanderings, and to have come out of his body, being very anxious to make him return. At Ununtumur he came up with him, and, standing by his side, lifted up his arms and struck the snake on its head as hard as he could, in the hope of making him dive down. The two human footprints, side by side, close to the head of the snake, indicate the man standing by the latter, while the two large curved bands, attached to the circles, represent his arms lifted up to strike the snake. Each man performing in the ceremonies of the Wollunqua totem wore a tall conical white helmet, decorated with a circular red band "—*i.e.* Crown of the land of the South or the White Crown, and the "red band" would represent the Crown of the North—Teshert Crown in its earliest form. There is no doubt that the building of the mound and stroking it is to please the snake, and the covering over of its remains "when the old men heard it growling in the distance," for fear lest it should come out and eat them all up, points to the idea of propitiation, the same as the Tordites throw food and bodies into the Lake Crater in Central Africa. Fundamentally similar are all tribes of natives: that the man coming out of the body of the snake would mean

FIG. 29.—Preparing the Wollunqua Mound. Warramunga tribe.

Reproduced by kind permission from "Native Tribes of Northern Australia," by *Prof. Baldwin Spencer* and *F. J. Gillen*.—Published by Macmillan & Co., London.

that at one time he was part of him, as Horus and Sut, the latter in earl.er times, being the associate of Horus, but after his position

FIG. 30.

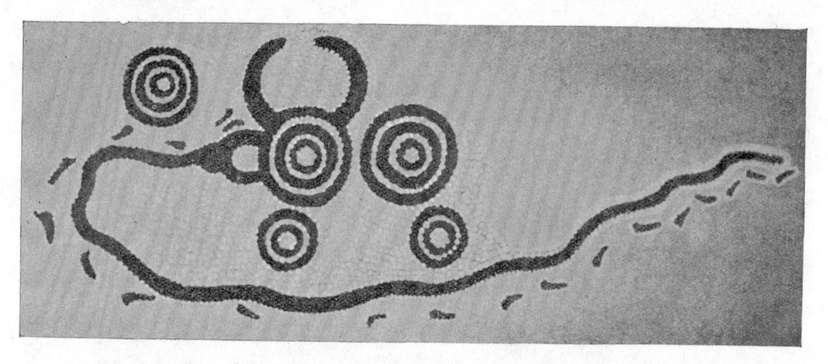

FIG. 31.—Ground-drawing associated with the Wollunqua Totemic ceremony of a place called Ununtumurra.

Reproduced by kind permission from "Native Tribes of Northern Australia," by *Prof. Baldwin Spencer* and *F. J. Gillen*.—Published by Macmillan & Co., London.

as a god was lost, he became the type and symbol of all ev'l. See photos of "Sut and Horus."

We give here these illustrations from the Australian aborigines, performing their totemic ceremonies, and the ground-drawings: also a drawing of the serpent mound in Ohio, North

FIG. 32.—Serpent Mound of Loch Necl, near Oban, Scotland (a drawing), by *Dr Waddell.*

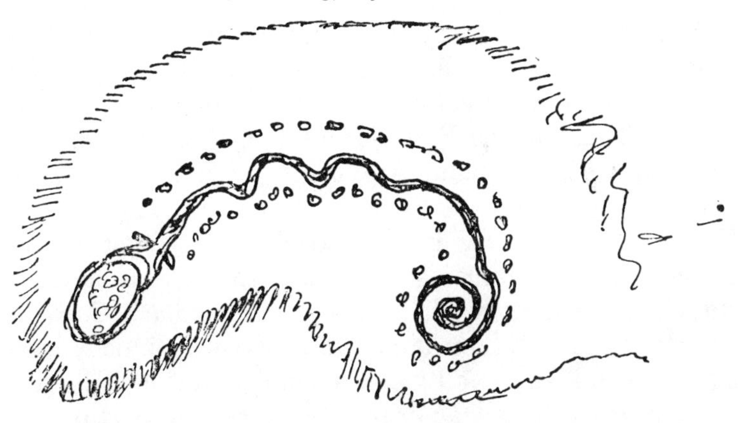

FIG. 33.—Water Creek. Precipice. Serpent 600 ft. long. Great Serpent Mound, Ohio, U.S.A.

America, and one in Scotland drawn by *Dr A. Waddell.*[1] This so-called *chamber of worship*, shown at the head of the snake in the latter, is not to represent that at all, as stated by those who believe in serpent worship, but represents the hole wherein the great

[1] The Wollunqua, in its wanderings, *meets two hawks*, named Warapula and Kirkalanji, and these two hawks made fire for the first time.—Native word for Fire is the same as the Egyptian—Mahateti: fire. Minurka signifies giving of fire and warmth;

snake dwells—"The Hole of Sut,"—and has been handed down as the *Devil's Hole.* With the Australians it represents the same, but their explanation is that it is the hole where the snake goes into the ground, so as to resume its travels *underground.* A most striking feature of the designs is the tracks of a man following until these have reached the head, and then the two raised hands and arms in the attitude to strike and kill the monster: we have them here depicted in each case. These track-steps represent the footprints of Horus, when he pursued the monster, as the Egyptian text tells us "that Heru-behutet and Horus, the son of Isis" (the two "hawks" of the Australians), "together pursued the foe. Sut changed himself into a serpent, which loudly hissed, and he sought out a hole for himself in the ground, wherein he hid himself and lived, and Horus, son of Isis, set himself above his hole in the form of a pole, on the top of which is the head of Horus in the form of a Hawk, so that he may never again come forth," etc. And here we have these poor aboriginal Australians practising at the present time the Totemic Ceremonies of this myth their ancestors brought with them from Egypt, ages ago, and from the other great serpent mounds, found in Ohio, Scotland, New Zealand and other parts of the world, so precisely similar, that there cannot be any doubt that this was the universal practice at one time, and that the origin of it can only be found in the Egyptian text, as we have stated above. The one at Glen Feechan, Argyllshire, is a huge serpent, 300 feet long.

Dr C. W. Andrews, in *The Geological Magazine,* vol. 8, 1901, describes the remains of a huge snake that he found in Egypt, to which he give the name of *Gigantophis Garstini.* It was related to the Python family, but of a very much larger size and more formidable; all the vertebræ were much larger than those of any existing *Ophidean,* and if the proportions of this snake were the same as the existing *Python-sebæ,* it would reach a length of 30 feet or more. This huge snake would therefore be a terror to the earliest inhabitants of these parts, and would always be looked upon as something to dread and avoid, and would become an evil import to them. Isaiah lxvi. 24, says:—"Their worm shall not die, neither their fire be quenched." This passage is a direct allusion to the great serpent of the Egyptian underworld—of the Tuat. In all periods of history, the dread and terror of the great serpent have been handed down under various names, and the Pre-dynastic and Dynastic Egyptians made it to represent the Great Evil One in their Eschatology, but the original, no doubt, was a great serpent, which lived in the Nile valleys in Prehistoric times. We must remember that these Ancients first mapped out or "dug out," so to speak, the Tuat and Amenta in a celestial form, and then mapped this out in Egypt and the Nile valleys to represent it. Commencing with the delta of the Nile as the entrance to the Tuat, they worked the various divisions and inhabitants therein to the South, from whence man originated, dividing the whole into twelve divisions. There is no doubt that the Hebrews and the Christian Copts both borrowed their Hell from the Egyptian Tuat, and that the Hebrew Gehenna was divided into seven divisions or Halls instead of twelve, would mean that they borrowed this at the time Egypt was divided into seven divisions instead of twelve, which it was at first. (*See* Appendix.)

We must recognise that all these Totemic ceremonies of the Australian and other natives, are performed here on Earth in the totemic stage of sociology, and that in Egypt, knowledge continued to advance, whilst these natives stood still or retrograded; and so the Egyptians worked out Amenta, and the Mysteries thereof, in the phase of their Eschatology, whilst those who had gone out of Egypt, and were cut off from intercommunication, never advanced.

CHAPTER VI

On page 271, figure 59, "Mexican Antiquities," published by the Smithsonian Institute, what *Dr Edward Seler* calls "the Twenty-Day Signs," giving his explanation of the same from the BORGIAN

FIG. 34.—The Twenty-Day Signs, from the BORGIAN CODEX. *Dr Edward Seler's* "Twenty-Day Signs." From "Mexican Antiquities," published by the Bureau of American Ethnology, Smithsonian Institute, Washington, D.C. We take this opportunity to thank *Mr W. Holmes*, Chief of the Bureau, for his courteous letter and kind permission to reproduce the plates from the above work.

CODEX, is in our opinion a type of Horus and Sut, illustrating many passages in the *Ritual* of ancient Egypt, belonging to the time of the Stellar Mythos. We cannot accept nor recognise anything in *Dr Seler's* interpretation. The face represents the

"Blind Horus," as we see a net drawn over the right eye. In the "History of Creation" we have a very interesting reading as regards the "Father Nu"—*i.e.* here represented in the Mexican (Horus I.), in which it declares that his eye was covered over with a large number of *bushes* for an indefinite number of periods, each containing sixty years—"They covered up my eye after them with bushes twice for ten periods" ("History of the Creation of the World," version B.)—bushes here may be translated a "hair" net drawn over the right eye, otherwise clouds, which hang around the earth and obscure the sun's rays—and the meaning is that it was impeded for centuries. The nose is represented by the hieroglyph Apt, and on it are the two feathers—*i.e.* the brow of the God Horus or Iu, representing the two lives, earthly and spiritual, and on the left side this is again represented by the Ḥawk's or Eagle's head, the one as "spiritual form"—Amsu, above: the one below, Horus, terrestrially. On the right, with his back turned, is the zootype for Sut. Over the head of Sut is the old Egyptian hieroglyph ,[1] to tie in a knot, to bind, to tie up. Sut is here depicted bound or tied up or chained—see *Ritual*—"Horus succeeded in fettering Sut and binding him in chains"—parallel to Satan being bound in the Christian doctrines. When the Solar took the place of Stellar doctrines, Sut then became the type of the Great Fiend, Apepi, and had other serpents under him—Rerek, parallel again in the Christian doctrines to Beelzebub and Satan. (In *Dr LePlongeon's* work, "Queen Moo," plate 52, is clearly shown the battle between Horus and Sut, and the binding of Sut with chains, or rather with rope, and also shows Sut changed into a serpent and Horus setting a pole over the hole, where Sut has taken refuge. This plate is divided into three parts: the upper, showing the commencement of the battle; the middle the binding of Sut, and Sut changed into a great serpent. In the lower part, Sut has taken refuge in a hole, and Horus is seen planting a pole over it. Although this is Mexican, it is precisely similar to the Egyptian text.) Over the centre of the body is the head of Horus, and beneath this a wide band bears hieroglyphics for five different names or attributes of him. The "dark face" on the right is the "dark face in its hour"—*i.e.* the Seer of the night. See *Ritual*. Below this is the phallus, showing that the rite of circumcision

[1] Also this is well shown in fig. 100, page 381.

was practised here: also that of sub-incision, as we see the drops of blood falling. The two primary gods formed Shu (the Sun), and Tefnut (the Moon)—see part of "The Story of Creation."—Shu was formed first, as may be seen from the position it occupies here. On the right he is crushing the great evil fiend with his left foot—see overthrow of Apepi—and then is chained, as is represented by the tail coiled around the serpent, and this hieroglyph on the top. Note left foot. In his right hand he holds light and splendour and division of time: in his left, darkness and night. He is seated on the throne of the two lands.

The head in the centre, as here depicted, is Horus (not a monkey's head as *Dr Seler* states). Having his mouth open and tongue out signifies, in Mexican sign language, that he is speaking: it is Horus, "the Sayer of the Sayings" and the "Word made Truth" or law by Horus the victorious, the father's own anointed son who fulfilled the word of power in the Eschatology, here shown in the Stellar as the victorious, having bound Sut. In chap. vii. of the *Ritual*, Horus says: "I am the one who presided over the Pole of heaven and the powers of all the gods are my powers; I am he whose names are hidden and whose abodes are mysterious for all eternity." That this is Horus and the same as the above "Eagle head," and that they are types of each other, is demonstrated and proved by the hieroglyph ⊙ being attached to each, in the same position anatomically—*i.e.* at the junction of the lower jaw and the ear. The five different characters represented on the "band" are five different attributes of him—Shu, Amsta, Hapi, Kabhsenf—and the "dark face" Anup—is the dark face in its hour or Seer of the Night—see *Ritual*. These=the five supports which when added to the seven glorious ones of the Pole Star constituted the twelve pre-zodiacal divisions or domains of the heavens. Five houses were assigned to them which are frequently seen in the Central American pictures. Horus is thus represented as Heru-Khent-an-Maati. In two plates, given in *Mr John L. Steven's* work: "Incidents of Travel in Central America, Chepas and Yucatan," published in 1848, there are two figures, which represent the Egyptian Taht-Aan, the bearer of the symbolic Uat. He is portrayed carrying Horus in his hand and holding him aloft as the True Light of the World, and a symbolic likeness of a soul in human nature, that was begotten of

Ra, the Holy Spirit, as the Father in Heaven, precisely as we find shown in the Egyptian monuments.

The pictures shown here, therefore, depicted Horus in spiritual and terrestrial form; he having overcome the great Evil One, bound him in chains, placed him underneath his left foot and consigned him to Hades. Horus is now supreme and reigns as the Everlasting Light and Saviour of the World. It gives also one version, in picture-sign language, of the creation of the world, which corresponds in every particular with the Egyptian—it is parallel with the Christian doctrines.

Dr Seler's decipherment, or rather attempted decipherment of the stone Tablets, found built in the South wall of the Temple Pyramid of Tepoxtlan, is very amusing. We quote what he says:—"Mexican Antiquities," page 347—"One figure (c. figure 86) contains the hieroglyph of King Ahuitzotl, who derived his name from a small ghost-like water animal, which, according to Mexican tales, played the rôle of a sort of nixy, and was represented in this form: On the other slab a rabbit is shown and beside it are *ten circles*, which would indicate the year, 10 Tochtli, *corresponding to the year* 1502 *of the Christian chronology* [Italics are ours], the last year of Ahuitzotl's reign, or the year of his death. *Saville* has interpreted these two tablets quite correctly, and he concludes that the year of the erection of the temple and its builder were thus immortalised. ——— The ancient temple of Tepoxtlan would be the only aboriginal structure, still standing in Mexico, to which we can with probability assign certain date."

Drs Edward Seler and *Saville* will have to go back some thousands of years before this (allow us to tell them) for the date—go back to see the Egyptian Pyramids (see Pyramids) where they built the names in the wall both North and South, and after East and West, the guardians of the four quarters, children of Horus, under various names, according to the dynasty; and also learn that the king of each dynasty associated himself and took on a divine title, as well as the high priests, of one of them; and that the ten circles are the ten divisions of heaven, which he will find fully set forth in the Litany of the 18th chapter of the *Ritual* of ancient Egypt, and shown elsewhere in this book very characteristically.[1] *This temple was dedicated to the Great Chief of the*

[1] The Celestial and Terrestrial divisions of Heaven and Earth are well shown in the SAHAGUN MANUSCRIPT and BORGIAN CODEX.

Hammer or "Great Seer," as Ptah was at Memphis, and *not to the Gods of Drunkenness and* 400 *rabbits ! ! !*—see God of the Axe. *Dr Seler* and others can only read these correctly through the *Ritual* of ancient Egypt. His "God of the Night" is Anubis, also his animal Xolotl the same. His "figure of a blazing star" (which he wishes the hieroglyph ce Acatl "reed" to represent, but which is absent) is the representation of the Egyptian "Sothos," and is shown by his "God of the Night" Anubis, who guided the soul through Amenta ; and let us assure him that these people of Yucatan and Mexico reckoned as did the Egyptians.

In plate vi. fig. No. 9 of the Vignette of "The Book of the Dead," chap. xvii., we see that in the Solar Mythos Osiris was Great Chief of the Axe which the Priests had brought on from Horus I.

"Thus we find that by earthquakes and other convulsive agencies the 'Blazing Star' has been eclipsed, their Altars thrown down and destroyed, and their Cubic Stone—always in the centre of the temple, has poured out all its 'blood and water,' and all the sacred words have been lost with the Great Seers."[1]

The different names of the four children of Horus we give in another part of this work—the four Bacabs of the Mayas. In the temple of Copan, *Prof. Dieseldorff* describes the representation of a battle between the Vampire God and Cukulcan, the God of Light, which he is inclined to regard as the struggle between darkness and light—yes, this is the representation of the battle between Sut (the Vampire), the King of Darkness, and Horus I. (Cukulcan), the God of Light—as is described and shown in this work elsewhere.

Amongst the Zapotecs they have a record of a deity of the name of Xipe, who came down from heaven in the form of a hawk. The Mexicans also have this deity under the name of Macuil-Xochetle, "who had a dark brother," to whom the name of Ixtlilton—the little black face—was given. The former has the "Horus Lock" plainly visible. These two brothers are shown in the AZTEC SAHAGUN text, and are the same as the Zapotec Xa quie ; they are found given in many forms amongst all the Nahua tribes as Xolotl and his twin brother Quetzalcoatl. These are all forms

[1] All these temples are now in ruins, note 18°.

and types of Horus and Sut, and in the paintings of Mitla we recognise the illustration of the Stellar Mythos of the Egyptians. The most famous city in old Yucatan, and the most famous ancient seat of its rulers, was Chichen Itza, and the sculptures in the ruins of this town are of a somewhat different form, bearing a greater similitude of likeness in the various characters to the ancient Egyptian than those of the great ruined cities of the West. In the traditions of the Mexican and Central American races there is mention of a civilised nation, said to have been in the country—or to have arrived in the country—a very long time ago—viz. the Toltec nation, "and that they carried their books with them on their migration, and were led by their wise men—the Amoxhuaque —who understood the books"—*i.e.* the picture writings, their sacerdotal wisdom, which was the hieroglyphic language and system of divination, learnt by these Amoxhuaque—the High Priests from Egypt or their descendants. The ancient temple of Tepoxtlan contains the representative of Horus I. and Sut, and many other Egyptian deities, Stellar, Lunar, and Solar, and the division of heaven into eight parts. We cannot agree in any way with *Edward Seler's* reading of the Central American, Mexican and Maya remains. His "Gods of Drunkenness," which he calls Totochtin (rabbits), is too ludicrous to discuss, as is his account of the Earth Goddess wearing the Golden Huaxles, shaped like a crescent moon, etc. He must go to ancient Egypt, then he will find that these are types representing Horus I., Sut—Anubis, and Hathor—Isis. It is immaterial whether we find the goddess Hathor in one form or the other: as the Moon Goddess, the great mother of the light of the night, or as an Earth Goddess, the great mother of those on earth, or as Goddess of the Pole-star, the great mother of the light of the North, or as the mother suckling the child Horus—"the divine mother." These are all one and the same, only representing different ages and types. For a true explanation we must know and recognise that it is one and the same. In the Christian doctrines we have the Madonna and Child.

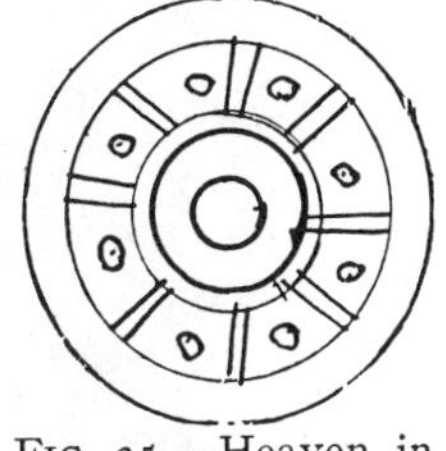
FIG. 35.—Heaven in 8 divisions.

We are enabled to give two figures from photographs of "Two Gods" recently discovered near the ruins of Mitla, by *Professor Marshall H. Saville.*

These two figures are symbolically typical of the Egyptian Horus, in two of his characters.[1]

The one on the right has a Crown on his head, with four Ears of Corn, two on each side, and between these the Hieroglyphic for running water. In front, between his arms, is the Egyptian ideograph hieroglyphic Rhi—" Garden of Earth." His tongue is hanging out, apparently as two tongues, symbolically uttering or saying that he is the Lord and bringer of food and water; this is identically the same as the Egyptian at Phila, where " the Corn Spirit " is represented by Stalks and Ears of Corn springing

FIG. 36.

from its mummy near running water—*i.e.* Horus as represented as a bringer of food and water; which must be interesting to Freemasons as being the origin of " an Ear of Corn near a fall of water."

The figure on the left is one of the Mexican depictions of Horus as " the Light of the World." He has a Crown on his head surmounted by several (there should be seven of them) " Three Rods " or " Rays of Light " \|/. This is the same as our

[1] " The grain-god " is well represented in the tomb of Seti I. (*Lefebvre*, La Tombau de Seti I. in the " Memoires de la Mission Française," Vol. II. pt. iv. pl. xxix. 2nd row, pl. xxxi. 3rd row) as a man wearing two full ears of wheat or barley upon his head. Maspero calls him " Naprit," but naprit simply means grain, the grain of wheat (*Brugsch, Dict. Hieroglyphique*, pp. 752-753). It is a type of Horus as " the bringer of food."

DESIGN ON A VASE FROM CHAMÁ.

This graphically portrays part of the ceremony of —— degree. The "signs" being given here are identical with those of Hu and Sa in J. L. Stevens' work. "Bes-kuȧ ȧbu ȧāā (n) u" *(MS: Nebseni)*, also *Ritual*, ch. lxxx; for Symbol on Nose, ch. cxxv and Notes.

Druids and the Egyptian (see later explanation).—In front, between the arms, there is a head with a rope around the neck, which passes over the shoulders of the god. Symbolical of a Power bringing death, darkness or ignorance to the Light Eternal, through or by Horus. The one Power through whom you are led from death to the mansions of the Blessed.

In each case the figure is seated on a Throne—4 stones of equal size, and symbolises the 4 Powers or Children of Horus (names and explanation of these given later). The 4 Powers or Supporters of the 4 Corners, all Egyptian originally brought here by the old Priests of Egypt.

Mr Salomon Reinach in his "Orpheus" has fallen into the same error as most other writers on these subjects, he, like them, being quite ignorant of that which they write about, when he states of the old Mexican nations that—"Although they worshipped gods in animal form, birds, and serpents, they also adored some in human form,"—but as these were only Signs and Symbols of the Powers, or Attributes, of the One Great God, first expressed by zootype form, and afterwards anthropomorphically, it could not be the Signs and Symbols they worshipped but the One Great God.

Photographs of these, reproduced here, must be conclusive evidence that wherever found it is one and the same, and this applies to Horus I. as well as others.

Again, *Dr Edward Seler* reads the PEREX CODEX, the Mexican manuscript of the BIBLIOTHEQUE NATIONAL, at Paris, from *right to left*, and we presume all others, and although he notices that the hieroglyphs, unlike most of the writings employed elsewhere in Maya manuscripts, these face backwards, that is, face to the left instead of to the right, he translates from right to left!! How can he expect to get a true rendering?

The Mayas copied the Egyptians, who sometimes wrote with the face of the hieroglyph to the right, and at other times they faced the left. The reading of these, therefore, must follow the same rule as the reading of the Egyptian—*i.e.* when the hieroglyph faces the right, the reading must be from right to left; when facing the left, the reading must be from left to right, otherwise you get about as true a conception of the real meaning as you do in the decipherment of the wall paintings at Mitla published upside down in the "Mexican and Central American Antiquities," by the Bureau of American Ethnology, Smithsonian Institute, U.S.A.

This design on a vase from Chama must be of great interest to all students of Freemasonry, as it portrays very graphically one of our ceremonies, although the attempted explanation by *Mr E. P. Dieseldorff* and *Mr Forstemann* is, in our opinion, entirely misleading and erroneous.

The flabellum or fan seen in the hands of A and C and under

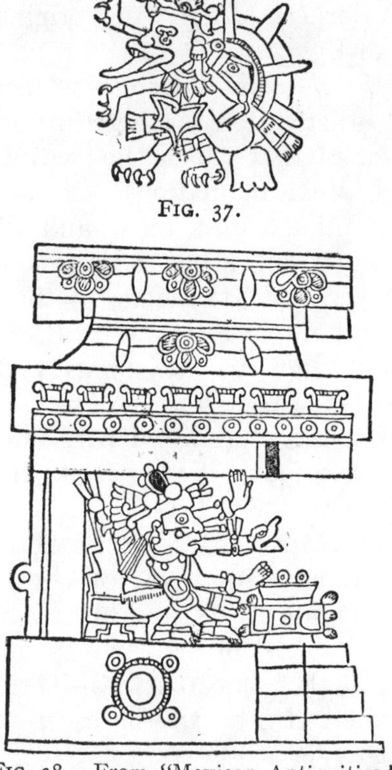

FIG. 37.

FIG. 38.—From "Mexican Antiquities."

the arm of G (who is holding up the sign), was a mystical emblem in the Egyptian mysteries, for one thing it signified the "Shade or Spirit" and in the above picture is portrayed for "a Soul of a primitive type" or Soul about to enter the mysteries.

The Jackal-headed man here represents Anup. It was the Jackal as Anup who carried Horus, the young Sun god, and he became the bearer and supporter of souls, as stated in the *Ritual*, which speaks of this subject: "Anup is my bearer"—chap. lxiv.

Anup is here represented as coming forward to "raise or bear" the soul of the I in the same way as the R in our ceremonies; he bears or raises and conducts the I through the valley of the Shadow of Death—through D D and D to the region of the Blessed.

The Red God of the Mexicans is the representation of Horus[1] as the divine avenger of the suffering Osiris. He is also the just and righteous Judge who does justice in the judgment hall of Mati on the day of doom, and in the *Ritual*, chap. lvii., he is thus addressed: "O fearsome One, thou who art over the two earths, *Red God* who orderest the block of execution to whom the double crown is given" as "Horus at his second coming." Another form of the Red God as Egyptian was *Har-Tesh*, a form of Anhur, passed into the Greek mythology as the great warrior Onouris= Anhur. Shu-Anhur is addressed under various names connected with his deeds:—"Thou wieldest thy spear to pierce the head of the serpent Nekan in that name which is thine of the god provided with horns"—"Thou seizest thy spear and overthrowest the wicked (The Sebau) in the name which is thine of Horus the Striker. Thou destroyest the An of Tokhenti in the name which is thine of the Double abode of Ra (=2 Earths=2 Caves). Thou strikest the Menti and the Seti in the name which is thine of 'Young-Elder.' Thou strikest upon the heads of the wicked in the name which is thine of Lord of Wounds. Mag. Pap. pp. 2 and 3."

The "prominence on the Nose" (monstrous wart on the nose) which is seen in this picture from Chama, and which *Prof. Dieseldorff* cannot understand or account for, is the symbolic representation of the "Nose or Neb of the Ibis," the Egyptian "Knowing One" or the "One with Knowledge." The larger the prominence represented, the greater is the knowledge of that Priest of the Mysteries, and one can almost define to what degree the Priest belongs by observing his nose only; the largest being

NOTE.—Perhaps it is as well to state here that all through this work we have adopted the name "SUT" as the opponent of Horus, instead of "Apepi," the former being the Anthropomorphic. That the two are one and the same is shown and proved in chap. cviii. of the *Ritual*. We wish to make this clear to our readers, because some might ascribe the "Vampire," the "Great Dragon," to Apepi and not Sut, but the Great Vampire or Great Dragon or Great Serpent (Apepi), whose length is given in the above chapter of the *Ritual* as 500 cubits long, is only a first type of Sut; so these are identical. The primary was the Zootype.

[1] Figs. 37 and 38.

that of the High Priest who had the greatest knowledge, representing also in this form Khenti-'Kâs.

The Ibis was considered the "Knowing One" in Egypt, and is thus symbolically represented in the Mexican picture. The Ibis was also the typical bird of Taht-Aan who was the sacred Scribe to whom the 36,000 books on papyrus rolls were attributed, he was the pre-Christian John the Divine. He was bearer of the Symbolic Utat, carrying Horus in his hand, holding him aloft as the True Light of the world, and the symbolic likeness of a soul in human nature that was begotten of Ra, the Holy Spirit and Father in Heaven.

As before stated, *Stephens* gives a plate in his book of this figure from Central American States, and it is precisely similar to the Egyptian. Taht-Aan, as the Sacred Scribe, wrote the *Ritual*, the book which contains the Divine Word, that brings about the resurrection to the glory of Eternal Life. It is the book of the Mysteries, in which this picture shows part of the revelation, that is here seen dramatically enacted in Mexico (*Ritual*, chap. cxxv.).

In figures B and C we observe that both have the Cable-tow around their necks, and B is being "held" or "led" by A. D is proclaiming to G (W M), and holds in his left hand —— and in his right hand has ——. E is being initiated into this degree, of which hitherto he has been "blind, speechless and ignorant," and is learning and copying the sign —— from G (W M). F is seeing that this is properly performed and instructing him in the sign. Our brethren may take D and F as the representatives of the two. D and G as W M, A as S W. This will be sufficient explanation to all Masons, who have obtained this degree, without exposing that which we should not.[1] The different grades of degrees are here plainly shown on their "aprons" and other symbols attached to their persons, which are unmistakable. Be it understood that this is a "prototype of this degree." The North and South is here depicted by the "Lotus and Papyri Flowers" or representatives of the same on the headdress of A and G, A being Upper Egypt, G Lower Egypt.

To our brother Masons, who may not understand why more

[1] Those of our brothers who have taken all up to the 30° will recognise it. R here is represented by "Anubis," and M one of the children of Horus. We have here the "yellow and black Bacabs," as is explained by the "Glyphs." The picture is so true as a prototype we refrain from giving all or any more of the "Secrets."

than one should wear the Cable-tow around his neck, we would explain to them that originally there was only *one*, which was the "rope" of Min or Amsu, or the risen Horus, and represented a power or attribute. Afterwards there were six others added, making in all seven, representing the seven powers. This can be seen from the *Ritual*. It was one of the types of the seven powers, and then they, who represented these powers, were distinguished by the Cable-tow or Rope around their necks, as some are seen in this picture. Masons will understand, even those in the R A degree, that each chair *represents one* Great One, each having or holding the emblem of the office which he occupies, the emblem being the sign or symbol by which they are known—see Cable-tow.

The Zapotec and Mexican conception of the Deity, according to *Father Juan de Cordova*, was "God without end and without beginning," so they called him, without knowing whom, "Dios infinito y sin principo llamavanle sin saber à quein."—The uncreated Lord, who has no beginning and no end (el Senor increado, el que no tiene principio y fin)—God, of whom they said that he was the Creator of all things and was himself uncreated—(Dios que decian que era creado del todo yel increado). If you compare this with the Egyptian you will find it identical.

The Mexican Tlanezcalpan Tecietli—the Lord of the Dawn and the Evening Twilight: the first light which illuminated the earth, is the representation of Horus I. In the Zapotec he was called Coqui-Zee Coqui-Cilla, which means the same thing, and is represented in their Calendar opposite the day which begins with "1 Snake." We see in their Calendar, then first represented, the beginning of the days by the sign of the crocodile—as the denominating sign, which proves that they represented and believed that Sut, the King of Darkness, was first or primary, and that Coqui-Zee or Horus I. deposed him, which is identical with what we find in the Egyptian primordial.

Dr Edward Seler is certainly under the impression that their year began with the Quaintlena—the feast of the Rain God (Tlalogue)—"Mexican Antiquities," page 22—and that the sign for the first day of the year was the sign of the Crocodile = Great Water Lizard.

In this he is perfectly correct (page 38), but he cannot make out how this should fit in with the rainy seasons of Mexico,

Yucatan, and Central American States, etc., and tries various and many ingenious ways to make the rendering agree, but he does not know the key, so cannot unlock the riddle.

We will give him the key and the explanation, and he will, we think, have no further difficulty in arriving at the correct solution, or in fitting in his various gods and deities in their proper places and order. To do this, we must give the Egyptian rendering of the commencement of the reckoning of time pretty fully; he will then understand why many old nations thought the world began their first year with the inundation (although it might not be their rainy season). They brought it from Egypt, and it is part of the Stellar or Lunar—Stellar Mythos—and will also explain the Mayas' "Renewal of the House" or "renewal of the Temple" (page 27).

Time was first kept in Egypt, and the year began, when the tail of the great Bear pointed South. That was the commencement of the year, and the time was kept by Tekhi—the Goddess of the Inundation, and the first month of the year was called Tekhi (oldest table of time found at Ramesseum and Edfu).

The year of the Great Bear was Stellar. Then came Lunar time, or Lunar-Stellar: twelve months of thirty days, each with five added, by Taht, the Moon God. The origin of these days as an Egyptian legend is repeated by Plutarch.

The seven Astronomes in the Celestial heptanomes of the seven Egyptian nomes were first mapped out in Egypt, and then figured in the heavens. The names of these in Egypt were: Memphites, Heracleopolites, Crocodileopolites, Aphrositopolites, Oxyrhynchites, Cynopolites and Hermopolites. The Goddess of the Great Bear, who as Khebt, or Apt, was mother of the fields of heaven when they consisted of the seven Astronomes.

The fields of the Papyrus reed, (the Papyrus reed or young shoots of the same, and water, were the original food of life symbolically,) were figured within the circle made by the turn round of the seven Stars about the North Celestial Pole. This formed the enclosure of the River of Life which was planted in the garden or on the Mount, the Tree of Life or food in the Celestial waters—otherwise the Tree of the Pole, in the Astronomical Mythology; therefore the Constellation of the Female Hippopotamus (or Great Bear) was the Mother of the time circles. It was a clock on account of its wheeling round the Pole once every twenty-four hours.

The Great Bear was also a clock of the four Quarters in the Cycle of the year. As the Chinese say: "When the tail of the Great Bear points to the East, it is spring; when it points to the South, it is summer; when it points to the West, it is autumn; when it points to the North, it is winter." In Egypt when the Great Bear pointed to the South, or, astronomically, when the Constellation had attained its Southernmost elongation, *it was the time of inundation, or the birthday of the year, which was also the birthday of the world.*

The tail stars of the Great Bear were pointers to the South—where the birthplace of the waters was—(African Lakes) which brought salvation to the people of Egypt, with Horus in the Ark as the Deliverer of Drought (Sut), and hence, doctrinally, as the Saviour of the World.

The inundation was a primary factor in the establishment of time in Egypt, and the foundation of the year (see Hymn to the Nile); also as Teacher of time. The Nile was the inspirer of Taht, who was the Measurer of time.

Under the name of Tekhi, the Old Great Mother was the giver of liquid and the supplier of drink; as Khept or Apt, she was the water cow, with a woman's breasts; as Neith, she was the suckler of crocodiles; as Isis, she was the Milk-mother; and as Menat, she was the wet-nurse, typical provider of plenty; and primarily, she was Mother Earth, and fundamentally related to the water source of the Egyptian inundation.

This was the Old First Mother, who was given the Great Bear as her Constellation in the Northern heaven, when she became the Maker of the starry revolutions, or Cycles, and the Mother of the earliest year in time, which year was dependent on the inundation, and determined by the birth of Horus, as the Crocodile-headed Sebek, the Son of the Great Bear, otherwise the Crocodile or Water Lizard of the inundation.

The birth is represented in the Astronomical fragment from a Theban tomb. On this the Old First Mother has just given birth to her young crocodile, and dropped it in front of her. Thus we behold the birth of Sebek which, according to sign language, is equally the birth of another year at the moment when the Great

Bear's tail is pointing to the birthplace—to the Great Lakes in the South.

The year of the Great Bear, and the inundation, or of Apt and Sebek, was found to be wrong in time, and this was righted when Taht Hermes, the Measurer of time by the Great Bear and the Moon, had added the five additional days to the earlier Stellar year, and thus established the truer Cycle of 365 days in the place of the 360 days.

When the Bear was pointing to the birthplace of the water in the South, the Festival of the Tail was celebrated for the coming inundation. There was a Set Heb Festival also, which was celebrated every thirty years as the Festival of the Tail, which was the anniversary of some special year of years, and the Lord of the thirty year Festival was, at one period Horus, and at another, Ptah.

Here is the reason why the Central American States, and all those old countries where we find the Stellar and Lunar Mythos, commence "their time" with the *inundation and have the sign of the Crocodile or Great Water Lizard as the first day of the first year.* The inundation in Egypt was the time in all these countries —(and roughly the opening or commencement of the year, coincides with the summer solstice—when the solstices had at length been recognised in the Solar Mythos).

In the Mexican Calendar, we have the four Quarters with the names of the four children of Horus, and the seven divisions of the Astronomes with the one added = eight, and also the seven primary ones, six with the centre = seven.

That the Ancient Egyptians knew that the Great Lakes in Central Africa were the sources of the Nile, and the cause of inundation, is proved by the *Ritual*: "I know what is written in the book-store kept in the library, that *whenever the Nile cometh forth from the two fountains* the offerings of the Gods are to be plenty."—R. of the *Ritual*, chap. lxii. These two great lakes were figured in heaven as the two Great Lakes, one on the North and one on the South of the Mount—the Baku hill, on which heaven rested—the Lake of Kharu and the Lake of Ru—*Ritual*, chaps. cviii.-cix. They are also represented in Amenta and in the Mexican painting—see HUMBOLDT, FRAGMENTS.

On page 372, fig. D represents Horus walking on the Sea or Lake, his headdress and crown represent The Lord of the four

Quarters and "Light to lighten the Way," the four symbols of the same are raised above.

Fig. 77, page 312, which is called by *Dr Edward Seler* "a dancer," represents Horus crowned with "The Three Rods," or

Horus, who is here represented as speaking to his Father in Heaven. Horus wears the Crown with the "All Seeing Eye," and above this 3 Rods or Rays of Light. His Serkh is behind with the 3 Rods on the top, also 3 on his feet. He is giving the sign of — and his Father in Heaven who is represented above is returning the answer—Horus is shown wearing the chain of the 33° with the emblem of the same, as used during the Stellar Mythos.

FIG. 39.—From "Mexican Antiquities."[1]

Rays of Light—The Light of the World. He also has a staff with this symbol raised above, behind him—these signs and symbols represented here, are the same as those we find amongst the Druids and in Egypt. His face is raised and he is speaking to "His Father in Heaven"—Ra (see *Ritual*, chap. 173).

Horus addressing his father, Ra—exclaims: "Hail, Osiris, I am thy son Horus, I have come, I have avenged thee, I have struck down thine enemies," etc.

Ra is here called Ra-Unnefer-Osiris Ra, who has the Royal Uræus on his head, and other emblems of attributes and sovereignty.

The Egyptians celebrated ten great festivals or Mysteries each year, and we find the Mexicans-Zapotecs did the same, also that the Mexican and Central States of America ideographed their Astro-Mythology in Uranographic mode, as did the Egyptians.

The Elements themselves, were the earliest superhuman powers, equivalents and these were thought of, and imaged by, superhuman in the Stellar Mythos in the same way as the Egyptians did.

The different gods we find here, correspond in every particular to those of Egypt :—

MEXICAN	EGYPTIAN	
The God of Fire	Khabsenup	We have given the equivalent names, in Mexican Zapotec, etc., in other parts of this work.
,, ,, Darkness	Sut	
,, ,, Light	Horus	
,, ,, Water	Nu or Hapi	
,, ,, Earth	Tuamutef or Seb.	Two lists of names for the 7 are given in the *Ritual*, chaps. xvii. xcix. cvii.
,, ,, Blood	Child Horus	
Breathing power of Air-Lifter of Clouds of Darkness, etc.	Shu	

The Frog or Toad is frequently portrayed in the Central American Codices, and the tradition in N. America (amongst the Indians) that a Frog in the Moon was followed by a devouring Wolf who was in love with the Frog, means the Frog was a type of transformation, and was applied to the changing moon in sign language :—Ptah was depicted as a Frog, and a Lamp was found in Egypt, with a Frog on it, with this written in hieroglyphic : "I am the Resurrection" (*Lanzone Dizionario*, page 853).

The Lamp here is equivalent to the Rising Sun, and the Frog on it is the type of Ptah, who in his Solar character was the Resurrection and the Life in the Mythology before the image passed into Eschatology, when the god who rose again as Solar, became the Light of the World in a Spiritual sense. The Frog here was a Zootype representation of Ptah in Amenta, or the Lower Earth, or Nether World, or Earth of Eternity. The Tortoise was another form frequently found depicted in these Central American Codices, as in Egypt.

It is by means of this sign language that this Egyptian wisdom keeps the records of the prehistoric past. The Egyptian Hieroglyphics shows us the connection between words and things, also between sounds and words, and a very primitive range of thought, and there is no other such a record in all the world, and this sign language includes the gestures and signs by which the mysteries were danced or otherwise dramatised in Africa by the Pygmies first, others following. They consisted largely of human gestures and signs, and the sounds first made by animals—as for instance, "ba," the goat, "meaou" for the cat, "su" for the goose, etc., and the living ideographs and zootypes were primarily of, and can be traced to this original home, and not anywhere else on the face of the earth.

These Zootypes were extant in nature as figures and pictures ready made, hieroglyphics and ideographs that moved about alive, living nature types that were employed when no others were known to art.

Mr Spencer is entirely wrong when he states that mythical representation began with "stories of *human adventure*," and that every kind of creation may be transformed into any other. The above proves that he is absolutely wrong.

The Frog in Egypt was a sign, also, of "Myriads" as well as "transformation." In the Moon it would denote "myriads of renewals" when periodic repetition was a mode of immortality.

The Goddess Heket (Frog) represented the Moon and its transformation, amongst the Andaman Islands and Australian aborigines, and also the Irequois N. A. I. They make the Frog "The Great Monster which drinks up all the waters"; hence the Frog plays the part of the Apap Monster, and we see thus that the idea was also held by the Mayas. See fig. and hieroglyphics, "Mexican Antiquities," page 425.

SYMBOLS AND SIGNS OF TALE OF BIRTH OF HORUS, SON OF ISIS, AND MACHINATIONS OF SUT

1. Large Scorpion representing Sut guarding the house wherein

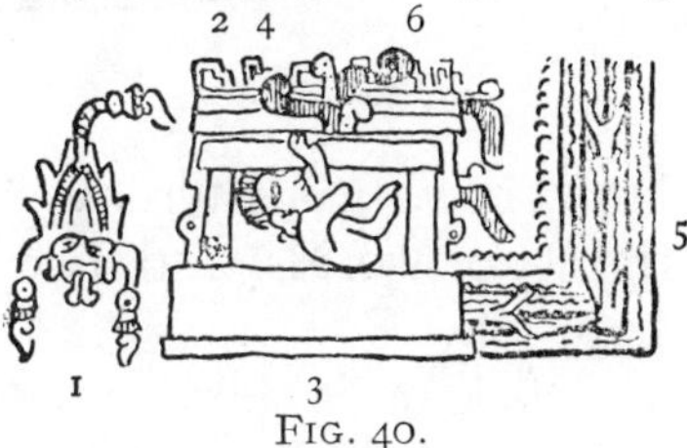

FIG. 40.
From "Mexican Antiquities," Bul. 28, page 179, fig. C.

he had hidden Isis and Horus (Sut changed himself into a Scorpion).

3. House with child Horus hidden therein by Sut.

2 and 4. Hieroglyph (Egyptian) for Isis and Nephthysis. Nephthysis came with Serquet and besought help from heaven, and Ra came with his "Boat of Millions of Years," and stopping the boat, and Thoth, by means of words of power, restored Horus to life again after he had been stung by the scorpion and died.

5. Water, with Papyrus plant growing, representing the Papyrus Swamp where Isis fled to hide herself when she brought forth Horus.

6. These hieroglyphs (on the authority of *Champollion*, in foreign names) represent the two feathers—Maat.

Horus as Lord of the Double-Horizon

Horus, he who made the pathway, not only between the two horizons, but to eternal life as son of Ra—the *Holy Spirit* in the Eschatology, the intermediate link in the Mythos which

Fig. 41.

"connects the Solar orb with yesterday," is now the intermediary betwixt the two worlds and two lives in time and eternity—*Ritual*, chap. xlii.

Horus (as Horus-Sebek he is represented as the earliest fish-man). He is here seen emaned from the great Fish mother, Apt — Nina was another form — Primarily he issued from the female fish—*i.e.* the Crocodile Apt (female) as her son Horus-

Sebek or young Crocodile. Jonah being ejected from the great fish's mouth is only an exoteric rendering of the above. The figure k represents Mythological and Eschatological part of the *Ritual.*

FIG. 42.

Reproduced from "Mexican Antiquities," published by the Bureau of American Ethnology, for which I have to thank *Mr W. H. Holmes.*

HORUS THE LIGHT OF THE WORLD IN TEARS

This figure depicts "Horus in Tears"—"Ye are the tears made by my eye in your name of men."

FIG. 43.

Reproduced from "Mexican Antiquities," published by the Bureau of American Ethnology, for which I have to thank *Mr W. H. Holmes.*

His Crown (emblem of light with three feathers) represents him as "The Light of the World" as witnessed by Taht-Aan—who carried the Eye of Horus in his hands and testifies that Horus is the true light of the world as son of Ra, the solar God, and of the Holy Spirit in the Eschatology (see *Ritual*). Taht-Aan was the primordial John, but far anterior and just as personal, as he carried in his hands the papyrus roll—" the word of life " and the eye of light, the Talismanic " Maatkheru " as seen portrayed here on the head of Horus.

The papers in this work, " Mexican Antiquities," by *Seler*, *Forstemann*, *Paul Schellhas*, *Carl Sapper* and *E. P. Dieseldorff*, all follow on the same lines in their arguments and explanations; nevertheless we cannot agree with them, and boldly accept the challenge thrown down by *Mr Forstemann* on page 541.—" You can make an hypothesis on anything, but the true meaning of all these codices can only be made by taking into account the Mythos of Egypt and the exodes thence," which these gentlemen have entirely ignored. The differences which we find, and have not been explained by these writers, can only be understood by a knowledge of Totemism and the Stellar, Lunar, as well as the Solar Mythos, and *Ritual*. In these myths and legends, and in their hieroglyphics, there are the same tales throughout—Horus I. as the Eagle or Hawk ; the God of the Pole Star : *The One* added to the Seven Glorious Ones : the Little Bear—not the Southern Cross ◎-◎ ◎ ◎ ◎ ◎ ◎-◎, and Sothos, as represented by the dog Anubis.

And O O O OOOOOO Mexican, is equal to No. 9 Egyptian, representing the nine circles of heaven, or the Put Cycle of Ptah.

SUT BOUND AND CHAINED AND WOUNDED BY HORUS' SPEAR

FIG. 44.
Reproduced from "Mexican Antiquities," published by the Bureau of American Ethnology, for which I have to thank *Mr. W. H. Holmes*.

This figure represents the Great Apap monster bound and chained. The text (*Ritual*) states that " he has a chain of steel upon him" (Ba metal) and "Thou art pierced with hooks" (chap. cviii.), etc.

We see here the Mount of Heaven, with the Double Holy House of Anup and the Sacred Word exposed in the Temple of the same, and the M W X, with his attributes, giving the — sign. Supported on two squares, or double squares, with four steps—*i.e.* earth and heaven or the two earths or Earthly life and

FIG. 45.

Spiritual life—four steps = four supports or children of Horus, with the Egyptian Hieroglyphic "Mes" in front = to be born again, etc., and the Put cycle of Ptah underneath and the "5 mysteries sign" and indication below on the right.

In the centre, below the Sacred Word, is the "Tree of Life," with seven branches and the Food of Life portrayed in its fruit.

In Egyptian the Tree of Hathor was the Tree of Life, and it was the Sycamore Fig Tree, from the fruit of which a divine drink of the mysteries was made and drunk at a certain part or time of the ceremonies, therefore it was the typical tree to make one wise, and it became a tree of abnormal knowledge. The divine drink is still made and used in the 18°.

The tree of Nut was the Tree of Heaven and Eternal Life, hence it was designated the Eternal Tree, as shown in the vignette of

"The Book of the Dead"—the tree or eatable plant and the water supplied the elements of life to the Manes in the lower paradise—*i.e.* Amenta—Arru-Garden. The tree of Nut was Stellar; the tree of Hathor, Solar. Uaxtepcatl Petlacalctl is the Mexican name for Lord or Keeper, Mount and Tree of Mount-Horus. Anauaacatl, Mexican name for Ear of Corn by a stream of water and God of Ear of Corn Cinteotl—Horus.

They have published this figure upside down, we have corrected it.

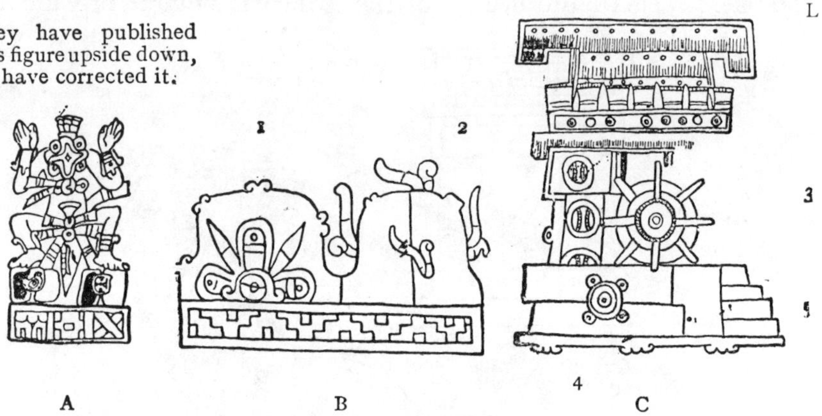

A B C

FIG. 46.—From "Mexican Antiquities," published by the Smithsonian Institute, Bureau of American Ethnology—Bul. 28, page 310.

The above must be interesting to brothers of the 18°.

A is the prototype of M W S with the sign H or A, with all his attributes attached, before the sacred name.

B. We have here on the left (1) the sacred name exposed to view. *A* is looking on it, with the sign. On the right (2) the sacred name is guarded within two closed doors with flames of fire—or the holy spirit guarding it—from the eye of the profane.

C is the figure of the Temple with the "Lights 33" Heaven in eight divisions (3) and one of the names of Horus (Amsu), the risen Horus in the centre of this. On the pedestal (4) is another name of Horus. "The Lord and Giver of Light and Life," or the "Diffuser of Light to the World" or "Giver of Rays of Light to the World."

The four steps (5) denote the number of supports or four children of Horus—Imexayacatzin—Mexican for The Children of the Thigh.

Their different coloured gods, seven in all, denote different elemental spirits in nature—seven colours—seven spirits—not human, but contained in their totemic zootypes (not ancestral spirits), and is the representation here and all over the world of the seven superhuman powers or the gods and the glorified, and the names are those of the Egyptians. The Aztec, Mexican and Peruvian legends must be read through the Astro-Mythology and *Ritual* of ancient Egypt, and only by so doing can you understand them.

This does not refer to a battle on earth or Mexico, as *Dr Edward Seler* states, but the mythical battle between Sut and Horus in one of its phases, and the hieroglyphics of the two names. It portrays Sut and Horus contending for the supremacy in the equinox on the mount, with Shu as arbitrator.

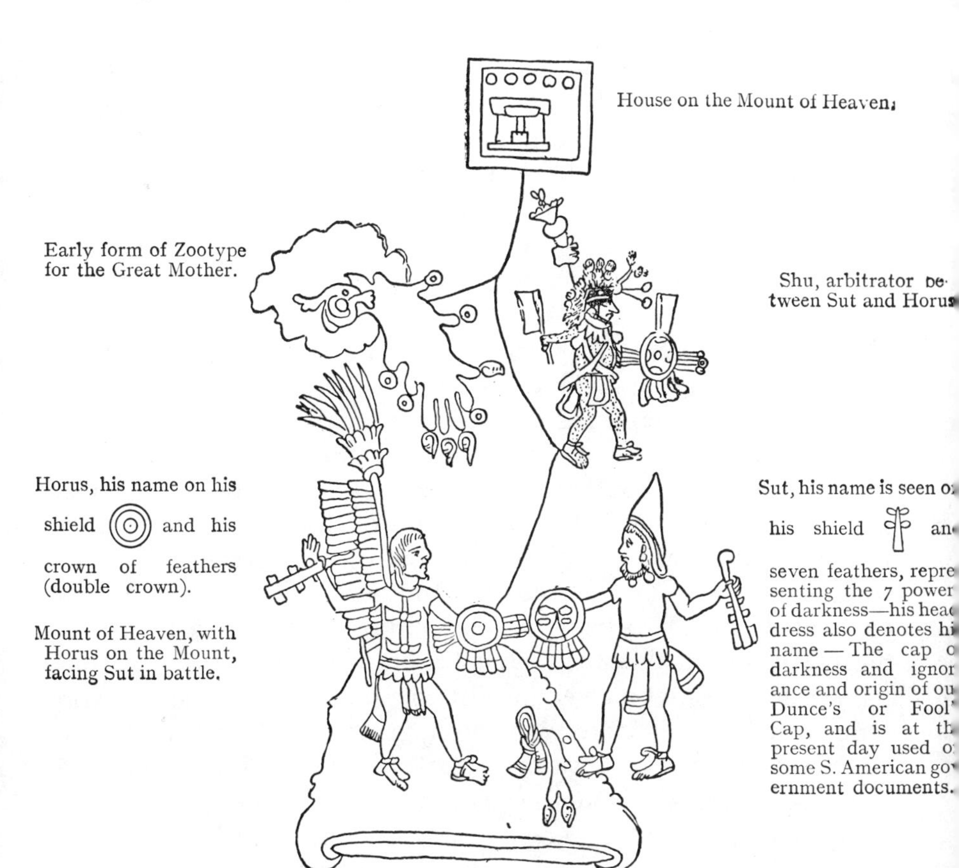

FIG. 47.
From "Mexican Antiquities," published by the Bureau of American Ethnology—Bul. 28, page 263.

[1] The Father in Heaven was not individualised at this early period and primitive man had not yet been able to impose the human likeness on the mother nature or nurse, so they portrayed her as "the suckler"—that in zootype form—which was the same as in Egypt—a living Ideograph.

It was on the mount of Hetep at the equinoctial level that the quarrel of Sut and Horus was settled for the time being by Shu. Law and order was established between the elemental forces which had hitherto been ever fighting for supremacy (light and darkness) and bounds to the contentions of these powers were established by dividing the whole universe from zenith to Nadir into the two domains—one for Sut—the South and night, and one for Horus—the North and light (*Ritual*, chap. cx.). This was the first in Stellar, and Shu was the arbitrator. In Lunar it was Taht, and in the Solar, Seb. The Great Mother, here depicted in zootype as the great many-teated suckler, shows her as the mother of the first three elemental powers. The Japanese have the same prototype. The uranographic symbol was constellated in "Triangula," composed of three stars, held in the hand of Horus.

On pages 378 and 381, "Mexican Antiquities," *Dr Edward Seler* reproduces many figures and symbols, Maya and Mexican. His Maize Goddess, fig. k, p. 378, and again in fig. a, 381. Fig. 99 k (p. 105 here) is the representation of Horus—the two fishes in Pisces—the fish-man. Horus is seen kneeling on the right knee with the sign—— holding a fish by its head, or food of life[1]; underneath are the two monster fishes, here shown identically as the ancient Egyptian hieroglyph; one represents the Southern Fish and the other Ketos. The Southern fish on the Celestial globe is portrayed in the act of emaning a stream of water from its mouth. The other monster, Ketos, as the "breather" out of the water, as is shown by the air issuing from his nostrils and bubbling on the surface of the water; the two being a representation of the earth as the mother of life in the water called the abyss—known by various names in the different versions of the Mythos. In the Sut and Horus Mythos they were twins born, because the conditions were co-extant in earth and water. In the course of time everything that was hot and dry, like the desert, was ascribed to Sut; whereas the products of water—green trees, life, etc., were assigned to Horus; hence the two monsters here were continued as types of the twins, and as born from water. One name of the Egyptian god of the inundation was Bahu—called the "Power of the

[1] The Zapotecs have, like the Egyptians, represented the Crocodile or "great water Lizard" as one name for the highest being and have portrayed it in the Glyphs as "the giver of food of life." The Zapotec name for this Crocodile is Tlaloc and ce Cipactli = the one.

Southern lakes"—*Rec.* vol. x. p. 149—and "I am Bahu the Great" is said four times over in the MAGIC PAPYRUS. The sign of the fish, enclosed in Egyptian hieroglyph, signifies An—to appeal to, to show, to teach. An in Egyptian is also the name of the teacher, the scribe, the priest. Horus, as Sebek, was the great fish of the inundation—typical of food and water. In the Stellar Mythos the deceased assumed the form of a fish to cross the waters in the nether-world; he had to swim around the under-world and across the Nu to the Celestial Pole or Mount of Heaven, and it was Horus, as "teacher," who showed or taught the way, and he is here depicted as the "teacher of the way." Horus is seen here with the two crowns on his head—spiritual and earthly. Fig. 99 g on the same page (104 here) represents Horus as "Lord of the Double Horizon." He is kneeling on one horizon with his right leg, and his left foot is placed on the other horizon; his hands and arms raised in the same sign ——. On page 381 (105 here) Horus is represented with the same sacred sign—in tears. "Horus in tears."—He says:—"Ye are the tears made by my eye in your name of men." He wears the crown of the three feathers and has the symbol of Light—thus represented as "the Light of the World." Fig. a (p. 381 m.a) on the same page represents Horus as "the Young Ear of Corn," here represented by Maize. He is giving life and plenty, the bringer of food of life to the world. On page 604 he is represented as Sebek, precisely as on the Egyptian monuments. The foregoing is *Dr Edward Seler's* "Goddess of Maize"!!! On the same page, 381, fig. h (p. 106 here), is represented Sut, as bound and chained by Horus. The chains are around him, the Egyptian hieroglyph "a to be tied up" is over his head, and Horus' spear is in his vital parts, which he is vainly endeavouring to remove. Fig. g on the same page: also on page 377 a is a representation of "Shaat, the Great Mother," both in Zootype and anthropomorphically.[1] The many-teated sow, or Hathor or Isis—all one and the same. On page 377 a it is Isis above, anthropomorphically, with the two feathers Maat: with the symbol of Shaat below, and on page 381 it is the Mexican bird representing "Mut," the Great Mother,

[1] The plate, The Goddess Nut, is from *Dr E. A. Wallis Budge's* "The Gods of the Egyptians," published by Messrs Methuen & Co. We are much indebted to these gentlemen for their kind permission to reproduce these beautiful plates from *Dr Budge's* great work and take this opportunity of returning our sincere thanks for the same.

with Shaat below—all one and the same—showing the different periods of time. Fig. a, 377, is of a later date than fig. g, 381. The former shows Solar and divinised in the Eschatology, the latter Stellar Mythos, and therefore a zootype. On page 70 are the four children of Horus, mentioned elsewhere in this work. On page 303 (a) is a figure of Shu on the right and the symbol of the Put cycle of Ptah, with Horus seated in front: also on page 372 Shu is depicted. *Stephens* gives several plates taken on the spot at Palanque and those of the Casa de Piedra, Nos. 1, 2, 3 & 4.—"Incidents of Travel in Central America, Chepas and Yucatan," 1848, are identical with those at Mariette, "Abydos," 1 pl. 10, 1 pl. 29, and are connected with, or rather are Vignettes of chaps. cxii. and cxxiii. of "The Book of the Dead."

The fact *that the Temples at Uxmal face East by South or are oriented E. by S.*, are of a much higher type of architecture, *and have no so-called idols, prove that these were of much later date*, were copied from the *Egyptians at the time that the pyramids in the Sudan were built* (*which are all oriented East and South*), *and must rank, as regards time, with the Druids, whose circles are oriented East by South* — *i.e.* during the Solar Mythos; whereas those at Casa de Palanque, the ruins at Copan and Quirigua, all are oriented North, like the Great Pyramid; have so-called idols and rude figures (zootypes). This will be easily understood, and accounted for the different Mythos (Stellar) in vogue at the time they were built. The ruins at Quirigua are undoubtedly the oldest of all the above. The huge snake and other animals here depicted were the earlier representatives as zootypes and symbols of the attributes of the "Great One" before the divination of the powers had been completely worked out, or the anthropomorphic had come into existence to take their place as representatives of these types. *Bernal Diaz's* description of beautiful temples, with huge serpents in some parts of them, is indicative of their origin being Egypt: the original being at "Pithom" and representing the "god of the gate of the East." The "huge serpent," a representation (symbolically) of the "god Tmu"—see later chapter on the Cross—and therefore the dedication of these temples must be attributed to Tmu or Tem. The reason why we find the name sometimes written Tmu and at others as Tem, was because one represented "the child" and the other "the man," but these were identically the same = to and

THE GODDESS NUT HOLDING A TABLET ON WHICH STANDS HARPOCRATES.

She is portrayed as the Goddess of Heaven, as the bringer-forth of a new life, *i.e.*, Horus being carried aloft as the True Light of the World, and a symbolic likeness of a Soul in human nature begotten of the Holy Spirit.

other names for the child Horus of twelve years old and Horus of thirty years old. That different animals or zootypes were used in different countries would naturally arise from the change of fauna as primitive wisdom passed from land to land, thus accounting for the different animals here represented in America to portray the various parts of the *Ritual* of ancient Egypt, both in the Stellar, Lunar and Solar Mythologies and their Eschatology, the latter in a limited area, comparatively.

At an early period we have the serpent, Sut, represented opposite to Horus I., as may be seen by the type of bird above his head. This serpent represented their old god, Ueuetcotl, who already existed in twilight—*i.e.* before the sun's rays had penetrated the watery vapour surrounding the earth, and the ultimate battle between the two. The Heaven, shown in eight divisions, is precisely as we find it amongst the Druids, Chaldeans, and, as we know, from the original Egyptian; the Great Mother suckling the child, as Isis did Horus, and so on. Throughout all this work, there is no difficulty in following the one, in comparison with the other, and although the Mayas had less of the Stellar and Lunar Mythos associated with the Solar, it was no doubt through their frequent intercourse with the Egyptians, they probably, like Moses, would wish to blot out and abandon as much of the Stellar doctrines and beliefs as they found consistent to carry on the later pure Eschatology or the Solar; whilst those of the Chipas, Guatemala, Honduras and Nicaragua, etc., would not be in such an advanced state, and the "overlapping" would not have been fully completed—as we find—and those of the North and farther West would have still less of the Solar and more of the Stellar. Other tribes, like the Seri, would date still further back and have the earliest Stellar and Totemism only, whilst there would be no mixture in some.

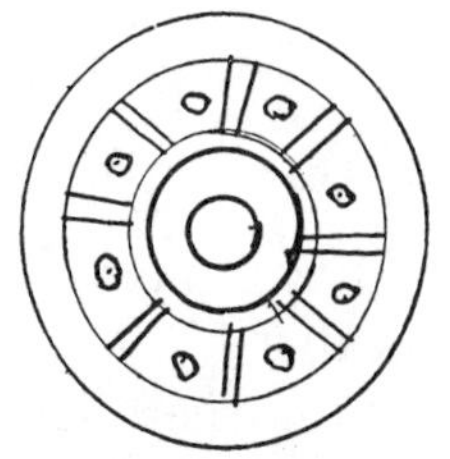
FIG. 48.—Heaven in 8 divisions.

Dr Edward Seler, in his attempt to decipher the HUMBOLDT FRAGMENTS, has fallen into the same error as *Dr Le Plongeon*, and has vainly endeavoured to assign all therein to places on this earth, —*i.e.* Mexico, etc.; but these fragments do not represent any map or picture of this earth; it is a part of the Tuat and Amenta and all therein, that is portrayed here. His eldest Motechuhzoma, which he describes and translates as "*the fire god*," is the representation of Ptah, the first Solar god, who, with seven assistants, formed Åmenta or built the underworld for the passage of the manes, sun, moon, etc. *His younger*, for whom he cannot assign any name or place, is Tem—Horus, the child of twelve years, or Temu—Horus, of thirty years of age. His mountain in water or water mountain, and the god thereof, was, at a later period, ascribed to Osiris. One of the names given by *Dr Brugsch* to Osiris was "the Great Water god," but primarily it was Horus of the mount of the North, surrounded by the celestial waters of the universe. His Xilotl or Cacamatl or "*Young Ear of Corn*," was one of the names of Horus, and his Zipe, with "flayed human skin," and was their representation of Ptah-Seker-Ausàr—the Triune God of the Resurrection. On page 65, fig. A, is depicted another type of this—Amsu the risen Horus, his name ☩ is twice portrayed on this figure — Amsu is again figured in another form—on page 616, fig. H. He is here rising from the Tomb where he lay in the *Thrice bent position*, his right hand and arm are free, his hand pointing upwards, his left arm still bound to his side with hand pointing downwards — he descended—he ascended. This was Amsu in the Stellar Mythos, the same as the Egyptian. Horus and Sut are also shown on page 377 fig. I. as in the Egyptian back to back—the black god and the white god. Quauhtli—eagle, Mexican, name of Horus. Cozcaquauhtli—vulture, same as the above, only older, sometimes, however, applied to Isis. His Acatl, Calli, Tecpatl, Tochtle, which he ascribes to the names of the commencement of days or periods, are the four children of Horus, gods of the four quarters—East, West, North and South.

The Mexican Calendar on page 29, here shown, is a Swasticà Cross, showing the four quarters with the names of the four children of Horus on it. His god of the earthquake is Shu or An-Heru, the lifter up of the heavens. Chibirias or Ixhebelyoxor or Zac Zuhuny—the White virgin, a name of Isis. His Toci or Teteo-innan or Mother of the gods as he calls it, is right, because she is always represented with the Chicautztle or "rattle-board,"

HUMBOLDT FRAGMENT FROM "MEXICAN ANTIQUITIES"

[*Facing page* 114

which is the same as the Egyptian Isis, with Sistrum. Moan—i-m-p 39, is Anubis—"*one who smells out the way*" in the underworld, to guide the manes to "the seat of the weighing of souls." Coatl or Cizuij sor Zee—Snake, the evil one, the troubler,

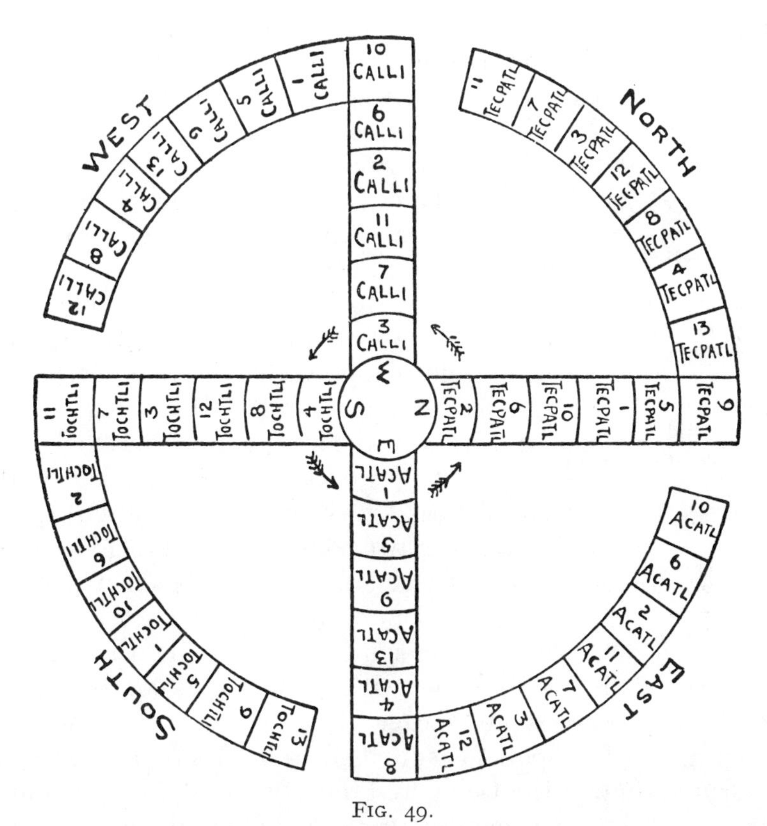

FIG. 49.

The Mexican Calendar in form of Swastica Cross, from "Mexican Antiquities," p. 29, with the names of the Four Children of Horus as gods of the four corners, at N. S. E. and W.

the one who brings misery, the deceiver, layer of snares, one who brings trouble, was their representative of the great Apap fiend.

On page 159 S, Ta-Urt, here shown, is so well depicted that it cannot possibly be mistaken by any Egyptologist or anyone else if they will compare this with the plate in the Book of "The Gods of Egypt." Mictlampa is the Aztec name for North, *and also the direction of the Realm of the Dead*. It was at the North that paradise was situated, and on the Holy Mount, situated at the North, surrounded with the waters of the universe, was the Great House or Holy City. The spirits of the departed had to pass the waters of space—in Stellar Mythos—carried from the underworld by "a zootype form," and in the Solar, after emerging from Amenta by a boat. This was the belief of these people, the same in every particular as the Egyptian, from whom they learnt their Mythology and Eschatology. On page 179, fig. c, b and a, we have part of the tale of the birth of Horus, son of Isis.[1] In fig. c, we see the child Horus hidden and secured in a house, surrounded by water and plants, with the great scorpion on the left (Sut), guarding the same. Above fig. b is seen the scorpion Sut in battle. He is pierced by two spears. Opposite, in another parallel passage of the same manuscript, there is again drawn, opposite the fire god, instead of the war god, merely a scorpion, a stream of water, and a burning house. c, Teoatl Tlachinolli—the symbol of war. In the Egyptian we learn that Isis became with child, and her son Horus was born in a secret place, where she suckled him and reared him. The spot was supposed to be situated amongst the papyrus swamp of the Delta, and the event is alluded to in many scenes in which is the goddess, suckling her child, amidst a dense mass of papyrus plants. Soon after the birth of her son, she was persecuted by Sut in the form of a great scorpion, who kept Isis and Horus prisoners in a house, but by the help of Thoth she eventually escaped with the child, etc.—For further information on this point and the stinging of the child Horus to death by the scorpion, and bringing to life again of Horus, and fight with Sut, see EGYPTIAN TEXT.

FIG. 50.—Ta-Urt giving birth to her son or the birth of a new year.

This is the Mexican representation (from "Mexican Antiquities," p. 159 S.) of the Old First Mother giving birth to her young Crocodile, precisely similar to the Egyptian here mentioned; also on page 99.

The foregoing picture-signs of the Mexican are most dra-

[1] Page 103 in this book.

matically and truly a portrayal of the Egyptian episode, and we contend that *Dr Edward Seler* is entirely in the dark, and has missed the key for the true decipherment of all these hieroglyphs and picture-signs. His seven warriors here represent the seven Scorpions, called Tefen, Befen, Mestet, Mestetef, Petet, Thetet and Metet, who protected Isis, with her child, when she escaped from the Papyrus swamp and fled to Per-Sui or Crocodilopolis, and then to the city of the Two Sandals—Goddesses.

In the HUMBOLDT FRAGMENT xvi. we see the beginning of the evolution of Christianity amongst these people, precisely similar to the earliest Christian Copts in the first part of the FRAGMENT. They have converted Amsu into

to represent Jesus Christ, and have given his age as thirty-three at time of resurrection and fourteen as the Child Jesus.

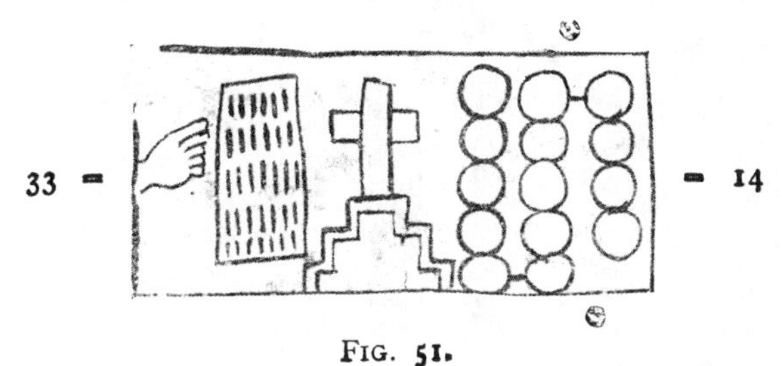

FIG. 51.

FIG. 52.

This plate is from J. L. Steven's work (" Central America," p. 311), published 1849, taken from a stucco bas-relief at the temple of Palenque. It shows an early type of the resurrection, namely, the raising of the Tat pillar, this being a type of the Pole or the pillar that sustained the universe, and also as a pillar of the four corners, based on the tree as a type of the Pole. The picture is pre-Osirian, and the central figure standing erect raising the Tat pillar is Atum-Ra. He is accompanied by his two sons Hu and

Sau. These two sons in the pre-Osirian mythos accompany their father in his resurrection, which it is shown to be here by the ithyphallic condition, as the prototype of Amsu (*Ritual*, chap. xvii.), and they are saluting him with the well-known signs used by us in the O degree.

It will be noticed, also, that this is the same sign used as those portrayed on the vase from Chama, except that in one case it is the R.S.L.H. and in the other L.S.R.H., the difference being in the degrees.

FIG. 53.

This plate is from J. L. Steven's work ("Central America," p. 318), from Palenque, and represents Horus of the Double Horizon or of the Double Equinox, who was termed the Double Harmakhu, and this duality was imaged in the two-foldness of the Sphinx, or the two Lions, which expressed the Double Glory of Horus, who was Lord of the Solar forces, that was double in the vernal equinox. In the *Ritual* (chap. xxxviii.) it is said of Horus of the Two Lions, "I am the Twin Lions, the heir of Ra." In chap. lxii. 2, "I am the Twin Lions." In chap. lxxii. 9, "I am the Double Lion." One title of Horus of the Double Horizon is Har-Khuti-Khepera. This is the Horus-Sun, and the two lions he is sitting on image the double strength of glory of Horus in the sign of Leo. The above shows one of the phases of the double character of Horus. Some others were, "He of the Double Crown," "the Double Feather," "the Double Uræi," "the Double Life, earthly and spiritual," etc. In front is Shu presenting him with the emblems of the two Lands, earthly and spiritual, and making him Lord of Heaven and of earth, symbols of which Shu is holding in his hands, the lower part representing the lands of the earth, and the upper part the spiritual. This picture is a representation of the Egyptian pre-Osirian character.

It shows the old sign of F—expressing his acceptance of the trust conferred.

Dr Le Plongeon, in bringing forward the results of his travels and studies amongst the Mayas, and trying to show that these were the "first people" who taught others, and the first people of the earth, takes no account of those who were much older than the Mayas, and had the Stellar Mythos; takes into account nothing of the anatomical conditions of previous inhabitants. Like *Dr W. Budge*, he commences very late "in his points of the Primordial," but his writings and photographs help to prove our contention: "that the Mayas obtained their knowledge of the Solar doctrines from the Egyptians, and were probably the first of the American nations who practised or believed in this," and although he mentions some of the Totemic Ceremonies of the Nahutls, he is apparently quite ignorant of them, or how these Nahaults obtained their Stellar Mythos. His signs and photos, which he found here, are valuable, but his interpretation quite wrong. We give a few for example, showing the true explanation. His sign of the Land of the Scorpion of the Mayas is the Egyptian sign of "Zodiacal West." His is Khui Land, a part of the Egyptian Amenta. ∩ is the Egyptian numeral for No. 10. is a pair of arms with hands outstretched, is a negative Egyptian sign to stop, to arrest, no or not, or to embrace. is a boat stand. ◎ his Tza, which he translates as "That which is necessary," is one of the Hieroglyphic signs for Amsu (the risen Horus). the tail he calls "Ain," the Maya *for Crocodile*, but this is wrong; the tail reads: "Ka or Kam, whence Kamit for Egypt." Kamit is the black night—death-darkness, and was depicted by the *Crocodile's tail*, not the *Crocodile*. His is fully explained on page 66 (explanation of this Hieroglyph on the body of the Australian Aboriginal). Horizon and a country or people, are purely Egyptian, as all Egyptologists know, and [1] is Ta the earth. His plate ii. represents Sut chained in the underworld, after the great battle with Horus, and Horus is represented here as King of the North and South. The serpent, with inflated breast, is the representation of the Egyptian Uræus. Plate v., the Scorpion with Apt, the brow of the God "I am," chaining Sut the Evil One. What he terms the very interesting ceremony, called "Hepmek," practised only amongst the Mayas, let us inform him, is still practised by the Burmahen women and some African tribes, and for quite a different reason to his interpretation.

We think the above examples sufficient for our proof, but the true explanation can only be obtained through the Egyptian. Throughout his book, "Queen Moo," he frequently mixes the Egyptian Celestial and tries to prove it Maya Terrestrial, but it will not pass. He must go back to the origin of the little red men or earth men, then follow the next exodus from Egypt—the men of the Stellar Mythos. He will find abundance of remains of these Astro-Mythological beliefs in North, Central and South America, and finally those of the Solar doctrines, of whom probably those Mayas of Yucatan were the first to bring it to America from Egypt. Let him compare all these with what we find in other parts of the world—Totemic ceremonies connected with the Stellar Mythos and Astro-Mythological beliefs, in only one place can the centre of origin be found—Egypt.

[1] It is written , which probably is the Mexican way of writing Taui, the two lands, but it might represent : Ta the earth, would therefore mean "the two Earths"—that is, the same as the two Lands—*i.e.* the Celestial and Terrestrial.

How the Stellar and Lunar Mythos were carried here, whether from Asia, via Japan and those parts North of it, (there being some reason to assume that they advanced from the Pacific—see later,) or whether they came from North Europe, via Greenland, it is not possible to say, probably both ways, but there is no doubt in our mind that the Solar doctrines were brought to Yucatan by the Mayas, direct by trading ships. It would occupy more time than we have at our disposal to go through all these codices, to interpret each one, and render what is, in our opinion, the true meaning and explanation of each. In the "Ritual or Book of the Dead" of ancient Egypt, lies the "key" to the true rendering of all. In the future decipherments of these "glyphs" they will recognise the hieroglyphic and picture scenes of these Egyptians, but they must make allowance for the different "Scribes and Artists" who have here thus written the copies of the original.

We contend that what is written in this work is sufficient to prove all that we advance as our strong belief, and that until the Primordial Mythology of Egypt is taken into account and acknowledged to be the origin of all, translators will often be falling into "pits" that only Egyptian ladders can extricate them from. In differing from the hypotheses advanced by these learned and distinguished writers, we have, we contend, replaced by another and stronger argument and reason, that which they cannot overthrow. If they will study the Egyptian *Ritual* and the primordial myths from the beginning, and follow and trace the exodes, we feel confident that they will arrive at the same conclusion, and give us much more valuable information in the future than they have done in the past.

FIG. 54.

Mexican Representation of Isis suckling Horus ("Mexican Antiquities").

This picture is taken from "Mexican Antiquities," published by the Bureau of American Ethnology, Smithsonian Institute,

THE GODDESS SEBEK-NIT SUCKLING HORUS.

This goddess and the goddess Sekhet-Bast were very early types of Isis and Nephthys, pre-Lunar and pre-Solar. The Ritual states, "she was uncreated by the Gods" and "who is mightier than the Gods," and to whom the eight gods offered words of adoration; therefore this was before the Put cycle of 9, *i.e.*, Ptah, and consequently a representation of the Great Mother during Stellar mythos.

Washington, D.C. This is a type of Isis suckling the child Horus, and we note the Hieroglyph of her name Ka-t which is sometimes painted  in the Egyptian.  This Hieroglyph is always associated with Isis or a type of Isis, and is seen shown in her name as the Goddess Sesheta—*i.e.* the Goddess of the Pole Star, in one of the oldest forms.

We have here, therefore, the representation of Isis as the great Mother, in the Anthropomorphic form, and also on the left, we have the Zootype of the same portrayed as SHAAT, the many-teated Sow, or Hathor the Cow, a pre-Anthropomorphic type. With the Babylonians, Nin-Ki-Gal, the Great Lady, is thus of the same type as the above Isis here.

Nut or the "Cow or Mother of Heaven" was the giver of liquid life, was the earliest "Mistress of the Mountain," the divine "Lady of the Mound," and when the zootype of the good nurse, the suckler, was changed into the anthropomorphic, the udder of the cow was superseded by the mamma of the human mother, as Rerit, the sow, she was the suckler or as "Many-breasted Menal" as the typical provider of plenty—zootypes. Isis suckling Horus —anthropomorphic type. Nut or Milch Cow Hesit is the Mes-Khe-n. The Meskhen, womb or rebirthplace in the heaven of eternity is portrayed by the "haunch." "I shall shine above the haunch as I come forth in heaven"—*Ritual*, chap. lxxiv. It is situated within the seven Pole Stars—*i.e.* Little Bear and not the Great Bear. The Great Bear is the cow Apt or the Water Cow, or the Great Earth Mother, or the Mexican type, "many-teated." These were the most ancient types of all and these were female.

Gerald Massey has been kind enough to write me his opinion on the subject of these types, viz.:

"The child born in the Totemic Group had no father and therefore in their first mythology the first mother was represented as being fertilised by her child in utero like Ptah the God in embryo—and was called the Bull of his mother. Why? Because this was not the human child—it was Horus or the Calf, born of the Cow and a pre-human type when the fatherhood was not yet individualised. The Solar God at sunset made its entrance into the breeding place of the nether world and is said to prepare his own generation for rebirth next day—but not in human form—the Bull of his mother is shown on the horizon next day as Horus the Calf.

"These were Zootypes, but, when this is presented anthropomorphically in accordance with the human terminology, the calf which had no father, but was his own Bull, becomes the child without a father. Thus the Elder Horus, who was the child of the Great Mother Apt, was the child of his mother who was born but not begotten—the original in mythology or sociology at the time of the Stellar Mythos; and in the Stellar-Lunar Mythos it was Horus the child of Light that was born of Isis in the Moon, when the Moon was the Mother of the child, and the Father, the source of Light, was unidentified, but later it was shown —in the Lunar-Solar Mythos—that Horus was not without a Father, but that Ra was the true Father as established by the evidence of Taht. It is the Lady of Light in the Moon (Isis) who pursues and seduces the Solar God in the darkness of Amenta, and who exults that she has seized upon the God Hu and taken possession of him in the Vale of Abydos where she went to lie down and sought to be replenished with his light (*Ritual*, chap. lxxx.). In the Solar Mythos the Mother is done away with as primary and the Father takes the place as supreme. In the Eschatology Horus is born in his first advent as the heir of Seb (Seb was the Father on earth). Horus says, 'I am come as a mummied one'—that is, in his embodiment when made flesh, the Hamemmet being the unmummied ones (*Ritual*, chap. ix.). 'I come before you and make my appearance as that God in the form of a man who liveth as a God'—or as Iusu, the son of Atum-Ra (chap. lxxix.). 'I repeat the acclamations at my success on being declared the heir of Seb' (chap. lxxxii.), 'Osiris in Amenta, and Ra in heaven.' 'I descend to the earth of Seb and put a stop to evil' as a bringer of peace, plenty, and good-will on earth (*Ritual*, chaps. xxii., xxiv., xxvii., xlii.). The *Ritual* proves that Seb, the god of Earth, was foster father of Horus when he was the child of the virgin mother only. In *Ritual*, chap. lxxxii., Horus says that as the heir of Seb he was suckled at the breast of Isis, the spouse of Seb, who gave him his theophanies.

"After the life with Seb on earth Horus is reborn in the earth of eternity for the heaven of eternity (*Ritual*, chap. lxxviii.-xxv.).

He is divinised with the substance of God (chap. lxxviii.) by means of Horus, his manifester Osiris is said to relive, Horus is Osiris in his rebirth—Horus rises as a god and is visible to the divine spirits in his resurrection (chap. lxxix.). He is the living soul of Ra in heaven. Horus was the only one of the 7 great spirits born of the Mother who was chosen to become the only begotten son of God the Father when he rose up from the dead. This is he who says in the *Ritual*: 'I am the bright one in glory, whom Atum-Ra hath called into being and my origin is from his eye. Verily, before Isia was, I grew up and waxed old and was honoured beyond those who were with me in glory' (*Ritual*, chap. lxxviii., Renouf). Those who were with him in glory were the 7 Great Spirits, the Khuti or Glorious Ones, and amongst these Horus became the divine heir of all things, the Son of God who claims to have existed before Isis his Mother and was the manifester for the Holy Spirit Ra in all things. In *Ritual*, chap. lxxxii., Horus says: 'I have come forth with the tongue of Ptah and the throat of Hathor that I may record the words of my Father Tum with my mouth.' 'I am Horus, prince of eternity' (chap. xlii.). 'I am yesterday, to-day, and to-morrow' (chap. lxiv.). Tum, as the earlier form of Atum's name in the *Ritual*, is pre-eminently 'the Lord.' In one chapter, lxxix., he is addressed as 'The Lord of Heaven,' 'The Lord of Life,' 'The Lord of all Creatures,' 'The Lord of all.' He was also the patron of builders and architects, and his symbol is the masonic square."[1]

In Egypt, Mother Earth was also represented by a Suckler as renewer of vegetation in the Goddess Rannut. Isis was represented as Mother Earth in another form as Sekhet (or field). Mamapacha was the name of the Great Mother amongst the Peruvian tribes.

In Mexico, they called Calalepec Mountain—the Mother, and the Quichè legend in which the human race descended from a Cave dwelling woman is only a type of Mother Earth as the Great

[1] The God Seb is the Egyptian Priapus who might be termed a Phallic Deity. But he is the Earth-God and Father of Food: the God of Fructification associated with plants and flowers, and foliage, which are seen issuing from his body. He is the Lord of Aliment in whom the reproductive powers of earth are ithyphallically portrayed. But the potency represented by Seb was not human, although the human member is depicted as a type of the begetter or producer (*Ritual*, xxxix.). It was also identical with the lion as a solar type (*Ritual*, xvii.), and took a first position in the most ancient places, being shown like a light set upon a candlestick, and is carried down to the present day by the Ritualists as evidenced by their long sperm candles mystically set up.

Mother. The Mount with a Cave was a natural figure of the Earth Mother, the same as the Tree and the Mount and the "Stone with a hole in it"—types in sign language; and the "Sign and Symbol" of the woman portrayed upon Rocks and Caves all over the world, is not a symbol of wickedness in all these lands—nor yet an object of worship (Zechariah, chap. v. 8).

It is a Symbol of Superhuman type of Motherhood depicted in primitive art by the Aborigines, who had no other way to

FIG. 55.—This is the Christian;

express their ideas, and a stone or tree was a symbol of the mother—the primitive birthplace.

Cæsar and *Lucanus* state that the gods of the Gauls were pillars—stones—or tree trunks, but they were not gods—but were images of the Mother Earth. The Stone or Tree were types of the Divine Abode which represented the Great Mother, or Bringer-forth. (*See* Appendix.)

There is a tribe, called the Seris tribe, who live in the remote wilds of Mexico; whose stronghold is Tiburon Island, who possess many of the same ceremonies that we find amongst the Aboriginal Australians of certain tribes and Nilotic negroes.

1. The women have the two incisor teeth knocked out to show that they are "open."

2. They are Totemic, with the Pelican as the tutelary deity, who protects from accidents and arrow wounds ; from the fangs of beasts and the firearms of the white man ; having the Pelican for their Totem, who made all things.—Zootype for Mut, [hieroglyphs] the great Mother of the Egyptians.

3. Marriage with any but a Seri is not permitted (no half-bred Seris have ever been known).

4. Women of one tribe must not marry the men of the same—*i.e.* a Pelican woman must marry a Turtle man or *vice versa*.

5. Every clan or tribe have their Totems, the Pelican and the Turtle being considered the oldest ; and the women have vertical bands of pale blue, white and rose red painted down the forehead and right across their cheeks and nose, and on the cheeks is painted, in a curious design, the sacred and totemic emblem of the clan—to distinguish their Clan or Totem. "Hindoos do this to show their cast."

6. Descent is always recognised through the female and not the male. This is the case with the Urabunna and other tribes in Northern Australia. No male is painted but wears a green stone in the cartilage of the nose. Women here rule, men having nothing to do with the organisation of the tribes or arrangement of marriages, and they settle all disputes, the elder women joining the councils that are held by the men. Women make all the crude pottery, baskets and "tents," and all ornaments, which consist of coloured stones, shells, etc., and they *prefer human hair* to anything else to make strings—they never use or barter for white men's beads. When women die they are given burial with food and water for the soul's journey, and their spirits are feared as more powerful and more likely to return than those of the men. No white man, as far as is known, can speak their language or ever knew the name of any of their men or women. They use stone axes, poisoned arrows and spears ; and for cutting up animals use their teeth and hands. They can run forty to fifty miles in a night and can overtake the fastest horse. Their food

consists of large sea turtles, shell fish, snakes, game and fruit of the Cactus and Mesquite. They seldom cook their food and steal all

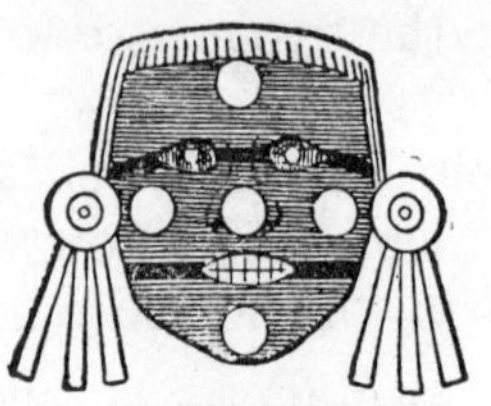

Fig. 56.

We see from this photograph that the Mexicans and Zapotecs painted their Totems across the face in earlier times, as above. This also has the Egyptian hieroglyph for daylight, splendour, etc. The five O denote the five mysteries or powers. The women of the *Inoit tribe* of the *Esquimaux* do the same. It is their Totemic sign and name, which is given them at the time of puberty, as before explained.

the animals they can for food from other Indians and the Spanish-Mexican Ranches.

The principal points to notice here are:—1. That they are divided into Totemic Clans or Groups. 2. That the men and women of one Clan must not marry each other. 3. That the men of one Clan, say Turtle, must marry a Pelican and *vice versa.* 4. That all the women have the two incisor teeth knocked out. 5. That they provide food and drink for the dead, believing that the Soul and the Spirit require it, and that they believe that these can return and work them good or ill, thus showing propitiation. 6. That the line of descent is through the female, and that the "Pelican" is the symbol for the Great Mother—(Mut, Egyp.). Probably there are many more interesting points if one could dwell amongst them and find them out, but at present they kill and eat all strangers.

Baron Nordenskjold, in his travels in South America, visited and dwelt for a time with the Quichnas and Aymaras Indians, living round Lake Titicaca and the fells of the Andes. He states that "these Indians often worship Christ and the Virgin Mary by dances, in which the Sun is used as a symbol of Christ and the Moon for the Virgin Mary, showing how they confound the old religion with the Christian faith"—but it shows and proves more than this—and that is, that the Virgin Mary has taken the place of Hathor or Isis, the Moon Goddess of the Egyptians, and Christ that of Horus I. or Osiris, or Ra and Horus the Child. Here we find another link to forge the complete chain of the past, only waiting for someone to go amongst these people and gain all the information of their past customs, as *Spencer and Gillen* did with the Australians—with plus a knowledge of Egyptology. The *Baron* has so far given very few particulars—very little—and yet so much; so great a point has it revealed and added to our knowledge that these Indians have undoubtedly the doctrines of the ancient Egyptians, whether direct descendants of the Incas or not is not of much consequence. The Moon Goddess, Hathor or Isis (two names for the same), becomes the type of the Virgin Mary, and the Christ, now symbolically the Sun, has taken the place of Horus I. or Osiris or Ra, which, we cannot say without more particulars, but the evidence is quite clear it is the one or the other, and as these evidently practised so-called "Solar Mythos" it would be Osiris or Ra.

It is another proof of the "Egyptian origin," and another nail driven into the coffin of the Aryanists, and it opens a door for such a wealth of knowledge to be gleaned upon this subject by anyone who can go and gather the remnants of the past which are still extant amongst these poor Indians. Thus it would add greatly to the elucidation of the mystery of bygone days, but we doubt if this can be achieved by anyone unless he has first made himself acquainted with the Egyptian primordial and their Eschatology; knowing this, he can with confidence expect to obtain all other points that are here awaiting him, as well as proving how much of the "Stellar Mythos," if any, remains or is practised still here—or if there be none. Our opinion is that much of the Stellar will be found mixed with the Solar, and merged in with their present Christian faith. These can be traced back to Central America, the Zapotecs and Mexicans—the Solar to the Mayas of Yucatan.

THE SECRET TRIBAL SOCIETIES OF WEST AFRICA

In his very interesting paper *Brother Fitzgerald Marriott* brings forward a list of Secret Tribal Societies of West Africa. Many parts of their ceremonies are analogous to those of the aborigines of Australia, which show that they have a common origin, although the secret tribal societies of West Africa are of a higher order and have a Mohammedanism added to them. There are also amongst the Puro these five mysteries:—

The first or lowest is called Yáyá.

The second is called Woodya—this is the Messenger or Entrance Keeper.

The third is called Bénima—he commands the Devil and is a Superior Messenger.

The fourth is called Konimahoohn—he explains the law.

The fifth is called Miseri—the word means a " Church," also a " Bookman."

The highest rank or the chief of the Circle, Guild or Society, is called Mama Koomé.[1] There are seven grades altogether in Purrohism.

1. Bangan—a Probationer (Loocumba).
2. Pornor—or fully Initiated.
3. Lakka—who is the Herald.
4. Bé Kesey—the Lawyer.
5. Famanja—the Moderator.
6. Negebana—the Revenger.
7. Svekoi or Sopivewi—the Chief of the House.

The West African tribes, Tshi, like the Australian, Nilotic and Bantu negroes, are divided into Totemic families and named after some animal or plant, such as the Leopard family, Bush-cat family, Dog family, Parrot family, Plantain family, etc. The members of these families are prohibited from eating the Totem, whether animal or plant, after which they are named, though, owing to the importance of the Plantain as food, coast natives do not recognise the rule as applying in that case.

A Purroh man has six small marks cut in his back, each in the form of an equilateral triangle, having the vertex in the centre of the spinal vertebræ and the base on both sides of the ribs; he has also concentric circles round the breasts. This sign we also see clearly shown on *one of the stones at Ollamh Fodhla,* as can be seen in the photo (Fig. 72) and the meaning is *the Khui Land of Egypt,* a region of Amenta—land of the Spirits and Gods.

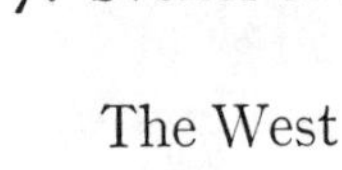

We have drawn particular attention to this, because it is a very important fact, and one which alone will prove the connection between these ancient rites and their origin.

[1] This is the same as the Egyptian " Maa-Kheru."

Initiation into one of the secret societies of these West Africans will pass you amongst nearly all the various tribes found on the West coast or in South Africa ; even if the tribes that you have to visit or pass through are at war or deadly enmity with each other, you are helped on and passed through unmolested, as many white men can testify who have experienced the same.

In West Africa, the Old Kongo was divided into seven districts or provinces, with a Prince over each and one Over-lord or King over all—the Bini and Yorba were the same, and the original Pygmies. They all believed in the seven powers representing the attributes of Nzambi—God on Earth, and their figures of so-called "fetish," simply represent these powers in sign language. Like the old Egyptians (see later), they believe that man has

A Soul—they call Bakuhu.

A Shadow—they call Dundu.

A Ka—they name Zidundu.

They divide things of the body into three parts, and

Things of the spirit into three parts.

When you ask a native of West Africa to what family he belongs, he answers by giving the name of his mother's family, showing that *they reckon in the maternal line*—the oldest form.

Like the Australians and other native tribes, the spot where they bury their dead they never visit again—it is tabooed—made sacred. They have their "sacred groves" and "sacred trees," animals, etc.

The Bini, when they build their houses, build in a sacred figure *in* the wall. This figure is important to students who wish to obtain the origin and meaning of their old religion and government.

Mr R. E. Dennett has done good work in studying these things in detail. He states that :—" on the top of the figure is a *bird*," meaning to represent "Ifi,"—the Son of God—I.U. or I.A.U. "Immediately underneath this are four parallel lines with sixteen marks or holes in each ; then a space is left, and then two parallel lines, with eight marks or holes—*i.e.* twenty-four marks or holes in all, with a distinct gap between the first and second lines—*i.e.* the first four and the last two."

Here we have a representative bird for Horus I.

The four first lines, representing the four children of Horus, who are called :

Ibara,
Edi,
Oyekun,
Ogbe,

and the sixteen marks or holes, representing the powers or attributes of each, in sign language, as we find in the *Ritual* of ancient Egypt. Of the two lower lines, we have not been able to ascertain the names, but we have no doubt that these would represent the two lives—Earthly and Spiritual, and the eight marks or holes the attributes of the same, as the Seven Glorious Ones, with The One added—*i.e.* eight.

All the people of Bavili, Bini, and Yorba possess the same. One of their sacred symbols is the triangle, resting on a Crown, with the "All Seeing Eye" in the centre, and feathers on the outside of the triangle, representing the Rays of Light or Delta.

In the centre of the triangle is a piece of looking-glass, or something bright to represent "Light"—"Light of the World." This distinctly shows that these people have brought on all their myths, sign language, etc., as above, from the ancient Egyptians, thousands of years ago, somewhat altered now, but there lies the origin, and to these we must return if we wish to find the key to their religion, philosophy and forms of government—a much more moral and higher type than most suppose, both in their religion and form of government, but which, unfortunately, the white intruder does not recognise or know, and so classes in entirety as "idolatry and ignorance."

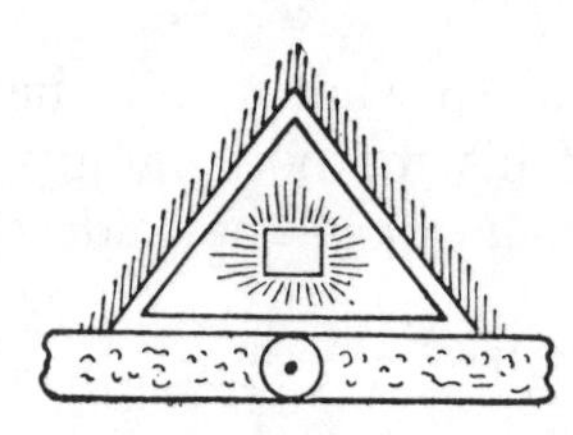

Fig. 57.

Mr R. E. Dennett has evidently devoted much time, study, and accomplished some good work, but we are of opinion that if he had studied the Egyptian Primordial, he would be in a position to give us much more information on the subjects he has written upon ; and we hope that this work may induce him to do so.

It is to be regretted that at present we have not a fuller description of the secrets and mysteries of the West African tribes, but there is sufficient for a student to see that they originated in ancient Egypt, and no doubt in time the whole of these secrets will be unfolded.

CHAPTER VII

We do not agree with *Sir Harry Johnston* ("The Uganda Protectorate") in his statement that "the Negro race certainly originated in Southern Asia, possibly in India, not far from the very centre where man himself emerged in some form similar to the Pithecanthropos Erectus, from a branch of the anthropoid apes." Our belief, from the anatomical and other studies of the various races, is that the original home of man was in the Nile valley and its sources, and not Southern Asia, the original inhabitants of which came from here, it being the centre of exodus for the world. Here we still find the four different types of Lemur, from one branch of which, no doubt, man descended—an anthropoid ape—which may still exist in the Congo forest, and from this the prognathous type of pygmy, and from this pygmy "the Masaba negroes, ape-like men; strongly projecting superciliary arches, low brows, flat noses, bulging nostrils, long upper lips, receding chins, broad in zygomatic measurement, cranial development very poor; stumpy individuals with much prognathism. The hands and arms long, the feet large and clumsy, the knees turn in, and the shins are much bowed." It has been said that *neither these nor the Pygmies circumcise, nor do they decorate the body with any pattern or scars or weals.* They are the most primitive and fundamental negro race, an aboriginal race, in fact, that has not as yet evolved any of those Totemic ceremonies that we find in the higher developed negro, which emanated, so to speak, by evolution from these. These spread N., E., S., and W. throughout the world, and we still have remnants left. The Viddas of Ceylon — the race that the Ainu drove out and destroyed in Japan—the earliest race in Mexico, and after them, developed by evolution, the types of "hairy men." The Nilotic negroes, who possess "Totemic Ceremonies," are a higher type of negroes than the Masaba, and by evolution were developed from them. From the earlier Nilotic negroes we can trace the Masai, a fine race of men, developed from the early Nilotic source, and we can see how much further these have progressed towards civilisation. They have in their texts the same Cosmic myths, moral and religious tales, and religious notions and traditions which we find in the old Egyptian papyri of the Stellar Mythos. Their physical and mental characteristics, their social and military institutions, show what progress they have made to reach a higher state. On many of the ancient tombs and mural sculptures the faces and forms of the oldest Egyptians that we find are undoubtedly similar to these Masai, who are now fast dying out. It is a question in our mind if some of these did not emigrate south and form the nucleus of the great Zulu tribes.

The Ainus, Australian and New Guinea aborigines descended from the Nilotic negroes, have still many of the forms, rites, and ceremonies of the early Totemic age. It is only necessary to place the Australian aborigines and the Nilotic negroes together and then examine them anatomically to establish their identity, to say nothing of the deductions to be drawn from the similar features in all their present rites and ceremonies.

The cranial capacity of the Pygmies is very low wherever we find their remains, about 960 c.c., and the sutures close early, thus preventing the further development of the brain, and retarding learning. As a result, progressive evolution would be slow. To understand evolution fully, one must go back to these primitive people of small stature and great muscular development: the first little earth-men or red man—*i.e.* Paleolithic man. As these spread farther north, the cold northern climate would cause their muscular tissue to develop greater strength, and they would become hardier than those of hot climates. The whole world was probably peopled by these "negroids" first, certainly long before the last glacial period. As the cold became too intense to live in the northern latitudes, they were driven back south again. Some, no doubt, went farther south than others. The cold would induce them to live in caves and underground places, and they had to think how they could keep warm and procure food, how to fasten skins together to wear and enable them to retain their natural warmth, and a commencement of mechanical devices to suit, and thus they would have to use their brains more and more, which would gradually tend to increase therein in size and cell development. As soon as the extreme cold had passed away they would spread northwards again, and would be followed by those who had developed both in stature and brain-power in Egypt and the Nile valleys, as we find that these were a taller, more energetic, and more warlike people—these were of the Neolithic age and brought the Stellar Mythos with them. They drove out and exterminated the first primitive people, as we find the Ainu and Australians did in Japan and Australia, and as the Neolithic did the Paleolithic here in these islands and Europe generally. This probably took a very long time, as all would not be at first exterminated. Some would, no doubt, mingle with the conquerors, but in many cases they would naturally die out. Marriages and inter-marriages must be taken into consideration in the further developments and evolution, as well as environment.

As far as the evidence that has been left us shows, the Paleolithic man lived simply by hunting and fishing. How long these little people existed before the Neolithic age it is impossible to say, probably 100,000 years, and so far there is no evidence of their having any Mythos.

Zaborouski attributed to *Sergi* a statement that the Egyptians are diffused through Asia Minor, Southern Russia and elsewhere, which *Sergi* does not claim to have stated; nevertheless it is quite true. *Sergi*, however, does not go back far enough for the Exodus direct. Of these the first was Paleolithic man, remains of whom have been found sparsely, the second was Early Neolithic. Their skeletons, burial places, etc., are many. The ethnographic observations of Herodotus and other classic writers are much too late to be taken into serious consideration when proving the origin of the human race, although interesting as to the facts they observed as regards the customs of the people they visited. *Professor Sergi* agrees and proves by anthropology, "that the origin and migration of the African racial element took place in primitive times from the Souh towards the North." The types of Cro-Magnon and Homme-Mort, and others in French and Belgian localities, as well as the oldest remains in these Islands, bear witness to the presence of an African stock in the same region in which we find the dolmens and other megalithic monuments erroneously attributed to the Celts. All these were widely extended over the world and had the same primitive funeral customs, shaped skulls, long forearms, etc., until they were modified by men and stronger influences, and only in Egypt can we find the centre from which these originated and migrated. The remains found at Harland Bay, Cornwall and Naqada are typical (see later). The "Celts" were those who came after and modified their funeral customs by introducing cremation.

One reason why Blonds are found in North Africa may be determined from the retrograde movement of the northern people through being driven back again during the Glacial Period; that only a small percentage of Blonds are found in North Africa would prove that only a few "crossed back again" during this intensely cold epoch when life could not exist farther north than about the centre of France. The skulls and physical types of these in North Africa have so many characters similar to the Finns (a northern people) that it amounts to positive proof when joined with others brought forward in this work.

Various authors have given from 70,000 to 200,000 years for the Neolithic age. When their culture was greatly advanced, they cultivated the soil, bred animals, understood the art of spinning, weaving, of pottery making, also working in copper, tin and gold, and had the knowledge of the Stellar Mythos. In some parts of Europe, at least, the gap between the Paleolithic and Neolithic is so abrupt and striking that it is only by assuming an entire or nearly entire disappearance of the former, and a subsequent re-peopling by the latter, who came up from Egypt and the Nile valleys, that one can understand the past, because, while primitive man was still struggling for existence with the mammoth and other animals, a relatively advanced degree of culture had already been developed in the Nile valleys; and this exodus spread all over the world. In tracing the evolution of man, there is one particular point of considerable importance we have not been able to find any author dilating upon, and this is, the development and evolution of the *Hair* from the short, "pepper-corn" character, which we find in the Pygmies first, and then on to the people who have long straight hair. We have given photos here of the Pygmies, Tasmanians and Bushmen, who have characteristic "pepper-corn" hair; but as one fact to add and prove with others in the development of the hair of the human race, it must and ought to be taken into account.

FIG. 58.—Man of the Kaitish Tribe.

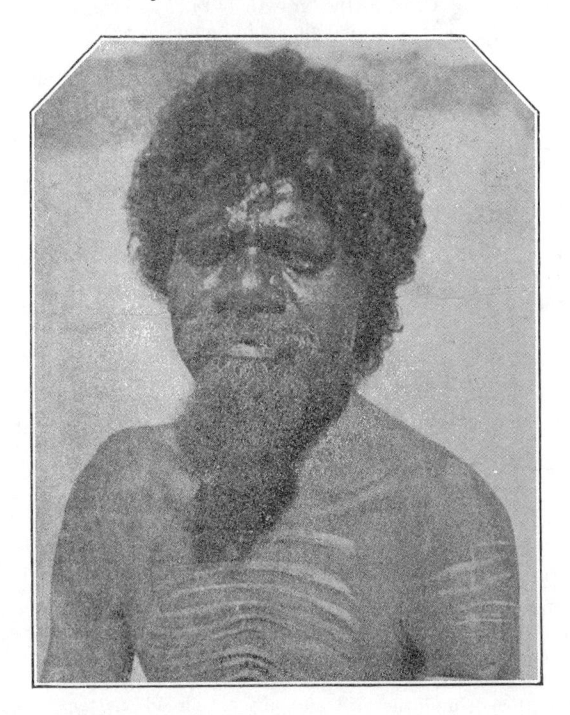

FIG. 59.—Man of the Tjingilli tribe, showing the curled nature of the hair. Full face. Photograph from "Native Tribes of No thern Australia," by *Spencer and Gillen*, published by Macmillan & Co., to whom we return thanks for the permission to reproduce it. Shows the curled nature of the hair, wide-spreading alæ of nose and depressed root of nose. Lips showing half development between pygmy and negro, also well marked cicatrices on lower figure.

In the Pygmies we have the first form of hair of primitive man, then, as evolution took place, we find certain modifications

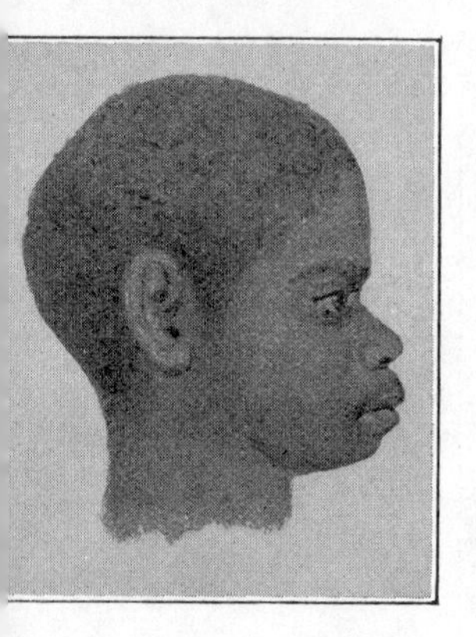

FIG. 60.
A Tasmanian Native.
Compare Amooriape with this one's face, nose, lips, hair, eyebrows, etc.

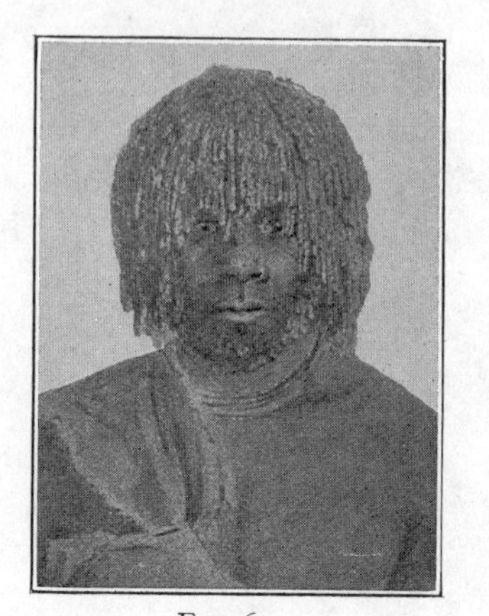

FIG. 61.
A Tasmanian Native.
Observe the growth of the hair, having the same characteristic pepper-corn elongated, which was that which preceded the "curly" hair of the negro.

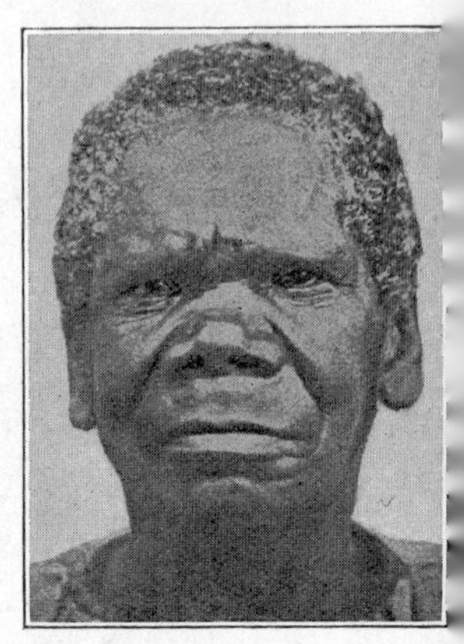

FIG. 62.
A Bushman of South Africa.[1]
Compare Bohani, Pygmy. Notice lips, nose, hair, etc., which are identical anatomically.

FIG. 63.—A Tamahu from Egypt.
From *Professor Sergi's* "Mediterranean Races," page 56, fig. 1.

coming to pass in the character of the hair along with other

[1] *Mr Tovey Cozens*, who lived some time amongst these people as well as the Pygmies, stated that the Bushmen told him that their ancestors were connected with the Pygmies. It will be observed that the lips are not those of the negro type, but have the same characteristic as the Pygmies. The root of the nose is very much depressed and flattened, and the tips and alæ are broad, flattened and greatly expanded. The hair is the same peculiar "pepper-corn" character.

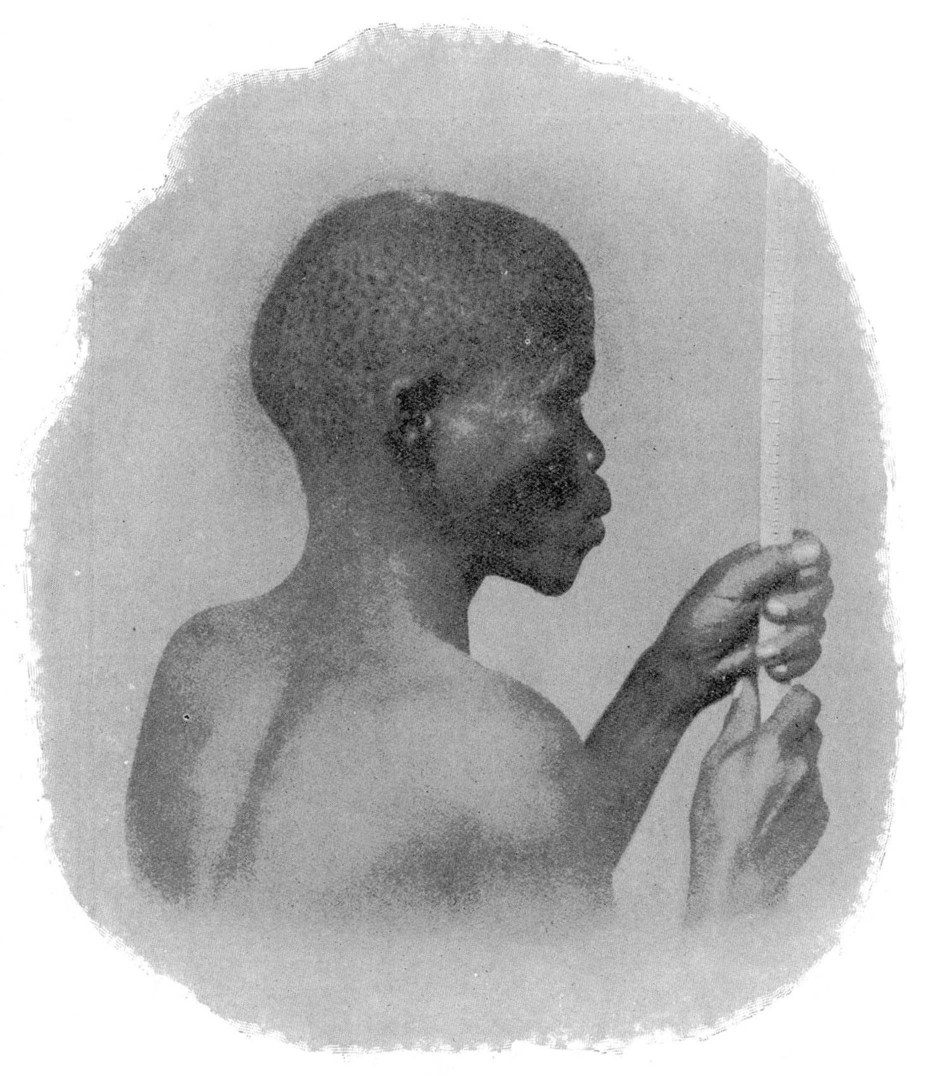

BUSHMAN OF THE 'GARIEP

(*From Stow's "Native Races of South Africa"*)

[*Facing page* 138

anatomical conditions ; and those tribes nearest allied to the Pygmies have the nearest approach to the same characters. In the Bushmen we have it almost identical, and from photographs still extant of the exterminated Tasmanians, it is very characteristic, with other anatomical conditions. It is only necessary to look and compare the photos here produced. As can be seen from these photos, the anatomical condition of the nose, lips, shape of the head, etc., are the same, and also the *hair*, as shown when it is short. In one photograph of the Tasmanian we see that the *hair* has been allowed to "grow long," and gives a very peculiar appearance. From this to the hair of the various other tribes, further removed by higher development of their anatomical features—Zulus, Negroes, etc., there is, and can be traced a gradual loss of the pepper-corn to the "curly" hair of the negro and other tribes. In the photographs of the Australians, we see that there is much of the "curly hair" still amongst some of these people, which helps to prove their origin ; others have it much straighter, and some have lost the curly nature. Much might be said on this subject, which is one of those we have studied, but what we have mentioned we consider sufficient for this work. To all those who are interested in this point we feel sure, if they will study the Ethnol, they will find in each race peculiarities—the hair, and its development, along with other anatomical developments—which must be taken into consideration, and that all the primary or Paleolithic people who went out from the Nile valleys, had this "pepper-corn" hair, remnants of which may be found all over the world, altered by time, evolution and environment to the straight.

Some further information may be gained, by those who wish to ascertain the truth, by studying the physical characters offered by the Egyptian monuments—the types represented under the name of Tamahu. The oldest has the characteristic long, "pepper-corn" hair as we see in the Tasmanians, lips are thin and not negro's, little beard, etc., with the Horus lock and two feathers on his head. In the next type we find the lips thick, like the negro's, and hair much longer and wavy or curly. For further information on this point *Professor Sergi's* "The Mediterranean Race" is valuable.

The Pygmies

Since writing the foregoing, by kind permission of the Manager of the London Hippodrome, *Mr Fred Trussell,* and *Colonel Harrison,* who brought them over from the forests of Ituri, in the Congo Free State, we have been able to examine the Pygmies here in London.

These Pygmies are primitive men—the little earth men. They are not negroes but are negroid, and many of their ana-

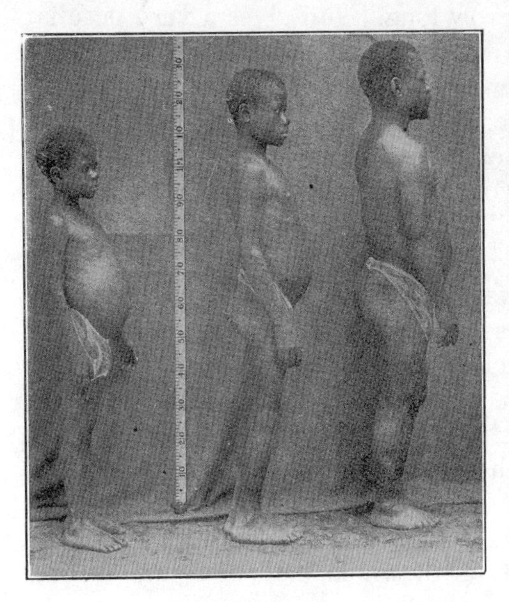

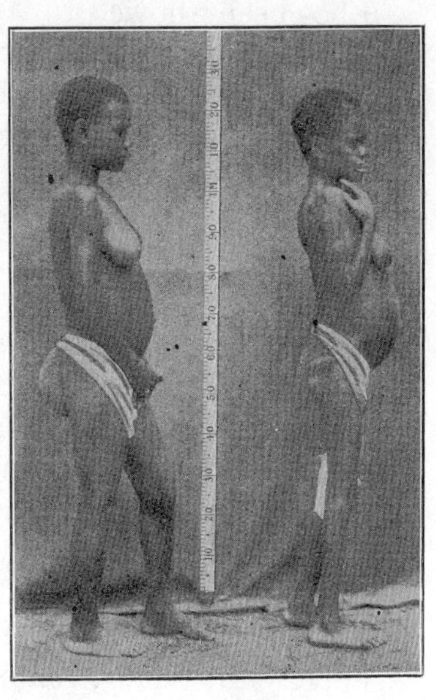

Fig. 64. Fig. 65.

Mongungu. Matuha. Bohani. Kuarhe. Amooriape.

Reproduced by the kind permission of Dr G. Elliot Smith and *The Lancet.*

tomical features show the near relationship they bear to the Pithecanthropos Erectus. The height of these Pygmies ranges from 1·378 metres, the tallest, to 1·158, the shortest; and they weigh from 7 stone, the heaviest, to 3 stone 7 pounds, the lightest. The average height of thirty-eight Akka Pygmies, from the Monbuttu country, is given as 1·378 metres by *Deniker*, and thirty Akkas, measured by *Emin Pasha*, gave an average height of 1·36 metres. It has been stated that these Pygmies marry at about eight years

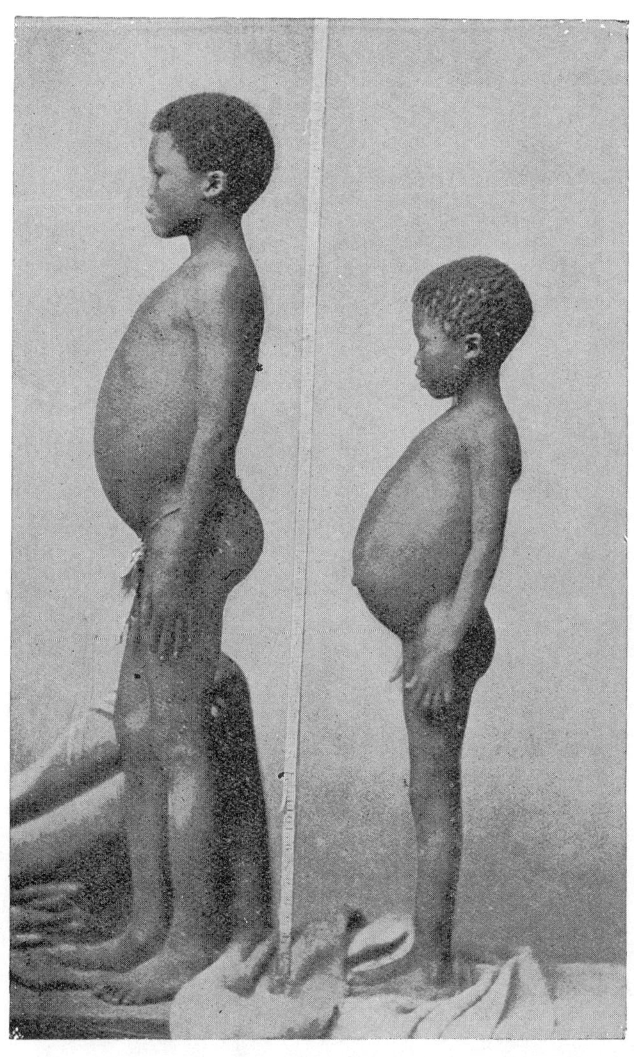

BUSHMAN CHILDREN

From Stow's "Native Races of South Africa")

[*Facing page* 140

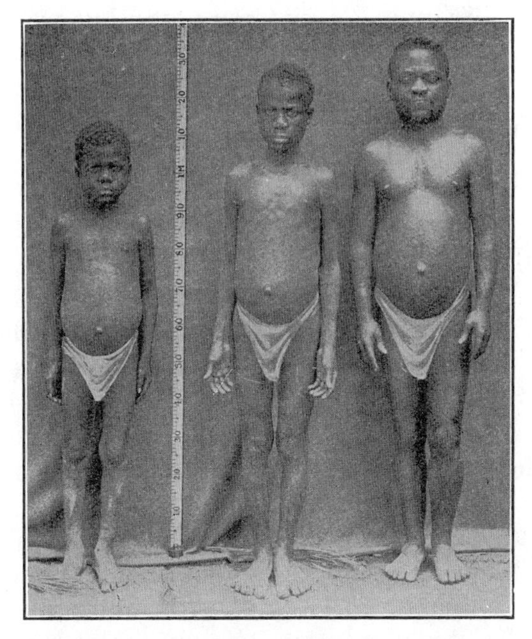

Fig. 66.

Mongungu. Matuha. Bohani.

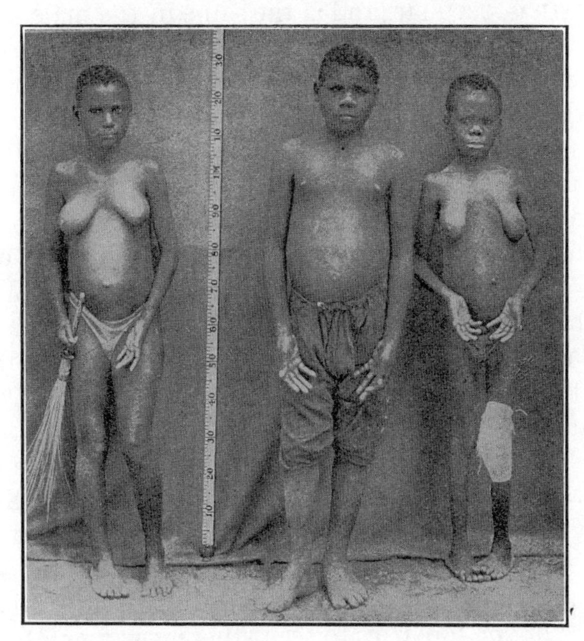

Fig. 67.

Kuarhe. Mafutiminga. Amooriape.

old and do not live much over forty years, but we do not think there is sufficient data to prove the ages of these little people, one way or the other. The people themselves have no idea whatever of their age, and the statements made concerning them are obviously mere guesswork. *Mr Geil*, when he asked the oldest Pygmy he saw how old he was, received the answer "many moons," and the Pygmy opened and clasped his fingers several times, so that he thought him to be about fifty years old. A very able article has been written on these Pygmies by *Dr G. E. Smith*, in *The Lancet*, 12th August 1905, to whom we are indebted for the reproduction of these photographs.

Their COLOUR is chocolate-brown—rather of a reddish tint.

The RITE OF CIRCUMCISION appears not to have been definitely settled by those who have seen most Pygmies—some state that they do not circumcise, others (*Sir Harry Johnston*, Uganda Protectorate) state that the males of all the Congo Pygmies seen by them were circumcised. In the case of these in London, only the chief was, and therefore it would be an important question to know if all the chiefs only are, or only males when they have become fully developed men.

Their HAIR is peculiar, and is the same in the male and female as regards length, colour and character. *Colonel Harrison* states: "Hairdressing is a great art among them; nearly as many patterns are cut on the head as there are grades of colour." The bristles of the red pig form their favourite headdress and earrings; these they twist up into small bunches and tie in tufts to the hair. It is closely rolled, and has the characteristic discrete pepper-corn balls, and of a peculiar dull, lustreless appearance, not what one would call black, but of an indefinite greenish-grey tint. *Mr Cozens* stated to the author that he has seen them shave "all over" with pieces of glass, and they told him it was done to protect them from the "Matakania."

They are BROAD-CHESTED, SHORT-NECKED, STRONG-LOOKING, MUSCULAR, AND WELL-MADE. The arms gave one the impression that they were much longer than the European. *Dr Smith's* accurate measurements give the "forearm" as being on the average 1 per cent. longer, but the upper arm and legs about the same as in Europeans. We were sorry we could not obtain a "raidograph" of the bones of the forearm, to see if there was a greater distance between their bones than the average European. We noticed

Matuha

Bohani.

Matuha.

Bohani.

Kuarhe.

Amooriape.

Kuarhe.

Amooriape.

FIG. 68.

several "scars" on the upper arms, on the left side, but could not get any definite answer as to their meaning. The general contour of the head is well depicted on the plates here produced. We give *Dr Smith's* measurements, as we had not a suitable opportunity to measure them ourselves, as stated in our article, "A Study of the Pygmies," in *The Standard*, 7th July 1905. *Dr Smith's* able article in *The Lancet*, 12th August 1905, is very accurate and important as regards measurements :—"All the heads are ovoid in norma verticalis, and the length-breadth indices are respectively 76·5, Mongungu; 77·7, Bohani; 78, Mafutiminga; 78·7, Amooriapee; and 79·1 both in Matuaha and Kuarhe. The heights of four of the crania are almost identical — 135, 137, 139 and 139, the two old people having much the loftier heads, the woman Amooriape's cranial height being 144 millimetres (head length, 174), and the man Bohani's 155 millimetres (head length, 184). The horizontal circumference of the heads are: 514, 544, 533, 518, 514 and 505 millimetres, respect vely. As a measure of their prognathism, the indices expressive of the proportionate length of the nasal and prosthionic radii are 111, 104, 115, 110·5, 107 and 108. Bohani s the least progenathous and Mafutiminga the most."

Nose.—The root of the nose is exceptionally flattened and very broad—from 40 to 49·5 millimetres. The characteristic Pygmy type of nose is well seen in the illustrations; the tip is broad and flattened and the alæ greatly expanded, although they vary a little in some particulars.

Eyebrows.—Well formed and different from the negro.

Teeth.—*Colonel Harrison* states :—"They are blessed with wonderful teeth, being able to crunch up bones with ease—a pastime they are particularly fond of. We noticed that their teeth were large, well formed, and of the 'animal type.'"

Mr Cozens states that he has seen some of the Pygmies "file their teeth."

Lips.—Are quite characteristic. They have not the massive, fleshy, everted lips of the negro. The Pygmy has long, rather narrow lips; the upper has a noteworthy sub-nasal projection, and when drinking or speaking, the combination of the flattened nose and the lips gives a strikingly Simian appearance. The lips of one woman had been perforated in three places. (See photograph of Kuarhe.)

EARS.—The ears are small ; the lobules not well developed, and in Matuha the pinna is crudely formed. Some of the ears are pierced, but not in all. The chin is small in all, and the mandible is narrow and pointed. Bohani alone has a beard ; it consists of a small stubbly growth of short close-rolled hair on the chin and upper lip, and the hair is the same on the chest and abdomen. The pubic and auxiliary hair in all the others is the same, and the same in the women. They shave part of the head at times, as may be seen in the photos, sometimes on one side and sometimes on the other, and others again only to leave a fringe. This, probably, is connected with some sacred ceremony unknown to us at the present with our limited knowledge of their habits.

ABDOMEN.—In all Pygmies there is an extraordinary prominence of the abdomen, which is not the result of over-feeding, but is owing to the cœcum being placed high up in the lumbar region, from it the colon is bent downwards to the right, and the iliac fossa, thus becoming largely distended, pursues a sigmoid course across the abdomen, and this prominence is not owing to the liver being enlarged, as *Mr Geil* states in his book.

STEATOPYGIA.—In some of the younger women and in Kuarhe there is a distinct Steatopygous condition.

BRAIN.—The average weight of the brain in a healthy Pygmy is about 900 grammes.

MUSIC.—Their music is similar to the Soudanese negroes. *Mr Geil*, who visited them, says :—" They are fond of dancing, very merry, and laughing and singing, continually at jokes. Their voice is really very melodious." *Lieut.-Colonel Harrison* says " that he has seen natives dance in all parts of the world, but nothing to surpass the agility of these little people, *who are taught to dance almost before they can run.*" He states " that it is wonderful to watch seventy or eighty men, women, and children circling in and out, round and round, always keeping the tom-toms in their centre, every foot along the whole line moving together, and every toss of the head and every twist of the body being executed with military precision." *Col. Harrison* adds : " How interesting it would be to follow them, in their own dialect, through all the plays and scenes their dances depict ! ! ! There are funeral and wedding dances, the hunting and wrestling dance (a curious dance, in which they try to throw each other by the interlocking of legs)."—*We have seen this and drawn attention to the same.*—Then they have the fetish dance, war dance, monkey dance, executed almost in a sitting position, and many more. Dancing seems to be their only source of pleasure, and many an hour is passed in its indulgence.

LANGUAGE.—Their language is not a language of "clicks" only, as we have seen stated; many of the sounds are quite soft, and mostly labial and lingual, and not so many lingual-dental; neither do we agree with what we have seen stated by *Sir Harry Johnston*, viz.:[1] "That they have no language of their own, but only spoke the words they had learned from surrounding tribes." We do not say that the Pygmies have not acquired some words from surrounding tribes that they have been in contact with, but we have not the slightest doubt that they possess a monosyllabic language of their own, and one of the principal proofs lies in the fact that they speak words which have the same sound as the ancient Hieroglyphics of Egypt, as we pronounce them, and our contention is that these are the "originals." There may be few words to express all their meanings, but we must call this "the first and oldest language of primitive man," and that the tribes who use the same and the old Egyptian, which is the same, must be original Pygmy words. No doubt many more words have been coined by surrounding tribes, as we ever find a progressive people coining words; and so words and language grew, as the mode of articulation for different sounds became easier with the practice of those they had. There cannot be any real argument that these Pygmies had learned these words from the old Egyptian Hieroglyphics and surrounding tribes, because it would involve the acceptance that long ago some ancient Egyptians, in a much higher state of civilisation, had been driven back, lost all the records of the time, and *degenerated to the Pygmy*, which, taking their anatomical condition into consideration alone, would be impossible; but the more we study

[1] We made this statement from seeing it in a daily paper, but *Sir Harry Johnston* has since in a letter in *The Lancet*, in answer to one we wrote, stated that he does not hold this dogmatic view. *Mr R. Tovey Cozens*, who lived amongst the Pygmies for many months, informed the writer that he was quite sure the Pygmies had a language of their own; at the same time, they could speak the language of the negroes surrounding them. They had burial grounds, which, however, they took great pains to keep secret; they only buried their dead here at night, and it was by following, unknown to them, that he discovered this. They bury their dead in the thrice-bent position, laid on the side. At the same time he agrees with Mr Geil in that they do not always bury their dead in their "burial grounds," but sometimes as Mr Geil has stated, but he never saw any "iron bracelets" put on the graves. He is of opinion that the Pygmies, as a rule, do not circumcise.

the facts that are already brought to light, the greater proof is there that the Pygmy is the oldest and first man, and with him language originated, and the first sacred ceremonies, as we shall prove later. We have learned some of the Pygmy words and give them here with the old Hieroglyphics, and only regret that we have been unable to obtain all their words. They are written phonetically, as *Mr F. Trussell* (to whom we are indebted for the same) states that he has used the French etymology, as he could not get the sounds in English. *Mr Geil* states that they have a sign language of their own, which all understand. This is very important, as all negroes have not, although the Aboriginal Australians have. It is also stated that they stick a small stem of fern through their noses sometimes.

It is important to note these points with regard to the Pygmies :—

1. They have a Sign Language of their own. This we proved, as we could make them understand many signs we knew and understand their signs to us.
2. They build Spirit Houses.
3. They sometimes use the "Nose Stick." *Mr Cozens* states that this is sometimes a bone.
4. They have Sacred Dances.
5. They mark the Forehead and Cheeks with Red Paint and sometimes smear blood on.
6. They believe in Spirit Ancestors and Re-incarnation.
7. *They have always been in the forest from all times.*
8. That when they die their Spirit enters a Great Serpent, which comes and visits the camp for a little time and then goes away; never does them any harm, and they never molest it.
9. Their Hair, Lips, and Anatomical Conditions generally—as "primitive man," not developed by evolution to the extent of the negro.
10. Their Method of Existence—by living by the Bow and Arrow and Spear, etc., and not cultivating the ground or domesticating animals as Neolithic man.
11. Nomad, but Paleolithic and not Neolithic.
12. Not intermarrying with any tribes, but amongst themselves —this we also find is the custom of the oldest tribes of Mexico, the Seri; and the smallness of stature. They

have no common burial-place for the dead, but each one is buried in earth where the camp is, and then the camp moves on. This last, however, *Mr Tovey Cozens* refutes by his observation.

SOME PIGMY WORDS

PIGMY	EGYPTIAN HIEROGLYPHICS		EQUIVALENT IN ENGLISH
O-be		ànb	to dance, to rejoice
Mai		mu	water
A-do-da		āx or za	to sleep
Bacchaté		baak	grain, fruit, bread, food
Massouri		maau	good, right, to be good, to do well, to be straight
Tzi-ba		Xerpu-baa	a bow, a piece of wood, etc.

PIGMY	EQUIVALENT IN ENGLISH
O-be	A Dance
Maria-ba	Pipe of Bamboo to smoke
Tath-bà	Whistling into a reed
Oct-bà	Wood
Di-pé	Spear
A-do-da	Sleep
A-pé	Arrow
Tzi-ba	Bow
Mai	Water or drink
Massouri	Good, well
Kon-pé	Clothes of any nature
Ma-di	Hunting horn
La-gou-ma	Bristle head-dress
Kalli-Kélli	Native bell
Bacchaté	Bread. This word is sometimes used—macchaté, the "ch" hard
A-foie	Dagger

They can count up to 100, have a particular sign for 50, also for 100. They reckon time by "Lunar" time—they have no "days," but have "seasons" and "moons." Most, if not all, have only one wife, and rarely more than two or three children. They have the most wonderful knowledge of poisons and counter-poisons, and the negroes around come to them if poisoned by bites of snakes or other reptiles. They bury their dead the same day they die with the bark cloth worn in life, cover it with green leaves and earth, and put on the grave a pair of iron bracelets (?). The corpse is buried close to or under the central fire in the encampment They mourn for a few days. They sing and weep for three days, but do not dance, and then leave and build a new camp. They are nomadic, and their average stay in one place is about three months. They build their camps in the form of an ellipse and their huts in the form of a half-moon, all facing inwards, with a large central fire, and small fires in front of each hut. *Mr Geil* states "that the Pygmies live in little huts, to the boughs of which large leaves are attached with fibre. Inside the leafy huts are little couches of the same large symmetrical leaves, laced together, making 'elfin beds fit for a fairy goddess.' Unlike so many native dwellings, the Pygmy hut is clean, and the Pygmy is clean also in person, and is a good hunter." *Lieut.-Col. J. J. Harrison*, who penetrated into the great Ituri forest, and made friends with the Pygmies and brought a number of them here to England with him (see photographs) says "that the whole Pygmy nation seems to be split up into small tribes of say sixty or seventy, each obeying its own chief. They live an entirely wandering life like our gipsies. Their huts, made of branches and leaves, measure about 7 feet in diameter and 4 feet high; they are hidden away in almost inaccessible places, so that no one could ever approach them unawares. They never steal from each other, but rob the negroes and Belgians with impunity." Pygmies say that they never intermarry with the negroes or others, only with themselves—*i.e.* with other Pygmies.[1] *Mr W. E. Geil* says that he asked the Chief of the Pygmies about the spirits of the Pygmies in the future, and all the answer he could obtain was: "We do not know about spirits. When we bury a man, the body of that man will enter a great serpent, and the serpent will come and see us. It will come near to us and coil up, but it will not bite us." I asked a second time about this, and the Chief persisted in saying "that the serpent would come and see them, and would not bite them, and they would

[1] From information that we have received it is probable that some Pygmy women have been given or sold to some of the negroes in their near vicinity, and *Mr Tovey Cozens* has informed us that their practice in this respect to strangers who come amongst them is the same as with the Australians and others.

do it no harm. That is all, it will go away afterwards." *Mr Geil* states that Pygmies believe in a good spirit and a bad one, and some in the finger of fate; "that they have a weird and mysterious air, which he attributes to their religious belief." He mentions the name of one tribe of the Pygmies as "Ti Kiti-Ki," which would mean in ancient Egyptian, "men of the double cavern." It is important to note that the Egyptians later used to think and believe that the Sun God—" Osiris in mummified form "—or the flesh of Ra was reborn into the life of a new day *only after he had been drawn through the body of a serpent*, and came out in the Double Cave on an Island in a Lake in spiritual form (see later). Thus we see that the Pygmies' idea of the spirit first inhabiting the body of a large serpent was brought on and made use of in their Solar mythos—it was a reincarnation of the spirit, and they probably adopted the serpent as a type because they noticed that it cast its skin once a year, and so came forth as a "new serpent," and thus they associated it with the regeneration of the spirit. We feel that to obtain the truth of all the past origins of mythology and all that followed, some capable person should go and dwell amongst these Pygmies, gain their confidence, and study them as *Spencer and Gillen* did the Australians; then many points would be undoubtedly cleared up, and the "book of the past" could be read and would be open to those who studied and understood. How much of the "original past" of the Pygmies remains at the present day or how much is "lost" is an open question, even when we gain all the knowledge that is possible now, because the ages and ages these little people have lived in their great forest would naturally tend to efface or alter some of their ideas and customs, even if only in a modified form at first, as we see in the Australians. We cannot agree, therefore, with *Dr Wallis Budge* in his statement in The Gods of the Egyptians, vol. i. p. 27: "There is no reason whatsoever for doubting that in Neolithic times the primitive Egyptians worshipped animals as animals and as nothing more: the belief that animals were the abode of spirits or deities grew up in their minds later, and it was this which induced them to mummify the dead bodies of birds and beasts and fishes, etc., in which they thought deities to have been incarnate." Now the Pygmies, from whence all sprang, do not worship animals, but they believe that the spirit inhabits the serpent for a time after death—reincarnation—but they do not worship it. They believe in a great spirit, as is seen and expressed in their care for one who is "defective." It simply represents a type, as in like manner the Apis Bull and the Ram of Mendes were *representative types of the attributes of the One Great God*, and they were only looked upon as this ; not worshipped as beasts and animals.

One of the most interesting and important points we found was that when we drew the oldest Hieroglyphic sign for Amsu they recognised it. In the Book of the Dead, chap. clxiv., we find that Mut the Great Mother of us all (a form of Isis), is associated with two Pygmies, each of whom has two faces, one of a hawk and one of a man, both have an arm lifted to support the symbol of the god Amsu, and wears upon his head a disk and plumes of the same form as we find "Bes" and others, associated with Central Africa, wore, according to *Dr Budge*, but which we associate with those of the "Lakes of the origin of the Nile and Nile valleys." The difference is really one of not much importance—it is simply a question of one or two degrees of latitude. All authorities are agreed that they are able to recognise photographs and pictures, and will themselves readily draw them, if given a pencil and piece of paper, and also draw figures to express what they have no words for. When we drew this sign and asked the chief if he knew what it was, he smiled and pointed to Matuha and Mafutiminga and told them to tell us what it was. They answered, "That is him," pointing to their chief, mentioning his name. That they recognise this sign, the most ancient sign we have for Amsu—or Horus I. risen—is very important to Egyptologists, because it was the first sign used by primitive man to represent the chief—a great one—and it was the sign of the Chief of the Nomes. It is found depicted on the oldest Australian Boomerangs and on the ivory tablets found in the tomb of Naqada. A full description and explanation of it is given later on.

Sacred Ceremonies.—It has been stated that they have no religious ideas at all, but this is evidently a mistake, as, before they "dance," they take off their ordinary head-dress (La-gouma) of light feathers, or that which they have to represent the same, and put on the representation of the "Horus Lock," also a

Leopard's skin, with the tail hanging down behind, and they tell you that this is *part of their sacred ceremonies.* This dance, which is "part of their sacred ceremonies," consists of a series of more or less zigzag movements in more or less of a large circle; the chief in front, and one following close behind imitating all his steps and actions. Suddenly the chief stops, faces round and wrestles with the other with his feet and legs. The one behind, having disengaged himself, the chief resumes his dance around in a large circle with the fantastic movements. Again he faces around as before, still followed closely by the other; again he stops and repeats the former action. This occurs three times, and on the third occasion, he, the chief, throws the other, and the dancing ceremony is ended. They do not use their hands or arms, but only the right leg, and it is a "good throw." Whether this is the first and typical representation of the "fight between Horus and Sut" we are unable to say, but it is very suggestive—the chief representing the day and the other the night, and the chief overthrows his enemy who is following him. The weird music is being played by those around, similar to the "Soudanese Tom-Toms," and as soon as it has ended they take off the Leopard skin and tail and Horus head-dress and put on their ordinary head-covering. Naturally one does not expect to find all the ceremonies of "Ancestor Worship" amongst these Negrilloss; we can only find the *commencement of the originals,* but there is a great deal more to be learned and studied yet; therefore, to say that these little men and women have no idea of a future or any religious ideas at all, is, in our opinion, incorrect. We believe that as we are able to gain their confidence, and to speak to them in their own language, we shall find that we are right. We must remember that all native tribes guard most jealously anything pertaining to their sacred ceremonies, and often pretend not to understand. *Spencer and Gillen* have proved this, perhaps more than any other men, in regard to the Australian Aborigines. The fact that the Pygmy considers that a man who is foolish has been sent down by the Great Spirit, and that he must be cared for and respected or the Great Spirit will punish them, and that they believe in the spirits of their ancestors, build little spirit houses about eighteen inches high, with a small opening, inside of which they sometimes place fruit and have one side of the head shaved during certain sacred ceremonies; must all be taken as a further proof that they have some religious belief. They also believe in charms, make marks down the middle of their foreheads and cheeks with a red substance, obtained from trees and sometimes smear black liquid on the face. The belief that the Spirits of their Ancestors are supposed to inhabit rocks, trees and stones, etc., we find has been carried all over the world. The so-called worshipping of spirits in trees, as amongst the gipsies of Germany, or about the trees as with the Shans in Western China, or occupying houses as prepared by the Wanandi, the Australian Aborigines, the Ainu, the natives of New Guinea, the Indians in Mexico and N. and S. America and the Esquimaux, must all have originated primarily from these little people. How long ago the first exodus from here in Pygmy Land took place it is impossible to say ; if you ask a Pygmy how long he has been in the forest and where he came from, he answers :—" Always here, came from nowhere, always have been in the forest."

Also *Major P. H. G. Powell-Cotton* states as follows, which is a further proof of their belief in a Supreme Spirit :—" It was during a forest storm that I received my first inkling that the Pygmies believed in a Supreme Spirit. One evening, about five, as they came to fetch me, after lying throughout the day in the forest, a wind got up and dried twigs and leaves came rustling down, while every now and then a dead branch or limb crashed to the ground. With quick glances to right and left at the tree tops, my head tracker hastened his steps ; then, uttering a shrill whistle, he placed his left hand to his mouth, made a sneezing sound into it and threw it above his head in an attitude of supplication. As the storm grew and the thunder came nearer I saw him darting anxious looks on either side, till he espied a little shrub, with leaves like a willow. Gathering a bunch of these, he pressed them into the palm of his hand, sneezed over them and again extended his hand in supplication over his head. Presently a tremendous thunderclap burst overhead, whereupon he hastily plucked a larger leaf, wrapped the other up in it, and tied them to the top of a stick, which he then held aloft, and every now and then, to the accompaniment of shrill whistles, waved it round his head. On return to camp I obtained from him an explanation of these strange proceedings. The first part of his ceremonies was an appeal to the Supreme Spirit to send away the tempest, but, as the storm continued, he besought protection for us from falling branches torn off by the wind." Here we have the Pygmy "offering propitiation to the elemental power"—the first origin of religion. The earliest mode of worship recognisable was in propitiation of the superhuman power. This power was elemental of necessity, a power that was objectified by means of the living type; and of necessity the object of propitiation, invocation, and solicitation was the power itself and not the types by which it was imagined in the language of signs. If we use the word worship, it was the propitiation of the power in the thunder and the storm; not the thunder or storm itself.

Since writing the above, we learn from *The Standard*, 19th February 1907, that *Major Powell-Cotton* has returned from a visit to Africa, where he spent some time amongst the Pygmies with his wife. We quote from *The Standard* the result of a correspondent's interview with him, and this proves what we have written before to be correct. "During our wanderings in the forest we came across many curious little structures—diminutive dwellings, which we were told were ghost-houses. These were built to propitiate the shades of departed chiefs, who, until a resting place is provided for them, nightly disturb the Pygmy villages. There the people sacrifice and place food for the spirits of the departed. We obtained much interesting information regarding the existence of religious beliefs, even amongst these Pygmies, and learnt that in some spot in the innermost recesses of the forest an imposing religious rite takes place on certain occasions, in which an altar is erected, whereon offerings are laid while the Pygmies arrange themselves in a semicircle and perform their devotions."

In Egypt the oldest god of all was Bes as is well shown in *Dr Budge's* last book, "The Gods of the Egyptians,"[1] vol. ii. p. 286, and anyone seeing this and the Pygmies, even if he were not an Egyptologist, would not fail to identify the two in form, figure and dress. Bes here has the same type of face as the Pygmy; the yellow plume of feathers, *La-gou-ma*, is worn on the head, and the "Horus Lock," the green and yellow "dress," are also worn, and the tail of the Leopard hangs down behind: in fact, these little people have some of the principal features of the

[1] We are much indebted to *Dr W. Budge* and Messrs Methuen for being allowed to reproduce these beautiful coloured plates in this work, and take this opportunity of sincerely thanking them for their kind permission.

THE GOD BES.

The first god anthropomorphically depicted; it is the primitive human form of Horus I., Bes-Horus being the earliest type of the pygmy Ptah The human type was not given to any before Ptah, so that the above shows that the ancient Egyptians left an indelible proof in their mythology of their descent from the first human, which was the Pygmy.

earliest mythology of old Egypt, and no doubt Bes, who was at the later date made to represent a type of Horus I., was at first their "*Chief of the Nomes*," and it was from these Pygmies that the first mythology of Egypt sprung. All have been brought on, added to, and made use of in the various types from the earliest mythos—astronomical, stellar, lunar and solar mythology, and finally the Eschatology which we know so well.

Although the Pygmies are now only found in the Congo forests and in proximity to the sources of the Nile, it is well known that their domain extended over a much wider area in former times, and there is no doubt, from the close anatomical relation, as well as by the similarity of their "sacred ceremonies," that the "Bushmen" are very nearly related to these Pygmies. We cannot agree with *Maspero* that the Egyptian Hieroglyphic which he states represents "dwarfs," not pygmies, is a correct view. It represents "a race of people," and there could not be any race of dwarfs in the true acceptation of the term. These old Egyptians would have no words, signs or symbols to distinguish between the two; they would simply represent them as "little people," and that must be the Pygmies—and thus we find out that they come from the South of the land of Punt. *Maspero* tells us that "all that lay beyond Punt was held to be a fabulous region, a void or intermediate boundary land between the world of men and that of the gods—the island of the Double"—land of the Shades, where the living came into contact with the souls of the departed, and, following the accounts given by *Schiaparelli*, *Erman* and himself, *Maspero* says further:—"It" (the Land of the Shades beyond Punt) "was inhabited by the Dangas, tribes of half-savage dwarfs [1] whose grotesque faces and wild gestures reminded the Egyptians of the god Bes—none knew better than they the dance of the god. We find that King Assi of the 5th dynasty, B.C. 3000, procured one which a certain Biûdri had purchased in Punt. His wildness and activity, and the extraordinary positions which he assumed, made a lively impression on the courtiers at the time, and nearly a century later there were still reminiscences of him." Seventy years after King Assi, an officer, Heru-Khuf, was sent by Pepi II., 6th dynasty, to bring back a Pygmy alive, and in good health, from the land of the great trees, away to the South. That the Danga came

[1] Probably this was the "Ti-Kiti-Ki" Men of the Double Cave. We shall draw particular attention to it later.

from the South is proved by a later inscription at Karnak, and that the word meant "dwarf," or "short or stunted person," is clear from the determinate of a short person or one of stunted growth. The whole of this account is perfectly straightforward and of indubitable reference to the Pygmies. *Professor Maspero's* argument about these not being Pygmies will not "hold water" when we take all into consideration. The "Land of the Shades," which he calls a fabulous region, was the "Khui Land"—the Land of the Spirits and Gods, and was depicted by Hieroglyphics thus: ⊙⧗⧗⧗⊙ which was first mapped out in the Heavens, and after as part of Amenta and was represented terrestrially by the Egyptians by the islands and lakes at the head of the Nile, where these men, so to speak, first sprang forth, and it was here again that the souls would return. This Khui Land sign is very old, and is found in evidence all over the world—on the Australian boomerangs—on the stones in Ireland—on the backs of negroes in West Africa belonging to the secret tribal societies, etc. All this we shall fully explain later on.

We believe that "the Island of the Double,"[1] except we use the term "the Double Cave," is very much later and does not date further back than the Solar mythos—the "Khui Land" dates back to the stellar. Until *Maspero* understands the primordial, as well as other Egyptologists, we are afraid he will always be going off the line and missing the track. We must go back to the beginning of these Pygmies and learn all that they can teach us, then all the totemic ceremonies of the Nilotic and other aboriginal negroes, before we can get to the origin of all. These Pygmies were the first inhabitants of the world—time, different environments and climates would affect this race in many ways, but their anatomy and sacred ceremonies would be

[1] We are uncertain what *Maspero* really means by the expression of the "Island of the Double." If he mean the Double Horizon, that was when Shu lifted up the Heavens, and came into existence during the Solar Mythos. We have no doubt that the text means the "Island of the *Double Cave*," where the mummified Osiris came forth in Spiritual form, as Ra, originally Horus I. in the Stellar Mythos. It was the Khui Land—the Land of the Spirits, because it was here that the dead emerged from the Amenta in *Spiritual form*, after passing through all the dangers and difficulties of the Tuat. It was the opening after the last hour of the night and the passage of the twelve divisions. This Island of the Double Cave is found amongst the Central Americans and in our 30°.—Full explanation, see later.

the least disturbed or different from the original, and this is what we find: many authorities, *Deniker* amongst others, express an opinion that there is no relation between the Pygmies and the Bushmen. One cannot judge by language alone. The fact that the Australians are composed of a number of tribes, each of them occupying a definite tract of country, and each speaking a dialect so distinct that a member of one tribe cannot possibly, without learning its dialect, understand a member of the next tribe, is a sufficient example. More than this must be taken into account. Whilst words can be modified and changed with more or less ease, in savage tribes it is quite otherwise in the case of customs and beliefs, more especially with those associated with sacred matters. When once these have become settled, they are of all things, amongst savage people, the least liable to change. What was considered right and proper by their forefathers, it was only right and proper that they should do. As example: although the organisation of the tribes Dieri and Urabunna, in Northern Australia, amongst whom the two exogamous intermarrying groups still persist, there is no evidence of any kind to show that the practice is an abnormal development; it is the oldest, and although the central tribes have been split into four or eight, this still indicates the retention of the ancient customs, but may be considered as a step in the evolution from the oldest towards our present state of marriage laws.

We are glad to see, from a letter published in *The Lancet*, 14th October 1905, from that great Egyptologist, *Dr Edward Naville*, that he agrees with us[1]: he states that the Danga of the Kings of the Sixth Dynasty must be Pygmies; at the same time he states that from the Egyptian texts there were also "dwarfs," the deformed, who would be kept in the houses of the rich for amusement. He states that the Danga must belong to an African tribe which had a special propensity to dancing. *Colonel Harrison* tells us how fond the Pygmies are of dancing in most grotesque attitudes, in which they also invite their women to join, and he was unable to restrain himself from boisterous laughter at the sight of their gyrations. *Dr Edward Naville* further states: "If the case of the Danga is still doubtful I can quote two instances in which it seems to be certain that the in-

[1] In answer to our letters we had written in *The Lancet* in August and September 1905.

scriptions mean Pygmies. In the sculptures, which describe a great festival, in the temple of Bubastis, we see a procession of priests, among whom are three small men, marching along, and holding long canes. They have a title, which *Brusgel* translates 'guards,' 'beadles,' something connected with the police of the temple. *These guards are neither children nor dwarfs*; they are well-proportioned, and are certainly Pygmies. They are probably not Egyptians, for we find in the same ceremony another African population—the Anu or Anti of Nubia, coming from the South. A third extraordinary figure is a man having a face like 'Bes' but a well-proportioned body. The inscription, which is above the figure, cannot be understood, it ends with 'nanasu nana,' which may be this man's language. Another instance, where we find the Pygmies mentioned, it is a nome or district inscription from the temple of Philæ, of the time of Ptolemy IV. It begins with the nome of Nubia, when we find the words: 'I give my bow to His Majesty that he may subdue the Anti . . . the dwarfs of the countries of the South bring their tributes to his palace.'" Now, it is clear that here we must translate *pygmies* and not *dwarfs*. Dwarfs could not pay tribute, it must be a settled population. Here again, as at Bubastis, they are quoted with the Anti and are said to come from the South, where we expect to find the Pygmies. We know of what a value the Pygmies' bows and arrows are, and even with their small bows and little poisoned arrows they are a terror to all their foes, and so they would bring these to His Majesty to help him in his wars, as the greatest gift they had to assist him, and we know that they are well-formed little men and women and not a distortion or dwarfs. The word Anti . . . would probably refer to the An-Rut or Ante-Rut, a people older than the Dynastic Egyptians but later than the Pygmies.

Pygmies and Bushmen

They have in common:—

1. Projection of the jaws and lips.
2. The flatness of the nose and the broadness of it.
3. Lobeless ears—ill defined.
4. The elongation of the palate.
5. The large size of the teeth.
6. The same character of the hair—pepper-corn.

7. The smallness of stature, and show the same skill in drawing, which the negroes do not possess (negroes having more articulate sounds to express their meaning would not require picture language).
8. The convexity of the sub-nasal space.
9. Occasionally and mostly in young women—Steatopygia.
10. Many words are the same, weapons are the same—small bows and poisoned arrows and small spears.
11. Sacred ceremonies are the same as far as is known.
12. Long forearm.

We contend that our opinion is conclusive of what we have stated; that there is a very close racial affinity, and that the Kattea and the Bushmen are an offshoot, and the latter, perhaps, of a little higher type than the Pygmy. *Deniker* and others do not appear to have studied their "languages" and "sacred ceremonies," which we claim as absolutely conclusive, *with the anatomical conditions.*

They live on roots, insects, and largely on snakes; fruit, when they can get it, nuts, and small animals. Their weapons consist of small spears and bows and arrows, the arrows having poisoned tips. They also make large strong wood-fibre nets with which to catch animals.

The Pygmies represented the earliest *human form* of the *seven* primal *powers—not giants*; the giants were the zootypes of the superhuman powers—not human, but the Pygmies are. In the Egyptian Mythos, Ptah was the Great Architect of the Universe, but not the universe as a cosmological creation. Ptah was a Pygmy and with his assistant Pygmies created Amenta or the lower earth, which was represented by a passage hollowed out of the earth, as an ideograph of the earth that was formed by Ptah and his Khenemmu—formed for the passage of the "manes" and the sun and moon for the first time—in Solar Mythos—*through the earth,* and *not around* as formerly (in the Stellar and Lunar Mythos). In the Stellar and Lunar the manes or soul had to *pass around the earth,* and was carried to the Celestial North by *a superhuman power that was preanthropomorphic,* represented by *zootype giants.* Now Ptah, with his assistants, formed or completed Amenta *through* the earth, thus forming a lower earth or creation which the manes had to pass through before emerging as a Spiritual body. Before Ptah and his Put-cycle of powers there was a secret earth conceived in the new, where nothing grew and no evil or sata had yet been formed, and no light had appeared; but this earth of eternity was not the world of human life, and no human beings were created there. There was no man or woman in the true Mythos. This second earth, created by Ptah and his assistants (Amenta), constituted, with the earth, "the double earth," which was different to the division of North and South in the Stellar Mythos. This upper and lower earth each had a sky, represented thus in the *Ritual*, and the Tatt symbol was here erected in Amenta as a type of eternal stability, and it was portrayed to form the gateway of eternity in the region of Tattu. This double Tatt, represented in the Solar Mythos, the pillars of Sut and Horus—or South and North—the sun and moon, revolving, passed through Amenta, giving light to the passing of the manes. Ptah thus created the circle, of which the egg is the Hieroglyphic sign. *M. Maspero* is wrong in his decipherment when he represents the earth as an oblong box ("The Dawn of Civilisation"), his oblong box being that part of Amenta represented by the Nile valley. He has left out the sky of Nut, and does not conceive the "*double earth*," which was created by Ptah and his assistants as a tunnel for the passages of the heavenly bodies and manes, which were now (in the Solar Mythos) to make the passage *through* the mount instead of *around*. Now that there was a different arrangement when the double earth was formed and built by Ptah, Seb made a treaty between Horus and Sut and called them from their two stations, North and South, to the mountain of the middle earth, the Solar mount in Ainnu, where the two earths met. This is Ptah's house of the two earths in which is the boundary of North and South—the meeting point of the two earths, upper and lower, and the junction of the domains of the North and South in the earlier division of the whole. As soon as Amenta was finished, the East and West were added to the North and South, and the heavens in the four quarters or the square were established on the solstices and equinoxes as the house of Ptah. The two earths are the upper earth of Seb and the lower earth of Ptah—Tatanen—Lord of Eternity. The inheritance of the earth was now given to Horus, "so Horus became Chief of the Land," which now for ever consisted of two lands. He wears the double diadem as ruler of the double earth ; he is now traverser of the two earths as well as uniter of both horizons.

Amenta consisted of a world of various states and many parts, including an Upper and Lower Egypt—the 7 nomes of the Heptanomes, the 14 domains that were based upon the lower half of the Lunar cycle, and the 15 domains that belonged to the Solar reckoning—*Ritual*, chap. cxlii. In the Egyptian divine dynasties Ptah is God the father in one character and Iu, the son, in the other. In the person of Iu he is the youthful deity who rises from the dead both as the Sun-god and as the soul in the image of the Sahu-mummy risen, with the Solar-hawk for its head as a symbol of the soul issuing from the body of Kheper-Ptah. Iu, as the son, is also representative of the Put-cycle or company of creators. *Here the gods were the powers gathered into One God as Supreme.* These were first 7—Stellar ; they became 8—Lunar ; they are 9 in the Put-cycle of Ptah—Solar ; they were 10 as the sephiroth of the Kabalists, and they are 12 in the final heaven of Atum-Ra. Thus *we see the old wise men of Egypt first represented the Solar in human type, and that type was primordial man, represented by the Pygmies*, the old Egyptians knowing that they originated or descended from them.

We have entered into larger details with regard to the Pygmies because we think it is important, these being the first or "primitive man," from whom all others sprang and first peopled this world. They were the founders of language—sign language first, with few articulate sounds ; as time went on more articulate sounds were formed and learnt, and also the beginning of mythology. All originated here in the Upper Nile valley and forest and spread N. E. S. and W. over the world.

At the present day these Upper Nile negroes and many of the Bantu tribes, Masai negroes, the Seri of Mexico, the Australian Aborigines, American Indians (N. and S.) and others

1. Practise knocking out the front teeth.[1]
2. Practise circumcision and some partial subincision, but this ceremony is not performed until the boy is seven or eight years old ; neither is it carried out in the camp but in a secluded spot in the bush, and the boy has to remain there some time.

[1] In some of the tribes one or more of the customs have fallen into disuse or altered a little, but in all sufficient remains to prove one common origin.

3. Practise cicatrisation on the body or raise scars, and on the female some of these tribes excise the clitoris at puberty.
4. Practise Ancestral worship, so called.
5. Have Totems, which are beasts, birds, reptiles, fishes and vegetables, all of which are held sacred by each clan or class.
6. Hold Taboo as regards relations in marriage laws, even to the mother-in-law. The Maories have some totemic rites and ceremonies, and many words of Egyptian origin.
7. All the negroes in Unyoro and Uganda have Totems, and these are divided into twenty-nine classes or clans, each with a Totem. Every family has its place of origin clearly written in the memory of the nation, and each clan holds one special Totem sacred, in so far as they will not eat or destroy it. In every tribe, without exception, there exists a firm belief in the Reincarnation of Ancestors.
8. All have the same tradition about the Great Evil Serpent.

These sacred ceremonies, however, have not yet been studied or observed so well and accurately as *Spencer* and *Gillen* have those of the Arunta tribes, but the reader has only to compare the rites and ceremonies of each and all to see that they are identical and must have emanated from one original centre. No doubt some of the Nile negroes were either driven back as they went North in their numerous wars that occurred at various periods, or remained in their primitive state here in the forests, never having had the chance of developing by evolution into a higher state. Thus we find that these are like the Australian aborigines who apparently never have improved because they have been cut off from all those sources which tend to develop, enlighten and produce a higher type of being, and some of the higher types of negroes may also have been in former times driven back from the North, when those of their descendants evolved into a still further enlightened condition—as, for example, the Masi, who are of a higher type of features. We see, on some of the monuments of ancient Egypt, figures depicted which may well be taken for these.

Dr Morton, recanting an earlier opinion, says :—" I am compelled by a mass of irresistible evidence to modify the opinion expressed in the 'Crania Egyptiaca,' namely, that the Egyptians were an Asiatic people. Seven years of additional investigation, together with greatly increased materials, have convinced me that they are neither Asiatics nor Europeans, but aboriginal indigenous inhabitants of the Nile or some contiguous region—peculiar in their physiognomy, isolated in their institutions, and forming one of the primordial centres of the human family." The Nile negroes were probably one of the first of the "An-rut race," the race that was the first and oldest race of men, after the Pygmies, as both *Eusebius* and *Syncellus* state that amongst the Egyptians there was a certain tablet, called the "Old Chronicle," containing 30 dynastics in 113 descents, during a period of 36,525 years ("Eusebius Chronicles," "Syncellus Chronicles"). The Ruti are those of monumental Egypt, and as An is the Egyptian for old or the oldest, or first, so the An-rut means the first or oldest race of men.

Haddon's description of the natives of the Papuan Gulf district of New Guinea is strikingly suggestive that they have ceremonials and sacred symbols which correspond to those of the Australians and therefore the Nilotic negroes, and that they have the same concentric circles and spirals painted on their bodies like the Australians ; as those of the Secret Tribal Societies of the West coast of Africa, described by *Brother Fitzgerald Marriott.* These, no doubt, were all of the same-time exodus, the Ainu being driven North and the other South as they were pushed on by those coming out after them in a higher state of evolution.

Since writing the foregoing, we find from *Dr C. G. Seligmann's* paper, read before the *Geographical Society* and published in their Journal, March 1906, further confirmation of our opinions. *Dr Seligmann* accompanied an expedition to British New Guinea, and when speaking of the Toro, which appeared to be the tribal name of the Bensback natives, he states that "one of their favourite attitudes was to stand on one leg, with the sole of the other applied just above the knee of the leg which supports the weight of the body," *in fact the same attitude that we still find used amongst the Dinkas of the swamps of the Nile at the present time.* The various tribes that he visited, he says, "are totemic folk," with descent in the male totems in some, and female totems in others. Marriage laws and burial customs are the same as we find amongst the aboriginal Australians. They also use the "bull-roarers" in their initiation ceremonies. Their hair also must be classed as the same—frizzly-curly-wavy and some almost straight. Their calaphic indices are the same. From photographs produced it would be impossible to say that these were not aboriginal Australians. There can be no doubt that these people are of the same "exodus" as the Australians—*i.e.* Nilotic Negroes. It is a pity that more of their sacred ceremonies were not observed; time, however, will give us all.

Captain Macdonald states that in several islands, belonging to the Solomon group, there is said to be a small race of men, about 4 ft. high, who inhabit the mountains of the interior, and will not have any intercourse with the "natives." They go in "families" and roam from place to place, and do not build houses. They have only bows and arrows, the latter deadly poisonous. Probably these are the remnants of the Pygmy race of the first exodus—Paleolithic man, who have not yet been exterminated by the Neolithic, who now form the "Nations of the Isles," and whose customs and totemic ceremonies are identical with these of the "Australian aborigines" almost in every particular. No doubt, in years to come, much more will be known about these people.

All these ceremonies are the acting of the drama of the Egyptian mythology—the survival of the myths in ceremonies, games, usages, is totally independent of the proverbial short memories of savages; the thing that had been they repeated, like any other act of nature, without troubling themselves about the origin or end, and these customs carry their message more simply than any written record in the world, when we know the clue to their primordial character.

It is only by taking into account the ages of time that have elapsed since the origin of primitive man and his evolution, and various exodes that must have taken place from Egypt and the Nile valley at different periods, that one can grasp the history of the past. Even in these islands, geology teaches us that at least two glacial epochs have taken place—*i.e.* twice 25,827 years and how many more no one can say.

Evolution is slow and gradual, but probably the second exodus was that when man had arrived at the totem state, present living descendants of which are found in the Nilotic and other negroes in N.E. Africa, and of which the Australian, Solomon Islanders and New Guinea aborigines are, at least, remaining descendants, still practically in the same state as their ancestors at the time of migration from Africa. Remains of these have also been found in Cornwall (see later), also in Southern Europe. This must have occurred long ages before the other exodus took place, because after Stellar mythos, the Lunar and Solar followed, and then exodes took place, as may

FIG. 69.—No. 1. A hairy specimen.

be seen depicted by the remains of the temples of the Druids, people of Yucatan, India, China, etc. No doubt one of the reasons why we still find some of the original descendants of early man in Central Africa, is, that some of them were "driven back" by those who had further evolved in a higher state, and have so remained buried in the "depths of darkness" that it is only now they have come to light through the explorer and civilisation. Also; we must not forget that when two savage peoples, at anything like a decidedly different level of culture meet, there is some small amount of amalgamation, and although the men of the lower grade would not be allowed to marry the women of the higher grade, on the other hand the women of the lower would be lawful prey to the men of the stronger nation.

Against the argument that we are not right in stating that man originated from here, and that all primal exodes took place to other parts of the world from here, the only one that could be advanced is that there were more centres than one from which

FIG. 70.—No. 2. Another hairy one.

Ainu, or Hairy Man of Japan. No. 1—The hair is somewhat straight; but in No. 2 we note the curly frizzly hair. Compare these with Australian natives and Nilotic negroes. Anatomically they are the same. Skulls are the same—1220 cc.

man emanated—in other words there were several, which, so far as we know, have never been advanced, nor have we been able to find any reasons for supposing that such was the case. That the various races of aborigines have evolved all their "Totemic Rites" from their own surroundings, would, to our mind, be impossible, seeing that all these are practically identical all over the world. There have been changes in the forms and ceremonies from the original by additions and eliminations, which can be easily accounted for by time, evolution, climate and the different surroundings in the countries they found themselves in, but we feel sure that is enough, if the order of nature and evolution be but observed, in making the knowledge of these things depend on the knowledge of the things which have gone before.

CHAPTER VIII

Of other exodes, which we know went out from Egypt at the time of the Solar mythos, one, we are told, went to the North and Isles of the West. Some of these people came to Ireland and Cornwall, and in Ireland we find the tomb of Ollamh Fodhla in the form of the hieroglyphic Kha or Cross.

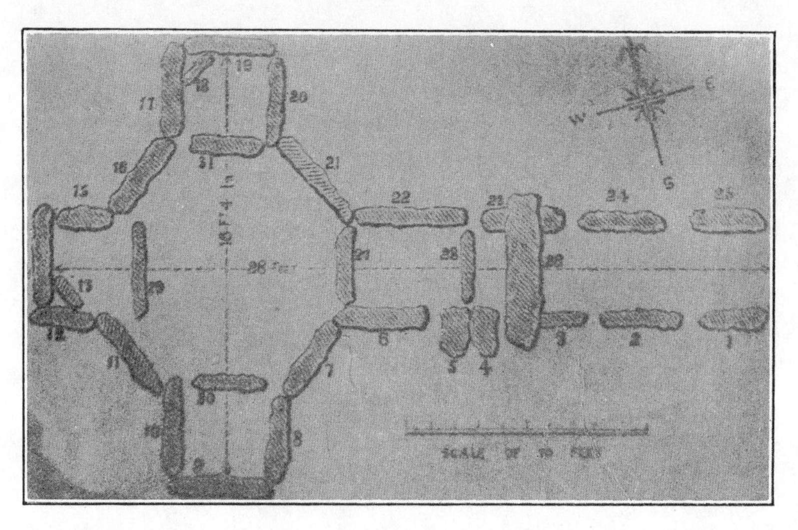

Fig. 71.—Ground Plan of the Interior of Ollamh Fodhla's Tomb.

It is a sign of the birthplace which is identical with the temple built in Upper Egypt, at Medum, called the tomb of Rahotep and Wife. This tomb of Ollamh Fodhla is only one of the Druidical temples which we find all over the British Isles, one of the greatest being Stonehenge, on Salisbury Plain.

A religion of the Cross was first of all established in the Mysteries of Memphis, as the Cult of Ptah, and his son Iu-em-hetep, otherwise Atum-Horus. There is evidence from the Pyramids of Medum that from eight thousand to ten thousand years ago the dead in Egypt were buried in a faith which was founded on the Mystery of the Cross, and this Mystery was the

Great Mystery of Amenta, and from the photograph we see it was the same in Ireland.[1]

The orientation of the "tomb" is very nearly East, though not quite, for it is a little South of East, and this orientation shows that at the time it was built they had reached the stage of Lunar or Solar mythos and had passed the era of Stellar mythology; whether Lunar *or* Solar it is difficult to say.

It would be a question of interest to know for certain whether all the temples we find oriented South of East were built at the time of Lunar mythology, and those due East of Solar, but at present we have not the means to elucidate this point.

It is also important to note that the Druids had only lintels, not arches, but that the tombs of Yucatan and the Incas possessed arches, therefore a later exodus than the Druids.

There are one or two writers who have distinctly stated that "Salisbury Druidical remains" were not erected by the Druids but by a much older people. These writers, let us assure them, are entirely wrong to make such statements and have no foundation for this assumption, which they evidently believe to be true. The proof that the Druids erected these lies there for anyone to see who understands and can read the records of the past left in stones. *The orientation is East or East by South, and these temples were built at the time that the Solar mythos was practised*, and the Druids were the first to bring this doctrine to these Isles; before they came it was Stellar mythos, the remains of which may be seen by anyone at Harland Bay, Cornwall. The orientation of the "tombs" here is North and the burial custom "the thrice-bent man" of the Neolithic age, with a triangular stone over the body with the apex pointing to the Northern or Pole Star and the face also set to the North, as will be shown later on.

The Druids (High Priests from Egypt) brought the Solar mythos with them, and much of the Stellar mythos they found here they merged into and made use of. They never lost anything, but brought all on under different names, and in some cases added to it.

We would particularly draw the reader's attention to photograph I., as it is a very important photograph of a relic of the past, which, in our opinion, should be carefully removed to a museum where it could be properly taken care of. This photo-

[1] The lesser Mysteries were Astro-Mythological, the greater Eschatological.

graph from Ireland is taken from a plate in *Mr E. A. Conwell's* book, and it is a pity the artist could not enlarge it in order to show some of the markings more distinctly ; as it is, one has to study it through a lens. However, we have been able to trace the following distinctly :—

I

Taking the large upper stone between the two lintels we find engraved on the facing edge this ⧻ which is an ideo-

FIG 72.

graphic sign for a nome, a district, a field, a vineyard. On the right lintel at the base we see ◎ a syllabic sign, *sep* or *an* and (, which is only a part of the hieroglyphic, the remainder having been destroyed by time or other cause. This is a Lunar sign. Above this we have the sign of the four quarters and immediately above this ideographic sign ⋀⋀⋀⋀ ; the back to cut in pieces. On the large stone between the two lintels the most striking hieroglyphic is at the upper part on the right half of the stone. Here we have three triangles with their bases one way, and three triangles with the r bases the other, and a number of concentric circles. These we have already shown are also found on the Boomerangs of the Australians, and amongst the Tribes of Mexico and Central American States.

As stated before, the most important fact connected with this hieroglyphic is that *Mr Fitzgerald Marriott* found the same sign on the backs—the apex of each triangle on the spine and the bases extending around the ribs, and concentric circles in front of the men belonging to the Secret Tribal Societies in West Africa, of which no explanation could be given (page 130).

This is the hieroglyphic sign for the "Khui Land," a region of Amenta, Land of the Spirits or Gods. And this is most important to know; because it enables us to say with certainty where was the origin of each—Egypt.

On the right side of the same stone, near the base of the lower right triangle, we see seven ◇ depicting the seven Bright or Glorious Ones (Lesser Bear), the top one representing the pole-star, and put across to show it is the "Head One"

There is also one to the right and one to the foot of these, the hieroglyphic (em)—from, in, into, on, at, with, out from among, etc.

In the centre of the stone we find Heaven depicted in ten divisions and to the right of this in seven divisions. To the left of the outer ring of the great circle—the Heaven in ten divisions—one can see the hieroglyphic sign of the Land of the Scorpion—*i.e.* Zodiacal West. Although very close to the outer circle this is still very distinct.

The Heaven in ten divisions may also be seen depicted on photograph, as well as the hieroglyphic sign of the Land of the Scorpion—*i.e.* Zodiacal West.

To the left and lower part of the great circle we find two serpents (Rerek). These are placed precisely as are those in the photograph from Australia. *Cf.* Fig. 31.

To the left of the base of the lower left triangle we have the ideographic sign ⊠ denoting a town or inhabited place, also ⊙ the Sun, Ra, Light, division of time. an egg, feminine gender.

At the lower part of the great circle part of the ideographic sign ⊔ Ka (qa) is found.

At the bottom is the ideographic sign ≋ for water, any liquid, basin, a lake, a river, the sea of water, etc.

The following are decipherments of some hieroglyphics on the other photographs; but it must be understood and remembered that syllabic signs have various interpretations according to the determinative ideograph, so that those are only some of many and various interpretations:—

1. The hairy net, which is renewed in the shadow which passes for a time over the heavenly body.
2. It has been granted (to the Speaker) by those who are in Tattu to destroy by fire (the souls of) his adversaries.
3. The backbone, the back, to cut in pieces.
4. The Sun, light, divisions of time.
5. An island, a shore, a maritime country.
6. To die, wickedness, misfortune.
7. The nose or nostrils, to breathe, to smell, to move, to rejoice, to delight, to shut up.
8. An egg, feminine gender.
9. Any serpent or reptile.
10. The moon and her phases.
11. Corn, wheat, crops, nourishment.
12. A town or inhabited place.
13. Bronze and iron, and objects made of these metals.
14. M.
15. His journeys.
16. His chariot.
17. a r, if, now, to tie together.
18. pet, the sky, heaven.
19. n e b (neb) each, every, all, any, master, etc.
20. r e r (keb) great, deep, name of a god, to resolve, to round, about.
21. am, kem, to go abroad and forget people.
22. mu, water.
23. set, she, it, its, mountain, to break, they, them, their, etc.
24. am, dweller in, in, with, among, through, upon, around, etc.

25. hammemet, the coming generations.
26. (hu) to taste, to speak, to eat.
27. (am) (xu) daylight, splendour.
28. (seb) a star, a constellation, a god.
29. (es) (is) S.
30. (un) when.
31. men.
32. The Tank of Flame is represented several times, part of the vignette relating to chaps. cxxv. and lxxxvi. in "The Book of the Dead."

FIG. 73.—Egyptian Tank of Flame with Swallow.

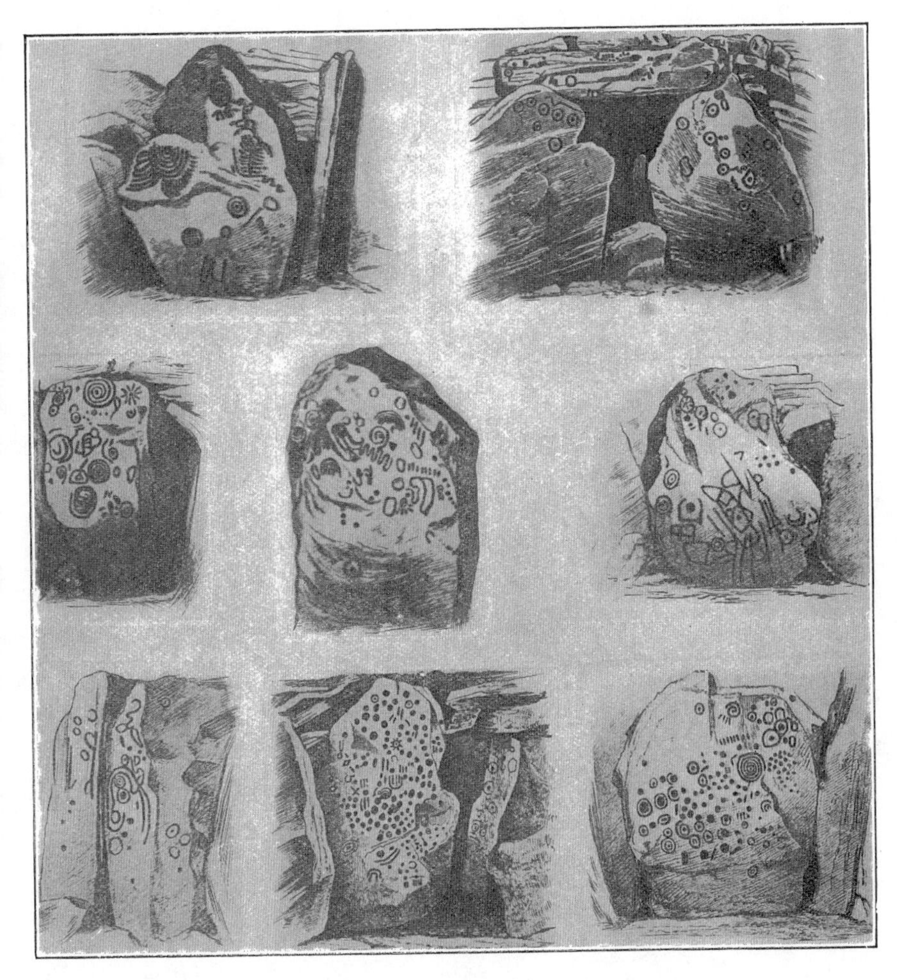

FIG. 74.—Photographs of Stones at Ollamh Fodhla, Ireland, with Egyptian Hieroglyphics.

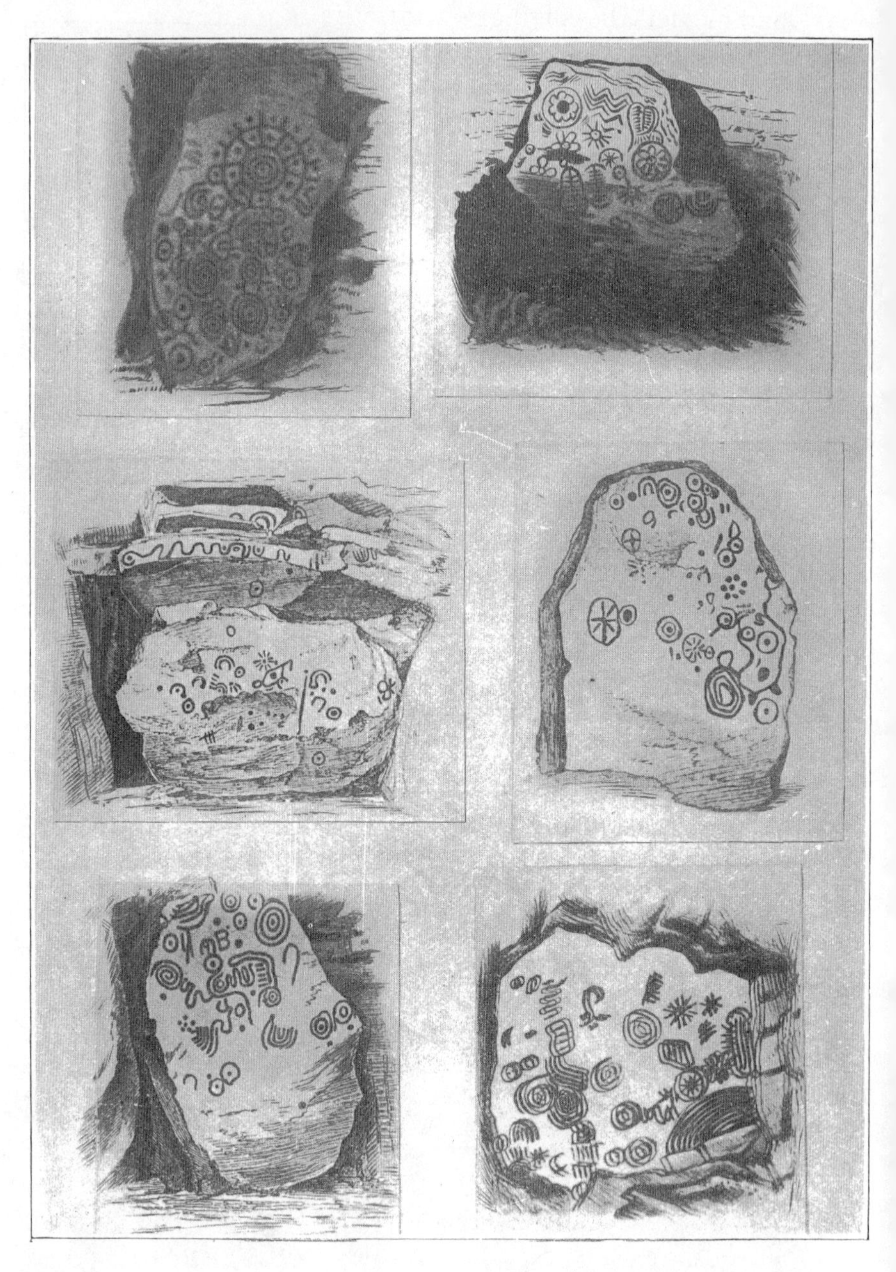

Fig. 75.

Fig. 76.

This sign on the apron of W.G.M.'s, the meaning being well known to Freemasons, is clearly depicted on photograph and on the apron worn by the god Heru-netch-Tuf-Ra (*Budge's* "Book of the Gods of Egypt"); it is also one way of writing Amsu, the Great Master.
The Land of the Scorpion—*i.e.* Zodiacal West.
Amsu the risen Horus. Horus in the resurrection.
The Shining One. The Divine Being.
The Serpent Rerek.

The Celestial World of Heaven or the universe in ten divisions is represented very distinctly, the earliest thus:—

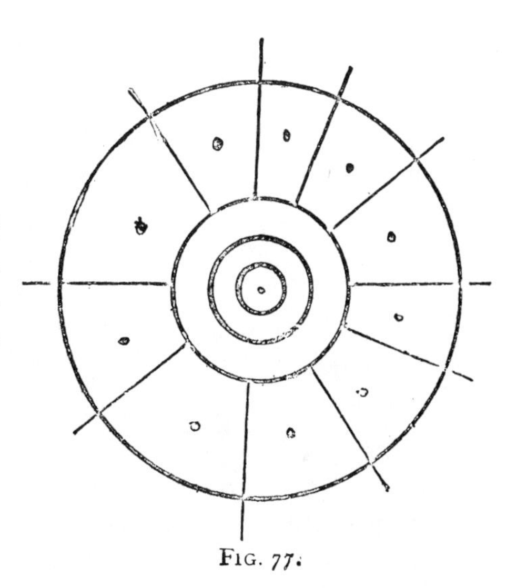

Fig. 77.

Later, the outer circle was omitted in depicting the same, thus:—

Fig. 78.

The Mayas and people of Central America had the same both in the eight and ten divisions.

Celestial and terrestrial division.
Heavens in eight divisions (Lunar).

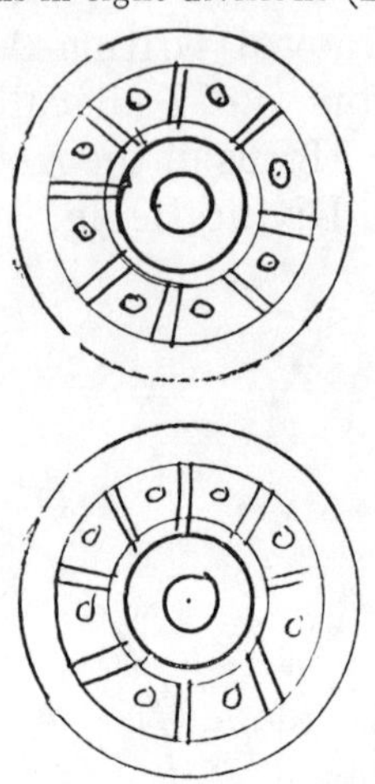

FIG. 79.

These two designs are in the SAHAGUN MANUSCRIPT and BORGIAN CODEX. The upper represents heaven in eight divisions and the lower the earth in the eight divisions.

In the Knight of the E degree, the 70 lights in 10 groups originally represented the Heavens, is 70 *sub-divisions of the* 10 and is much earlier than the 72 sub-divisions of the 12. Of course the Jews, who borrowed this from Egyptians, gave their own version, *re* 70 years of captivity and Cyrus, etc., which it is not necessary to give fully here, we only wish to show the *origin* of this.

We have found more than 150 of these ideographic and phonetic determinatives and syllabic signs, identical with those found amongst the Mayas of Yucatan and the aborigines of Australia.

We would here draw attention to the photographs (page 179)—two from Ireland and one from the central tribes of Australia. It must be noted that the explanation of the markings on the Churingas, as given by the present natives, is not the true meaning, and that they have had these concentric circles in use for long ages, and that these have always been associated with the oldest traditions. The true meanings have been lost to them, and furthermore, the natives state that originally all totem groups had stone ones and that those who have not them now have lost or have had them stolen. These concentric circles, as we have stated before, are associated with the six triangles which is the Egyptian hieroglyphic for the Khui Land or Land of the Spirits. We have these Churingas as sacred stones, with concentric circles on them, as a form or symbol of the everlasting spirit and emblem of the mysteries of the same. The Mayas have also a similar one, which is somewhat different in shape, but has the same significance.

This complex Maya sign represents the deity, the universe ; and these five radii stand for the numerical five. Taken altogether it represents the five mysteries.

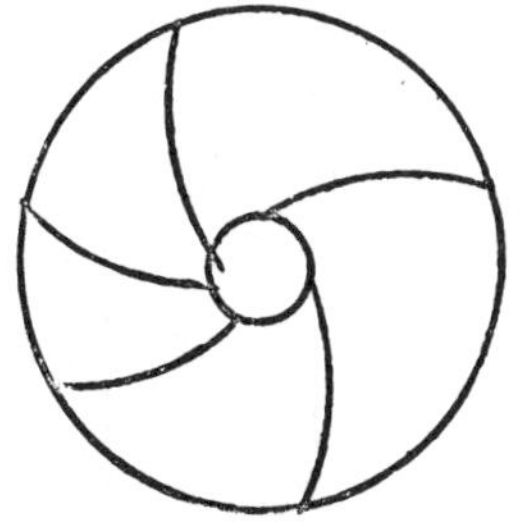

FIG. 80.

A plate in *Mr Conwell's* book represents the five mysteries,[1] which are also depicted by the markings on the Churinga in the photograph taken from *Spencer* and *Gillen's* book on the Australian aborigines.

1. The Purification.
2. The reception of Sacred Rites.
3. Epopteia or reception.
4. End and design of the Revelation, the building of the heap and fixing the Crowns.
5. The friendship and interior communion with God, the last, most powerful and awful of all the mysteries.

Apparently they only knew five of the mysteries, although there were thirty-three in all, the secrets of which up to the present time have, we believe, not been discovered and all had not been evolved at the earliest time (Neolithic age), only completed when the Egyptians had finally worked out their Eschatology.

The characters found on these stones are both symbolic, phonetic and ideographic, and are undoubtedly ancient Egyptian hieroglyphics, and many are identical with those depicted in

[1] In the mysteries of Mizram there are 90°. These have been concentrated to 33° in the English-Scottish and American chapters, but the whole represents the divisions of the Tuat and Amenta in the Ancient Egyptian Eschatology.

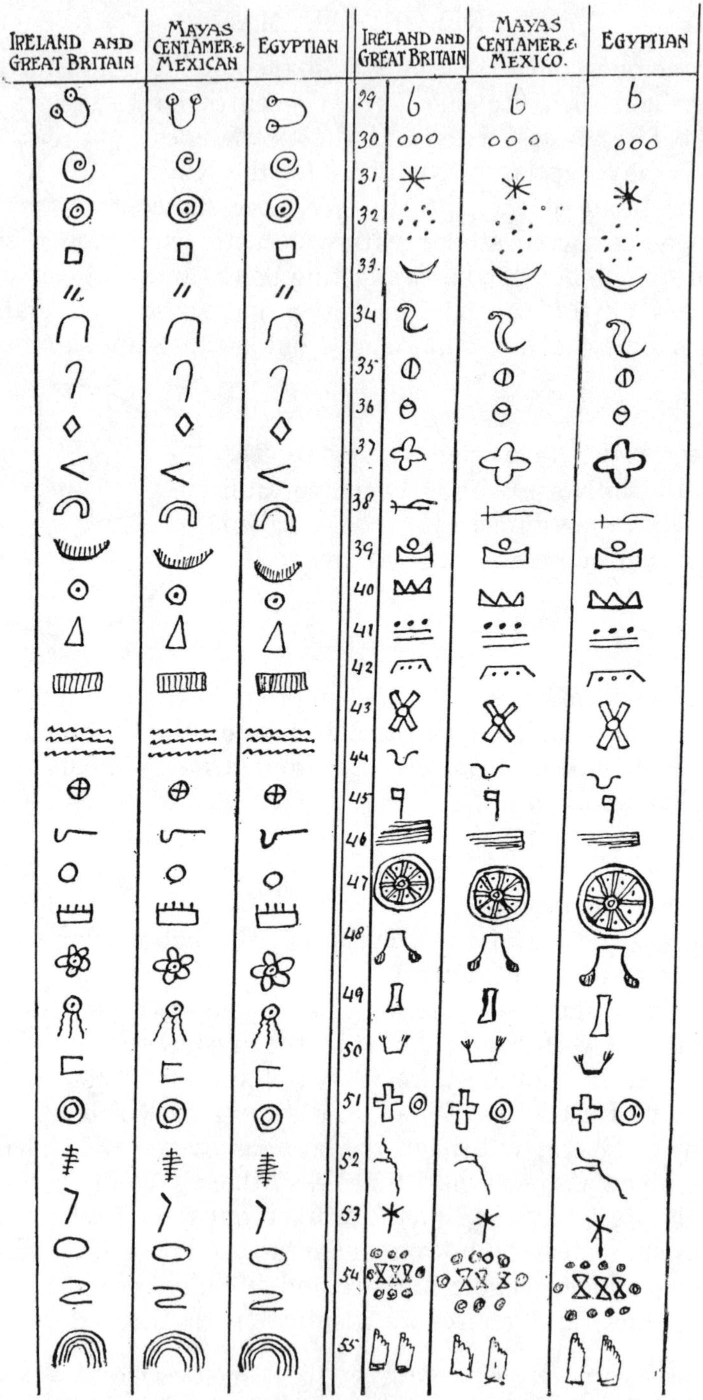

IRELAND AND GREAT BRITAIN	MAYAS CENT. AMER. & MEXICAN	EGYPTIAN		IRELAND AND GREAT BRITAIN	MAYAS CENT. AMER. & MEXICO.	EGYPTIAN
			29			
			30			
			31			
			32			
			33			
			34			
			35			
			36			
			37			
			38			
			39			
			40			
			41			
			42			
			43			
			44			
			45			
			46			
			47			
			48			
			49			
			50			
			51			
			52			
			53			
			54			
			55			

FIG. 81.

We show here 55 true Egyptian Hieroglyphics found by us in various parts of the world. Altogether we have discovered over 150.

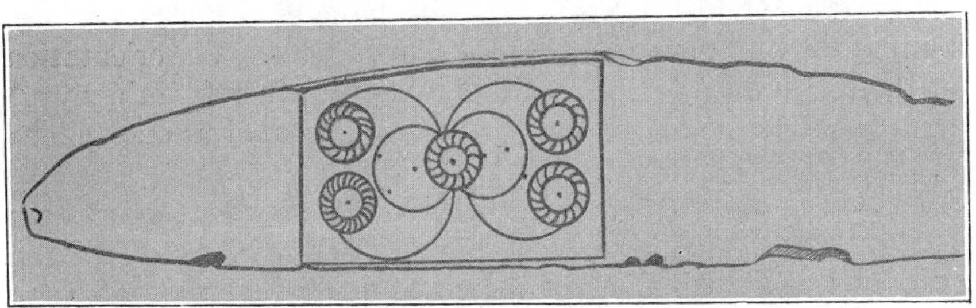

FIG. 82.

Spencer and *Gillen's* book, but although some words and sentences are clear, these writings in stone are so fragmentary and disjointed that it is impossible to decipher them all correctly or to form an interpretation of the whole.

We have given the decipherment of many of the hieroglyphics here, but there are several others which are the oldest form of hieroglyphic, so-called indigenous, and are of Neolithic origin, identical with those found on the ivory tablets and pottery from Naqada and Abydos.

Many readers would no doubt contend that the linear characters found on some of these stones have no relation whatever to the true Egyptian hieroglyphic, but at Naqada and Abydos in the tombs of the earliest dynastic period we find these linear characters side by side with the pure hieroglyphic. In several cases, however, the apparently linear forms are badly scrawled hieroglyphs, and we know from marks on Vases and Pottery found in the royal tomb of Menes that a transition stage had commenced even in indigenous Egyptian Neolithic times in their writings, and that these " linear signs " were the commencement of the same and of purely Egyptian origin and wherever the hieroglyphic for the name of Ptah or Amen Ra is found we know that it must be at the time, or after, Solar Mythos had been instituted, that the exodus of these Druids took place.

We have given photographs here, and if the reader will carefully compare them, he will doubtless arrive at the same conclusion. Of course, a few of the signs appear to differ somewhat, whilst others are identical, but this can be accounted for by the fact that they were inscribed by various scribes.

There is also another proof that the Druids were of a later exodes date than the Egyptians who built the pyramid of Gizeh, the orientation of which is North, and which therefore must have been built at the time of the perfected Stellar Mythos. The orientation of these Druidical temples is East by South, therefore they were built in the time of the Solar Mythos, which confirms our opinion of their Egyptian origin.

Professor Sergi, from his anthropological studies, confirms our opinion that the Druids and inhabitants of these Isles came from an African stock originally, yet there was a still earlier exodus than the Druids in these islands, as is proved by the recent finding of the remains of early Neolithic man in Cornwall, having the practice and belief in Stellar Mythos (Harland Bay, Cornwall) see later on.

CHAPTER IX

DRUIDS AND ISRAELITES

The religion of the Druids was similar in all particulars to that of the Israelites and Mayas. If we compare the recorded practices of the ancient Israelites with the remaining relics of Druidical customs, both internal and foreign evidences prove their similarity. They both believed in one God, the Creator, Preserver and Ruler of all things, the life and soul of the world, who endures for ever and exists throughout space.

The names given to the Supreme Being by the Druids and Hebrews point out in a still more definite manner the identity of the two Deities. The Israelites were accustomed to adore God under the title of Bel or Baal—the original name for Jehovah—"Thou shalt call me Ishi and shalt call me no more Baali"—Hosea ii. 16. With the Druids Bel was the Supreme God. The sacred name of the Lord להוה had also its equivalent term amongst the British Druids: Hu was an epithet of Bel, signifying the self-existent Being:—"He that is." The similarity in sound of the two names and the near relation between "He that is" and "I am that I am" must be evident to the most superficial student (see further chapter on Cross).

The great similarity existing between the Druidical, Maya and Israelitish rites will appear from the following:—

Grove worship was equally prevalent amongst the Israelites as amongst the Druids: it was in the recesses of groves that the Druids exercised some of the mystic rites and taught their votaries the worship of the true God. Abraham planted a grove in Beersheba and called then on the name of the Lord: and after, when the family of Abraham had greatly increased, journeying Northward after leaving their native country, they were strictly commanded to cut down the groves of the people whom they destroyed:—"Ye shall destroy their altars, break their statues and cut down their groves" (Exod. xxxiv. 13), which shows the time that the Stellar doctrines were changed into Solar and the Eschatology.

Their kings, in numerous instances, worshipped in groves. Though the practice was afterwards discontinued, yet there is sufficient to show that the custom had formerly been prevalent. "The Lord God appeared to Abraham by the Oak of Moreh." The word ארדה should be translated "oak" not "plain" as in our version, see Gen. xii. 6. "He pitched his tent by an oak tree." Jacob adored his God through the same medium, and buried his dead beneath an oak, and this mystic adoration of the oak survived after many centuries had elapsed. "Joshua took a stone and raised it up under an oak that was by the Sanctuary of the Lord" (Joshua xxiv. 26). *Pliny* mentions the high esteem which the Druids had for the oak.

In very early times the Deity was adored only in the open air: the worshippers' astronomical acquirements had taught them that certain stars rose when Spring, Summer, Autumn and Winter commenced, while their acquaintance with various astronomical occurrences led them to commemorate them by raising up stones, which were generally in a circular form. "And Moses rose up early in the morning and builded an altar under the hill and twelve pillars, according to the twelve tribes"—twelve signs of the Zodiac. The manner in which these stone temples were erected may be more fully gathered from other parts of the Pentateuch (Deut.). "So Joseph was buried in the temple of Gerizim." See also temple of Gilgal—Joshua iv. 5.

Stonehenge may be said to be analogous to one of these temples: its stones are arranged in the same manner as were those of the Israelites and its magnitude and rude grandeur proclaim that the people who raised the ponderous blocks of stone here, as well as in other parts of Britain, were both learned and powerful.

Joshua, the builder of the structure at Gilgal, assembled the Israelites in the new temple. He said, "When your children in future ages shall ask their fathers *what mean these stones?* ye shall tell them that these were erected as an acknowledgment to the Almighty God, that ye might fear the Lord your God for ever."

The seven stones set up at Stonehenge and elsewhere represent the seven giants who were petrified and changed into enormous stones. These also stood for the seven stations of the pole in the circuit of precession or the circle of Sidi. Under one title, Stonehenge was called the circle of Sidi or the circle of the seven. The Mexicans also have a class of gods who had been turned into stone. These powers could resume a movable shape when they pleased. Becoming petrified as stones would denote the condition in which they stood as fixed figures of the pole, and known to the astronomers that all in turn would resume a movable shape as gods of the pole stars. They constituted the typical foundation of the heptanomis that was built in the heavens and repeated by the mound builders in many lands on earth. This was part of the Stellar mythology brought on and merged into Solar.

In Ireland, as well as in England, a vast number of these monuments exist, but it is in the Scottish Islands that they are discovered in their finest preservation. In France, as well as in other parts of the Continent, they are also to be met with. A very little thought will show how well they were calculated to obtain the end desired. The feelings of the devotee on entering these mystic temples must have been indescribable; the solemnity of the surrounding scenery, the vast and silent concourse of attentive people, the rude, romantic, imposing magnificence of the structure, the Arch-Druidical prophet, emerging from beneath the mysterious trilithic altar and announcing to the wondering multitudes the answer he had heard in whispers from his God;—all this must have created a religious exaltation, intense and overwhelming.

It has been said that when the ancients experienced any signal favour or received any gift at the hands of their Deity, it was their usual custom to erect a stone in remembrance of the blessing. In the British Isles pillars of this description are very numerous, and this practice in our Isles was just as prevalent amongst the Israelites.

We wish to point out here that the religion as practised by the patriarchs differed somewhat from that which Moses afterwards taught. The old patriarchs worshipped God under the name of Baal, sacrificed in high places, adored in groves, planted oaks, intermarried with their immediate relatives, all of which was afterwards forbidden by Moses; in other words, it was a change from the Stellar and Lunar into Solar Mythos.

We mention this because some divines have stated that there was no connection at all between these religions, but that the Druids were infidels. They quote Scripture of much later date to try and prove their statements. They have, however, either ignored the first part of our volume of the sacred law or overlooked it in their anxiety to prove that these ancient people were idolaters. The above will prove the contrary.

Bel—when the Druids and others fell from their original purity of manners—became, as it did among the Israelites, a title with a different meaning, and the reason for the change was that at first it was the Stellar mythos of the Egyptians, and as the Egyptians changed this into Lunar and Solar, and finally formulated the Eschatology, so all those who had intercommunicated with them did the same, and everything was gradually brought up to date—no doubt it took many years to achieve. Bel or Set Anup or El Shaddai was the primary Pole Star God South until he was deposed by Horus I., God of the Pole Star North.

Their sacrifices were the same. The mensuration of time by night and day was the same. The Israelites kept their Sabbath from sundown (Levit. xxiii. 32). *Cæsar* says the Druids did the same. "*Galli se omnes, ab Dite patre prognatos predicunt, adque ab Druidibus proditum dicunt. Ob eam causeam, spatia omnis temporis non numero dierum, sed noctium finiunt, dies natales et mensium et annorum initia, sac observant at noctum dies subsequatur.*"

The manner of the burial of the dead was the same among the Druids, Israelites and Egyptians.

In fact, we find that the ancient Egyptians, Israelites and Druids all adored the same God and the rites of all were similar. The Egyptian PTAH—I am all that has been, is, or shall be—to whom they ascribed every attribute of nature, is the same God as the God of the Israelites and Druids, and all had the same religious ceremonies.

Brother Gould, in his "History of Freemasonry," vol. ii., says: "The connection of Druids with Freemasonry has, like many other learned hypotheses, both history and antiquity obstinately bent against it, but not more so, however, than its supporters are against history and antiquity, as from the researches of recent writers may be easily demonstrated."

It is obvious that *Brother Gould's* "researches" must be

altogether too recent for him to be able to discuss the question he here makes bold to dispute, for all facts show that some of the assertions contained in his work are "fables."

We have only brought forward facts to prove the connection of the ancient Egyptians and the Druids, which no one can dispute, because these facts exist.

Brother Gould also states that Julius Cæsar did not mention the British religion (Druids) at all. The above quotation from *Cæsar* has evidently not come within *Brother Gould's* "researches." He cannot have made any deep study of the antiquity of the subject, for the monuments that still exist and the decipherment of the hieroglyphics on the same distinctly prove that the views we have stated are correct: nevertheless, his recent history of the craft is certainly most elaborate and complete to date.

When the Romans, under Julius Cæsar, invaded Britain, the inhabitants were famous, even among foreign nations, for the superior knowledge of the principles and the great zeal for the rites of their religion. History informs us that the Druids, the Gymnosophists of India, the Maji of Persia and the Chaldeans of Assyria had all the same religious rites and ceremonies as practised by their Priests, "who were initiated" to their order, and that these were solemnly sworn to keep the doctrines a profound secret from the rest of mankind. They never committed anything to writing and were the same as the Priests of Egypt, from whom they obtained them, and their laws were the same as the so-called laws of Moses. The fact that the similitude or rather identity of their opinions, institutions and manners of these orders of ancient Priests, though they lived under different climates and at no great distance from each other, without intercourse, amounts to this:—that all these opinions, institutions and beliefs simply flowed from one source—Egypt. *Cæsar*, *Diodorus* and *Mela* all agree to this, and *Mela* tells us that they taught the doctrine of the immortality of the souls of men—it was the Eschatology of the Egyptians.

It is of no use to take into account what all of these "preached to the public." It is not possible to bring women and the common herd of mankind to religious piety and virtue by the pure and simple dictates of reason; it is necessary here to call in the aid of superstition, which must be nourished by fables and portents of various kinds, and this we find the Druids did, and possessed unbounded power, before the advent of the Romans, over all and everything ; but as the Romans gained control in this island, so the power of the Druids gradually declined, until it was quite destroyed as a civil factor. Those, however, who would not submit to the Romans, fled to Ireland, Scotland and the smaller isles, where they supported their authority for a long time after, up to the eleventh and twelfth centuries A.D. This we see from the following law made by Canute :—" We strictly discharge and forbid all our subjects to worship the God of the Gentiles." The Druids had one chief or Arch-Druid in every province, who acted as High Priest. These had absolute authority over all the others and he was elected from amongst the most eminent by a plurality of votes. *Cæsar* acquaints us that they taught their disciples many things about the nature and perfections of God, and that there was only one God, the Creator of heaven and earth. One name, under which they worshipped Him, was Esus or Hesus or Harits, which is their name for Horus. But their secret doctrines were never communicated to the bulk of mankind ; these were carefully kept concealed. The consecrated groves, in which they performed their religious rites, were fenced around with stones, to prevent any person entering, except through the passages left open for that purpose, and these were guarded by some inferior Druids to prevent any stranger from intruding into their mysteries, in the same way that we find the ancient Egyptians all had their entrances guarded by the " Cutters " (Tylors). The Druids taught the wisdom of Egypt in the British Isles ages before the present volume of the Sacred Law was heard of. They had the Ark of Nu as the ark of the seven Kabiri and the seven Hohgates the seven who were companions of Arthur in the ark.

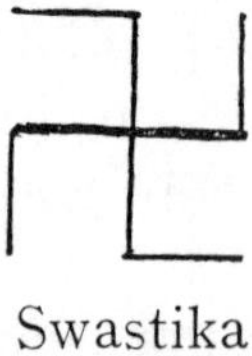

With the general consent of the whole there were three orders. The Arch-Druid, who was elected to that position by all the other Druids, it not being a hereditary office, fixed on the most beautiful oak-tree in the grove and then performed the rite of consecration. All the side branches having been first cut off, he proceeded to join two of them to the highest part of the trunk, so that they extended on either side like the arms of a man and formed in the whole the shape of a cross Swastika. Above the insertion of these branches and below they inscribed in the bark of the wood the word "Thau" and before it performed their most ancient rites. This sign is also found occupying the centre of the triangle

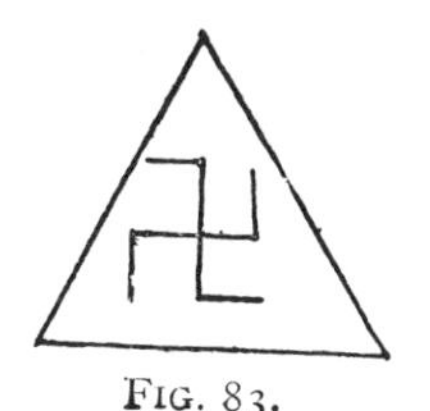

Fig. 83.

That this sign of the Swastika was found in Britain, 3000 B.C. until 300 A.D. will prove pretty conclusively that the time of the exodus of the "Druids" from Egypt was at the time they had the Swastika, after they had converted this from the figures of the four quarters and before they had changed the same into the Ankh Cross by evolution, probably more than twenty thousand years ago if *Flinders Petrie* is right in his dates as to his recent discoveries at Abydos. The meaning of each is the same. The conversion of this sign—"Swastika or Gammadion," another name of it, and there are a great many different names for the same sign in various parts of the world—into the Latin Cross was effected by the Christians in this way, as may be seen on a Runic stone from Sweden.

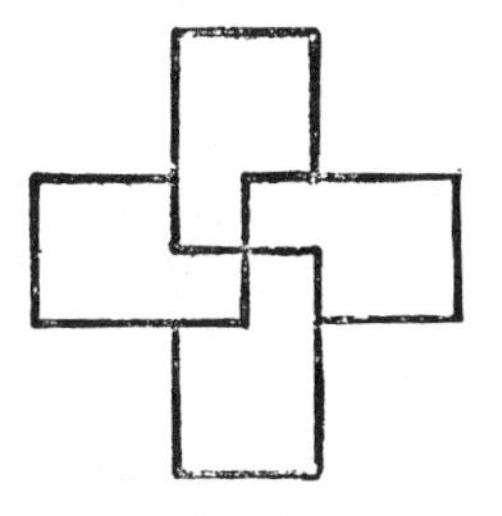

Fig. 84.

Thus we see how one form of the Cross, now used amongst the Christians, originated direct from the sacred symbol of the Swastika, without following the evolution of the Ankh Cross which some others have, in those countries where the practice of the Osirian doctrines had been in progress for thousands of years after the exodus of the Druids from Egypt, probably at the period when they had just evolved the Solar mythos from the Stellar and Lunar; and the above would lead us to believe that there was little intercommunication, eschatologically, or any interference with them until the time that the Romans brought the doctrine of Christianity amongst them, then converting their long-used ancient and sacred symbols into an "up-to-date" form of the time.

We think that this must be so, because of the very important figures of the earliest form of the Swastika, in the form of four Human Figures, which is still preserved and can be seen in Scotland as shown here (see chapter on "Cross"). And the god of the 4 quarters is depicted as Atum-Ra in the *Ritual* (chap. lxxxii.). The divine man described by Plato was bicussated and stamped upon the universe in the likeness of a Cross. The new heaven in the book of Revelation was formed according to the measure of a man (Rev. xxi. 17), which was the old Stellar heaven founded on the 4 cardinal points represented by the Swastika Cross of the 4 quarters, as seen here in Mexico and many other parts of the world.

Probably this is of much greater importance in deciphering the true meaning and origin than any other form we have met with. The Egyptian original of this will be shown later on, and there cannot be any question of identity between the two. If formed during the Stellar mythos it would mean or represent the four quarters. (*See* Appendix I.)

This is also represented by another sign—viz. two triangles—as follows, which has the same meaning and is well known to all R.A.M.'s, and has by some been named the Seal of Solomon (see origin of triangles). The origin of the double triangle was the double triangle in "Ares," therefore Celestial, as may be seen on any celestial globe. The Druids had the three feathers in use amongst them in the form of \|/ or \|/ called "three rods or rays of light," signifying the eyes of light or the radiating light of intelligence shed upon the Druidical circle It is also the name "I.A.U." I.A.U., the son of PTAH—*i.e.* Jesus, son of the Father, so the three rods stand for "The Light of the World," and the Druids used it as a sacred sign and symbol, the same as the Makalanga use and recognise it. The Makalanga, the children of the Sun, in South Africa, have this sign carved or tattooed on their bodies, and consider it a most sacred sign, and "the name of the great giver of light." They do not know the origin of this, but their ancestors handed it down to them, and so they still mark their bodies with this device and treasure the meaning and name in a most sacred and solemn way. Jesus tells his disciples, "Ye are the light of the world" (Matthew v. 14). He himself was called by Simon "a light to lighten the nations" (Luke ii. 32), and he assumed the name of "the light that is come into the world" (John iii. 19); and in another place he says, "I am the light of the world" (John viii. 12), and again, "yet a little while is the light with you" (xii. 35); "I am come a light into the

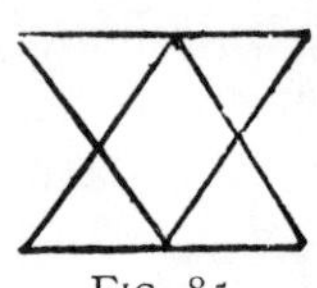

FIG. 85.

world, whosoever believeth in me should not abide in darkness" (xii. 46). The Central Americans also had the three rays of light to represent the same, and four rays of light in this form

to represent the four children of Horus.

The symbol was appropriated by King EDWARD III. and adopted as one of his badges. It was borne by his son, the Black Prince, and by other Princes of Wales, and still is as the three feathers, which was the original, and is seen as this.

These feathers are also a sign of ancient Egypt (Pierret 754). I.U. is older than I.A.U.; in fact, it is the oldest Egyptian name of Jesus. See later on how this has been altered. Two feathers first represented I.U. and then three as I.A.U.; also the two lives—spiritual and earthly: and it is a significant fact that I.U. or I.A.U., the son of PTAH, should have the original handed down and adopted here, as an earthly type of the son of the King.

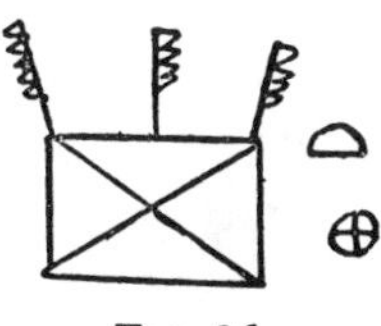

FIG. 86.

The fact that these rods are rods in one case and feathers in another, does not alter the meaning or change the original. The Broad Arrow occurs as a mark of the Royal Household in 1386. It also shows that the Druids, although practising and belonging to the doctrines of the Solar mythos, had brought on with them and used the symbols of the first or Stellar mythos. Another important sign, and the most sacred amongst them, was the first evolution of the Cross—viz. the Swastika, as we have shown.

These three \|/ rods or rays of light or symbol for I.U. are still worn and used by *our present Druids*, and anyone can see the symbol on the Caps worn by those of the highest degree; how many of them know its meaning? It has identically the same meaning as the supreme council wear on the Caps the triangle; how many of the S.C.'s know this or what its signification is? but the S.C. should have the triangle with the apex downwards to be correct, as the triangle as they wear it was originally the name for Sut or El

Shaddai or Bel; it was certainly appropriated by Horus later, but the triangle belonging to Horus only was ▽ apex downwards. (*See* Appendix 2.)

As regards some of the other signs and symbols that we use and which we find amongst, and in use as sacred symbols by, the Druids are the rough and smooth "A." The cube  was used by them first to signify truth and it was also a symbol of mercury. They represented the northern Heavens by a circle

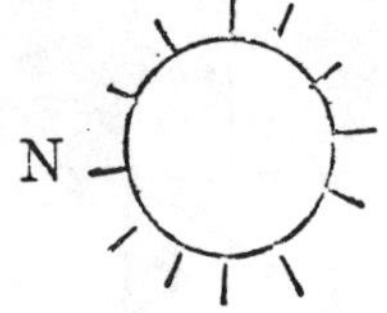

with twelve pillars, also the southern Heavens

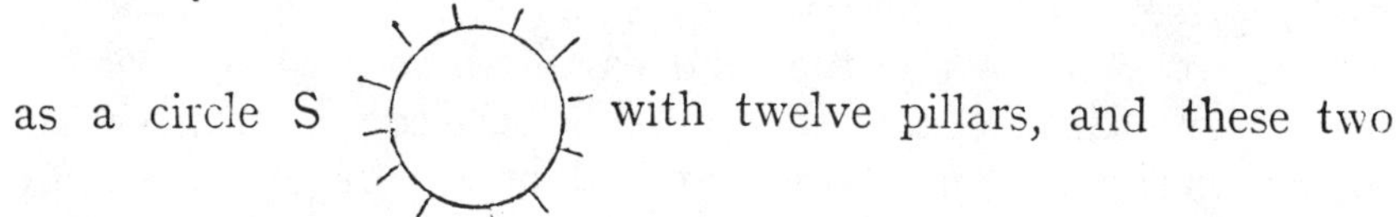

as a circle S with twelve pillars, and these two circles were intersected in their centres by another smaller one

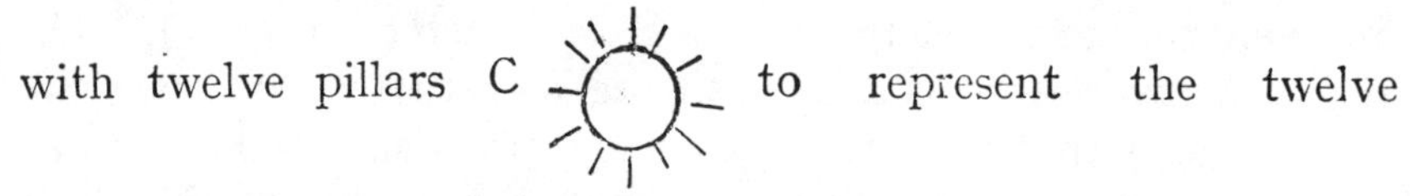

with twelve pillars C to represent the twelve signs of the Zodiac. The twelve in the north they called "Tywysogaethu"—"Leaders or Councillors," and the twelve in the south Heavens, "Cyfiawneon."

N. Heaven with twelve pillars. Small circle with twelve pillars to represent the twelve signs of the Zodiac.

S. Heaven with twelve pillars.

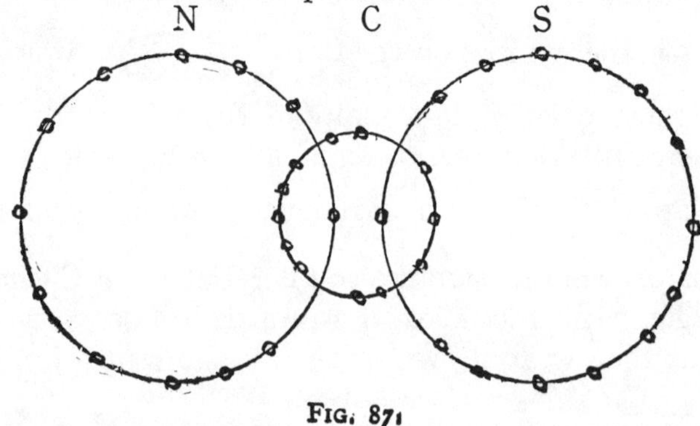

FIG. 87

Heaven in thirty-six divisions also represented the thirty-six gates of "the Great House of him who is on the Hill"—*i.e.* the Great House of Heaven based upon the thirty-six gates or duodecams of the Zodiac.

When we were in Cornwall in 1904, inspecting some old Druidical remains, we came across a typical specimen, still existing, at Rough Tor, and took drawings of the same as here

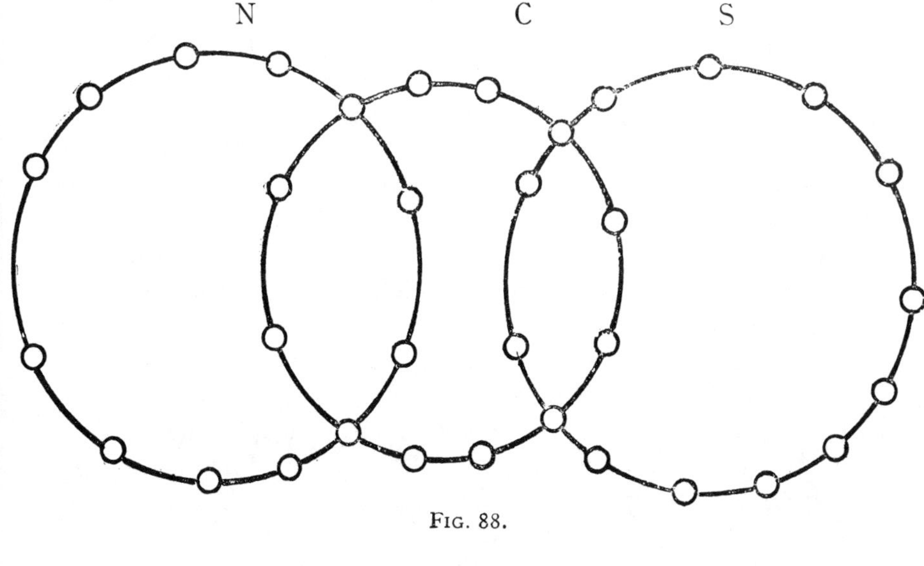

FIG. 88.

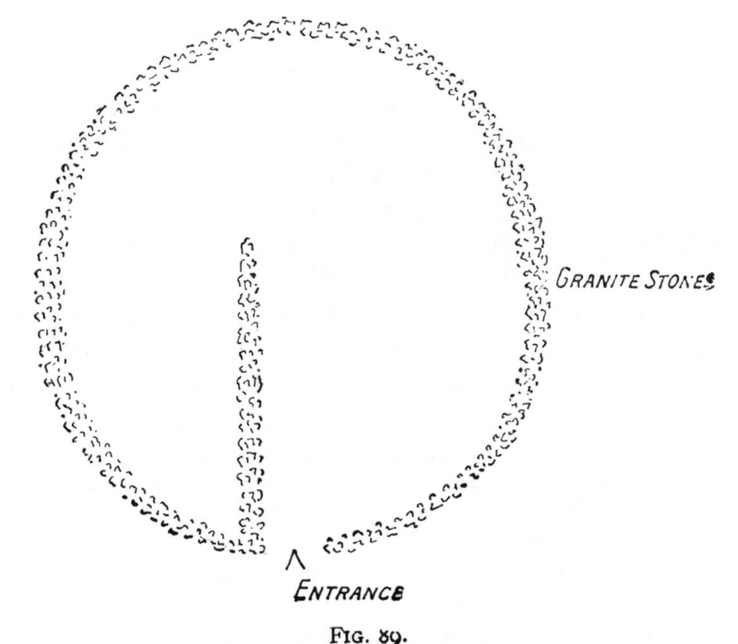

FIG. 89.

depicted—two large circles, N. and S., and one smaller one intersecting these. Each had the so-called twelve pillars, and here they are called "Huts." A good specimen of one, almost perfect, still exists here; we give the drawing of this also, taken on the spot, and it shows the entrance E. by S. of all the smaller circles or Huts, so called, or "Pillars." All these we found at Rough Tor, in Cornwall. It appears to us that *Sir Norman Lockyer* (in his article in *Nature*, April 1906), in speaking of *two* circles at Tregeseal, has overlooked the lesser, which must have bisected the two greater circles. In all our researches in Cornwall we have been able to trace the remains of the *three* circles, and at Rough Tor these are very distinct. It is quite possible, however, to overlook the three here if you have not the "key," but to anyone who will mount Rough Tor some fifty or a hundred feet above the circles and then look down, the three can be seen quite distinctly. Then, if we count the "Stone Huts" [1] of each, and can understand the meaning and reasons for which these circles were erected, we shall know that they represented the three divisions of the heavens celestially, and the thirty-six nomes of Egypt terrestrially, which, of course, is a somewhat different view from that of *Sir Norman Lockyer*. Of course, his third circle may have been destroyed, as the farmers make hedges with these stones.

These three stone circles of the Druids must not be confounded or associated in any way with the "artificial mounds" we find throughout the world, all of which bear a striking resemblance. There is one at Salisbury Hill, at Avebury, 170 feet high, which is connected with ramparts—avenues 1480 yards long, circular ditches or "Dew Pans," and stone circles. Many of these are to be found in England, Ireland, and North and Central America, which are almost precisely similar. These are the remains of the "Towns" or dwellings of Neolithic man, situated on hills or downs, and ramparts were thrown up to keep off wolves and other wild animals from their cattle. The "avenues" were made for their cattle to pass through, morning and night, as they were driven to and from their pasture. The stone circles marked the places of the "huts" for the "keeper and look-out," and the

[1] We found that it was a good thing to "whitewash" these stones first. Of course it must not be forgotten that they also portrayed the Heavens—first in the seven divisions, then in eight, nine, ten and twelve—so we may find amongst the more ancient remains stones only of one of these divisions of the Heavens approximately giving the date of erection.

"dew pans," which were a peculiar construction, were made to contain their water supply. Early Neolithic man thus lived and protected his cattle from the ravages of wild animals, he having only stone axes, clubs, arrows, flint-heads and spears to use against many ferocious beasts, therefore many would dwell together on the top of the down or hill, throwing up ramparts of earth and digging ditches under them so that wolves and other animals could not easily get up to their flocks, which they drove in at night to keep secure. Here we see the first formation of "Towns" and "Cities" and man beginning to settle down in one place, instead of leading the nomadic life of their Paleolithic fathers. We draw attention to this as we have seen it stated that these "Mounds" have been attributed to the Druids by some writers. They are anterior to the Druids and are only to be associated with Neolithic man, and at the time of Stellar mythos; whereas the three circles were erected only by the Druids during Solar mythos, and are of much later date.

Diodorus Seculus gives the number of the nomes in Egypt as *thirty-six*. This symbol of the three circles of the Druids, therefore, would also represent the thirty-six nomes of Egypt at the time the Druids left Egypt *during the Solar Mythos*, and somewhat approximately fixes the date, as we know that the Egyptians were continually adding and increasing the number of nomes from the original seven up to forty-six. Historians have differed as to the number of nomes in Egypt and the reason is that with the Astral Mythology they mapped out seven in the heavens first of all and depicted the seven in the earth, and from them circles of twelve divisions, each of which, no doubt, was first astronomical, the three twelves had gradually increased from seven, ten, twelve to thirty-six. We know that not only did they map out the Northern division of the heavens but also the Southern and Central, therefore it is quite certain that here we find that they divided the North into twelve, the Central into twelve, and the South into twelve, making in all thirty-six; and, as they mapped out the heavens in a Celestial form, so they depicted the same in Terrestrial form.

That the Druids brought this with them from Egypt is also certain, because they could not map out the Southern heavens here—*these could not be seen here*, and it would only be possible to do this when near the Equator—here only could the Northern,

Southern and Central heavens be mapped out by the ancient astronomers, and this we know that the Egyptians did very thoroughly, and their Priests took this knowledge with them to whatever part of the world they went; hence the remains of these ancient monuments we find in various parts of the world and the true explanation of the same. We challenge anyone to gainsay and prove differently.

These three circles are not only found in the British Isles, but in various parts of the world, and these are proofs alone which suggest how many thousands of years before the Babylonians and Sumarians ever existed that the knowledge of the architecture of the heavens, North, Central and South was worked out and known to the old Priests of Egypt; and how any man, of such eminent knowledge as *Dr W. Budge,* should state "that the Egyptians borrowed their knowledge of the signs of the Zodiac, together with much else, *from the Greeks, etc.,*"[1] is beyond comprehension!! Even the Mayas had the knowledge before the Greek nation or Babylonians existed, and it is a question if the Druids were not much older than the Mayas. Numbers of these circles may be found in Devonshire and Cornwall, especially Cornwall, and because the Greeks, at the latter period of the Egyptian Dynasty, were employed to paint Dendera and perhaps some other temples, is no reason or proof to any thinking man, who has such contrary and conclusive facts still extant, that the Greeks introduced the signs of the Zodiac into Egypt, and we feel sure, from the great knowledge that *Dr Budge* possesses, that he really does not believe it to be a fact. Perhaps he is afraid, if he published the whole of his knowledge on these subjects, "that he might be placed in a similar position as *Dr Ray Lancaster* has been."

These must not be confounded with the two circles ○ ○ which were pre-Solar however, and twelve stones erected to form each—one to the north and one to the south representing the 24 zodiacal stars, and as characters in the Egyptian learning these earliest pre-Solar powers constituted "the old ones" or "the Elders." These are Egyptian wherever found and are traceable to two different groups of 12=the 24 mysteries of the Stellar Mythos. These were the 12 who had their thrones as rulers

[1] "The Gods of Egypt," vol. ii. page 312.

(or æons) in the Zodiac and the 12 as spirits with Horus-Khuti, Lord of the Spirits in the heaven of eternity. In the papyrus of Ani and of Nunefer we see the Judges in the Maat appear as 12 in number sitting on 12 thrones and we find these two circles in Cornwall distinguishable from the three.

"Where did our ancient brethren meet before lodges were erected? upon 'holy ground'; on the highest hill or lowest vale or any other secret place, the better to guard against cowans and enemies"; and we have distinct records left that when St Augustine came to these Isles in the sixth century to convert the "*Heathern Natives*" to Christianity, he found numerous priests and their disciples here, and who had *been* here "for all time that was known," who were distinguished for the pure religion which they practised and professed. These were the so-called "Culdees," and many joined the "Christian Church" and became priests of the same, and were merged into it after the close of the twelfth century, although many kept themselves aloof for a long period after. These were the last remnants of the old Druid Priests—descendants of their Egyptian brethren—who practised the pure Eschatology of their forefathers. Gradually they all died out as a separate and distinct class, and those who remained were merged into "Christianity," but they brought on all the doctrines with them and practised these in secret places, in so-called lodges, and these exist to the present day as "Freemasons." The ceremonies have been somewhat changed, and innovations have been made to suit the evolution of the times, but still Freemasonry is the purest of all the relics of our forefathers, and in Egypt alone do we find the origin. (*See* Appendix 3.)

No regular history of the order at this time can be found, nor is it necessary to our purpose. We know that their open worship was prohibited by this edict of Canute here in England, who reigned from 1015 to 1036. Some time, therefore, during this period, the edict was issued, and they were forbidden to perform their devotions. To evade the minions of the law, they resorted to private meetings and secret celebrations, and we do not entertain any doubt that these formed the first so-called "Lodges" in England, as a cloak to screen their religious rites and ceremonies and to keep them pure as they had received them originally from the parent sources in Egypt. It is impossible to state if this took the form of "Craft Masonry" first in England or Scotland. The Druids were first persecuted and driven to secret meetings in England, as may be seen from the above edict, but all that is immaterial to us, and we only mention it because the Scotch people claim to be the "oldest masons." Our contention is that the Druids were the direct descendants of the High Priests of Egypt, who came over here. Their beliefs, forms, rites and ceremonies were the same, and our brotherhood—Freemasonry—has been carried on ever since, and is one and the same thing.

The allied Degrees—Degrees are quite arbitrary—contain much innovation in some of the parts, and many of these have been interpolated by members who have travelled and been initiated in the so-called "Eleusinian Mysteries," which were those founded in various centres of the world by men who had been to Egypt and had learned some of the doctrines of the Priests there. When they returned to their own country they founded so-called "Schools" and sects of the order. Hence, to gain the correct knowledge of the whole of our degrees, it is necessary to know these and the Egyptian *Ritual*, and the knowledge of their progressive evolution for the development of their mythos to Astronomical Mythology, Stellar, Lunar and Solar; and finally their Eschatology, to appreciate the knowledge of all our signs and symbols, etc., taking into consideration at the same time what evolution and time have brought about.

What is that which is lost? And where do you expect to find it? The reason that we go from East to West in search of that which is lost is because, when Osiris lost his life by the machinations of Sut, like all the Manes he travelled from East to West to enter Amenta. There, in Amenta, after passing through difficulties, dangers and darkness, his Manes was regenerated or raised again in the form of Amsu, or Horus, in spirit, and he came forth from Amenta after entering the West, to the glorious gate of the East again, as a raised Manes or glorified spirit in the form of Ra ⊙.

He *returned to the East with all the secrets of Amenta.* Here it was, in Amenta, that the Tatt Cross was thrown down; here it was that the Veil of the Temple was rent asunder and the C. S. poured forth blood and water, and all was reborn; here he was shown all the signs and given or taught those passwords, or words of power and might that kept evil and the powers of darkness away, and enabled him to advance from one Aāt to the next.

The Tatt Pillar was re-erected and the dead Osiris was reborn as the Child Horus, and came forth as the glorified spirit Ra ☉; or the dead man had here been raised to this glorious resurrection in spirit form. The final password and sign had been given him, the highest degree conferred, and to him who was in possession of [hieroglyphs] all doors were open, both in this life and the life hereafter.[1]

Ta-Ua to Am-Ur is the Egyptian for E. to W.

Here we have the answer which solves the question of "who and what were our ancient Druids?" They were undoubtedly descendants of the ancient Egyptian priests, who came over and landed in Ireland and the West of England, and who brought with them their religious doctrines and taught and practised them here. The Tuatha-de-Dananns, who came to Ireland, were of the same race and spoke the same language as the Fir-Bolgs and the Formarians, possessed ships, knew the art of navigation, had a compass or magnetic needle, worked in metals, had a large army, thoroughly organised, and a body of surgeons; had a "Bardic or Druid class of priests." These "Druids" brought all their learning with them, believed and practised the Eschatology of the Solar doctrines, and all came from Egypt. That their temples are older than those found in Uxmal, in Yucatan, in Mexico (which are stated to be 11,500 years old) and those amongst the Incas in South America, and some of the Zimbabwe in South Africa, is clearly proved by their want of knowledge in building an arch, although we find in the oldest remains amongst the Zimbabwe lintels at Umnukwana, and no doubt there are others in South African ruins, but successive immigrants have obliterated most of the original, which was the old Egyptian, as can be proved by other facts.

The Incas had the same wonderful and skilful way of building as the Egyptians—that is, they so prepared and finished huge blocks of stone, and fitted them so accurately, that it is almost impossible to distinguish where the joints are. This was done by a very fine cement, made with granite, which blended with the blocks, and made it perfect. This we also find amongst the ruins

[1] The word, sign and T. of the 30° was taken from Anhuri. An interesting plate of this in Egyptian is shown in Maspero's work, "Dawn of Civilisation," p. 99.

Satit presenting Pharaoh Amenôthes III. to Khnûmû, from the Temple of Khnûmû at Elephantine, shows precisely the S—— of ——?.

at Umnukwana and all the *ancient* part of the ruins called the Great Zimbabwe.

But the ancient Egyptians did not build arches until a later date. The first true arch is found in a Fourth Dynasty Mastaba, at Medum—one always finds lintels. This is the case with the Druidical temples ; but at Uxmal we find that the arch has taken the place of the lintel. We have no doubt either, from the character of the hieroglyphics and their significance, that this temple or tomb of Ollamh Fodhla was built at the time of the Lunar or early Solar mythos. The arches we find in Central America are built in the same way and form as we find the Egyptians and early Greeks built them—that is, *one stone overlapping the other*. This may be proved by comparing those of Las Monjas, Palenque, with the Egyptian Fourth and Fifth Dynasty arches, and "The Treasure-House" at Athens.

In "Neu Manners and the Auld of Scottis," *Boea* says the old inhabitants used the rights and manners of the Egyptians, from whom they took their beginning. In all their secret business they wrote with cyphers and figures of beasts, made in the manner of letters.

The ancient Britons buried the beetle with their dead, the same as the Egyptians, and the same genus—the *Dermestes*. It was the emblem of time, ever renewing—a symbol of eternity. The scarab not only represented the circle of the sun, but the renewing cycles of the soul.

The Hebrew Gev is identical with the Egyptian Khef and the children of Khef. The Æthiopic Genetrix are designated the Gentiles, who went northward out of Egypt and carried with them the primordial name of the birthplace in the Celestial North—the race of Japheth is the same as the race of Kheft, and we learn from CANUTE'S EDICT that the Druids were called Gentiles here at that time.

How many years the Druids lived and practised their ceremonies and religious rites in Britain is not known, but when Christianity was introduced into these isles there would be, no doubt, a "war waged" against "the heathen," and as the former spread and increased, so the other would naturally die out as Druids, but the few who remained would still carry on their mysteries secretly, and as many of their signs, symbols and rituals were the same as taught by Moses, naturally they would become absorbed into the later doctrines.

According to *Cæsar*, the Druids taught the Gauls that they were all descended from Dis Pater, the Demiurge—that is, from the god of Hades, or Amenta, who is Tanan, as consort of the goddess Tanen, and whose name was taken by Ptah-Tanan, the better known Dis Pater who was earlier than Osiris, in the Egyptian Mythology, and from whom the Solar race *ascended*, whether from Puanta, or the Tuat.

To understand this, it is necessary to know that Egypt represented the Tuat, and Amenta geographically. Lower Egypt was the representation of the Tuat, and Upper Egypt, of Amenta.

Thus interpreted, the Tuatha, or tribes who brought the *Ancient Solar wisdom out of Lower Egypt, or the "Tuat of Egypt," were genuine Egyptians*, and must not be confounded with the *manes* in Lower Egypt, in the book of Hades, which was not a geographical, but a mythical locality, in the earth of Eternity: the lower domain of the double earth, the country of the manes.

The wise men of Old Egypt understood that this was made by Ptah, and their religion at this period was the commencement of the Solar, and the exodus at this time bore the names here as it did in Egypt—*i.e.* what they portrayed celestially, and in the earth of Eternity, in their religious doctrines, they mapped out geographically.

Cæsar tells us also that Manannan, son of Lir, was patron of roads and journeys, and he was worshipped by the Gauls above all other gods. This is the Egyptian Ap-Uat, a form of Anup—the guide through Amenta, and was a god of the Pole Star, and lord of the Polar Paradise, before he fell from heaven, thus showing that previous to the Solar, they had the Stellar mythos. Another name for him was El Shaddai.

There are two points always to be considered in the departure of the human migrations from Egypt: one is from the summit of the Celestial Mounts—the other from the hollow underworld, beneath the Mount, or inside the earth, as these from the Tuat.

The races who *descended* from the Mount were people of the Pole, whose starting point and reckoning time were from one or other stations of the Pole Star, determinable by its Zootypes—these were Stellar.

Those who *ascended from* the nether world were Solar. Taking this point in conjunction with the others we have brought forward, we can trace approximately the time of the exodus from Egypt of the different tribes from all over the world, by tracing their Zootypes to the Constellation of the Pole Star, corresponding to it, but prior to the time that the Pole Star passed into the Constellation of Herakles, or the Man—or at the time of the Great Deluge of Manhu—*i.e.* when Herakles was replaced by another Pole Star.

Previous to this, the races were imaged by pre-human types, and the Great Mother was the origin of all; all was Stellar mythos, or Stellar-Lunar; after the Constellation of Herakles arrived, the Man superseded the Woman; Solar doctrines took the place of Stellar and Lunar, and the Fatherhood replaced the Motherhood.

The time of the exodus of the North American Indians and Samoans must have been at the time of the change of the Pole Star from Cygnus to Vega, in the Constellation of Lyra, about 18,000 or 20,000 years ago, according to their traditions and the Zootypes of their tribes or about 26,000 years before that.

All such origins as found in their Marchens are of course mythical and not historical or geographical, although the mythical land gets localised on the surface of the earth, geographically.

In explaining the story of the Deluge from tales found (from all over the world), there was not one, but seven—one at the change of each Pole Star, the hitherto reigning star sank down into the waters of space, and gave precedence to the next one in the cycle of precession, and therefore there was a deluge at the change of each Pole Star, 6—and the Great Deluge of all. The One=6+1=7, was when Herakles, the Man, sank down and was drowned in the Celestial water of space, the end of the Great Year, when all the Zootypes—the Tortoises, Apes, Bears, Serpents, etc.—were transformed into human beings—*i.e.* the creation of man, and the cycle of precession recommenced again. And the seven primary powers which had hitherto been portrayed by Zootypes, were now imaged in the earliest human form of man—as Ptah and his pygmies.

Here, then, we have the original ● dot, or "point within the centre of the circle, from which the M.M. cannot err" if he believes and so acts, etc.

First the dot ● or point is in the centre of a star with seven Rays ✵ or its summit. It signifies "The Supreme One," and the seven glorious ones—The Master and the seven wise men. The seven Powers sustaining The One :—Horus, in Heaven situated at the Pole Star, with the seven glorious ones circulating round—*i.e.* the Stars composing the Little Bear. Heaven was, at this period, divided into two divisions, North and South—Light and Darkness, with Horus representing the North and Light, and Sut, the South, Night and Darkness ○○ sometimes represented by two circles with ◎ above, with emblems of regal power—One name of Amsu, the risen Horus.

FIG. 90.

FROM MEXICAN CODICES

With the Ancient Egyptians, the highest land or summit of the Earth was at the Equator, called Ap-ta, and was then rendered mythically as the highest point of the Northern heavens —as the Apta in their Astronomical representations.

The Sources of the Nile—Equatorial provinces—where the great Lakes and the Papyrus swamps were, was their Ta-Nuter, or Holy Land—*i.e.* "The Land of the Spirits or gods," and the chief features of this earthly Paradise were repeated in the circum-polar high land.

The Sky, as the great Celestial water, was also divided into two great Lakes, one to the North and one to the South of the Mount of Bekhu on which heaven rested ; these are mentioned in the *Ritual* as the Lake of Kharu, and the Lake of Ru—chaps. cviii.-cix. No doubt this was founded on the two great Lakes in Central Africa.

In Equatoria the two Pole Stars are seen resting on the horizon ; the only two fixed stars in the firmament, and these were seen there, resting on the Poles or summit of the Mount, never setting—the two eyes or Merti, and were represented sometimes by two Jackals in the Kamite Astronomical Mythology—but first as the two Pillars, North and South.

As man travelled North, the Star and Pillar of Sut (South) sank down into the dark abyss, or the Nether World, and so Sut became the Power of Darkness in the Nether World—or Amenta. Travelling North, they would see the Stars of the two Bears, circling around the Pole Star, fixed on the Summit of the Mount of the North—the farther North they came, the farther these would be lifted up, and it is here that Shu lifts up the Heavens (Mythically). The Pole Star for ever rested on the horizon at the Equatoria, and so Shu lifted up the heavens, as the nomads travelled North.

There were no Solstices in Apta, it was equal day and equal night, so that when Shu upraised the sky, it was equally divided into two parts, between Horus and Sut. The rising and setting of the stars were vertical, and the two fixed centres of the Poles, were on the two horizons ; or, as the Egyptians explained it, on the North and South of the Mount of the Earth.

The Pole Star was a type of the Eternal because, apparently, it never changed with time ; it was the earliest type of supreme intelligence which gave the law in heaven which was unerring, just and true, and it became a standpoint in the heavens for the mind of man to rest on at the centre, and radiate to the circumference, "a point within a circle from which you could not err."

The Eye on the Mount, or the point ● within the centre of the circle, was a type of Anup, and the earliest law in heaven was given on the Mount because the Mount was an image of the Pole, and Anup administered the law as the Judge—the Jackal in Egypt was a Zootype for the Judge.

Gerald Massey has attributed Anup (Jackal) on the Mount to a form of Sut at the North, but we differ from him, and for this reason. On the planisphere of Denderal the two Poles are represented by two Jackals, or two Eyes, the North that of Horus and the South that of Sut ; therefore we attribute the Anup of the North to a type of Horus and not Sut, who was the first god of the Pole Star which was South (the Southern Heavens were mapped out first, as proved by the *Ritual*) and as the Southern Pole Star sank down into darkness and was lost to view as they migrated north, so the Northern Pole Star would rise and supersede it in the Pole Star of Horus—Anup, and it was only the Northern migration, people who at this time advanced in stature and wisdom, and spread over the world. There is sufficient evidence in the *Ritual* to prove this as well as tracing the people of the various exodes. A type in the Egyptian may be variously applied, and may not always determine the nature of the deity, but the Jackal denotes the Judge, and the Judge in heaven here, in the North, was Horus: of course it was not the Mount which was the divinity, or the Jackal, but the power which dwelt upon it, as portrayed by the type.

The power of stability, fixed as the centre of the Universe, was the typical Eternal, and the Stars—*i.e.* Ursa Minor (The Stars which never set — Rit) constituted the circumpolar ○, the starry types of eternal powers.

In all Mythologies, the Pole Star is an emblem of stability, a seat, or throne of the Power which is the highest god—Anup or Horus in Egypt, Sydik in Phœnicia, Anu in Babylonia, Tai-Yih in China, Avather or Zivo in Mesopotamia, Ame-No-Foko-Tachi-Kami in Japan and various other names for the same in different parts of the world.

In Rig-Veda the habitation of the one god is placed in the highest North, "beyond the seven Rishes"; these are by some supposed to be represented by the Stars of the GREAT BEAR, but it is not so; these seven Rishes—Urshi, or Divine Watchers—were grouped in URSA MINOR, "the Stars of which constellation never set." These were the chief of the Akhemu under Anup, the god of the Pole Star, the Subbas, or Mandozs, "the Ancients of the Mesopotamia," who are still followers of the old Egyptian Stellar Mythos.

FIG. 91.[1]

In the next progressive evolution, we have the Sacred Triangle as the Emblem of Heaven in three divisions, with Shu added at the Equinox to the North and South, thus forming the original Trinity. The above was all formed and worked out by the old wise men during the Stellar Mythos.

Progressing further, we find that they had now mapped out Heaven or "Built the Heavens on the Square" with the four children of Horus at the four corners, as the supports thereof, and finally Ptah completed the tunnelling through the Earth and formed Amenta as a passage for Ra the Sun, Taht the Moon and the Manes. In the complete Put-Cycle of Ptah, we have the Heavens in a circle in nine divisions, then in ten divisions, and finally in twelve; and then twelve signs of the Zodiac were com-

[1] Triangle associated with Horus only.

pleted and filled in. The Heaven in eight divisions was formed when Taht was added to the seven Stellar, and was therefore Lunar.

As the Sun, or Ra, rose in the East to diffuse Light and Glory to men on this Earth, so when it "set in the West" it entered Amenta—"the land of the Nether World" to diffuse its light and glory to "the Manes there"; it made its passage from West to East, rising again at the East here, ever completing its circle as time rolled on.

This was Solar Mythos, and the Eschatology which follows is explained, separately, in other parts of this work.

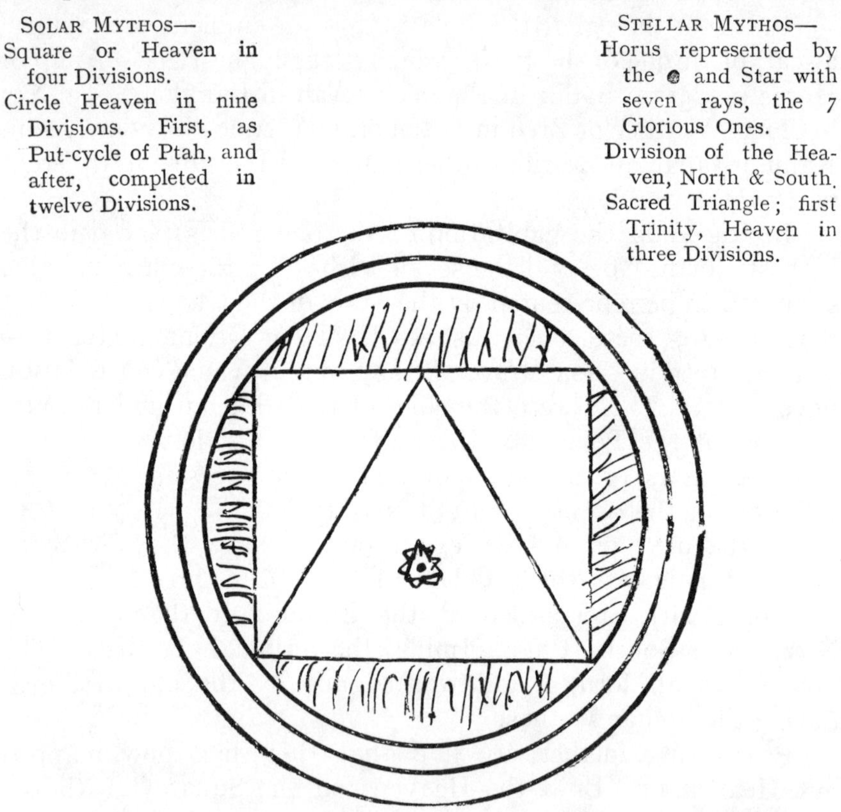

FIG. 92.

The mysteries of Osiris, Isis and Horus, though the latest in evolution, have been given the foremost place in the *Ritual*, and have somewhat obscured the pre-Osirian Mythology, but Atum was the Great Judge upon the Mount of Amenta at a far earlier period than Osiris.

THE GOD AMSU.

The rising spirit of mummied Horus in the Mythos, and of Osiris in the Eschatology
He holds the whip of power– the Egyptian Khu—in one hand pointing above, H.A
The other is not free yet from the swathing bandages, and is pointing downwards, H.D.
The Good Shepherd

The Cable-Tow

How many of our fraternity know the true import and meaning of the " Cable-tow " ? Originally it was a chain or rope, of some kind, worn by the I. or those about to be initiated, to signify their belief in God and their dependence on Him, and their solemn obligations to submit and devote themselves to His will and service, and the fact that he is neither naked nor clothed is an emblem that he is untutored—a mere child of nature—unregenerate and destitute of any knowledge of the true God, as well as being destitute of the comforts of life. This is the state in which we find all candidates. The chain was used by the Druids and Egyptians as a symbolism, as stated above. Also that he was being led from darkness into light, from ignorance to knowledge of the one true and living God, Creator and Judge of all things in heaven and earth. Here we have the origin of the Cable-tow in the Eschatology.

Father Burgo's description of the Zapotecs, Mexicans and Mayas, and also *Juan de Cordova*, speaking of " Tola, a grass-like plant, (una yerva de los ervazales), out of which they made a straw rope, (una sozuilla o' tonuza), which they brought to confession and laid down on the ground before the pijana and confessed what sin they wished to confess, etc," gives you a very wrong impression, and their translation is not correct, because " Tola " here they make the meaning of as " sin " and " lao-Tola " place of sin or confession, but this is wrong ; the meaning of the word is " a dark place," and the ceremonies observed and described by the above show how ignorant they were of the true meaning of the ceremony, which was the same as that of the first degree in Freemasonry, and the " rope of straw was not to hang the young man with," as all I.'s well know—although in some Glyphs the rope appears around the neck.

That the rope appears around the neck of more than one, in these picture scenes (seven in some) is only a symbol of the seven powers—as " the seven ropes," and each one of the wearers of these represents one of the seven powers or attributes of Horus I. in their sacerdotal duties. Originally it was one only which was associated with Horus I. and Amsu (the risen Horus or Horus in the Spirit). This is well depicted in the accompanying photograph of Amsu. The Cable-tow is seen hanging down his back; it has been removed from the neck (earthly type). Horus, having been led or passed through dangers, difficulties, darkness and death in the underworld, emerges as Amsu, the first risen man-God, and attached to his crown of two feathers (denoting the two lives, earthly and Spiritual) is this Cable-tow or rope—as a symbol that it is "a power" which has led him through from earthly to Spiritual life.

In the same way was the boat of Osiris dragged through the underworld by a rope, by the "powers" we find mentioned in the *Ritual* as he was dragged in, led through darkness into light, came forth in the double cave, and emerged as Ra in a Spiritual form—one and the same—the former being the Stellar and oldest, and the latter the Solar or Osirian: in our case we apply it symbolically in the Christian.

The origin of the "Blazing Star" was the Egyptian "Sothos," and shown as Anubis, who guided the soul through Amenta, and its allusion as the star which guided the "wise men," etc., is a recent version of the old, and one which does not require further explanation (see *Ritual*), and which is found many times in the Mexican and Maya pictures and glyphs. (*See* Appendix 4.)

"The Bright Morning Star," the Star with eight rays, also represents Horus of the resurrection or Jesus. It originally represented "Orion," the eightfold one—the highest. The seven, with the essence of these added to make "THE ONE"—*i.e.* eight.

In Revelation the Son of God promises to give the Morning Star to him that overcometh, "as I also have received of my Father: I will give him the Morning Star," Rev. ii. 28. The Morning Star was equally identified with Horus, "I know the power of the East, Horus of the Solar Mount, the Calf in presence of the God and the Star of Dawn," *Ritual*, chap. cix.; henceforth the Morning Star was given to the followers of Horus, therefore we use it.

It was the Star of Horus and his guide which led him to Paradise when he seated himself upon his Throne, and then Horus gave his Star as a guide to his followers (see *Ritual*).

Perhaps nothing shows or demonstrates so well the universal evolution and the origin of all our Signs, Symbols and PW's, and how they have been brought on from the primordial and the ancient Egyptian Stellar, Lunar and Solar Mythos, added to when necessary, or altered in name to suit the Priests of various ages, as the SSW of the so-called 90° of the Mysteries of Mizram (Hebrew for Egypt). These mysteries are the same as the Mysteries of Memphis, all of which we know and are perfectly acquainted with. They are somewhat similar to our Freemasonry in all its degrees; but we have compressed their 90° into 33°. The Egyptian PW and A are "I and O" in the highest degree, but the English Freemasons do not recognise any connection with these. We are of opinion that our Freemasonry is purer and a truer copy of the *Ritual* than the others, which contain innovations.

The original Pole Star with dot ✵ represented Horus I. This, with Triangle, was Stellar. The square was Solar, first portrayed at the time of Ptah when he completed Amenta and built the heavens on the square by adding E. and. W. to N. and S. with four supports—the four children of Horus.

CHAPTER X

THE Chaldeans, who were a College of Priests connected with the Babylonian empire, were celebrated for their extensive learning. It is said that they took their origin from Zeratusth, an Egyptian Priest, and the mysteries instituted were the same as those of the Egyptians at the time of Isis, Horus and Osiris, and, like the Greeks, very few were ever initiated into the full secrets, and it was only by passing the most terrible ordeal that anyone could be permitted to learn them all.

Josephus, as well as other historians, agrees with the above.

Their first map of the Celestial Universe—in clay tablet—was depicted thus,  which is the same as the seven nomes of Egypt. Egypt was originally divided into seven nomes—this was the first division into nomes—and represented the seven Celestial Glorious Ones, (Little Bear) in a Terrestrial form, in the Stellar Mythos, thus 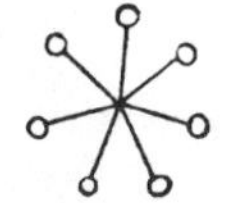

Afterwards they added a central one—THE ONE—around which the seven others revolved in the Celestial Heaven, and THE ONE who governed the seven in the Terrestrial. The Great or Mighty Prince who ruled over this other seven, which they depicted by eight divisions. The Chaldeans followed this also, which can be proved and seen by their tablets, where they show the heavens in eight segments, with diameters running from the four cardinal points thus, 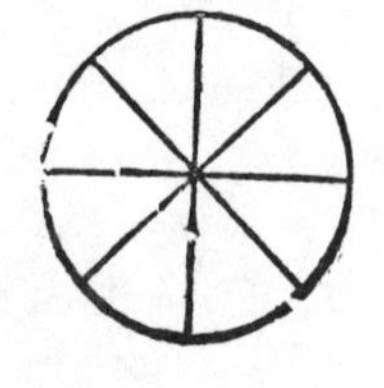 the external circle of which they afterwards omitted and symbolised thus, 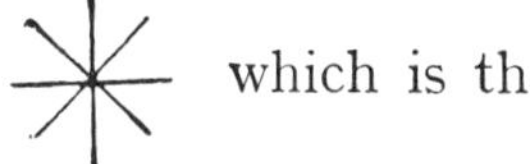 which is the same as the Egyptian 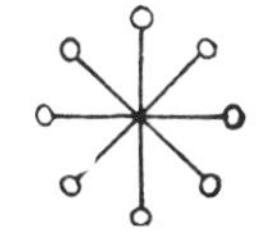 The Sumarians, Chaldeans and Babylonians, in fact, obtained all their laws and learning from the Egyptians. The Code of Hammurabi the Sumarians copied from the Egyptians and handed on to the Chaldeans.

Their old company of primeval gods, mentioned in the "Seven Tablets of Creation," were eight in number and may be classed as four pairs, the same as the Egyptians, for instance:

Apzû-Rishtû—Mummu-Tiamat
Lakhmu—Lakhamu
Aushar—Kislar, correspond to the Egyptian
Nu—Nut
Ḥeḥu—Ḥeḥut
Ḳerḳui—Ḳerḳuit, etc., etc.

Later on the Egyptians added four more and mapped out the heavens in twelve divisions—the twelve signs of the Zodiac. The Chaldeans did the same, or rather copied them. Their history of Creation is a copy of the Egyptian; also the great battle between Horus I. and Sut, and their underworld or Hell. But these gods were not eight or twelve different gods but attributes of THE ONE. This is clearly shown in the Egyptian Texts. When they first divided the heavens into four divisions they assigned four different powers or attributes to these and four consorts for the same:—

Nu, name of a god or attribute of God, represented the great watery vapour from which this world consolidated primarily.
Nut was the female counterpart.
Heḥu represented the fire and heat of the Sun.
Heḥuit was his female counterpart.
Ḳeḳui, represented light and darkness or night and day.
Ḳeḳuit was his female counterpart.
Ḳerḳ, powers of nature at rest; these were the attributes of the two forms or first.
Ḳerḥet was his female counterpart.
And were divided further into eight and twelve, the Chaldeans did the same, and each different name of the powers or attributes

have been called separate and different gods and goddesses by those who should know better, and thus may Egyptologists "have become mixed," because they have not traced all these "powers" back to "THE ONE," and perceived that by evolution different names had to be added and given to the various powers which dawned upon them, and which they recognised, as their brains expanded in knowledge and observation, as the only way that their true idea and meaning could be expressed, having only a rudimentary language at the time.

The Babylonian Tiamet, which waged war against Marduk, the Champion chosen by the gods, was held to be the incarnation of all evil. This monster was 300 miles long, and had a mouth 10 feet wide, and moved in undulations 6 miles high, and was 100 feet round his body, corresponds to the great serpent of the Warramunga of the Australian Aborigines, which was a copy of the Egyptian Sut, when he battled with Horus I. The tales are the same in each instance and he is the same as "the Leviathan" of the Hebrew—the "serpent of many twistings and folds" (see Job xli.; Jeremiah li. 34; Isaiah xiv. 29). He was hunted for slaughter by Gabriel, and with the assistance of Yahweh was slain by him. Gabriel here is the counterpart of Marduk, Yahweh taking the place of Anshar as the head of the gods. Although the *Hebrews obtained their Hell direct from the Egyptians they took their "Leviathan" from the Babylonians*, but these latter obtained it direct from the Egyptians at a much earlier date, and we must not forget that this great serpent, Apep of the dynastic and Solar-worship time, took its origin and was brought on from the pre-dynastic Stellar Mythos—Horus I. and Sut—the first fight between light and darkness. When this earth was surrounded by thick watery vapour so that the sun's rays could not penetrate, Sut was the primary—the god of darkness—but as soon as this vapour cooled down and the sun's rays penetrated to the face of the earth, then light superseded darkness—Sut was deposed and Horus I. became primary. When this was brought on in dynastic times, Ra took the place of Horus I. and Sut that of the great Apep, and the fight was day and night—Ra overcoming the darkness of night each day.

The seven-headed dragon and beast of the Book of Revelation, like the seven-headed basilisk serpent mentioned in "Pistis Sophia," have their origin in the seven-headed serpent which is mentioned in the Pyramid Text, and in Revelation ix. 19 horses are referred to which had "tails like unto serpents, and had heads," which is a copy of the monster which inhabited one of the Pylons of the Tuat.

The Babylonians made offerings to the dead in the same way as the Egyptians did; in fact, all nations did, and *Dr W. Budge*, speaking of the offerings taken to the tombs of the dead in his "Book of the Gods of the Egyptians," page 86, says:—"It is possible that certain simple folk may have been led to believe that because meat offerings and drink offerings in abundance were taken to the tombs, the deceased must naturally partake of them, and it is more than probable that the Egyptians, in a semi-savage state, made such offerings because they believed them necessary for the dead." But this practice was simply a continuation of the customs of the earliest Egyptians—earliest man—the Pygmies, and still is amongst them and all native tribes all over the world—"offerings to the spirits of the departed," as a *propitiation*, so that the spirits may not come back and work them any harm. These nations still believe, as their forefathers did, that the spirit may return and do them "good or ill," and so you find "spirit houses," with food placed inside, to propitiate them. This was the original, and the Egyptians worked out from this first two things—that is, the Ka, the Spirit, and the Ba, the Soul. The Ka or spirit after death separated from the Ba or soul and went before the Divine Creator to be judged, and, if justified, then returned to the soul and could travel after throughout the universe. After it was justified the spiritual body was called the Sāhu. All these things took a long time to work out, and many Egyptologists have overlooked this: also their names as well as others which were afterwards added. These "offerings" are still carried on in the Christian Church, but by evolution they are now called "Offerings to the Church"—"Easter Offerings," "Christmas Offerings." One has only to go into a Roman Catholic church to see the abundant offerings to "the Saints," or walk into any churchyard of orthodox Christians and still see the flowers, etc., on the graves of the dead—the remnants of the evolution of past ages—the offerings to the Spirits. The foregoing will answer *Dr Budge's*[1] questions on page cxi. "as to when this spiritual body

[1] "The Gods of the Egyptians," by *Dr E. A. Wallis Budge*. Published by Methuen & Co.

began its existence. Unfortunately no satisfactory answer can at present be given to it, for no text yet discovered supplies the necessary information." No text gives it because it existed long before ; how far back it would be difficult to say, but as we find the Aboriginal Australians and all native tribes throughout the world and the Pygmies still believe and practise this rite, it would date long before the "Dynastic Egyptians." The skeletons of man, found in the earliest quarternary period or *Pleistocene age*, and also in the upper quarternary period, have been few. Apparently the mode of burial of the present Pygmies was followed—*i.e.* they had no "burial ground" but buried them where they died and moved on, and so we know little or nothing about their weapons, mode of life or ideas; but in the later Paleolithic age we find some evidence. In the Neolithic, ample evidence of the commencement of their Mythos, when it must have existed.

The Babylonians copied the Egyptians but they confounded the "good Zootypes" of the Egyptians with the "bad ones" and made them all bad, perverting the whole Eschatology because they did not understand their uranographic creation, and the Hebrew legends are mere drivelling nonsense rendering their Zootypes anthropomorphically.

We cannot agree with *Dr Budge* that "the Egyptians borrowed their knowledge of the signs of the Zodiac, together with much else, from the Greeks, who had derived a great deal of their astronomical lore from the Babylonians" ("The Gods of the Egyptians," vol. ii. page 312). He says further: "It is at present a subject for conjecture at what period the Babylonians first divided the heavens into sections by means of the constellations of the Zodiac, but we are fully justified in assuming that the earliest forms of the Zodiac date from an exceedingly primitive time." Why, the knowledge of all this was "old" in Egypt before the Babylonians even existed or knew anything about it, as we shall prove later in this work. The Egyptians had worked out all the architecture of the heavens, and their priests had carried the same with them to all parts of the world—not only the Northern heavens, but the Southern, as well. Probably they worked out the South before the North, and the Druids and the Mayas and the Incas knew it all from the Priests of Egypt, the earliest probably thousands of years before the Babylonian nation existed. The Babylonians copied and obtained all their knowledge from the Egyptians, and we are surprised that *Dr Budge* should write that they borrowed from the Greeks; they were old and degenerating and in decay before the Greek nation was born!! Well may he say that "it is a subject for conjecture at what period the Babylonians first divided the heavens into sections, etc.," because they never did; what they knew they borrowed either *direct from the Egyptians* or Sumarians—the latter obtained it from Egypt. It was the ancient Egyptians who mapped out the heavens into 12 divisions in the North, 12 divisions in the South, and 12 in the centre, making 36 in all, and the twelve signs of the Zodiac. To whatever part of the world the Priests went they carried this knowledge with them; this proof lies more in the ancient remains that we find in various parts of the world than anything else—the 3 circles, the 2 greater bisecting the middle and lesser, and each divided into 12 parts—*these are much older than the seven tablets of Creation by thousands of years.* If this is not so, how can *Dr Budge* and other Assyriologists explain or get over the facts we bring forward in this work? It is very well to say that "whether the Babylonians were themselves the inventors of such origins—*i.e.* (the Zodiac), or whether they are to be attributed to the earlier non-semitic Sumarian inhabitants of the country, cannot be said"; and when he states "that the Greeks borrowed the Zodiac from the Babylonians, and then the Greeks introduced it into Egypt, probably during the Ptolemaic period,"[1] it appears to us that *Dr Budge* must have left this part of "the Gods of Egypt" to be written by one of his assistants, who knew nothing about the history of the past. We should be grieved to think that *Dr Budge*, in all seriousness, believed and thought as the Aryanists and Assyriologists of the past have done. Surely, researches into recent discoveries, at least, must convince him differently, or how does he account for even the various three circles of stones found throughout the world, each divided into twelve parts, the two greater bisecting the less? The "Photographs of the Nomes of Egypt, representing the divisions of the heavens," which the old Priests had worked

[1] Herodotus considers that the names of the gods of Greece are derived from Egypt, the Pelasgians being the intermediaries who brought them to Greece, and he attributes absolutely to the same Pelasgians the carrying there the "*Cabiric Mysteries*," which he considers and believes were brought by them from Egypt. Even at this time Egypt was old, and it was late in her history.

out and carried with them in the various exodes throughout the world, besides other mural and " Pietra Libra " evidence, must be acknowledged to be thousands of years older than the Babylonians or Sumarians ! ! These latter cannot be overlooked or passed over if we wish to elucidate and obtain the true history of bygone ages of the life on this planet—its origin and evolution.

And surely, because the Egyptians, when they were decaying as a great nation, employed some Greeks to paint some Mural scenes for them, it cannot be in any manner of way a proof that these men introduced the Zodiac !

The twelve legends of the solar hero, Gilgames, relating to the twelve signs and the twelve labours of Hercules, are comparatively late, as they are based upon the Zodiac of twelve signs, which belongs to the final formation of the heaven that was preceded by the heaven in ten divisions, and earlier still in seven. The Greeks, with their indifference to facts and their fondness for figures and fancies, played pranks with the Astronomical Mythology, and mixed the crocodile, which was a good dragon, with Apap, the reptile. The blind god, " hungering for the morn," is a Greek figure of Orion, which does not explain anything—but Orion is the Stellar representation, by night, of Horus, the Solar god in the darkness of Amenta, who is An-er-f, the blind Horus, whose sight was restored to him at dawn.

In the Babylonian astronomy, Saher-Sahu is identical by name with the Egyptian Orion—that is, Horus in his resurrection as the Sahu or glorified likeness of the risen god or soul—the Sahu in the planisphere, who represents the manes rising from Amenta to paradise above. The planisphere contains a number of Egyptian deities. They are the gods and goddesses of Egypt —the mythological personages and zootypes that make up the vast procession which moves on for ever round and round, according to the revolutions of the earth or the apparent revolution of the sphere—at least a dozen can be identified.

1. The Ram-headed Amen—with the constellation Aries.
2. Osiris, the Bull of Eternity—with the sign of Taurus.
3. Sut-Horus—Twins with the Gimini.
4. The Beetle-headed Kheper-ptah—with the sign of the Beetle, later, Crab.
5. The Lion-faced Atum—with the sign of Leo.
6. The Virgin Neith—with the constellation Virgo.

7. Hur-Makhu of the Scales—with the sign Libra.
8. Isis-Serkh, the Scorpion Goddess—with the sign of Scorpio.
9. Shu and Tefnut, figured as the Archer—with the sign of Sagittarius.
10. Num, the Goat-headed, who presided over the abyss—with the sign of Capricornus.
11. Menal, the Divine Wet Nurse—with the sign of Aquarius.
12. Horus of the Two Crocodiles—with the sign of Pisces.

It is not possible that all these gods and goddesses and nature powers of Egypt were constellated as figures in the universe by any other than the Egyptian mystery teachers of the heavens.

The deity of the Pole Star was known to the earlier Chinese and Japanese as the supreme god in nature, who had his abode on the great Peak or Mountain; this god the Chinese called Tien-hwang Ta-Ti—god of the Pole Star ("Religion in China," page 109).

Shang-ti, the supreme ruler, was the highest object of worship. His heavenly abode, Tsze-wei, is "a celestial space round the North Pole," and his throne was indicated by the Pole Star (*Legge*, "Chinese Classics," vol. iii. pl. 1, page 34, and "Chinese Repository," vol. iv. page 194).

This is the most sacred and ancient form of Chinese worship: a round hillock is the altar on which sacrifice was offered to him. In the Archic Chow *Ritual* (Li) it says:—"When the sovereign worshipped Shang-ti, he offered up on a round hillock a first-born male as a whole burnt sacrifice."

Both the Mount and the first-born male are typical. Anup was the first male Ancestor. The hillock is an image of the Mount. This deity was also known to the Chinese as the "Divine Prince of the great Northern Equilibrium" who promulgated the laws of the silent wheels of the heaven's palace," or the cycle of time determinated by the revolution of the stars (*De Groot*). This was the Stellar Mythos of the Egyptians.

It is stated in a very ancient Chinese manuscript, called Pih-Kea-Sing, the date of which is said to be 3000 B.C., that the Chinese originally came from the North-west as colonists, the whole number of whom did not amount to more than a hundred families, whose names are still preserved in this manuscript, and are the same as we find in China at the present time. They came over the heights of Kwan-lun towards the borders of Hwang-ho, subdued and perhaps exterminated in succession the barbarous clans which they found in the country. In this manuscript is shown the head of the first Buddhist, called the "Messenger of God," and of him it is said, "The Holy One appeared from the West." The head of the same shows "two horns," symbolical of Solar descent, which the Israelites assigned to Moses, Mosheh or Amosis, the regenerator of their creed.

These people had considerable knowledge in the arts necessary to social life. They could write, but their writing was in hieroglyphics. They knew the course of the stars, and had the same astronomical knowledge as the ancient Egyptians; also the same ideas of symbolism and a similar Eschatology, and they had made out the same cycles in time. Their Y always had the same meaning as the Egyptian ☥ ank or Hebrew T Tau. Christian X. How far all their hieroglyphics correspond to the ancient Egyptian we are unable to say, except that we know that these hieroglyphics were the images of the things represented in life, and many that we have seen are identical. They were the first or original writings, and they have been altered at the present day by the addition of a number of straight lines which have gradually obliterated the original. Only on such monuments as those of Yu and Mount Thraé-shan, in the province of Shan-tung, can we still see the original images, and in these characters one may yet trace a great similarity to those in use amongst the ancient Egyptians. Also on some very ancient Chinese coins Egyptian hieroglyphics have been found.

Tai-Hao, the great celestial, was the first mythical or astronomical ruler in the Chinese divine dynasties. With him *commenced* the mystic diagrams called Yi or changes, which were eight in number. These were revealed to him by the dragon-horse that issued from the yellow river, or the (representation) Milky Way. Tai-Hao corresponds to Anup, the inventor of astronomy and first ruler of the Pole Star. The dragon-horse is the same as the Egyptian water-horse that was combined with the crocodile in Apt, goddess of the Great Bear and mother of the seven rulers. According to *M. Philastre,* in his version of the Yi king, the name of the Chow dynasty and of the Chow Yi divinising-book, signifies circular movement, the revolution embracing the whole universe, the movement of the Pole. Chow Yi would mean the changes of the Pole and the Pole Stars in precession. Thus the Chow dynasty of the sons of heaven would be the seven successive rulers of the Pole who reigned for 25,827 years—a scientific fact.

Anyone who can write Symbolic Chinese, can, even at the present day, travel all through China, Japan, Chinese Tartary, Siam, Java, Corea, in fact, throughout the whole of Eastern Asia, and with this symbolic language, make himself perfectly understood although he may not be able to speak a syllable of any of the languages of these countries.

Sir C. Alabaster, who was a great Masonic student and had much insight into China, says:—"Going back to the earliest historic times in China I find a clear evidence of the existence of a mystic faith, expressed in allegorical form and illustrated, as with us, by symbols. The secrets of this faith were orally transmitted, the chiefs alone pretending to have full knowledge of them. I find, moreover, that in these earliest ages, this faith took a Masonic form, their secrets being recorded in symbolic buildings, like the tabernacle Moses put up in the desert and the temple, his successor, Solomon, built at Jerusalem; that the various offices in the hierarchy of this religion were distinguished by the symbolic Jewels, held by them during their term of office, and that, as with us, at the rites of their religion they wore leather aprons, such as have come down to us, marked with the insignia of their rank. The compasses and square, used as the symbol of right conduct. The man who had the compasses and square and regulated his life thereby, being then, as now, considered to possess the secrets and to carry out the principles of true propriety." We find one of the most ancient names by which the Deity is spoken of in China is that of "The First Builder" or, as Masons say, "The Great Architect of the Universe." The original from which these sprang was the Egyptian PTAH, who built the heavens with his seven assistants, but at the present time the mysteries of this ancient faith in China have become lost or obscured, though attempts at a revival may be traced in the proceedings of existing brotherhoods, whose various rituals and signs are supposed to be, in some measure, founded on ancient rites and symbols, which have been handed down from earliest ages. Here we see the degeneration that has crept in and gradually contaminated, debased and obliterated the true Masonic rites and ceremonies which their forefathers carried with them out of Egypt and established in this country.

The Ainus,[1] the aboriginals of Japan, "the hairy men," are a very old people, and came out of Egypt in the earlier times, or before their Stellar Mythos, or as their name implies—"The Children of the Bear,"—the children who went out of Egypt at the time that they first made out in their Astronomical Mythos that the seven pole stars circulated round the Pole Star, that is—Seven Glorious Ones—the Seven Lights. Probably these people first inhabited Persia, India, China and Asia generally, but were driven out farther and farther east by a superior race, which took their place from the centre, until now we only find the remnant of the original in the Far East, north of Japan and Northern Asia. They still practise some of the earliest Astronomical Mythological rites amongst themselves, having the Bear as their "first" Totem.

The Ainu say that their forefathers drove out and exterminated with clubs a race of dwarfs who were there before them; they say that these dwarfs were only three or four feet high.[2] They describe them as being of a red colour and having very long arms in proportion to the rest of the body, and that they used flat stone knives, scrapers, and other implements of stone.

These Ainu are of the same original race and type as the Australian Aborigines, and the story of Abydos and their beliefs—*i.e.* future state—correspond with the ritual of ancient Egypt. They are not really Polytheistic and do not believe in the existence of gods innumerable, as has been stated by some writers. The so-called different gods are names only of the various attributes of the One Great God. Their skulls are of the same shape and average capacity as the Australians and Nilotic negroes.

The fact that the name *Ainu* is found on the stone of black diorite, containing the Code of Hammurabi, at Susa, may have some connection with these ancient people. *Mr Stanley Cook*, like a good many others, is in doubt as to the origin of this Code and from whence it was originally derived. His able

[1] Probably these Ainu came from that domain of Egypt which Maspero calls the "Haunch," opposite Aûnû, the "Haunch" here representing the Great Bear. It is situated to the N. of Memphis and Pyramids of Gizeh, and W. of the Nile.

[2] Recently some of them have been found living amongst the mountains in China.

arguments leave it an open question, but the more one studies it the greater is the conviction that it was originally Egyptian and brought from there. Assyriologists generally agree that the dynasty, to which Hammurabi belonged, was associated with immigration, and if we take it as pretty well proved by the various words, the origin of which is Egyptian and not Arabian, except as "carriers" of the same, we can understand why there is such a close resemblance of "The Laws of Moses" to this Code. Moses lived about 1000 years after this Code was engraved on this stone, but he was one of the High Priests of "On" and well versed in all laws and doctrines both of Amen Ra and Osiris, and he no doubt made use of as much or as little of their laws, or modified them, as circumstances required when he left Egypt with his followers. We must remember that after the ancient Egyptian language died out Aramaic intervened before the earlier Coptic, Moabite or Biblical Hebrew. Iau is Iu of the Egyptians, and Yahu is certainly an earlier form than Yahwè. Iu dates at least 6000 years B.C., as can be seen on Egyptian Papyri in the British Museum, and abandoned later on. Iu was the same as Tmu, the son of Ptah, and Iu is therefore the son of Ptah. It was written later by the Phœnicians in Greek, Hebrew, etc., in various forms, such as Iau, Iahu, Ias and after as Yau and Yahu, Y being of much later date than I, and we have no hesitation in stating that the Iau here referred to—and of still later date as the Chinese Y—is the same as Iu in the original, and that all these laws of Hammurabi were those which had been in use in Egypt thousands of years before the existence of Hammurabi.

South Arabian and Phœnician were simply copies of the Egyptian. *Erman* states that the administration of justice was centralised under the old empire. The old empire, from recent discoveries, dated at least 10,000 years ago, probably much longer, and until those who are studying this subject recognise the facts that have been brought to light by discoveries in recent years, they will always be falling into a pit which they cannot get out of, for words and names can be traced to the Egyptians long before the name of Moses, although it is more than probable that, as he was a learned High Priest, he made use of this code for the Israelites. As stated before, the Chaldees were from Egypt originally, and obtained their learning from there centuries before the existence of Israelites in Asia.

Seven Footsteps of Buddha denote the seven steps in precession which are a co-type, equivalent to the seven stations of the pole, and a footprint on each peak is the symbol of a station in precession. Thus, the footprint of Buddha upon Adam's Peak in Ceylon shows that this was one of the seven annular Mountains in its sevenfold system of Mount Meru.

The two feet, as found on rocks and in caves in Australia. From *Prof. Spencer* and *Gillen's* "Native Tribes of Central Australia," published by Macmillan & Co.—by permission, with our thanks, and two feet in Mexico and amongst the Zapotecs. See pictures of the Rock Drawings of the Australians and Humboldt Fragment of the Mexicans (pages 66 and 114).

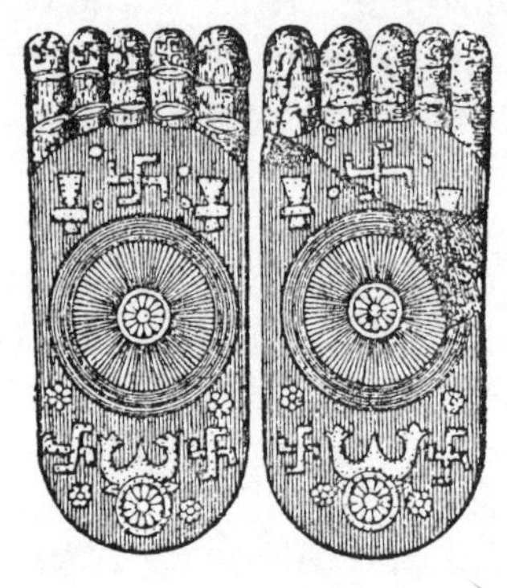

The Two Feet of Buddha.

Feet of Horus from MEXICAN CODICES, with the three Rods or Rays of Light symbol.

FIG. 93.—Two feet of Horus I., as shown in the Vignette—Plate ii., "Book of the Dead"—*Renouf's*.

The two soles of the feet of Buddha, here shown, held as sacred by the Buddhists, represent the soles of the feet of Osiris. Osiris was stated to have been mutilated into fourteen parts—some versions give sixteen—viz. his head, *the soles of his feet*, his bones, his arms, his heart, his interior, his tongue, his eyes, his fists, his fingers, his back, his ears, his body, etc., and these were buried in different parts of Egypt. In the *Ritual* we are told "that the soles of the feet, which had trodden the earth, were removed in order that Osiris might tread the Hall of Judgment with pure feet, and that *his feet were bathed with milk that the pain thereof might be assuaged, etc.*": and we find one or more representations of these parts held sacred in many lands, which probably date further back than the time of Osiris, in fact, to Horus I. Amongst the Australian natives we find these soles of the feet shown upon various rocks and cave-walls, where they are regarded as "*sacred*," although you cannot obtain any information about them except that "they have always been," which is as far as the natives can tell you: also on the rock drawings from the sculptured stones from Dolmens in Brittany, which we show here from *Professor G. Sergi's* "The Mediterranean Race," page 313, fig. 93. They are also shown at Palenque and several other places in Central America. They are all identically the same, and it is only by going back to the Stellar Mythos of old Egypt that you can discover the true meaning and origin. These two feet are well shown in the vignette, plate ii. of "The Book of the Dead," which refers to chap. xvii.: "I have come upon earth and with my two feet have taken possession. I am Tmu, and I come from my own place." These soles of the feet were therefore considered sacred objects, and as we find them shown on the Dolmens of Brittany, the rock-drawings of the Australian Aborigines, at Palenque in Central America and in the HUMBOLDT FRAGMENT. They must date back to the Stellar Mythos, and first and primarily refer to Horus I., although they were afterwards brought on in the Solar doctrines and then refer to Osiris, as we see from the Buddhist records. Then we have the parallel in the Christian doctrines, being washed, bathed in RA°, etc. Another proof that it was originally Horus is found in the great Harris Papyrus, 15-3, when the God Ra-Tem-Neberter is restored to his first condition, after having been dismembered and cut to pieces; "he is then the God who is the possessor of completeness, integrity, hence inviolate." Most Egyptologists have ascribed the name to Osiris, but it was Horus I. primarily, and the above name, Ra-Tem, shows the transformation from Horus to Osiris—Tmu was another name for Hours, and Ra was Osiris in spirit.

There is a tradition amongst the North American Indians that all the tribes were formerly one and dwelt together, and their tradition is that they came across a large water towards the East or sunrise. They crossed the water in canoes, but they know not how long they were in crossing, nor whether the water was salt or fresh. The Dakotes possess legends of "huge skiffs," in which the Dakotes of old floated for weeks, finally gaining dry land—a tradition of ships and a long sea voyage. Their language was the same as the Welsh. We have here two different traditions, one leading to the supposition that they came *via* Japan, and the other *via* the British Isles, Greenland, etc. If we take the anatomical conditions, as far as we can find, all our ethnological studies prove that first the inhabitants of Copan, Palenque, and still many tribes in South America and Western North America, deformed their skulls, had squat figures, coarse features, large noses, thick lips; or were short-statured individuals with round heads, oval faces, high cheek bones, flat noses, large mouths, small oblong eyes—types of the Tartar or Manchurian. All these had, and those that still remain have, the Stellar Mythos only. In the Mayas we find regular features, good-looking small figures, with well-proportioned limbs, finely-formed heads, high foreheads, well-framed noses and small mouths with firm lips.

Eyes, open, straight and intelligent. These we see depicted on sculptured frescoes, etc., and amongst the Incas. All these had the Solar Mythos; but there is a very clear line of demarcation between these people and some earlier races. From the ethnological conditions found, and their practice of the Stellar doctrines, one can trace the early exodus through Asia to Australia, New Guinea, Japan, all Northern Asia, across to North America, and also from North Europe to Greenland, and across to America by way of the North there.

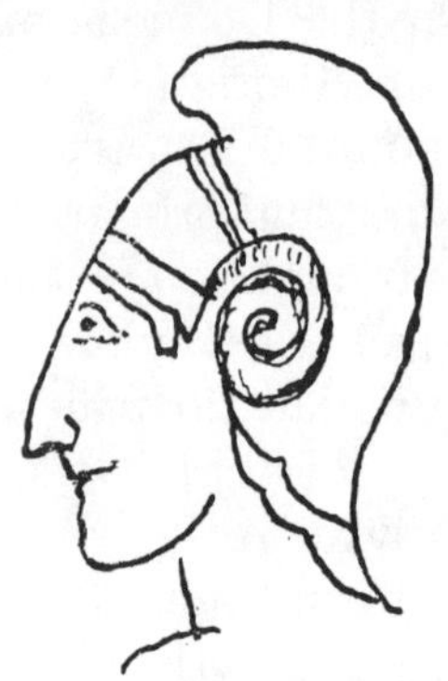

FIG. 94.

We give here a drawing from a stucco-relief found in a temple at Palenque, Central America,[1] which shows that these people also wore the "Horus Lock" of the Egyptians. Amongst their carvings we find representations of the Elephant and Lion, animals which did notexist in America.

Solar Mythos, and the exodus that followed, one traces

[1] The Tablet of the Cross Palenque is the Mexican representation of the Egyptian *Ritual* of Raising the Tatt Cross and the birth of Horus from the Great Mother—Mut. It is not a great sacrificial scene as Professor Forstemann states. The Divine Babe who maketh his appearance in Chemunnu, the place of the 8 gods, the Babe of "the God of longstrides" (Ra), of the God "of Lion form" (Shu), of the Goddess Bast, of Nefer-Tmu, of the Striker (Ahi, a name of Horus), and of Nehebkan and others (see *Ritual*). In the centre is the Tatt Cross or their representative, surmounted by a Zootype of the Great Mother, who is giving a New-Heart, or Soul, to the child held aloft by the figure on the right, with the emblem of a new-birth in his left hand. As the *Ritual* states—the divine Babe was lifted up into the upper world by two divinities (see *Ritual*, chap. cxxv.),[1] here represented. The decipherment of the whole of this important Tablet is reserved for another book.

[1] Mariett's "Monuments Divers," plate 46, gives a fine picture of this.

through Europe, Persia, India, China, and part of Japan, where it ceased. The Mayas probably came across direct from Egypt or North Africa and spread South to a certain extent, and to a smaller extent to the North and West, because to the North and West we see how far the Solar Mythos was carried, comparatively no great distance. This is proved by the fact that the Mayas had the Solar doctrines and had absorbed into them part of the Stellar: the countries bordering to the North and West had a little of both, but more Stellar than Solar, and then, still farther away, only the Stellar: therefore the Solar did not come to America *via* Asia, but *via* Africa or Europe.

This will clearly prove that all these people at one time had a common ancestry, whose writing was symbolic and whose language was of the hieroglyphic type. It also proves that *Max Muller's* theory of "Roots" is wrong. Throughout all Eastern Asia, however much the dialects and syllabic or oral sounds and spoken language may differ, the written symbolic language is understood by all.

Their Eschatology was pure original so-called Monotheism, which corresponds in all ideas, forms, ceremonies, symbolisms, etc., to those in use amongst the ancient Egyptians.

The followers of the messenger (Sinphos) in Assam preserve traditions of their forefathers, which connect them with the earliest ages. They are divided into twelve tribes, in commemoration of the twelve Elders (twelve signs of the Zodiac), and worship one Supreme Being. In Ceylon we find that the Buddhists have the same belief.

The tribes of North America are divided into Totemic divisions, and the Crow tribe has two interesting "signs"—tokens of friendship and brotherhood, and, if given and answered by strangers, you are a "safe brother" amongst them, which is important to those brothers of the 18°.

1. In crossing their arms on the breast L U
2. In raising the R H to the side of the H, with the I F pointing to the Great Spirit, and then reversing H A and H D.

As we have shown by photographs from Mexico and Central America, this sign was a "sacred sign," used there during the Stellar Mythos, because we find it depicted here before the Solar arrived, and in some ruined cities that the Solar doctrines never reached; at least, there is no evidence of its having done so (see

"Mexican Notes"). These signs are plainly shown in many of the Vignettes of the Egyptian "Book of the Dead" and connected with the *Ritual* of their Sacred Ceremonies. Another important point to prove that these people came from Egypt during very

Fig. 95.
Swastica Totem of Tribe of North America.

early times is that of the oldest tribes known—one has the tortoise for their totem (the oldest) and another the Swastica, as may be seen from the photograph taken from a drawing in "their camp" many years ago. This is the "Swastica Totem," and is made up of the Swastica above two circles, with another Swastica and a Disk in the centre. This Disk represents "Aten" and was an ancient form of Her-Mahu (Horus) god of the double horizon in Egypt. It was not a worship of Solar-deity, but was an emblem of the circle made by Aten as the god of the double horizons, lifted up or made by Shu. From recent inquiries we have made, we are given to understand that this tribe has "died out," and that very few, if any, of the Indians belonging to it exist at the present day.

The same custom found amongst the Jews and Hindoos (as in Egypt) for a man to raise up seed for the deceased brother by marrying his widow, was found amongst the Central American nations: also, none but the High Priests might enter the Holy of Holies. All ate the flesh of the sacrifices of atonement (analogous, see 18°), and poured the blood of the sacrifice on the earth; they sprinkled it, they marked persons with it, they smeared it upon the walls and stones (brought on from the Totemic ceremonies, see description of same in *Spencer* and *Gillen's* books). All their temples faced the East, showing that they had passed the Stellar Mythos. They all had the ark as a portable temple, and all held it in the highest veneration. It was thought too sacred to be touched except by the Priests: all offered water to a stranger that he might wash his feet, used dust as a token of humility, anointed with oil sacrificed prisoners and hung up their heads—and the Lord said unto Moses:—"Take all the heads of the people and hang them up before the Lord against the Sun, that the fierce anger of the Lord may be turned away from Israel." And Moses said unto the Judges of Israel:—"Slay ye every one of his men that were joined unto Baal-peor" (Numb. xxv. 4-5). And they all practised baptism, as is proved by the following:—"Then the Mexican midwife gave the child to taste of the water, putting her moistened finger into its mouth and said: 'Take this: by this thou hast to live on the earth, to grow and to flourish; through this we get all things that support existence on the earth; receive it.' Then with moistened fingers she touched the breast of the child and said: 'Behold the pure water that washes and cleanses thy heart, that removes all filthiness; receive it; may the goddess see good to purify and cleanse thy heart.' Then the midwife poured water upon the head of the child, saying: 'O my grandson, my son, take this water of the Lord of the world, which is thy life, invigorating and refreshing, washing and cleansing. I pray that this celestial water, blue and light blue, may enter into thy body and there live. I pray that it may destroy in thee and put away from thee all things evil and adverse *that were given thee before the beginning of the world.* Wheresoever thou art in this child, O thou hurtful thing, begone! leave it, put thyself apart: for now does it live anew *and anew is it born,* now again is it purified and cleansed: now again is it shapened and engendered by our mother the goddess of water'" (Bancroft's "Native Races," vol. iii. page 372). Here we find many resemblances to the Christian ordinance of baptism; the pouring of water on the head, the putting of the fingers into the mouth, the touching of the breast, the new birth and the washing away of the original sin—all part of the *Ritual* of Egypt referring to the passage of the manes in Amenta.

The Christian rite, we know, was not a Christian idea, but was borrowed from ancient times. The original name for the goddess of water was Nut, afterwards she became Isis. Isis and Horus were the mother and divine child, the divine healer, and the Romans brought them with them to Rome and they were worshipped there by the Romans, the Roman women more especially. Anyone going to Italy now may see many of these figures in black basalt, which were brought there from Egypt. On this the Roman Catholic religion was founded, and that is the reason why the Virgin Mary (Isis brought on in the Christian doctrines) has so much adoration paid to her. The Roman Catholics did not have the Father at first, who was brought on by the Jews, and thus we see that the Eschatology of the Solar was practised by all when Solar Mythos had perished. All these customs, etc., were the same in N. and S. America, Europe, India and some other parts of Asia. The primordial came from Egypt.

Language

We have made some remarks on the origin of language to show how, in all probability, our present use of signs and symbols has originated, and how these have been handed down from generation to generation, time and circumstances modifying the original to the present interpretation.

Tracing the origin of the ancient Egyptians from the origin of language, *Gerald Massey*[1] says that "concerning the origin of

[1] "Natural Genesis."

language very little is known and hitherto nothing absolutely established. All theories on the subject are chiefly negative. The 'science' has been founded and its 'origins' have been discussed without the ideographic symbols and the gesture-signs being even taken into account. These must take their root from Inner Africa and not, as the Aryanists have laboured to show, in Asia."

The Inner African languages prove that words had earlier forms than those which have become the "roots" of the Aryanist. There is no way of getting back to an origin of words except by learning once more to think in things, images, ideographs, hieroglyphics and gesture-signs; and the primary modes of expression must be sought in their birthplace, for in Africa only shall we find the earliest rudimentary articulation of human sounds which accompanied gesture-signs and preceded verbal speech. The clicks, the formation of words by the duplication of sounds and all original types of expression must be allowed to have been evolved in Africa until it can be shown how they came otherwise.

Gesture-signs and ideographic symbols alone preserve the early language in visible figures, and we are unable to get to the roots of all that have been pictured, printed or written, until we can decipher the figures made primarily by the early man. The latest forms of these have to be traced back to the most primary before we can get to know anything of the origins. These are the true radicals of language, without which the philologist has no final and adequate determinative; and yet these have been left hitherto outside the range of discussion by the Aryan school. But the doctrine is prevalent in current philology, whilst the earlier sign-language has been ignored altogether.

Whenever the ideographic signs of the oldest civilised nations can be compared, evidence of the original unity becomes apparent, and if we take the earliest inhabitants of any part of the world, we find from the skeletons that these were all of the same class—Negroid, just as we find in gesture-language that the further we go back the nearer is our approach towards some central unity.

The "Origin of Language" itself is not a problem to be attacked and solved by the philosophical speculator. To know anything with certitude we must go back the way we came, along the track that only the evolution is free to pursue and explore. We know now that the dumb think, and that man had a gesture-language when he was otherwise dumb. And in common with the lower animals he still uses inarticulate cries to express his meaning, aided by gestures and the movements of the muscles of the face.

Speculation, without the primary data, cannot establish anything, but when we have the data we find that development was, from the very first, in accordance with the laws of evolution, and that there was but one beginning for language, mythology and symbolism, however numerous their intermediate forms or widely scattered the nearest links.

Fortunately, Nature is very careful, and a type once evolved is never entirely lost, nor altogether effaced, but unity of origin in language was only possible when the human intelligence was too limited to disagree and diverge, and the race a mental herd making the same signs and sounds for ages and ages without choice in the matter or desire to differ.

Be it noted that at the present time there are many signs, used with the hands and fingers, both by deaf and dumb people and aborigines when at a distance from each other. *Roth*, in his book, gives 213 such signs to communicate their wishes or thoughts. A good example is that used by our navy and army. Many a time have we watched with interest our bluejackets, leaning over the side of a man-of-war talking to another, perhaps 500 yards off, only with his hands and fingers, after the order has been given to "cease signalling." In one case the bluejackets and soldiers, deaf and dumb, use an alphabet, and in the other, the native, being ignorant of alphabets, uses the signs with his fingers, showed to imply sentences which have been prearranged and stand in the same sense as the alphabet to him.

Thus we see that the primary forms of language, so to speak, signs, symbols, ideographs, etc., were first written as a visible means of expressing articulate sounds. This hieroglyphic language became afterwards a secret language, known and carried on from generation to generation, with secret meanings, the interpretation of which at the present day, as of old, is only known to those who have worked and passed through the necessary examination to enable them to obtain that knowledge. But, inasmuch as we find the same hieroglyphics, signs, symbols, etc., in various parts of the world, also that the earliest race of beings were Negroid, it is but natural to believe that at one time these were universal, and that their birthplace must have had one common centre, which must have been Africa. Throughout the whole world, where the ossified remains of earliest man have been found, we find the same type, which is Negroid. This is proved by the shape of the bones, the flattened fibia, the shape of the skull, etc., and the long forearm with wide space between the two forearm bones (Ulna and Radius), the discussion of which would be outside this work. At the same time, for those interested in the argument, we would draw attention to *Professor G. Sergi's* work, "The Mediterranean Race," and to the various "finds" that have been well described by many able writers. These point to the conclusion that primitive man emanated from the continent of Africa, and could not have been evolved from anywhere else.

Of course much of the original meaning and interpretation has been lost and others substituted, still the true originals remain engraved on monuments and stones, because language, like a species, when once extinct, never reappears ; the same language never has two birthplaces. Distant languages may be crossed or blended together ; we see variability in any tongue, and new words are frequently being "coined." But as there is a limited power to man's brain capacity for remembering single words, like whole languages, these gradually become extinct, although in the spelling of new words letters often remain as the rudiments of ancient forms of pronunciation, and dominant languages and dialects, naturally spread widely and gradually extinguish other tongues.

As far as possible, we only bring before our readers those facts and remnants of antiquity which still exist and which all can verify, pointing as they do that the conclusions we have arrived at, and which every earnest student can prove for himself, are not "visionary" but are existing facts.

Whilst candidly admitting that there still remain many broken links, we contend that in the chain of evidence which we have helped to forge there is more than sufficient to prove to all students and thinkers the truth of what we advance ; at all events the *fact* that we find the same signs, symbols, doctrines, etc., practised throughout various parts of this world would lead us to conclude that they all had one common origin, and all our research proves that in Egypt was the birthplace and nowhere else can it be found.

In using the term "in Egypt" we include the Nile valley and its sources.

CHAPTER XI

It is well known that the Buddhists and Brahmins, in many of their religious ceremonies, make use of words that are not Sanskrit but are said to belong to a very ancient form of speech, now dead, the ancient Egyptian.

Their traditional history tells us that they came from the North and West, and pushed down through the mountains to the Ganges and base of the Himalayas, South and East, and formed settlements by the great rivers of the Punjaub ; but they never forgot their former home, as may be seen by the Vedic hymns (Rig-Veda), which are the same as those beautiful hymns we find in the *Ritual*—very little "editing" has been done—and are of Egyptian origin—undoubtedly.

Professor Max Muller's idea that the names of the gods, representing the different attributes of the One Great God, were first taught by the Veda, and that each god is separate and worshipped as supreme and absolute by the followers of the Hindoo religion, only shows that he was not acquainted with the *origin* of the Veda, or the Eschatology and *Ritual* of Egypt (from whence the Hindoo religion originated), because their creed was pure Monotheism, and all these supposed "different" gods were in reality only the *attributes of the One Great God*, who created the heavens and earth and all therein. *Professor Tiele* has also missed the point when he expounds the Egyptian religion ; first, "as a lively sentiment of the spirituality of God, united to the coarsest materialistic representations of different divinities," and secondly, "a sentiment, not less lively, of the unity of God united to an extremely great multiplicity of divine persons."

Many books have been written to try and prove that the ancient Persians, Buddhists and Brahmins obtained their religions from our ancient Druids in Ireland and the British Isles ; and others, that ancient Britons were simply Buddhists, on account of many similarities which may be traced ; but we cannot discover anything to support these theories, on the contrary, there is everything to prove that all religions had their origin in ancient Egypt.

It is true that in all and every one of these, instances are recorded of the falling away from the original Eschatology, and in its place various other practices and doctrines have been introduced, so that at the present day there is little of the original left, and there is so much diversion of opinion and so many different sects that it requires a large amount of study and research in order to unravel the tangled skein.

Only in the rites, ceremonies, signs and symbols of Freemasonry at the present time do we find the purest types of the original, and these are as similar as possible to the perfected Eschatology of the ancient Egyptians, even to the 30°—over which some of our Brethren would cross swords with us, and which our present *Ritual* gives as "*recent*." We feel confident in stating, without a semblance of doubt in our minds, that these traditions have been "brought on" and have emanated from the Egyptian originals, the whole of the symbolisms, ceremonies, passwords, etc., being identical.

The ancient Egyptians had no other way of demonstrating their ideas except in what *Professor Tiele* calls "coarsest materialistic representations." They had not the words that we now have, and although apparently they made use of a coarse form, the meaning was not such. It was their only means of representing the *spiritual attributes* and not *different divinities*; not "the unity of God with an extremely great multiplicity of divine persons," but "the great number of attributes or powers that the One Great God possessed." And it was by forms, symbols and dramatic actions that they taught their doctrines; but they never believed in more than one god, under whatever name they worshipped him—and there were many during the Stellar, Lunar, and Solar Mythos—as the *Ritual* proves very clearly indeed.

Moreover, there is no evidence that the Egyptians, predynastic or dynastic, ever believed or practised Polytheism. On the contrary, there is every proof that from the earliest predynastic times they believed in and practised Monotheism, and that this Monotheism from the first they represented as "God in mummified form," a "Man-god," and "God in Spirit" or "the risen Man-god." The more we study the *Ritual* and Papyri, and other evidences which still remain, the more certain it becomes that from the first it was one and the same god through all ages, pre-dynastic and dynastic. At various periods, exodes went from Egypt, carrying their then knowledge with them, and forming colonies in all parts of the world, and it is only by thus following them that anyone can get a true idea and unlock those hidden secrets of the past.

Throughout all the *Ritual*, papyri, monuments, etc., and in fact every evidence that we can look for and see, pre-dynastic and dynastic, there is only one conclusion that we can arrive at in studying this question, and that is: "The ancient Egyptians only believed in One Great God, who was Immortal, Uncreated, Invisible, and hidden in the inaccessible depths of His essence; He is the Creator of the Heavens and of the Earth; He has made everything which exists, and nothing has been made without Him, who existed before all things, and who represents the pure and abstract idea of Divinity," and *only the highest of the initiated of the Sanctuary were taught all the powers and attributes which He possessed and all His names attached thereto.*

The conclusion that these old Priests arrived at in their Eschatology—"That God is a Person," in the sense that He is "self-conscious and intelligent will," is at one and the same time the most original and fundamental form of religious belief, and the most mature and conclusive tenet of scientific and philosophical Theism. Among such predicates as the foregoing, the following five must stand out first: Omnipotence, Omnipresence, Eternity, Omniscience and Unity. These qualifications must be characteristic of an "Absolute Self," of whatever form, Spiritual or otherwise, which conclusion they had arrived at and thoroughly believed in at this early period, and which has never been improved upon since.

We differ from a great many scientific men and Egyptologists in our opinions expressed in this work, but we are convinced and feel as sure as we are now writing, that future generations will find the truth of that which we now state and will prove it more conclusively than we have done, and some perhaps will wonder why so many eminent men had wandered away from "the original" to a "foreign land" for their "origins." The answer is that they could not read what was written in stone and papyrus, countless ages ago, left and preserved to be rediscovered and re-read, as a guide to reform into one universal brotherhood the various sects of the different religions of the present day, which have all taken their origins from this one source. Also, priests of many and various religions have gone on perverting the original for ages past, and those of the present day have followed in a blind lead those who had lost the true Eschatology and were ignorant of the Mythos, Astro-mythology, Eschatology and the *Ritual* of ancient Egypt. Hence the schism which still increases! Hence the uncertainty of " thinkers," the disagreement amongst various sects, both in the Christian and Buddhist doctrines, and the numerous religions scattered all over the world at the present time. Some have one part of the Eschatology, some another, but all have been changed from the original. We feel, however, that one day all these religions will be reunited into one again. It is so written; but whether this will be done by the Japanese, who are now introducing Freemasonry into Japan, or by the Anglo-Saxon race, or by the two races combined, no one can say; but in the Japanese religion of the *Ancient Sect* there is much of the pure Eschatology of Egypt remaining, which will not be difficult to amalgamate or blend with our doctrines and thus form one, and so lead to the true Christianising of the whole of Japan. Although there are in Japan various sects of the Buddhist doctrines, *they were all originally one.* The ancient inhabitants brought with them out of Egypt, at the time of the Solar Mythos, their present Eschatology, only Japan, like others, has suffered from perversion of the original, which has been split up into various sects by the different priests for ages. Still, one " ancient sect " preserves more of the original than the others, and we believe that this will blend with our *Ritual.* When we speak of the present inhabitants we do not include the Ainu, as these were there ages before the Japanese, so-called now; the Ainu had brought with them the Stellar Mythos out of Egypt and not the Solar. This accounts for much of the Stellar Mythos that we find at the present day in the beliefs of some of the sects which are supposed to be of Buddhist or Brahmin origin, and in the beliefs of the people who belong to these various sects, as, for instance, " ancestor worship," which is a very strong characteristic in these people, is of Stellar Mythos and not Solar, although one was blended with the other. Most, who now have the remnants of the Solar, have lost this particular characteristic, as may be seen from the Buddhists in India, etc., whilst the present

Japanese have developed it to a greater Eschatological point than they of the original Mythos, and at the same time we must not overlook the fact that before "ancestral worship" was evolved, so-called "spirit worship," or the divination of "nature's powers," had existed for ages and ages.

Amongst the Mayas, Mexicans, Zapotecs, and all the people of Central America and some parts of N. and S. America, we find from the inscriptions still extant, that their one belief was in One God, and described him as "God without end and without beginning, the Uncreated Lord, who had no beginning and no end; God, who was the Creator of all things, and was Himself uncreated—Lord, Leader, King, Great God—the Great One, Strong, Powerful, He who is the Great, the Strong, Powerful Living Spirit."

The whole of their customs, literature and traditional history point out that these came out of Egypt at the time of the Stellar or Solar doctrines.

Cows are accounted sacred in India, and the reason is that the ancient Egyptians held them sacred to Isis (the Moon Goddess, represented with horns—Hathor), and the people in India object to kill them as food, as did the Egyptians—another proof of their having obtained originally their Eschatology from Egypt.

Time and evolution have changed the original, but Brahminic philosophy has distorted it more than anything else.

Their divinities (Devata in Sanskrit) literally mean "the Shining Ones." There were no castes at that time, and they treated their women as did the Egyptians, allowing them to enjoy the same high position as themselves.

The reason why the "Emerald Stone," or green stone (Jade), as found amongst the Maories and various tribes in North and South America, Mexico and other parts of the world, is considered and looked upon as a "sacred stone," is because it represents one of the names of Horus I.—viz. "Her-uatch-f-" *i.e. Prince of the Emerald Stone.* It was for this reason that it was sacred and carried by those throughout their wanderings into countries where it could not otherwise be found, and so we find it amongst them at the present day. In Central America it is found depicted in various forms connected with Horus I. as the Giver of Rays of Light, and a representation of Eternal Youth.

It was not until a short time before the period of the Greeks and Romans that Egypt began to decay, when their priests became degenerate, and their downfall has progressed in one

FIG. 96.—High Priest, without Breastplate.

continuous line ever since, until the British and Freemasonry came to their rescue. Lord Kitchener, a Freemason, acting thus —perhaps unknown to himself—has laid the foundation of a college at Khartoum, on almost the identical spot of the first Temple of Learning.

The Jews—if we take it in a broad sense—never had any ethnology as a nation, but only as a religious sect. *Manetho* states that Moses, who received his priestly education and learned all the wisdom of the Egyptians in the city of Heliopolis, in the Delta—the Biblical city of On or Beth-Shemesh, the House of the Sun—left Egypt with his followers and went to the East and founded Jerusalem, the history of which is too well known to need repetition here. It is more than probable that he brought on the Eschatology of the ancient Egyptians, in which he was

FIG. 97.—High Priest, with Breastplate.

learned. *Manetho* states that Moses was one of the priests and was learned in all the Osirian and Amen-Ra doctrines, and changed his religion twice, or rather, forms of his religion, although time and evolution have doubtless changed a good deal from the original, and many other ceremonies have been introduced to suit the requirements of the gradual evolution of civilisation. The ornaments of the ancient Druid Priests—*i.e.* Breastplate, Gold Girdle and C (the L) are precisely similar in every point to those worn by the High Priests of the Children of Israel, as may be seen at the present time in the Dublin Museum and Truro

Museum, in Cornwall, these having been recovered from the tomb of Ollamh Fodhla, and near Rough Tor, in Cornwall; one of these was the same as worn by the ancient Egyptian priests.

FIG. 98.—Full Dress of the High Priest of the Egyptians, Israelites, Druids, and Mayas. They all wore snow white. Breastplates—and the above various Head Dresses—some modified.

The Maya, Central American and Inca priests all wore the same, as far as we can trace, from historical records.

Many people think, and the Jews themselves believe, that they are the "chosen people." Yet, it is distinctly recorded in the old Papyri that the Egyptians used to believe and say that they were *the chosen people* of the Lord. Those who may believe in either of the above, should distinguish between "Jews" and "Israelites." The Jews, strictly, are of the tribe of Judah, the Israelites, as we have shown elsewhere, were from Egypt. Thus

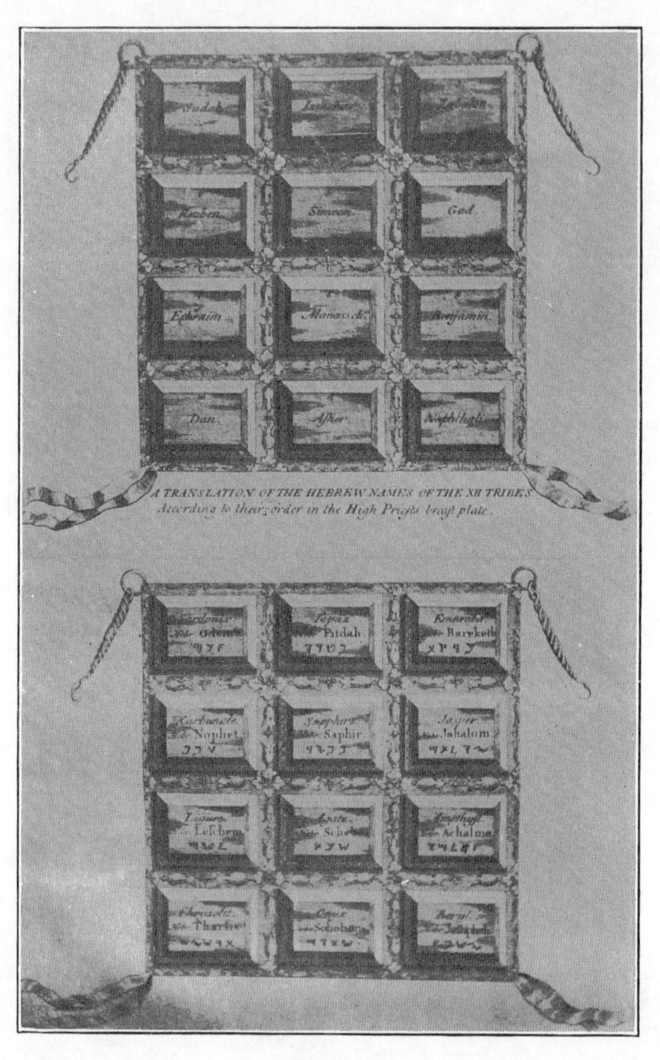

FIG. 99.

Israelites are not Jews, although some Jews may be Israelites. Their whole history, laws and traditions prove that they borrowed very largely indeed from the Egyptians, and the "Laws of Moses," which they consider and believe their own specific laws, were the old laws of Egypt, given to them by Moses; laws which had been in existence thousands of years before Moses lived, as is proved by the *Stalæ of Hammurabi*. In fact, the exodus, etc., must, to be understood, be read *through the Egyptian Mythos alone*, because, only in one place and at one time do we find that the Jews were mentioned in the old Egyptian records, and that was at the time of "Meru Ptah," when reference was made to their having been driven back and utterly routed by the Egyptians, so that we must come to the conclusion that never did a large body of them come to Egypt.

Volney states that "in vain did Moses proscribe the worship of the symbols which prevailed in lower Egypt and Phœnicia, and in vain did he wish to blot from his religion everything which had relation to the stars." In other words, he was a priest of the Solar Eschatology of the Egyptians, and knew that this was brought on from the Stellar. Yet the seven luminaries or seven Glorious Ones of the Pole Stars were represented by the great candlesticks, and the twelve stones or signs in the urim of the High Priest and the feast of the two equinoxes—entrance and gates of the two hemispheres—were the same as the breastplate worn by the hierophants of Egypt, which had inscribed upon it the twelve signs of the Zodiac. Moses wished to keep the doctrines up to date, and we find that the Mayas did the same. When they brought the Solar doctrines to Yucatan, they obliterated as much of the old Stellar Mythos that was being carried on and practised then, drove as much as possible back to the West, and conquered those tribes they were able to, replacing the old Stellar by the new Eschatology. This can be accurately proved by studying the "remains of the past," which are still to be found in great abundance in these countries at the present time.

The Jewish religion is founded on the Mysteries of the double horizon of Ra Harmachis; they still celebrate the Mystery annually *as Mystery*, and *their two times* remain equinoctial, and has never been changed to the winter solstice and Easter equinox. They killed the "Old Mother" and "the young child" and did away with them altogether, but *kept the father*. Their religion is an exoteric rendering of part of the *Ritual* of Ancient Egypt instead of an esoteric representation, hence the similarity of all these religious doctrines.

With regard to the question of the earliest Egyptians being of the tribe of Dan, as contended by the Anglo-Israelite Society, these were called Danites, but their origin was from N.E. Africa—sources of the Nile and valley of the same. *Rawlinson*, however, mentions an exodus of Black Jews from Upper Egypt to the East, who settled in India and are still there, practising their ancient forms of religion; but they have not the Pentateuch. We find that in Southern India they are locally called White Jews. At what time the exodus took place we are unable to say, but not at a very early period in comparison to the Australians and Druids.

The Pentateuch,—from a very ancient Egyptian text we learn that amongst the 36,000 books ascribed to Taht, there was a particular collection known as "The 4 Books," these had the titles of—1, The Old Book; 2, The Book to Destroy Man; 3, The Great Book; 4, The Book to be as God. These four books were probably in the Temple at Annu or On where Osarsiph, or Moses, was a priest who was profoundly learned in the wisdom of Egypt, and these books formed the basis of the Hebrew Pentateuch, and although the number now (5) does not coincide, yet the books originally assigned to Moses were 4 in number only, and not 5.

Probably the difference was brought about in the translation, as the original would naturally be written on rolls of Papyrus in the library at Annu from whence it was carried forth in one of the exodes from Egypt.

The original of the Hebrew collection consisted of "the precepts of the Pentateuch," which may be said to be the Jewish Torah, which signifies or denotes the whole law, and in the Egyptian Teruu signifies all, entirely the whole laws.

Shu-Anhur was the giver of laws to man as revealed by Ra, and is mentioned in the *Ritual* as the author of writings called "His rules and laws and his papyrus" although *Renouf* is of opinion that the God Taht is meant R. B. of D., chap. cx.), but *Renouf* is wrong in this as Shu is said to work in the abode of the books of Seb—*i.e.* of earth (*Ritual*, chap. xvii.). This can be identified with the Great Library at Annu, "The papyrus Mahit of Shu" as mentioned in the *Ritual*—"I am in unison with his successive changes and his laws (or rules) and his writings" (*Ritual*, chap. cx.). The Book of the Laws is the Book of Ma or Mati, which was presented by the duality of Shu-Anhur, the Lord of Truth or Mati. The writings of Shu-Anhur were preserved at Annu amongst the 36,000 books that were traditionally ascribed to

Taht. He wrote them at dictation from Ra or Atum-Huhi, the Father of Iu, who was carried into Judea as Ihuh and brought on the sacred writings that had been placed in the temple of Atum-Ra-Har-Makhu to be transmitted from generation to generation for time and eternity.

The human race therefore had its origin in Africa, and that by gradual development and evolution some of them settled in Upper Egypt and along the banks of the Nile, gaining here the first knowledge of Nature's Laws, and gradually acquiring a mythology—later an Astral mythology—and finally the perfected Eschatology.

That some remnants of their Astro-mythology, as well as their Eschatology, were scattered over various parts of the globe is clearly shown by the totemic ceremonies still in existence in Australia, New Guinea, Java and West Africa ; and these secrets can yet be traced in the ruins of the temples and cities found amongst the Mayas, Incas, Druids, early man (Neolithic) in Cornwall and other parts.

The exodes, at the time of the Druids, however, are of much later date than those where we find the totemic ceremonies were practised.

Whether the remains of the temple in North America, mentioned by *Gerald Massey*, were of totemic or eschatological origin, the author is unable to state, but it is quite certain that all those who practised the totemic ceremonies date back to an extremely early period, because this exodus from Egypt must have taken place whilst the Egyptians still practised and believed in their Stellar Mythology, or before this was fully developed, and had not by evolution entered upon the Solar Mythos or perfected their Eschatology. The subsequent evolution of their Astronomical Mythology shows that Egypt was the progressive centre. The accurate observations of their High Priests as to the precession or rather recession of the Pole Stars, which they must have made at least once, if not twice. The time it took to be accomplished, and the changes that occurred before they had begun to record the same, show how patiently they worked for 25,000, if not 50,000 years.

Reasoning from these various points and the different times of exodes that we find occurred, one can, to a very great extent, clearly understand the record of the past.

We know that there was inter-communication between Egypt and Mexico. We have shown the totemic ceremonies existing and still practised by the Arunta tribes in Australia, and probably those of Java and New Guinea were precisely similar to those in use in Egypt. We know of the exodus to the Northern and Western Islands (Cornwall and the British Isles), where we find, first, Neolithic man and Stellar Mythos, and after, the Druidical temples and doctrines, the same as those at Medum ; we read also of the exodus of Moses to the East. His subsequent history is too well known to be repeated here. The Buddhists also obtained their Eschatology from the Egyptians and have the White Stone and the Ten Circles of the universe, or ten Heavenly Worlds.[1] They also know the secret sarcophagus in the pyramid of Gizeh, as may be seen from the following.[2]

Maspero says that this great Pyramid concealed a black and white image seated on a throne and invested with the Kingly Sceptre = Sut and Horus.

Certain totemic ceremonies which were practised by many tribes in various parts of the world are identical in their symbolism, and they must all have had one common origin, which can be definitely traced to Egypt at the time of the Stellar, Lunar or Solar Mythos. We find many of the same signs and symbols both in Lunar and Solar Mythology, but they were brought forward from the earlier Stellar Mythology. We date the origin of Freemasonry at the time of Ptah, the Great Architect of the Universe, who, with his seven assistants, built the heavens on squares, and from whose date we may practically determine the commencement of the Solar Mythos, for at Memphis a magnificent temple was raised by the pious Mena, called Ha-Ptah, the abode of the Creator, in honour of the Architect-God, Ptah, and that the signs, symbols, etc., which were in use and recognised by the earliest Egyptians long before this date, were brought down and made use of as part of their Astral Mythology.

From all this mass of evidence it would appear that from Ancient Egypt originated Stellar Mythos—the totemic ceremonies

[1] "And he said, by the mystery of the White Stone, by the Stone of Black, by the Gloomy Sceptre of Terrors, by the Holiness of the 'Prophetic Coffer,' I pray thee, I abjure, I give command, reveal not unto mortals the secret of God ; let it be hidden in the glens of thy soul, as the Queen Bee within the hive."—BUDDHIST THEOLOGY.

[2] Particulars of these are given in the Litany of the eighteenth chapter of the "Ritual or Book of the Dead."

and customs, still found amongst,—and practised by, the native Australian aborigines and the aboriginal inhabitants of Java, and many tribes in Africa. Following this was Lunar and Solar Mythos, and from these was evolved one of the most perfect eschatologies as regards moral and social life, to say the least. The various exodes that went out of Egypt caused this to be spread throughout the world, and under various names the same religious beliefs were practised and carried on.

The Druids—the original Buddhists, the Chaldeans, the people of Yucatan and the Israelites had all the signs and symbols originally used, which were brought down and made use of symbolically.

We fail to see the utility of *Ignatius Donnelly's* comparison of the Maya alphabet with the *Egyptian Hieratic*, to try and prove that the Maya was "the older" and original, and not the Egyptian. He must go back further than the "Solar Mythos" to prove this, and take the above into consideration, and the other proofs we have brought forward in this work; then he will find that the Mayas obtained their characters from the "Egyptian Hieroglyphics," and all their astronomy, learning, and religious doctrines and ceremonies, pyramids, etc., from the Egyptians. There are more than four hundred pyramids in Mexico, built of huge stones and faced as the pyramids of Egypt. As a matter of fact, pyramids are found in many countries, but they are copies of the Egyptian, and all *Ignatius Donnelly* states about "Atlantis, the Antediluvian World," goes no further back than "Solar Mythos," and the parts of RIG VEDA that he quotes are copied, nearly word for word, from the old Egyptian *Ritual*, which dates from the Stellar Mythos. He confounds the Egyptian hieroglyphics ⊙, ◎, —— Ra, Sep or An, Ta, etc., with *letters* of the alphabet, instead of what they are—Syllabic signs.

Such numerous and striking similarities between these ancient totemic rites and early religions, whose relics are to be found all over the world, conclusively prove that they must have been derived from one original, Egypt, and there is no logic, fact, reason, nor any argument to be advanced which could prove that any native tribes or the Australians or West-Coast tribes evolved their religion and religious ceremonies from their own surroundings and experience. In the case of the Australians their traditional history alone is sufficient to prove the negation to this as well as all the others if we study them.

Also, in the Secret Tribal Societies of West Africa the mark of the "Khui Land" of Egypt, with concentric circles, cut on the back of the Purroh man and the fact that the same is depicted on the Druidical stones, is still another proof which cannot be lightly cast aside; in fact, we cannot too strongly emphasise this sign which is of so great an importance in unravelling the mysteries of the past. For those of our readers who may doubt, these still exist for them to see and study if they feel so inclined.

There can be no reasonable doubt that some of the Egyptian priests emigrated to Ireland and the British Isles and brought their religion with them, and here, in the British Isles, they founded and built temples and carried on their religious rites and ceremonies. As it was only the priests who were learned enough to know the hieroglyphic characters and writings, and as these are very distinctly shown engraved on the stones at Ollamh Fodhla, this must have been either the tomb of one of the original immigrants, or of descendants who were learned in their doctrines, as well as those found on the Granite Stone in South Tawton Church, in Devonshire.

The Papyrus of Nesi-Amsu is an important one for Freemasons to read, as the reason for and origin of "left foot first" is given. In the destruction of Apep—the great serpent of evil—the greatest in fact of all the Evil Fiends, the left foot was first placed on him; and his destruction and how this was accomplished is described; therefore symbolical of commencing our journey through life by putting all evil thoughts or actions under and away from us, we should tread down the great evil which besets us through life. The great fiend was to be wiped out of existence in every form. After the various modes of his destruction having been described, it says "he was to be burnt to ashes and these ashes strewed over the face of the earth so that no trace of him could be found." These are the actual words in this papyrus. *Dr Budge* says: "In the Egyptian text we have at present an account of the first fight which took place between Ra and Apep, but it is clear from several passages in the 'Book of Overthrowing Apep' that such a thing must have occurred, and that the means employed by the Sun God for destroying his foe resembled those made use of by Marduk in slaying Tiamat, and that the original of the Assyrian story is undoubtedly of Sumerian origin and must be very old, and it is possible that the Egyptians and the Sumerians derived their version from a common source." We are pleased to see that *Dr Budge* acknowledges so much, and, if he would study the primordial, he would, we think, find the solution of the question, the original being Egyptian, which was that great fight at the time of the Stellar Mythos between Horus the first and Sut—the great fight between light and darkness. This was the original of the story, and has been handed down in various forms through the people of all nations, and although in some countries and descriptions there is a little variation (Bel and the Dragon—Satan being chained, as in the Christian doctrines) so in the latter text of the Egyptians we find that various editings, etc., by the Scribes, have differed, but the story is the same throughout all ages and all lands, and it is not difficult to see how the priests of Egypt and others grafted new religious opinions and beliefs on old ones and changed their names. We would wish to draw *Brother Gould's* attention to this Papyrus.

Note [1913].—On p. 242 (ll. 24 and 25) *read* "the origin of the higher degrees of Freemasonry" for "the origin of Freemasonry." And after "Stellar Mythos" (l. 35) *read* "following after and evolved partly from the totemic ceremonies."

CHAPTER XII

THE day is dark and the night
To him that would search their heart ;
No lips of cloud that will part
Nor morning song in the light
    Only, gazing alone
To him wild shadows are shown,
Deep under deep unknown,
And height above unknown height
Still we say as we go :
" Strange to think by the way
Whatever there is to know
That shall we know one day."

DANTE ROSSETTI.

FURTHER EVIDENCE RECENTLY FOUND, CONNECTING PREHISTORIC MAN WITH ANCIENT EGYPT AS HIS BIRTHPLACE, DATING FROM THE NEOLITHIC AND PALEOLITHIC AGE, AS PROVED BY THE IVORY TABLETS FOUND IN THE TOMB OF NAQADA, ETC., AND OTHER RECENT DISCOVERIES IN EGYPT, UGANDA, CORNWALL, ETC.

FIG. 100.—Ivory Tablets found in the Tomb of Naqada.

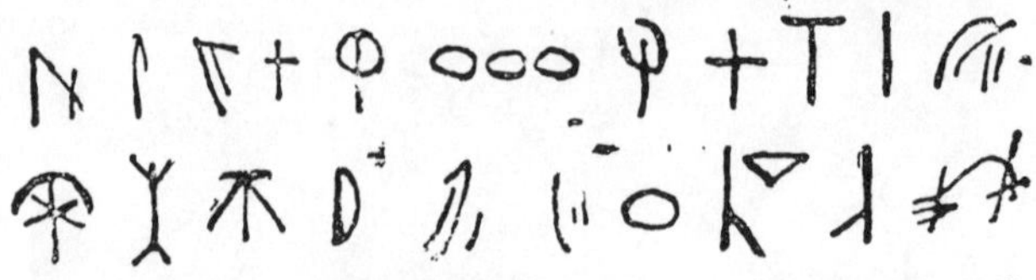

FIG. 101.—Linear writing signs on clay vessels (*De Morgan*).

WE give here a photograph of Linear writings, found on clay

vessels in Egypt, dating back to the earlier Neolithic times, and Ivory Tablets, showing so-called Linear writings, found in the royal tomb of Naqada, which *Professor Sergi* thinks have nothing in common with the Egyptian ideographic characters,[1] but which we consider one of the most important discoveries that have ever yet been made, because they give the names of six "Kings of the South," with the length of the reign of each, before the time of Meni, the supposed first king of the first dynasty. Having been found in his tomb they must have lived before him. They reigned :—

The 1st	...	...	97 years.
,, 2nd	...	...	85 years.
,, 3rd	...	...	23 years.
,, 4th	...	...	64 years.
,, 5th	...	...	76 years.
,, 6th	...	...	23 years.
		Total	368 years.

We see here the earliest beginning of the Linear writing, which was a commencement of the progressive form from their hieroglyphic system. We are convinced that these so-called proto-Egyptian writings were simply the earliest attempts to form writings into "an alphabetical form," an improvement upon the ancient and true hieroglyphics. Exodes took place out of Egypt during this period of their evolution, carrying the knowledge which they possessed, and the various writings (or rude marks) which we find in other countries—Britain, Yucatan, N. and S. America and Australia, also Cretan and Ægean—were and are all identical. Their birthplace was Egypt.

It will require very little study to compare the writing of this country a thousand years ago with the highest Lithographic Art Writing which can now be produced, to show what time and evolution will do for a progressive people ; therefore, to say that these signs or "rude marks" have nothing in common with the

[1] From *Professor Sergi's* book, "The Mediterranean Race," published by the Walter Scott Publishing Company Limited, by whose kind permission we reproduce it here, and for which we here express our thanks.

Egyptian Ideographic characters is not, we think, correct; in fact, we read them as the same, though the one may be looked upon as "crude" and the other as "artistic"; otherwise we find no difference. This also applies to the Cretan, Ægean and Libyan inscriptions, tabulated by *Evans*, as well as others, in different parts of the world.

The discovery made by *Piette* at Mas-d'Azil simply shows and proves that there was a period of transition from the one to the other. In these Alphabetiform signs of *Piette* there are a great many true and pure Egyptian hieroglyphics of the old type mixed with those of "transition stage." Seh, Mes, the serpent Rerek, the same as we found at South Tawton, in Devonshire—the sign for backbone, to cut in pieces—the sign for water, and the same kind of Ank Cross as we found in Cornwall, also the same cross enclosed  as we find at Palenque in Central America. The signs from the French Dolmens, which are given

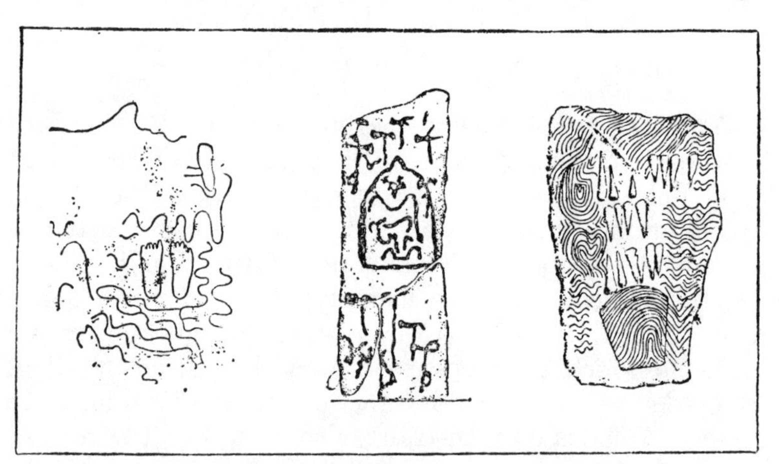

(See two feet, page 220.)

Fig. 102.—From the Dolmens of Brittany—the two feet—there are also some Egyptian hieroglyphic figures, very distinct—Apt, twice repeated—Zodiacal West. Serpent Rerek—Meu. S. I. N., etc.; although *Professor Sergi* calls these Alphabetical Signs.

Reproduced from "The Mediterranean Race," by *Professor Sergi*, published by the Walter Scott Publishing Company Limited, to whom we are much indebted for this privilege.

in *Professor Sergi's* book (page 290, fig. 79), which he calls

"Alphabetiform signs," contain nearly all true Egyptian Hieroglyphics—badly written. We can decipher the whole of them, from the "Tank of Flame" to the "Ank Cross," the latter being identically the same as that found at Llantagloss. Speaking of fig. 93, which is a production of one of these carvings from Brittany (fig. 102 here) he states: "Here are found *human feet, primitive* axes and other designs, which must indicate implements or other objects of *unknown significance*." The same may be said regarding the carvings found on Swiss rocks, the date of which is undetermined, and is indeed difficult to determine. If *Professor Sergi* will read this work, he will find he can trace these all over the world, as we have done, and we have given the meaning and decipherment of the same—it will help him to arrive at a more definite conclusion that his opinion, stated in his Italian edition, was the correct one, and that anthropology must not be relied on solely, although a great factor to be duly taken into consideration. All these signs and symbols have *a definite meaning, and prove that there must have been a "common origin," and only in Egypt could that be.* The fact that these relate to their religious ceremonies is sufficient reason for one to understand that they are found universally—that the origin and date of the exodus of these people must have been about the same time, comparatively. Their religious ideas, signs and symbols would remain to them as the most sacred, and liable to less change than anything else.

In many instances we can approximately give the date that these people left Egypt by the decipherment of the hieroglyphic denoting the name of the god delineated on the stones and other objects. We cannot agree with *Professor Sergi's* opinion that Copper was first imported into Egypt from Cyprus, where he supposes it was first used, any more than we can that the cultured races originated from here in the Eastern Mediterranean basin, because in the tombs found at Naqada and Abydos many Copper instruments were found, showing that these ancient people were well versed in its use; and if we turn to the Cretan and Ægean writings and signs at this period, we find the Egyptian Ptah clearly depicted in the hieroglyphic for his name (fig. 83, p. 295, S.M.R.), *therefore these were brought forth from Egypt at or after the time of Ptah.*[1] Now Ptah did not exist, nor was he brought into

[1] See fig. 23, page 43 in this book.

being in Egypt until the time of the Solar Mythos—*i.e.* after the Stellar and Lunar Mythos. This would give therefore, approximately, the time that these people migrated from their Egyptian home and brought all they knew with them, very late in comparison to the first commencement of their Stellar Astro-Mythology, but probably fifteen or twenty thousand years ago, as we know that the Solar Mythos was in existence at that time from what has recently been discovered there. Neither can we agree with *Montelius*, who writes as follows:—" It is evident that the Mycenæn civilisation in Greece is due not only to an influence from another country but to the immigration of a new people. That this people—or at least the great majority of the immigrants—came from Asia Minor is proved by the important fact, which, however, has not been sufficiently noticed, that the Mycenæn tombs are the same kind as those common in Asia Minor. *The lions on the famous gate of Mycenæ and numerous objects point also in the direction of Asia Minor because similar remains have been discovered there that do not exist in Phœnicia or Egypt*" (italics are ours). *Montelius* has here made a statement which is absolutely incorrect. " The lions and numerous other objects " are purely Egyptian and nowhere else can we find the original. We have already shown that these not only exist there but also in the Central States of America (see plate 54, page 119), and we have explained in other parts of this work the interpretation and meaning of the same. Until *Montelius*, *Reinach* and other learned men have mastered the correct decipherment of the Axe—the double Axe—the lions—the tree, and the hieroglyphic names of the gods of the Egyptians found here and elsewhere throughout the world, and Symbols and Signs of their astronomical mythos — Stellar, Lunar and Solar — they will never be able to correctly interpret the various problems that come before them. " That the scenes found depicted on vases, walls and other objects, etc., are similar, if not identical, to those found in Nineveh and Babylon " is not evidence that the origin was from there, because the same are found, as we have shown, in Central America and various other parts of the world, and only through Egyptian wisdom can we i terpret their meaning.

In writing on this most important subject the aforementioned and other Archæologists are apt to treat as facts what they merely imagine to be true and to base their arguments on suppositions. Unless they are in possession of the "Alphabet," here plainly portrayed, and the knowledge of the Wisdom of Ancient Egypt, their suppositions must be erroneous. The people of Nineveh and Babylon obtained their knowledge from the Egyptians, hence the similarity

We do not consider that the order in which *Professor Sergi* gives from *De Morgan* these Six Ivory Tablets is correct. The first and last are certainly earlier than the other four, and indicate that the Governors were then styled Lords or Princes or Conductors of the Land of the South. In the other four there is an Ideograph, indicating that they had reached another stage—*i.e.* Crowned Kings, which may be seen by the hieroglyphics on them. The reading of the two end tablets is Lord or Prince or Conductor of the Land of the South, who reigned, in one case, 97 years, and in the other, 85 years.

o Neb, Lord of, or Prince or Conductor of the Lands of the South or "Lord of the Nomes" would probably be the correct term found on these two tablets, and would indicate, in our opinion, that there must be five others, as from the *Ritual* we find that there were "Seven Lords of the Nomes" in the very earliest times, unless we look upon the four others as part of these, in which case there would be one missing. o would be equivalent to the later or more developed hieroglyphic Suten-Ra ⊙ but as Ra did not exist as Ra at this time, the dot was representative of Horus the first. It was the top of the triangle of their first or Stellar Trinity Horus Sut Shu Ra ⊙ circle with dot was brought on from these when the Solar Mythos took the place of the Stellar. We shall explain this later on.

Dr Wallis Budge, in "The Gods of the Egyptians," vol. i. p. 499, finds this triangle associated with many names of Horus, and ascribes the symbol to the god Sept or Set, and states that "up to the present no satisfactory explanation has been given of the object which is the symbol of the god Sept, but it appears to have been *some kind of triangle* (the italics are ours), a figure or model of it was preserved at Amen-Kheperutet, which is described in the Edfû list as [hieroglyphs] *i.e.* the hidden [hieroglyph] of Khas (?) en Sept." We think, if *Dr Budge* will read what we have written, he may find a little light on this point. It was the sacred triangle, as we have stated, and we will explain the meaning of "the hidden of Khas," but we must go back to the Stellar Mythos, and also study the primordial, since he will find no solution of his question by the Solar alone. Then he will find that at the time this earth was enveloped in a thick watery vapour—when the sun's rays could not penetrate through it, that Set or Sept was the "primary," and at the head or apex of the triangle. That is why this triangle [hieroglyph] stands as the symbol for his name; but when Horus I. fought him, and he was deposed, then [hieroglyph] became the Sacred Triangle, with Horus I. as the primary and "THE ONE." The symbol was then attached to and appropriated to the name of Horus I. Horus became the god of the Pole Star at the apex, and Sut was put at the bottom, South; *hidden in the hole of Sut*—thus the association it bears to the two names. Set having been first primary, it would remain as the symbol, or one of them, for his name, but as he was overcome by Horus in the fight between light and darkness, or sunk down out of sight as they came N., all was therefore subject to Horus, so it would become associated with Horus I., and then the dot ● or star ∗ was added in many cases to denote that he was god of the Pole Star, and it became the Sacred Triangle, with Shu at the Equinox. The ● was afterwards assigned to Ra in the centre of the circle ⊙, when the Mythos became Solar and Ra became the head of all—"THE ONE" in the Solar, as Horus was "THE ONE" in the Stellar.

The sign [sign] is the earliest form of [sign] or [sign] which are ligatures of [sign] and [sign] and is one way of writing the name of Amsu—the risen Horus.[1] This sign, we have shown before, is still found on the oldest boomerangs in Australia, and was recognised by the Pygmies in London as the sign of their Chief.

[1] We see from *Ritual*, chap. cxv., and elsewhere, that names were sometimes written without their phonetic value, probably this was the original custom before the time of Menes.

THE GODDESS MESKHENET.

An early type of Isis as the Goddess of Birth with the two feathers Maat.

In the seventeenth chapter of the *Ritual* we find as follows :—"I am Amsu in his manifestations, here have been given to me Two Feathers upon my head." These equal the Urei upon the forehead of Tmu, although later texts ascribe the Two Feathers to Isis and Nepthys, or as two kites.[1] In the recently unearthed Amen-Ra at Karmah, Amen-Ra is represented with Two Feathers. Here Amen-Ra and Tmu would be the same identical god under different names, and the Two Feathers would represent the two lives—Earthly and Spiritual.

As we know the Kings of Egypt took divine titles, it is more than probable that here we have in the beginning the first kings styling themselves Amsu or Horus, more probably Horus. Amsu is another name for Horus—he is the risen Horus. We find that Usertsem II. had a Horus name, as may be seen inscribed upon his "Serekh." This displayed their names as the descendants of Horus I. and gave them their Horus name. This seems reasonable, because they were undoubtedly in the Stellar or first Mythos, and Horus was at the "Pole" or Mount of Heaven, and Sut Horus Shu it is here that the *Ritual* will considerably help us to understand the latest discoveries of *Professor Petrie* and *De Morgan*. This sign indicates that now they had adopted a so-called "Crowned" King and definite name, and the crown was of this form . This was the earliest form worn by the ancient Egyptians, long before the two feathers and Atef crown came into existence. We shall have more to say about it, because it is significant that it is the same shape as that used by the Aboriginal Australians in their Totemic Ceremonies, which we have previously shown were identical with those of Egypt. This Crown is also the same form as that depicted in the PAPYRUS OF ANI, after his Spirit has been justified and united with his Soul and presented to Osiris when his hair had been made white and a Totem or Crown had been placed on his head. This will be of some assistance, as it shows that the *Alcheringers* of the Australians left Egypt about this period. All their Totemic Ceremonies correspond with those in use in Egypt at this time, before the Egyptians had made further progress in their Mythology or

[1] This plate of the Goddess Meskhenet showing the two feathers is reproduced from *Dr E. A. Wallis Budge's* "The Gods of the Egyptians," published by Messrs Methuen & Co. We are much indebted to these gentlemen for their kind permission to reproduce this beautiful plate.

Eschatology. It also proves that there was an exodus at the earlier part of their Stellar Mythos, and another at a later period, when they had further progressed, as seen by the remains we find in Central America.

The shape of the skulls of the Aboriginal Australians and Ainu correspond with the Nilotic Negroes found in N.E. Africa. The mean internal capacity of the Australians measures 81·9; Nilotic Negro, 80 cubic inches; Europeans, 92·3; Americans, 87·5; Asiatics, 87·1; which proves to us what progressive education will achieve in the development of brain cells and tissues, etc. We are unable to state if the Mayas do or do not correspond, as we have no data to assist us, although, from the photographs taken by *Le Plongeon*, some at least appear the same. *Professor Sergi* has shown that the skulls of the Druids and Welsh were undoubtedly the same, although he gives a wider latitude for the Egyptians than Egypt and the valleys of the Nile, and calls them Aboriginal Libyans; but to our minds his arguments and researches would apply better if he had confined himself to the original inhabitants of Egypt and the Nile valleys, as his first opinion was. *Professor Retzine* ("Smithsonian Report," 1859) says: "With regard to the primitive dolichocephalæ of America, I entertain an hypothesis still more bold, namely, that they are nearly related to the Guenches, in the Canary Islands, and to the Atlantic population of Africa, the Moors, Twarscks, Copts, etc., and which *Latham* comprises under the name of Egyptian Atlantida." We find one and the same form of skull in the Canary Islands, in front of the African coast, and in the Carib Islands, on the opposite coast, which faces Africa. The colour of the skin in each case is of a reddish-brown. *Evans* would also be right if he would understand the term he uses—proto-Egyptian—for these, the originals.

We fail to see the arguments of *De Morgan* and others, trying to show the importation from Asia. To us there is no proof on any point for their conclusions, but there is every proof that these people were the oldest, and that from here Asia and the rest of the world obtained their original learning. The arguments, as well as the comparison, show most clearly their relation, and cannot be separated or distinguished by their writings alone. This must depend on other facts also. For instance we find in Naqada and Abydos undoubted proof of a Neolithic age with writings of a very distinct character, and also remains of a Paleolithic age that existed ages before the Neolithic age. This, with many other points, shows that this was the first, or rather the one, progressive centre of the earlier inhabitants of this world. The whole anatomical remains that we can discover are also conclusive on this point. The skulls of Neolithic man, found at Harlyn Bay, in Cornwall, correspond to those of the earlier Egyptians brought forward by *Professor Sergi*, and those of Wales correspond with the Dakote and North American Indians, therefore, with the Egyptians.

It would be useless to bring forward any argument whatever for the entire civilisation of historical Egypt without taking into consideration the fact of pre-existing indigenous inhabitants, which must now be admitted as proved.

The Aboriginal Australian Alcheringa ceremonies are probably the truest copy we have in existence of the Totemic Ceremonies of the ancient Egyptians at the time of the *earliest* Neolithic age, as, up to the present date, those of the Nilotic Negroes and others surrounding them, from whence these Aboriginal Australians came, have not been studied sufficiently to say how much still remains here at the present day. Of the forms and ceremonies of these very ancient people we have not much to guide us except the *Ritual*, their " rude marks " and the fact of dismemberment at the time of burial. This dismemberment would be indicative of the dismemberment of Osiris or Horus the first, and would be practised during the early times of these people, later than the Paleolithic Age. We are led to believe that they had worked out their Stellar Mythos from the fact of the ceremonies of the Alcheringa of the Aboriginal Australians, as well as from the shape of the Crown or Totem ; all of which is plainly shown in " The Book of the Dead." *De Morgan's* attempt to show, by the aid of Anthropology, that this prehistoric people were different from the historical Egyptians (whom he wishes to prove came from Asia) is bad logic, because if he only argued from his own great discoveries and the records of the past he found, he could only form but one conclusion, which must be that these Neolithic people were descended from an earlier race—*i.e.* the Paleolithic, remains of which have been found here ; and furthermore, the objects he found show that they were a progressive people. *Wiedemann's* argument that because their burial customs were different therefore they must be a different race, will not, we think, be borne out by anyone who studies the question seriously.

But, on the contrary, we find that these old Neolithic people had, in fact, already commenced in a primitive way to embalm their dead or in some way to preserve them. This is plainly shown by *Fouquet* in his craniological examinations. He states that there exist, in the skulls of the rude stone epoch in Egypt, deposits of bitumen mixed with cerebel substance, and this bitumen could not have been introduced by the nasal passages, the brain not having been removed, but only through the occipital foramen after the head had been cut off, and *Professor Petrie* tells us that this custom of cutting off the heads was common.[1] We see this dismemberment also amongst the remains of those found at Harlyn Bay, Cornwall.

But a still earlier form was that of anointing with Red Ochre, this being probably the first substance employed for preserving the bones of the dead and sacred emblems, which were exhumed periodically, scraped and reanointed. This is still practised amongst the Aboriginal Australians, Maori and other native tribes, and, as may be seen from the human bones in the British mounds of Caithness, it was the custom in these isles at the time of the later Paleolithic Age.

The form of burial in use at present amongst the Australian Aborigines and the Ancient Mayas is also the same as we find in the Neolithic Age—"The Thrice-bent Man." This form of burial was probably the one adopted by all people of the late Paleolithic and Neolithic Ages, and is still practised by many tribes in Africa and Australia. We also find that it was the custom in Yucatan at an advanced period of civilisation, as may be seen from the carvings over some of the tombs, one of which is very distinct. The inscription reads thus: "The Thrice-bent Man." The Altar welcomes the crushed body, lying face downward, of the man from Uxmal. This in Maya is: "Ta ox uuɔ u Tem Kam uuc noocal Oxmal."

[1] In *Ritual*, chap. clxvi., it states: "Thou art Horus, the son of Hathor, the flame born of a flame, to whom his head has been restored after it had been cut off. Thy head will never be taken from thee henceforth. Thy head will never be carried away." This shows and proves that the custom originated during Stellar Mythos.

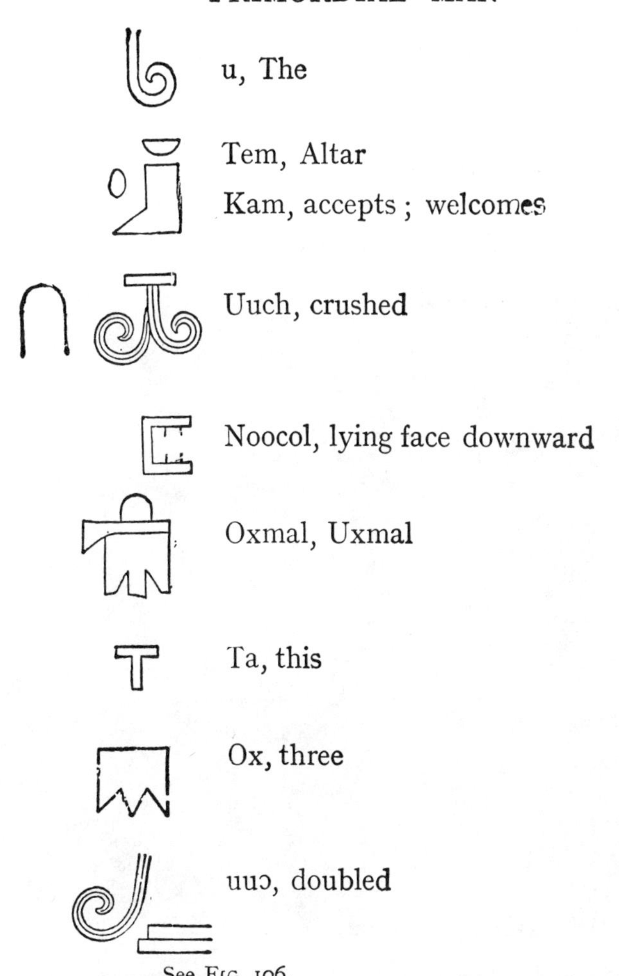

See Fig. 106.

"The Thrice-bent Man"—that is, the thighs bent up on the body and the legs again bent on the thighs. In Cornwall also, at Harlyn Bay, there have recently been discovered early Neolithic remains in this position—*i.e.* "the Thrice-bent Man," and those in the Round Cist show that this is the earliest form of burial that we find practised by the human race all over the world—*i.e.* a round hole and the body as a "Thrice-bent Man" placed in it. In an ancient graveyard, 6 acres in extent, found in Tennessee, from 75,000 to 100,000 were found buried in this form—round cists with thrice-bent position. From the length of bones it was estimated that these people were about 4 ft. high.

We must add that *Mr Walter E. Roth* mentions in his book,

"Ethnological Studies Among the North-West Central Queensland Aborigines," 1897, that the mode of burial is recumbent, but that the face is always towards the North, although the practice is dying out where they have been much in contact with the whites. They could not give him any reason for this except that it had always been so from the time of their ancestors. The meaning of course is that they came out from the original land at

FIG. 103.—Skeleton in Cist : Characteristic Position.
Reproduced by kind permission of *Mr Reddie Mallett.* Found at Harlyn Bay, Cornwall.

the time of the practice of the Stellar Mythos, over 20,000 years ago certain—after the recent discoveries at Abydos perhaps more than 100,000.

The fact that these were buried facing North—*i.e.* facing the Pole Star and with a triangular stone placed over them with the apex pointing to the Pole Star—would, in our opinion, be an indication that they or their ancestors came out of Egypt at the time of the practice and belief in the Stellar Mythos, and that these people practised the rites and ceremonies, and had their beliefs in the same, and that they are of a much older date than the Druids. The Egyptians, at the time that they sent out the colonies of these people, had not yet evolved the Solar Mythos,

FIG. 104.—Cist and Skeleton in Situ.

Reproduced by kind permission of *Mr Reddie Mallett.* Found at Harlyn Bay, Cornwall.

which they had done at the time that the Druids left Egypt. Thus Egypt, ever progressive, and losing nothing, certainly brought the triangle on into the Solar Mythos, and then the Eschatology after ; but with these early people the triangle represented the first or Stellar Mythology, with Sut, Shu and Horus the first as the primary trinity.[1]

Therefore, taking into consideration what *De Morgan* and *M. M. Amelineau* found at El-Amrah—*i.e.* a number of oval graves sunk in the stony soil to a depth varying from five to six feet, wherein were the skeletons of human bodies lying upon their sides, face to the North, hands crossed before their faces, and knees bent up on the body upon a level with the chest, and with them were buried flints, small bronze implements, pottery, stone

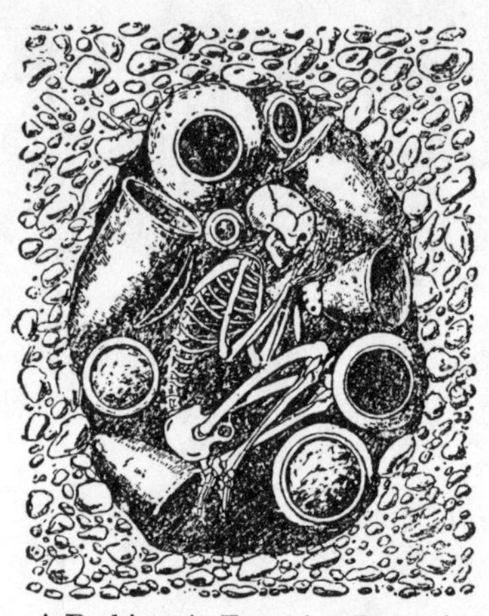

FIG. 105.—A Prehistoric Egyptian Tomb (*De Morgan*).

Reproduced from "The Mediterranean Race," by *Professor Sergi*; published by the Walter Scott Publishing Company Limited, to whom we are much indebted for this privilege.

vases, shell ornaments, etc.—the mode of burial practised by the Makalanga, natives of New Guinea, Solomon Islanders, and natives of Australia at the present day, and many other native tribes still extant, and then, at the time of the first of the fourth dynasty, we find the body laid upon its back as at present with us, and arms laid on the body, we must come to the conclusion that:—

1st. At the earliest date of Paleolithic man we have no record of any burial ground, but from the knowledge of the customs still in practice amongst the Pygmies, it is probable that they buried their dead as the present Pygmies do, either where they died or in burial grounds, where they placed them under about a foot of earth and leaves, on their sides, in a "bent-up" position.

[1] At Chichen Itza all the principal figures (Priests) wear on the forehead a headband with a triangular plate of turquoise mosaic—the zinh-intzolli of the old Mexican Kings.

2nd. At a late Paleolithic, and all through the Neolithic age, they had recognised "burial places," and buried their dead either in a 'hole" or "cist," in the "thrice-bent" position, or on the side, with face to the North, which was the custom all through the time of the Stellar Mythos and early part of the Solar.

3rd. During the Solar Mythos, dating from the third and fourth dynasty, the body was laid on its back, flat, as at present

FIG. 106.
From "Queen Moo," by *Dr Le Plongeon*. By his kind permission. Found at Uxmal, Yucatan.

with us. This we find throughout all the world, wherever remains have been found, not taking into account what may be termed "accidents" or cremation, which came into use "later."

(Mention is also made of a find of spindle-whorls in Harlyn Bay, but nothing is said about any markings, etc. It would be interesting to know if the "Swastika" mark was found here, but one of the most interesting points about this find of prehistoric things is that there is evidence of a long occupancy of this district by Neolithic man. The Swastika is found frequently on Stones in Devonshire, and a good specimen is in the Museum at Torquay.)

That this "thrice-bent" position form of burial was the common practice amongst the early races of man will not admit of any doubt, and that it had sprung from one original, and was taken from the knowledge of the position of the *fœtus in utero* ; they believed that the spirit entered the body of the child in this position, and when the body died it was placed in the same position for the spirit, until it left again. The burial customs, rites, and ceremonies, one and all, from the remotest times, were founded in the faith that the departed still lived in the spirit ; in the earliest mode of interment known the dead were buried for rebirth. The corpse was bound up—the "thrice-bent position"—in the fœtal likeness of the embryo in utero, and placed in the earth as in the mother's womb ; it did not denote a resurrection of the body, but was symbolical of rebirth in spirit ; not only were the dead elaborately prepared for the spiritual rebirth, but many symbols of reproduction and resurrection were likewise buried in the tomb, as amulets and fetish figures of a protecting power.

What then does this indicate ? Undoubtedly that here we have a progressive people ; and this custom, like the hieroglyphic language, was simply the beginning of that higher and more perfect state that we find in both—that is, the one brought to perfection in embalming ; the other—those artistic hieroglyphic writings—which perhaps took many centuries from the time they commenced to record their "rude marks" and "crude embalmings" to the time those Egyptians whom we now know so well excelled in a perfect Eschatology.

We have no doubt that some parts of the "Ritual or Book of the Dead" have been worked out and carried on, orally at least—if not written anywhere—for ages, and this, it appears to us, was the time of the first Horus and the Stellar Mythos.

Fishes, crocodiles, lotus sprays, birds, etc., were the original hieroglyphics, and were of an indigenous Paleolithic or Neolithic origin, and also the means first used to express ideas. Before the language of speech was developed to express thoughts and wishes orally, the early man could only do so by means of rude drawings of what he saw, and thus convey the meaning required. These drawings had been improved upon for centuries, and at the time of Abydos we find sufficient progress had been made in the art of writing to add linear signs to these originals. Other types followed. *Sir Harry Johnston* states that the Pygmy is very apt and quick at drawing, and with a reed or piece of stick will mark on the ground a figure or sign to convey his meaning, having no words to represent what he wishes one to understand ; and which we proved to be a fact.

CHAPTER XIII

At Abydos, *Professor Petrie* has been excavating and found remains, well preserved, of ancient cities, which he dates at least 15,000 B.C., and which show clearly that the people practised the Osirian religion at that time in its full forms and ceremonies. This is the so-called birthplace of the Osirian religion, which came after the doctrines of Amen-Ra, practically the same, developed under different names, and before this there was the Stellar Mythos of Horus: thus we see how old this country is.

Although writers on this subject have used the term Neolithic (age of polished stone instruments), but are silent about the Paleolithic (unpolished), which preceded that by centuries, and which we know existed by the implements found here, later discoveries will no doubt assist us in connecting the limits of the Paleolithic age with the Neolithic, although, of course, the one gradually overlapped the other, as in all other higher developments of evolution.

The remains in the immense tomb, discovered by *Professor Petrie*, prove that these very ancient people lived here, and by their "rude marks" it is seen that they had made considerable progress in their evolution, and that they certainly may have existed here long before the last glacial epoch, when every place was frozen and uninhabitable, from the North Pole to 53° or 56° latitude—(South of France). The conclusion he arrives at by summarising the characters of these ancient people and comparing them with those of the Egyptians of the time of Pharaoh, shows how much progress these latter had made by working out their own evolution. Their civilisation was anterior to that of the Pharaohs in its definite and well-known form, and the whole of the arguments brought forward by *Petrie, De Morgan and Wiedemann* really furnish the proofs that these were all one people of African origin, and that time and evolution had worked the different advancements we find amongst the Pharaohs.

The writings found amongst the Aborigines of Australia, the

Mayas, and the people of the Canaries, the Druids and Cretans, and others, show a similarity, and must have had one common origin. In Egypt we find the key. The earlier Egyptian characters were primarily identical with these, as may be seen by comparison, and craniology must be taken as one of the proofs which cannot be left out of consideration: taking all, therefore, it is quite conclusive.

If we study the Seven Tablets of Creation, which are written in cuneiform, and contain the views and beliefs of the Assyrians as to the origin of the gods, and of the world, and of mankind, and then compare these gods with those of Egypt, there is but one conclusion to arrive at—they were all of them copied from the Egyptians. Their Apzû-rishtu and Mummu-Tiamat are the exact equivalents in the Babylonian cosmogony of Nu and Nut in the Egyptian, and so on throughout them all, not all direct; some were borrowed from the Sumerian,[1] but these were obtained from Egypt, and no one can show any proof to the contrary. The Syrian god Bar-a-Pa-Bar was identical with Sut[2] of the Egyptians and Baal of the Hebrews. In whatever form or under whatever name we study the origin and trace back the religious beliefs, origin of words and symbolisms of the people of Asia, we can only arrive at the conclusion that they came out of Egypt. Some of the earliest, as the Ainus, have the totemic ceremonies, and others, Buddhists, Chinese, Persians of the Stellar and Solar Mythos. Even the present writing of the Chinese and Japanese are only the old Egyptian Hieroglyphics with linear signs added. It was by them that Babylonia and Asia were colonised and fertilised with Egyptian culture, and it is thus only that the correspondence between Babylonian and Asiatic knowledge and institutions became intelligible. The pictorial writings forming the basis of the cuneiform and Chinese characters is unmistakably only a species of the hieroglyphics; their astronomy is only a copy of that of Egypt. The Babylonian unit of measure—that is, the royal or architectural ell of 0·525—is completely identical with that of Egypt, which we find described on the walls up to the fourth millennium, B.C. Its temples and its pyramids and obelisks are an imperfect imitation of Egyptian originals, and so

[1] Cuneiform Text from the Babylonian Tablets in the British Museum.

[2] Ueueteotl was the Mexican name of the old god who existed in the period of twilight, when as yet no sun illuminated the world. This is identical with Sut of the Egyptians, and Ometecutli Omeciuath = "The Lords of duality"—*i.e.* Horus and Sut, as brothers, represented as the deities dominating the beginning.

with the other arts. At every step one meets with traces of the Egyptian models.

Dr Budge, in speaking of the Assyrian and Babylonian cuneiform texts, states that "these must be of Sumerian origin and must have been formulated in remote antiquity," and he is surprised to find so much similarity existing between the primeval gods of Sumar and those of the Egyptians, and he adds, "especially as the resemblance cannot be the result of borrowing," and that "it is out of the question to assume that Ashur-bani-pal's editors borrowed the system from Egypt"; but that is just what they did do, and we cannot agree with *Dr Budge* in his conclusions more than we can with those who have stated that all t e aborig nes of the world who have the same Egyptian hieroglyphics, the same Totemic ceremonies, the same signs and symbols, and many words which are of Egyptian origin, the same ideas of life and birth, regeneration, and of the life to come, the same as we find amongst the earliest Nilotic Negroes at the earliest Stellar age, that all evolved them separately and from their own surroundings. The recent discoveries will prove that the above statement is the correct one, and that the primeval gods of Sumar were taken from the Egyptians, the same as the laws of Hammurabi, some of which Moses made use of when he left Egypt, and had been in use for thousands of years, and that the Jews are wrong in supposing that these "laws of Moses" were invented and promulgated "as original," and for their own special benefit, and given by God direct to Moses for them, because, the fact that these laws existed for ages before proves the contrary, and however much it shocks them, it is impossible to gainsay the fact that they did exist, because we have the STALÆ OF HAMMURABI, which dates ages before Moses lived.

Also the discovery of the hieroglyphic "Khui land" and "Zodiacal West," Land of the Scorpion, amongst the Druids and Central American and West African negroes, and on the Australian Boomerang, must be evidence that cannot well be contested, and undoubtedly shows that at a very early period man began to learn in the land of his birth (Egypt) and emigrated into other countries, taking with him all the knowledge he then possessed.

Professor A. H. Sayce, in the "Proceedings of the Society of Biblical Archæology," writing on *De Morgan's* work, states that he has long been interested *in the sealed cylinders of "Babylonian type which have been brought from time to time from Upper Egypt"*

—at the end of the article he says "In the Green Stone." We thus have probably a monument of the conquest of Upper Egypt by the Pharaohnic Egyptians, and the establishment there of a monarchy of kings whom later history knew as the Hor-Shesu or followers of Horus. Why does not *Professor Sayce* put this down as records of the past, distinctly and clearly prove that here, in Upper Egypt, were the originals, and that the Babylonians and others only copied them and that that is the reason why he finds them in Babylon? He has to acknowledge the fact that "We detect upon it the Egyptian hieroglyphics in the process as it were of formation, and can form some idea of the long development that was needed before they became the characters that were used by Menes and his successor." Yes, quite so, and if he and others would only drop Babylon as the original, and could see that from all evidence, both positive and negative, we have it clearly shown that here, in Upper Egypt, we have the remains, first of an age of Paleolithic man, followed by Neolithic, a progressive knowledge and civilisation being evolved before Meni and other dynasties, which are now comparatively well known, continuing until that high state of culture was arrived at, the remains of which undeniably still exist, proves their errors and that our contention is right. We should then obtain definite knowledge of the past. The Babylonians and others of Asia copied and obtained their knowledge from these Egyptians, and that is the reason why we find them there.

In the "Proceedings of the Society of Biblical Archæology" (vol. xxii., 30th Session), *Professor A. H. Sayce* gives a head-dress of a human or divine figure, and a part of one of the shells which are frequently met with in prehistoric graves of Egypt. This is very important, and bears out the above in a lucid manner, showing the evolution that was then taking place, because it was further advanced and certainly later than the above. The name of the King is here given in a cartouche. This is what *Professor Sayce* says:—"The head-dress is of black stone with a perforation for attaching it to the head of a figure; at the back it is inlaid with an arc of ivory, under which lines are drawn to represent hair. On the front is an inscription, exceedingly well engraved, which is given as No. 1 in the plate. The greater part of the same inscription is repeated on the shell (No. 2 in the plate), where, however, the mace and hawk are rudely drawn. The King, whose cartouche is thus twice repeated, is new to

Egyptian history, as also are his titles the 'Horus-Hawk' and 'the Mace.' He is not even 'King of Upper Egypt.' But the cartouche itself, of which this is the earliest example, in no way differs in form from that of later times, and so throws no light on the origin of the hieroglyph. Underneath the hawk the character intended must be the diadem khâ and not the cake **t**. To the left of the mace, which, it must be observed, has the prehistoric shape, we have the Uraeus. The Diadem and the Uraeus are omitted on the shell. How the name of King S was pronounced it is impossible to say."

We have already given the answer—*i.e.* (?) Horus I. or Amsu name, another link connecting their progressive evolution from the Neolithic age to that of Meni. On Cylinder, No. 4, *Professor Sayce* says "the Hieroglyphics read 'Nekhet-Khen (?)—s—the governor of the two lands, a title not met with elsewhere.'" Then we have the name and picture of a dog, Unsh (u) and of another animal, perhaps the Ichneumon, called the Zenef. As we have pointed out before, "the *Ritual*" helps us—the "Lords of the Nomes" were the "Lords of the Two Lands," and here we have a definite fact in this form on an ancient seal that these existed, which assists the reader of "the *Ritual*" to understand more clearly how accurately and faithfully these ancient people recorded everything, and clears up the true meaning, definitely, of various points of argument of many able writers and observers who have held different opinions on the subject. *Professor Sayce* has evidently overlooked the fact that the earliest kings took the name of Horus, and that the Horus-Hawk and the Mace were the symbols of the same. The proof of this is seen in the "Serkh of Usertsem II.": also in the "Serkh of Rameses II." we find there is an inscription of the Horus name of this king—viz. Ka-Neckht-Meri-Maat, and in the "Text of Unas" the meaning of Ashem and Ashemu, etc., is undoubtedly Hawk of Hawk—the Great Hawk of the Hawks—and means Amsu, the risen Horus. We have no doubt if *Professor Sayce* will refresh his memory by looking at the above-named Papyri, he will have no trouble in finding that it is not a new name, but the oldest, and existed long before the "Dynastic Kings," and here is that which proves it, but which he has failed to decipher, or overlooked.

It is not difficult to trace and follow the primordial if one will take a little trouble and see how Horus I. was brought on from the Stellar to the Lunar and then merged into the Solar. In the city of Tchert, "Menthu" was worshipped under the form of a man, with the head of a bull, but instead of the Solar disk he wears on his head the "Lunar" crescent and disk. This is Horus brought on in their Lunar Mythos and shows one of the connecting links—when the Lunar was merging into the Solar he was given the name of "Menthu-Ra."

FIG. 107.[1]

The Priests added Ra after Menthu. That it is Horus I. is proved by the pictures reproduced by *Lanzoni*, where he is represented standing upright, with the "head of a hawk," and he holds in his right hand "*an ear of corn*." Another name for Horus during the Lunar Mythos was Khensu-Tehute —the twice great, the Lord of Khemennu, and as Khensu-Pa-Khart was Khensu the Babe, and Khensu-Hunnu—*i.e.* Khensu the Child. This was brought on into the Solar Mythology as Horus the Child, son of Isis. The *Ritual* states: "Khensu-Pa-Khart caused to shine upon the earth the beautiful light of the Crescent Moon, and through his agency women conceived, cattle became fertile, the germ of the egg grew, and all nostrils and throats were filled with fresh air." He was also called "the messenger" of the Great One and Lord of Maat, like Ptah: also Great God, Lord of Heaven, etc. The forms in which Khensu is depicted on the monuments varies, but, whether standing or seated on a throne, he has usually the body of a man, *the head of a hawk*, and wears on his head a *Lunar Disk in a Crescent, or the Solar Disk with a uraeus, or the Solar Disk with the plumes and uraeus.* As Khensu nefer-hetep, he appears on the Stele of Pai in the form of a mummied man, seated on a throne. Over his head is the uraeus of royalty, and by the side of his head is the Lock of Horus or the

[1] Serkh of Rameses II., on which is inscribed the Horus name of the King—*i.e.* Ka-Nekht-Meri-Maat.

Lock of Youth ; in his hands the Flail, the Crook, a Tatt and the Sceptre, and wears the crown of the two feathers .

The Priests of Heliopolis had brought on the Lunar and Stellar doctrines with whatever there was of the Solar from Henen-Su, and although their doctrines had changed now from Stellar and Lunar into Solar, they still attached the Horus name to the Kings, as the descendant or servant of Horus, and it was not until User-Ka-f, the first King of the fifth dynasty, that the Horus name, showing that he was a descendant or servant of Horus, was omitted. This man substituted the title of "Son of the Sun" in its place for the Egyptian Kings, which was adopted by every King of Egypt afterwards.

It was the legend set abroad by the Priests of the first King of the fifth dynasty that Ra took upon him the form of the King and visited the Queen's chamber, and became the actual father of the Child, which is parallel with the Christian "Immaculate Conception."

A study of Khensu is important, because it gives the key to how these old Egyptians merged the Stellar into the Lunar and the Lunar into the Solar Mythology. This is one of the great connecting links which must be studied if one wishes to know and understand how they brought on all the first Trinity in the Stellar Mythos and added to it in the Lunar and Solar doctrines. Volumes might be written on this subject, but we feel that what we have brought forward is enough for this work, both for Freemasonry and the Christian doctrines. At the same time we must not lose sight of the fact that although various and many names were given him, and various and different attributes attached to each different name, it was the one and the same god, from the time we first recognise him as Horus I. and Amsu, to Osiris and Ra. We dissent from *Dr Brugsch* when he says : "The two Bulls, mentioned in the texts of the late period, are Osiris and Khensu, and they represent the Sun and the Moon." *If he means by this that they were different*, we contend that Khensu was Horus I. brought on from the Stellar, and was now Lunar, and Osiris was the same, brought on in the Solar doctrines. This applies also to Khnemu, the first member of the great triad at Abu. Although he is represented in various forms—in one example, quoted by *Lanzoni*, he has *the head of a hawk*—Stellar Horus I.[1]

It was probably at Henen-su that the doctrines of Solar

[1] Khnemu, or Her-Shefi of "The Book of the Dead," means "he who is on his lake" or "he who is on his island."

Mythos, in place of the Lunar, were first established. It was undoubtedly much older than Heliopolis. The head-dress here of the goddess Anqiet, who was associated with Khnemu, shows an original type, much older than those we find at the latter, and one that must have taken its origin with that of the God Bes. Sati, it must be noted also, wears only the crown of the South. We are of opinion that these were taken from the Pygmies, who dwelt at the sources of the lakes and around, at the head of the Nile (" Pygmies of the Two Caves "—see Pygmies). The Island of the Double Cave must be referred to here, and not at the first Cataract, as is *Dr Budge's* opinion. We must remember that the Nile was the typical representation in the terrestrial of the " Milky Way " in the celestial, and also that the ancient Egyptians knew quite well that the Nile came from and took its origin from the Lakes, and that the gods of the Nile here would represent types of the gods of the Milky Way celestially.

In the seventeenth chapter of the *Ritual* it says: " I am purified at the two great and mighty lakes at Sutenhunen," and " these were approached by the road that leads to the Land of the Spirits." " Eternity is the name of one and the Great Green One that of the other." These were, of course, celestial, but what the Egyptians mapped out celestially they depicted terrestrially, and therefore it is only reasonable to assume that they knew the two great lakes were the sources of the Nile, and were the representation of the above: also that the Land of the Spirits was situated on the islands of these lakes at the source of the Nile—the Khui Land.[1]

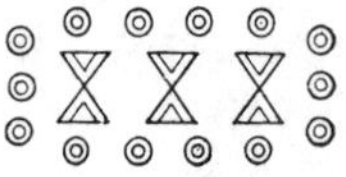

In the seventeenth chapter of the *Ritual* we find the names of the two lakes:—" Endless Time and Eternity "—Endless Time is Day, Eternity is Night—spiritually applied. It is interesting to note that on this point the Zapotecs, Mexicans and Mayas had also their " deep and exclusive cave " on an island in a lake, as may be seen from *Fathers Juan de Cordova* and *Bungoa*'s works. They state that in the neighbourhood of Theuantepec, upon an island in a lake, was a deep and extensive cave, strictly guarded, where the Zapotecs had one of their most important and most reverent

[1] This is proved because one is salt water and the other fresh water. The Albert Nyanza is a salt-water lake, and would therefore represent a primitive lake for purifying, healing, etc., and in the *Ritual* we find one is salt and one fresh water. *Sir Le Page Renouf* in his translation, *Ritual*, p. 251, supposes that the Ancient Egyptians placed the source of the Nile in the neighbourhood of Elaphantine—the Cavern of the Double Well of Elaphantine—but it was not so, it was the two Great Lakes of Inner Africa, as we have elsewhere stated.

deities, which they called "Soul and Heart of the Kingdom,[1] because these barbarians were persuaded that this fabulous deity was Atlas,[2] upon whom the land rested and who bore it on his shoulders, and when he moved his shoulders the earth was shaken with unwonted tremblings, and from his favour came the victories which they won, and the fruitful years which yielded them the

FIG. 108.—Symbols and Figures of Deities, from MEXICAN CODICES.

An-her "Lifting up the Heavens," forming the double Horizon of East and West.

From "Mexican Antiquities," published by the Bureau of Ethnology, Smithsonian Institution.

On Right—The Double Holy House of Anup, with the ten ○ of Heaven (divisions).

On Left—The representative of the Sun with nine ○ ; representation of the nine circles of Heaven, or the Put-Cycle of Ptah.

To the left of the House of Anup—The Heavens portrayed in two divisions, North and South, with "The One" ◎ as God of the Pole Star—*i.e.* Horus ; "The All-seeing One," with Emblems of Royalty.

means of living." This is the version and explanation given by the "Christian Fathers," who did not know anything about their Eschatology, probably more ignorant than the "barbarians," certainly more so than their Priests and Holy men. There was an oracle, connected also with this temple, but when *Fray Bernardo de Santa Maria* sought out the island and forced his way into the cave, he found there a large quadrangular chamber, carefully swept, with altarlike structures, and on them many incense vessels and necklaces of gold ; *but he found no Idol.* At Yucatan

[1] Alma Coragon del Reyno.

[2] Atlas was Shu-Anhur, the lifter up of the heavens when the double Horizon of Horus, East and West, was first formed in the Stellar Mythos and became the arbitrator of Sut and Horus as to the domains of each—*i.e.* Horus to the North, Sut to the South. Shu-Anhur was a duality. As Shu he lifted up the "Celestial Sky," as Anhur he lifted up the "Sky of Amenta," and was not an earth god, as *Maspero* supposes.

there was also a sanctuary, consisting of a great cave, etc., of a similar kind. The meaning and decipherment of these, which are known to all of the 30°, are set forth in the *Ritual* of Egypt, and were taken from the "Islands and Double Cave" of the Egyptians. In "Mexican Antiquities," page 307, published by the "Smithsonian Institute," there is a fine representation of Shu lifting up the heavens, and the formation of the Double Holy House of Anup or Heaven to the right, with ten great circles (see "Book of the Dead," Litany, chap. xviii.).

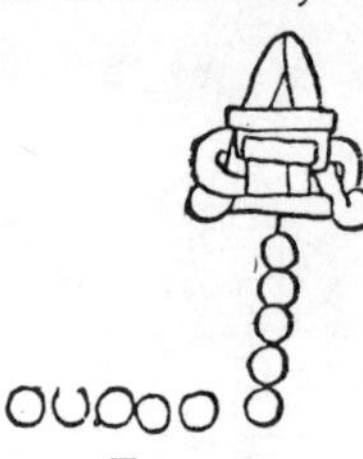

FIG. 109. Double Holy House of Anup.

Between the Double Holy House of Anup and Shu is seen the first symbolical division of heaven into two parts ○ ○ North and South, with the god of the Pole Star symbol above ◎ *i.e.* Horus I. and his royal symbols of power and might. On the left of Shu is represented the first Solar god — Ptah, with his Put-cycle of nine divisions of the heavens. Shu is here portrayed as lifting up the heavens and forming the double horizon — *i.e.* the heavens in three divisions (as explained in another part of this work, forming the ▽ (Horus triangle). The heavens above Shu are represented by a canopy of twenty-six lights or stars, and the seven glorious ones, thirty-three, with the eight added, and THE ONE. An-Heru or Shu is also shown with a crown with nine o's on it — the Put-cycle of Ptah. The above shows how far these people had advanced, at least, in their Stellar and Solar Mythos of the Egyptian "Religion."

FIG. 110. — Ptah and Put-Cycle.

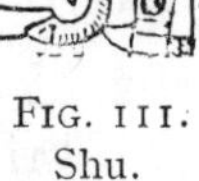

FIG. 111. Shu.

Shu-Anhur was the giver of the laws to man as revealed by Ra and is mentioned in the *Ritual* as the author of writings called "his rules or laws and his papyrus."

Shu is called An-Heru, the lifter up of the heavens

An-her, the lifter up of the heavens, was assigned (primarily) the place of the God of the Underworld, before Osiris. As he lifted up the heavens he would naturally be beneath them, and so was given the place of the god of the dead or mummified. "He was chief of the unseen land, the hidden

[1] Quetzalcoatl = the God of Wind, was one of the names of Shu here.

place,"[1] but afterwards, in the Solar doctrines, Osiris took his place.[2] We know that they commenced the entrance of the Tuat terrestrially (first division of the Tuat and first hour of the night) at the delta or mouth of the Nile, and that it ended in the "Island of the Double Cave." That was the island situated in the Great Lake, the source of the Nile—*Victoria Nyanza.* This was the "Khui Land," the exit of the twelfth division of the Tuat and the twelfth hour of the night. To reach this the boat *Sektit*, containing the mummy form of Osiris, in passing through the last division, entered the tail of a great serpent, *was drawn through its body* and came out at its mouth, and thus was born anew. He had passed the "border land and the bowels of the earth" and came forth in a spiritual form—regeneration had taken place. In chapter clxxxiii. it says: "I have given him to enter the mysterious cave, where is revived the heart of the god whose heart is motionless—Unneferu, the son of Nut the victorious" and "as he came forth in this celestial and spiritual form as Khepra" we see "the goddess Nut (Mut, the Great Mother), with hands stretched forth to receive him."[3] The "Island of the Double Cave" was one of the most sacred, if not the most sacred, sanctuary of these ancient people, both here in Egypt, as well as amongst the Central American natives, and was guarded more jealously than all the others—it was the place from whence their risen Lord had "ascended." "He descended" in "mummy form" at the commencement of the Tuat at the delta of the Nile and "he ascended" on the "Island of the Double Cave," at the source of the Nile, having passed through the twelve divisions of the Tuat and all the difficulties, dangers and darkness therein. One of the Mexican versions is that when Quetzalcoatl died his ashes immediately flew upwards and were metamorphosed into birds of all kinds, but the *heart* flew up to heaven and became the Morning Star—*i.e.* became "Lord of the Dawn," but for eight days before he went to heaven "he descended" into the underworld and wandered through this for four days, and for four days more he was "being born dead" or was transformed. Regeneration into Spiritual form took place, and he then emerged from the under-

[1] Old Text of "Coming Forth by Day."

[2] "Book of That which is in the Tuat" and "The Book of the Pylons."

[3] In the later text it gives Isis and Nephthysis waiting to receive Osiris or Shu regenerated as he came forth from the Cave—prototype of Christ issuing from the Tomb and being met by the two Marys.

world and "he ascended" the Throne as God—Horus I., called here Ce Acall and in their text is hieroglyphically depicted as the numeral one—*i.e. The One* (Horus I., God of the Pole Star)—*i.e.* the eighth, added to the Seven Glorious Ones, as we have shown elsewhere in this work. It was in the Double Cave or the "Mysterious Cave of the *Ritual* that the heart of the god, whose heart was motionless" was revived into Spiritual life and born anew, and that Citlalxonecuilli, the curved S-shaped constellation, shown in the text as 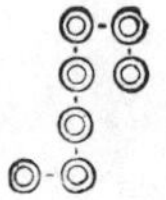 is the Little Bear—the Seven Glorious Ones, circling round THE ONE—the Pole Star—Horus I. The Lord of the Northern Lights and god of the Pole Star is the true decipherment of this text, and has nothing to do with the Southern Cross, as *Dr E. Seller* translates and deciphers it. *Dr Budge* is not correct, in our opinion, when he states, "As if *the dead body of Ra* passes into our world, etc."[1] It is not *the dead body of Ra*, it is *the mummified Osiris*, which passes through the twelve divisions of the Tuat, and emerges then in a *Spiritual form, after regeneration, as Ra the Spirit*. In some texts it is in the form of Khepra, which is an earlier type or form of Ra, and it is not to be wondered at when he says, "These two works represent two opposite and conflicting theories as to the future life."[2] If he mix the whole up, as one would suppose from reading his great work, to us the only conflicting theories would be in *Dr Budge's* mind, they are certainly not in either of the books, because the versions are very plainly set forth. We have given the translation of the oldest as Horus I., as the man God, and Amsu as the Spirit or risen Horus, and the latter was Osiris in mummified form, entering the Tuat and emerging in Spiritual form under the name of Ra. The one was Stellar and the other Solar Mythos. The semi-circular wall of thick darkness, which forms the end of the Tuat, and the division between it and "this world," as published by *Seignor Lanzone*, is the representation of the "Mysterious Cave" of *the Ritual*, where the soul, regenerated, emerges into the Spiritual world. The *Ritual* states: "The tunnels of the Earth have given me birth." The whole of the passages of the *Ritual*, referring to this, must be full of interest to the members of the 18° and all those up to the 33°. This is the prototype of the Christian doctrines, which are

[1] "Gods of the Egyptians," page 200.

[2] "Book of the Pylons" and "Book of That which is in the Tuat."

too well known to need repetition here. "The pylon of the twelfth division and twelfth hour is called Tesert-baiu—*i.e.* Red Souls, and the serpent God is Sebi, and its two guardians are Pai and Akhekhi, in Egyptian."

The Cave and those who guard the same, etc., etc., and other points connected with this, we must refer our readers of the 30° to the *Ritual*, which is directly associated with this subject; but we must guard the secrets from those who are not initiated and therefore not entitled to know them, although all the brotherhood may learn if they so desire.

FIG. 112.
From the MEXICAN CODEX. M. W. S. instructing I. how he "descended" and "ascended."

The text wherein it says that "*Osiris enters the tail of a great serpent, was drawn through its body and came out through its mouth, and was then born anew*" must be read and understood through Sign language. The Serpent was a sign and symbol of regeneration, the renewal of life, and therefore, in this case, of transformation from the mummy Osiris, to Amsu-Horus, and Ra, the Spirit.

In the Eschatology, Osiris represents, in Amenta, the dead man who was torn in fourteen pieces by the machinations of Sut. As a mummy he enters the Tuat in Amenta, and then he rises from the tomb in spiritual form as Amsu-Horus, who has burst the bonds asunder and is regenerated as the Sahu of Osiris; he was transfigured and transformed from the Osirian dead mummy, into the luminous body which still retained the mummy form—*i.e.* Amsu-Horus at his rising from the sepulchre.

Osiris, the hidden God in the earth of Amenta, does not come forth at all, except in the form of the risen Horus, who is the Manifestor for the ever hidden father.

To issue thus, he makes his transformation which constitutes the Mystery. The mummy, as Corpus, is transubstantiated into the Sahu. The Mortal Horus, by the descent and union of the Holy Spirit Ra into the Immortal, the physical mummy of the mortal Horus disappears instantly; the *Ritual* says: "He is renewed in an instant in his second birth" (chap. clxxxi.).

When Horus rent the veil of the Tabernacle or Temple, he became Hawk-headed, a spirit in the divine likeness of Ra, the Holy Ghost. Therefore the veil of the Tabernacle, or Temple here, would denote the body or mummy, "the veil of flesh" from which he had emerged. The *Ritual* (chap lxxi.) states: "I am the Hawk in the Tabernacle, and I pierce through the veil"—*i.e.* when he is invested with the soul of Horus, and disrobes himself of the mummy (or the veil which represents the flesh, as did the veil or bandages of gauze, which were folded round the mummy).

It is one of the Ten great Mysteries of Amenta, which were celebrated on ten different nights of the year.

1st. Was the night of the evening meal—the last supper and the laying of offerings on the altar—the night of provisioning the Lord's Table. Osiris had been overcome by Sut and the Sebau, and they had renewed their assault upon Un-Nefer, but were defeated and exterminated by the faithful followers; it was the night of the great battle, when the Moon God Taht, and the Children of Light, overcame and annihilated the Powers of Darkness.

2nd. Is "the night of hiding the body of him who is supreme in attributes." The mystery is that of collecting the mutilated and scattered body of Osiris, and of hiding it.

3rd. Is the Mystery of Anup, the Embalmer, the anointer of the mummy; this is Rusta, the place of resurrection from Amenta.

4th. Is in the region of Rekhet, and the Mystery is that of the two sisters, with Isis watching in tears over her brother Osiris, and brooding above the dead body to give it the warmth of life.

5th. On this night the overthrown Tat-Cross, with Osiris on it, was again erected by Horus—Prince of Sekhem, in the region of Tattu, when the Holy Spirit Ra descended upon the mummy, and the two became united for the resurrection.

6th. Here the scene is in Sekhem, where the Mystery is that of the blind Horus, or Horus in the dark, who here receives his sight, and it is also the Mystery of dawn upon the coffin of Osiris—the Mystery of Horus, the Mortal, transfiguring into Horus the Immortal.

7th. On the 7th night, the four Pillars are erected, with which the future Kingdom of God the Father is to be founded; it is called "the night of erecting the flag staff of Horus," and of establishing him as the heir to his father's "property."

8th. The Mystery of the 8th night, was that of the Great Judgment on the highway of the damned, when the suit was closed against the rebels, who had failed and were defeated—the verdict of the avengement.

9th. The great hoeing in Tattu, when the associates of Sut are massacred, and the fields are manured with the blood.

10th. On the 10th the glorious ones are judged, the evil dead are parted off, and joy goeth its round in Thinnis. It is the great festival night, named Ha-k-er-a, or "Come thou to me," in which the blending of the two souls is solemnised.

Amenta, the Earth of Eternity, is the Land of the Mysteries, where Taht, the Moon God, in the nether night, was the great Teacher of the Sacred Secrets, together with the seven wise Masters. The passage through Amenta is a series of initiations, for the Osiris deceased.

He is inducted into the Mysteries of Rusta (1, 7, 9).

The Mysteries of the Tuat (27, 130).

The Mysteries of Akar (2, 3, 148).

The Mysteries of Nekhen (1, 113).

Chapter clxii. contains the most secret, most sacred, the greatest of all Mysteries. Its name is "The Book of the Hidden Dwelling"—*i.e.* the Book of Amenta, or the *Ritual* of the Resurrection.

But the meaning of the Mysteries could only be known whilst the genuine gnosis was authentically taught; this had ceased when the Christian Sarcolatræ literalised the mystical drama of Amenta, the Earth of Eternity, as a more tangible-looking human history, and a new revelation sent from God. Yet it is at least 15,000 years old—probably 50,000 or more.

And from these Mysteries the ceremonies of the Masonic Brotherhood have been handed down from generation to generation, re-edited and altered only to conform with our present religious ideas.

The six periods of the world's existence—now about to close with the second advent—when time will be swallowed up in Eternity, has no meaning, nor has it any origin, without the Egyptian Mythos—no more than the Sun, Moon and 7 Stars, which we find frequently grouped together on Assyrian and other monuments, and which the Chinese call the 7 Lights of Heaven. It is parallel with the same grouping of the 9 Pyramids of Mexico: One for the Sun—One for the Moon and 7 for the Stars—symbolically.

The great Pyramid of Egypt and Stellar Mythology explain the Mystery. The great Pyramid is in itself a sign of the 7 Stars comprising, as it does, the Square and Triangle in one figure, and the other two Pyramids near this One, represent the Sun and Moon.

The key to its meaning is the 7 Pole Stars, and the Periods of the same which were also figured as 7 Eyes, or 7 Circles, in consequence of these being a figure of a Cycle. This type is presented to Joshua in the Book of Zechariah in the shape of 7 Eyes upon a stone: "Behold the stone I have set before Joshua—upon one stone are 7 Eyes." These are the Eyes of the Lord, also the 7 Lamps, the same as in the Book of Revelation (Zech. iii. 9; iv. 1-12).

As a mode of measuring time and period on the colossal scale of the Great Year, the Eye or Circle came to the full "as at first" 7 times at 7 stations of the Pole, in the Cycle of precession. As a type the Eye might be full, once a month, once a quarter, once a year, once a 1000 years; in 2,155 years; 3,716 years, or in the Great Eye of all—the Eye of the Eternal, about once in 26,000 years (the correct time was 25,827 years) (*Ritual*, chap. cxl.-cxiv.).

The submergence of 7 Pole Stars involved the same number of deluges, and marked the periods of the world's existence in the Cycle of precession, which culminated in the great deluge of all, not to be swallowed up in Eternity, but to recommence again (to be swallowed up in Eternity when the 7 Pole Stars cease to exist). The advent of Horus as the young Solar god in the Mythology, and as Horus of the Resurrection, in the Eschatology, changed the reckoning of time, and therefore, when he came, Stellar time was no more, and came to an end as "Stellar time reckoning" or periods of 6 and 1 = 7 circles.

The mystery of the 7 circles is the same as the mystery of the 7 Stars in Revelation, it is the mystery of the celestial heptanomes in the astronomical Mythology, and proves how some of the Stellar Mythos has been brought on and mixed with the Solar and Eschatology, and gives the reason and meaning to this part of the ceremonies, and *without which* it is meaningless.

The "Second Advent" marks the time of origin of this, which must have been at the time the Old Mystery Teachers had marked the end of the second revolution of the 7 Pole Stars, from the time of the first observing and recording, the proof of which they have left in Egypt on monuments and in the *Ritual*. Observations for 50,000 years=two revolutions.

It was asserted by Martinus Capella that the Egyptians had secretly studied the science of astronomy for forty thousand years before it was made known to the rest of the world (Lewis, "Astronomy of the Ancients," page 264).

Therefore the six periods of the world's existence were represented by the six pole stars in precession, with the 7th added, which, when ended or about to change to re-precession, represented the great deluge or eternity of the great year—*i.e.* all is at an end, to recommence again with another life. It was astronomical mythology at first, a deluge being an ending of a cycle of time. It became a natural type of an ending of time in the uranographic representation, but in no other than in an astronomical sense of a rebeginning at the same point of departure as in the beginning. It will rebegin again in the great circle of precession, but only as a matter of chronology. In the great year of precession there were seven stations of the celestial pole, in these constellations: 1, Draconis; 2, The Lesser Bear; 3, Kepheus; 4, Cygnus; 5, Lyra; 6, Hippopotamus; and 7, Herakles (the Man). These were the seven sustaining powers of the heavens; the seven pillars; seven mounts; seven divinities, called Lords of Eternity, etc., etc. The seven periods in precession corresponded to seven stations of the pole in their Stellar Mythos, and Horus I. was the God of the Pole Star. He was the great power who presided over the pole, and the Pole Star symbolised the Lord of Eternity. The circuit of precession first outlined by the movement of the celestial pole was the circle of the eternal, or seven eternals, which they imaged by the Shennu-ring. The end of the great year, determined by the great deluge of all, occurred in the sign or constellation of the Man; hence, when they converted their mythology into Eschatology—the explanation given to Brothers of the 18°.

The evidence of these facts has already been discussed here and in other works, and the proof can no longer be doubted. We should make more definite progress, and with greater celerity in unravelling the mysteries of the past, but for those who have so persistently, without any positive evidence of facts, but only on the various hypothetical translations and versions of the volume of the Sacred Law, claimed that the human race had originated in Asia.

The whole of this article otherwise simply shows most conclusively that at the time these hieroglyphic writings were made the Egyptians were in their "Stellar Mythos," and at the time of the first Horus, and that undoubtedly an exodus or colonies went out from Egypt at this period N. S. E. and W.

The figure of the giraffe, which is so frequently represented in the rock drawings of Upper Egypt—which *Professor Sayce* mentions, and does not know the meaning of—is their representation of Sut, one of their original Trinity. The emblems of Anubis, twice repeated, Thoth, Horus and Min, seen on standards, on the lower end of which is a hand grasping a rope, should be translated Ha-Ka-Amsu.

We quite agree with *Professor Sayce* that the character underneath the hawk is not the cake t. It is the same as the first form of crown or diadem above ⌒ badly written (or Neb, Lord of the North and South—Horus I.). The Uraeus has been added to those found, which we see above, and is probably the seventh King or Lord of the Nomes, which was missing when we wrote the former part of this *re* Ivory Tablets. We are of opinion that at this early period there were no letters but that each sign or hieroglyphic signified more than a letter—it was ideographic.

Professor Sayce says: "How the name of King S was pronounced it is impossible to say." So far as this he is perfectly correct, and he might have added that we do not know how they pronounced any of their hieroglyphics.

Amsu was Horus I., risen from the dead, and he was the first "man God." Osiris was only the same, years later, under a different cult. The text says: "Horus rose from the dead and established himself for ever."[1] I-em-Hetep was another form of him—"The Divine Healer.' *Dr Budge* is rather amusing when he suggests: "If we could trace his history to its beginning, we should find probably that he was originally a *very highly skilled 'Medicine Man' who had introduced some elementary knowledge of medicine amongst the Egyptians, and who was connected with the practice of the art of preserving the bodies of the dead by means of drugs and spices and linen bandages*." If *Dr Budge* will go back to the primordial we think he will have little difficulty in understanding that all these gods were not different gods, but all the powers and divine attributes of "Atum" depicted in various ways which they could

[1] The coloured plate is reproduced from *Dr Budge's* "Gods of the Egyptians," by kind permission of Methuen & Co.

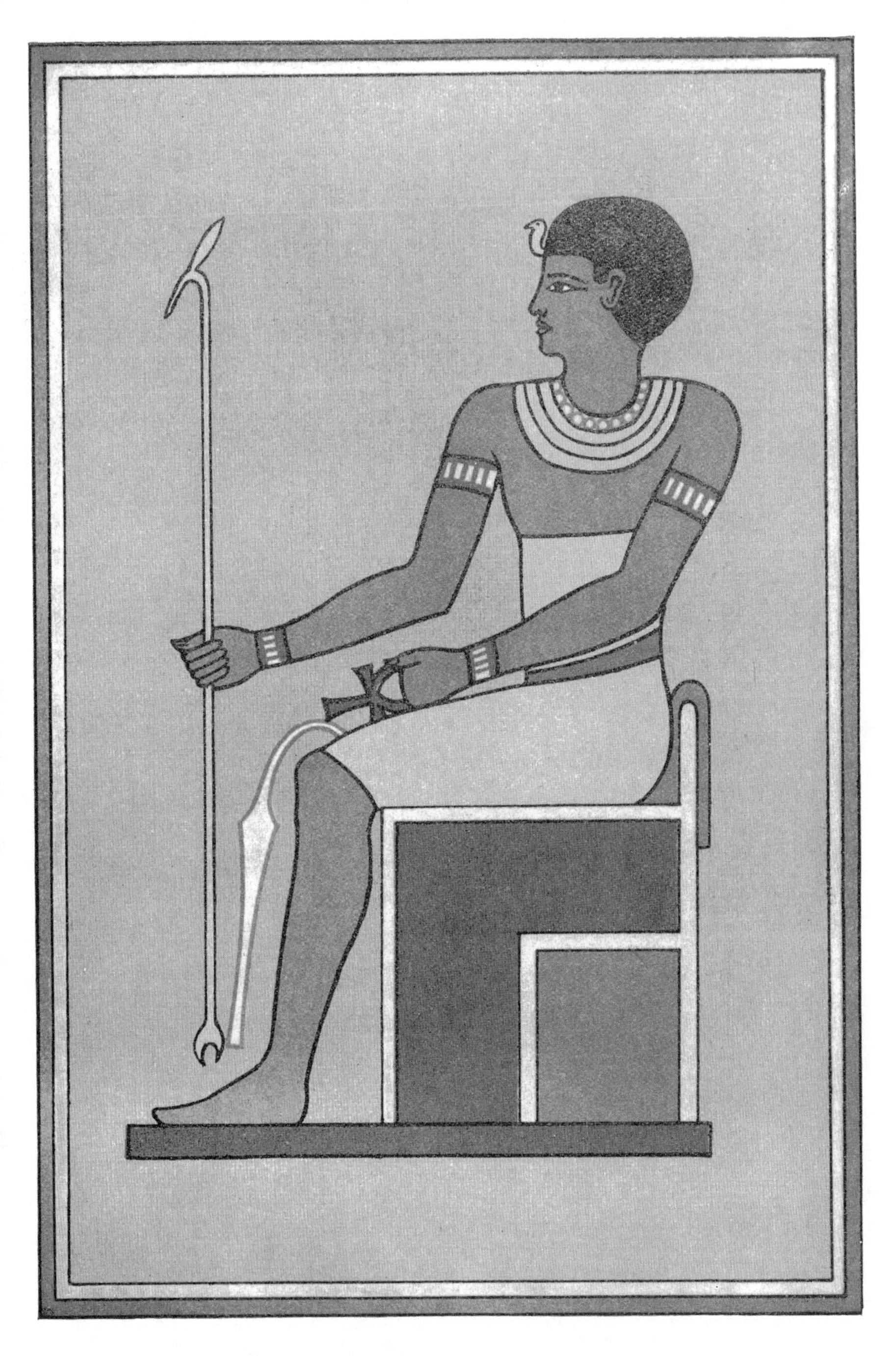

THE GOD I-EM-HETEP (IMOTHIS).

One of the eight gods. Son of Ptah at Memphis, son of Atum at Annu, Builder of the Temple of Heaven, Bruiser of the serpent and Conqueror of the dragon, Prince of peace and goodwill, Teacher of twelve years old in the temple, the Divine healer.

understand. He it was who destroyed all evil and brought light and dispersed darkness, healed all those who were ill, and caused light to shine to bring forth all life—The Divine Healer, The Good

FIG. 113—Ixtlil.o.i.

The Mexican representative of I-em-Hetep (Egyptian). It is one form of Horus as the divine healer, the Good Physician, etc., and is portrayed here with a crown and 4 feathers—*i.e.* the God of the 4 Quarters—also with the Star with 7 Rays—*i.e.* God of the Pole Stars. He has the Horus Lock and is further represented as the "Dark face of the night"—the original prototype of R. in the 18°—An-er-f of the Egyptians, the one who leads you from Darkness, Death and Dangers, etc., into Light and Glory. The Ancient Mexicans turned to him when sick or afflicted and implored his aid to heal them of their diseases. He is shown here "as preaching, or Sayer of Sayings in the Temple." He has the Emblem of the A.S.R. on his arm and the Horus sign of the "Two feathers" on his feet. His Left hand and arm point to the passage of "The Tuat" and in his Right hand he holds "The Mount of Paradise."

Physician—and the young teacher of Divine gospels in the Temple (see *Ritual*).

Nothing that we have written as regards the great antiquity of ancient Egypt and the Nile valley demonstrate that here primitive man first began to learn and observe nature's laws, and progressed in all forms of knowledge until a great civilised people was formed, from whom emigrations took place to all other parts of the world, carrying all they knew up to the times of the various exodes, is altered by the recent discoveries of *Flinders Petrie* and *De Morgan*. There is no doubt in our minds that *Flinders Petrie's* view that there were two races at least which inhabited Egypt—one African and indigenous, the other immigratory from Asia, bearing with it the civilisation of the Pharaohs, and subjugating the first indigenous and savage population—is an entirely erroneous idea. There is absolutely nothing to prove that either the ancient Egyptian knowledge, or the people, came from Asia, and the fact that *Flinders Petrie* discovered an immense tomb at Naqada, revealing a civilisation unlike that of the Pharaohs, and showing a genuine Neolithic civilisation, with some copper objects, and graves similar to those of the same epoch in Europe —that is, with shrivelled corpse buried in the position of the fœtus *in utero*. The thrice-bent man of Uxmal and Cornwall, and dismemberment of some parts of the body, etc., shows by other discoveries of *De Morgan's* at the same place, and at Abydos, that these were the older inhabitants.

In our opinion, *De Morgan*, who found new graves, including a royal tomb, presenting data of great importance for the primitive history of Egypt, is quite right in interpreting the facts differently from *Petrie* and in regarding these as the "old race," representing the Aborigines, the earlier inhabitants of these parts. *Professor G. Sergi*, in his Anthropological Studies, proves more conclusively than anything else—outside our statement of the facts which we have brought forward—that we are correct in placing Egypt and the Nile valley as the birthplace and centre of civilisation, from whence various emigrations to other parts took place, and as the dates of these exodes varied, so did the customs, etc., which they carried with them, remains of which still exist in various parts of the world.

The argument which *Petrie* uses that the Egyptians were a new race of emigrants, conquering those of Neolithic civilisation, which can be seen by the writings of the former, and because the latter had none, "only rude marks, not grouped," will not be borne out by any argument if we go into the facts. It is true that the "old race" had no writings, as *writing* is now understood, but they had their "rude marks," which may be taken as linear alphabetical signs, and may be seen by *Petrie's* plates, also in the examples given by *De Morgan.*

Now, although these "marks," without having any alphabetical significance attributed to them, are really writing signs, many of which still remain in the alphabets of existing races, shown by *Evans*, which would be brought into line with the pre-Phœnician writings, found in the Mediterranean, and the pre-Neolithic of other parts of Europe, Australia, Canary Isles, Yucatan, in Mexico, Europe, and other parts of the world, carried out of Egypt no doubt by exodes at this period, for it is distinctly shown that they were used here at this date, and further, at the epoch of Abydos and Naqada they were used cotemporaneously with writings of Egyptian type—hieroglyphics. It is proved by the pottery and ivory tablets found in the royal tomb at Naqada that a large portion of the hieroglyphic signs, which at the time of Meni were conventionalistic types, are of indigenous Neolithic origin, and shows more conclusively that the elements of hieroglyphic writings had been growing here on the banks of the Nile long before the time of the first historic dynasty, from the time that the first Pygmies invented the first sign language, and which they still have and use amongst themselves most proficiently, because they had not, and have not words enough to express all their meanings and ideas.

The Egyptians were a progressive people from the first, and as they acquired more knowledge their modes of expression by signs and symbols would naturally improve, they never lost anything, but preserved and improved it, merely altering to suit the times. Their writings were altered and added to afterwards as is plainly shown in the Hieratic and Demotic. One has to consider that probably the work of centuries had been carried on from the time when the first man made his "rude mark" until even the time of Meni.

Diodorus Siculus declares that the Egyptians claimed to have sent out colonies over the whole world in times of the remotest antiquity. They affirmed that they had not only taught the Babylonians astronomy, but that Belus and his subjects were a colony that went out of Egypt. This is also supported by the book of Genesis in the generations of Noah. He was greatly impressed with the assertions of the priests respecting the numerous emigrations, including the colonies of Babylon and Greece, but they named so many in divers parts of the world that he shrank from recording them upon hearsay and word of mouth. He tells us that they had sacred books transmitted to them from ancient times in which the historical accounts were recorded and kept, and then handed on to their successors (see Book I. 28, 29, 44, 81). It is much to be regretted that he did not record what the priests told him, because his writings are still extant; but we fear that the records of the priests are for ever lost with those and many non-historical facts which might have helped to link the broken chain "in the records of the past." Thus we see that colonies went forth and settled in all parts of the world, leaving the proofs in language, myths, and the hieroglyphics in religious rites. The symbolical customs and ceremonies in far-off lands are still extant amongst races by whom they are no longer read or understood, but which can be read in Egypt.

Crowns

The Crown is a symbol in the 33°, the highest we have, and because of its importance we have taken some considerable trouble in searching the records of the past to find why the Egyptians attached such great importance to it and from whence they took the origin. We believe that this can only be traced back one way, seeing that one form of crown at the time of their Solar Mythos represented Zodiacal Light, it must have been brought on from the Lunar and previously from the Stellar Mythos. Now we know that the Pole Star (one) represented Horus I.—*i.e.* the Light of the World. That was one, but there were seven Pole Stars in the circle of recessional movement:

There was one in the Dragon,
" one in the Lesser Bear,
" one in Kepheus,
" one in Cygnus,
" one in Lyra,
" one in Herakles,
" one in Corona Borealis or the *Northern Crown.*

The Crown, being a symbol of the highest, which, being the Pole Star, would be the highest point and the Star Alpha in this constellation is called "Clava Corona," which means the key of the Crown; also the seven Pole Stars in their circle formed a

Crown for the Supreme Being, of whom it is said: "His diadem predominates at the zenith of the starry heaven, which was the Crown upon the summit of the Stellar Mount of Glory" (*Ritual*, chap. cxxxiii.). This is the origin of the eternal Crown in the Eschatology, having been carried on from the seven stars of the Stellar Mythos. In the *Ritual*, chap. cxxxi., it says: "He arriveth at the aged one (Horus I.) on the confines of the Mount of Glory (Pole Star) where the Crown awaiteth him."

From the very earliest times crowns were used by rulers to denote their rank and position, and from their shape we learn the period in which they were worn. The earliest, shaped thus adopted probably during the Stellar Mythos, can be seen on the Ivory Tablets found at Naqada, Australian Aborigines, PAPYRI OF ANI and "Book of the Dead."

At a later period Atum is depicted wearing a crown with two feathers, thus , Ptah is also represented as wearing this crown. There were other forms as well, but these two feathers represent the two lives, temporal and spiritual. The yellow plumes, still worn by the Pygmies and other natives of Central Africa, must be associated with the Stellar Mythos. We see these adorn the head of the god Bes, also the goddess Anqiet, and are still worn by the Inner African natives at the present day. These after were reduced to two feathers in the crown of the Two Feathers in the Solar doctrines, and signified the two lives, earthly and spiritual; what the original signification meant—if any more than a simple adornment, we are unable to say. At the time of Solar Mythos we find the Atef crown. Many have sought the reason why the Egyptian kings adopted this crown, which is very remarkable in its form. It adorns the figures of Ra and Osiris, and was worn by the kings of Egypt to denote, symbolically, that they were the representatives of Ra and Osiris. The shape might have been taken from one of the projections in the corona of the sun.

On page 220 of "The Story of the Sun," by *Sir R. S. Ball*, this Illustration,  which is identically the same as the Atef crown or Crown of Zodiacal Light of Supreme

Heaven, can be seen. The Atef Crown represented Zodiacal Light and not the triangle of Horus, ▽ as some Egyptologists have stated, and this Atef Crown is frequently seen shown on the sculpture scenes amongst the Mayas and people of Central America, and the first to wear the Atef Crown was Atum-Ra, "the Father in Spirit."

The earlier priests and astronomers of Egypt, at the time of the Solar Mythos, saw that Ra (the Sun) was adorned with this crown, and adopted the same for the King, who was the head and symbolical representative of Ra. If this were so it shows their remarkable knowledge and the accurate observations they made of the heavenly bodies, as well as proving that this projection in the corona of the sun also had this shape at the time of their observations, which would be interesting to present astronomers. There were, however, very many different forms of crowns, which may be seen on the monuments of Egypt. We know from records left that they had worked out the transcendental relation between radius and circumference and used it. They had an accurate knowledge of the motion of the earth, the sun and moon and all the planetary system, and had worked out a correct calendar, based on the full knowledge of the motion of the earth ; in fact, nothing is more astonishing to those who study the records of the past, than the knowledge of science which the ancient priests of Egypt possessed, much of which has been lost, but which our own scientific men have rediscovered, to find that it was all known so long ago by these old Astrologers, and left written in signs and symbols, on stones and papyri, which we are now enabled to read, and which prove the truth of that which we have written. No doubt the reason was that all the secrets of nature and their theology were carefully hidden from the uninitiated, and it was only those who could go through the severe ordeal of training to the highest degree who had the full knowledge of all these divine religious teachings. As internal wars, etc., occurred, these became less and less until the true light became lost or perverted, and as they could only use the heavenly bodies and their unerring laws as a perfect example, we thus find that everything was first worked out astronomically and then depicted in earthly form.

"The White and Black Eagle" date back to the Lunar

Mythos and originally represented the white bird of the new moon and the black bird of the old moon.

In "the Destruction of Mankind" Ra says to the moon god, "Thou art my abode, the god of my abode (The Lunar Ark)—behold thou art called Taht, the abode of Ra, and there arose the Ibis. I shall give thee to raise thy hand in the presence of the gods. And there arose two wings of the Ibis of Taht. I shall give thee to embrace the two parts of the sky." The one white and black bird as representative of the moon, in the Egyptian rendering, was therefore the white bird of the new moon and the black bird of the old moon. In different countries different birds have been used to represent this. In some a white dove and a black, others the Martin or Swallow, which combines the two, and with us the White and Black Eagle.

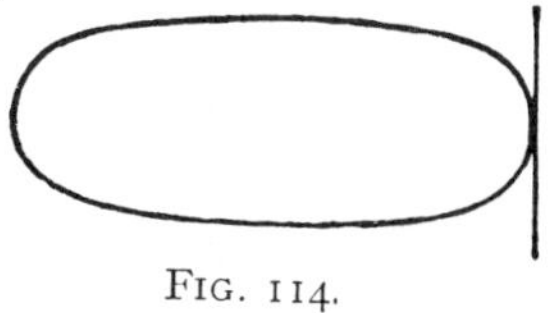

FIG. 114.

Mr Marsham Adams' opinion of the origin of the form of the Royal Cartouche is that it was taken from the course of the Sun; as follows:—"At the present epoch, the earth reaches the apsides or turning points of her orbit, that is to say, the greatest and least distance from the sun, a few days after passing, respectively, through the summer and winter solstices; but, inasmuch as these

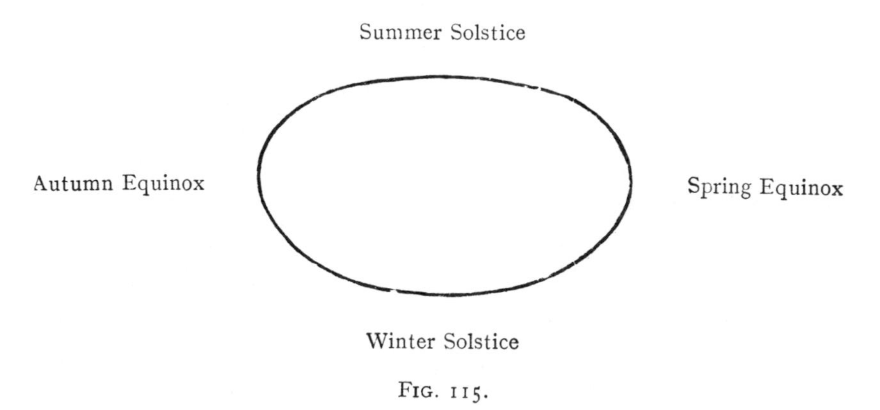

FIG. 115.

points have a slow relative motion round the orbit, the period of the year at which they attained thousands of years ago, took place about the time of the equinox. Hence, if we represent the orbit in its true elliptic form, a tangent at the extremity of the major axis will define both the point of equinox through which it passes, and the direction of the minor axis or line of solstice to which it will be parallel, thus indicating the relation of the universe, and the figure thus described exactly gives us the royal cartouche, always encircling the names of the Egyptian Kings, which thus images forth the celestial foundation and universal jurisdiction of that monarchy, so long as the earth preserves its divinely appointed course."[1]

[1] "The Book of the Master," by *Marsham Adams.*

CHAPTER XIV

THE ORIGINS AND EXPLANATIONS OF OTHER PRINCIPAL SIGNS AND SYMBOLS USED AMONGST US

TAKE the oblong square first (a Masonic term). The form of Lodges is oblong Square; the length thereof is as great as the breadth; the length, and the breadth, and the height thereof are equal. This was the Heaven of Atum based or founded on the four quarters of the Solstices, and the equinoxes which followed the making of Amenta. (*See* Appendix.)

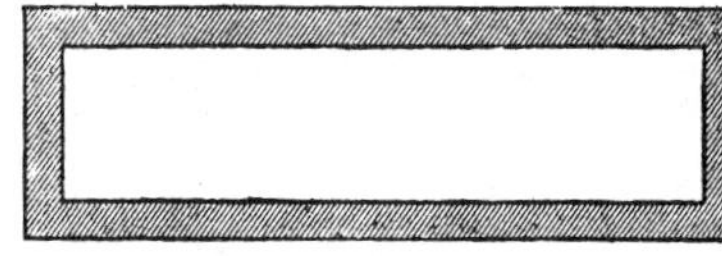

FIG. 116.

This sign or form was first used to represent the Zodiac, and is found at Esnè and Denderah, and may be considered, therefore, as the origin or oldest form of our lodge. (Plates may be seen in Brugsch.)

The Square 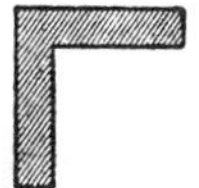 is also very clearly depicted, symbolically, in the Egyptian *Ritual* and is plainly shown in "The Book of the Dead," with three figures seated on it—two represented by the figure of Maat or Mati—Truth, Justice, Law, etc., the third figure being Osiris, seated on the Square in the Judgment Hall. The Egyptian name is Neka.

This Square you find depicted in many of the ancient temples and in the Great Pyramid, as two seats, one for Osiris and one for Maat—it is the Masonic Square.

This is portrayed as the corner-stone of the building, and the foundation of Eternal Law in the Court of Divine Justice.

The figures here exhibited are taken from the Egyptian Hall of Judgment or Righteousness—PAPYRUS OF ANI.

One of these is, as you see, the great Judge Osiris, and his Judgment Seat is modelled on the Masonic Square.

Much is made in Masonry of "Acting on the Square," and here is the foundation of the whole matter.

FIG. 117.

Maat or Mati, and Osiris, seated on Masonic Square.
(From PAPYRUS OF ANI.)

In the Egyptian Maat or Hall of Judgment, sits Osiris judging the dead upon the square that is imaged by the Masonic Square, which was first employed in squaring the stones of the builders, and next in squaring the conduct in the sphere of morals of the Masonic Brotherhood, which in Egypt was as old as the brotherhood of the seven Khemmu or the seven Masons who assisted Ptah in building the heavens on the Square, of which the ideograph, in hieroglyphic language, is the Mason's square.

Ptah, in Egyptian mythology, was the first great Architect of the Universe, which he built with seven assistants, the Heavens *on the Square*, previously it was in the form of a triangle, and the "*Stone-Squarers*" date from this time. Ptah was the very great God who came into being in the earliest time: "Father of fathers, Power of powers, Father of beginnings and Creator of the eggs of the Sun and Moon, Lord of Maat, King of the two lands; who created his own image, who fashioned his own body, who hath established Maat throughout the two lands. Ptah it was who fashioned the new bodies in which the souls of the dead were to live in the underworld; he was the great artificer in metals and he was at once smelter and caster and sculptor, as well as the master architect and designer of everything which exists in the world and the universe—I-em-Hetep was Horus, brought on as the son of Ptah, the divine healer, the good physician, the healer of the bodies of mortals during this life, and through him the good spirits were brought and presented to his Father"—I. U. is the same, but another name for him. In Ptah is the commencement of the Fatherhood, all was Motherhood before.

Ura Kherp Hem, who held the highest sacerdotal office in Egypt, as the High Priest of Ptah at Memphis, is also spoken of as the Arch Craftsman "tes." He raised up the body as well as the soul, and, in conjunction with Sem and Hen nutar (prophet) exalted and anointed with oil. The *Ritual* says:—, —"I lustrate with water in Tattu and with oil in Abydos, exalting him who is in the heights" (in excelsis).

A great ceremony consisted in a grand procession round the walls of the Great Sanctuary of Ptah, conveying upon a sledge the "Bark" (or Ark) in which the coffin of the god was supposed to rest, and the mourners sang the song: "To the West" to help them on their way to the gate of fair entrance in Amenta.

The "Coffined One" and the "Seven Glorious Ones" who followed the coffin of "their Lord," were brought on from the Stellar Mythos, and there the "Coffined One" represented the Pole Star, and the Seven Glorious Ones, the stars of the *Little Bear*, constantly circling around the Pole. That it must have

FIG. 118.

The First or "The Maatit Boat."[1]

From photo by Emil Brugsch-Bay. Original found at Meir is now at Gizeh. The only boat which has preserved its original rigging. Dates from eleventh or twelfth Dynasty. The dead man is sitting in his cabin wrapped in his cloak.

been the Little Bear and not the "Great Bear," may be assumed, because the former could always be seen and was always under observation, whereas the latter, at times, dipped so far down the horizon, that at certain periods it must have been lost to view to those in Egypt.

Sir L. Page Renouf, in his translation of "The Book of the Dead," is of opinion that the "Coffined One" and the "Seven

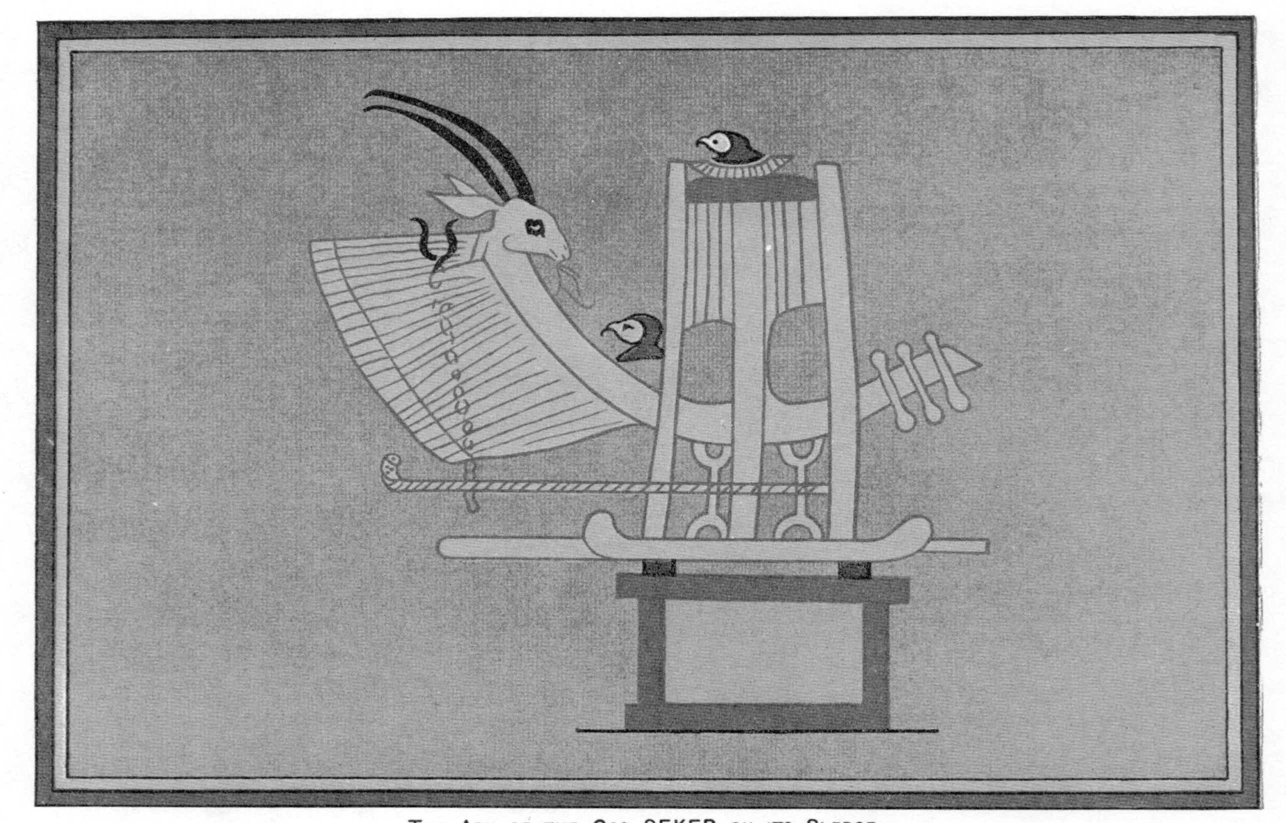

THE ARK OF THE GOD SEKER ON ITS SLEDGE.

The Sekru-Sledge or Ark which preceded the Boat or Ark before Ptah had completed Amenta, and the Boat of Ra or Osiris came into being

Glorious Ones" who follow, represent the Pole Star and the *Great Bear*, but he evidently overlooked the fact that at times the Great Bear dropped below the horizon in Egypt and could not be seen, yet the "Seven Glorious Ones" always remained visible. Hence our opinion that it was the *Little Bear*—Ursa Minor (*Ritual*, chap. lxxii.), "The 7 Stars which never set."

In the depiction of these seven that we find in Central America the form of the seven stars would apply equally to

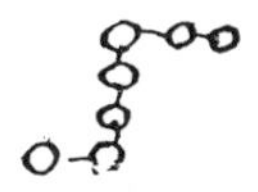

either but certainly not to the Southern Cross, as the German translators have assigned them, and whose decipherment of the same we cannot agree with.

The first "boat" or ark is called Maatit, and the second is called Sektit in the Egyptian language.

The Sektit or the Seher boat or Hennu boat[1] was not made in the form of an ordinary boat, but one end of it was very much higher than the other and was made in the shape of the head of a gazelle. The centre of the boat was occupied by a carefully closed coffer, which was surmounted by a hawk with protruding wings stretched out over the top of it. This coffer contained the body of the dead Osiris, and it rested upon a framework or sledge which was provided with runners. The support of the sledge was made in the form of lotus flowers, which are well-known types of the dawn and renewal of life. Papyrus plants are emblems of the South—Lotus plants of the North. It was in this boat that the mummy form entered the Tuat, was drawn through, and, finally entering the tail of a large serpent, was drawn through its body and came forth as a new or regenerated soul at the Double Cave on the island in the lake. It is of great antiquity and pre-dynastic.

As Egyptian, the ark and shrine of Ra-Harmakhu represented the double equinox in the two horizons. The double abode of Ra (in Solar Mythos), in the dual domain of light and shade—the same model was in Hebrew, which was to be erected equally in sun and shade—the open part to the rays of light was to be exactly

The coloured plate represents the second or "The Sektit Boat." Reproduced from *Dr Budge's* "Gods of the Egyptians," by kind permission of Methuen & Co.

the same to balance the veil or shade of the covering, and not to have more sun than shade.

It was the custom of the Egyptians to represent heaven in miniature, as an ark of so many cubits, and inside, there was a shrine for the deity, and a figure of the God, within the Sanctuary, so that the sacred ark shrines of the Egyptians dated back to the earlier Stellar Mythos, and consisted of a boat and shrine, and the images of the god were placed within the shrine, and borne on the shoulders of the priests around the Temple, on certain festal days.

There was an ark of 7 cubits (Stellar), and one of 8 cubits (Lunar), and one of 4 cubits (Solar). The 4 cubits represented the four quarters of heaven; the one of 8 cubits, the octonary, and the one of 7 cubits, the Heptanomes.

The Ark of the Israelites was brought out of Egypt by Moses, and probably used by him as High Priest at On, and the two Cherubim, which were afterwards adopted, with wings (here shown), were prototypes of the Egyptian beetles.

The name of the beetle in Egyptian is Khepr, and in the Hebrew the Mercy-Seat is the Caphoreth, לפךח rendered "the Cover of the Ark," that was formed by two cherubs, which are Beetles in the Egyptian prototype. The Beetle-headed Solar God was Khepr, and the two Beetles formed the Caphoreth in the Egyptian Ark as the cover of the Mercy Seat. The Beetle was Khepr, and the Beetle with Atum-Iu was Khepr-Ra. This identifies Iu with Iahu as Khepr-Ra, who is a form of Atum in the scarabæus sign of the Zodiac: so that Atum-Iu is the sign of the two Beetles.

Khepera is much older than Ra, because he is sometimes represented as a Hawk (the Spirit) issuing from a mummy. This would mean a type of Horus I., and, coming forth from the mummy as a spirit, would indicate and prove how old is their Eschatology. As the doctrines of Atum were in existence ages and ages before the Osirian, it will give one some idea how old these people were, and the advancement they had made and worked out in their religious beliefs at this very early period.

The first "Bark," or Ark, is that in which the soul proceeds on its journey from this sublunary abode. First, it travels from the East to the West until Ra sets in the West; then the soul has to disembark from this ship and has to enter, by a ladder of seven steps, another Ark, the Sektit Boat, which takes the soul across the firmament after passing through Amenta, it travelled to the North, with Horus, the Sun-God, at the prow, "until the stars which set in Heaven are reached." This is called the "Land of Life." Hence the origin of the song: "To the West, to the West, to the Land of the Free." In chapter lv. of the *Ritual* we read: "See thou Horus at the Look-out of the ship, and at his sides Thoth and Maat. All the gods are in exultation when they behold Ra coming in peace to give new life to the heart of Chu"—*i.e.* Horus the Son with Truth and Justice bringing Chu, the new-born soul to Osiris (God) to be received by him and all the angels with joy and exultation into the Land of Life.

The song: "To the West, to the West, to the Land of the Free" was sung as a "Funeral Song" or "Dead March." It was sung at the obsequies of all the dead at burial, having their belief as before stated. As regards this having been written by *Russell* and referring to the United States, it could not be so. In Ireland there is a very old song to the same effect, probably handed down by tradition from the ancient Druids—Egyptian Priests. *Russell* may, and probably did, use part of this, but *Maspero* gives the whole translation from the hieroglyphics, which is sufficient proof of its origin and meaning. The Egyptian Lands of the West were not geographical, they were in Amenta, the nether world of the dead. The dead, on their way there, were called "Westerners."

Dr Le Plongeon, in his works on the Mayas, confounds Amenta —"the Land of the West" of the Egyptians—which was celestial, and a figure of Sign Language to teach the Mysteries only, with the terrestrial, and misunderstands *Proclus* and *Plato*, who were quoting the Egyptian High Priests. If he would read and understand the 110th chapter of the *Ritual*, he would see that it was "not geographical knowledge of the earth," but that which they had worked out in the heavens, and had nothing whatever to do with the land of the Mayas, whom they knew and called Haûi-nibû (people beyond the seas).

He mixes Amenta with the Mayas as geographical, puts an exoteric rendering and does not understand the uranographic and esoteric representation.

THE ARK OF THE COVENANT

The Ark of the Covenant, built and set up by Moses in the wilderness, according to the Sacred volume—and which has not been seen—is precisely similar in all measurements to the "Stone Chest" still to be seen in the King's Chamber of the Great Pyramid, and which is undoubtedly the original, although the contents are gone. According to the *Ritual* it should have contained the "Coffined One," and we know that miniatures of this used to be carried around the Egyptian temples at Memphis on stated occasions during their religious rites.

FIG. 119.

THE HOLY OF HOLIES IN THE TEMPLE OF SOLOMON

The "Ark of the Covenant," showing the bars on the side, according to I Kings viii. 8. The Cherubim above on the covering, each with two wings, without hands, and a cloud above between the Cherubim, which seems to shine and to be, as it were, embraced by the wings of the Cherubim.

FIG. 120.

The Holy of Holies in the Temple of Solomon, and *The Ark of the Covenant*, showing the bars on the side, according to 1 Kings viii. 8. The Cherubim above on the covering, each with two wings without hands, and a cloud above between the Cherubim which seems to shine and to be, as it were, embraced by the wings of the Cherubim, and we give the origin and history of the Ark, as it may be interesting to those who belong to the Grand Council of Royal Select and Super-excellent Masters.

The Latin word *Arca* הארון (Hebrew, Aran, Arca) signifies

properly a coffer, and this is the true meaning of the Hebrew *Aran*, which Moses makes use of to denote the coffer or chest wherein the Tables were deposited upon which the words of the Covenant or the principal Commandments of the Law were written. This Coffer was made of *Shittim* wood, covered with plates or leaves of gold, being two cubits and a half in length, a cubit and a half wide and a cubit and a half high. Upon the top of it there was all round it a kind of gold crown and two Cherubim were fastened to the cover. On the two sides of this Coffer there were four rings of gold, two on each side, through which staves were put, by the help whereof it was carried as they marched through the wilderness. This was " the Ark of the Covenant," a Chest or Coffer of great value, wherein the two Tables of Stone were placed.

After the passage of the Jordan the Ark continued for some time at Gilgal. From thence it was removed to Shiloh. Here it was when the Israelites took it thence to carry it to their camp. They gave battle to the Philistines, and the Ark of the Lord fell into the enemy's hands. The Philistines, oppressed by the hand of God, which lay heavily upon them, sent back the Ark, and it was lodged at Kirjath-jearim. It was afterwards, in the reign of Saul, at Nob. David conveyed it from Kirjath-jearim to the house of Obededom, from thence to his palace at Zion ; and last of all Solomon brought it into the temple which he had built at Jerusalem.

It remained in the temple, with all suitable respect, till the times of the last Kings of Judah, who gave themselves up to idolatry, and were so daring as to put their idols in the very Holy Place itself. The Priests, being unable to endure this profanation, took the Ark and carried it from place to place that so they might preserve it from the fury of these impious princes. Josiah commanded them to bring it back to the sanctuary, and forbade them to carry it, as they had hitherto done, into the country.

Some time before the captivity of Babylon, Jeremiah, foreseeing the calamities which would happen to his nation, and enlightened in a supernatural manner, removed the Tabernacle and the Ark of the Covenant into a cave of that mountain which Moses ascended some little time before his death, and saw from thence the heritage of God. To this mountain Jeremiah went, and in a hollow cave of it concealed this sacred depositum. The

Priests who accompanied him intended to set a mark upon the place in order to remember it, but never were able afterwards to find it. The prophet reproved them for their curiosity, and declared that this place should continue unknown till the Lord should gather together once more His people that were dispersed, and should be reconciled to them. It is questioned, with good reason, whether the Ark was placed again in the temple after the return of the Jews from the captivity of Babylon.

The Talmudists relate that Solomon, having learnt by revelation that the Assyrians would one day burn the temple lately built by him, and carry away all the rich materials which he had placed there, took care to have a private hole made underground where, in case of necessity, he might conceal the most precious ornaments and most sacred things belonging to the temple from the knowledge of any enemies. Josiah, having a foresight of the calamities which were upon the point of falling on the Hebrew nation, hid here the Ark of the Covenant, together with Aaron's Rod, the Pot of Manna, the High Priest's Pectoral, and the Holy Oil. But during the Babylonish captivity, the Priests having lost all knowledge of the place where these things had been concealed, they were never afterwards seen, and were not in the second temple.

Others affirm that Nebuchadnezzar conveyed the Ark to Babylon, and that it was among the rich vessels which were carried off by him from the temple. Some are of opinion that King Manasseh, having set up idols in the temple, took away the Ark, which was not settled there again during his reign. The author of the fourth book of Esdras represents the Jews lamenting that the Ark of the Covenant was taken by the Chaldeans in the plunder of the temple. The Gerama of Jerusalem, and that of Babylon, both acknowledge that the Ark of the Covenant is one of the things which was wanting in the second temple after the return from the captivity of Babylon. The Jews flatter themselves that it will appear again with the Messiah who is expected by them. But Jeremiah, speaking of the time of the Messiah and the calling of the Gentiles to the faith, says that they shall neither talk nor think of the Ark, nor remember it any more. Esdras, Nehemiah, the Maccabees and Josephus never make any mention of the Ark in the second temple; and Josephus tells us expressly that when Jerusalem was taken by Titus the sanctuary was empty.

St Epiphanius relates, without doubt from some ancient tradition of the Jews, that Jeremiah, foreseeing the approaching ruin of the temple, carried the Ark of the Covenant into a cave, and by his prayers prevailed that it might be sunk and swallowed up in the rock so that it never more might be seen. This done, he addressed himself to the Priests and Elders, who accompanied him in the following words: "The Lord is ascended from Zion into Heaven, from whence he must one day descend with His celestial host: and it shall be a sign of His coming, when all nations shall adore the Cross. No one shall discover the Ark except Moses, the prophet of the Lord; and no priest nor prophet shall open the tables which are inclosed in it, except Aaron, the elect of God. But at the second resurrection the Ark shall be raised and come forth out of the rock, it shall be placed on Mount Sinai, and all the saints shall be assembled about it, waiting for the Lord's return, and endeavouring to defend themselves from the enemy who would take it. Jeremiah, at the same time, sealed the stone, writing with his own fingers the name of God upon the place, in like manner as if it had been cut with iron. From this moment a dark cloud was spread over the name of God and has kept it concealed to this very day, so that no one has been able to discover the place nor read this divine name. This cloud appears every night with great brightness over the cave, to show, as it were, that the glory of the Lord does not forsake His law. And the rock, before mentioned, lies between the two mountains where Moses and Aaron died."

Josephus, the son of Gorion, who had seen the books of the Maccabees, having first related that Jeremiah had concealed the Ark and the veils of Moses' Tabernacle, put these words into the mouth of Jeremiah, to the Priests who followed him and desired to know where those things were hidden: "The Lord hath sworn that no man should know this place, nor discover it, till the Prophet Isaiah and myself return to the world; then we will lodge the Ark again in the Sanctuary and under the Cherubim's wings." Lastly, the Rabbins agree in saying that the Ark no more was seen after the captivity of Babylon, and that the Foundation Stone, which they believed to be the centre of the Holy Mountain, was placed in the Sanctuary in its room. The Fathers and Christian Commentators agree generally with the Jews on this point, that the Ark was never found again after the Captivity.

Besides the Tables of the Covenant, placed by Moses in the sacred Coffer, God appointed the blooming Rod of Aaron to be lodged there, and the Omer of Manna, which was gathered in the wilderness. *Tertullian* is of opinion that the twelve Stones, taken from the bottom of the Jordan when the Israelites passed this river dry-shod, were likewise placed there. The Mohammedans assure us that Moses' shoes, which he pulled off before the Burning Bush, were likewise preserved there ; that besides these, Aaron's Pontifical tiara was kept there, and a piece of wood, called Alouah, which Moses made use of when he sweetened the waters of Mara. They also add that the Ark was given by God to Adam ready made, and that it passed from hand to hand, and from Patriarch to Patriarch down to Moses ; that all the portraitures of the Patriarchs and Prophets were represented about the Ark ; and that Shekinah, or the Majesty of God, rested upon it : that in times of war an impetuous wind rushed out of the Ark, which blew fiercely upon the enemies of Israel and entirely defeated them : and that for this reason they often carried the Ark of the Covenant at the head of their armies. There are some who believe that the Ark was brought to Ireland by Jeremiah and that it still lies buried there at Tara, but we must turn to the Mythology and Eschatology of Egypt to learn the true meaning of all this, and the solution of the question is the esoteric representation in the *Ritual*.

In 1877 William Simpson called attention to the Japanese Ark—shrines or mikoshi—which have many points of likeness to the Jewish Ark of the Covenant, and which was "carried on men's shoulders by means of staves." Mikoshi signifies the high or honourable seat of Temo-sama, or " Heaven's Lord."

The first lord of heaven in the Astronomical Mythology was the ruler of the Pole Star, whose high and honourable seat was at the Pole—Anup on his Mountain.

In some of these arks is the small figure of a deity, which is the representation of "Heaven's Lord." There were seven of the lords of the Pole Star altogether—one for each star in the cycle of precession in succession. Now there are seven of these arks preserved in the Temple of Hachiman at Kamakura, Japan. They are said by some to be state-norimans, but as these shrines are connected with the deified Mikado, they are mikoshis as well as norimans. " The mikoshis Themselves being eight," the eight seats or ark shrines answer to the Kami when the eighth one had been added to the seven, as overlord, but seven was the primary number in the Kami as of the Egyptian Akhemu, or Never-setting Ones. Israel is charged by Amos with having borne an ark shrine which was obviously the Tabernacle of a Star God, as Gods were once the Elohim (Amos v. 26).

The Heathen likewise had in their pagan rites little Chests or Cistæ, wherein they locked up their most sacred possessions. *Apulius* says that in certain profane processions made in Egypt, there was a person whose office it was to be Chest-bearer. He held a box, containing the richest things for their religious uses. *Plutarch*, in his book entitled " Of Osiris and Isis," tells us almost the same thing. *Pausanias* speaks of a Chest in which the Trojans locked up their mysteries, and that, being taken at the siege of Troy, it fell to Euripilus' share. The ancient Hetrurians had also Cistæ among their sacred vessels. There was the same custom among the Greeks and Romans. These boxes often enclosed things of a lewd, profane, superstitious and ridiculous nature ; whereas the Ark of God contained the most sacred and serious things in the world, such as the Table of God's Law, etc.

As among the Egyptians and Jews the Ark was a kind of portable temple, so among the Mexicans, the Cherokees and the Indians of Michoacan and Honduras, an Ark was held in the highest veneration, and was considered an object too sacred to be touched by any but the Priests. Amongst the Mandan Indians, in N. America, we find the image of the Ark preserved for generations, and religious ceremonies performed, similar to those in Egypt, connected with the same. In Mexico and Central America we find the Ark preserved in the most sacred part of the temple, and some of them in a most perfect state of preservation, viz. at Copan and at Palenque in 1848 (see *Stephen's* travels).

The Osirian religion is at least 20 thousand years old, and may be 50 thousand for aught any Egyptologist knows to the contrary. This has been proved by the recent discoveries at Abydos, showing that the Osirian doctrines existed there in all their glory and perfection more than 15 thousand years ago, and before this the Egyptians had the doctrine of Atum, etc. ; but the masonry of Ptah is infinitely earlier than that. Freemasonry may be said to have arisen at the time of the " Stone-

Squarers"—*i.e.* at the times they had "worked out" the "double horizon," and squared the heavens, which was done by Ptah, the Great Architect of the Universe.

The double horizon was formed by Shu when he lifted up the heavens, but was not squared.

Ptah was the builder who wrought in conjunction with Ma or Mati, the goddess of law, justice, truth, etc., and we mention this to show that Ma or Mati was also founded on the Masonic square.

We have no doubt that our saying, "to act on the square—Masonically"—is from the Egyptian: "to act rightly, to act justly and truthfully, or according to Maat." Working with Ma or Maat donotes creation according to eternal laws or understanding rule.

The ┐ is the seat of Osiris in the Judgment Hall, from which place all are judged as to the past, and must be found perfect before they could proceed further.

Symbolically, therefore, it shows that it was first emblematically the seat for judging right from wrong, so to speak; "to bring the material into perfect form, and to reject that which was not perfect," and to build on the square as a fourfold foundation is to build for ever. Paul speaks as a mason when he makes Christ "The Chief Corner Stone" in the Temple that is builded (Ep. ii. 20-22).

We must date the origin of our Ceremonies in Freemasonry back to the time when the Egyptians had perfected their Eschatology; in fact, it was and is their Eschatology, practised in a dramatic form, the more so to impress upon the I. and those of the various degrees, as they pass from the lower to the higher, to instil into their minds the whole of the doctrines of final things. These were the Priests and learned men only, who knew all things, and the common herd of mankind were never taught all the forms, ceremonies and doctrines. The Priests, who formed a distinct brotherhood amongst themselves, kept the knowledge and powers as a close secret, and only taught the common people as much or as little as they thought fit; but, although we date our *ceremonies* only as far back as this, we must go back thousands of years before to find *the origin of most of the signs and symbols.* Some of these date from the earliest Mythos, but more from the Stellar Mythology.

These were brought on and used in their Eschatology, symbolically, as we have brought it on in the Christian doctrines in the same manner, *therefore, the origin of the signs and symbols would be much older than the form of our ceremonies.* We would impress again upon our readers that the *word Freemasonry* was not used then, but that Freemasonry, in all its degrees now, is the purest form that is in existence of the old Eschatology of ancient Egypt, and that the more one studies the records of the past, the greater proof there is that we differ very little, even in the form of our lodges and all pertaining thereto in each degree. The study of the ancient remains of the writings and temples, found in Central America and Yucatan, and other parts of the world, prove how universal this was, and how exact the copy ; and because we find different names in different parts of the world, and different names in the same countries through the various ages of this earth's existence, even up to the present day, *it was the same Great God from the beginning until now*, the same attributes, and the same trinity in unity. Evolution and time have changed much as regards names, and various Priests have made innovations, but from the time of Horus I., the first man-god who lived and died and rose again as Amsu, it is all one and the same, however much the various cults have made innovations.

"The situation of the Lodge—due East and West"—proves that our Brotherhood was founded at the time of the Eschatology of the Ancient Egyptians, and not from the Stellar or Lunar Mythos, as it would then have been North and South ; but, taking all the various degrees of the Brotherhood into consideration, it is astonishing how little has been obliterated from the Astronomical Mythology, not only in signs and symbols, but also, that part of the *Ritual* has been retained from the earliest date ; and although we have "substituted words and explanations" for all our ceremonies, so much of it has no real meaning for those who are Students of Freemasonry, because we only repeat it like the poor Aboriginal Australians : "it has always been" ; there can be no wonder, therefore, that many Brothers have looked for the true meaning and origin for years, without being satisfied that the present one is right, nor can they ever do so without returning to Old Egypt, for it is here only that the birthplace of the Brotherhood can be found. The legends which have been founded on the Astronomical Mythos, and *Ritual* of Egypt, will find their explanation here only, and nowhere else. It is useless to try and continue an exoteric rendering in the place of the true esoteric representation; science and knowledge in the end will prevail, ignorance and false beliefs must give place to scientific truths.

Origin of the Twenty-four-inch Gauge

The 24-inch-gauge or cubit is the hieroglyphic ▭ and has the phonetic value of Maat and indicated, primarily, "that which is straight," and was the name which was given to the instrument by which the work of the handicraftsman of every kind was kept straight and measured: metaphorically, a rule or law or canon by which the lives of men and their actions were kept straight and governed, belonged to the Egyptian word Maat. The Egyptians thus used the word in a physical and moral sense as we do in all our ceremonies connected with this instrument, as their naming it Maat clearly proves, therefore, it is a very important instrument used by our Brotherhood; much more so than the majority would at first conceive. The British inch was the unit of linear measurement used at the building of the Great Pyramid, or at least it is the nearest standard in existence, as it has lost 1 one-thousandth part of itself, after being carried from land to land through all these thousands of years. There is, therefore, more in it than being an instrument to "measure our work" and being "symbolical of time." One inch is the time representation of the Great Year prophetically. Five hundred millions of the Pyramid inch is the length of the earth's Polar diameter.

Twenty-five inches give the length of the Sacred Cubit ($5 \times 5 = 25$ angles of the Pyramid). The absolute length of the Sacred Cubit is the same used by the Israelites and spoken of in the volume of the Sacred Law as the one ordained by God, and was brought out of Egypt by Moses, who, being one of the High Priests of On, no doubt knew and understood all the mysteries and secrets of the Great Pyramid and sacred doctrines. It was different in length to that of the Greek, Roman, and later-day Egyptian cubit. Freemasons, perhaps unknown to themselves, have been the custodians of the secrets connected with it from the original, through ages of time, bringing on from its origin how much of the original secrets connected with it ? ? ?

Thus we see that the standard and unit of linear measurement, used at the building of the Great Pyramid, from which the British inch was derived in primeval days of purity and Eschatological worship, before the people fell away from their true doctrines, has been handed down by us pure and unsullied. The measurements of the Mayas were the same as the Egyptians in all particulars, reckoning by 5 and 20.

The great attempt of the French people to abolish alike the Christian religion and hereditary weights and measures of all nations, to replace the former by a worship of philosophy, and the latter by the Mètre—French mètre scheme depending, in a certain manner of their own, upon the magnitude of the earth, as well as the substitution of a week of seven days by an artificial period of ten days—is not very old nor yet an improvement upon the exactness in measurement of these ancient people ; because, by assuming, as their unit and standard of length, the one ten-millionth of a "quadrant of the earth's surface" that took a curved line drawn on the earth's surface in the place of the straight axis of rotation it could not be so exact, and in fact is far inferior in measurement. The British hereditary inch, therefore, is much nearer and more exact to an integral earth measure. As long as one retains a power of geometry, so long will the diameter be thought of greater primary importance than the circumference of a circle, and when we come to a sphere in motion, the axis of its dynamical labour shall hold a vastly superior importance, especially when the earth's equator is not a true circle. Yet all this was taken into account and provided for by the builders of the Great Pyramid and the references for the grand unit—the ten-sevenths or ten-millionth part of the earth's Polar semi-axis—then adopted, is now shown to be the only sound and scientific one which the earth possesses. Through all these years the British inch has only lost 1 one-thousandth part of its length—and that we are aware of. Who shall say that this has not been caused by a Divine will ?—you ask why—because, as years go on the interior of the earth cools down, earthquakes take place and the outer crust falls in and the circumference would lessen, and in time so would the earth's Polar semi-axis. If the Pyramid was built by Divine Inspiration, we may be sure that the Great Architect of the Universe has provided in some way—His way—to keep all correct, even to the smallest detail. For those who believe in the Divine Inspiration, there is something for them to think about and ponder over before any change is made in our standard.

Origin of the D.C.'s Symbol

The symbol of the dove on the white wands of the D.C.'s is very ancient, and dates back to Stellar Mythos. These white wands, surmounted by a bird, were the symbols carried by certain of their priests, certainly as far back as the time of the Temple of Pithom and probably much earlier, and are still used as they were thousands and thousands of years ago by the priests of Egypt, and those of the Central States of America, by the Yezidis around Mosul, who have carried them down, with all the ceremonies of their ancient religion, from generation to generation to the present day. The dove is a symbol of the soul. *In the Stellar Mythos it was always the dove, because it was the representation of the soul of the mother—that was primary.* It was the bird of soul, when the soul was first attributed to the female source, but when the Solar Mythos took the place of the Stellar we find from the *Ritual*, that the transformation from the mummy was made in Amenta, the deceased became " bird-headed " as a soul, and thus assumed the likeness of Ra, the Holy Spirit, in the form of a hawk, as it was in their later Eschatology, the sign of the soul that was considered to be male, the soul of God the Father—the Holy Spirit. There can be seen in Egyptian drawings, the soul portrayed in the process of issuing from the mummy in the shape of a dove instead of the usual hawk: both are emblems of the risen soul, but the dove was the earlier type of a soul derived from the mother. The hawk was the symbol of the Father and Son—*i.e.* of Ra and Horus, so that, wherever we find these symbols used, we know the origin of the date and meaning attached thereto. The divine Horus rises again in the form of a dove as well as in the shape of a hawk. " I am the dove! I am the dove! " exclaims the risen spirit as he soars up from Amenta—*Ritual*, lxxxvi. 1. Here the dove (of Hathor) is also the bird of Ra, and thus the dove becomes the bird of the Holy Spirit, female in the mother and male in the divine Horus, and finally in the Father. On the tomb of Rameses IX. the dove appears in the place of the hawk, as a co-type of Horus at the prow of the Solar boat, which shows how they made use of and brought the oldest symbols on. The Holy Spirit was always represented by a bird, which, in the Egyptian symbolisms, was the dove or hawk. We find also that two birds (symbolically) *acted as " conductors."* The *Ritual* says :—" Ye two divine hawks upon your gables, who are giving attentive heed to the matter—*ye who conduct the ship of Ra, advancing onwards from the highest place of the ark in heaven* " ; also it is said to Osiris : " Thy two sisters, Isis and Nepthys (represented by two birds), *come to thee and they convey to thee the great extent—(of the waters) in thy name* of the great extender as the Lord of the Flood "—TETA, 274.

These allusions prove that there was " an ark " *to which the two birds were attached as " conductors."*

CHAPTER XV

THE ORIGIN OF THE TRIANGLE

Triangle of Horus I. which Shu lifted up on the Seven Steps.

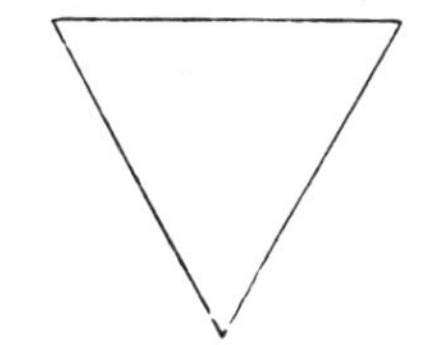

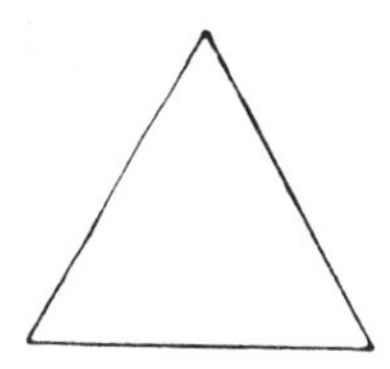

Triangle, Pyramid or Cone of the God Set, God of the South Pole Star and Primary.

THE Triangle was a primary form of the Pyramid and a sacred symbol, because the Pyramid was typically the Pyramid of Heaven; therefore this triangle is typical of Heaven.

In the Egyptian Stellar Mythology, Shu, standing on seven steps, first lifted up the heaven from the earth in the form of a triangle, and at each point was situated one of the gods, Sut, Shu, and Horus.

The triangle, therefore, was one of the most sacred emblems. The definition of Sut, Shu and Horus, in the Egyptian, is identical with L.A.B., as demonstrated in R.A. chapter, the apex being at the Pole Star, where Horus was situated.

Horus was the first god of "the Pole Star North," with attributes of Set brought on. In chapter vii. of the *Ritual* it says: "I am the one who presided over the Pole of Heaven, and the powers of all the gods are my powers. I am he whose names are hidden and whose abodes are mysterious for all eternity."

No. 3 was a sacred number, because it represented these three. They are the Trinity in its very earliest form, which was Stellar.[1]

In some of the oldest papyri and monuments we find the original triangle of Horus I. thus ▽ *i.e.* with the apex downwards. This has wrongly been associated with the zodiacal light, but it has nothing to do with it or its meaning. It is in the

[1] An oath taken on the Triangle was never known to have been broken.

FIG. 121.

FIG. 122.

form of this triangle that Shu lifted up the heavens, standing on the top of the "Seven Steps," and the apex of the triangle rested on them (Fig. 121).

The uranographic symbol, which was constellated in "Triangula," was composed of three stars held in the hand of Horus (Fig. 122). Drummond, Od. Jud. pl. 3.

The Triangle, which was thus constellated in "Triangula," is the tripartite division of the Ecliptic, and the triple seasons of the Egyptian year :—

The Water season being represented by Horus ;

The season of Wind and the Equinoctial gales by Shu ;

The season of Dryness and Drought by Sut ;

otherwise, "the water season," "the green season," and "the dry season," the three signs of which are :—"water," "growing plants," and a "barn" or storehouse.

Four months for the water season gave the correct length of the inundation, and the Egyptian harvest occurred in the eighth month of the year ; then followed four months of drought and dearth, which came to be assigned to the destroyer Sut. These three seasons can be traced as a basis for the Zodiac, which was afterwards extended to one of four quarters and twelve signs.

Horus of the Inundation was given the Lion as a Solar Zootype ; the Archer, four signs farther round, was assigned to Shu, and four signs are a correct measure of one season, or a tetramine.

Sut was continued in conflict with Horus in the Constellation of the Twins, the power of drought which was opposed to the power of life. Shu was the reconciler of these two continually warring powers, and in the Zodiac he represents the green season of vegetation and breathing life, which came betwixt the seasons of water and drought.

The Egyptian month was divided into three weeks of ten days each, which obviously corresponded with the heaven of the triangle, the tripartite Ecliptic, and the three seasons in Egypt. Then followed a heaven of four quarters or four sides, in which may be traced the houses of Sut, Horus, Shu and Taht ; but the division of the month or moon, and the Ecliptic in three parts, equated with the three seasons in a circle or Zodiac, which was measured monthly by the Lunar god Taht, with his 3×10, thirty days.

This mound or pyramid of seven steps is called the staircase or ladder of Shu, and *Maspero* says it was famous throughout all Egypt. The event (as supposed history) took place at Hermopolis, the city of which Taht was lord, therefore it was during Lunar Mythos that this originated. In the *Ritual*, a figure of this mound, with seven steps, called the ladder or staircase of Shu, is frequently portrayed. The moon fulfilled its four quarters in twenty-eight steps, fourteen up and fourteen down. In the first quarter the moon took seven steps upward, from the underworld to the summit, which, in the annual reckoning, was the equinoctial mount. There are two sets of names in the *Ritual* given to the seven steps, as the seven primordial powers in two of their Astronomical characters in Egypt. In the first :

1. An-ar-f, the Great.
2. Kat-Kat.
3. The Bull which liveth in his fire.
4. The Red-eyed One in the House of Gauze.
5. Fiery-face which turneth backwards.
6. Dark-face in its Hour.
7. Seer in the Night.

Different Names or Attributes of Horus.

In the Second :

1. Amsta.
2. Hapi.
3. Tuamuteef.
4. Habhsenuf.
5. Maa-tef-f.
6. Karbek-f.
7. Har-Khent-an-maa-ti.

We give the original Egyptian names ; all brothers of 30° know our present ones.

The first four of the latter seven are the gods of the four quarters, who stand on the papyrus of earth and who become the children of Horus in a later creation.

We must remember that Shu upraised the heaven of day in one character and the heaven of night in another.[1] He is a pillar of support to the firmament as founder of the double equinox. He sustains the heaven with his two arms. It was at the equinoctial level that the quarrel of Sut and Horus was settled

[1] Shu upraised the heaven of day and in his other character was Anhar who upraised the heaven of night.

for the time being by Shu, and therefore Shu stands for the equinox as the link of connection betwixt Sut and Horus in the North and South.

The heaven in two parts, South and North, as the domains of Sut and Horus, was now followed by the heaven in three divisions that was upraised by Shu, as establisher of the equinox in the more Northern latitudes. This heaven in three divisions was the heaven of the Triangle, which preceded the one built on the square by Ptah.

Horus and Sut had been twin-builders of the heaven and the founders of North and South (South first by Sut) and established the two poles or pillars, situated at the North and South, which afterwards were placed at the Porchway entrance of the temple of Ptah, Amenta, Solomon's Temple, etc.—the two Tatt pillars. Shu followed with the new foundation in the equinox, which was double—East and West. Sut, Horus and Shu then founded the heaven of the Triangle, based upon the twofold horizon and the crossing: Shu, as the equinoctial power, is the third to Sut and Horus of the South and North. With him the first triad was completed, and the two pillars, with a line across, would form the figure of the triangle ▽ (*Ritual*, chap. cx.).

The meaning of this triangle is well known to those of the 33°, and it is associated with this degree where the apex rests on the † which surmounts the Crown, which is supported by the double-headed eagle, holding the sword in its talons. This crown would be the representative crown of zodiacal light — (see CROWNS) — not the triangle, the highest crown of illumination in the highest degree—*the Atef-Crown* which was first assigned to Amen-Ra.

FIG. 123.

We draw particular attention to this form of the triangle, as it is very ancient, and because this form was associated *with Horus I. only*, and is one of the symbols which stand for his names, and is different from the Pyramid Triangle.

As we have stated elsewhere in this work, this triangle △ was the first hieroglyphic for the name of Sut or Sept, but after the great fight it was associated with the name of Horus I. and was appropriated to him. We see in this papyrus that Shu lifted up the heavens with his hands, hence the base of the triangle above. If he had done it with a stick or prop he would have had the apex above, but we see from the drawings left us that he did not do this, and the apex rested on the top of the seven steps where Shu stood. Much more might be written as an Egyptologist on this triangle, which has been a great stumbling block to all Egyptologists hitherto, and no one, as far as our researches have gone, has given the true meaning of this particular hieroglyphic. From the base of the triangle thus lifted up, the square of the heavens was afterwards worked out, and the four children of Horus were assigned as its supports. This could not have been done if the triangle had its base at the bottom. After this triangle △ was assigned to Horus we frequently find them blended together in this form (upon which we have already written), or in this form ⧗ as we find among the oldest Mexican Indians, and those of Central America and Australia. These two triangles, thus depicted, we find, as may be seen in Egypt, Assyria, Mexico ; all over the world, in fact.

We refrain from giving more particulars of this ▽ and its meaning, as we are not a 33°, but only a 30°, and therefore only "on the summit of the seven steps," but those who are interested will find amongst all the oldest tribes throughout the world the two triangles on all their sacred ornaments, depicted thus ⧗. Afterwards it was blended into this form . The former is much more ancient than the latter, and we cannot find any reason for *Brother Gould* calling it "Solomon's Seal." Solomon was not born when this was first used as a sacred sign, and as far as our researches go, we have not been able to trace any facts or reasons to support the assertion that Solomon ever used it as a seal, though possibly *Brother Gould* may have some authority with which we are not acquainted. However, whether he used it or not, this sacred sign is much older than Solomon, and the origin and meaning was as we have given. It is widely dispersed all over the world, and is often to be found in connection with the "Khui Land," and they probably took and adapted it from the sign in Aries in the above way. In the Royal Arch degree we have also these two triangles interlaced, surrounded with the circle and with the triple tau in the centre, the meaning of which is known to Royal Arch Masons.

The Royal Arch Degree Symbol

Fig. 124.

9
8

7
6

5
4

2 3

This ▽ , with the numbers, will also be interesting to

1

those of The Royal Ark Mariner's degree. (*See* Appendix.)

The earth or house of Anup was then completed by the Square or base of Pyramid, at the four corners of which, as keepers, were the Divine Powers—the children of Horus :—

			Hebrew		Christian
In Egyptian :	Amsta	..	Man	..	Matthew
"	Hapi	..	Lion (Ape)	..	Mark
"	Tuamutf	..	Ox (Jackal)	..	Luke
"	Kabhsenuf	..	Eagle (Hawk)	..	John

Adapted as the signs of the four banners of the Children of

Israel when they left Egypt, and the explanation of which all R.A.M.'s are well acquainted with. We give here a photograph taken from a copperplate engraving over one hundred years old.

These "four children of Horus" are very important in tracing back the origin of the present Eschatologies to the past, as they are the prototypes of our present four Evangelists. We have stated before, these four children of Horus are the same which we find amongst the Mayas under the names of

1. Kan-Bacab—The Yellow Bacab, who stood at the South,
2. Chac-Bacab—The Red Bacab, who stood at the East,
3. Zac-Bacab—The White Bacab, who stood at the North,
4. Ek-Bacab—The Black Bacab, who stood at the West,

and in Central America, Mexico and amongst the Zapotecs these names are:

Acatal	Beeu	Kau
Tecpatl	Ezanab	Muluc
Calli	Ahbal	Lx
Tochtli	Lamal	Cauac

These all represent the four children of Horus, and until those who are working on the Antiquities in Mexico and Central America recognise Sut, Horus, Isis, Anubis and others in their mural paintings, they will never be able to interpret or decipher the meaning of the same.

It is stated that in remote ages the Maya's ancestors imagined that the vault of Heaven was sustained on four pillars, placed one at each corner, on each cardinal point, and that the Creator assigned the care of these to the before-mentioned four brothers. Their traditional history and duties here are the same as we find stated in the Egyptian *Ritual*, from whence they obtained their knowledge, their sacred books being a copy of the *Ritual* of Egypt. If *Drs Edward Seler*, *Forstemann*, *P. Schellhas*, *C. Sapper*, and *E. P. Dieseldorff* and others will turn to the *Ritual* of ancient Egypt, and recognise that the Primordial was there, and that all these are copies, carried out by various exodes at the time of the Stellar Mythos, and after the Solar Eschatology was brought here, they will have no difficulty in their decipherment, and will be in a position to write something that is worth studying, and will be able to solve all those points which they are at present unable to do.

Second: The four principal Protecting Genii of the human race amongst the Chaldeans were named:

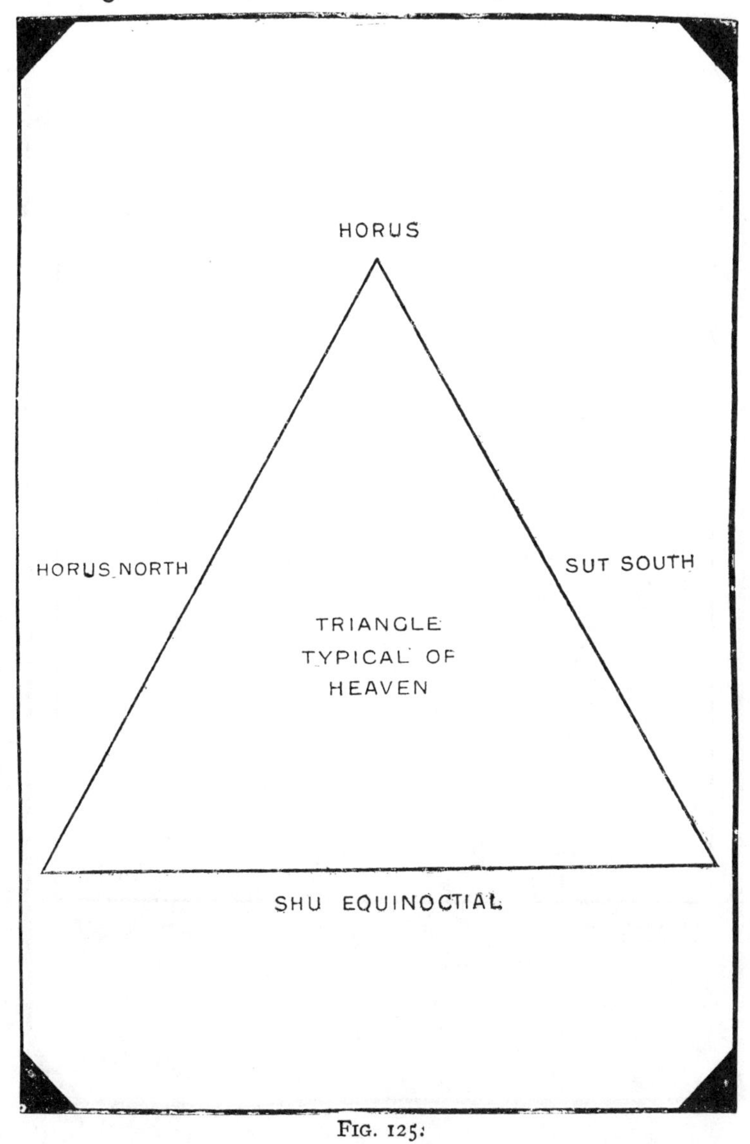

FIG. 125.

1. Sed-Alap or Kirub, represented as a Bull with a human face,
2. Lamas or Nirgal, as a Lion with a human head,
3. Ustur, after the human likeness,
4. Nattig, with the head of an Eagle,

and were said by Ezekiel to be the four symbolical creatures which supported the Throne of Jehovah in his visions by the river Chebar.

AMSTA

HAPI

HOUSE OF ANUP OR EARTH

TUAMUTF

KABHSENUF

FIG. 126.

Third: These four are known to the Hindoo occultists as the four Maharajahs or great kings of the Dylan Cholans:

1. India, the King of Heaven to the East,
2. Kowvera, the God of Wealth to the North,
3. Varouna, the God of the Waters to the West,

4. Yama, the Judge of the Dead to the South.

Fourth : Also amongst the Chinese, the four quarters:

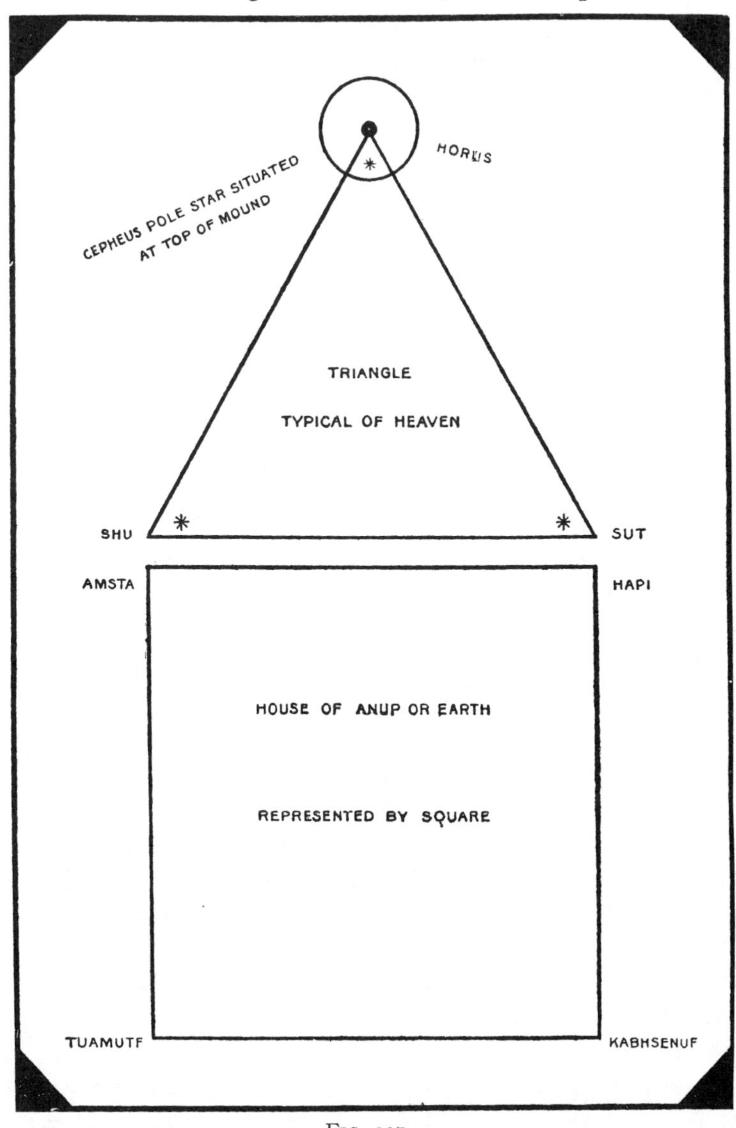

FIG. 127.
The Double Holy House of Anup. Origin of Temples found by *Dr Le Plongeon* at Uxmal.

1. Tai-Tsong—East,
2. Sigan-fou—West,
3. How-Kowang—South,
4. Chen-si—North,

which represent the four Great Powers or Mythical Mountains in China.

Fifth: Amongst the North American Indians they are known as the "Four Powerful Ones." These people supposed that these heavenly architects emanated from "the Great Infinite One," evolved in the material universe from chaos, and they represented them by a square within a circle and by joining the ends of the vertical and horizontal diameters, in some cases with an erect pillar in the centre of the square to represent the Great Infinite One, the origin and centre of all.

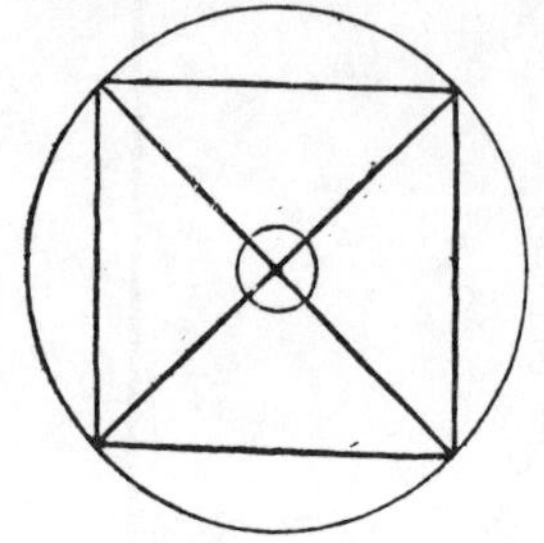

FIG. 128.

Probably this figure may be the same as those found, one in Java and the other in North America, mentioned before; but we are unable to say for certain as we have not seen any photographs of them, and have only the description given by *Forbes* and *Gerald Massey*.

Sixth: The people of Bavili, Bimi and Yorba, West Africa, have the same under the names of

1. Ibara,
2. Edi,
3. Oyekun,
4. Oz-be,

and build these names, with the name of Ifi, the Son of God—*i.e.* Horus—into the walls of their houses.

Seventh: Revelation iv. 6.—And in the midst of the Throne, and round about the Throne, there were four beasts, full of eyes before and behind:

The first was like a Lion,
The second was like a Calf,
The third had the face of a Man, and
The fourth was like a flying Eagle.

This photograph shows the four Evangelists, St Matthew, St Mark, St Luke and St John, depicted here as a Man, Lion, Ox and Eagle, and must be conclusive evidence to the reader, showing him how the Egyptian prototypes have been brought down and adopted by the Christians. These also may be seen in many churches here in England at the present time, one of the finest specimens, perhaps, being over the altar at South Tawton

Church, in Devonshire, where also may be seen a granite stone in one of the aisles over a grave, with some very clear hieroglyphics (Egyptian) cut on it ; which probably was taken from one of the Druidical remains on Dartmoor.

FIG. 129.

The Christian form of symbolically representing St Matthew, St Mark, St Luke and St John. Brought on from the old Eschatology of the Egyptians and represented throughout the world as we have shown.

The foregoing, we think, is sufficient proof that mankind emanated from one common centre, and for this we must go back to Egypt, for mankind existed here long before they had evolved their Eschatology, at the time of their Mythology. Nowhere else have we been able to trace Stellar Mythology proper, except in Egypt, and all have their origin in the *Ritual* of ancient Egypt ; nowhere else can it be found.

ORIGIN OF THE TWO COLUMNS I AND B AT ENTRANCE OF TEMPLE

In that beautiful PAPYRUS OF ANI, the original of which is in the British Museum, you see the entrance to their temple shown thus :

We find at the entrance two pillars. The four lines at

the top represent four sides of a square, because the ancient Egyptians always drew on the flat, as they did not understand

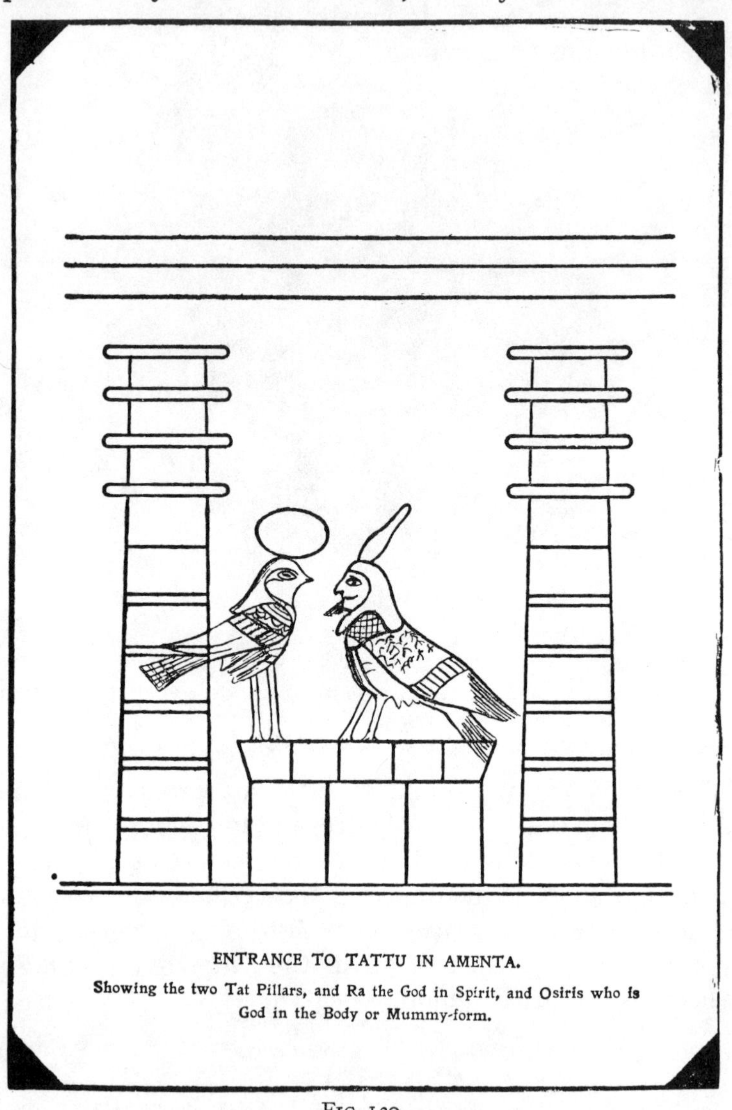

ENTRANCE TO TATTU IN AMENTA.

Showing the two Tat Pillars, and Ra the God in Spirit, and Osiris who is God in the Body or Mummy-form.

FIG. 130.

perspective. The squares here represent the Terrestrial and Celestial Globes.

The two figures shown here between the pillars are, (1) Ra, the God in the Spirit, and (2) Osiris, who is God in the body or mummy form, as the Initiate, claiming entrance to Amenta; but according to the *Ritual*, questions are asked, which must be answered satisfactorily as regards his conduct during life, before being admitted to that immortal region ; and many trials have to

FIG. 131.

We give here a photograph from a copper plate which is over 100 years old, showing the Pillars of I and B at the porchway entrance of King Solomon's Temple, of which a full description will be found in the volume of our Sacred Law, and although some may think that these differ materially in shape and form from the Egyptian, their meaning is the same.

be gone through and passwords be remembered—see "Book of the Dead," chaps. xcix. and cxxv.

Creation is of two sorts, (1) such as that of the Spirit, which is everlasting and can never pass away ; (2) visible creation, which is material, finite and perishable.

In many papyri, two figures, "each holding a knife," are seated before or on each side of the door. One is the Watcher and the other is the Herald—see *Naville, op. cit.* Bd. 1. BI. 154.

The Circle or Arrcts are 7 in number—7 Arrcts or Lodges or Mansions, also the names of the "Doorkeeper," the "Watcher," and the "Heralds."

These pillars, which are ornamented octagonal columns, were

placed at the Porchway entrance of the temple in Amenta. One was called in Egyptian "Tat," which means in their language, "In strength"; the other, "Tattu," which in Egyptian is "To establish." The word "Tattu" also denotes the two Tat Pillars; this means in Egyptian "The place of establishing for ever."

The explanation of the ornamentation you see on these, is symbolically the same as the two pillars at the Porchway Entrance to King Solomon's Temple. The Tat is a figure of stability; it supports the four corners and is equal to the square.

The original "Two Pillars" was brought on from early Totemic Ceremonies, and represented Horus in the North and Sut in the South, and was always erected in the ceremony of "making the boy into a man," an establisher, a creator, etc., as may be seen amongst the Australian Aborigines and other native tribes at the present day, after it was brought on in the Stellar cult; and when the Egyptians had worked out Amenta, then the two pillars were brought on and placed at the entrance of Amenta as above and became eschatological. There were two pillars of the gateway of the house of Ptah. These represented Horus and Sut.

Two Tats form the entrance to Tattu—a Double Square—Tattu is the entrance or gateway to the region where the mortal Soul is blended with an Immortal Spirit, and is established for ever in the mysteries of Amenta.

According to the Egyptian Creed all these temples were simply representatives, so to speak, of Amenta and Heaven: their priests were human representatives of the Divine Master, and bore Divine titles. All these "Types" were a dual of their belief of the same in Heaven and life hereafter; their teachings, forms and ceremonies, representing their beliefs as to the life that must be led on this earth to attain the "Throne of Glory," and the trials the Spirit would be subjected to until that was accomplished.

"Never the Spirit was born, the Spirit will cease to be never:
Never was time it was not: end and beginnings are dreams!
Birthless and deathless and changeless remaineth the Spirit for ever;
Death hath not touched it at all, dead though the house of it seems."

CHAPTER XVI

ORIGIN OF THE CIRCLE AND THE POINT WITHIN A CIRCLE

THE point within a circle 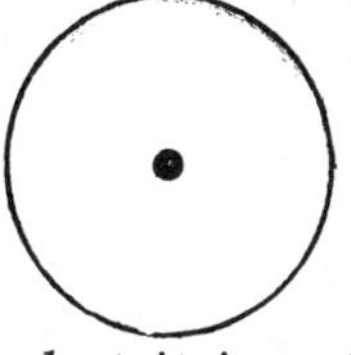 is one of the hieroglyphic signs of the Sun-God, Ra, but it is not merely an image of the solar disc. For one thing it is a Masonic symbol, and *H. A. Giles*, the Chinese scholar, who is himself a Mason, tells us it is held to represent the One Supreme Power, whatever that power may be, the Great Architect of the Universe, recognised alike by ourselves and our brother Masons of every religious denomination—see *H. A. Giles*' "Historic China," page 389.

The earliest supreme power figured in Heaven in a masculine shape was the Power of Stability and Equilibrium, associated with the fixity of the Pole Star. This was first assigned to Anup, in the form of a Jackal; then to Horus I., to Ptah, the Great Architect, and finally to Osiris, the power that held all things in equipoise.

The Pole Star is the first fixed point within a circle, not the Sun, and the earliest Supreme Being at the head of the seven primary stars was the god of the Pole Star. Therefore we claim the Glyph of Ra to have been the Ideograph of the Pole Star at the centre of a circle.

And as the sceptre of Anup and the Jackal itself was assigned to the latter Solar god when he became supreme, as the one who presided over the Pole of Heaven, it follows that the sign also was transferred to Ra.

The Great Architect of the Universe began to build the House of Heaven with the Pole Star for foundation stone, or rather, for the coping stone of the cone, the Ben-ben, the House of the Mound, when the circle was the enclosure of Am-Khemen.

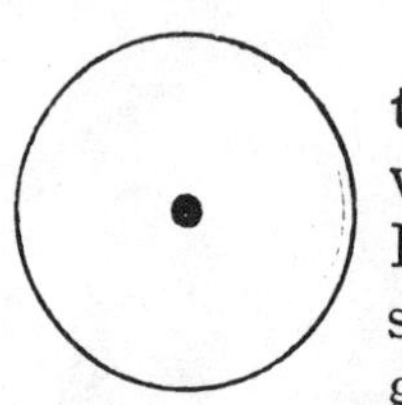

The dot in the centre of a circle is equal to the point at the top of the cone that was crowned with the star at the summit. In this circle of the Pole Star there were seven gods or glorious ones grouped together in the constellation of the Lesser Bear, revolving round the Most High, the Great Judge, the All-Seeing Eye who saw by night, and who is the figure of Anup at the Pole in the Planisphere of Denderah.

The circle of Precession, or rather, Recession, takes 25,827 years to perform its cycle, and each one of the Pole Stars (7) could be seen shining down the passage opening to the north in the interior of the Great Pyramid in its turn.

The Divine Circle 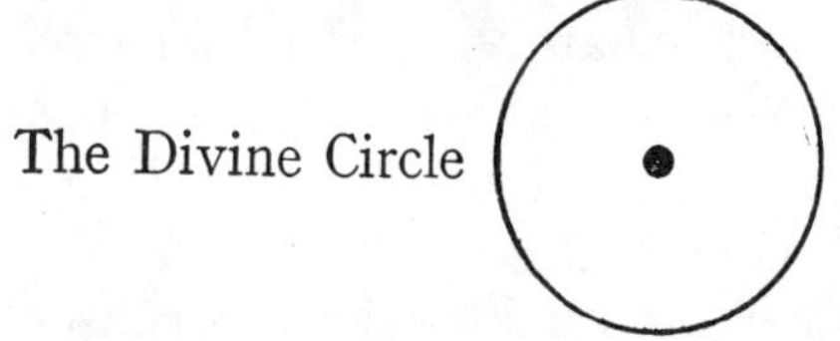 became the sign of Ra in his Zodiacal Circle, but there is no such standpoint for its origin as a Solar symbol that there is for its having been the star at the centre of the Circumpolar Enclosure. Moreover, the Glyph

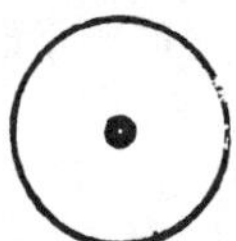 is an equivalent for the Eye, and the two are co-types.

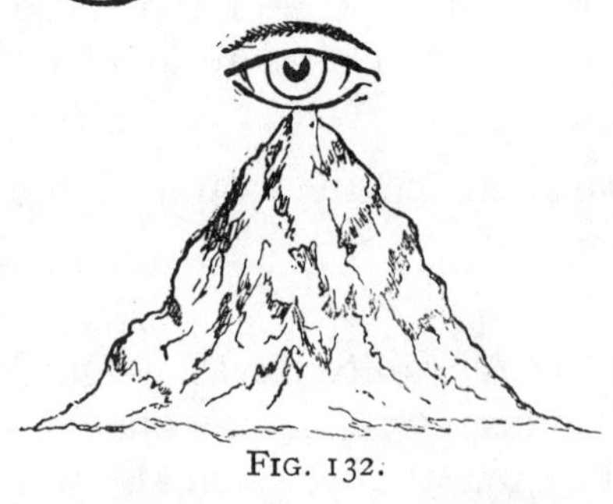

FIG. 132.

Therefore it may be inferred that, as the fixed star at the centre, it was the Primordial All-Seeing Eye in the Astral Mythology. The Pole Star, considered as an eye upon the summit of the mountain, explains the Chinese name of the "Heaven's-Eye Mountain." We find the same equivalent in the States of Central America.

The gods are described as being in their circles according to their numbers, and the god of the Polar Circle was A 1 or the One, the Supreme One. When the sign was given to Ra it denoted the One Supreme Power in his Circle; then his Circle was astronomically the Circle of the Zodiac or eschatologically the Circle of the Universe. The Pole being at the centre, served to determine the four quarters and the eight semi-cardinal points.

Taking the sign  for the Pole Star Circle,

we may infer that the wheel with eight spokes or the star with eight rays is the figure of Am-Khemen, the Paradise of the eight gods—that is, of Anup and the seven Glorious Ones.

The sign , familiar to all R.A.M.'s, combines the enclosure of the Pole Star with the Triangular Heaven of Sut, Horus and Shu. The Triangle, united to the square of the four quarters, formed the double Holy House of Anup. The Mountain of the Pole was the Mount of the Seven Stars, the Seven Stairways, Seven Steps and other forms of the Mythical Seven. It is on these Steps that Shu is said to have stood when he upraised the Heaven of Am-Khemen, the Paradise of the eight gods which succeeded the Circle of the Great Bear, and the seven in the Lesser Bear. Thus Am-Khemen was the Circle of Enclosure of the Seven, with Anup of the Pole Star added to complete the Eight. This is the Circumpolar Paradise, upraised upon the summit of the mount that was a figure of the Pole: the Mythical Mountain of the North which was figured in the artificial Mounds, Round Hillock, Cairns, Beehive Huts, Pict Houses and other Conical structures in all lands and from remotest times, as burial places for the dead that where to rise again upon the Mount of Heaven. We are unable to get back to the time when the work of the Mound Builders had no religious or eschatological significance. The first Mound of Burial also denoted the Mount of Resurrection, and it is the Mount which led up to the Paradise upon the summit, first uplifted by Shu-Anhar as the Heaven of Am-Khemen.

The seven candlesticks with lighted candles we have no doubt

FIG. 133.
The Seven Golden Candlesticks.

were introduced by Moses as a representative type of the "Seven Glorious Ones"—*i.e.* the seven stars of the Little Bear, originally in Stellar Mythos. We have at the present time the same in use amongst the Christian Churches representing the mystic seven which are the prototypes of the Seven Glorious Ones. Also the 7 Pole Stars each in turn represented The One—and these became the origin of the 7 Powers, 7 Great Princes, etc.

Nothing can be plainer, more definite or more convincing than this :—

Revelation ii. 28.—I will give him the Morning Star.

Revelation i. 16.—And he had in his right hand seven stars.

Revelation i. 20.—Mystery of the seven stars—and seven golden candlesticks. The seven stars are the angels of the seven churches. The seven candlesticks are the seven churches.

Revelation iii. 1.—Seven spirits of God and the seven stars.

Revelation iv. 5.—There were seven lamps of fire burning before the throne, which are the seven spirits of God.

In furnishing the Ark of testimony according to the pattern seen in the Mount, instructions are given for the Lampstand to be made with Six branches giving out of the Candlestick. But it is added: "Thou shalt make the lamps thereof seven"—Ex. xxv.

This therefore was a figure of six encircling the one that was a fixture in the centre—*i.e.* The Seven Pole Stars.

Houses of Heaven

When the four quarters were filled in with the twelve signs, the circle surrounding the Mount or Pillar of Earth was the Zodiac. Thus, when Moses "Builded an Altar under the Hill and Twelve Pillars, according to the twelve tribes of Israel"—Exodus xxiv. 4—these were an image of the Mount, and the twelve signs which marked the twelve divisions of the Celestial Circle. This Astronomical Circle was also figured in the Hebrew Gilgal, formed with twelve pillars or stones. Joshua is said to have taken twelve stones out of the Jordan and set them up in Gilgal. These were landmarks in the waters of Heaven, not in the waters of Jordan below. The Gilgal, or circle of revolution, then, was a figure of the Zodiac, and the twelve erect stones or pillars represented the twelve Celestial signs ; and an erection in the centre of this circle, a Stone, a Cairn, a Pillar, an Altar or a Mound, would signify the Mount upon which the four supports were set up at the four cardinal points in the Circle of Heaven.

According to Mohammedan tradition the Kaaba at Mecca had been constructed ten different times. It was first built in Heaven, when the angels circled round it in procession. This shows it to have been an image of Heaven in ten different shapes, beginning with the Cone or Pyramidion of the Pole. All ten might be made out from the figures that survive as sacred emblems, such as the Cone, Triangle, Square, Pyramid, Cube, Octagon, Cross, Circle, and the rest. The name of the Kaaba, from Ka'ab, a cube, denotes the shape the building had assumed at the time that name was given. This would indicate the Heaven of the four quarters with Zenith and Nadir added to the Square. Naturally the primary figure drawn in Heaven was the Circle, which the Kamite record shows. This was made definite by the revolution of the seven great stars in Ursa Major—the constellation of the Ancient Mother, also known as the Thigh—Uterus—and the Mesken or chamber of birth. In this circle also revolve the seven stars of the Lesser Bear (as children of the Thigh), who represented seven primary powers here grouped together as the seven Glorious Ones. They circled round the Mythical Mountain of the North, which, as a figure in Astronomy, is the Celestial Pole, and in the Eschatology is the Mount of Glory. This Mount was imaged in the Conical Mound of the primeval builders. Two figures were established as the Circle and the Cone. Thus it was seen that there was a fixed point to this Circle of the Seven Stars, determined by one never-moving star, which we now call the Pole Star. This, to the early Astronomers, was the star that crowned the summit of the Mount, the Cone or Pyramidion, as the fixed point in the circle of the Bears—that is, of the Great Mother and her seven children. The Pole Star was assigned to Horus, who was added to the group of seven as the eighth child of the Ancient Genetrix. Horus became the first or supreme one, as highest and most stable of them all, and who, in the course of time, was looked upon as a father to the earlier seven. The earliest fixed point within the circle was the Pole Star. *Plutarch* speaks of the Egyptian Priests having a ceremony when they walk seven times around a circle, "seeking for Osiris," burning incense, resin and myrrh. They do not find him, but Horus, the Son, whom the *Ritual* says "has taken possession of the throne which his father had given him; he has taken possession of Heaven, and inherited the earth, and neither heaven nor earth shall be taken from him, for he is Ra, the oldest of the Gods."

The second chapter of the Aat tells of the difficulties, dangers and darkness that have to be traversed through the valley of death, in the following words :—"I am the man and clothe thy head—and after his two eyes are given to him, and he becomes glorious therewith." The book further says :—" I have come to see the princes, *uncover your faces and lay down your head-dresses when ye meet*, for behold I am a mighty one among you, and let me live upon the offerings among you," which may interest those of the 18°.

FIG. 134.

Prototype of part of the Ceremonies of the 18°. From "Mexican Antiquities," published by the Bureau of American Ethnology, Smithsonian Institution.

The 17th and 18th chapters of the *Ritual* must be interesting to those of the 18°, because here we find that the blind Horus, or Horus in the dark, or blindness or invisibility, had the veil of darkness (a net) over his head, so that he was unable to see, and had to pass through difficulties, danger and darkness, after which he was presented to the great circle of Chiefs or Princes, the veil being removed by Thoth, who restored him to light, life, health and strength, and all the glorious company of Princes, in which he was given a place.

He was first presented and conducted by An-maut-ef, who saith, "I am come to you, ye great circle of Chiefs and Princes in Heaven, upon earth, and in the world below. I bring to you N— void of offence towards any. Grant that he may be with you daily." He is then taken by Se-meri-f through the valley of the shadow of death, and after mounting seven steps is presented to the Glorious Princes with these words : "I come to you, O Circle of Princes"—*i.e.* Chiefs, in Restau—"and I bring N— to you. Grant to him bread, water, air (provender of the altars), and an allotment in the Sechit-hotep, like Horus." Thoth having removed the dark net, he is invited to unite or join in our circle and the feast. The oldest text gives it, "Come thou to me," which means an invitation to join in the circle and feast. Both names (An-maut-ef and Se-meri-f) are titles of

Horus. He states (*Ritual*, chap. cxxv.): "I have given bread to the hungry, water to the thirsty, clothes to the naked and a boat to the shipwrecked." It is the usual thing for the Egyptian Priests to bear divine titles, the *Ritual* observance being dramatic and symbolical representation of the actions of the gods. The above may interest *Brother Winn Westcott*, and we invite him to study the *Ritual* and "Blind Horus"—see A. 2. 2.

Fig. 134. This picture, taken from the MEXICAN CODEX, may be of interest to brothers of the 18°.

Practically it represents a part of the ceremonies of this degree. One figure depicts a representative of Xipe, "the flayed one," and is the same as the Zapotec "Teotitlan del valle," which means "the one who has passed through the valley and shadow of death, difficulties, danger and darkness," as depicted in other figures of this Codex.

A is a part of the ceremony which all will understand, and it is not necessary to give here too much information regarding the "secrets."—K. of E. and W.

B. Here we observe two figures; the first on the left is the candidate to be initiated into higher secrets, and he is giving his solemn promise, as seen by his left hand, to keep all secret and sacred. He has already attained to a certain eminence, as may be seen from the Horus lock and the apron he wears.

Seated on a throne before him is our representative or M.W.S. He has the sacred gold chain or collar round his neck and the sacred scrolls on his knees. He wears the Horus lock and has the Horus feathers on his head. By his hands it can be seen that he is telling his friend that "He Descended and He Ascended." Between them is the "food or provender of the altar" to be consumed later. The emblem of fire at the back of the cakes and wine denotes that all will be consumed. The crown and three feathers, also depicted, are ready to be placed on the head of the P.

The uniformity of the priesthood and ceremonial usages amongst the Zapotecs, Mexicans and Mayas is undeniable, and dates back to Egypt, whence they all obtained their doctrines and beliefs.

There was a distinction between the high and subordinate priests. Amongst the Zapotecs the former were known as Uigatas—*i.e.* "great seer," and amongst the Mexicans they were called Quetzalcoatl. They took divine titles of the gods, as did the

Egyptians, and this is a prototype here reproduced from Central America.

The figure on the right, B, in Mexican is called Piltzinteott or Piltzintecutli, "God of Princes" or "Master of Princes." The god of the Pole Star was called "god one" and "A 1," as we find in the early Stellar Mythos of Egypt. Examples of this are numerous in all the ruins of the ancient cities of Central America, and the Hieroglyphics are still extant for anyone to read who cares to learn.[1] Where *Dr Edward Seler* finds the type of the Crocodile (the hieroglyph representing A 1), it shows that this was erected and depicted on stone at the early part of their Stellar Mythos, when Anup represented the supreme power, and before he was deposed by Horus; they knew this and believed it because it was part of the *Ritual* of Egypt, from whence they obtained their knowledge.

The *Ritual* mentions ten great circles about Ra (Heaven divided in ten divisions), which, with Ra's circle, would make eleven

see this depicted on Druidical stones from Ireland, also from the Mexican and Central American, and in another part "I travel over the earth on foot (eleven to the N., eleven to the S., and eleven to the W.), returning to the E."—here was a ladder of seven steps leading to the Elysian Fields (or Heaven)—PYRAMID TEXT, plate of Ani—"furnished with words of might, after encountering 'impurities and abominations' to which the damned are liable in Amenta. After I come to you, O Circle of Gods or the Glorious and Great Ones, in Restau (or an association of persons, chiefs and princes), and bring to you N., grant to him bread, water and air, and an allotment with you." Certain words of might and the names of the Priests, "who present the manes of the dead, may be given here, as follows:— . Shah-la-mah, to salute or salaam in Egyptian. (Assyrian, Peace.) Make a peace offering . Se meri-f. Hebrew, Ab-. The Beloved Son or the Son he loves. Prince, Lord. The Great One, the Mighty One, the Ever-Coming One. The Great Prince who was at

[1] The Great Crocodile = the Great Water-Lizard, the first day sign here. The Mexican Chalchiuhtlicue—*i.e.* the Great Water-Cow or Great Mother = Apt who brought forth the first young crocodile—was her first-born. See page 116, fig. 50.

the head of the seven tribes of the Nomes or seven Astronomies in the Heavens. In ancient times Upper Egypt was divided into seven tribes, with a Prince over each, and one Great or Mighty One over all. The names of these we find on the so-called "Green Stone," now at Ghizeh, and are as follows :—

Seven Cities enclosed in fortified walls in Upper Egypt:

1. The City of the Eight Owls, beloved by Horus.
   (Khu, that is : the City of Seven Spirits.)
2. The City of the Seven Tebbirds.
3. The City of the Twins.
   (Taui, the ancient Nekker, opposite El Kab.)
4. The City of Kheperu—Ru or Kheperu.
   (This represents the City of the Beetle—Keper-Ru is a form of Atum in the sign of the Zodiac—or the City of the Ark. "Shadow of Wings."—Psalms xvii. 8; xxxvii. 7; lvii. 1; lxiii. 1.)
5. The City of Kau, beloved by Sekhat.
6. The City of Pu (Pa), beloved by Selk.
   (The Powers of Pu are Horus, Amsta and Hapi—chap. clxii. Those of the Red Crown.)
7. The City of the Kings, beloved by the Monarch.
   (This was the Royal or head of the Seven Nomes.)

Egypt was first mapped out in seven Nomes as the Heptanomes. The earliest heaven was formed in this figure with seven Astronomes in the waters of space. The seven Constellations with seven Rulers—the seven Khuti or Glorious Ones known as the seven Ali, under various names, the first and foremost of whom was Sothos, the leader of the seven in the circle of the year. This we see was also the custom of the Kingdoms of West Africa and amongst the little Pygmies before mentioned in the forests of the Congo.

[hieroglyphs].[1] An-Maut-ef may be translated :—"the column" or support of the Great Company of the Princes. With regard to the ten great circles, which, with "The One," made eleven, and which the ancient Egyptians, according to "The Book of the Dead," believed "that there were ten great circles in the universe circling around one great centre of all," making complete the Architecture of Heaven, shows how accurately the old "Mystery Teachers" had made and recorded observations for 50,000 years. Do the Astronomers of the present day recognise

[1] An-Maut-ef was also a title of Horus as ruler in the circle of the lesser year, and Se-meri-f title of Horus as traveller of the Heavenly road in the circle of Precession.

that ten separate divisions could be made to correspond to this ? We believe not. Moreover, it would be extremely difficult, if not impossible, from observation during one lifetime to define these. Stellar Photography has proved to us the millions of other stars that exist, which cannot be seen even with the most powerful telescope, as well as proving that constant changes are taking place, and the disintegration of the old and reforming of "new systems" ; so that it would appear the ancient Egyptians could not comprehend the vastness of the universe and space, and what existed therein. All they could have done would be to mark down through 50,000 years or more that which they could see by the eye alone, as far as we know. We also know they divided the heavens into thirty-six divisions after—twelve North, twelve South and twelve Central.

Herodotus says that the Egyptian Priests told him that they had recorded time for so long that during that period the sun had twice set where it now rises, and had twice risen where it now sets.

Drayson says the sun revolves around a centre as we revolve around the sun, and the sun travels at the rate of 40 miles per second, therefore it would travel through space 33,000,000,000,000,000 miles *in performing its one year.* As the Priests of Egypt made observations from one generation to another, tabulating the results for future generations, the question arises : "How much could they map out of the universe during this period, and how much came under their observation that cannot be seen either through the telescope or from Stellar Photography during a period of a present life ?" And yet we find that they did so ages before our present knowledge of photography —from ancient papyri, a free translation of which is :—

"Then God, seeing that they sought Him not, but longed after material pictures and attractions, sent forth His Edict unto each one of the Suns, and commanded them to emane worlds, and when the Suns heard this edict of God, they prepared themselves to do His bidding, and every Sun that was in the universe sent forth from his bosom a choir of planets. Thus began the Solar System that exists, each Sun being the centre of the planets which he evolved, and every planet revolving around that centre, from whose glowing bosom he had birth. Many and various were the planets evolved, according to the nature of the Suns from which they came, according also to the manifold existencies which

God foresaw would be produced thenceforth; wherefore the Earth-Sun is called Parent of the Earth of Man. From the body of the Sun Man's Earth came, and into the body of the Sun it shall be absorbed when the consummation of all things cometh. When the planets were evolved from the Sun they were sent forth at first in gaseous vapour, immense revolving spheres projected into space, but bound by laws unto the parent star. When this vapour subsided and condensed they became mighty spheres of water, whirling ever in their appointed circles and proceeding along their regulated paths. When ages and ages rolled into the gulph of ages and ages, and ages and ages vanished into the abyss of time, the Sphere became solidified with earthly particles and ceased to be a watery globe; and thus, as years revolved on years, and the forces of Nature exercised their powers, and heat contended with cold, and vapour with solid; there were volcanic changes and fiery revolutions and many deluges. Then the earth gradually assumed its present shape, having been the grave of successive generations, until the race that now exists upon it assumed unto themselves living developments."

Thus we see that what Stellar Photography has only now, within the last few years, "discovered" and demonstrated by photographic art to be facts, was known thousands of years ago by the Theopneustics. How could they have known these facts, as now proved by Stellar Photography? Had they the same instrumental means of finding out these things as our present astronomers, or was it Divine Knowledge imparted to them by the G.G.U., or recorded observations from generation to generation for at least 50,000 years? We believe the latter.

Note to Royal Arch Masons

The 64th Chapter and Rubric is a very important one to all R.A.M.'s. It commences with "I am Yesterday, To-day and To-morrow (Alpha and Omega)," etc., and is probably the oldest of all. Two versions seem to have existed in the earliest times. In the Rubric of one it says:—"This Chapter (Scroll of Papyri)[1]

[1] It is a chapter from the "Book of Life," "to be recited on coming forth to-day, that one may not be kept back on the path of the Tuat, whether on entering or in coming forth; for taking all the forms which one desireth, and that the person may not die a second time." If this chapter be known, the person is made triumphant on earth (as in the nether world) and he performeth all things which are done by the living, etc., etc.

was found in the City of Khemennu upon a Block of Iron of the South, which had been inlaid with letters of real Lapislazuli under the foot of the god during the reign of His Majesty the King of the North and of the South, Men-Kau-Ra triumphant, by the Royal Son Heru-Ta-Ta-f triumphant. He found it when he was journeying about to make an inspection of the temples. One Nekhit was with him, who was diligent in making him to understand it, and he brought it to the King as a wonderful object, when he saw that it was a thing of great mystery, which had never before been seen or looked upon."

In the other Rubric (Papyrus of Mes-em-neter) it says: "This Chapter (Scroll of Papyri) was found or discovered in the foundation, on a Plinth of the Shrine of the Divine Hennu boat (or Ark) by the Chief Mason in the time of the King of the North and of the South, Hesepti triumphant"; and it is there directed that it shall be recited by one who is ceremonially pure and clean.

This last Rubric dates B.C. 4266, and the other B.C. 3733. It is stated that it was "found." Also in the Demotic Tales of the Priests of Memphis we are told how it was found. R.A.M.'s are told the present tradition. Chap. cxlv. says:—

> I have washed myself in water—
> I have anointed myself with oil;
> I have arrayed myself in apparel of white,
> I have with me my sceptre of ——.

The 17th chapter is very ancient, more than 6000 years before the probable date of Moses. Although we take Ptah as the founder of Freemasonry, yet from the 17th chapter of the *Ritual* we can clearly see that this sublime *Ritual* or Doctrine must have existed earlier.

From the time of Ptah we date the orientation from the East and the commencement of the Solar Mythos.

The 17th chapter gives two lists of the Primordial, but Ptah is not amongst them. These must date back to the Stellar Mythos and the orientation North at the time of Sut and Horus I. We can see this by the name Men-Kau-Ra, because that shows the Horus or Amsu name of Ra, and *at a very early date of the Solar Mythos*—at the time they were changing from one to the other: *and also that Heru-Ta-Ta-f was Horus, then being brought on as the Son of the Father; a most important point in studying the Ritual and Eschatology which must not be overlooked if we wish to elucidate and trace accurately the evolution of their religion in all its mysteries, for here we see the evolution from Horus I., the first and One God, merged into Father and Son, the Father and Son being one and the same.*

"The new sayings of Jesus and fragments of a lost Gospel," translated from papyri found at Oxyrhyncus, is connected with this chapter. The translators of the above have rendered the fifth Logion as follows :—"*Raise the stone and there thou shalt find me,*" but in the *Ritual* it is "*shall find the word of God.*" It is Horus who speaks, who says it was a revelation made by Ra, the Holy Spirit. This was given to Horus the son who speaks with his father in heaven, and Horus speaks it as the word of God—he is the sayer of the sayings. The opening sentence, "Let not him who seeks cease until he finds," is on the same parallel. This fragment is a copy of one of the oldest parts of the *Ritual*, dating at least 10,000 years ago.[1]

Royal Arch Formation

When Shu lifted up the heavens, he formed the East and West divisions of heaven—*i.e.* the two horizons. Heaven had hitherto been divided into North and South only, and in doing this, standing on the equinox, he formed the Royal Arch (celestial) Catanarian. The North was represented by a pole or pillar, and the South was represented by a pole or pillar ; the former assigned to Horus and the latter to Sut.

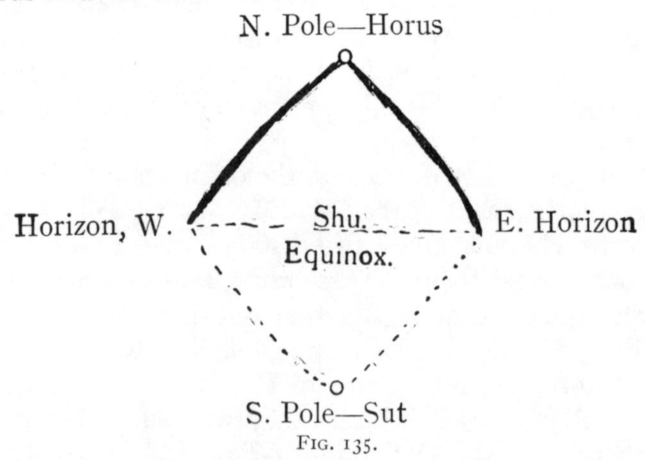

Fig. 135.

[1] There is no doubt that St Paul, Clement of Rome and Polycarp, knew the Egyptian Ritual.

These two pillars were afterwards brought on and assigned to the entrance of Amenta. They represent the two Tatt pillars =to I and B at the gateway entrance of the house of Ptah, and the Royal or Catanarian Arch was formed as represented above.

Note re Spade and Pick.—In the *Ritual*, chap. i. it states : " I have grasped the spade on the day of digging the earth in Suten-Henen," and is referred to again in chap. xvii. 49. We give the Egyptian Hier glyphics only, so that the secrets may be kept to those only who are entitled to know them.

The Origin of the Term " Companions "

This term or word dates back far away into the past, yet it is so distinctive that there cannot be any reasonable doubt as to its origin and meaning.

In Monumental times, Egypt had passed the stage of Totemic Sociology, but the evidences left of its prehistoric existence are still visible and extant in the place-names and in the mirror of Mythology : as the Nome of the Crocodile, Nome of the Hare, Nome of the Serpent, etc., and many others, still recognised.

The status of Totemic Sociology survived in Egypt when the Artisans worked together as " Companions " in " Companies." The " workmen " in the temples had the distinct name of " Companions " applied to them, and were a distinct body of men, possessing certain privileges. In the Egyptian these Companions are the ARI by name, and the Totemic ARI can be traced by name to Upper Egypt, where ARIU, the land of the ARI, is a name of the 17th Nome—*Brugsch.* Only men or Companions of this Nome had certain privileges connected with the Temple and the religious rites at this early period. They were of a lower order than the priests, but had the distinctive appellation of " Companions." (*See* Appendix II.)

" Most illustrious " is an Egyptian title used for the Master of Masters by the Osiris N. (*Ritual*, chap. xiv.). Other signs and meanings of the same may be found in Hymn 13, chap. xv. (*Ritual*), interesting to those of R.A.°

Notes on Different Signs, etc., in Several Degrees

To F.C. brother Masons it may be interesting to know that " their Sign " is much older than the traditional history that is given to it. If they will look in the Papyrus Leyden or one of the vignettes in *Sir Page le Renouf's* "Book of the Dead," P. V. B., or *Naville's* "Book of the Dead," 1 pl. 22, they will see that this sign was used by the ancient Egyptians "at the setting of the Sun." They will find the meaning in the 15th and 16th chapters of "The Book of the Dead." The original P.W.'s will be found here and allude to the R and SS. The intermediate is Horus-Behut (*Dr Budge's* blacksmith — 1st worker in metals). We, having lost the true meaning, although not the sign, have substituted the names of the TC of the PE, the original being the E of the S and S of the same. (*See* later.)

FIG. 136.—Origin of the H.S. of F.C.D.

In the 3rd or MM's degree, the death of HAB and the legend attached thereto is not borne out by facts taken from the Scripture history, which shows that the true history has been perverted or lost to Masons generally, as we see from 2 Chron. iv. 11 :—"and Hiram finished the work that he was to make for King Solomon for the House of God" *Josephus* mentions that he lived at Tyulong afterwards. The original was the prototype of the death, burial and raising of Osiris, and this legend differs very little, as can be seen in the Papyrus at the British Museum, from that which is now used and recited in our MM's Lodges. The traditional history must strike all MM's as being identical to that now in use. It is not to be wondered at, therefore, that "the true word has been lost and another substituted till time and circumstance shall restore the original" ; at the same time we can assure our brother Masons that the word now used by

NOTE.—The coloured plate represents Iris and Nephthys having failed to raise Osiris Anubis, with D.G. raises him and conducts him. From "The Gods of the Egyptians," by *Dr E. A. Wallis Budge*, published by Methuen & Co., to whom we are much indebted for this reproduction.

ANUBIS MINISTERING TO OSIRIS ON HIS BIER; AT THE HEAD KNEELS NEPHTHYS, AND AT THE FEET ISIS.

The raising of the body cf Osiris by Anubis, Isis and Nephthys having failed to do so. But it is not the body simply, *i.e.*, the dead body, cadaver. The true meaning is raising "the spiritual body, The Sahu." *(See Pyramid Text.)*

MM's is the Hebrew translation, but a bad translation of the same in the Egyptian papyri. It is the same as the reputed murders of "Chrisma" amongst the Hindoos and Prince Coh amongst the Mayas, who had it direct from the Egyptian tradition, which was handed down from the Stellar Mythos, the primordial being Horus I.

At Suten-Henen (or Henen-Su or Het-Henen-Su) we have the flight of seven steps thus depicted:—

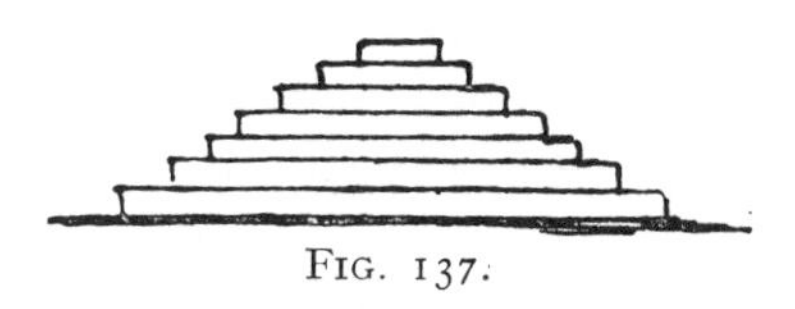

FIG. 137.

and before the first step are two watchers with cutters, or, as the text has it: "the bearer of the Hatchet and the supporter of the Scales," who demand to know the names of the Pylon on the right and on the left, and the names of all the steps before they let the *N* through, and who protect him when he passeth through darkness and shadows, and show what examination he has first to go through before he is admitted to advance to the above steps, etc., which must be interesting to members of the 30°, and if they will read chapter cxxv. of the *Ritual*, they will find the original words and not a bad translation into Hebrew of the same. The two names on the "pillars" on the right and left of the "steps" are the Hebrew names for two names of Horus I.

The chief one of the three was *Khnemu* as Her-Shef or Her-Sheft. "He who is on his Lake or He who is on his Island" that is, the Sacred Cave on the Island in the Lake. This we have shown before was the same in Central America as in Egypt. The Great Enemy who is wounded, but not dead—is Sut in his cave or Hole, whom Horus has defeated, and is now guarded.

That souls needed a ladder whereby to mount from earth to heaven was a very ancient belief in Egypt and a legend, current in early times, asserted that Osiris experienced some difficulty in getting to heaven, and he only succeeded in doing so by means of a ladder with which Ra provided him. Even then he found so much difficulty in mounting the ladder that he had to be helped to ascend it by Heru-Ur and Sut, who were twin gods.[1] In the text of Unus it is said: "Unus cometh forth upon the ladder which

[1] The Mexican Ometecutli Omeciuatl—Lords of Duality. Deities denominating the beginning.

his father Ra hath made for him ; and Horus and Sut take the hand of Unus and they lead him into the Tuat." The fact that Sut is here associated with Horus shows how old the belief in the ladder was—so far back that it must have existed before the battle or Horus and Sut, when the latter was deposed from being a "brother and equal to Horus." That it was afterwards associated with Osiris only shows how it was brought on from the primordial, and we see from Genesis xxviii. 12, 13 how the association continued. Much more could be written on the seven steps, etc., but we contend that what we have brought forward is sufficient to prove the Primordial.

"The Camps" and "Circles" of the gods will be found in the 18th chapter of the *Ritual.* We are not acquainted with the secrets of the 33° in the English Chapter, but one of the PW's for the highest degree we have no doubt is "Maa Kheru" in the Egyptian. No doubt we have a bad translation of the same in Hebrew or some equivalent. We only mention this, and then in Egyptian, because it may be "interesting to those who know," and it will not be giving any "secrets, signs or symbols away to anyone who is not initiated." As the *Ritual* states : before a man, who is "*Maa Kheru, every door in the Underworld opened itself, and every hostile power, animate and inanimate, was made to remove itself from its path." Those, like ourselves, who are "the Highest in the Mysteries of Memphis," will understand, and yet the secret will remain hidden from others.*

The 12 Camps and the 12 Banners of the Children of Israel represent the original characters in the Astronomical Mythology, that were given to the 12 Thrones under one name or another in the final Zodiac.

At first they represented 12 Stellar powers who were afterwards given Seats, Thrones, or Camps, in the 12 signs of the Zodiac or in Heaven—the 12 great spirits who are "Companions" with Horus in Amenta.

Originally they were first 7, as preservers of the Treasures of Light in the Celestial Heptanomes—whether as rulers of Constellations, or as Lords of Pole Stars, who first upraised the starry fires which were kindled on the 7 Hills of Heaven. To these 7, another 5 were added, to complete the first twelve Saviours of the treasure, and 12 orders of each of them, which are the 7 emanations of the 7 voices, and the 5 supports so that they should be kings with Horus, in his kingdom of Eternal Light; these were pre-Zodiacal, but were, in the Solar Mythos, stationed in the Zodiac or around the Mount of Glory.

The original characters in the Astronomical Mythology that were given the 12 Thrones or Camps, with separate and distinctive banners, or Totemic Zootypes, were:—

(1) Sut; (2) Horus; (3) Shu; (4) Hapi; (5) Ap-Uat; (6) Kabhsenuf; (7) Amsta; (8) Anup; (9) Ptah; (10) Atum; (11) Sau; (12) Hu.

These were the Kamite Originals.

FIG. 138.

In chapters clvii. and clviii. we find that a Vulture of Gold, with outstretched wings, holding the symbol of life in each talon, is to be placed around the neck by a chain of gold, to protect The Perfect One. The Vulture here represents our Eagle.

We have given the Egyptian representation of one of the Symbols of the "highest degree" and the 33° English, and it must be obvious to anyone that these are identical.

The foregoing is Nekhebt—the Goddess of the South, as one type of Isis—represented as a Golden Vulture—the Great Mother of us all.[1] The "Shen" or seal, held in each claw of the Vulture, in their Solar Mythos, represented the Sun's orbit or the "circle," hence as an emblem to secure life eternal, as we of the Christians have the Cross ☩ to represent the same—brought on from the circle of precession or rather recession of the Pole Stars or Seven Glorious Ones, and represented at times by the ▽ ("Triangle apex down"), sacred name of Horus I.

[1] The Mexicans had the same. The names in Mexican and Zapotec are Ixchel and Tonantzin, or Tetcoinnan, or Toci.

The sword held in each claw is also the same as in the 33°.

The winged disk or Horus I., under the name of Hor Behutet, to which sometimes the two Uraei are added, with the two crowns, represents the Lord of the North and the South. We are ignorant of the explanation as given in this degree here—if it be given at all—not being in possession of the 33° in England; but the origin is the representation of the Winged-Disk, with the Uraei of Egypt, the original of which we find in the text summarised by *Naville* in the "Myths of Horus," pll. xii. ff.:—"Horus commanded Thoth that the Winged-Sun-Disk, with Uraei, should be brought into every sanctuary wherein he dwelt, and into every sanctuary of all the gods of the lands of the South and of the North, and in

FIG. 139.

Amentet, in order that they might drive away evil from therein. Then Thoth made figures of the Winged-Sun-Disk, with Uraei, and distributed them among the temples and sanctuaries and places wherein there were any gods." This is what is meant by the Winged-Disks, with the Uraei, which are seen over the entrances of the courts of the temples of all the gods and goddesses of Egypt. *Mr I. L. Stephens* found a "Winged Disk" over the door of a Temple at Ocosingo, near Palenque, corresponding in every particular to those of Egypt.

Although this legend is of a very modern period (Egyptian), the fundamental facts of the story are very old, for they belong to the earliest period of the Egyptian history, and are derived from the old myth of the combat between Light and Darkness. Freemasons have taken our interpretation from the Hebrews; but we must remember that many of their laws and tales were derived from the Egyptians at a very remote period. In the 30°, our present supreme council do not attempt to give you any explanation of the meaning of the "R——" in this degree, probably because they are ignorant of its meaning.

The two Uraei are the same as the two feathers. The R H thrown over the L S and the L H thrown over the R S are two signs used by the Egyptians when approaching. These are both represented in the various vignettes from Egypt, the former was the sign seen during this life, and the latter after the soul had been weighed; and then, when he was presented to Osiris, this sign was given to him to use—see plate 33, "Book of the Dead." The former was the terrestrial, the latter celestial. The Mexican, North and Central American Indians still use the above signs, as well as crossing their arms L and U and the sign H A H D. If given and repeated to you "it is friendship and brotherhood," and you are safe amongst them as brothers, and is used and explained to all the initiated in their Totemic Ceremonies.

The "Pair of Scales" Makhaat, , which was presided over by Thoth, who from very remote days was known as Ap-Rehui—*i.e.* "Judge of the two combatant gods"—that is to say, "Judge of Horus and Sut," and as Ap-Senui, "*Judge of the Two Brothers*," was used "in the weighing of words and actions or deeds," and Thoth watched the balance—when words, these words and actions or deeds were being tried. The god, whose eyebrows are the arms of the Balance, is "he who lifted up his arm"—*i.e.* Amsu.[1]

Also the Scales or Balance is a Symbol of Maat and its oneness in duality, the balance being the Scales of Justice, and was erected in the Maat or Hall of Twofold Justice for the weighing of hearts and also of words. It was erected as a figure of the equinox, or the two balances of night and day at equal poise, being erected at the place of poise and weighing in the equinox.

This is fully depicted and set forth in the oldest or Pyramid Texts, and may be interesting to the brethren with the "Balance on the Collar." We refrain from further writing on this point, as we are not 31°.

The fact that many Masons state and think that no doctrines of Christian religion exist in Freemasonry, only shows that they have not taken the 18° and those above it. Without entering into the long argument of how much of the Christian doctrines were founded and brought on by the earliest Christian Copts from the doctrines of the Osirian religion; "the man God" and "Isis and the divine child, Horus" have been transformed into the "Virgin Mary and Holy Child, etc."; it must be clearly and

[1] Mexican name, Motecuhzoma Xocyotzin.

distinctly stated that the 18° and those above it are up to date by evolution, and that the professed principles and beliefs in the Christian religion are here insisted on.

The figure O or ⊖ given as one of the "Mason's marks" in *Brother Gould's* last work is the Egyptian Hieroglyphic Ru or Er, and is not the rough outline of a fish, but represents the fish's mouth, and means: at, to, with, among, against, from, according to, near by, towards, upon, concerning, more than; according to the other Hieroglyphics accompanying it—see also in Chapter on the Cross; probably copied or taken from the carp's mouth—or an allied species as a type—as these abound in the Nile rivers. It is also the emaning mouth of that fish which gives birth to water as the life of the world and to the saviour who comes to Egypt by water, as the water of the inundation in their Astro Mythology, represented terrestrially by the overflow or inundation of the Nile, which fertilises the seed planted to sustain life, and which would thus represent the water of life, the symbol and sign of the sustainer of new life and new birth. Hence this old symbol which is found amongst the most ancient ruins and stones all over the world, a symbol used amongst the ancient brotherhood but forgotten by most of the present, and the meaning lost to them, until now.

Another word used in one of our ceremonies is "Hoshea." We have asked more than a hundred Brothers, including those who "govern and are supposed to know," what was the meaning, and whence derived? but all the answers we received have been the same: "Don't know, we use it."

We will give the Brotherhood the origin and reason here now; guarding the secrets at the same time. Shu, as the son of Ra, is the great leader of the people to the Promised Land; Anup, the Jackal-Dog, was the guide, and these two are represented in the Book of Numbers by *Joshua, or Hoshea,* the son of Nun, and Caleb, the son of Jephunnel.

These two, the leader and the guide, both in the Astronomy and the Eschatology, are the only two in the Hebrew version, who are to go forth in the exodus from the wilderness and burial-place of the dead.

Shu was at first the son of Nun, the deity of the Celestial universe who was also called the father of the Gods. He afterwards became the son of Ra, as the supporter of the Solar disk on the Horizon, "with his two hands."

Joshua also had a double character, like Shu ; in the first he is called *Hoshea, the son of Nun.* In the latter role, Joshua becomes the upholder of Ihuh, and his change of name is connected with the change of character. The name of Joshua, or יהושע, contains the name of Ihuh, united to a word signifying assistance or help.

In the form שויא it denotes a lifting up, an upholding, as in the Egyptian name of Shu, to uphold which describes him in the character of the uplifter to Ra, the Solar God ; thus Hoshea is the uplifter of his hands in one character, in adoration of Ra, and in the other as the 7 powers: 6×1 (Joshua xxiv. 15, 16 et *Ritual.*)

This should suffice to demonstrate to all Brothers of this degree the origin and meaning of the sign and word, without exposing any secrets to those who are not entitled to know them.

The Hebrew name "*Abaddon*" was derived from the Egyptian Abut-Unti, which we learn from the *Ritual* was one of the Egyptian names of the huge typhonian reptile in the Abyss. Abut or Abtu was a form of the Apap which typifies non-existence or unti. In the *Ritual*, chap. xvii. lines 67-68, "The beast that was taken and cast alive into the lake of fire, or in the red lake, the pool of the damned in the fiery pit of the 'recess' in Amenta."

N. O. L. U. B. A. H. A. J., was another name for the Hebrew I. H. U. H., which was the Egyptian Atum-Huhi—Atum-Iu or Atum-Ra, and was known by the title "Ankhu" or the living one eternal God. "In the coming forth to-day from out of the dark of death"—which is the resurrection in the *Ritual.*

"The Ancient of Days" in the Semitic is Ra of the Egyptians, the Solar God who typifies the eternal in the *Ritual.* He is called "the aged one at the confines of the mount of Glory" (chap. cxxxi.). He is the aged one upon his throne, as in the Books of Enoch, Daniel, and John the Divine.

The Ancient of Days together with the Son of Man preparing for the judgment is described by Enoch, chap. xlvii. 3, and *Ritual*, chap. xviii.

In the earlier cult at Annu, Atum-Ra was the judge as God the Father with Iu-em-Hetep as God the Son. In the mysteries of the *Ritual* "He that sitteth upon the Throne" as the Great Judge in Amenta is Osiris with Horus as the beloved only-begotten Son—but this was a later cult, the mysteries of Osiris,

Isis, and Horus, although the latest Egyptian evolution has been given the foremost place in the *Ritual*, and has somewhat obscured the pre-Osirian mythology ; but Atum was the Great Judge upon the Mount of Amenta at a far earlier period than Osiris. Our Lodge likens Amenta. "It lieth 4 square, and the length thereof is as great as the breadth ; the length and the breadth and the height thereof are equal." This was the heaven of Amenta, based upon the four quarters of the solstices and the equinoxes which followed the making of Amenta. (Rev. xxi. 16.)

Explanation of the symbol of the Pelican or Vulture portrayed on the Apron of the 18°, as having pierced her own thigh to give her blood to her young for nourishment, has not any meaning as demonstrated ; nor does the "Church," where we see it sometimes depicted, know the origin or meaning—a fine specimen may be seen as a lectern in St Saviour's Church, Reading. It represents in Sign-language the first—*i.e.* the earliest soul considered to be human, being born of the mother-blood, the soul that was made flesh in the child Horus, who was born of the mother-blood—the blood of Isis—and as such was distinguished from the earlier elemental powers—otherwise the six Totemic and pre-human souls.

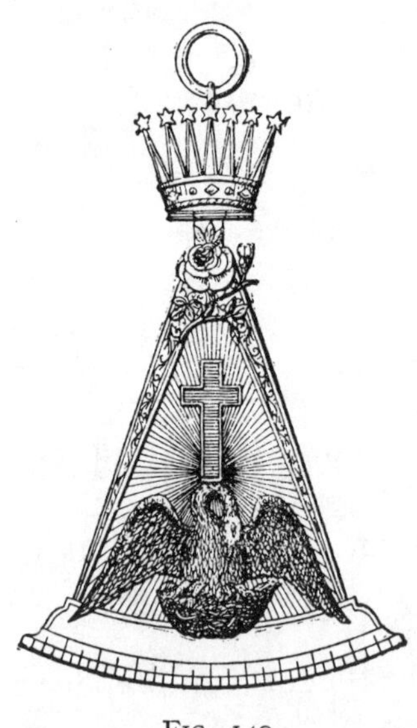

FIG. 140.

The picture itself is the earliest Egyptian zootype sign and symbol for the virgin Neith, and shows in Sign-language the conceiver of a soul that was incarnated by the Blood-mother.

The blood that was considered to be the soul of life, and in a series of seven souls, is the blood of the female and not the blood of the male. In the Egyptian system of representation there are seven souls or life-forces recognised in nature ; six of these were pre-human elemental powers, born of the primary Great Mother, when there was as yet no human soul distinguished from the six that were souls—the seventh alone was human, and the soul was brought forth by the goddess in human likeness, here depicted in Sign-language.

Of course this was Mythology, but it shows that the Totem

was first given to the mother and hers were the children—Blood-Motherhood, and their children were the Blood-Brotherhood. She was the mythical virgin mother, and had a very natural origin in their Totemic ceremonies, and was afterwards exalted in the Eschatology to the virgin mother, who in one character conceived and in the second brought forth. These two mothers were imaged by the Double Uraeus Crown of Maternity. Isis is at once the great mother and also the virgin mother who keeps the primary place in the Mythology, because the virgin preceded the bringer-forth of the child, as the source itself.[1]

It is parallel with the double motherhood, which is assigned to Jesus in the Gospels, with the two mothers as two sisters, the first being the Virgin Mary and the second the wife of Cleopas; thus we see that, although the present interpretation does not give any real meaning to the 18°, yet the Esoteric representation is most profoundly interesting and only applicable to this degree. (*See* Appendix II.)

[1] Gignuntur autem hunc in modum. Cum amore concipiendi vultur exarserit vulvam ad Boream aperiens, ab eo velut comprimitur per dies quinque. The doctrine is the same in the Christian phase when the Holy Spirit makes its descent and insufflates Mary with the dove for totem instead of some other type of breathing force or soul, the difference is that the Holy Spirit takes the place of the Spirit of air—otherwise Ra, as source of soul, had superseded Shu, the breathing force.

CHAPTER XVII

THE CROSS—ITS ORIGIN, DEVELOPMENT AND INTERPRETATION

Fig. 141.

This good specimen is one form of Cross, used and adopted by the Christians, showing original type of Ank Cross, and the four quarters and circle.

The Cross is another sacred symbol used amongst us. It is much reverenced by all nations, civilised and semi-civilised. Ages before the establishment of Christianity we find representations of it almost in every part of the world; from delineations scratched on stones and rocks to the most stately temples; on statues and

Egyptian Swastika   Egyptian Ank Cross   Christian   Hebrew Tau   Chinese

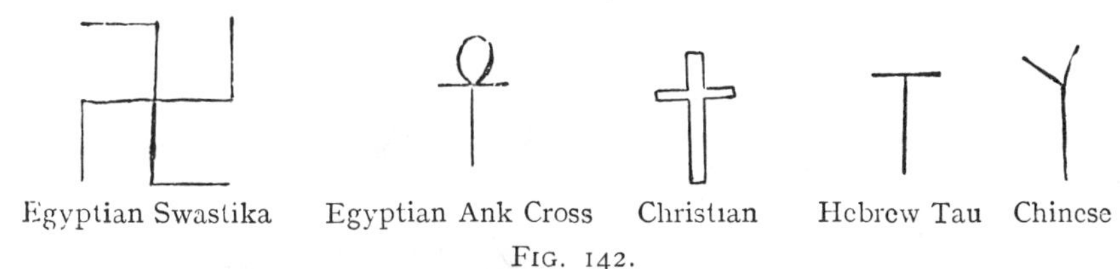

FIG. 142.

on statuettes in Palenque, Chopan and other cities of Guatemala, South and Central America, China, India and Scandinavia, and throughout all the civilised world.

Amongst the Bantu negroes several missionaries, who are authorities, attest that before Christianity was introduced the Cross was used as a mystic symbol by the Priests who directed the worship of the spirits. Amongst the Nilotic negroes at the present day a form of the Swastika is frequently shaven on men's heads —see Head of Negro, *Sir Harry Johnston's* book, "Uganda." Fig. 143.

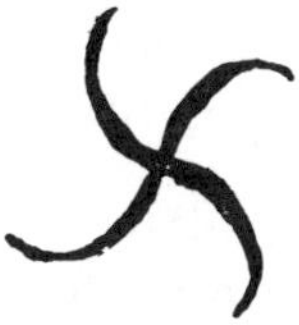

FIG. 143.

Also we find that in the practice of the sacred ceremonies amongst the aboriginal Australians a Cross is used. In the ceremonies of the Ulpmerka and the Iruntarinia ceremony of the Unjiamba totem of Urthipita they show the Umbalinyara Cross, and in the sacred ceremony of Waninga the double and treble Cross is often used, which may be interesting to members of the 33°.

There are several varieties of Crosses, some of which we represent here. All can be traced back to the one primitive form, which was two human figures crossed, and is first found depicted on one of the seal cylinders found in a prehistoric grave at Naqada, dating back to the Neolithic age. These figures, as here seen, first represented the four quarters, long before these ancient people even made out their astronomy. From these two figures other two figures were blended to form the so-called Swastika as here seen cut on a sepulchral stone found

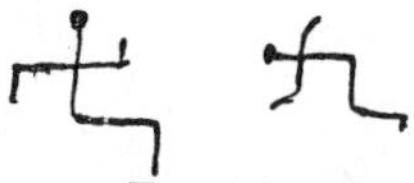

FIG. 144.

at Meigle, in Perthshire.

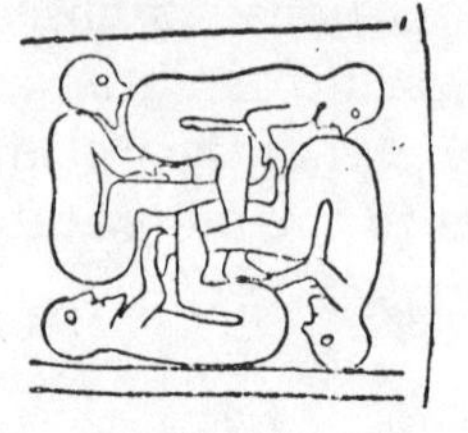

Fig. 145.

From this form was evolved the various other forms of the Swastika which we find throughout the world.

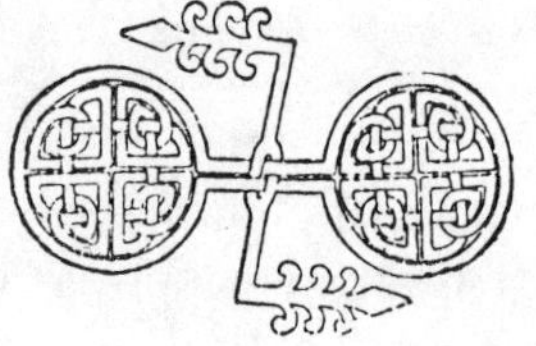

Fig. 146.

This is a sinister Swastika from a Cross at St Vigeans, in Forfarshire, and this

Fig. 147.

from one of the old Mahometan buildings of the Mo(n)gol period at Lahore. This is from the fourth city of Troy (Schliemann). From these four figures, then, it passed on to the so-called Swast ka which was carried out of Egypt at the time of one of the earliest exodes, when they had their Totemic Ceremonies and Mythology, and probably before they

Fig. 148.

had finally evolved their Eschatology, as at this latter time they had by evolution converted it into the Ank Cross ☥ The Swastika 卐 is also found widely distributed throughout the old and new world in various forms, and much has been written about its meaning and origin. We contend that what we have written is the solution and key to the whole matter. This symbol has probably a wider range than any other that has been preserved from prehistoric times. On looking over the entire present known prehistoric world, we find it used on small and comparatively insignificant objects, such as pots, jugs, implements, tools, household goods and utensils, objects of the toilet, ornaments, monuments, altars, etc., in America, Asia, Africa and Europe, and it is only by understanding the Egyptian *Ritual* and the evolution of their Totemic Ceremonies and Mythology into the perfect Eschatology, and the various exodes that took place at different periods, each time carrying all the various signs, symbols, etc., that had so far been developed or evolved, that anyone can find the real truth of the past. Knowing that nothing was ever lost, but all carried on and made use of in all the gradual evolution that has taken place, one sees how this was first carried out as the representation of fig. 84 (page 187), and how the various forms of Crosses have been evolved out of this. The definition and meaning of all are practically the same in whatever country or part of the world we find them, and it is the same as the Egyptian Ank. ☥ "The express emblem of Life to Come."

That a great number of these signs has been mere ornaments, monetary signs or trade marks (the Swastika appears upon a coin of Krananda, which is held to be the oldest Indian coin), is perhaps a fact which it would be idle to dispute, but the uses which have been made of the figure in all the various countries in all parts of the world, the nature of the symbols with which it is found associated, its constant presence on altars, tombstones, sepulchral urns, idols and priestly vestments—besides the various written documents upon it—afford more than sufficient proof that it partook everywhere of the nature of the amulet, the talisman and the phylactery. Moreover, for the Swastika to have thus become a charm it must first of all have been brought into contact with a being or a phenomenon, more or less concrete, and distinctly invested, rightly or wrongly, with some sort of influence on the destiny of mankind. We have therefore given its origin and its evolution into various forms, and different Crosses now used amongst the Christian world, which we think is quite enough for this work. The figure of the Swastika in the centre of the Sacred Triangle may be said to represent the highest and greatest of the Christian doctrines of the present day as preached and promulgated by our Priests: "That the spirit must be born again and will be everlasting, and that we can only attain this by believing in the Cross and Christ and the Holy Trinity." The Swastika here represents the regeneration of the life to come as evinced by its position in the centre of the Sacred Triangle, which is here the representation of the first Holy Trinity—(Stellar)—it shows their beliefs and the original doctrines of these ancient people were identically the same as what we now use, time and evolution having altered them very little, and that only to suit the exigencies of the times.

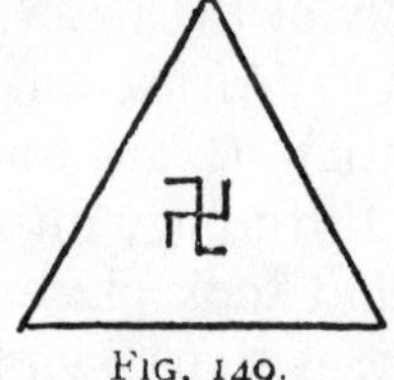

FIG. 149.

Here is a Cross we found in Lanteglos Churchyard, Cornwall (fig. 151). It is an old Druid Ank Cross, evidently removed from Rough Tor, near, and has had the Latin Cross cut into it and placed here. It is of the same form and shape as those found amongst the Dolmens of Brittany.

FIG. 150.

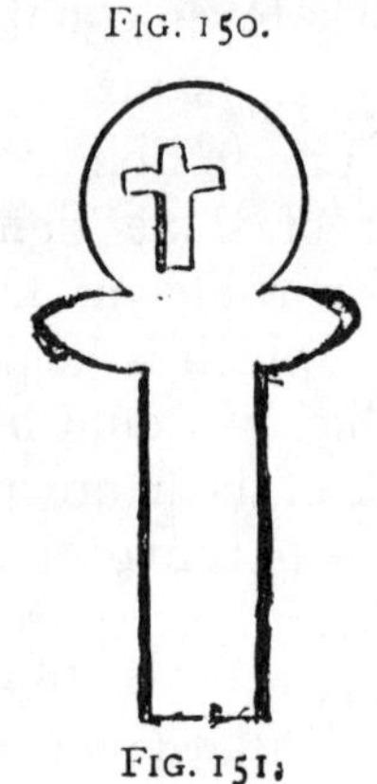

FIG. 151.

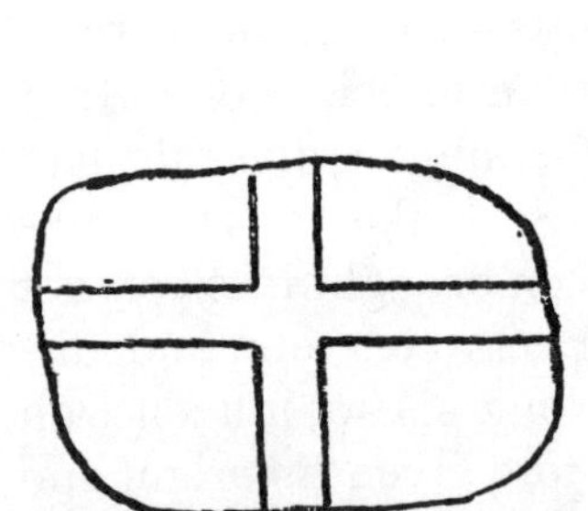

FIG. 152.

This is a Pre-Christian Cross, as found in Central America.

FIG. 153.

This Cross, from the monuments of Palenque, is also Pre-Christian, and found depicted on the Dolmens of Brittany, precisely similar in every particular, as we have shown elsewhere.

FIG. 154.
Pre-Christian Cross with the four corner supports (four quarters) from Central America.

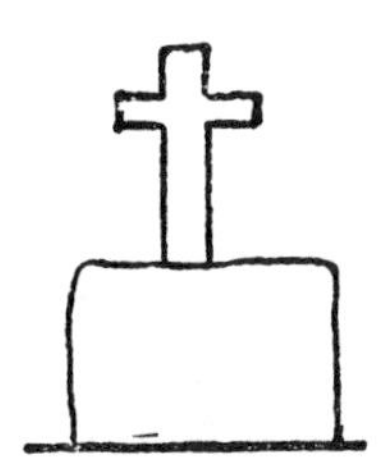

FIG. 155.
Pre-Christian Cross from Central America.

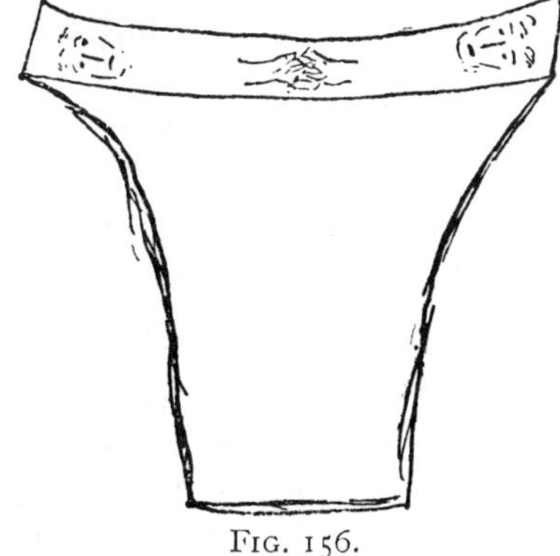

FIG. 156.
This is an Irish Cross—Pre-Christian—at Kiloraboy. The figures at the top must be interesting to Freemasons, as it shows the "hands grasp" in the same position as on one of the remains of a temple in Mexico. This Irish Cross is a typical representation of chapter clxvi. of "The Book of the Dead" and Head Rest—in form of ×.

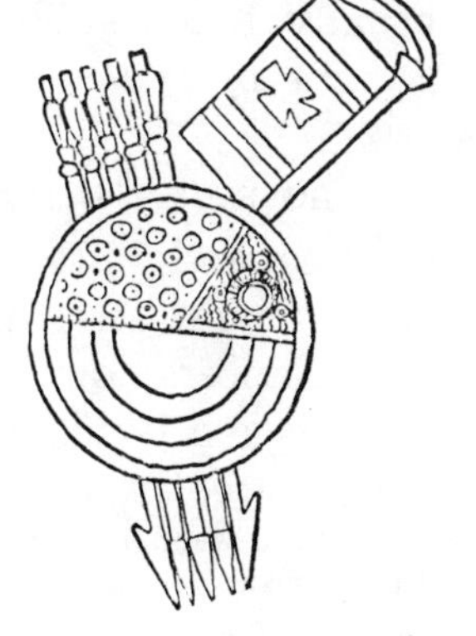

FIG. 157.

We find the Cross well shown in the god Zipe's banner, with the representation of the two feathers above and on the shield attached (fig. 7 c, page 62, "Mexican Antiquities"). Here we have the Hieroglyphic for the "Tank of Flame" and the Emerald in "mirror form," as *Dr Seler* correctly describes it, throwing glittering rays in four directions. It is used here as the West African tribes use it in the centre of the Sacred Triangle—see page 132. The whole is symbolic of Horus I., and indeed at Ocosingo, in Palenque, we have the Hieroglyphic for Horus risen (Amsu)[1] plainly shown in this form  as we have shown elsewhere. *Zipe* was one of the Mexican names for Horus I., here represented by a ✣ and as the risen Horus the same with two circles added. The four rays of the Emerald stone represent the four attributes or children of Horus as well as the "Light of the World." We see that the form of the cross is the same as the Egyptian, as the following descriptions will prove.

Perhaps one of the best examples that can be found of Pre-Christian Crosses is seen on the "God Bes," with a chain of beads around his neck, the same as the Roman Catholics wear round their necks. See plate, page 154.

This figure is a very important one to those who are interested in the history of the past.[2] Some authorities have placed "Bes [hieroglyphs]" amongst the foreign gods of the Egyptians, and state that he is of Semitic origin, but there is no foundation for this supposition, and we agree entirely with *Dr Budge* that he is purely Egyptian and very early Pre-Dynastic. *Dr Budge* says: "He is usually represented in the form of a dwarf with a huge bearded head, protruding tongue, flat nose, shaggy eyebrows and hair; large projecting ears, long but thick arms and bowed legs; around his body he wears the skin of an animal of the panther tribe, and its tail hangs down and usually touches the ground behind him; on *his head he wears a tiara of feathers*,[3] which suggests a savage or semi-savage origin."

The root [hieroglyphs] implies the idea of darting, springing forth, dancing, and we know that the Pygmies were very celebrated and much sought after in Dynastic times for their dancing—and are great dancers now. See chapter on PYGMIES.

This god Bes is pictured in many forms from the very earliest

[1] One of the old Mexican names was Motecuhzoma Xocoyotzin—*i.e.* the Soul of the dead warrior or King, that is the Soul of the dead or mummified Horus risen = Amsu.

[2] Reproduced from *Dr Budge's* book, "The Gods of the Egyptians," by kind permission of *Dr E. A. Wallis Budge*, the author, and Methuen & Co., the publishers.

[3] The italics are ours.

to the latest Dynastic times, and various attributes are apparently added to him as time proceeds. The figure of Bes shows that he was of a very early date and certainly an African Pygmy. *Dr Budge* says: "The figure of Bes suggests that his home was a place where the dwarf and pigmy were held in esteem, whilst his head-dress resembles those head-dresses which were and still are worn by the tribes of Equatorial Africa, and this would lead us to place his home in that portion of it which lies a few degrees to the North of the Equator. The knowledge of the god and perhaps figures of him were brought from this region which the Egyptians called the 'Land of the Spirits.'" To our minds this perhaps is the earliest form of a god that we find symbolised in human form, probably by the earliest Nilotic Negroes when they were changing and forming their Solar Mythos, they naturally would depict "their Father" in this form, knowing that the Masa Negroes and Pygmies were older than themselves. As seen at some places "he is the old man" and at others "the regenerated young man." Thus various attributes would be given him under different conditions. He would be "*the Father*" *and head of all and everything*, and after would merge into and be associated with Horus I. The *Father* here would mean two lives, earthly and spiritual *in the first form*. *Dr Budge* is right in our opinion in speaking of this land as the "Land of the Spirits" if he means the *land* before they had worked out *Amenta—the Land of the Spirits* of the Dynastic times. These early people certainly had a "Land of the Spirits"—"*The Khui Land*," which they illustrated by three triangles one way, and three triangles another, surrounded by concentric circles, which we have mentioned before. These were first in the heaven and second in the *Lakes and Islands from where the Nile takes its rise*. The Lotus flower held in each hand would show that the Southern parts of the Nile was the birthplace of this god. The Northern emblems had not yet come into use. Probably this part was at the time more civilised and was the centre which afterwards opened farther North, carrying everything with it and adding thereto. The "Old Father" never became lost but merged into Horus I., and was associated in some attributes and carried on to the latest Dynastic times. We see this in the various forms that Bes is depicted, and he was certainly associated with Horus I. As a

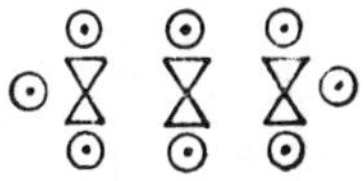

FIG. 158.

regenerator of "new life" he invariably figures in birth scenes in all the Mamisi of Egyptian temples.

Also on Nefer-Hetep (plate produced from *Dr A. W. Budge's* book, "The Gods of the Egyptians," vol. ii. p. 38, published by Methuen and Co., to whom we are greatly indebted for the privilege of reproducing same) we see the cross depicted, hung around his neck by a "collar." This was one of the "Gods of Egypt" as Khensu-Nefer-Hetep, brought on from the Lunar and Stellar Mythos, which we have mentioned before as being the original Horus I., now merged into the Solar—and would be the same as "Bes" originally, since Bes was a primary form of Horus I.; Bes being originally the first form in the Stellar it probably represented the Great One or Father among the Pygmies before Stellar Mythos was perfected; but in the Lunar Khensu-Nefer-Hetep took the first place, and Bes became another form. Khensu was deified under this name — *i.e.* as they worked out their mythos from Stellar and Lunar to Solar, many of the names and representative types of those who had gone before were "as primary," degraded to attributes of the One Great God, and a fresh name was substituted in the place of THE ONE, giving all the powers, etc., that he possessed from the former to the latter, and at the same time carrying on the latter as representing some attributes of the former. In the Roman Catholic Church doctrine it is somewhat similar: first, the bishop, then the Pope, with various powers and attributes attached to him, until the last, "The Infallibility" of the same.

To demonstrate this, take the word "Bishop," which was taken from the French évêque, which is borrowed from the Latin "episcopus" in the first part, and the old English "biscop" from the middle of it, and both from the Greek "episcopos," which signifies an overlooker or one who stands higher than his fellows and overlooks them. To this we may add, one who possesses several moral and intellectual ideas. In the next few generations we see that the Bishop has developed into a "Pope," and in a few more the Pope has been proclaimed and developed as an "Infallible." The present tonsure, worn by the Roman Catholic priests, only represents the disk of the sun ○, and if they had but left a small bunch of hairs in the centre they would then have retained the old ideal solar symbol ⊙ of Ra, whom they are supposed to represent as his servants or representatives. Their

NEFER-HETEP.

KENSU-NEFER-HETEP was a type of Horus I. as one of the seven great gods in Stellar mythos, and one of the Triad brought on in the Lunar as Khensu-Tehuti the twice great, the lord of Khemennu, and Khensu the child in Lunar mythology, was Horus the child in Solar.

stole represents the zodiac, and their rosaries are symbols of both Stellar and Solar Mythos. Such is evolution, but not Nature's ! ! !

Although the Pope was not the first man to claim "infallibility"—Augustus proclaimed himself to be not merely a human likeness but the very God himself on earth.

Tacitus ("Annals," 1-10) states: "The reverence due to the Gods was no longer peculiar, Augustus claimed equal worship. A mortal man was directly adored and priests and pontiffs were appointed to pay him impious homage."

As the Cross enters into the symbology of the 18° and higher degrees, we have given some of the history of it which is certain to interest the members of the 18°-33°.

The St Andrew's Cross—the Red Cross or Fiery Cross—is a very important one to Freemasons of the 18°, and it was originally formed from the four figures direct, without going through the evolution of the Ank ☥ as may be seen as follows:

FIG. 159.
On a Sepulchral Stone at Meigle, in Perthshire, there are four human figures in the form of the Swastika.

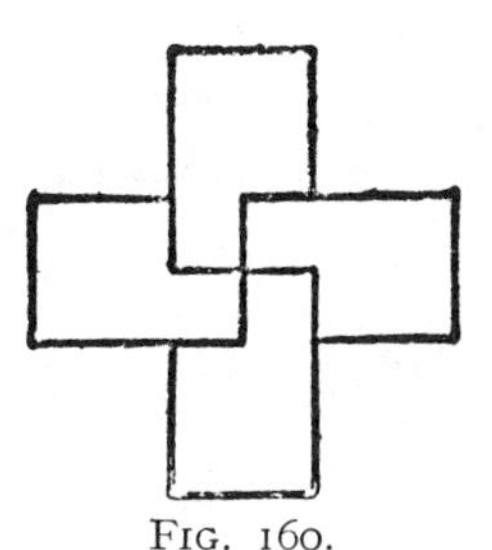

FIG. 160.
From this the St Andrew's Cross was formed direct, as may be seen from a Runic Stone from Sweden.

In the Papyrus of Nu (British Museum, No. 10,477, sheet 30) we have this St Andrew's Cross with these Hieroglyphics, date about 10,000 B.C., which are precisely similar in meaning to our 18°, and there cannot be any doubt that ours was copied and brought on from this. It is one of the Aats or Domains and reads as follows:—

"The brow of the god Hu=I-u." "The word and the name." The last figure is Ptah, the Great Architect of the Universe, as depicted in other Papyri, in this, the Lord of the heaven and the earth—ruler of the destiny of the world. I-u was the son of Ptah. In the code of Hammurabi we find the word I-a-u,

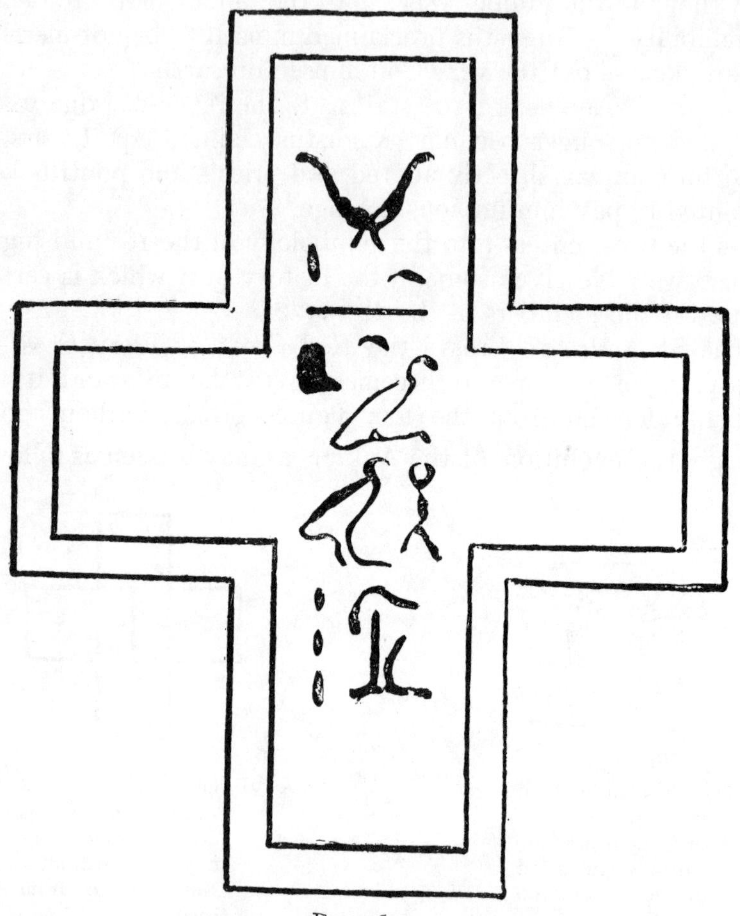

FIG. 161.

which was a later way of writing I-u, who is the same as Tem, the son of Ptah.[1]

Tem, Temu or Atem, son of Ptah, was Heru-Khuti—*i.e.* Horus I. Heru-Khuti (Egyptian) "Light of the World," was one

[1] The code of Hammurabi existed long before Moses and shows that the so-called laws of Moses were in use in Egypt thousands of years before he lived, but there is no doubt that these were well known to him and he made use of them to fit the requirements at the time, altering or supplementing as occasion might require. In this code the words used are :—be-el-sa-me-e-u-ir-si-tim, translated—Lord of the Heaven and the Earth, ruler of the destiny of the world. That is the same as we have above—Ptah.

of the names used for him intermediately between Horus I. and Osiris and Ra.

Dr Budge states that Tem was the first living Man-god known to the Egyptians; yes, as another name of Horus, but not human as *Dr Budge* implies. Tem-Asar and Tem-Ra were the Solar names for Horus and Amsu of the Stellar, and a link, showing the connection—the transformation of the one into the other. *M. Naville* found and proved that the temple dedicated to Tem was situated in the 8th nome of Lower Egypt under the form "Pithom," the sacred name of the City Pa-Atemt, spoken of in the volume of our Sacred Law. The inscriptions proved beyond all doubt that the Great god of Pithom was Tem, and from allusions which are made in them to the "Holy Serpent" therein, and from the fact that one part of the temple buildings was called "Pa-Qerhet" or "Ast-Qurhet"—that is, "the house of the snake-god Qerhet"—proves from this that it is certain one of the forms or types of Tem was a huge serpent. *The serpent was not worshipped, but was a representative type of an attribute.* If Tem were God and the serpent was the symbol, obviously it was the divinity that was the object of the worship and not the symbol. Their Eschatology had not at first been worked out from the primordial to those beautiful and lofty conceptions which we afterwards find. *Bernard Diaz's* description of the temples found in Mexico, in the first expedition under *Cortez,* describes *beautiful temples with figures of "huge serpents," in some parts of them. We contend that these must be attributed to copies of the original Egyptian at Pithom—"The God of the Gate of the East,"* [1] *and must therefore have been dedicated to Tem. "The Holy Serpent," or the House of the Snake-god Qerhet of the Egyptians. It is more than probable that all these temple-buildings, with representations of huge snakes, were built at the time of the Stellar Mythos and afterwards embodied in the Solar.* When they represented the Deity by some animal or bird, etc., it was simply a type of an attribute, *and we find these all over the world.*

These are the zootypes before the types were represented anthropomorphically. That we are right in our decipherment and contention is proved by a living remnant of past ages who still practise and believe in this cult—viz. the Yezidis, who inhabit the mountains around Mosul, in Asia Minor. These people number about 20,000 at the present day. They live among the

[1] One of the Mexican names was Cipactli—*i.e.* God of the East.

mountain fastnesses and own allegiance to one prince. The Turks have never been able to subdue them, owing to the inaccessibility of their homes. Like their old forefathers in Egypt, their priests are all clad in white, and each has *a wand of office, surmounted by a brass bird*, which is regarded as the most sacred symbol, and which these Yezidi say has never been lost. *At the entrance of their Chief Temple is the figure of a huge serpent*, which is looked upon as a symbol of great veneration, and each worshipper kisses the serpent before entering the temple. Their religious rites, which include the use of hypnotism, are kept secret from all those who are not initiated, and are only practised between sunset and sunrise. Their rites and ceremonies are the same as the ancient Egyptians during the time of the later Stellar Mythos and beginning of the Solar. Here we have still in existence the open book of explanation of those temples we find the remains of in Mexico, Central States of America and other places, the cult of which has hitherto been unknown or forgotten (for explanation of the wands of office, surmounted by a bird, see symbol of D C's). Some learned men, who have visited these people, have described them as "Devil Worshippers," *although they have to acknowledge that these Yezidi deny it*, and we have seen it stated that there is ample evidence to that effect—*i.e.* "Devil Worshippers"—which shows and proves how ignorant these learned men are of the past history of Egypt, of their Mythos, Eschatology and past history of the world, having here a living book, the alphabet of which they do not understand.

Dr Budge thinks, from a passage in THE PYRAMID TEXT (the oldest), "that the oldest form of the worship of Tem was Phallic," but as we have stated before, *there was not such a thing as Phallic worship, but only a Phallic festival*, dedicated to seed time—harvest, youth, etc., and our Maypole dance is a remnant of the same. Tem, in one form, would represent the "seed time," "producer," etc., just the same as Horus had previously been represented as a "young ear of corn." In the changing of one Cult to another they associated Tem with Osiris and Ra as Asar-Tem and Ra-Tem, and then after with Harmachis—*i.e.* the child Horus and Tem-Heru-Khuti (Tem-Harmachis).

The lifting up of the serpent in the wilderness by Moses, Numb. xxi. 9: "And Moses made a serpent of brass and put it upon a pole, and it came to pass that if a serpent had bitten any man, when he beheld the serpent of brass he lived"—would therefore be a sign for his followers as a type of Tem. They were commanded to look upon the serpent as a saviour, and all who did so escaped death. Moses fell back upon a symbol of the Stellar Mythos, of which he knew the meaning, and which, no doubt, his followers would recognise as part of their old religion, and this would be parallel again in the Christian doctrines, as we find in John iii. 14: "And as Moses lifted up the serpent in the wilderness, even so must the son of man be lifted up," etc., and all who looked upon him and believed would be saved. *Dr Budge* thinks "from THE PYRAMID TEXT that the attributes of Tem were confounded with those of Ra," but he does not appear to understand that Tem was a much older form, and that the priests appropriated all the attributes of "Tem" and gave these to the later name "Ra" in the same way as former priests had passed these of Horus I. to the name Tem; but these were all one and the same under different names and different dates—a study of the

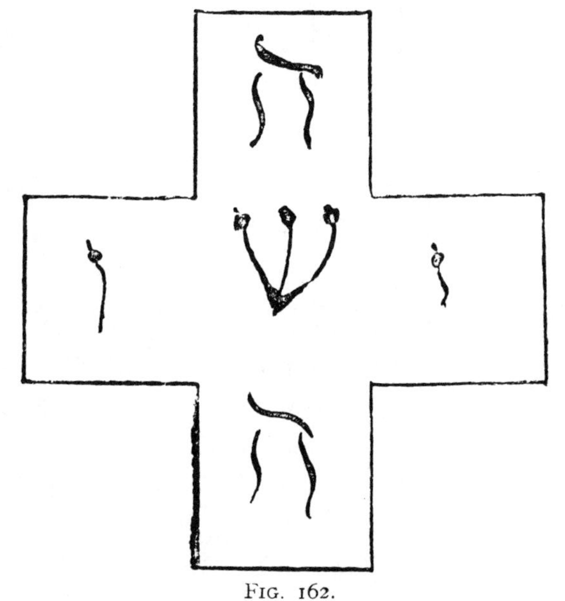

FIG. 162.

She-en or Se-en, the initial standing for The Almighty in Hebrew Shadai.

Note.—Readers must not confound the "Great Serpent fiend Apepi or Sut" with the "Holy Serpent" representing Tem. In the Egyptian Mythology there were many serpents, some types of "good" and some "evil."

Ritual proves this. As we have shown I U or I A U was the

"Light of the World"—*i.e.* Horus or Heru-Khuti and Tem or Tem-Heru-Khuti is the same, and in the Christian doctrines, Jesus is the "Light of the World"—different names for the same at various times of the world's existence. The attributes of each are identical, and one has only to place THE PYRAMID TEXT, the Hymn to Tem in the PAPYRUS OF MUT-HETEP, "The Book of the Dead" and the volume of our Sacred Law together, to prove what we have put before our readers.

We give here the St Andrew's Cross as used by the M W S 18°.

Jesus or Jesu or Saviour, Son of the Almighty. (In Hebrew—Shadai.) It is difficult to distinguish in some Jewels of the M W S if it be ה Hu or ת Tau, if the latter then it would stand for a Taw and not Hu as some have expressed it, therefore the Tau would mean a Cross like the Egyptian Ta or Tat, therefore ת = Tat and תת would be equal to two Tats—*i.e.* Tattu, and the Tat is the sign of stability. Tattu, the place of eternity, and the Cross is equivalent to the Tat as a four-fold foundation.

T.T. or תת or also denotes the Deity, who, as God of the Pole Star, was the stable, firm, just, righteous and unalterable One, because he represented the pole as the point of fixity in a moving universe. This Deity, as the God of Israel, was Jashar-El ישר-אל; The God of Jashar—Jeshurun or Baali (and the other form of the name) El Elyoun Phœnician.

But whoever were the members of the Supreme Council at the time when "El Shadai" was first put on the cross, were certainly ignorant of its real import and meaning, because El Shadai (which is Phœnician) in the Hebrew represents and is Sut-Anup or Sut or Seth upon his mountain at the Pole. *In the earliest Stellar Mythos he was the first Stellar god.* El in the highest being the Star-god on the summit of the mount, but, after his fight with Horus, was deposed and became the type of the evil one (god of darkness and ignorance), and Horus superseded him. Horus, here represented by ה Hebrew, Egyptian,

=Hu or Iu, became the son of his father in the Solar Mythos and Eschatology, but *his father was not El Shadai or Sut, but Ptah, who was the first father in the Mythology.* He could not be the son of the Devil (now represented by Sut), which he is here shown to be, *according to the Hebrew character and time,* although as primary Stellar he was brother to Horus. The explanation, as given, has no meaning (like many words in the 30th and other degrees), according to the Hebrew characters, and in fact is quite wrong, being a mixture of the Stellar and Solar Mythos with the Eschatology of which the writers were ignorant. (*See* Appendix I.)

The change in Israel from the worship of El Shadai to the worship of Ihuh (=Hu or Iu, Egyptian) from the Eloistic to the Jehovistic god, corresponds to the change from the Stellar to the Solar Mythos in their Astronomical Mythology and the Eschatology of Egypt, and can be seen and proved in the volume of the Sacred Law—in the book of I Chronicles xii. 5, in which we find that Baal-Jah, as divinity, supplied a personal name. Thus the Baal is Jah יח, who is one of the Baalim (the earliest Baalam were the seven elementary powers in the Astronomical Mythology). The One God in Israel was made known to Moses by the two names *of* רורח *and* יה, *Ihuh and Iah.* In the Egyptian the One God, Ptah or Atum-Ra, was Huhi—the Eternal, in the character of God the Father, and Iu in the character of God the Son, which two were one.

Gesenius derives the name of *Ihuh* from the root *Huh,* which root does not exist in Hebrew, but it does exist in Egyptian. Huh or Heh signifies ever, everlastingness, eternity, the eternal, and was a title which was applied to Ptah, Atum-Ra, and Osiris as Neb-Huhi—the Everlasting Lord or Supreme One, Self-existing and Eternal God, which each of these three deities represented in turn as one divine dynasty succeeded another in the Egyptian religion. Bel or Baali was El Shadai, or was another name for him, and when they changed from Stellar into Solar Mythos and the Eschatology, he was no longer to be considered the One God—see Exodus xxxiv. 13. "Thou shalt call me Ishi and shalt call me no more Baali"—Hosea ii. 16—and therefore to have the Hebrew El Shadai as the father and Hu=Iu, Iau, Ishi, Ihu, etc., as his son, is quite wrong and has no meaning, and no explanation could be given that would be correct with the Hebrew characters on the symbol as it is now, but the Egyptian is correct, because [hieroglyph] Hu is rightly the son of Ptah, who is represented at the bottom of the symbol [hieroglyph]. It also proves to us the great antiquity of this form of the symbol, because it is Ptah here represented, not Amen-Ra or Osiris. Now Ptah was the earliest and first god of the *Solar Mythos*, and thousands and thousands of years older than Amen-Ra, and Amen-Ra was thousands of years before Osiris. *Ptah was the first father god*, and therefore we have the son, Hu, Iu, Iahu and various other names for one and the same. In the Eschatology Iu was Amsu—Horus, the risen, Horus " in spirit form " who had been crucified on the Tatt Cross in Amenta, and had risen as the glorified spirit—the son of the father—both one and the same. Amsu, as portrayed in the Egyptian Vignette of the *Ritual*, is seen emerging as an immortal on the horizon of the resurrection, safe beyond the valley of the shadow of the darkness of Sheol. He uplifts his right arm from the swathing of the mummy as he rises from the tomb ; he has burst the bonds of death and conquered the grave ; he is the bearer of the crook ; he is *the Good Shepherd* who comes in that character to look after the father's flock—Psalm lxxvii. 20. His right arm raised portrays that " he ascended " ; his left arm, still shown, found bound to his side, not yet free from the swathing of the tomb, pointing downwards, indicates that "he descended." Thus he is shown as bursting from the tomb, rising to join his heavenly father for ever in a glorious and happy eternity—Exodus xv. 2 ; xvii. 16.

Here we have the name of Jesus, son of the Lord of the Heaven and Earth—the Almighty, written at a very early date, probably 16,000 B.C.—" The word and the name," interesting to those of the 18°. For obvious reasons we do not give fuller explanations or decipherments ; but the foregoing is sufficient answer to *Dr W. Westcott*, in his note in ARS QUATUOR CORONATORUM.

Much more could be written on the decipherment of this, but we refrain from doing so on account of " The Secret Word," but all who have taken the 18° will fully understand.

Though a single name certainly does not manifest to us all the parts of a " complex idea," yet it must be acknowledged that in many of our " complex ideas " the single name may point to us some chief " property " which belongs to the thing the word signifies ; especially when the word or name is traced up to the original through several languages from whence it is borrowed, although it may be very precarious and uncertain, and although our *words* which are applied to *moral and intellectual ideas* will, we venture to say, be read by those who are not initiated, they will be found to signify sensible and corporeal things which cannot be misunderstood by any student seeking the truth.

But the Cross of symbolism has no significance without the circle ; both go together and are indivisible.

The mystic chain of the Masonic and other mysteries, formed by making the circle with the hands of each person crossed, derives all its significance from the cross and circle being figured at one and the same time and in one and the same image. Interesting to brothers of the 18°.

The great Cross, which was discovered a few years since at Callernish, covered with a bed of peat-moss more than four feet thick, which must have taken ages to accumulate, was a chamber, sunken near a circle of standing stones. It was planned according to the four quarters with scientific precision, with the head to the South, foot to the North, and arms extending East and West —270 feet in length and 27 feet across.

"The Cruz Ansaia unites the circle and cross of the four corners. From this origin the circle and the cross came to be interchangeable at times."[1]

The Tat Cross consisted of a pedestal with four horizontal bars or shelves that are circular, constituting a kind of Altar-Cross. It was used in the temples as the pedestal and fulcrum for supporting the statues of the gods. The name signifies to establish, and it is the symbol of stability as the fourfold foundation of a world, or an order of things that was established upon the four quarters. The Tat-altar or Pedestal is the equivalent of the mount of the four corners, or the tree with four branches, or the Cross with four arms. The Tat is the special type of Ptah, the establisher of the four corners of the Solar Mythos ; but it existed as a lunar emblem for the moon-god. Tat impersonates the Tat and says :—" I am Tat, the Son of Tat, conceived in Tat and born in Tat"—(*Ritual*, chap. i.). As a lunar type it would represent the four quarters of the moon, for, whether the four corners may be those of the four stars or spirits, the four leaves of the lotus, the four lunar divisions of the four corners of the Solar Zodiac,

[1] Nat. Gen., Gerald Massey.

the Cross is everywhere the sign of the four quarters with one exception. The Tat was set up in Tattu, the established or eternal region corresponding finally to the zodiacal sign of the Fishes, the station of the Seven Great Gods of the Assyrians, the chief of all the four corners because of the Solar birthplace. A most curious form of the Cross is given in the *Journal of the Royal Asiatic Society*. At each of the four corners is placed a quarter arc of an oviform curve, and when the four are put together they form an oval ; thus the figure combines the cross with the circle round it in four parts, corresponding to the four corners of the cross.

The most sacred Cross of Egypt that was carried in the hands of the gods, the Pharaohs and the mummied dead is the Ankh ☥, the sign of life, the living, an oath, a covenant and a pair, or to couple and duplicate. The top of this is the hieroglyphic Ru O, set upright on the Tau-cross. The Ru is the door, gate, mouth, the place of outlet. This denotes the birthplace in the northern quarter of the heavens from which the sun is reborn. Hence the Ru of the Ankh-sign is the feminine type of the birthplace representing the north. It was in the northern quarter that the Goddess of the Seven Stars, called the "Mother of the Revolutions," gave birth to time in the earliest cycle of the year.

The first sign of this primordial circle and cycle made in heaven is the earliest shape of the Ankh Cross ∝, a mere loop which contains a circle and the Cross in one image. This loop or noose is carried in front of the oldest genitrix, Typhon of the Great Bear, as her Ark, the ideograph of a period, an ending, a time, shown to mean one revolution. This then represents the circle made in the northern heaven by the Great Bear, which constituted the earliest year of time, from which fact we infer that the loop or Ru of the North represents that quarter, the birthplace of time when figured as the Ru of the Ankh-symbol. Indeed, this can be proved. The noose is an Ark or Rek type of reckoning. The Ru of the Ankh-cross was continued in the Cypriote R, O and the Coptic Ro, P. The Ro was carried into the Greek Cross ⳩, which is formed of the Ro and Chi, or R-k. Thus the Ark (Eg.) sign of the circle and cross survives by name in the Ro-chi cross, and the connection of the Ru or Rk with the birthplace can be shown by this name. Ru (Eg.) is the outlet, and the feminine Kha determines its nature. Rak in Akkadian, like the Ru-Kha, is the vulva. Rakha, in Quichua, is the vagina and the woman. The Rak or Ark was the sign of all beginning (Arche) on this account, and the Ark-tie is the cross of the nor, the hinder part, which is represented by the Ru O.

A form of the Ankh-cross, found in the fourth pyramid, enables us to prove the origin of this cross as a sign of North and South, because the pillar and base are the pyramid of Sothis, the Dog-star. The Pyramid being both four square and triangular is a figure of seven. Hence its name of Hept or Sept (Sothis) is the name of number seven. Sothis was a masculine or southern type of the Goddess of the Seven Stars, who was thus represented by the Ru of the North and the Pyramid of the South. The top is the Ru of the birthplace in the North and the bottom is the symbol of the South. With the two arms it presents the figure of above (North) and below (South), with the crossing East and West or right hand and left. (This is the complete Ankh-cross of life—from the Swastika which was taken from the human figures as represented by fig. 159, page 359.) The inhabitants of the Isle of Anaa tattooed themselves with the cross. The people of Baratonga were in the habit of tattooing themselves with the cross and square, side by side; a double figure of the four corners. According to the Kahn the Hurons tattoo themselves on the thigh with black figures, sometimes of a serpent, at others of a cross. Both Protestant and Catholic missionaries, who first entered the territory of Hudson's Bay, found the adoration of the tree of the cross was quite common in those regions of North America as a magic talisman and emblem of fertility. According to the native Toltec historian *Ixtlilxochitl*, the deity, Quetzalcoatl, who was said to have introduced the cult of the cross, was adored under the sign of the cross, which was called the Tree of Sustenance and the Tree of Life. He was also portrayed in a robe covered with crosses. The hair of the Toze, the Great Mother (*cf.* Tes-Neith, Eg.), was carefully arranged on her forehead in curls and crosses; the curls being made to form the crosses. *Garcilasco* says that a great cross cut out of a single jasper was sacred to the Incas of Peru.

Dobrizhoffer tells us the Abipones were all marked on the forehead with the cross. They likewise wore black crosses in red woollen garments, a custom which was not derived from their knowledge of Christianity. The cross was discovered in the ruins of Palenque on the tablet of an altar with a bird on the top and a serpent at the foot. It was standing on the serpent's head. The cross being the type of stability, this would be the Evil Serpent, the representative of dissolution, the Dragon of Darkness conquered by the cross or by the bird-headed sun-god at the crossing.

The cross was used in Egypt as a protecting talisman and a symbol of saving power. Typhon, or Satan, is actually found chained to and bound by the cross. In the *Ritual* the Osirian cries, "Apophis is overthrown, their cords bind the South, North, East and West, their cords are on him. Har-ru-bah has knotted him." These were the cords of the four quarters of the cross.

From time immemorial the copper ingots of Central Africa have been smelted in the shape of the Cross. As *Livingstone* remarks :—"Not as a Christian emblem, certainly." They were so founded because the cross was a primal figure of the fourfold foundation.

The cross that was seen in heaven by Constantine was that of the four quarters ; hence he had himself represented in the solar character as the slayer of the dragon. After his victory over Licïnus he was portrayed at his palace in Nicomedia with the cross on his head and a transfixed dragon writhing at his feet.[1] This is the same imagery as that of the cross established on the serpent found in the ruins at Palenque. One of the coins of Constantine also shows the Labarum standing upon the conquered serpent. The meaning of this is simply the cycle founded for ever on the four quarters, and the cross is nothing more than a type of duration.

The Labarum was the Royal Roman Standard, which *Lactantius* calls "The ensign that was consecrated by the name of Christ" ; by which he means the monogram or "KR" upon the banner. No doubt this signification was being read into the sign on the standard of Constantine. But there was nothing new in it ; whether found in Rome or out of it, the tree and cross are identical, and, as a type, the one involves the other.

[1] The author has an old gold coin similar to this in his possession.

The Labarum was the tree from Laba—*Greek*—a staff. This is a common-type name for the tree. Llwyf is the Elm-tree in *Welsh*; Liobhan in *Irish*. Laban, a kind of wood, in *Malayan*. Lipa, a Plane-tree—*Polish*. Luban, a Conifer—*Arabic*. Labanah, a Poplar-tree—*Hebrew*. Labanj, a Plane-tree—*Persian, etc*. Lep or Rep (Eg.) signifies to grow, bud, branch and take leaf. The vine is a form of the Rep or Arp. The Repa personified was the branch of the ancestral tree, the shoot and offspring of the Pharaoh, called the hereditary highness, the prince, lord, heir apparent. Now, when Constantine is portrayed on the Labarum, with his child or children, he is the exact equivalent of the Egyptian Ra with the Repa; and the coins prove that he was assimilated to the Solar God, after the fashion of the Pharaohs.

The doctrine of the Repaship belongs to mythology, in which the Repa was the divine child, the KR or Khart, who is portrayed as Horus on the cross; at the crossing; the representative of the KR, a course or circle. Seb-Kronus is called the veritable Repa of the gods—that is, as the personified course of time—KR, for the course, being the monogram of Kronus. The latest form of the Repa was the lord of the solar course, the Kar, whose representative was the Kart in Egyptian, the Kurios in Greek, the god Har-pi-Khart, whose image is portrayed in the catacombs, or Her-Ma-Kheru. The cross goes with the tree of the four corners. The cross in inseparable from the circle, the Kar or course, and the maker of the course is intended by the monogram of KR, whether personified as the Kart, Kronus or Christ. The typology is so ancient that the Repa is found as Rupe in the Maori mythology—he who was fabled to have fallen from the cross or at the crossing; Ripeka being a name for the cross, the cross-roads and to crucify.

Wilkinson remarks upon the (to him) strange and startling fact that the first cross found in Egypt, belonging to the Christians, is not the cross which was substituted in after times, but the Crux Ansata, the Ankh-sign of life. "The early Christians of Egypt," he says, "adopted the Ankh in lieu of the Roman Cross, which was afterwards substituted for it, and prefixed it to inscriptions in the same manner as the cross in later times. We can attest that the Ankh holds this position in the sepulchres of the Great Oasis, and that numerous inscriptions headed by the Ankh are preserved to this day on early Christian monuments."

The origin of the cross, as a type of the four quarters, was probably dawning on the adapters. The Syrian liturgy prescribes thirty-six crossings, the same as the number of decans in the zodiac, which were first reckoned by thirty-six crossing stars. Here then we have the cross of the thirty-six decani (tekani or tehani, Eg.) of the early reckonings, continued in a Christian liturgy. It was prescribed in the Ordo Romanus that in consecrating churches the walls were to be signed with the Chrisma in the shape of the cross in twelve different places, the number of signs in the zodiac, and on the papal chair, which, according to *Bower*, was being cleaned, in the year 1662, when the twelve labours of Hercules were found to be pictured upon it.

If there be one thing considered more certain than another, it is that the cross, composed of the Chi and Ro, ☧ which reads Chr, must be the abbreviated name of Christ; and it is always taken to convey that meaning. Be it so. Yet it is not of Christian origin, and, to go no further back, it appears upon coins of the Ptolemies and on those of Herod the Great, which had been prophetically struck forty years before the Christian era. Chr answers to and represents the Egyptian Kher or Kheru, which means the word voice or the later solar logos. Chi and Ro are the cross and circle. The Egyptian Khi 𓐍, called the sieve, is a cross—the sieve being made by crossing (Eg. Teka). The Ru 𓂋 is an oval, as on the top of the Ankh ☥ These are continued in the Greek. ☧ The Kher then is a dual sign of the cross and circle. The sign ☧ appears upon a coin of the Emperor Decius with the letter A prefixed. Here the ARK is an abbreviated form of ἀρχοντος, which proves that the sign has the value of RK when read one way, and therefore KR the other. Kher and Rekh interchange in the hieroglyphics for the "Word": also Ker for the circuit, course or turn round, is identical with the Ark, a period or cycle of time. The KR and Ark, signs of the cross and circle, or the crossed circle, likewise correspond; and the Ptolemian or Greek form of the KR symbol is the later equivalent for the Ark-tie, ∝ which, from the beginning, contained both the circle (Ru) and the cross (Chi). The "Ark" was the sign of the annual circle when it was made by the "Great Bear." It denotes a lunar month in the Assyrian Arkhu. And the RK or KR is a circle or course of time. KR denotes a course in Egyptian and various other languages. For this reason the sign appears in Greek inscriptions as an abbreviation for Kronus, the monogram of Time himself. Further, Tek (Eg.) is a cross, and this explains one reason for the sign ☧ found upon the coins of the Armenian King Tigranes, which stands for the first letters (Tigr of his name or that of his capital, the city of Tigranocerta). In this the cross reads both Tau and Chi in one as does the hieroglyphic Tek X and with the Ro form TKR, whence "Tigr."

But to add the missing link and further proof one must go still back further than the Greeks. As we have stated before ⚹ or ⚹ was one way of writing the name in the very earliest times of Amsu—the risen Horus I. or Horus in the spirit. The Ru ⬭ was here in the above written and added to this, making ☧ so as to keep time with evolution and bringing on the original up to date, a very important point, taking all the above into consideration and which really explains itself, although no one hitherto appears to have really grasped or comprehended how and why this was evolved or for what reason ; but we will elucidate this :

We have given *Gerald Massey's* decipherment, reasons and explanations, because we believe that he has approached nearest the solution of the subject, but our opinion is that the *true solution* is as we have put forward before our readers—*i.e.* the sign ⚹ Amsu with the Ru, 0 (This cross ☧ is found depicted on many stones in Cornwall.) Now, the Ru 0 represents the fish's mouth ; it is also the emaning mouth of that fish which gives forth birth to water as the life of the world and the Saviour who comes to Egypt by water as the water of the inundation or overflow of the Nile. When the ground is parched and dry, the overflow or inundation occurs and thus brings life, gladness and plenty to all those who depend on the fructification of seeds, etc., planted to maintain life, representing symbolically "the water of life," "the saviour of life," etc., and in conjunction with, ⚹ would represent originally "the Great One,"[1] "the Great Saviour of Life," on which all must depend; hence this symbol, found amongst Masons, originally brought from Egypt, but the meaning of which hitherto has been lost to the Brotherhood, now restored to those who read this, which should interest *Brother Gould*.

Thus we see that the Cross originally represented the four quarters and was depicted in human form by two cross figures. After two others were added, making four figures in all; and afterwards in various forms as the sign of life and rebirth, etc. With the Christian faith the Cross generally is too well known to need any further remarks from us, therefore we may finally say that:—

In Egypt, Assyria and Britain, it was emblematical of creative power and eternity.

In India, China and Scandinavia, of heaven and immortality.

In North and South America, of rejuvenescence and freedom from physical suffering.

And in "all" the common symbols of the Resurrection, or the sign of life to come.

And in all "Heathen" countries, without exception, it was the emphatic type, the sole enduring evidence of the Divine unity.

In the Christian doctrines, all the above combined.

(*See* Appendix II.)

[1] The Zapotecs have represented the Crocodile or Great Water Lizard as one name for their highest being and have symbolised it in their Glyphs as "the giver of food of life." The Zapotec name for this Crocodile is Tlaloc and Ce Cipactli—"The One." This is the same as in the Egyptian, but which must not be confounded with the Great Dragon uranographically represented by the Constellation Hydra.

CHAPTER XVIII

THE GREAT PYRAMID

IN Egypt, we contend, is the key and cradle of the whole mystery of the Primordial. We disagree with *Le Plongeon* that Yucatan was a more ancient seat of learning than Egypt, and we also maintain that the Mayas, as well as all the other ancient nations

FIG. 163.
The Sphinx, with the Great Pyramid at the back on the right. Taken by *F. W. Collingwood, Esq.*, for the Author.

of the world, obtained their knowledge, either directly or indirectly, from the Egyptians. The Mayas, as their traditional history shows, certainly traded with the people of the Mediterranean, and there is reason to believe that they penetrated as far as the Himalayas. Probably these Mayas were the Egyptian Haûi-Nîbû (people beyond the seas), as it is stated that they were as civilised as the Egyptians about the time of the fifth dynasty, 3900 B.C. The texts show that these people were known long before this date. The translation is " People beyond the seas " or " the people from behind "—*i.e.* behind the setting sun. As the sun, setting in the West, went down into the sea, the Mayas would naturally be spoken of as people " beyond the seas " or " behind the setting sun." Further proof may be found in the orientation of their temples and from their possessing the knowledge of building arches. That the Druids also were evidently a more ancient people than the Mayas may be demonstrated from the fact that they had no knowledge of building arches, and other points we have brought before our readers.

The Pyramids of Egypt are well known by the descriptions that have frequently been given them both by ancient and modern writers. Some antiquarians think that they were originally intended for tombs for the ancient Kings of Egypt. The Mahometans pretend that they were built by the Preadamites. They mention particularly Gian-ben-Gian, the Universal Monarch of the World in the ages that went before Adam's creation. Ezekiel speaks of the Sepulchres of the Kings of Egypt, or rather he describes in a poetical manner the Deliverer of the Pharaohs going down to Hell, or into the deepest parts of the earth, with his army when put to death by the sword of the Chaldeans.

It was about the time of User-Ka-f that we find a number of shrines which united the chief characteristics of the low rectangular tomb, commonly known by its Arabic name of " Mastaba " —*i.e.* bench, and of the Pyramid, were built. According to *Prof. Sethe* this custom of building only lasted about 100 years —*i.e.* from the reign of User-Ka-f to that of Meu-Kau-Heru. This knowledge would be very important, if correct, as it would give a more reliable date when the Mayas took the Egyptian Solar Mythos into Yucatan, as we find this form of buildings there. Having seen them in Egypt they would take the copy back with them. We do not find these farther West than Yucatan and the lands of the Mayas. The remains of the Stellar Mythos are alone found beyond. Then we must not overlook the important point of orientation of these Pyramids and temples, the later in Yucatan are E. by S. and all the Druid remains that we have found are E. by S., and all the Pyramids in Tankasi, Kurru, Zuma, Gebel Barkel and Nuri, and the remains of the temples built by

Nubian Kings of the Sudan, on both banks of the Nile, near Meraiori, are all oriented E. by S., *but the Great Pyramid of Ghizeh is oriented N.*

The Mayas and the people of America had also copied these, as may be seen from the remains of their ancient monuments at the present time.[1] The Pyramid of Teotihuacan, Mexico, according to *Almarez*, has, at a point 69 feet from its base, an opening with a gallery large enough to admit a man crawling on his hands and knees, which extends inwards on an incline, a distance of 25 feet and terminates in two square wells or chambers, each 5 feet square, and one 15 feet deep. *Bancroft*, however, states that the gallery is 157 feet long, increasing in height to 6½ feet as it penetrates the Pyramid, extending (apparently) down to the base and up to the summit, and that other cross galleries are blocked with stones, and that the well is over 6 feet square (Tank of Flame). Nothing is mentioned about the *form of entrance* to this Pyramid, but from the meagre details it is evidently a copy of the Great Pyramid of Egypt with the details of their Eschatology written here also in stone.

It would be interesting to know if the entrance was at the North, and whether all other details of the internal construction were the same. Most probably we shall in time find this to be so, when it is thoroughly explored, and may also add something to our knowledge as to the full construction internally of the Great Pyramid in Egypt, concerning which we are still in doubt, and so enable us to find still another chamber. The one point, however, which impresses itself on the author is *that the external measurements differ, so far as we can ascertain*, but the site chosen is the same—*i.e.* the line through the centre of the structure is in the Astronomical Meridian, and the buildings are orientated with slight variation. The construction in grades and steps is the same. This points to the fact that the Mexicans copied the Great Pyramid but built theirs at the time of the Solar Mythos, and as the Egyptian Pyramid was erected during Stellar or when the Stellar Mythos was perfected, and the Mayas obtained their

[1] The picture seen on the pillars walling the entrance to the cella at the Pyramid of Tepoxtlan, part of a huge glyph of the chalchiuith, or "green precious stone," represents Horus as Prince of the Emerald Stone, Her-uatch-f—The Light of the World. As the Emerald Stone was an emblem used by the Zapotec and Mexican people to represent "Rays of Light," or "Diffuser of Light," therefore this would correspond in every particular to the Egyptian Heru-Kuti spoken of in the *Ritual* in connection with the Great Pyramid of Ghizeh.

doctrines from the Egyptians during the Solar Mythos, we should naturally find that the orientation was somewhat different. Of course, it is a question of orientation if built during Stellar or Solar Mythos, and this will account for all the differences we find in the other Pyramids in America as well, either with orientation N. or E. by S. There is no doubt, also, that they brought the *Ritual* with them as well as the " copy " of the Great Pyramid, but it was all the Solar doctrines that they brought direct and not Stellar, the knowledge of which they had obtained before from previous exodes, and they associated their Pyramids with the Solar alone latterly, whatever they did at first. We know that there was intercommunication between the two peoples at the time of the 4th and 5th dynasties—4000 B.C., and we know that the Solar doctrines were fully established 15,000 years ago in Egypt, and if we calculate that these Pyramids in Mexico are ten thousand years old, they must have been in communication and carried this over 5000 years before the fifth dynasty, which will probably be as near the correct date as we can arrive at, and they would have had time " to become as civilised as the Egyptians at the time of the fifth dynasty."

Their knowledge of the Stellar Mythos must have dated many thousands of years before this, and probably came from an exodus which went out of Egypt, travelling through Asia and reaching America, *via* the Pacific coast. We are of an opinion that they obtained their *Solar* Mythos direct from the Egyptians, through trading with them. This would explain why the Mayas had more of the Solar Mythos, and had obliterated much of the Stellar in comparison with those tribes farther to the West and North, who retained more of the Stellar than the Solar. All the temples at Uxmal face the East, those at Palenque, Copan and Quirigua, North. All the temples in these latter cities have zoo-types as Symbols of the gods in Sign Language, and must, therefore, date back to the Stellar, as the anthropomorphic dated much later. As stated before, both here in Mexico and Central America and other parts of the world and Egypt, from whence these were derived, the people did not worship these " great beasts "—these were *Symbols* of the Deity—and it must be obvious that it was the Deity and not the Symbols they worshipped, more than we do in the Christian doctrines the Lamb, which is a Symbolical representative of Christ. So in our lodges we have Symbols to represent the WM's ; these are not the WM ; but Symbols by which they are known. In "the Knight of the Serpent" we recognise the serpent only as a Symbol of Tem, the god of the East and West, as Horus as god of the North and South (Knights of the E. and W.).

Everyone knows, and some of our readers must have seen, that stupendous and most mysterious monument called the Great Pyramid of Ghizeh, not far from Cairo, which has been a subject of contention for years amongst scientific men, and has certainly no connection with any of the other pyramids which were built years after, except that of Teotihuacan.

The Great Pyramid, when understood, far surpasses and eclipses King Solomon's Temple as a building, or any other in the world, and the wonderful secrets and hidden systems, embracing absolutely mathematical precision and workmanship, can only be thoroughly understood by its co-relationship with the *Ritual*—THE PYRAMID TEXT—undoubtedly the oldest in existence that we are acquainted with.

The base is a true square and perfectly oriented, set due N. E. S. W., parallel with the equatorial line, absolutely no variation of points ; its base on a huge rock and that rock perfectly and truly hewn and levelled to the earth's curvature of 8 inches to the mile, the importance of which is evident—keeping it from convulsive damages as time goes on. The height of the Pyramid is 486·256 feet, and each side 763·81 feet. The height thus measures, with the radius of a circle whose circumference equals the four sides, this being exact when worked out by decimals, showing that the circle could be squared by these ancient architects which has not been improved on since. Its base side length is 365·242 sacred cubits, showing the number of days and fractional part of a day in a year. The slope of the angles are paralleled and commeasurable with the earth's pole and slope to the equinox, giving the angle, whence the sun's distance from the earth may be calculated at 91,840,000 miles, also it is twice recorded in the construction of the Pyramid, the period, called the procession of the equinoxes—viz. 25,827 inches, equal to 25,827 years—the one great year or the time the sun takes to traverse through space around its centre, and also for the recession of the 7 Pole Stars or the 7 Glorious Ones. By it we may discover how the planets move in their different orbits and mathematically demonstrate their various revolutions. The distance from the Pole is equal to the distance from the centre.

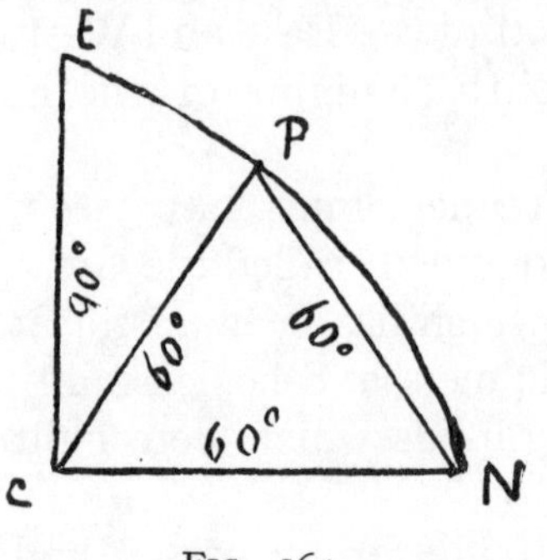

FIG. 164.

c Centre of Earth
p Situation of Great Pyramid
n North Pole
e Point where the Meridian of the building cuts the Equator, then *e c p* will be the latitude of the building — viz. 30° — and *c p n* will be an equilateral triangle, since the angle at *c* is =60°, and the radii *c n* and *c p* will be equal to each other, therefore *p n*, the distance from the Pyramid to the North Pole will be equal to *c p*, the distance to the centre of the Earth, and we have here three angles of 60° interesting to Freemasons.

Here, in the Great Pyramid, is the one material centre which gives the standard for those practical things—weights, measures, etc., and these were carried from land to lands, with the utmost care by the Priests who left Egypt, no doubt for some future purpose under divine will, which is not yet apparent. The builders of the Pyramid were masters of Astronomical and Geographical science, and it contains the minute measurements of the earth and heaven, far exceeding the scientific knowledge of any man in our own time, and this knowledge and the secrets thereof were known to the High Priests, and they carried out their then knowledge wherever they went. The Ark of the Covenant, built in the wilderness by Moses, Noah's Ark and King Solomon's Temple, all bear a true decimal proportion to the Pyramid, and "the Ark" or "Sarcophagus" in the King's chamber within the Pyramid.

It may be this Pyramid was built by Divine Inspiration to stand for all time as a record; as from Job 38, v. 5-7; Jer. 32, v. 18-20; and Isaiah 19, v. 19-20: "In that day there shall be an altar to the Lord in the midst of the land of Egypt and a pillar at the border thereof to the Lord, and it shall be for a sign and witness to the Lord of Hosts—until this day." What should make this a sign and witness? That it is a copy of the *Ritual* written in stone, and only in conjunction with the *Ritual* can we properly understand it. "And a pillar at the border thereof," what is that and where is the answer? The answer is the Sphinx, and a mighty pillar is this with all its secrets and hidden chambers still unread and buried in sand; nevertheless, in time "this mighty pillar" will be cleared, and its secrets, so long hidden, will be given up to future generations to read and to enlighten them upon the mysteries of the past. The *Ritual* will help them to decipher the meaning of these secret and hidden chambers and their contents written in stone.

The Sphinx at Ghizeh (in Egyptian, Hu [hieroglyphs]) *Dr Budge* regards as the symbol of the Sun-god Ra, Temu, Khepera, Heru, Kuti, and says, "it was made to keep away evil spirits from the tombs which were round about." We cannot agree with *Dr Budge* in the reason he assigns for its erection, since the names alone denote that it was erected as a monument to "The One Great God," and the "Seven Glorious Ones" and as a "pillar of the great wonder in Egypt," as we read in the volume of the Sacred Law; and also from the *Ritual* we find that Ra, Temu, Khepera are all one and the same—names of the great spirit under different dynasties in the Solar Mythos. "Hu" was also a name of Horus, as we find from the 80th chapter of the *Ritual*: "I have seized upon Hu from the place in which I found him," also "I am the craftsman who lighteneth the darkness and I come to dissipate the darkness that light should be." For Heru and Kuti we have to go back to the Stellar Mythos. Heru represents Horus I. and Kuti denotes the Seven Glorious Ones, the Shining Ones, light, etc., and combined as Heru-Kuti, "the Light of the World." Speaking of Heru-Kuti in the *Ritual*, it says, "I am the Light of the World," and the ancient sign is \|/

The Sphinx was most certainly erected in connection with the Great Pyramid of Ghizeh, though after the latter. This is most distinctly stated in the *Ritual* and the oldest Papyrus. It could not have been erected for the *abode* of the Sun-god, because it is typical as it stands of the *passage* of the Sun from West to East—*i.e.* from sunset to sunrise. The old Egyptians took the Sun as a type of the powers of Ra, Temu, Khepera, etc.—seven names in fact of the Great Spirit. Kuti would then mean that these represented the Seven Glorious Ones in the Stellar Mythology, but Kuti also means light, and therefore probably was used as "the light of the Glorious Ones," Ra having taken the place of the Seven Glorious Ones, as "The Light" in the Solar Mythos. To many there may be a difficulty of decipherment of all these names under the consideration of Solar Mythos, but to us there is not any difficulty, and the explanation is this: that the Sphinx was erected after the Great Pyramid of Ghizeh was built as a monument to Heru-ur or Horus I., and Heru-Kuti would mean a monument erected to Horus I., "the Great Light of the World" \|/—*i.e.* Horus. The God of the Pole Stars is the God of the Seven Glorious Ones—*i.e.* Horus I., and when the Stellar Mythos was merged into the Solar, Heru was brought on as one god, but Ra took his place, and Temu and Khepera, etc., were other names for the same in different dynasties as supreme for the time. The sun, representing Ra, rose in the East and set in the West, diffusing the light of day from its rising to its setting, and thus giving light to the world in the Solar.[1]

It is only by studying the *Ritual* of ancient Egypt, in connection with these ancient monuments, that we can arrive at anything like a true and clear conception of their ideas and beliefs, and we cannot understand the volume of our Sacred Law if we simply take a literal translation as we have it, hence the various and different opinions of many divines, who honestly believe in the Bible and Christianity.

The one point on which Egyptologists might differ from us is with regard to the position of the Sphinx. The Sphinx faces the sun at rising (East), and in our opinion this would indicate that it was built much later than the Great Pyramid, and at

[1] *Gerald Massey* is of opinion that it represented the double equinox or the double horizons—*i.e.* a monument that commemorates the founding of the equinox in the double horizon, and represented the passage of the sun from West to East in the under earth before they had worked out Amenta, but as we have shown from the *Ritual* the Sphinx was built *after* the Great Pyramid, but it is quite possible that *Mr Gerald Massey* may be right in his opinion, if we take it that this was built at the earliest part of the Solar Mythos or in the Stellar as the double horizon of Shu. It is made in a compound image—male in front, female behind—and if they built it to represent the passage of the Child Horus (Harmachus) entering the Sphinx in the West at sunset travelling through (representing Horus travelling the underworld) and coming out in the East as the rising sun—symbolical of the risen Horus—it would be symbolical of the passage of the Sun God or the Soul. Amenta was not entirely worked out at this time, in *Mr Massey's* opinion, but from the structure of the interior of the Pyramid we are of opinion that a great part, if not all, was worked out during the Stellar Mythos and when the Solar came in vogue they changed the God of the Pole Star (North) to the Sun God (East) as orientation of other Pyramids prove. If then we take it to represent the double horizon of Shu and the passage from the West (setting sun) through to the East and rising again in the East as a glorious light and body it would symbolise the risen Horus or Amsu and be one point of the commencement of the Solar Mythos.

the time when the Solar Mythos was taking the place of the Stellar, except *Mr G. Massey* is correct in his view. It would not alter the meaning or the reason, but only show how they brought on and made use of the Stellar doctrines in their Solar Mythology. It was evidently a connecting link between the two, and when the future has restored to us the hidden chambers buried here, light will be given to us. That these chambers are there the *Ritual* proves to us, and there is no doubt in our mind, also, that the ancient name of the Great Pyramid was "Khuti," which denotes the seven Lights or Glorious Ones, and not merely light as *Mr Marsh Adams* has stated ; it also signifies as Heru-Kuti, the representation in stone of Horus I., the Light of the World and all his doctrines, or the doctrines and divine message given to man at this early period to read and learn what he must do and what he had to pass through to attain triumph over darkness (ignorance), so that his soul and spirit, after this life, should find everlasting rest and happiness, and the presence of the Divine God of Light, and have a full knowledge of all things.

Therefore the ancient name of the Great Pyramid was "Khuti," which denotes the seven Lights or Glorious Ones, and not merely light. This most mysterious monument stands to-day almost perfect and intact, whilst of all other structures, which made the marvels of the ancient world, scarcely a vestige remains ; but the Great and Grand Pyramid of Ghizeh still stands undestroyed and indestructible, ages after the lesser structures have passed away, as it stood ages before they ever came into existence. Certainly more than fifty centuries, and how many more it is impossible to say for certain, have passed away since the building first concealed from view those secret chambers and hidden mysteries, of which no other building on the globe contains the equal. What the concealed significance may be of that secret masonry, by whom and for what purpose the complex plan was designed, has perplexed many minds and created a large amount of discord.

Maspero takes it for granted that the Great Pyramid of Ghizeh was built by Kufu ; most other writers have followed his example. In his well-written book, "The Dawn of Civilisation," he dilates upon what might have been, and draws a pretty picture out of his imagination : but are there facts for the foundation of his picture ? If we turn to the papyri we find that all the plans of the architecture of the building had been handed down to Num-Kufu (we do not like the word "Kheops," because it is the Greek, and why use Greek in Egyptology when we have the Egyptian, which to our ears is quite as euphonious, if not more so. Num-Kufu is certainly a softer and pleasanter sound than Kheops), and in all probability the Pyramid had been completed many thousands of years before Num-Kufu was born. The name Khufu or Kufu, King of the 4th dynasty, was found cut on stone dating back to the King of the 1st dynasty, at Bubastis. There is evidence that his grandfather had obtained these plans from his ancestors, and that they were handed down simply to give the "key of the building." The fact of the name being found written on the side of a stone built into the North wall does not necessarily identify the builder, for we find in the Papyrus of Nu that it was a part of the eschatological ceremony to engrave four different names on four stones, which were to be built into the North, South, East and West walls. The names on these stones were different names of the guardians who protected the North, South, East and West, and might have been changed with each "Grand Master" or dynasty. This has a very significant meaning to Freemasons, who will be interested in understanding the same if it were so, and we find that the temples in Central America had the same either written or depicted in Sculptured Figures. These four names, as we have stated before, the guardians of N. E. S. and W., are the four children of Horus. (*See* Appendix 1.)

The orientation of the Great Pyramid was undoubtedly made from Stellar observation (which is a very important fact to note) at the time when the Stellar Mythology had been perfected.

Proctor states: "It would seem that the builders of the Pyramid were anxious to place it in latitude 30° as clearly as their means of observation permitted. Let us consider what result they achieved, and the evidence thus afforded respecting their skill and scientific attainments. In our own time, of course, the astronomer has no difficulty in determining with great exactness the position of any given latitude-parallel. But at the time when the Great Pyramid was built it must have been a matter of very serious difficulty to determine the position of any required latitude-parallel with a great degree of exactitude. The most obvious way of dealing with the difficulty would have been by observing the length of shadows thrown by upright posts at noon in spring and autumn. In latitude 30° North at noon in spring (or, to speak precisely, on the day of the Vernal Equinox) the sun is just twice as far from the horizon as he is from the point vertically overhead; and if a pointed post were set exactly upright at true noon (supposed to occur at the moment of the Vernal or Autumnal Equinox) the shadow of the post would be exactly half as long as a line drawn from the pole to the end of the shadow. But observations based on this principle would have presented many difficulties to the architects of the pyramid. The sun, not being a point of light, but a globe, the shadow of a pointed rod does not end in a well-defined point. The moment of true noon, which is not the same as the ordinary or civil noon, never does agree exactly with the time of the Vernal or Autumnal Equinox and may be removed from it by any interval of time not exceeding twelve hours. And there are many other circumstances which would lead astronomers, like those who doubtless presided over the scientific preparations for building the Great Pyramid, to prefer a means of determining the latitude depending on another principle. The heavens would afford practically unchanging indications for their purpose. The stars being all carried round the pole of the heavens, as if they were fixed points in the interior of a hollow revolving sphere, it becomes possible to determine the position of the pole of the star sphere, even though no bright conspicuous star actually occupies that point. Any bright star close by the pole is seen to revolve in a very small circle, whose centre is the pole itself. Such a star is our present so-called Pole Star; and, though in the days when the Great Pyramid was built, that star was not near the pole, another, and probably a brighter star lay near enough to the pole to serve as a Pole Star, and to indicate by its circling motion the position of the actual pole in the heavens.

"This star, called Thuban, from the Arabian al-Thuban, the Dragon, is now very bright, being rated at barely above the fourth magnitude, but it was formerly the brightest star of the constellation, as its name indicates. *Bayer* also assigned to it the first letter of the Greek alphabet, though this is not absolutely decisive evidence that so late as his day it retained its superiority over the second magnitude stars to which *Bayer* assigned the second and third Greek letters.

"In the year 2790 B.C. or thereabouts, the star was at its nearest to the true North pole of the heavens, the diameter of the little circle in which it then moved being considerably less than one-fourth the apparent diameter of the moon. At that time the star must have seemed, to all ordinary observation, an absolutely fixed centre, round which all the other stars revolved. At the time when the pyramid was built this star was about sixty times farther removed from the true pole, revolving in a circle whose apparent diameter was about seven times as great as the moon's; yet it would still be regarded as a very useful Pole Star, especially as there are very few conspicuous stars in the neighbourhood. This was at that time and for many subsequent centuries the leading star of the great constellation called 'The Dragon.'

"The pole of the heavens, as we know, varies in position according to the latitude of the observer. At the North pole it is exactly overhead. At the equator the poles of the heavens are both on the horizon; and as the observer travels from the equator towards the North or South pole of the earth, the corresponding pole of the heavens rises higher and higher above the horizon. In latitude 30°, or one-third of the distance from the equator to the pole, the pole of the heavens is raised one-third of the way from the horizon to the point vertically overhead; and when this is the case the observer knows that he is in latitude 30°. The builders of the Great Pyramid, with the almost constantly clear skies of Egypt, may reasonably be supposed to have adopted this means of determining the true position of that 30th parallel on which they appear to have designed to place the great building they were about to erect.

"It so happens that we have the means of forming an opinion on the question whether they used one method or the other; whether they employed the sun or the stars to guide them to the geographical position they required. In fact, were it not for this circumstance, we should not have thought it worth while to discuss the qualities of either method. It will presently be seen that the discussion bears importantly on the opinion we are to form of the skill and attainments of the pyramid architects. Every celestial object is apparently raised somewhat above its true position by the refractive power of our atmosphere, being most raised when nearest the horizon, and least when nearest to the point vertically overhead. This effect is, indeed, so marked on bodies close to the horizon that if the astronomers of the pyramid times had observed the sun, the moon and stars attentively when so placed, they could not have failed to discover the peculiarity. Probably, however, though they noted the time of rising and setting of the celestial bodies, they only made instrumental observations upon them when these bodies were high in the heavens. Thus they remained ignorant of the refractive powers of the air. Even that skilful astronomer, *Happarchus*, who may be justly called the father of observational astronomy, overlooked this peculiarity, which *Ptolemy* would seem to be the first to recognise. Now if they had determined the position of the 30th parallel of latitude by observation of the noonday sun (in spring or autumn), then since, owing to refraction, they would have judged the sun to be higher than he really was, it follows that they would have supposed the latitude of any station from which they observed to be lower than it really was ; for the lower the latitude the higher is the noonday sun at any given season. Thus, when really in latitude 30°, they would have supposed themselves in a latitude lower than 30° and would have travelled a little farther North to find the proper place, as they would have supposed, for erecting the Great Pyramid. On the other hand, if they determined the place from observations of the movements of the stars near the pole of the heavens, they would make an error of a precisely opposite nature ; for the higher the latitude the higher is the pole of the heavens, and refraction, therefore, which apparently raises the pole of the heavens, gives to a station the appearance of being in a higher latitude than it really is, so that the observer would consider he was in latitude 30° North when in reality somewhat South of that latitude. We have only then to inquire whether the Great Pyramid was set North or South of the latitude 30° to ascertain whether the pyramid architects observed the noonday sun or circumpolar stars to determine their latitude ; always assuming, as we reasonably may, that those architects did propose to set the pyramid in that particular latitude, and that they were able to make very accurate observations of the apparent positions of the celestial bodies, but that they were not acquainted with the refractive effects of the atmosphere. The answer comes in no doubtful terms. The centre of the Great Pyramid's base lies about one mile and a third *South* of the 30th parallel of latitude, and from this position the pole of the heavens, as raised by refraction, would appear to be very near indeed to the required position. In fact, if the pyramid had been set about half-a-mile still farther South, the pole would have *seemed* just right.

"Of course such an explanation as we have suggested appears altogether heretical to the Pyramidalists. According to them the pyramid architects knew perfectly well where the true 30th parallel lay, and knew also all that modern science has discovered about refraction ; but set the pyramid South of the true parallel and North of the position where refraction would just have made the apparent elevation of the pole correct, simply in order that the pyramid might correspond as nearly as possible to each of two conditions, whereof both could not be fulfilled at once. The pyramid would indeed, they say, have been set even more closely midway between the true and the apparent parallels of degrees North, but that the Jeeseh hill on which it is set does not afford a rock of foundation any farther North. 'So very close,' says *Professor Smyth,* 'was the Great Pyramid placed to the northern brink of its hill, that the edges of the cliff might have broken off under the terrible pressure, had not the builders banked up most firmly the immense mounds of rubbish which came from their work, and which *Strabo* looked so particularly for 1800 years ago, but could not find. Here they were, however, and still are, utilised in enabling the Great Pyramid to stand on the very utmost verge of its commanding hill, with the limits of the *two* required latitudes, as well as over the centre of the land's physical and radial formation, and at the same time on the sure and proverbially wise foundation of rock.' (Peter-Cephas—a Stone.) 'Thou art Peter, and upon this rock I will build my Church' (St Matt. xvi. 18).

"The next circumstance to be noted in the position of the Great Pyramid (as of all the pyramids) is that the sides are carefully oriented. This, like the approximation to a particular latitude, must be regarded as an astronomical rather than a geographical relation. The accuracy with which the orientation has been effected will serve to show how far the builders had mastered the methods of astronomical observation by which orientation was to be secured. The problem was not so simple as might be supposed by those who are not acquainted with the way in which the cardinal points are correctly determined. By Solar observations, or rather by the observations of shadows cast by vertical shafts before and after noon, the direction of the meridian, or North and

South line, can theoretically be ascertained, but probably in this case, as in determining the latitude, the builders took the stars for their guide. The pole of the heavens would mark the true North, and equally the Pole Star, when below or above the pole, would give the true North, but of course most conveniently when below the pole. Nor is it difficult to see how the builders would make use of the Pole Star for this purpose. From the middle of the Northern side of the intended base they would bore a slant passage, tending always from the position of the Pole Star at its lower meridional passage; that star at each successive return to that position serving to direct their progress, while its small range East and West of the pole would enable them most accurately to determine the star's true mid-point below the pole—that is, the true North. When they had thus obtained a slant tunnel pointing to the meridian, and had carried it down to a point nearly below the middle of the proposed square base, they could, from the middle of the base, bore vertically downwards, until by rough calculation they were near the lower end of the slant tunnel; or both tunnels could be made at the same time. Then a subterranean chamber would be opened out from the slant tunnel. The vertical boring, which need not be wider than necessary to allow a plumbline to be suspended down to it, would enable the architects to determine the point vertically below the point of suspension. The slant tunnel would give the direction of the true North, either from that point or from a point at some known small distance east or west of that point. It would only be a lucky accident, of course, that the direction of the slant tunnel's access and that of the vertical from the selected central point would lie in the same vertical plane. The object of the tunelling would, in fact, be to determine how far apart the vertical planes through these points lay, and the odds would be great against the result proving to be zero. Thus, a line from some ascertained point near the mouth of the vertical boring to the mouth of the slant tunnel would lie due North and South, and serve as the required guide for the orientation of the pyramid's base. If this base extended beyond the opening of the slant tunnel, then, by continuing this tunnelling through the base tiers of the pyramid, the means would be obtained of correcting the orientation.

"This, we say, would be the course naturally suggested to astronomical architects who had determined the latitude in the manner already described. It may even be the only very accurate method available before the telescope had been invented ; so that if the accuracy of the orientation appears to be greater than could be obtained by the shadow method, the natural inference, even in the absence of corroborative evidence, would be that the Stellar method, and no other, had been employed. Now, in 1779, *Nouet*, by refined observations, found the error of orientation measured by less than 20 minutes of arc, corresponding roughly to a displacement of the corners by about $\frac{37}{2}$ inches from their true position, as supposed to be determined from the centre, or to a displacement of a Southern corner by 53 inches on an East and West line from a point due South of the corresponding Northern corner. This error, for a base length of 9140 inches, would not be serious, being only one inch in about five yards when estimated in the second way. Yet the result is not quite worthy of the praise given to it by *Professor Smyth*. He himself, however, by much more exact observations, with an excellent altazimuth, reduced the alleged error from 20 minutes to only 4-0, or to 9-40ths of its formerly supposed value. This made the total displacement of a Southern corner from the true meridian, through the corresponding Northern corner almost exactly one foot, or one inch in about 21 yards, a degree of accuracy rendering it practically certain that some Stellar method was used in orienting the base. Now, there is a slanting tunnel occupying precisely the position of the tunnel which should, according to this view, have been in order accurately to orient the pyramid's base, assuming that the time of the building of this pyramid corresponded with one of the epochs when the star Alpha Draconis was distant 3° 42′ from the pole of the heavens. In other words there is a slant tunnel Northwards and upwards from a point deep down below the middle of the pyramid's base, and inclined 26° 17′ to the horizon, the elevation of Alpha Draconis at its lower culmination when 3° 42′ from the pole. The last epoch when the star was thus placed was *circita* 2160 B.C., the epoch next before that was 3440 B.C. Between these two we should have to choose, on the hypothesis that the slant tunnel was really directed to that star when the foundations of the pyramid were laid, the next epoch before the earlier of the two named was about 28,000 B.C., and the pyramid's date cannot have been more remote than 4000 B.C."

We have given *Proctor's* statements thus fully to show that the orientation of the temple is *North*, and therefore must *have* been built during a period of Stellar Mythology. Why could this not be 28,000 B.C., and what reason and facts had he to corroborate his theory that the date of the Pyramid cannot have been more remote than 4000 B.C. ? We cannot find any facts to support this, but there is evidence of the greater antiquity. This Mythology preceded both Lunar and Solar, and we know that the Osirian was in practice 15,000 years ago, so that the Great Pyramid must have been in existence a long period before all the temples which were oriented East, according to Lunar or Solar Mythos, suchas those of the Druids, Yucatans, Incas, etc., and some of these we know to be upwards of 10,000 years old. We find that various writers differ a good deal in their opinions about the antiquity of many of these temples, consequently they disagree as to the date when they were built. But these writers only bring forward their own opinions without any facts to support their arguments. Our astronomers have never attacked the subject of the precession, or rather recession of the seven Pole Stars, as did the ancients. *Proctor* may be wrong in his date of 28,000 B.C. before a Pole Star shone down this slant ; if not, then it must be at least of this age. The recent discoveries at Abydos prove it over 15,000 years at the lowest estimate.

The one Great Year takes 25,827 years to perform its cycle, and during that time the Pole Star changes seven times—once in every 3700 years, roughly. The priests of Egypt recorded their observations from generation to generation at least for one cycle, if not more, and mapped out the heavens in seven astronomes—the origin of the seven heavens, seven mountains, seven lights, seven pillars, etc. Each Pole Star symbolised the Lord of Eternity—" The Book of the Dead," chaps. cxiv. and cxxiii., prove this conclusively.

Now, if our readers—we speak to those who are really interested in the subject—will but think and reflect for themselves—they will see that the date of the pyramids and of many of the very earliest remains which we find throughout the world, can be proved by their orientation, because the orientation denotes the mythology and beliefs which were extant at the time these were built, though this fact seems to have been overlooked by a large number of writers on the subject.

Thus we know that the orientation of the Great Pyramid of

Ghizeh is North, therefore it was built when the Stellar Mythology was extant. We also know that the orientation of the Druidical temples and tombs, still to be found all over the British Isles, the Mayal temples in Mexico, and amongst the Incas of South America, etc., is East or East by South, therefore the mythology at the time was Lunar or Solar, probably Solar.

At the same time we must always remember that one mythology overlapped the other, so to speak, because perfect evolution takes time ; thus, when Lunar Mythos was first established it would be long before this entirely supplanted Stellar, and in the same way, when Solar Mythos first came into existence and began its lease of life, the Lunar would overlap it.

The Egyptians never " lost anything," but brought forward and incorporated all the old with the new. A careful study of this, we venture to say, will tend to elucidate a more accurate date as regards the ancient monuments, wherever there are remains of past records to be deciphered. This is a point of great importance to the Antiquarian.

We maintain that the Pyramid was built at the time when the mythology of the ancient people became eschatological in its development and perfection—*i.e.* after the Grand Master or Priest had received divine knowledge direct from the Grand Master above. In its decipherment you will find the architecture of our planetary system, with its laws and movements, portrayed in minute measurements, and illustrating their belief in future life. Also in its interior is shown hieroglyphically and symbolically their belief as to what occurs to the departed dead before the soul is finally united to its Ka in the Grand Lodge above, which contains all as the " One Great Wonder out of Egypt."

Nothing could prove our argument more conclusively than to quote *Eratosthenes*, a most unimpeachable witness for the Egyptians. He was born in the year 276 B.C., and was keeper of the great Alexandrian library, and the most learned Greek in Egypt at the time. Amongst the subjects he wrote on, one was Astronomy, where he mentions this fact : " *that the festival of Isis was celebrated in his time at the Autumn equinox.* It had been celebrated when the *Easter equinox was in Virgo.*" This perfectly agrees with the position of Isis, the Virgin mother, in the Zodiac. During six months in the great year six signs receded in precession from Virgo to Pisces, and not until thirteen thousand years later did Autumn equinox coincide once more with the sign of Virgo. There is no meeting point of the mythology with the astronomy more obvious than these two signs of the zodiac. It is impossible that this imagery should have been constellated in the planisphere for the *last* time the equinoxes entered them, which was about the year 255 B.C., where they still linger at the present moment. The time before that, in round numbers, was twenty-six thousand years previously. It is equally a fact that when the "Solar Horus" had entered the zodiac, the birthplace was shifted from sign to sign, *according to the movements* in precession, from Virgo to Leo—from Cancer to the Gemini—from Taurus to Aries, and from Aries to Pisces. Now this *was all Solar,* as the *Ritual* proves, and Lunar and Stellar *were previous to this.* As we have shown, the Great Pyramid was built at the time of Stellar, therefore the most ancient date must be the correct one. The position of the equinox has to be made out according to the *precessional* year, not by *the lesser year.* This difference constitutes the difficulty of the reckoning. The time of the equinox was determined in the lesser year by the recurrence of equal day and night, but the *position* of the equinoxes in the great year was determined by the ruling of the Herald Star. The Egyptian founders of Astronomical science *did not begin with* mathematical calculations: they had to verify everything by observation through all the range of periodic time—it was the only method at first. It was by direct observation, not by calculation, that the wise men of Egypt obtained their knowledge of precession. By ages and ages of watching and registering they perceived that the backward movement of the equinox, as immense in time as it is slow in motion, had to be reckoned with as a factor of vast magnitude, and that this long hand on the face of the eternal horologue was a determinative of the highest cycle of all, so far as they could measure periodic time. By imperceptible degrees the movement itself had become apparent, and the point of equal day and night was observed to be passing out of one group of stars upon the elliptic into another *which coincided with a change of Pole Stars.*

It could only be in a climate like Egypt that this could be done, where the atmosphere was clear and no clouds to obscure their perpetual view and unceasing watchings and all the stars shone with that brilliancy we find there. What other country on this Earth has the same atmospheric surroundings?

CHAPTER XIX

Side by side with this Masonic mystery have come down to us various papyri of sacred writings, which have been called the *Ritual* of ancient Egypt or " The Book of the Dead," and it is to this we now turn for an explanation of the mysteries of the monument. Not only in the pyramid, however, were these rites and ceremonies practised and carried out, but at other temples in Egypt—Memphis, Heliopolis, the temple of the Sphinx; but none of these were perfect in later dynastic times, nor did they have the whole of the symbology like the pyramid itself. It is only the Temple of the Pyramid and the Papyrus that show any theopneusty. A number of different papyri that have been written at various times by separate scribes have been found. We believe if we could obtain the whole " Papyri of the Pyramid " we should find a perfect ritual of the various eschatological ceremonies. We have no doubt that a great part of the writings have been lost, but there is quite sufficient evidence extant to explain the secret. Although the language is symbolical to a very great extent, we have it on other evidence that the secrets of the Eschatology were not written, but were declaimed and learnt orally; all that they had written being recorded in the " Pietra Libra " or " Book of Stone," which the High Priests read once a year to the people. All the secrets were passed on from generation to generation, and taught orally by the priests alone. We can only conjecture that some explanation of these secrets was written on papyrus, symbolically, so that they should not be lost for ever, at some far remote period when internal changes were taking place in the country, which we read of in history, and that they might die without having transmitted them orally, being considered divine laws. *The " Ritual or Book of the Dead " is what is written and known as their religious belief, as far as their writings have been discovered.* At the same time be it understood that to understand the *Ritual* of the Resurrection you must go back for their Eschatology to the lesser mysteries of their Mythology and Astronomical Mythology, and even before, back to the original Sign-language, which was the language of the mythology, and which was the primitive mode of representing external nature and its animistic powers. The types here called totemic were extant as a means of rendering these powers when there were no gods or goddesses yet divinised. Powers of nature were perceived to be at work throughout all the earth and celestial bodies; their powers were superhuman from the first and they were represented by appropriate and equivalent zootypes, but the powers and not the types were the object of supreme regard. *The types were not the object of worship.* The Gods and Goddesses were after represented by totemic types, but they were not conceived to be the types, and in all cases there were obvious reasons for the representation, but *it was the powers and not the types* that were *ultimately divinised.*

In the Eschatology the same types were reapplied to the human soul which were imaged in the flesh by Horus, who died bodily, entered Amenta in mummy form, and rose again in glory as Horus the divine. The true interpretation of the Egyptian picture, copied by *Denon* at Philæ, is "*I am the Resurrection and the Life.*" From the beginning to the end of the *Ritual* it is based, first on the mythologies, and then the rendering of these becomes eschatological. We must recognise the different phases and discriminate these—to read the *Ritual* correctly and try and fathom the thinking minds of the old Egyptian priests. The main difference betwixt the Mythos and the Eschatology is that one is represented in the earth of time, the other in the earth of eternity. It is the Egyptian Book of Life, it is the Pre-christian Word of God, and it purports to contain the gnosis of salvation from the second dead, together with the ways and means of attaining eternal life, and these were enacted in the drama of the mysteries. After this life on earth there was a resurrection after passing the Tuat in Amenta—the earth of eternity for the human soul evolved on this earth. It was then that the claim to the resurrection in spirit and to life eternal in heaven had to be made good and established by many long and painful experiences, by which the soul was perfected eventually as an ever-living spirit. The words of promise had to be performed and made true before the Ma-Kheru of immortality could be earned and endless continuity of life be assured.

It is only by going back to the original and following on step by step that we can gain a true idea of what the Egyptian religion was at the time of its purest Eschatology. So many writers on this subject have simply described the "Osirian doctrines," and in doing this have followed the Greek and Latin writers, stumbling about in the dark and falling into holes they cannot get out of, until they call upon the Egyptians to bring them a ladder, therefore it is hardly to be wondered at that so little is known of the meaning of all the religious ceremonies and observances which were the dramatic performances of their belief in the resurrection of the dead, and everlasting life, and which were certainly carried on in perfect ceremonies in pre-dynastic times, perhaps more difficult to understand because the priests and scribes of the later dynasties had so altered and corrupted the original particulars—partly because the scribes at the time of the New Empire (B.C. 1700-700) were unable to read correctly the hieratic characters which formed the names of some of the kings of the early Archaic period, and partly because nearly all Egyptologists believe and are still under the impression that there were a large number of gods instead of the different powers and different types of the One God—God in the Spirit, Ra; God in mummy form, Osiris; and God as Son, Child Horus. This was the latest form of their Trinity, and the earliest, Horus I., Sut and Shu. But what ages had passed ere the Egyptian Mythology of Horus, Sut and Shu had passed by evolution into the higher Eschatology of Ra, Osiris and the Child Horus!! and how long, probably thousands and thousands of years, had it taken the earliest form of man to observe the powers of nature—to image these in sign-language—to formulate his totemic ceremonies into a mythology, and then astro-mythology, before this was perfect, and all these various types and powers of the One God, and not the many as most people suppose?

It is only by studying the "Ritual or Book of the Dead" that anyone can really understand the meaning and significance of the Great Pyramid—in fact, here lies the *Ritual*, written in stone. This *Ritual* of the Resurrection was the Egyptian Book of Life, and the account which this scripture gives of itself is that *it was a revelation made by Ra, the Holy Spirit.* It was given to Horus the

Son, who converses with the Father in Heaven. Horus speaks it as the word of God and as the Sayer of the Sayings to those who are living on earth and to the " breathless ones in Hades." " I utter his Word to thee," says Horus, who personates the Word in his first advent, and, in the second, is the word made truth as Horus-ma-Kheru. One of the most beautiful ideas of the Egyptians was that of representing the eternal Father by the ever-coming Son, as in the Child Horus, who was the type of eternal youth as an external child. This was the child of a mother who was the eternal virgin, and thus youth or youthfulness had been imaged by the pre-anthropomorphic types of the calf, the lamb, the branch of a tree and the shoot of the papyrus plant. The doctrines of the Incarnation, the Virgin birth, the Resurrection, the Father-God who is identical with his own son, and others, believed to be specifically Christian, were Egyptian ages and ages before the present era began. " The Book of the Dead " contains a true decipherment of the symbolic language found depicted in stone in the pyramid itself, teaching their belief as to what occurred to the spirit after leaving the body, and what it had to pass through before it could reach the Grand Lodge above, and thus pointing out and laying down a guide to our thoughts and actions while in this sublunary abode ; also in Amenta, so that the departed soul might be able to pass through the various ordeals encountered hereafter, namely, by learning to obey the principles of Truth, Justice and Morality in this life.

In Chapter XV., Hymn 3, of " The Book of the Dead," it says : " Freedom for ever from perdition is derived from this book, and upon it I firmly take my stand."

In the double symbolism of Pyramid and *Ritual* lie the chief difficulties of decipherment and the strongest evidence of their correspondence. For, as the departed in his progress was ultimately to become united in the fulness of intimacy with the Soul of All, his Creator, so it was necessary that he should progress in the knowledge of the mysteries which envisage alike the spiritual and material creation. To know Horus in his forms of manifestation was the secret of power ; to understand Horus in all his names, all his places, conferred the Crown of Illumination. But in the attainment of that knowledge there were many stages which must be traversed by the finite mortal ; many grades which must be achieved by the holy departed, when the mouth of the tomb, the Portal of Eternal Day, had been opened for him, and the catechumen of divine wisdom had been adulated as the Postulant of Immortality. The Postulant, with upraised arms, must be recreated in incorruption, and the soul must be born anew before the Postulant could be initiated into things divine ; or, as the *Ritual* says : " The Ka with upraised arms is the soul to be ultimately attained by the manes perfected." As we have it, the Initiate must pass through the fiery ordeal to be proved as adept, like Paul, who was *epopt* and perfect, thus showing that Paul was a Mason and initiated into the highest degree. The Adept must be justified in the Tribunal of Truth before he could emerge from the shadow of the Halls of Death into the immediate presence of the Source of Light. The Justified must become the Illuminate. The Illuminate must be consummated as master before he could obtain the innermost mansion in the divine house. For each of such grades, according to the creed of Egypt, the Creator has assigned a distinct locality in the universe of space, and each of these localities is described symbolically in "The Book of the Dead" or *Ritual*, and inscribed masonically in the features and dimensions of the Pyramid. Not to everyone, therefore, did the secrets of the Pyramid lie open, nor could there be a more unpardonable offence than the profanation of its secrets. And as it was the character of that religion to be concealed, and as the manifestations of the Creator are deeper and more secret yet than His works, so it was essential that the sacred symbols relating to Him should not betray their deepest mysteries, even to the Initiate ; but should reserve their most sacred meaning for the Illuminate after full probation. In other words, the Initiate was taught step by step, and it was pointed out to him that only by perseverance in a right and true line of conduct could he pass to the next stage, and finally obtain the Crown of Triumph ; he must lead such a life as corresponds with our tenets and teachings. Does not this point out to us the analogy between our teachings and our own forms and ceremonies, even all the various names of the G.A.U. in each degree as we advance ? The passage of the C—— in the 18° through the D.R. represents the passage of the soul through the Tuat and Amentet in the Egyptian Eschatology.

In studying the *Ritual* of ancient Egypt it is by the power of sense and reason, joined together, that we study the secret properties and powers which are therein expressed and portrayed, and though our senses are sometimes liable to be deceived, yet, when they are rightly disposed and fitly exercised about their proper objects, with the first assistance of reason, they give us sufficient evidence of truth; of course, many errors are derived from our weakness of reason and incapacity to judge of things either from a diseased or weakened brain through old age, or those whose genius is very low, whose judgment is always weak; who are "ever" indulging the dictates of "sense and humour," but "are simply large children"; these stand exposed to everlasting mistakes in life, and live and die in the midst of prejudices. The creed of Egypt, therefore, as taught by the Theopneustics, was this: that we have a body,[1] within the body a soul, and within the soul a spirit. The body entirely belonged to this earth, the soul and spirit to heaven; although the spirit had to join the Great Architect of the Universe first, before it could return to its soul. When the body or material part died, the soul and spirit were liberated, and had to travel through many dangers and difficulties, also to undergo various trials, as depicted by the symbology which we find in the pyramids and ancient stones, before the spirit could regain the Mansion of Bliss and the abode of the Great Architect of the Universe. The spirit became separated from the soul before divine judgment took place, and after the spirit was justified the regeneration of the soul took place. In the Eschatology of the Egyptians they had a Trinity and Unity, and they believed in punishment as well as Everlasting Happiness. The doctrine of Immortality and Everlasting Life, and the belief in the Resurrection of the "Spiritual Body" are the brightest and most prominent features of the Egyptian religion, and this we find was their belief before the time of the first King of the first dynasty. A study of the religious formularies of all periods proves that the great fundamental ideas of the Egyptians remained unchanged from the earliest to the latest historical times, and it seems that they must have been received by the earlier Egyptian priests of Dynastic times in much the same form as that in which they handed them on.

At first they were "recited" only and not written, and it

[1] *The Dynastic Egyptians believed in*:—

1. A Physical Body—The Khat. 2. A Soul or—Ba. 3. A Heart or—Ab. 4. A Double or—Ka. 5. An Intelligence or—Khu. 6. A Power or—Sekhem. 7. A Shadow or—Khaibit. 8. A Spiritual Body or—Sāh. 9. A Name or—Rem. *By some divided again or added to.*

is probable that they existed in this form for a very long period.

The variety of names given to God and the Holy Spirit has led persons, who ought to know better, to assert that in ancient Egypt each separate name indicates a separate god or goddess ; hence they stigmatise these early people as idolaters and image worshippers of many deities. These various names merely express the infinitely various powers and types of the divine. The reader need not be reminded that in the Jewish sacred books numbers of names are given to the Deity which appear in the Hebrew text, but are concealed from the English reader under the general title of God.

Their Priests, here on earth, did not worship images nor serpents nor bulls, as many have stated, which was an ancient error of the Greeks, made in complete ignorance of the primitive modes of representation ; these were only symbolical types, representing their belief in the great A O in Heaven. *It was by teachings, by signs, symbols and ceremonies that the soul and spirit were prepared here for the future, and taught dramatically what they had to encounter and pass through after the material body had ceased to exist.*

In the papyri of the old hieroglyphics we find the origin of all our sacerdotal stories and the manner of the evolution of the same. Then a blank occurs, and until the papyri, written in Hieratic and Demotic, containing the stories of the priests of Memphis and the sayings of Jesus, were found, we lost the thread that connects the old with the new Eschatology, but here, in the Demotic, more especially, we have the "bridge" which connects the Old with the New and Better Covenant. Many may contend that these are partly copied from our "New Covenant" ; but these tales in Demotic are simply the same as we find written in the oldest hieroglyphics, in every particular, and any student will perceive the fallacy of any argument against this, although we find that it is adopted by many writers, ignorant or otherwise, who appear anxious that the records of the past should not be solved, but to all earnest students the oldest tales in the ancient hieroglyphics and those found in the Demotic writings and the Eschatology of the present day, are identical. They are simply repetitions of the story, written thousands of years before the date when the supposed present covenant was made. That this is not mere supposition can be proved by the comparison of the one with the other, and the history of the same. The recently published "Tales of the Priests of Memphis," from the Demotic Papyri, prove that the missing link has been forged. There are many other papyri still in the British Museum, the translation of which, when completed, will demonstrate this fact more clearly. Certain religious texts are little more than transcripts of old Egyptian in Demotic spelling, and the present stories in Demotic are as closely related as possible to the new Egyptian of the 12th century B.C. as to the Biblical Coptic of the 4th and 5th century A.D.

The ancient Hebrews, Muhammadans and Syrians, borrowed from the Egyptians their ideas, but they never properly understood the Eschatology, which they most profoundly perverted from the original. *Dr Budge,* in his book, "The Gods of Egypt," says: "It cannot be too strongly insisted on that all the oldest gods of Egypt are of Egyptian origin, and that the fundamental religious beliefs of the Egyptians are also of Egyptian origin, and that both the gods and their beliefs date from pre-dynastic times, and have nothing whatever to do with the Semites or Aryans of history." He asks: What is the meaning of Ashem?[1] It has for its determinative a Hawk, perched on a standard, etc., and goes on to say that the Hawk was undoubtedly the first creature worshipped by the pre-dynastic Egyptians. We maintain that it was not worshipped by them. It was a type representing Horus I.—and moreover, these ancient people, at the time of their Eschatology, never worshipped animals or birds or serpents at all, and it is a great mistake to think so. *Dr Budge,* in the above-named book, commences very late indeed, and evidently does not understand the primordial or ignores it for reasons of his own. The early gods and their powers are evolved from their astronomical mythology, and without this it is impossible to understand or come to a true idea of how the Priests, in the dynastic times, changed names and added to the originals. The earliest Stellar Mythos, the *Ritual* and Great Pyramid must be studied together, to arrive at a true and correct value of the religion of these early people.

It is not of much use commencing with Osirian doctrines to get a true and definite knowledge of the gods of Egypt, because,

[1] We have already answered this in another part of this work.

before Osiris, they had the religion of Amen Ra, and before this that of Atum and Horus I. We must at least go back as far as then to obtain any originals. The hawk and other birds and animals, etc., were all depicted to represent the various attributes of "The Great God." They had no other way of doing it at that time. It would be the work of a lifetime to trace out all the proofs of the earliest people from the time they took the form of man by evolution; the lowest degenerate race of human beings, who had no idea of a life hereafter or a supreme being, and from that time onwards, formed a mythology and astro-mythology, totemic ideas and ceremonies, and Stellar mythos, etc.; and it gives a poor and incorrect idea indeed of these people when you commence with the latter part of the Solar Mythos, which is beginning to change and decay, as such, by the perversion of the texts by the Priests. That the earliest Egyptians had, and believed in, only One Great God is quite evident. As the text of the Creation says: "I am the Great God, self-created." Various names and attributes were given to all his members and his powers, which have been mistaken by Egyptologists as separate gods, which was not so, as the earliest texts will show. At the same time it is not to be wondered at as the scribes did the same in later times—*i.e.* they confounded the names of the various attributes of each member and each power to separate gods, and so the later texts have become somewhat mixed.

Devil Worship, Tree Worship, Phallic Worship, etc.

These are quite incorrect terms, and in this case "Worship" is a word employed by writers who are ignorant of Sign-language in general—such phrases as the above do not explain anything.

The tree was a type of the abode—the Roof Tree, the Mother of Food and Drink, the Giver of Life and Shelter, etc. Others we have explained previously.

The Egyptian *Ritual* is written in the language of animals, and never was it read in the past, and never will it be in the future, unless the thinking can be done in the Ideographic types of thought. Merely reading the hieroglyphics, as phonetics, is but a first lesson in Sign-language.

Dr Budge states: "The Priests and upper classes certainly held views and religious beliefs which differed from those of the husbandman, *but it is a significant fact that it was not the religion and mythology of the dynastic Egyptians, but that of the indigenous pre-dynastic Egyptians.*" [1]

The best educated Priests were as much attached to forms and traditional symbols as the people themselves, and they were most unwilling to give up any part of them ; but the symbolism was misunderstood by the ignorant classes, and produced serious errors. The uneducated loved a plurality of gods, whilst the Priests and educated people, who could read and understand books, adopted the idea of ONE GOD, the creator of all beings in heaven and on earth. But when all is said against the Egyptian religion which can be said, the fact remains that it is not the religion itself, but the myths, wherewith generations of foolish Priests obscured the pure beliefs in monotheism and immortality, which existed in Egypt from the earliest times of the pre-dynastic Egyptians. If modern religions were judged in the adverse manner in which the religion of ancient Egypt has been judged, none would escape similar condemnation.

The monotheistic character of the Egyptian religion rests on too firm a foundation to be overthrown, and notwithstanding the elaborate system of symbolic ceremonials, which was so prominent a feature of their worship, it has always maintained its place in the minds of those who were sufficiently educated to understand the ideas which the symbols thereof represented, and of which we have been the custodians, bringing them on to the present day in Freemasonry.

Many think that the god Ra was a different god from Osiris, but Ra was the spirit form, and Osiris the *mummified* form of the same god—both one and the same in two different forms—the same as Ra-Tem, the Father and Son, and an earlier form still, Ptah-Tem. The first form we have in the Stellar Mythos was Horus I. Later, his name became Amsu or the risen Horus. He was the first man-god, as he rose from the dead ; then his name was changed to Amsu, and he established himself for ever. Osiris was Solar and a much later cult. The different changes from the originals are not difficult to understand even in our day, when one thinks of the various sects and different doctrines preached by the Christian Priests, all under Christianity.

We must remember that the Priests of Heliopolis had lost

[1] Italics are ours.

much of the original meaning and key from those even at Henen-su, and the Priests of Thebes, who followed, still more.

In Horus I. we have the essence of the primeval god, Nu or Atum. He was the great spirit and divine body in heaven. He, it is stated, fought and vanquished the traditional fiend, Sut, who dared to wage war against him, and was the establisher of right and wrong throughout the world. He made the earth and the heaven and all that therein is.

Horus is here represented as Atum, the Son of Ptah, shedding his own blood and being portrayed as a Creator of mankind[1]—Atum, as shown here, was the Creator by the blood shed in a voluntary sacrifice, and superseded the Mother.

Ptah in the character of Sekari, the Silent Sufferer, "the coffined one," was the deity that opened up the nether world for the resurrection in the earliest Solar Mythos.

The original Trinity was first evolved at the time of Horus I., and all that followed were, and are, copies, prototypes, under different names, and there are no facts to prove this to be the contrary, and there is nothing that *Dr Budge* or any other Egyptologist can show to prove their assertions that Horus I. came to Egypt with his followers. The whole of the *Ritual* and other texts, taken in conjunction with the astro-mythology, prove what we state. We must remember that there is unquestionable proof to show that the pre-dynastic Egyptians had worked out and perfected their Eschatology 10,000 years before the dynasties began. One must go back to their astro-mythology to obtain the clue of all the meaning of what we read, as the Egyptians always brought on everything and made use of it in some way, and so knowing this from Horus I. and Stellar Mythos, we can trace all the other gods, so called, which had various names and attributes, back to the one original Trinity and the meaning and origin of our sacred Triangle. Upon the foundation of Horus I. all that followed must be built up.

The great fight between light and darkness arose at the time when the sun's rays were struggling to penetrate the thick watery vapour which surrounded the earth's surface before it had sufficiently condensed to make solid matter. In the earliest mythology Sut was first assigned the supreme power; he was indeed the king of darkness, and darkness was all that overspread

[1] The Mexican name is Zipe Totec, which means Our Lord, the flayed one.

PTAH-SEKER-AUSAR, THE TRIUNE GOD OF THE RESURRECTION.

The silent sufferer—the coffined one—was the deity who opened up the nether world for the Resurrection in the earliest Solar mythos. He is here seated on the Throne with all the emblems of sovereignty as a "spiritual body"; in front is the representation of his body and blood—*cadaver*—and emblematical of the change from earthly to spiritual.

the face of the earth ; but as time went on the thick vapour began to condense in solid form, and the sun's rays penetrated farther and farther until they reached the solid crust and turned all the darkness on the face of the earth into light and day. The battle between Horus I. and Sut had commenced and ended in victory henceforth for Horus I., and he was the supreme power, and Sut was cast out into utter darkness (night), and so, as Horus was assigned the place of the god at the apex or top of the triangle, Sut was placed at the bottom or South.

The reason why the great serpent fiend was chosen as a type to represent the evil and wicked one was because these huge reptilian monsters were numerous at that time, and primitive man must have felt the great danger he was always exposed to from these reptiles. He also observed that they came out at night in the darkness, and sought for prey and food, and when the sun arose and drove away the darkness, these fiends also retired to sleep and disappeared until the night again returned ; and of all these they probably chose the biggest and most dangerous one to themselves as a type of "The Great Evil One," and as there were others of less size and less danger, these were chosen to represent the lesser "Evil Ones," so we have Beelzebub, the Chief of the Devils, and Satan as one of the lesser in the Christian doctrine. That primitive man did not exist at the time when the sun's rays first began to penetrate and fertilise the earth must have been a fact, but inasmuch as he afterwards knew how the world was created and the stages that intervened from the time that it was given off by the parent Sun, until his time, as records stated herein show ; all the above would be associated with his mythology, and after that his astro-mythology. Hence the origin of the legend which has been handed down from time immemorial by all nations and all creeds, differing perhaps a little in names and circumstances as time and evolution have progressed, but in essence the same, and the foregoing is the origin. Many writers have not understood that most, if not all nations, at all times, have made animals as symbols of gods and divine powers, and still do, as we see here in our own churches. The figures of a lamb, lion, eagle, ox, and others, in the sculptured work of our churches, is sufficient proof alone, and any future generation, finding these, might say with just as much truth as these Egyptologists and others have, that we worshipped animals, etc., and that it must be so, because they were found depicted in the remains of our churches and sacred books.

In tracing from the foregoing the history of man and the creation of this earth from its parent sun, which no doubt was evolved from its sun, and the evidence of the history as we find of the past, be it on written papyri, or marks, signs or symbols, wherever found in any part of the world, delineated on stones or otherwise, proves that at first man could not write, and had but few words to express his thoughts ; he could only think in things as he saw them—and draw them. Analysing the oldest records of creation we can find, we come to the opinion there is a very definite statement, as one would have expected primitive man to have handed down orally from generation to generation. Taking the oldest records of the history of the creation we can find and our present scientific knowledge, which we know from actual observation and proofs, we can but arrive at the conclusion "that there must be some one great eternal power who governs the universe, a divine being whom we call 'God,'" and of whose form or power we have no conception ; that by His will He created all things ; that our parent sun was at first a huge mass of fiery vapour given off from another sun, around which it travels and takes 25,827 years to do so, and as it has been cooling it has given off our planetary system, all ever rotating at immense speed. This earth, as well as the other planets, have given off other bodies as adjuncts of themselves for purposes which the divine Creator foresaw—the moons. The earth, when given off, was one huge mass of fiery vapour, which went whirling round and round for countless ages until the heated vapour condensed to water, and this watery mass to solid crust, the interior gradually cooling, which it will continue to do until the whole is one mass of solid matter. As soon as this heated watery vapour had cooled sufficiently to allow the sun's ray to penetrate it and fertilise any organic matter, the Great Almighty, by His divine power and will, created germs of life, which fertilised and increased from the lowest form of organic life to the present highest cultivated man and woman. The oldest hieroglyphic texts of the creation tell us that vegetable and creeping things existed first, and science and evolution teach us the same. Man was not evolved from the Lemur for ages and ages, and at first he had no idea in his primitive state of a superior being or life hereafter.

Examples of these primitive little red men may still be found in the Congo Pygmy, Veddah of Ceylon, the Pygmies in forests of South America and mountain fastnesses of China, and lowest form of Negro. Gradually man began to observe and think and to work out a mythology, and as he progressed in this, an astro-mythology, ending in their Eschatology.

That the ancient Egyptians believed in evolution there can be no doubt, for in the " Story of the Creation " Khepera is made to say :—" I made a foundation in (or by) my own heart, and then came into being multitudes of things, of things from things, of what was produced from the things which they produced," which is a most emphatic manner of stating that everything that is came into being as a result of the act of the God in laying a foundation in his own heart, and that when once the creative process had been set in motion they continued the operation of their own accord, apparently without any direct interference from the original creative power, by spiritual and natural laws made by the Divine Creator. They mapped out the celestial heavens and depicted them by terrestrial ; they used various animals and compounds of various things they could see and observe to express the different powers, etc., because they had no words or articulate sounds to otherwise express their meanings ; often we find a compound animal to show the various powers they wished to express that this was symbolical of. They were too great observers of all nature to make symbols of anything without a meaning.

At this time we find the records of these very ancient people tell us that they knew the whole planetary system, the distance from the earth to the sun, the precession or rather recession of the Pole stars, or Little Bear, etc., and left full records of the same in the building of the Great Pyramid. The time that it took these people to do this must have been at least the observing of the sun to travel twice around its centre—two great years—over 50,000 years, and how much more it is impossible to say. After this we have the Lunar and Solar Mythos, and from the latter practically all our different religions have been evolved ; the difference from the original being principally substituting one name for another and adding to it, to suit the exigencies of the times and will of the Priests. Now we know that the old originals were right in their calculation of the heavenly bodies, and ideas of how worlds are emaned, much more accurately than our astronomers of 100 years ago, therefore, whence all this correct knowledge? Was it by evolution into a very high type of man who possessed the power of observation, and had obtained the powers of calculation, the same as our highest scientists of the present day, and who died out, or was it that the divine G.A.U. gave divine inspiration to the highest class of man then existing, for a guide to future generations, that they might know that there is a life hereafter, and that we on this earth are only a minute speck, an infinitesimal part of the universe, of which the One Great God is the centre who governs all things? To our mind the latter must have been so, but at what time or what age of the life of the earth we cannot tell, probably during or at the time of the so-called Stellar Mythos did the divine Creator give His message to man, and that a chosen people should continue to possess the true knowledge and secrets through all time and all lands, although often separated by wars and other causes; yet the sacred symbols have lost nothing of their lustre; they are all religiously preserved, and although many writers and critics have said that as our ceremonies, now worked in allegory, are all of modern delineation, yet we find in the oldest ancient Egyptian *Ritual* the ceremonial working of the Brotherhood very little different, and that from the most ancient times the Brotherhood have been knit together in one indissoluble bond, and so met, taught and instructed their successors in the wisdom they had acquired by and through the G.G. and that means have been adopted for the preservation of these throughout all time, and it is worthy of remark here that Freemasonry conforms to the practice of the Egyptians in prohibiting to slaves a participation of its mystic rites. The Romans brought many of their forms, ceremonies, signs and symbols to Italy when they took Egypt. But the Romans never understood or knew the true Eschatology of the *Ritual*. Many of the Christian Fathers gave to the Virgin Mary the title of "Theotokos," or Mother of God, forgetting no doubt that it was an exact translation of Neter Mut  a very old and common title of Isis.

No doubt the Romans took their canonising of Saints from the Egyptians, who used to "canonise" their kings, but they did this because he was the *representation* of Horus I. He was not believed to be of *the seed of the God Horus*, but was set up as the *type of the earthly representation.* We must differ in this from *Dr Budge.* In Abyssinia, where the oldest Christian churches are and the earliest Christian doctrines are found, it is of importance to note that the priests use the Fly-flap (it is an exclusively sacerdotal privilege to carry one) the same as the Egyptian priests, which can be seen from monuments still extant in Egypt (Egyptian Frescoes), and almost everything in fact connected with religion here, has its prototype, in ancient Egypt—the Sistrum—the Fly-flap—the Crutch and others are all brought from the valley of the Nile, and are still preserved here at the present time, although Western Christians have altered or ceased to use them. Even the custom of painting all the faces of pictures the same as we find amongst the Central Americans, Zapotecs and Mexicans—the good in white and the bad in black—the prototype of Horus I. in white—light and day ; and the bad in black, representing Sut—night and darkness—good and evil. Their churches are also built to represent the ancient Egyptian—the outer part for the common people, an inner part for priests and high personages, and a still inner—Holy of the Holies—for the High Priests alone. The Jews copied these also from the Egyptians, and still use the double triangle as a Sacred Sign on their Holy Vestments and Sacred Scroll. The cross on the church of Amba Derho is a form of the Ank-cross, with the Seven Glorious Ones. The seven ◯ being Ostrich eggs and representing the Seven Pole Stars of the old Stellar Mythos — the Seven Lights — Seven Golden Candlesticks.

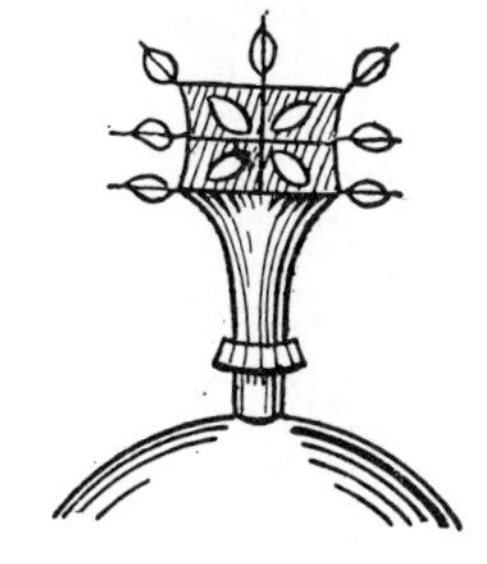
Fig. 165.

There are sacred groves surrounding the churches, and the priests dance and play the Sistrum, and carry the Ark as did the old Egyptian priests. The Abyssinian Christians still cling with extraordinary tenacity to the very earliest rites and ceremonies of their doctrines, and neither Jesuits nor Roman Catholics have been able to make the least impression on them to fall into line with the up-to-date doctrines, etc., now preached by the Western Christians. Their word "Tabout" or "Ark of the Covenant" is the Egyptian "Tebut" (Egyptian for Ark). *Bent*, in his book, writing on the sacred city of the Ethiopians, describing the houses at Aksum, says that they are round, and about twenty feet in diameter, thatched roof, and in nearly every case surmounted by an ornament, which he saw only at Aksum (the oldest sacred city in Abyssinia). It looks like a huge raspberry growing on a stalk out of a plate, with a handle at the top and a cross surmounting it. He also states that he has no doubt that it has some symbolical and religious meaning, *but could not tell what it was*—it is the Egyptian Ank-cross.

We abstain from any theological arguments because we contend that Masonry is the pure Eschatology of the originals, which has survived all the upheavals and battles of the past, and has been brought down from generation to generation, pure and unsullied, and is now once more being spread over land and sea to the good of all those who believe in it. The ancient Egyptians never lost anything, but " brought on " all their doctrines, adding new ones as evolution took place, and we have done likewise, simply supplying new names for the old, but leaving the essence the same. Further than this, we can only say that no amount of research nor any discovery has, as yet, yielded any information about the home, origin and early history of "The Book of the Dead," more than that which we have given.

CHAPTER XX

From all the evidence we have brought forward there is, in our opinion, but one conclusion to be drawn :

1. That our sun was thrown off from another sun, around which it revolves, taking 25,827 years to perform its cycle of one year—the one great year. That evidence remains, geologically, that at least three cycles have taken place—how many more we cannot say, probably many.

2. From our sun, this earth and other planets, forming our Solar system, have been thrown off as superheated vapour, gradually cooling down, ever revolving on their own axes around our sun, in their allotted space and time. This was known to the ancient Egyptian astronomers, and now proved by Stellar photography.

3. That as soon as the crust of the earth was cool enough, the Great God created the first cell of life by His divine will. From this, by the laws of evolution which He created, all other living matter has been formed, each generation being gradually succeeded by a higher type, as environment was favourable, until we find the first primitive man evolved. As time has continued, so has generation succeeded generation, gradually passing to a higher type as ages followed ages, where favourable circumstances have been encountered. That in some places we find this has not been, and so we still find " primitive man " and different grades from him to the present highest type in various parts of the world. These primitive people have still all their ideas, religious beliefs and totemic ceremonies, which were practised by their forefathers thousands of years ago, and the reason or cause, no doubt, has been because they have been cut off from inter-communication with others, who were advancing in knowledge and development, anatomically, like the Tasmanians, Australian aborigines and other islanders we find in this primordial condition. Others would be driven to the fastness of forests or mountains,

where those of a higher type could not, or did not follow to exterminate them, as the Pygmies, Viddas, Pygmies of the New Hebrides, and Bolivia in South America, living in forests, and probably many other remnants of these not yet discovered. They were all nomadic, possessing bows and arrows, small spears, stone knives, with only a limited articulate language, *but having a sign-language* ; no totemic rites or mythos, as far as is known. Some circumcise, others do not, *yet all believe in a Great Spirit*, and *have spirit houses as a propitiation for the departed spirits.*

4. That the first man was the "little red man" or earth man, as proved by his remains found all over the world. These universally correspond in their osteo-anatomy, wherever found, and correspond to the Pygmies of the present day. Some of these are still found in Central Africa and in the mountains of the New Hebrides, and in Bolivia, South America ; probably we shall find some in New Guinea and other parts of the world, where they have not been exterminated by the Nilotic negro type, who followed them. In Tasmania they have all now been exterminated. These could not have been a degenerated race from a higher type, *because nature does not and could not degenerate anatomically.* However much a tribe or section of the human race may degenerate in manners and appearance, *his osteo-anatomy could not* ; that would be contrary to the laws of evolution and therefore impossible. What religious beliefs they had we have no knowledge to guide us, and can only partially form an idea from those of the present Pygmies—see PYGMIES.

That the origin of Spirits and religion commenced with these Pygmies, and was of a twofold nature—at first a propitiation of the elemental powers (see PYGMIES), and then the Spirits of their Ancestors were also propitiated or worshipped (as may be seen by the Spirit houses and food put there for their Ancestral Spirits who might return), as we have proved.

5. These were followed by a higher race, more developed in every way, physically and mentally. Ages must have passed whilst these little men had been making progress here in the Nile valley and developing their brain power, forming a mythos and then astro-mythology ; developing in stature and evolving their totemic ceremonies, and then an exodus of these followed "the little red man" throughout the world, carrying all their totemic

ceremonies and sacred signs and symbols with them. These spread N. E. S. and W. all over the world, carrying their Stellar Mythos, which they had evolved out of the mythos and totemism, which must have taken thousands of years, exterminating the little red man and ever driving him farther and farther away; no doubt taking some of the women and intermarrying. As the nucleus of the cell of life comes from the male, and as the nucleus is dominant as to the determination of the future individual, naturally as man became of a higher type, so the nucleus of the cell of life would become of a higher type also. Science has taught us that the properties which distinguish the individuals of any race or family from the individual of any other race or family are to be traced back to the constitution of a single cell, the fertilised ovum from which that individual has been developed—the "new cell of life," inheriting properties and characteristics of the original nucleus of each cell, from each parent; thus we get various types of men, as we find at the present day. From ancient remains we arrive at the conclusion that there must have been at least two exodes from the Nile valley during the period of Totemic Sociology, an early one, with Totemic Ceremonies, in a primitive form, having no Mythology and no Hero Cult, followed by a later exodus, who possessed Hero Cult and Mythology. The next exodus which followed were the Stellar Mythos people, but these did not go to Australia, New Zealand, New Guinea, extreme North of Asia, extreme North of America, or farther South than Chile. These people spread all over North Africa as well as South and West. Probably North Africa was peopled by a dense population, if we may judge by flint knives, arrow heads, etc., still to be found in the Great Sahara, and some may have crossed to Europe by way of Spain and thence to the North. Others spread over Asia and Europe, the British Isles and across to America; probably to America by two routes, one *via* Greenland and N. Europe, and the other North of Japan and Eastern Asia to America, and then spread South. From South of Asia they spread to New Guinea, Australia and other parts which are now islands. The remains of these people are found in all these countries, and the remains of their sacred signs and symbols, totemic ceremonies and mythology are all identical and all identical with those found and evolved in Egypt and the Nile valley. Although nomadic at first, we find remains in various parts of the world where they began to form their "first towns or cities," generally situated on hills, with ramparts and fosse to protect them and their cattle ; and they worked in metals. In their later time they built cities and temples, and fashioned beautiful sculptures, at first wrote in picture sign—hieroglyphics, and afterwards commenced a written language by adding alphabetical or linear signs to their hieroglyphics in some cases, and new ones in others. Amongst those who formed the first exodus from Egypt at the time of the earlier Totemic Ceremonies (the Arunta and other tribes of Australia, New Guinea, Hebrides, and some tribes in America, North and South) in their state of mythical representation, there are no gods or goddesses. The powers of the elements had not yet been divinised, they are only known, like the human groups, by their Totemic types. In the wisdom of ancient Egypt, we can identify the elemental powers and trace them in nature and name, into the phases of their gods and goddesses, the superhuman powers in totemism preceded these divinities in the Mythology. The elemental powers are propitiated, next the Ancestral Spirits are worshipped.

The great Mother Earth—the giver of life, food, water, etc., who was represented by Zootypes, etc., these were the spirits of the elemental powers, and were propitiated and invoked, but not worshipped, and were not human, they never had been, and never could appear as human, which these natives knew and understood.

The other Spirits—the Ancestral, were propitiated and worshipped—not to return to do them harm, but to assist them in danger and help them when called upon ; these spirits had been human—the body was dead but the spirit lived, was seen by their Seers, and could be communicated with by their initiated Clairvoyants and High Priests. They recognised the difference between the two spirits—the totemic type and the ancestral human. The animistic nature powers were typified ; the Ancestral spirits, personalised.

Although the Arunta Alcheringa are called the "Ancestors" (who reproduced themselves by incorporation in the life on earth in the course of becoming man or animal) these spirits of the elements—air, fire, water, etc., may be called in a sense *Ancestral*, but not *Ancestral Spirits* ; the one was pre-human and the other originally human. The confusion arises from the lapse of the primitive wisdom—forgotten.

The Snake, Lizard, Lion, etc., were totemic types, not only of the human brotherhood, but also of the elemental powers ; as an example, there was an elemental spirit of the snake-totem and also an ancestral spirit of this totem, and the snake remained as a representation of both, to the confounding of the animistic spirit, with the Ancestral spirit, at a later stage.

The superhuman powers in totemism, preceded the gods and goddesses in Mythology, and therefore in the earlier exodes we find that the tribes who went out of Egypt all over the world, have the same Mythical Ancestors who were Snakes, Lizards, Lions, etc., as totemic representations of elemental forces, but have no gods or goddesses.

In the Egyptian Eschatology, these primordial powers finally became the Lords of Eternity, but from the first they were Ever-living ones, under totemic Zootypes.

Different colours were also assigned to totemic spirits, and became associated with the Totems ; these were afterwards assigned to the different gods when divinisation took place, and in Egypt were as follows :—

Horus was the	White god, sometimes depicted as Red, as the Blood of Isis.
Osiris	Black god ; sometimes Sut was thus represented.
Shu	Red.
Amen	Blue.
Num	Green.

Yellow also represented Corn, which gave the name to the Yellow Neith.

These colours we find associated with the same, or the representation of the same, all over the world, and are plainly depicted in the Mexican Codices which *Dr Edward Seler* might study, with advantage to himself and others.

It is a great mistake to assume that these early people began by fashioning the nature-powers in their own human likeness. Totemism—first commenced after the Pygmies—was formulated by myth-making man with types that were the very opposite of human. In their mythology the Anthropomorphic representation was preceded by zootypes ; in this way the powers of nature were first portrayed as superhuman powers by means of living superhuman types. Paleolithic and Neolithic man was too poor in possessions to dream of shaping the superhuman powers of nature in the human likeness—he simply could not, and it is because of this that we have the zoomorphic mode of representation as the Sign Language of Totemism and Mythology. In every country and on every line of research we discover the representation of nature was pre-anthropomorphic at first if we go back far enough, and on every line of descent the zoomorphic passes ultimately into the human representation. Modern metaphysicians have so developed the faculty of abstraction and the disease of subjectivity that their own mental operations offer no true guidance for generalisation concerning primitive or early man *who thought in things.* Ignorance of primitive sign language and the want of knowledge of reading the hieroglyphics have been and are a great source of false statements and beliefs, begun by the Greeks and continued by the Romans. One of the greatest mistakes of the past has been made in misapprehending this primitive sign language for what is designated *worship—Sun Worship—Serpent Worship—Tree Worship—Phallic Worship*; but these were only *types of powers,* and it was not the types that were worshipped—it was a mythical mode of representing nature; it was not an *explanation* of natural phenomena, but a *representation* by such means as primitive man had to express his thoughts, not having the words or language in articulate form to do so, and sign language included all their gesture signs and ideas of thought, as in dancing or otherwise dramatised shape. The serpent represented the god Tem as a type, but it was not the type that was worshipped, it was the god. Later on, when they had developed their ideas, etc., this type was carried on and applied to the human in sign language. This is proved by the *Ritual,* as when Osiris in the Tuat exclaims, "I am the Crocodile in the form of a man"—*i.e.* a soul of which the Crocodile had been a symbol. It was not the belief that the Crocodile was the soul of the man, but only the sign or symbol, hence all these signs, figures of various animals and symbols, etc., we find throughout the world and in their ancient temples. These *represented zoomorphically the powers, and were not worshipped* as has generally been stated.

6. The people of the Stellar mythos were followed by a still higher type and race of men, who had developed great learning in all branches of art and science. Their Stellar mythos

was now evolved first into Lunar and then into the Solar, and after they perfected their Eschatology or doctrine of final things. An exodus of these took place, but only we find to a limited extent in comparison to those of the Stellar.[1] The remains of these are found in Europe and the British Isles, Asia, except the extreme N. and N.E. In America, only in Yucatan, amongst the Mayas, and the Incas of South America. In the Islands of New Guinea, Australia, New Zealand, extreme North of Asia, and some parts of North, South, and West of America, the Solar doctrines never reached, or if so, we have not found any trace of their existence ; but so far as these went, they, like their predecessors drove out, exterminated, intermarried and absorbed all that went before. How long this took to accomplish it is now impossible to say and we must take into consideration "overlapping time."

These latter were of the highest type of Egyptian exodes, and wherever they went they have left the marks of their immense knowledge and wisdom in all its forms, and all these are universally the same. The doctrine of the immortality of the soul had been worked out gradually by the pre-dynastic Egyptians, and was not, as is assumed by many writers, founded first at the time of Osiris ; no doubt it was at its perfection at the time of the earliest Osirian cult, and continued thence to the early Christian Coptic times, and so onward to the present day. The Greeks and Romans, after them, obtained all their beliefs from the Egyptians, which the Romans carried with them wherever they went throughout the empire, even to the remotest provinces of the Danube and the Rhine, which can now be proved by the remains of altars raised

[1] *Dr D. R. O'Sullivan Beare*, H.B.M.'s Consul at Bahia, Brazil, has recently informed the writer that through an Indian he has discovered the ruins of a large ancient city, situated three days' march through dense forest, in Brazil, which was not known, nor has it ever been seen by a white man before, to the best of his knowledge and Indian reports. He visited these ruins and describes immense walls of granite and huge blocks of the same, beautifully fashioned, and one tall Pillar with a figure, surmounting it, pointing to the North. This is a very important find and no doubt much information regarding the forgotten history of South America will be found here if someone who explores it understands Stellar Mythos, as from what he has told the author there is little doubt that these are the ruins of one of the great cities of South America which flourished before the Solar doctrines were introduced, therefore prior to the Incas and Mayas. It would be a great pity if anyone not conversant with Stellar Mythos and the contents of this work were sent to explore, as it must be a question of deciphering Ancient Signs and Symbols, the language of past ages now forgotten and only known to a few.

to Osiris—to his wife, Isis—and to his son, Harpocrates or the child Horus, and although neither the Greeks nor Romans were ever admitted into all the sacred mysteries or understood the Eschatology of the Egyptians, still the doctrines of the Osirian faith so influenced both the Greek and Roman philosophers that it became the precursor of Christianity—a foundation upon which it was possible to erect the Christian edifice; but the error into which many have fallen in supposing that the "Osirian doctrines" took their foundation from Osiris, and that Osiris was the first man-god, who lived here on earth, was murdered and rose again, having triumphed over evil and death, and ascended the throne of God, shows that they are ignorant of the primordial. Osiris is only a very late representation of Horus I. and the risen Amsu. The history of Horus I., his death and resurrection as Amsu, is thousands of years older than Osiris, and all was worked out by the pre-dynastic Egyptians, including the immortality of the soul, at this early period. The *Ritual* proves this. The earlier Egyptians worked out the doctrine of the immortality of the human soul, and it was from an exodus of these that the Semites, Indo-Germans, Turcomans, and Mongolians obtained their knowledge and learning. Osiris was not the first divine king of Egypt who reigned in true human likeness, civilised the Egyptians, instructed them in agriculture, gave them laws and taught them true religion; it was Horus I., who, after a long and blessed reign fell a prey to the machinations of his brother Sut, and, having been slain, descended into the underworld, and rose again as Amsu—but these were not human.

But let us not be misunderstood: what we contend we have proved in this work from the *Ritual*, and other facts we have brought forward, prove that it is the same tale and history, as far as we can discover, and that the primoridal is the Egyptian Horus and Amsu. The same tradition has been brought on through countless generations, that during these periods names have been changed and one substituted for another, until at last it is Osiris in Egypt. Then followed the Christian doctrines in some countries; the Copts first and Europe generally; after these N. and S. America and other parts of the world, where at the present day we find the beliefs and practices, under whatever denomination. Rev. xi. 8: "The great city, which spiritually is called Sodom and Egypt, where also our Lord was crucified" (in

Amenta). The angels in the Christian doctrines have taken the place of the "divinated powers" of the Egyptians—they are one and the same. The four archangels of the Muhammadans—Michael, Gabriel, Azrael and Israfl—are the representative types of the four children of Horus. The story of Cain and Abel and the murder of Horus by Sut are prototypes, and others have been shown throughout this work.

Gerald Massey writes to me:—"In studying the '*Ritual* of the Resurrection,' we find it is based upon the mythical representation which was the primordial. This mythical representation was first applied to the phenomena of external nature; and this manner of representation was continued and re-applied to the human soul in their Eschatology. Egyptian myths are not inventions made to explain the *Ritual*. Totemic representation was first, and was continued in the mythology. The *Ritual* was founded on the rendering becoming religious in the form of their Eschatology, and did not arise as an explanation of totemism and mythology; for example, in the mythology, the primary Solar God, Ptah, is the maker of a complete circle for the sun as founder and *opener of the nether earth*, this solar road *being a figure of for ever a type of the eternal working in time*. In the Eschatology, the god in spirit, Ra or Amsu, is the god who has created (or opened the road) eternity—*Ritual*, chap. clvii. The one is on the physical plane, the other on the spiritual. In the mythology the seven primordial powers that pass through various phases, elemental, stellar and lunar, always in a group of seven, finally become the seven souls of Ra as the holy *spirit*—the seven souls of man as seven gifts of the holy spirit. In the Eschatology, Horus. 'The Lord of Resurrection' in mythology became the Lord of Resurrection of ever-living souls in the Eschatology. The difference between mythology and Eschatology is that the one is represented in the earth of time, the other in the earth of eternity, represented by Amenta. It was there that the resurrection of eternity for the human soul, evolved on earth, took place; it was here that the claim to life eternal in heaven had to be made good; it was here that the soul was weighed in the balance and had to pass through many trials and judges, and, in order to pass, must have lived a righteous life, and been just, truthful, merciful, charitable and humane—*Ritual*, chap. cxxv.

"The most primitive imagery was sacredly preserved in Amenta, which makes 'The Book of the Dead' an eschatological record of the beginnings in mythology, that is unparalleled, and not until we have mastered the wisdom of Egypt, as recorded in Amenta, shall we be able to read it on the surface of the earth. First comes the natural fact, next the mythological representation, and lastly, the eschatological application of the type; all these phases have to be studied, collated and compared, and for this purpose the Egyptian 'Book of the Dead' and of Amenta is worth all other sacred writings in the world.

"The story of the voluntary victim, who in a passion of divinest pity became incarnate and was clothed in human form and feature for the salvation of the world, did not originate in a belief that God had manifested once and for all as a historic personage; it had its roots in the remotest past, and the same story was repeated in many lands with a change of names, but none of the initiated in the esoteric wisdom ever looked upon the many saviours as historic in personality—they had been taught the truth."

Mythology was earlier than Eschatology, and the human form was preceded by the zootype, and that first rendered mythology was not manifested in the human sphere.

Horus I. represented the soul of life, which came by water to a dried up world, upon the verge of perishing with hunger and with thirst. Here the fish, as the first fruit of the earth, was a sign of his incorporation in matter; hence the typical shoot, the green ear of corn, or the branch that were imaged in Child Horus—the Saviour who came by water.

The Saviour who came in fruit as a product of the tree was the Natzar. The Saviour who came by spirit was the soul of the sun. This was the earliest rendering of the incorporation of Horus, as the primary life and light of the world, before the doctrine was applied to biology in the human domain, when Horus came by blood as the wonder of incarnation in the human form.

Horus not only warred against Apap, or the Great Dragon, for light but also for water. The Great Dragon who drank up all the water, and converted everything into a desert. The type is not always the Dragon, in Mexico it was the Frog who drank up all the water—"Mexican Antiquities" (page 291).

Uranographically, the Constellation Hydra represented the Great Dragon.

Sothos, in its helical rising, was the Star of the Annunciation at the birth of Horus the Child. Farther South, Phact represented the Dove as the Harbinger of Inundation, and still farther South, Canopus the pilot of the Argo, the starting point of the water of the Nile at the Great Lakes, and Horus came by water as Ichthus the fish before there was a boat or Ark.

But when the Ark had been built, Argo is constellated as the Ark of Horus, and the figure in the planisphere is the Child on board the Ark with the Great Dragon coiling around seeking to kill or destroy the Child—the infant saviour of the world who brings the food and water, as the Lord of Life.

In the later Solar Mythos, Apap, the enemy of Ra, is the blind devourer of darkness; but as the adversary of the elder Horus—he of the inundation—Apapa Hydra is the Dragon of Drought. Drought in "Old Egypt" was the "curse," and the evil dragon as its deadly image was the primitive type of physical—not of moral—evil, and the inundation was the source of the life of Egypt. It was her annual salvation, and Horus or Sebek, the fish-man, was her Saviour.

We give here some of the different names and attributes of Horus, which, if compared with the volume of the Sacred Law, will speak better than our poor pen.

Horus I.—The different Names or Attributes of Horus and Amsu, the Risen Horus or Horus in Spirit

Horus—The first Man-God
Horus—I. U. or I. A. U. = Jesus.
Horus—The Light of the World.
Horus—God of Life.
Horus—God of the Four Quarters, N. E. S. W.
Horus—God of the Pole Star.
Horus—God of Light.
Horus—Creator of Himself and Heir of Eternity.
Horus—Child of Isis.
Horus—King of the North and South.
Horus—Guide of the Northern Horizon.
Horus—In Spirit (Amsu).
Horus—Guardian of Sut.
Horus—Lord of Dawn and Evening Twilight.
Horus—The Mighty One of the Teshert Crown.
Horus—In the Resurrection.
Horus—The Child-suckling.
Horus—The Great Spirit.
Horus—The Seven Powers of.
Horus—Of the Two Horizons.
Horus—As Hawk or Vulture or Eagle Hawk.
Horus—As Young Ear of Corn.
Horus—As Her-Shef or Khnemu—He who is on his Lake.
Horus—The Anointed Son of the Father.
Horus—The Red Calf (Type of Horus the Child).
Horus—In the Tree.
Horus—On the Cross.

Horus—Lord of the Northern and Southern Horizon.
Horus—Fettering Sut (or binding or chaining Satan).
Horus—Prince of the Emerald Stone.
Horus of the Triangle.
Horus—The Great One — The Mighty One.
Horus—The Great Chief of the Hammer or Axe.
Horus—Lord of Tattu.
Horus—The Blind.
Horus—The Tears of.
Horus—The Followers of.
Horus—The Feet of.
Horus—The Divine Healer.
Horus—The Master.
Horus—In the Tank of Flame (Baptiser with Fire).
Horus—The Good Shepherd with the Crook upon His Shoulder.
Horus—With Four Followers on the Mount.
Horus—With the Seven Great Spirits on the Mount.
Horus—As the Fisher.
Horus—As the Lamb.
Horus—As the Lion.
Horus—Of Twelve Years.
Horus—With the Tat (Cross).
Horus—Made a man at 30 years in his Baptism.
Horus—The Healer in the Mountain.
Horus—The Exorciser of Evil Spirits, as the Word.
Horus—Who gives the Waters of Life.
Horus—In the Bush of Thorns (as Unbu).
Horus—The Just and True.
Horus—The Bridegroom with the Bride in Sothis.
Horus—As "I am the Resurrection and the Life."
Horus—Prince of Peace.
Horus—Who descends into Hades.
Horus—Lord of the Two Eyes or Double Vision.
Horus—The Manifesting Son of God.
Horus—As Child of the Virgin.
Horus—The Sower of Good Seed (and Sut the Destroyer).
Horus—Carried off by Sut to the Summit of the Mount Hetep.
Horus—Contending with Sut on the Mount.
Horus—One of Five Brethren.
Horus—The Brother of Sut, the betrayer.
Horus—Baptised with water by Anup.
Horus—Who exalted His Father in every Sacred Place.
Horus—The Weeper.
Horus—The Lifted Serpent.
Horus—In the Bosom of Ra (his Father).
Horus—The Avenger.
Horus—He who comes with Peace.
Horus—The Afflicted One.
Horus—The Lord of Resurrection from the House of Death.
Horus—As the type of Eternal Life.
Horus—The Child Teacher in the Temple (as Iu-em-Hetep).
Horus—As Ma-Kheru (the Witness unto Truth).
Horus—As the Lily.
Horus—Who came to fulfil the Law.
Horus—Walking the Water.
Horus—The Raiser of the Dead.
Horus—One with his Father.
Horus—Entering the Mount at Sunset to hold Converse with his Father.
Horus—Transfigured on the Mount.

Horus had two mothers: Isis, the Virgin, who conceived him, and Nephthysis, who nursed him.
He was brought forth singly and as one of five brothers.
Jesus had two mothers: Mary the Virgin, who conceived him, and Mary, the wife of Cleophas, who brought him forth as one of her children.
He was brought forth singly and as one of five brethren.
Horus was the Son of Seb, his father on earth.
Jesus was the son of Joseph, the father on earth.
Horus was with his mother, the Virgin, until 12 years old, when he was transformed into the beloved son of God, as the only begotten of the Father in heaven.
Jesus remained with his mother, the Virgin, up to the age of 12 years, when he left her "to be about his Father's business."
From 12 to 30 years of age there is no record in the life of Horus.

From 12 to 30 years of age there is no record in the life of Jesus.
Horus at 30 years of age became adult in his baptism by Anup.
Jesus at 30 years of age was made a man of in his baptism by John the Baptist.
Horus, in his baptism, made his transformation into the beloved son and only begotten of the Father—the holy spirit, represented by a bird.
Jesus, in his baptism, is hailed from heaven as the beloved son and only begotten of the Father, God—the holy spirit that is represented by a dove.

The ancient Egyptian code of morals, as may be seen from chap. cxxv., was the grandest and most comprehensive of those now known to have existed amongst any nation.

The "Recension," no doubt, was drawn up by the priests of On or Heliopolis (Moses was one of them), and it contains the views held by the priests of the colleges of that very ancient city. All the texts, however, have not yet been discovered, in fact, only five, and as there is considerable evidence that the priests of On did much "editing," it is also undoubted proof that these texts had been edited several times before. It would be out of place to say more here. For those deeply interested, "The Ritual or Book of the Dead" is always open, for therein you will find that the soul declares its innocence in language whose moral tone has never been surpassed, and throws light on the virtues and vices of old Egyptian Society, which makes clear how poor a guide to the past are its monuments compared with its literature, but this can only be read through sign language and astro-mythology.

And now let us draw your attention to the map of the interior of the Great Pyramid, as well as to the door of entrance. You see that the door of entrance was placed at the north and was concealed, so that when looked for it could not be seen, and was only accidentally discovered. This stone was in the form of an equilateral triangle, surmounting a square, and revolving on a pivot or apex. We lay the cornerstone at the north-east, and you will also perceive at this entrance you have a square with a triangle above it, typical of heaven and earth. Through these the Postulant has to pass, for they symbolise the passage from this to the future life. The *Ritual* shows that there were twelve entrances to pass through before you could attain to the Grand Orient, with secrets and trials restricted to each. The first could not be seen;[1] it was apparently a blank and was guarded by

[1] The entrance to the valley of the Tuat was concealed by "a walled up doorway"—*i.e.* no visible door, but the means of entrance through "what appeared a blank wall" was by knowing the secret of the nicely adapted triangular stone over a square

Horus, the Son—*Inner Guard*. It was a blank of nothingness, because the Postulant was blind and bereft of all his senses, except that of motion; which you see is identical with the

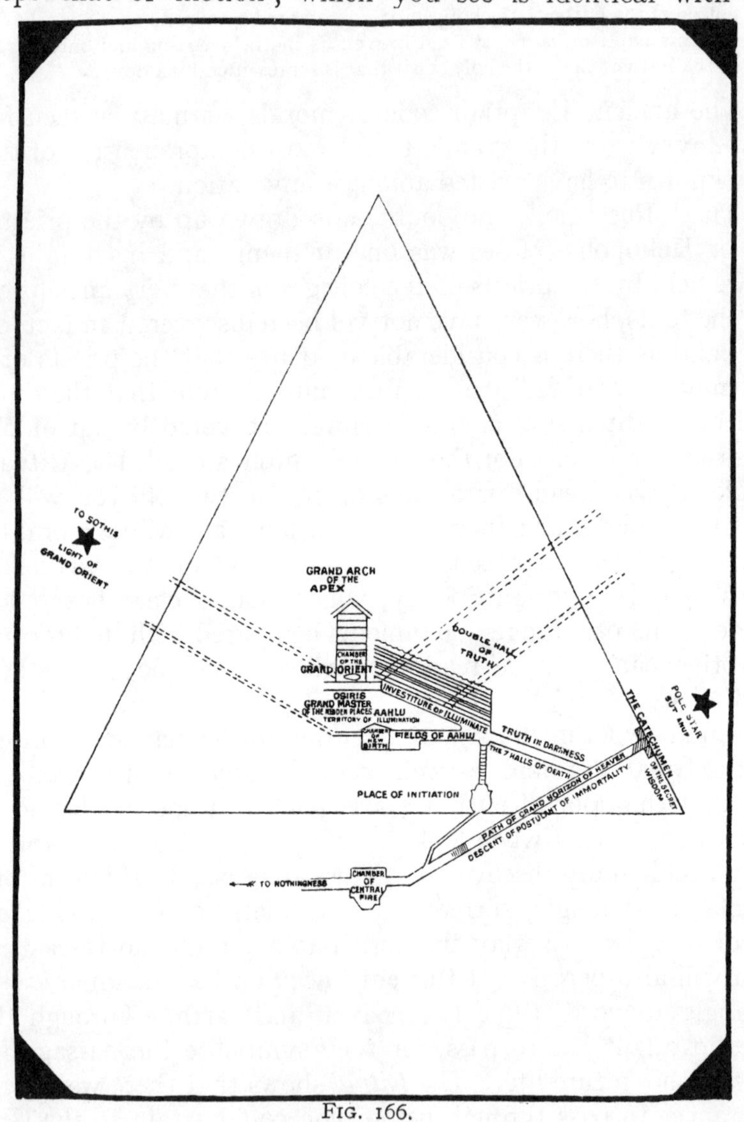

Fig. 166.

position of our I——. This portal has to be passed through with the aid of a friendly spirit, who has led him to the portal where questions are asked. Having passed through the portal, he is one, and the secret was communicated to the I. with a password in the mysteries. The password for this "door" in Egyptian was "Ra-gririt."

conducted down these passages by the same friendly spirit, whom he cannot see, and taken to the place of initiation, where his manes is regenerated by the descent of the soul to expecting Postulants;

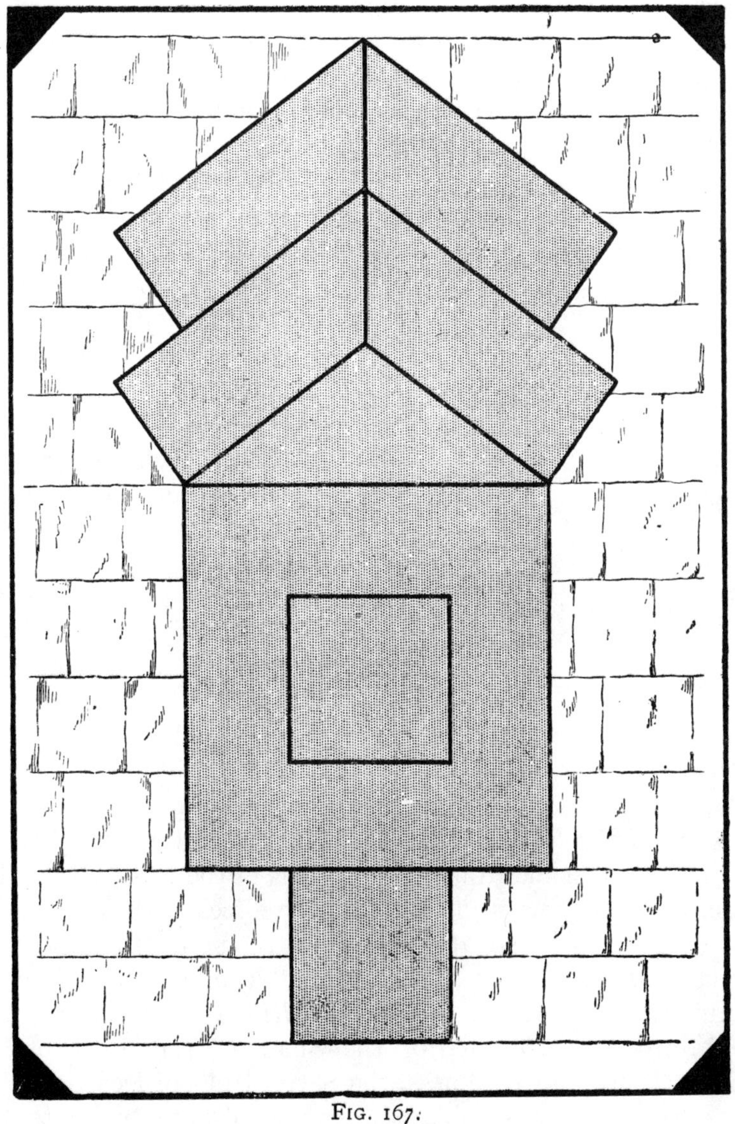

FIG. 167.

he is then conducted to the Chamber of Central Fire, which he passes through successfully. This Chamber of Central Fire is "the Tank of Flame," is very important, and is spoken of in the *Ritual* in chap. i. 22 and 86, and shown in the PAPYRUS OF

LEYDEN and PAPYRUS OF ANI; plate xxii. of *Sir Le Page Renouf's* "Book of the Dead." The *Ritual* says: "I enter in and come forth from the Tank of Flame on the day when the adversaries are annihilated at Sechem." It is where the second baptism takes place—the baptism of fire—where the raising up or resurrection takes place in their Eschatology, not only to represent the Spiritual resurrection of the soul but of the Spiritual body also. The baptism with water took place as a child, and after the child had become twelve years old or upwards, then this second baptism took place in their eschatological doctrines, which took the place of the initiation ceremony in their Totemic times, when the *boy was made a man* and a begetter or raiser up of future generations.

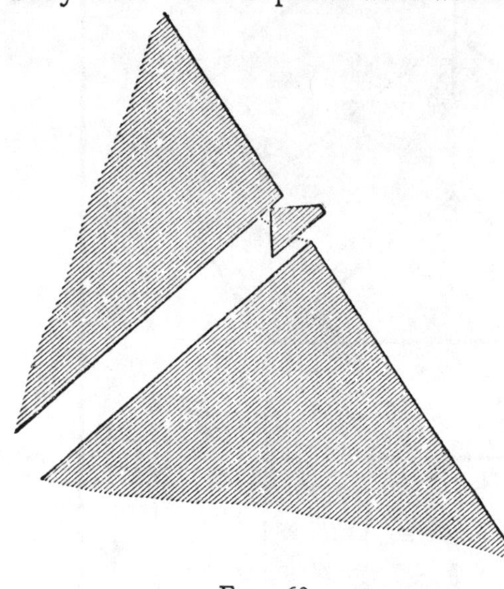

FIG. 168.

Then he is conducted up the grand horizon of Heaven, and reaches a portal; questions are asked, which he answers, and then he passes through and is able to see: light is given to him and he can see his guide and friend who is conducting him. In chapter x. of the *Ritual* I. N. speaks of the desire for light, and later on, "Deliver me from the Wardens of the Passages." The Wardens are the powers who keep off the forces of the adversaries of Ra or Osiris, who sit at the head of the stairs to receive the Postulant after he has been tried in the "Tank of Flame," which he puts out (see plate xi. chap. xxii., *Ritual*). He is now conducted into the Chamber of the Shadow, Judgment of the Justified, Truth and Darkness, the Seven Halls of Death. Here he has to pass his examination, and words are given to him which he must remember, before he is led to the second portals, where he has to give answers also before he can pass through them. Having passed through the second stage, the adept is allowed to enter the hall, which is called the tenth hall of Truth or Trial Scene, and is depicted by ancient brethren in black and white—the tessellated pavement, Right and Wrong, Truth or Lie—and is conducted to the Chamber of New Birth or place of coming forth with regeneration of soul. Here, in this chamber, you will observe the emblem of mortality, the sarcophagus, empty —corresponding to our coffin. You will also see the small opening admitting the light of that bright morning star, Sothis, shining down the line into the chamber. All the rest of the chamber reminds the adept of what he has passed through: he now emerges from the tomb. Then he is taken to the Throne of Regeneration of Soul, and Investiture of Illumination takes place, and he has to pass through more ordeals to attain to the Chamber of the Orient, to the Throne of Ra, to become a Master. The uncreated light, from which is pointed out the whole happiness of the future, he can see for himself in the distance. After passing through another portal, where he has to bend, he is conducted to the Chamber of the Grand Orient. In all he has to pass through 12 gates or doors—the first being closed, and which he cannot see, all the others are open—the last being a double gateway or door.

Can anything be plainer from the brief description and passages from the *Ritual* we have given, than the ceremony of our E—— A—— Passing, Raising, M.R.A., and to 18° and 30°. Are not these identical? Do not the principles and tenets of the craft correspond in almost every particular? Our passwords differ somewhat, and yet the translations are symbolically identical. We are not giving you question and answer, verbatim, as they appear in the *Ritual*, but any brother can read them; the sense and meaning are identical with what forms our bulwark—Truth, Justice, Morality, Charity. We have, however, given you words and symbols which will be sufficient for all M.M.'s, R.A.M.'s and others to understand the similarity of these to our own, up to and including 18° and 30°.

In the Egyptian, the word "Mati" means Law, Justice, Truth, etc. To us it teaches this lesson:—that our brotherhood will exist as long as this world will last, because we have the essence of what our Divine Creator set down as a guide for our forefathers, in the most perfect form, in comparison with all others, at the present time.

Our principal tenets are the same. We have a monument

with the mysterious secrets written in stone, which dates back to remote antiquity, and yet remains to the present day, with writing as fresh and clear as fifty centuries or more ago; and we Freemasons have practically the same signs and symbols in use now as the Egyptians had. We have the different degrees, with knowledge and secrets restricted to each, and before passing from one to another, questions and teachings have to be gone through, as well as certain ordeals to prove that the faith of the brother is identical with our own.[1]

The principles and tenets of our craft are the highest principles of Morality, Charity, Truth and Justice, which we have received as a sacred legacy from our forefathers, teaching us by sign and symbol those duties we owe to others and ourselves, to guide us through this dark life into everlasting light and happiness.

We find some of the signs and symbols in and near the ruins of ancient temples in Mexico and other parts of the world; and can we doubt that these signs and symbols represented the universal beliefs and principles practised by our forefathers? We date our first Temple or Lodge to have been formed at the foot of Mount Horeb, in the Wilderness of Sinai, with Moses A. and B. as the first G. P.'s. At what date this occurred we have no authentic record, and we contend that we have shown that Moses became initiated into and knew the whole of the Egyptian mysteries. He was one of the priests of Osiris, and also of Amen-Ra, according to *Manetho*. When he left Egypt with his followers[2] he handed down the principles, tenets, sacred signs and symbols, to future generations, and these were brought on by the Israelites from generation to generation, up to the present day; and therefore we have it clearly in a direct line from the Egyptian originals, as well as from the Druids, as we have shown before, ever remembering however that our volume of the Sacred Law must be read by symbolism and the *Ritual* of ancient Egypt.

Although there are some writers who have expressed their

[1] The different degrees and ceremonies that we have are not all in chronological order, and there is a repetition in many, but as we have stated it is the representation of the final Eschatology of the Egyptians and portrays the passage of the manes through the Tuat and Amenta from the time of the death of the body (Earthly) to the final resurrection of the soul and its glorification in the Eternal Paradise situated in the North (Spiritual).

[2] Two numbers are given by different writers: 80,000 and 250,000. To be read as esoteric representation.

views as follows: "Whatever may have been the conduct of some of its deluded members, impelled by a fanatical zeal for the preservation of its supposed secrets, or whatever innovations may have beeni ntroduced by aspiring political demagogues, adverse to the established principles of the order, and that moral actions can never be taught without the aid of the mosaic or musaic pavement, the tessellated border, the square, the compass, the beehive, the plumb-rule, etc., and as to any useful art or science, about which great parade is still made in masonic books, nothing of the kind is now practised in lodges," *let us assure him that he has entirely missed the "word," he has failed to unlock the door, and thus, until he finds the "word and the key," he, like many others, will still remain "blind and without light."* How long it will take future generations to see and find "the Eschatology" is beyond our powers of divination; but we have no doubt that it will be so and that there will be "one universal brotherhood, which will be evolved from our Masonic Brotherhood." Although we acknowledge that at the present day, out of the many thousands who are Masons, few are "students," yet our opinion is that these few will increase year by year and generation by generation, and will ultimately work out the great destiny that is before us—nothing will stop or prevent this—it is so written: "Strange to think, by the way: whatever there is to know, that shall we know one day," but at present we have to contend against the blind, ignorant, and dogmatic principles of those who are in power, who take no interest in the Eschatology of our rituals—in the origin of the same—nor who appreciate the power for good to humanity generally that is in their hands, but prefer to continue in their blind and ignorant dogmas, explanation and meaning of which they cannot give. Like the poor native savages, they do it because their forefathers did it.

The present position is one of Office and the Churches, both excellent in their way, but it is not all or half or a hundredth part of Freemasonry. We say finally to our brothers, who have the good welfare and interest of our brotherhood at heart: study the Eschatology of the Ancient Egyptians, which was their final evolution "of all." You will find, like science, it is not bent against the religion of the present day, rather, it will strengthen it, it will place you on surer ground. The Eschatology of the ancient Egyptians, which was the final evolution of all their

Totemic ceremonies, Mythology and Astro-mythology, and upon which all other religions throughout the world have taken their origins, and upon which our Brotherhood is founded, and we have it more perfectly—in our rites, forms and ceremonies, etc.—than all others combined, yet it is in the higher degrees alone we find the perfect and dramatic forms of the passage of the Tuat and Amenta. Therefore study and learn the whole. That it has been Christianised will not interfere with the truth or your faith. You will find all " dates " wrong, but that is of very little consequence, the principle and essence you will find true, and it will increase your faith, both as to your duties to your fellow-creatures in this life, and what you have to pass through in the next, before you come before the Great Judge of All, to answer and to be weighed in the " scales " for " deeds and words " in this life.

We contend that Freemasons will fulfil the prophecies of Isaiah, Ezekiel, and Jeremiah. You may ask how and why ? In a few words this may be answered, and we only wish that our Brothers would ponder and think a little more over the grand inheritance which has been left them, and learn to solemnly appreciate the same.

1. *Who are Freemasons in this world ?*—Principally British and American, scattered over the face of the globe : " And when two or three are gathered together, I will be with them " ; for whereever we go we carry this creed with us, and every year our brotherhood increases in numbers.

2. *What is the destiny we have to fulfil ?*—To govern this world by advancing knowledge and Fraternal Brotherhood, and equal rights to all ; in short, carrying out all those principles and tenets belonging to the craft, rendering homage to the One Great Eternal Lord God of all the Universe. " In the North East (Africa, Nile sources and valleys) God first planted man—from here all knowledge was derived and here it shall return."

3. *How long has Egypt remained down-trodden and in darkness ?*—England now has altered that, and Lord Kitchener of Khartoum, a Freemason, has already commenced the building of a university at Khartoum. Britain's sons are now forming a great kingdom from the Cape to Cairo. The only other countries of importance in which Freemasonry exists, and which have their temples and lodges (whose members may not be classed as British) are the United States and Germany. Many of the latter are now English

and American subjects ; perhaps in time all will be. Many of the former are of British descent, and in our opinion the prophecies point to the ultimate union of these before the time of the next glacial epoch. When these islands will become cold and buried under ice, *where will be the centre of learning and knowledge?* Egypt—Khartoum.

It would take up too much of your time to investigate this interesting subject further. It points to the ultimate unity of England and America. In all other countries, as yet, Freemasonry, as we understand it, does not exist. It is a significant fact, that in the Transvaal *all* the members of the only National Transvaal Lodge, "The Ermelo Netherlands Lodge," were killed at the commencement of the war, and all the remaining Masons in the Transvaal and the Orange Free State are now British subjects (*Standard*, 27th Dec. 1899).

No doubt much has been lost which we shall never recover ; but we contend that we have shown enough to prove that our rites and ceremonies, as well as the principal tenets of the craft, have descended from remotest ages. Some of our signs and symbols are those used to represent the astronomical mythology of the ancient Egyptians and the whole of the world, as far as can at present be traced, and afterwards as sacred symbols, when the mythology was perfected in their Eschatology ; and that the Great Pyramid of Ghizeh was the first and still remains the greatest Masonic Temple in the world, open to all Masons who can read symbolically what was written in stone ages ago ; teaching the principles that we teach—that to all just, upright and true Masons there is nothing to fear, and that the Grand Master waits above ready to receive with joy the souls of those who failed not in the hour of trial.

According to Christianity and its ethics, regeneration must come from within, must begin in the heart and mind of the individual. Socialists, on the contrary, look for regeneration from without, from natural conditions and a levelling of social life. They seek not the ideal society through the ideal individual, but conversely, the ideal individual through the ideal society, the primary condition and the end of individuality. In the former case they hold that the highest morality consists of a continual mortification of self, utter contempt for nature and reality. But by killing of oneself, he is only doing this at the instance of another and still more exacting self, his object being only the individual in another form; the taint of introspection vitiates his view of life, and he must seek by sophistry to poison life for himself and others in a way that is aptly illustrated by *Punch's* joke of the little girl who directs her brother "to go and see what baby is doing and tell him he mustn't." But it cannot be denied that the aspect of the world and this country, to those who have faith in the Spiritual nature of man, is at this time changing, one of the causes being the recent discoveries of science, which are frequently believed to be inconsistent with our long-received convictions, as to the relations between the Creator and the created. One of the consequences of the divine government of the world, which has ordained that the sacred purposes should be effected by the instrumentality of various human races, and the revelation entrusted to a particular family, must cause jealous discontent amongst those races; but there is no cause for this scientific invective, and truths thus demonstrated have always gone on simultaneously with the revelation of Spiritual truths. Scientific, like Spiritual truth, has ever from the beginning been descending from heaven to men, and the word of God is eternal and will survive the spheres, but the effects of the discoveries of science and the uneasy feeling that they cannot co-exist with our religious convictions, have their origin in the circumstance that the general body, who have become conscious of these physical truths, are not so well acquainted as is desirable with the past history of man. In the Church schism has perverted and discouraged many; it has caused differences in many and grief in us all, and yet sedition still continues.

A broader intellectual grasp of subjects has opened the eyes of men to the weakness of the foundations on which the Church, for so many generations, has endeavoured to maintain itself. One looks back with horror to the days when men were burned in Smithfield and elsewhere "to the honour and glory of God." On tracing the work of the Church since then, we see the effects of its despotism, its lack of that great virtue, *Charity*, and its badly concealed hatred of all who have differed from its dogmas.

Schisms have led to a display of bitterness and hatred which have been the means of alienating thousands who believe that *Charity* and forgiveness should be the principles of the Church and Christian doctrines. The cause of the falling away and schisms in the Church and Christianity is in the Church itself. Follow the people who come from these places of worship—listen to their conversations and their comments, and you will soon find how little of true Christian charity is in their hearts. The tyranny in the ranks of the Church is shocking. By the Church we mean all denominations of so-called Christians.

God is the principle of Christian science. He is not the imaginary being who holds heaven in one hand and threatens hell with the other, but the undying principle of Life, Truth and Love, right thinking and right doing, and a knowledge of that divinely harmonious and scientific principle which holds the world together, giving us Faith to support us when tempted to despair, Hope to console us in all our afflictions, and Charity to sustain us in every trial. "Charity envieth not, vaunteth not itself, seeketh not her own, is not easily provoked, thinketh no evil, rejoiceth not in iniquity, but rejoiceth in truth" (1 Cor. xiii. vv. 4, 5, 6).

It is the jealousies of the different sects of Christianity amongst themselves which throw the great difficulties in the way of bringing about one great conversion to the true doctrines of religion and religious beliefs—in the West, and yet this is not worse than the various schools of Buddhism which we find in the East. Bigotry and ignorance denouncing each other in such a way that causes one to wonder if these priests *ever think*: do they grasp how few years their lives are here on this earth, and that after this there is another life for *eternity*?—a term very few can comprehend the meaning of. Do those whose duty it is to teach the general masses of mankind ever ponder over their words and actions, and recognise how blind and ignorant they are themselves when denouncing their fellowmen to Hell and Perdition if they do not follow their blind and ignorant lead: preaching and outwardly acting as if they were the only true disciples of the Great God, possessing divine inspiration. Nature's Laws—the laws of God, they utterly ignore and preach as if the one Great Divine Lord, who created the millions, only did so to punish and everlastingly destroy all except their own "flock," which will be saved. What a monster they make the Divine Creator! yet they preach of His divine love. How can they wonder or be surprised that thinking men have such a great contempt for them that they abstain from joining their churches. If these only studied more what is still extant in various parts of the world; *learn to read what has been written in past ages; learnt he origin and meaning of the religious doctrines of those whom they condemn as infidels and idolaters*, they would find that from all these *Idolaters and Infidels* they might learn the great lesson that all originated from one and the same, and that although we still *find many names in different parts of the world*, there is but one whom all profess to worship. Recognising and knowing the above, there would be less difficulty in re-establishing one universal religion—one universal brotherhood—the same doctrines, forms and ceremonies of worshipping the One Great Creator of all, under the one name now brought on by evolution—Christianity.

The science of Evolution, which is God's law, never fails. It is true nations grow, advance and become great, then fall away, degenerate and are practically wiped out—why? In the history of the rise and fall of all nations we find the same answer—that the primary cause has been the falling away from true religious doctrines—collectively and individually—Schism, discontent, degrading influences of the Priests, their teachings or want of teaching pure religion leading to Socialism and revolution and disobedience of nature's laws in some form or other, yet evolution does not stop. If one nation decay another rises and advances to a higher type, and yet you constantly read from the writings of some "supposed authorities" of "the perils of the black and yellow man." These are types of a lower order than the white man, and must eventually give place to him. How many Red Indians are in North America now—how many Aboriginal Australians in Australia—compared with 100 years ago—and how many will exist there in another 100 years? Where will the black man be when the next glacial epoch has driven the whole of the white population from the North down to 56° latitude to the South of this? It is only a question of time, and because a small community of a lower type may gain an advantage for a time, eventually they must, by the laws of evolution, which are immutable, disappear or become absorbed, and only the higher type of white man will exist. Socialism *is not an advancement*, it *is a throw back* for thousands of years. Those who advance the cry for such, are people "whose brains are thrown back," the same as you see in some individuals a strong type of the Simian. This part of their anatomy has retrograded. It is an exception to the rule individually, but does not occur to a nation generally, and those who are striving for socialism are striving to go back to their ancestors when they were in a state of Totemism and Clans, when no one individual had any particular right except that which was common to all the tribe, but as surely as a nation becomes socialistic entirely, so surely it will be wiped out or become absorbed into another nation which is not so. The white man, by evolution, has passed that stage, and so we proceed to different grades, the result of education and brain expansion, distinguishing the difference in these. Many people have an erroneous idea that Freemasons are "levellers," like the Socialists, who would reduce all to the primitive element, disorganise society, and abolish all human distinctions, and so produce "chaos." But although Freemasons are all "brothers," there is no existing government or institution of any kind where the grades of rank are better defined or more correctly preserved; each has a particular duty, which is punctually discharged; some govern, others obey, in pursuit of that common object, carrying out all the laws and tenets to the good and advancement of the common brotherhood, all worshipping the one Great God, and rendering homage to Him according to ancient forms and ceremonies.

If those who govern use their powers only for their own aggrandisement, then the nation or community, over which they preside, suffers. They should only use their powers for the good of those they are set over, or if not, should be removed and others should take their place. No one has a right to accept power except he is prepared to sacrifice his own interest, if necessary, for the good of those who have placed him in that position. By the acceptance of office he has pledged himself to act thus.

What a power do the brothers united possess to-day! They have the future destiny of governing the world for the good of all; and there cannot be a higher or more noble, or more moral creed than we possess in all our teachings through the various degrees—that of our forefathers, from the earliest times, handed down from generation to generation, pure and unsullied from the Primordial.

The time of the fulfilment of the prophecies in the volume of the Sacred Law cannot be determined, but we have no doubt that eventually those prophecies will be fulfilled, and through us.

The fulfilment of the prophecies by us will enable Isaiah,

Psalms, Zechariah, Daniel, as well as other parts of the Sacred Volume, to be read as Paul, who was learned in all the mysteries of ancient Egypt, interpreted them; these will eventually be understood and read, not as a literal fulfilment to be on this earth, but "as the Manes in Amenta." "The pictures of these Prophecies" were pre-extant long ages earlier than these prophets—as Egyptian.

The Jews' prophecy is terribly misleading for those who are ignorant of the Ancient Egyptian Wisdom, and much of it has no meaning literally, without the *Ritual* as guide; an exoteric rendering has taken the place of the esoteric representation, which contained the only true interpretation, and by establishing this truth, one religious doctrine only, will remain.

At present this world is divided into various religious factions and sects, but time and evolution will again bring about those laws which, socially, morally and politically, will be the same for all, and the dissensions among the various religious bodies will end, and one universal brotherhood will prevail.

"So Mote It Be."

"God calls man to universal brotherhood;
Wherefore God's religion is also universal;
Reason not of His designs from what thou seest;
For on earth all is imperfect.
Wouldst thou judge of a temple by its wreck?
Neither shouldst thou of the spirit of man,
For that, verily, is not what it was;
But it has fallen down into a ruin.
Like a wandering leaf blown hither and thither,
It rests in no place, nor for any time;
Seeking peace, the repose of Heaven,
In a thousand conflicting systems."

Therefore

"Be innocent; take heed before thou act,
Nor let soft sleep upon thine eyelids fall
Ere the day's action thou hast three times scanned
What have I done, how erred, what left unwrought?
Go through the whole account, and if the same
Be evil, chide thee; but, if good, rejoice.
This do, this meditate, this ever love,
And it shall guide thee into virtue's path."

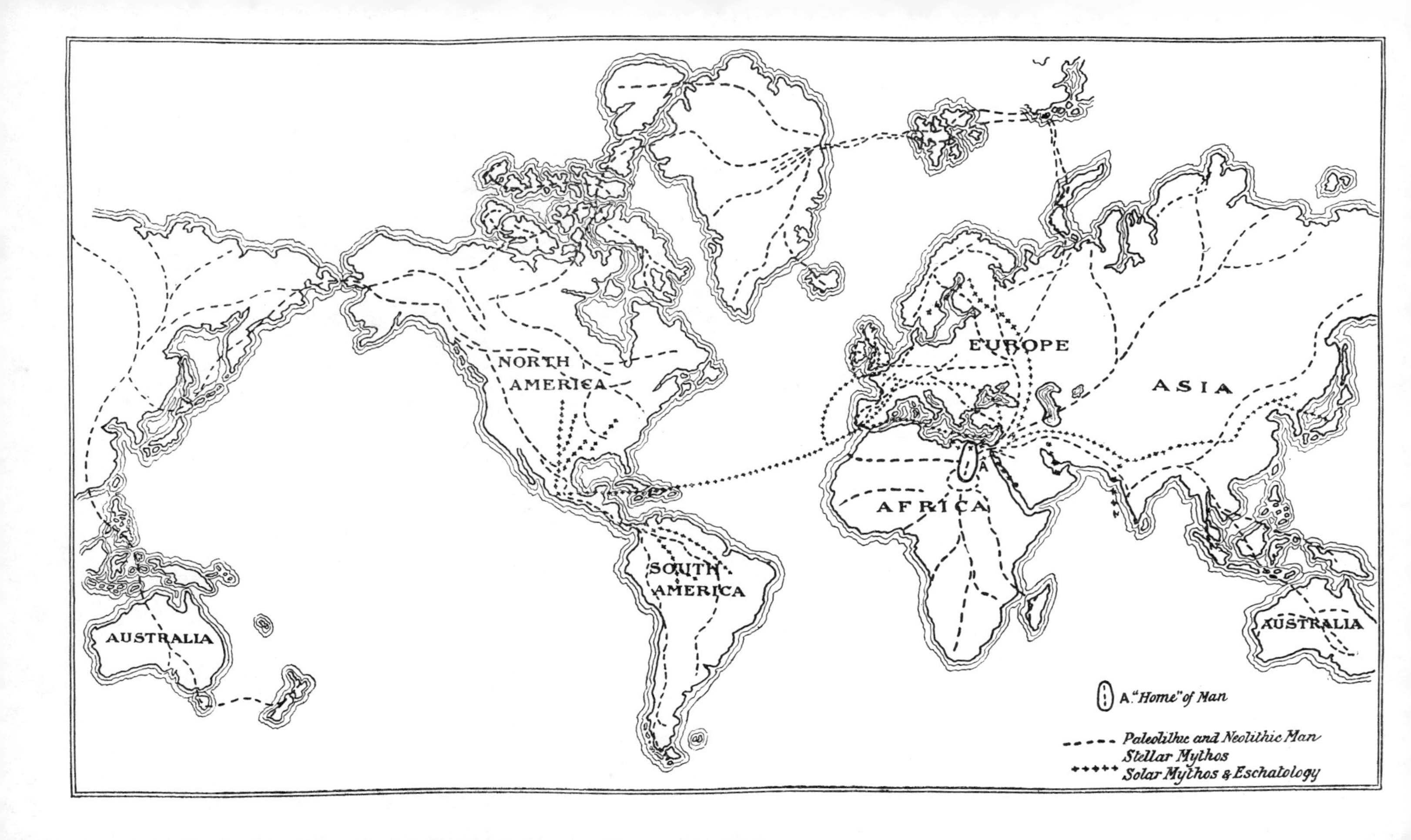
NORTH AMERICA
SOUTH AMERICA
EUROPE
ASIA
AFRICA
AUSTRALIA
AUSTRALIA
A
A. "Home" of Man
Paleolithic and Neolithic Man
Stellar Mythos
Solar Mythos & Eschatology

EXPLANATION OF MAP

The Red Man or "the little Earth Men"—as some authorities object to the term "Red Man" or paleolithic Man (rough stone age)—made the first exodes from Egypt and the Nile Valley. These were negroid pygmies such as we find in the Congo Forest and near the sources of the Nile. Remnants of them still exist in various parts of the world. The Tasmanians were of this type, and the inhabitants of Australia and New Zealand before they were exterminated by the present Aborigines; also the people who occupied Japan before the Ainu, remnants of whom are still found as "Tree Men" in various parts of the East of Asia and the Viddas of Ceylon. We find them also in Mexico and some parts of South America and remains of them are still to be found in the British Isles, North America and other parts of the world. They had an idea of a future life and of a divine being, but as far as can be traced they certainly had no Totemic Ceremonies, these were pre-Totemic.

In whatever part of the world we find the remains of these ancient people their Osteo-anatomy are all alike and correspond to the present pygmies. They are the oldest inhabitants of the world and belong to a primitive African Race before the last glacial period. They were a people of small stature and great muscular development. The suture in the frontal bone closed at an early age which prevented subsequent brain expansion. Thus their progress towards civilisation was slow. Their average cranial capacity was about 960 c.c. The oldest remains that have been found of the skeleton of man dates back as far as the pliocene period—from 650,000 to 800,000 years ago. In them we find the skulls dolichocephalic with markedly prominent superciliary ridges, receding brows, flattened vertex and projecting occiput, whilst the massive mandible sloped downwards and backwards anteriorly and was moreover wholly destitute of a chin. Later, in the skeletons that were found in the upper quaternary age, we find the receding forehead has become more prominent, less prominent supraorbital ridges and the flattened vertex higher, and we also find a well-marked chin;

all are of short stature and have marked prominences of muscular attachments, which proves them to have been endowed with great muscularity. Throughout the whole of the paleolithic age, man had time to mount up the ladder of evolution, and his skeleton which remains, as well as his industrial relics, furnish unmistakable evidence of that evolution.[1]

Of the exodes after the Pygmy there were at least two of the Nilotic Negroes, the first without Hero Cult, and the latter with Hero Cult.

The instruments found with the remains of these people are "chipped on each side, but not polished," as distinguished from those of the Pygmy race, whose instruments were chipped on one side only.

All these Nilotic Negroes had Totems and Totemic Ceremonies. They had no gods or goddesses, but believed in elementary powers with a Great Mother who brought them forth, believed in a spirit life hereafter, propitiated these elementary and ancestral spirits. After these came the Stellar Mythos people. There were at least two exodes of these; the first having Set as Primary God (God of the South Pole Star), and the second having Horus as Primary God (God of the Pole Star North). These divinised the elementary powers into gods and goddesses and gave them stars on high. Their primary implements are chipped on each side and polished. These were the first people to reckon time, which they did by observing and recording the precession of the 7 Pole Stars in Ursa Minor. Their buildings can always be distinguished from the Solar people who came after, *as the Stellar were iconographic, the Solar not.*

Whilst the Totemic people are found all over the world, the Stellar Cult people did not reach Australia, New Guinea, New Zealand or Tasmania, or extreme North of Asia, or North America, or farther South than Chile in South America; at least no remains of these people have yet been found in these countries. The Stellar people divinised the great Mother Earth and the 7 elementary powers of the Totemic people into the Great Mother Apt, who brought forth 7 sons which were assigned to stars in heaven as gods and were given consorts as goddesses, and later worked out the early part of the Christian doctrines—(as proved *supra*).

[1] See "Origin and Evolution of Primordial Man."

These are the people who left Egypt at the time of the Solar Mythos and perfected Eschatology, and were a higher developed race in every way. The Druids, Priests of Yucatan and Incas were some of them, and later Moses and his followers. Progressive evolution had developed in Egypt all the great civilisation which we know they possessed. Their mental and physical culture were at this time the highest type this earth had seen. These in their turn gradually obliterated and drove farther and farther away all those of the Stellar Mythos or absorbed them, wherever they came in contact, and the Solar thus superseded the Stellar. The reader must remember, however, that the " lines of distinction " were not made suddenly; it was only by progressive knowledge and development that the changes took place, and that the one always overlapped the other, carrying the earlier signs and symbols with them. Their average cranial capacity was from 1220 c.c. to 1500 c.c.

Also these exodes may be divided into two, roughly classified :—

1st. Those of the Stellar Mythos having legends and myths of having *descended* from the Celestial Mount, or the summit of the Mount which was an image of the Pole.

The races of man who descended from the Mount were people of the Pole whose starting point in reckoning time was from one or other stations of the Pole Star, determinable by its type—as the Tree or Turtle, or other image of a first point of departure, and their traditions, found in various countries, are that they were born when no Sun or Moon as yet had come into existence —*i.e.* they were pre-solar and pre-lunar in reckoning of time, and in their legendary lore try to tell us from which of the 7 stations they descended, as a time-gauge in the prehistoric reckoning of their beginnings, and which can be worked out fairly accurately by Astronomers who can understand their Mythos, and recognise their Zootype totem astronomically.

2nd. Those of the Solar Mythos *ascended* from the hollow underworld, beneath the Mount, or inside the Earth, which had been hollowed out beneath the Mount for the passage of the Sun by Ptah and his 7 Assistants, the human ascent being figured in the upward pathway of the Sun.

They were the Solar race who came into existence with the Sun as it is represented in the legendary lore—*i.e.* when the Solar Mythos was established.

Thus then, are two points of departure in the Astronomical Mythology, one from above, one from below. The oldest races that have kept their reckonings are *descended* from one or other of the 7 stations in the Mount of the North, and in the later Mythos men *ascended* from the earth below, or from below the earth.

All this can only be traced back to the Ancient Egyptians, and explanations found only in the *Ritual,* and Monuments. No other origin can be possible.

In this map the present positions of lands and water are depicted as we now know them, but no geologist, or we suppose anyone else would overlook the fact that ages ago the earth's surface was different. Geology proves this most conclusively and shows us that at one time the continents of Africa and South America were connected.

APPENDIX TO CHAPTER II

At the same time, no doubt it will be interesting to my brother Masons for me to give them a short review of the ideas and beliefs of other Masonic authors.

There are authors who attribute the origin of modern Freemasonry to the followers of *Pythagoras*, because some of the speculations of that philosopher concerning the meaning of numbers are to be found in the esoteric doctrines taught in Masonic Lodges. Others, on account of the Christian symbols that have been incorporated in the decorating of things pertaining to Masonry, follow the Swedish system, and say that the Essenes and the first Christians founded it. Others, again, make it originate in the building of Solomon's Temple; many Jewish names, emblems, and legends, taken from the V.S.L., have found their way into the rites of Initiation in several degrees. Others state that it goes back to Adam; ask why—they do not know. *Thomas Payne* and those of his school say that the Druids were the fathers of the Craft, they being *supposed* worshippers of the sun, moon, and stars, these jewels of the firmament being represented on the ceilings of the Masonic Temples.

Dance of Villoison speaks of Herculanæum as its birthplace, because of the many similarities that existed between the collegia of the Romans, and the Lodges of the operative Masons of the Middle Ages. *Michael Andrew Ramsay*, a Scotch gentleman, in a discourse delivered in Paris, in 1740, suggested the possibility of the fraternity having its origin in the time of the Crusades among the Knights Templar, and explains it in this way: The Pope, Clement V., and Phillippe-le-bel, King of France, fearing the power of the Templars and coveting their immense wealth, resolved to destroy the Order. When, in 1308, Jacques de Molay, then Grand Master of the Order, was preparing an expedition to avenge the wrongs and disasters suffered by the Christians in the East, the Pope, the only Sovereign Power to which, in the spiritual, the Templars owed allegiance, enticed him to France. On his arrival he was received with every mark of friendship ; but soon after the King caused him to be arrested, together with some other dignitaries, accusing them of the most heinous crimes, imputing to them the secret rites of their initiation. By order of the Archbishop of Sens and his provincial council, Jacques de Molay, Guy of Auvergne, and several other officers of the Order were burned alive on 18th March 1314.

The Pope, by a Bull, dated 2nd April, and published on the 2nd of May 1312, that he issued on his own responsibility—the Council of Vienne, in Dauphiné, being averse to hasty measures—declared the Order abolished throughout the world. The execution of the Grand Master and his companions gave the *coup de grâce* to the Order, but some of the Knights who had escaped to Portugal continued the Order. They assumed the title of Knights of Christ, which the Order still bears. Jacques de Molay, before his death, had appointed Johan, Marcus Larmenio, as his successor to the office of Grand Master. The Knights, who, fleeing from the persecution, had taken refuge in Scotland at the Court of King Robert Bruce, refused to recognise his authority ; and pretending to re-establish the Order of the Temple, under the allegory and title of Architects, protected by the King, laid the foundation of the Order of Free and Accepted Masons of the Scottish Rite, in 1314.

The new society soon forgot the meaning of the execratory oath that the members were obliged to take at their initiation ; the death of Clement V., of Phillippe-le-bel, of the accusers and enemies of Jacques de Molay, and the other Knights who had been executed, having removed the object of their vengeance. Still they continued to decorate their Lodges with tokens commemorative of the death of the Grand Master, and to impose on all new members the obligation of avenging it, which they signified by striking with an unsheathed dagger at unseen beings, his supposed murderers. This allegory is well known to the Knights of Kadosh. A century had scarcely elapsed when this idea was abandoned—the founders and their disciples having passed away, their successors saw only allegories in the Symbols of the Order—and the extensive use of words and texts taken from the Bible was then introduced. Little is known of the work until the reign of Charles I., when their mysterious initiations began to attract attention.

The enemies of Cromwell and of the Republic, having in view the re-establishment of the monarchy, created the Degree of Grand Master to prepare the minds of the masses for that event. King William III. was initiated.

Masonry, says *Preston*, was very much neglected as early as the reign of James II., and even after this period it made but slow progress until 1714, when King George I. ascended the throne. Three years later, in February 1717, the first Grand Lodge was established in London. A committee from the four Lodges then existing in that city met at the tavern of the "Apple Tree," and nominated Anthony Sayer, who was elected Grand Master, on the 24th of the following June, the day of St John the Baptist, and for that reason St John was selected as the patron of the Order.

This origin of the Craft is credited by many authorities on the subject. They found their opinion on the fact that many of the ceremonies practised by the "Architects" are still observed among Masons, and that the Grand Lodge preserved the fundamental laws, together with the spirit of the ancient Brotherhood. Others, who claim to be well informed, are of opinion that it did not originate in any Order of Chivalry, but in the building fraternities of the Middle Ages.

From 1738, however, Lodges sprang up over Europe at a rapid rate, notwithstanding the bitter opposition of the Church of Rome, which fulminated against it in most terrible anathemas, as early as 1738, at the instigation of the Inquisition. Pope Clement XII., on the 28th of April of that year, caused a prohibitory Bull to be issued against Freemasons, entitled, "In Eminenti," in which he excommunicated all Masons; and the Cardinal Vicar of Rome, by edict, in the name of the High Priest of the God of Peace and Mercy, decreed the penalty of death against them in 1739; and in May 1751 Pope Benoit XIV. renewed the Bull of Clement XII. by another, beginning with these words: "Providas Romanorum Pontificum."

Lodges were established in France in 1725, and on the 14th September 1732 all Masonic Associations were prohibited by a decree of the Chamber of Police of the Châtelet of Paris.

In 1727 Lord Coleraine founded a Lodge in Gibraltar, and in the succeeding year in Madrid, the capital of Spain, the stronghold of the Inquisition.

In 1740, in consequence of the Bull of Clement XII., King Philip V. of Spain promulgated an order against Masons in his kingdom, many of whom were arrested and sent to the galleys. The Inquisitors took advantage of the opportunity to persecute the members of a Lodge they discovered in Madrid. They caused them to be loaded with chains, to be obliged to row in the galleys, with a scanty supply of food of the poorest quality, but plenty of bastinado. King Fernando VI. renewed the ordinance on 2nd July 1751, making Masonry high treason.

In 1735 a Lodge was established at Lisbon, the capital of Portugal, by some of the Knights Templar who fled there, under the title of "Knights of Christ." These have kept alive the ancient Order in defiance of the Pope's Bulls.

In 1730 a great many Germans were initiated in England. In 1733 the Grand Master, Lord Strathmore, authorised eleven of the Brotherhood to open the Hamburg Lodge. In 1740 B. Puttman, of the Hamburg Lodge, received a Patent of Provincial Grand Master from England, and the Lodge assumed the title of Absalom. King Frederick II., who had been initiated when Crown Prince of Prussia, continued to give support, and assumed the title of "Great Master Universal, and Conservator of the Most Ancient and Most Respectable Association of Ancient Freemasons or Architects of Scotland." He cemented together again the Order, which had become scattered, so far as he was able, and signed the Constitution in his Palace, at Berlin, 1st May 1786, which saved Freemasonry from annihilation in Germany.

I. G. Findel was a great advocate that Freemasonry was not derived from the mysteries of the ancients ; he says : "Seeing that the ancient symbolical marks and ceremonies in the Lodges bear very striking resemblance to those of the mysteries of the ancients, some have allowed themselves to be deceived, and led others astray, imagining they can trace back the history of the Craft into the cloudy mist of antiquity ; instead of endeavouring to ascertain how and when these ceremonies were introduced into our present system, they have taken it for granted that they were derived from the religious mysteries of the ancients."

Now I propose to take *I. G. Findel* at his word, and trace these mysteries, for the information of the Brotherhood throughout the world; and having done so, I feel sure that he will modify his expressed opinion.

"The cloudy mists of antiquity" may no longer remain; within the past few years we have discovered how to decipher and read the ancient writings on the walls of old ruined temples and cities in Africa, Asia, and North, Central, and South America, as well as the ancient writings on papyri, and these give the key to unlock the mysteries of the past and reveal the origin of our Signs, Symbols, and Rituals; and these I trace back to Ancient Egypt, and in no other part of the world can the origins be found.

If we take the theory propounded by *Krause*, what do we find? He has endeavoured to prove that Freemasonry "originated" in the association of operative Masons, who, in the Middle Ages, travelled through Europe, and by whom the Cathedrals and Monasteries were built. Granting that these associations spring from the building Corporations of the Romans, to what does it point? The initiates of the Architectural Colleges of the Romans did not, however, call themselves Brothers or Companions; they were styled Collega or Incorporatus. These Colleges held Lodges wherever they established themselves, had signs, symbols, tokens, and passwords, which they had learnt and received from the Chaldean Magicians who flocked to Rome at the beginning of the Christian era. These Chaldean or Turanian Priests, nevertheless, were of inferior order, and had been initiated into part of the lesser mysteries of the Egyptians only. In fact, they were the working or operative Masons of the old Egyptian Stellar Mythos Cult, from the seventeenth Nome of Upper Egypt, and were styled Craftsmen (see *Ritual*). Many of these working or operative Masons still exist here in this country; they were initiated in the 1st and 2nd degrees only of the old Egyptian Cult, because they, and they alone, were employed to look after the building of the Temples and keep the secrets of the same.

These Turanians, who were called "Craftsmen" in Egyptian, only knew the secrets of two of the degrees out of the Seven Primary Mysteries, which were Astro-Mythological. We ordinary Masons, M.M. and up to P.Z., only have these Seven

Mysteries. The Greater Mysteries belong to the Egyptian Eschatology, and were ten in number. (See later.)

If we trace these old Turanians (operative) back to Egypt, we find them well established at the commencement of the Stellar Cult—but it is possible to trace them farther back than this, even to Early Totemic Sociology.

In Africa, at the present day, there exist some of the Nilotic Negroes, descendants of those who first formed the "Nomes" in Egypt; those who formed the seventeenth Nome are now "the Elgunono." These tribes still, at the present time, are mostly formed into a "secret brotherhood," and by some are called the Blacksmiths. "Horus-Behutet," the first worker in metals, is their chief or head Deity; our word T.C. is thus a substituted word. Their chief priest is called Ol-Aibon, and they still have many of the primary Symbols and Signs we use. These, with the Madi (who were the first builders) and Masai, ultimately all settled in Egypt and formed the early Stellar Mythos people. The early exodus of these tribes, to other parts of the world, were the old Turanians.

The Stellar Cult existed for at least 300,000 years, as witnessed by records found and still extant; they travelled and went out over Europe, Asia, part of North and South America, Central America, and the Islands of the Pacific, as well as Africa. The remains and ruins of the large cities and Temples found throughout the world were mostly built by these people. The Solar, who came after, built some, but the buildings of each are easily distinguished one from the other. The former were iconographic, the latter were not. They worked out all the revolutions of the Sun, Moon, and Stars, and the *Ritual* of Ancient Egypt upon which all doctrines throughout the world have been founded. So that for the oldest records of our Brotherhood we have to go back as far as Totemic Sociology over 800,000 years. This is proved by the fact that six skeletons of Stellar Mythos people were found in Lombardy in the Pliocene strata—and the above is a low estimate for that.

Now we find from these old Temples that all our Signs and Symbols were in use then just as we use them now; there is no difference, except that in some cases we have slightly modernised them. Their Rituals, with slight modifications, were the same as ours. (Proofs later.)

Here we see *Krause's* theory not without some semblance of plausibility, as Rome, during several centuries, held sway over Gaul and Britain. Roman colonists settled in various parts of these countries, and with their language and customs they imported many of their institutions and associations. That of the Builders, or Collegia, held their Lodges wherever they established themselves, and no doubt initiated new members, and as these countries freed themselves from the yoke of Rome the associations would still remain in these countries. But these at best were only carriers of the " operative masons "—Egypt was their birthplace, and we can identify the Nome as the seventeenth Nome from the *Ritual*, these names, for instance, " Craftsmen "—carried out of Egypt by the Turanians, who spread over Europe ; Asia, except the North ; lower part of North America, Central America, South America, as far down as Chile, in the Caroline Islands of the Pacific—but not in North of Asia, Australia, Tasmania, or extreme North America.

Chevalier Ramsay stated that modern Masonry had its beginning in the Society of Architects founded in Scotland under the protection of King Robert Bruce, and the title of " Ancient and Accepted Masons of the Scottish Rite " may possibly have been formed in Scotland there and then, but, if that is so, we must trace the origin of this to the Order of Knights Templar, who fled to Scotland (see *supra*), and through them to the Ancient Mysteries practised in the East. From whence did these Templars obtain them ? It is well known that one of the charges made against Jacques de Molay and his associates by their accusers was that " they used sacred rites in their initiations." Their four oaths are well known, but who knew their rites of initiation ? The aim of the Society of Architects was to perpetuate the ancient Order of the Temple, and they continued to use their initiations of members, symbols, signs, and some parts of the initiatory rites, which had been obtained in the East, but they only knew three degrees out of the seven lesser and ten greater. The next question is, From whence did the Templars receive those symbols, and their esoteric meaning, in which we plainly trace the doctrines of the old Egyptians ? No doubt from the Christians, who, like the Emperor Julian, the Bishop of Synnesius, Clement of Alexandria, and many other philosophers, who had been initiated to some of the mysteries by the

Priests of Egypt before being converted to Christianity. In this way may be traced how part of the religious mysteries of Egypt, signs and symbols, etc., came to Scotland.

We must remember that the mysteries practised by the Samothracia Greeks, Romans, Pythagoreans, the mysteries of *Eleusis*, the mysteries established by *Zoroaster*, and the Mahatmas, or Brothers of India, all took their origin from the Egyptian Eschatology. We see also from the above how, in one way, the so-called Higher Degrees (The Ten Greater Mysteries) were introduced here in Britain.

The reluctance of the Egyptians to admit strangers to the holy secret of their mysteries was for a very long time insuperable. They, however, at intervals, admitted to the 1st and 2nd degrees personages noted for their wisdom and knowledge. They admitted the great philosopher *Thales*, who went to Egypt to learn Geometry and Astronomy about 587 B.C., and *Zoroaster*, 5000 B.C. Another was Eumolpus, King Eleusis, who, on returning to his country, instituted the mysteries of that name, which he had learnt from the Priests of Egypt. *Orpheus*, the Greek poet, was also initiated into the 1st degree. *Pythagoras* was initiated, but had not the courage to go through to the 3rd degree, only the 1st and 2nd. The Pelasgians had initiated to the 1st and 2nd degrees the Samothracia. These Pelasgians obtained their knowledge from the Egyptian Priests direct.

We must remember that from the downfall of the old Egyptian Empire, five thousand years ago, up to within the last two hundred years, we have passed through a dark and degenerate age. There was no history that we could read; our History of the World is quite recent, all the rest is tradition only. Therefore, if you do not read the Hieroglyphics and Glyphs, "The Writings on the Wall," you still remain in ignorance of the history of the human race, and of the origin and antiquity of Freemasonry. There were no records left otherwise than these. But these records have been left for the future student to decipher and translate. What records will be left in these Islands after another twenty thousand years have passed, or less?

One might say that for five thousand years there was no literature left that could be read and properly understood. The Greeks, who have been much over-estimated, and who obtained their knowledge partly through the Pelasgians and

Samothracia, and partly through a few of the best-informed Greeks, who went to Egypt, and were there initiated into the 1st degree of the Lesser Mysteries by the Egyptian Priests, never understood the Eschatology, could not read or speak the Egyptian language, and in their ignorance perverted all that had been told to them. Then, as far as our Sacred Volume is concerned, you must remember it was not until *Luther's* time did we have, speaking generally, any of these Esoteric writings to study, except a few extracts given out by the Roman Priests, and even then the Esoteric representations were not known, and it is only during the last few hundred years that we have kept written records of anything.

The word "Freemason" is not met with in MS. until 1376, and the oldest Lodge records in 1598, in this country. Again, is it reasonable to suppose that the huge continents of North and South America have lain incognito by the great communities of Europe, Asia, and Africa until the yesterday of Columbus; unknown throughout the ages of vast time that man has existed? Columbus reached America less than five centuries ago, and Eric the Red and his early Norsemen in 983. *The Chinese have written records of trading with America in* 500 B.C., *and sending some of their Buddhist Priests there, who returned with the news that they had met Priests with religious writings, signs and symbols similar to their own,* which, you may see by my "Origin and Evolution of the Human Race," had been established in America at least 300,000 years before this. Let me also state here that there is no question of "having one's faith shaken," as I heard one Brother remark to another after my lecture before the Dorset Masters' Lodge. What I write and state for all my Brothers throughout the world is *The Truth. That is what you want to know; that is what you are all striving to obtain,* and if you follow the evolution of the human race in all its phases, you will obtain it, but not otherwise. Then, instead of having your faith shaken, you will find, on the contrary, it will be considerably strengthened.

Many of our Brothers, some of them very eminent and learned divines, have stated, and no doubt they would not make the statement if they did not believe it: That Freemasonry is not a religion. My contention is that Freemasonry is the greatest, truest, and purest religion in the world, for these reasons: (1) Religion proper commences with, and must include, the idea or desire and belief for another life; (2) This belief in another life is founded on the belief of the resurrection of the spirit; (3) We all believe in one great God, Divine Creator of the Universe—The Great Architect of the Universe; (4) Therefore, we all believe in the rising again of the human soul, emerging alive from the body of dead matter. This body of dead matter could not come back or rise again, but the spirit could; (5) In our teachings, in our forms and ceremonies, which are dramatically performed, we are taught how we should live in this world, and how we should die, to attain that great and everlasting life and happiness which is the one object all the brotherhood profess and desire to attain. Therefore this is the greatest, truest, and purest religion in the world, void of all dogmas; one on which humanity can work together in perfect harmony, and one on which there cannot be any dissensions to disturb the fraternal feelings which should always exist between the brotherhood. May it ever continue to be the same.

By going back to primitive man, the Pygmy, we find the first symbol we use. He believed in a Supreme Spirit and propitiated elemental powers. In the next stage of the Nilotic Negro we find more of our Signs and Symbols originated. In the next stage of Totemic Sociology, and the commencement of the Stellar Cult, we have still many more Signs, Symbols and Rites of our Order, and the whole tale of the Christian doctrines founded. Because it was amongst the Masai group in Inner Africa that the tradition arose, and *is still extant, that the Man-God came from Heaven, suffered, and was crucified and rose again.* We must remember that man at this time had very few words to express his ideas and beliefs; it was done by signs and symbols, and Sign Language, and although this has been lost for thousands of years, it is now being rediscovered by men who can read this Sign Language. The Solar Cult and the Christian Cult, which have followed one another, have not in either case altered the tale, it is all one and the same from the beginning; that names have altered is nothing, different languages have different names for the same idea, and because the attributes of the One Great God were expressed in "Zootype form" during the Stellar Cult, and "Gods and Goddesses" in the Solar, whilst at the present day these are expressed in words, does not alter the meaning, ideas, or beliefs ; these are only altered and misunderstood by men who cannot read and understand "The Writings on the Walls" ; and as regards dates, few, I believe, now would even think or believe that man has only existed about six thousand years, as assumed from Biblical tradition, when we find the skeletons of the present type of man in strata of the Pliocene age, 800,000 years old at least. Therefore whatever Cult our Brothers may have belief in, the knowledge of the evolution of the human race would only be a greater factor to strengthen his belief. If we take the Chinese, and there are many Brothers amongst them, we know that they went out from Egypt during the Stellar Cult, and they have never risen in evolution since. The Hindu left at the time of the Solar Cult ; he has always remained the same. The white race, generally, left at the end of the Solar and beginning of the Christian. The early Copts were the first of the Christians in evolution, and the white man has gradually developed into a higher type of the human. With this development into a higher type of man, so have his spiritual ideas developed into a so-called higher type of Christianity than that which we find at the commencement of the time of the early Copts. Yet it is all one and the same from the beginning, under different names. The original Signs and Symbols which our early Brothers had to use in place of words, which they had not, have now given place to expressions in linguistic and grammatical form, of which he was, at that time, still ignorant. I am bound to bring this before my Brothers because I wish to assure them that I have no intention or wish to shake their faith in the Volume of the Sacred Law, but, quite on the contrary, wish to establish their faith still firmer, more especially those who profess the Christian doctrines, by proving that these are the highest point of the religious conception of the human in his progressive evolution. At the same time I would say to my other Brothers who do not yet believe in the Christian Cult : Continue in your faith, it is one and the same as ours, only in a more primitive form. Now let us consider the proofs of the same.

APPENDIX TO CHAPTER IV

I QUOTE from my late dear friend, *Gerald Massey's* great work, "Ancient Egypt," as regards circumcision and subincision: The change from the human descent from the Mother-blood to the Father-blood is obviously commemorated in the Mysteries or ceremonial rites of the Arunta. In the operation of young-men-making two modes of cutting are performed upon the boy, by which he becomes a man and a tribal father. The first of these is commonly known as circumcision, or lartna, by the Arunta; the other ceremony of initiation which comes later, is the rite of subincision called ariltha. The second cutting is necessary for the completion of the perfect man—with this trial test the youth becomes a man; a fathership is founded, and as certain customs show, the Motherhood is in a measure cast off at the time, or typically superseded by the fatherhood. Nature led the way for the opening rite performed upon the female, therefore we conclude that this preceded the operation performed upon the men, and we suggest that this was a custom established, like the couvade, in the course of commemorating the change from the Matriachate to the Father-right,—When the Arunta perform the rite of subincision, which follows that of the primary operation (circumcision), a slit is cut in the penis right down to the root. (The natives have no idea of the origin of the practice—N.T.P. 263). But as the practice proves it is performed as an assertion of manhood, and is a mode of making the boy into a man, or creating man. Now, at this time it was customary to cast the Motherhood aside by some significant action, that is at the time when the fathership is established in the initiation ceremony. And in the Arunta rite of subincision the operating Mura first of all cuts out an *oval-shaped* piece of skin from the male member *which he flings away*. The *oval shape* is an emblem of the female all the world over, and this we take to be another mode of rejecting the mother and of attributing begettal to the father, as it was attributed in the ceration by Atum-Ra who was both male and female (as the one " All Parent ").

From the " cutting " of the male member now attributed to Atum-Ra, we infer that the rite of circumcision and of sub-incision was a mode of showing the derivation from the human father in supersession of the Motherhood, and that in the Arunta double cutting the figure of the female was added to the member of the male. Nor is this suggestion without corroboration. In his ethnological studies (p. 180) *Dr Roth* explains that in the Pitta-Pitta and cognate Boulia dialects, the term Me-ko ma-ro denotes the man with a Vulva, which shows that the oval slit *was cut* upon the penis as a figure of the female, and a mode of assuming the Motherhood. In the Hebrew Book of Genesis this carving of the female figure on the person of the male—in the second creation—has been given the legendary form of cutting out the woman from the body of the male. Adam is thus imaged as a biun parent=Atum Ra.

APPENDIX TO CHAPTER V

To understand the interpretation of this Totemic ceremony we must go back to old Egypt—the primary fight between Light and Darkness, when the latter is represented by the zootype of a gigantic serpent, which hides within the earthly Nile and devours the banks during inundation, coming forth at times from the depths of the waters to rise in the path of the God of Light.

At the turn of the eclipse men cried aloud, they were beside themselves with excitement, beating their breasts, sounding their instruments and striking upon all their drums, throwing their spears and shooting their arrows into the air, etc., that their clamour might terrify the monster, so as the eclipse passed away the monster fell back into the abyss of water again, until the next period. This monster serpent dwells in the bottom of the river. The tradition or belief still exists amongst some of the people in Egypt at the present day. *Maspero* states: "In Upper Egypt there is a widespread belief in the existence of a monstrous serpent which dwells at the bottom of the river, and is the genius of the Nile. It is he who brings about the falls of earth at the decline of the inundation which often destroys the banks and 'eat' whole fields. At such times offerings of dura, fowls and ducks are made to him, that his hunger may be appeased, and it is not only the natives who give themselves up to these superstitious practices."

Part of the grounds belonging to the Karnak Hotel at Luxor having been carried away during the autumn of 1884, the manager—a Greek—made the customary offerings to the serpent of the Nile.

This is the Great Apap or Great Gigantic Serpent which hides within the earthly Nile, and devours its banks and comes forth to war against "Light," so they propitiate the power of darkness.

This Great Evil Serpent of Totemic Sociology must not be confounded with the zootype serpent which represented Rannut, as the Mother Earth, found amongst the Dinkas, Masai and other tribes throughout the world, which afterwards, in Stellar Mythos, was brought on to symbolically represent Tern.

These Australians use the words, " Ara Tapa tyiri ai," which they have forgotten the meaning of (S. and G. U. T.). This is pure old Egyptian ; and means " The Chief of the Red Crown made, or constructed, another burial place for the Snake."

This photograph should be interesting to Brothers of 18°, as it shows the primitive origin of part of one of their ceremonies.

The above shows part of an initiation ceremony called the " Bora " of the aboriginal tribes of New South Wales ; all the members of this society are pledged to secrecy. The penalty for any breach of its rules is death. We see here several members with spears and boomerangs or clubs, etc., " forming an arch over a representation of a dead body," a " valley of death as here represented." At the far end is the " Conductor " of the Initiate (who is not here shown). The Initiate is conducted through this Valley of Death and has to undergo trials, etc., as he passes through or by each Brother. His conductor carries implements of power and might to ward the danger off. As he comes to each they say: "I will not let thee pass until you give me the word"—with threats of death. The word is given and passes. It is a primitive, symbolic and dramatic form of passing through the underworld. He is initiated into the passage of the dead to the Spirit world, a Totemic form of the "abyss" of the Stellar and Lunar Cult people, and Amenta of the Solar. This picture depicts the first primitive form of the ideas and beliefs which were afterwards, during the evolution of the human race, finally formed into their Eschatology.

APPENDIX TO CHAPTER VI

PERHAPS it would be more convenient for my readers if I put in a tabulated form the origin and evolution of "The Mother," it being understood that Totemism preceded Mythology.

Primarily it was the Old Mother Earth in Totemism and Totemic Sociology, which I have given; represented in the Egyptian by *Ta-Urt* (see *Dr Budge's* "Gods of the Egyptians," vol. ii. page 30). *Ta-Urt=The Great Mother Earth,* was the first form of Isis—the first and earliest mother. This is proved by *Professor Maspero* (see "Dawn of Civilisation," page 99):

"*Isis of Buto* denoted the black vegetable mould of the valley, the distinctive soil of Egypt annually covered and fertilised by the inundation which brought forth their food of life."

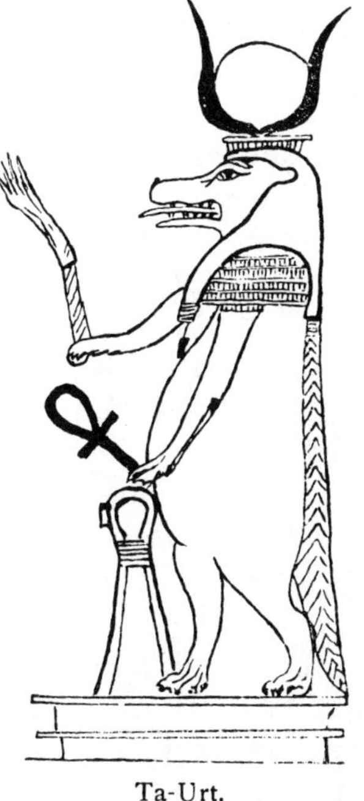
Ta-Urt.

As the *Goddess Mirit,* she represented the inundation or the water of life, so we have here Isis in her first forms as supplier of food and water of life,—she is also represented as goddess of Fire, Darkness, Wind, Light and Blood, in different forms under different names. Here she is represented as of no sex, and reproduces no children, male or female, but is the supplier of food and giver of life, as represented by the seven Elemental Powers:

1. Fire. 2. Darkness. 3. Light. 4. Water. 5. Earth. 6. Blood. 7. Wind, or breathing force of Air-Lifter of Clouds of Darkness, etc.

Ta-Urt=the Great Mother Earth. The primitive Earth Mother of African origin still survives in Africa as the Earth

Goddess *Nzambi,* "The Great Mother." Nkissi-Nsi or "The Mystery of the Power of Earth" is another African name=Kep (Egyptian)=name of the old Earth Mother—Ta-Urt.

Amongst the Peruvian tribes her name is *Mamapocha,* signifying mystery, mysterious, mystery of fermentation—fertilisation, etc.

Amongst the Moqui Indians—Mother Earth is the Great Mother.

Amongst the Finns—"*Ukko*" is their Goddess Mother Earth.

Amongst the Esquimaux—"*Gigone*" is their Mother Earth Goddess.

Amongst the Khonds of Orissa—"*Tari-Pennu*" is their Mother Earth Goddess.

Amongst the Greeks—"*Gae*" is their Mother Earth Goddess.

Amongst the Romans—"*Opus*"=to Apt Egyptian, is their Mother Earth Goddess.

With the Shawonees—"*Our Grandmother*" is their Mother Earth Goddess.

With the Karens in Burmah—"*Our Grandmother*" is their Mother Earth Goddess.

With the Arunta—the "*Erathepa-Stones*" are their Totem for their Great Mother.

With Figians—"*Pillar Stones*" are their Totem for their Great Mother.

With Babylonians "*Omoroca*" was their Totem for their Great Mother.

In the later part of Totemism and commencement of Mythology she (Ta-Urt), was divinised, and called Apt, and given a place on high, in heaven, situated at the Haunch (part of the Great Bear) and brought forth 7 children—three at first, Sut or Set, Horus and Shu; these then became the "Heroes" of *Dr Haddon,* and in those of the second, a last exodus of the Nilotic Negro, they play an important part in the folklore tales, which *Dr Haddon* has termed Hero Cult (personally I think it is a good term, because it coincides with the tradition of *Manetho* (see later). The Great Mother was now represented by the Egyptians as the Great Mother Apt or Mut: the Mythical Great Mother, also a type of Isis. Astronomically (see *Dr Budge's* "Gods of the Egyptians," vol. ii. page 29) Apt is represented as Male and Female, both in one, and her children are called "the Bull of their Mother."

All the 7 Elemental Powers were now divinised and represented by 7 gods. There are two lists of these, which I here give. These were given stars on high and represented the 7 Pole Stars, and were called *The Glorious Ones* in Stellar Mythos. So we have the *Heroes* and *Glorious Ones of Manetho*; as well as the *Glorified Spirits*, the latter who had once been men, the former were mythical, and had not, nor ever could be, human. The Glorified Spirits were the spirits of their ancestors who had lived here on Earth and risen again after the death of the corpus.

The Heroes and Glorious Ones were the Mythical Gods, or divinised elementary powers, who had never lived or reigned as man or woman, and never could, and it is in the mixing of these, without understanding the gnosis, that the Hindus have gone wrong in their decipherment of the *Ritual* of Ancient Egypt; so, too, the Hebrew translators of the Bible, when they mention that the "sons of God saw the daughters of men that they were fair; and they took them wives of all which they chose" (Genesis), and "the sons of God came in unto the daughters of men, and they bare children to them." He thus mixes the mythical gods with the human woman!

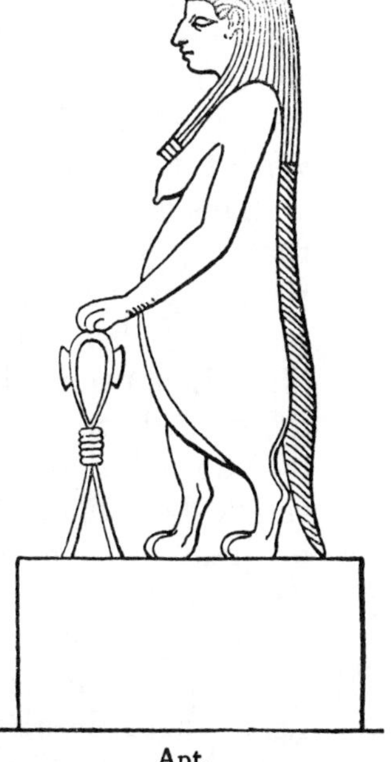

Apt.

The worship and the propitiation of the Glorified Spirits is what is called *Ancestral Worship.* One of the earliest phases of representation was the twins born of the Great Mother Apt—her two first-born, Sut and Horus: as the primary elemental powers, Light and Darkness. Sut was the Power of Darkness. Horus the Power of Light. These were first imaged in Zootype form as the black bird of Sut and the White Bird or Golden Eagle of Horus. *These are the two oldest types of the elemental Powers in universal Mythology* and were afterwards divinised as the two gods, Sut and Horus, with the two birds, dark and light, the Black Vulture and the Golden Eagle, depicted back to back as their two representative types of personal Totems.

The crow and eagle hawk are equivalent to these two birds of darkness and light amongst the Australians, and according to their traditions the eagle hawk and crow were first amongst the ancestors of the human race. These are the first two of the elemental powers which became non-human ancestors in Mythology. They are also known as creators who divided the Murry Blacks into two classes or Brotherhoods, Totems of which were the eagle-hawk and crow, and who now shine as stars in the sky (*Brough Smyth*, vol. i. pp. 423-431). In Western Australia these are represented as the Black Cockatoo and the White Cockatoo, the two Totems of the Mukjarawamt. Amongst the Zulu the legend is that two mothers in a bed of reeds brought forth two children, one black, one white. This is Mother-Earth who had been duplicated in the two mothers who brought forth in space, when this was first divided into night and day.

This is the earliest battle between Horus and Sut and shows that the beginning of Mythology had already commenced; this the Egyptians founded on facts that they had observed in ever-recurring phenomena of external nature, and then expressed in Sign Language. In the beginning was the void, otherwise designated the Abyss. Darkness being the primordial condition, it followed that the earliest type in mythical representation should be a figure of darkness. This was the Mythical Dragon or Great Serpent Apap, the devouring reptile, the monster which swallowed all the light and all the water, the prototype of evil in external nature which rose up by night from the Abyss and coiled about the Mount of Earth, to devour all light, and as the fiery dragon drank up all the water, whose voice was the thunder that shook the firmament (*Ritual*, chap. xxxix.). Other powers born of the void were likewise elemental wicked spirits called in the *Ritual* the Sami, demons of darkness or the wicked Sebau, who for ever rose in impotent revolt against the powers that wrought for good. These were of no sex and they supplied fiends and evil spirits to later folklore tales.

Sex was not introduced until later. As the first Great Mother Earth, her type was the water-cow and her children were the elemental powers or forces—wind, water, earth and fire, etc.—not to be confused with the evil progeny of Apap; both are elemental in their origin, but one is baneful, the later is beneficent.

Duff Macdonald found the same legend amongst the Central African natives. This is universally found throughout the world in many phases, but all represent the powers of darkness and daylight, portrayed in Egypt as the Sut and Horus twins, the two first souls that were derived as elementals.

The next elemental male soul was assigned to Shu, the God of breathing force. In *Ritual*, chap. lv.: "I am Shu, who conveys the breezes or breathings: I give air to these younglings as I open my mouth."

Messrs *Spencer* and *Gillen* have shown that the Arunta tribe of Central Australia do not, as yet, ascribe the begettal of a human soul to the male parent. They believe that the soul is incorporated from elements of external nature, such as wind or water—"Spirit children," derivable from the air—and on seeing a whirlwind if the native woman does not wish to have a child she runs away and hides. It is the same as we find in old Egypt, where the Goddess Neith was impregnated by the wind—the insufflation of the female by the Spirit of Air. It was the elemental powers that supplied pre-human souls in the primitive stage of man—Totemic souls—that were common to the Totemic group of persons, plants, animals or stones, etc., when there was no one soul yet individualised from the rest as the human soul. These could not be "the souls of men" that were supposed to inhabit beasts, birds, reptiles, etc., because in old Totemic times there were no souls discreted from the pre-human souls.

It is these elemental souls that have been mixed up with the human soul by Hindus, Greeks, Buddhist and Pythagorean, and mistaken for the human soul in course of transmigration through the series, which were but representatives of souls that were distinguished as non-human by those who understood the Sign Language. There was not and never will be any transmigration of human souls. This is where the book of Enoch is wrong: "The sons of God who cohabited with the daughters of men." The writer of this book mixes the 7 Elemental Powers which were divinised, or mythical gods, with the human woman (!!), not understanding the Sign Language of the *Ritual*.

The first seven:

1. Fire.
2. Darkness.

3. Light.
4. Water.
5. Earth.
6. Blood.
7. Wind, or breathing force of Air-Lifter of Clouds of Darkness, etc.

These are the later representations of the first seven:

First List

1. " An-ar-ef, the Great " is his name (Horus).
2. Kat-Kat.
3. The Burning Bull, who liveth in his fire.
4. The Red-Eyed One in the House of Gauze.
5. Fiery face which turneth backwards.
6. Dark Face in its hour.
7. Seer in the Night.

Second List

1. Amsta.
2. Hapi.
3. Tuamuteef.
4. Habhrenuf.
5. Maa-tef-f.
6. Karbek-ef.
7. Har-Kheut-an-maa-ti (Horus).

In a later phase, in 17th chapter of the *Ritual,* we find that these were represented by the Little Bear Pole Stars:

1. In the Dragon.
2. One in the Lesser Bear.
3. One in Kephus.
4. One in Cygnus.
5. One in Tyra.
6. One in Corona Borealis.
7. One in Heackles.

The first four of the second list are the gods of the four quarters, who stand on the papyrus of earth and who become the children of Horus in a later creation.

Different Names of the Great Mother

1st Form, Ta-Urt Pre-Mythological and of no sex	= Isis of Buto = the Mother Earth. = Mirit = the Mother of water of life. The Nile goddess of water. = Ranuit, the August Lady of the double granary.
2nd Form, Apt Mythological and of both sexes	Mut. Mirit was brought on from the first form into that of the second, as she then gave birth to Sa = Son of the goddess of water (Ka sa Mirit).

In the Stellar Cult it was Sekhet, the goddess who conceived and Sebek-Nit who gave birth to Horus the Child.

In the Lunar the two women were Sati and Hathor.

In early Solar it was Nebt, Hetep and Insaaset.

In the late Solar or Osirian it was Isis and Nepthtyses.

In the Christian it was the Virgin Mary and Mary the wife of Cleophas.

In the Stellar Mythos. The 7 powers are represented by the Stars of Ursa Minor, and are called the 7 Glorious Ones with Horus.

In the Lunar. The 7 powers are the 7 Taasu with Taht.

In the Solar. The 7 powers are the 7 Khammu with Ptah.

In the Eschatology. The 7 powers are the 7 souls of Ra the Holy Spirit and the 7 souls glorified with Horus as the 8th in the resurrection of Amenta.

In the Christian. The 7 mentioned in Revelation.

APPENDIX TO CHAPTER VIII

Note to Fig. 81 [1913].—Since writing the first edition of this work I have found the following pure Egyptian Hieroglyphics depicted on the old temples in Central and South America.

= Mra or Mr-tar. It is the name or one of the names of Egypt I found in Peru.

= Auk or aux = life, living.

= name of countries.

= Sxt = take, to net.

= Hr = to open, to fight, to bind.

= Ha = ah ! oh ! time day.

= An = abode, name of Amen. Horus was the eldest son of Amen depicted as here (*Bun. Dict.*, p. 102).

= N = Pole or Tank.

= Ht = a mace.

= A later form of = Amsu or Horus in spirit form

= Sn=to open.

= Celestial Paradise of the North (*Perolt Dict.*).

APPENDICES TO CHAPTER IX

1. The Swastika, one of the symbols the Operative Mason uses, is the older form of our Tau or Cross. *It does not mean axial rotation, with reference to the Pole Star, nor was it ever a symbol of God himself, as Dr Carr and the Operative Masons assert Neither has the Pole Star North anything to do with El Shaddai. Set, of the Egyptians,* was the Primary God, and was God of the South Pole Star. The Pole Star North was assigned to Horus, when Horus became Primary God ; the change in Israel from the worship of El Shaddai to the worship of Ihuh (Hu or Iu, Egyptian), from the Eloistic to the Jehovistic God, corresponds to the change from the South Stellar to the North Stellar, and, later, the Solar..

The Swastika was the earliest representation of the four quarters, or Cross, and can be traced back to the one primitive form, which was two human figures crossed ; it is first found depicted on one of the seal cylinders found in a prehistoric grave at Nagada, dating back to the earliest Stellar Cult. These symbols represented the four quarters after the division of the three. These two figures were then blended into four, as seen cut on a sepulchral stone found at Meigle, in Perthshire. (See later.) The Mexican calendar in the form of Swastika Cross has the names of the four brothers or children of Horus, one on each arm, and these represent the four quarters or divisions of Heaven into North, South, East, and West, and were the four supports of Heaven as portrayed by the Square. This Swastika, therefore, represented the four quarters and not axis of rotation of the Pole Stars (Ursa Minor). *Nor was the Swastika itself ever a symbol or Ideograph for God Himself,* and I challenge all Operative Masons to bring forward any proof that it was so.

One of the earliest Ideographs for Set, El Shaddai, and Horus were the two Eyes, symbols of the two Pole Stars, North and South, originating at Apta, or at the Mount of the Equinox—Equatorial Africa. Another Ideograph was the two Poles—the

Pole or Pillar of the South, assigned to Set, and the Pillar or Pole of the North, assigned to Horus ; two of the Tatt Pillars (Fig. 5). The Ideograph for the name of Set, as El Shaddai, was as No. 1,

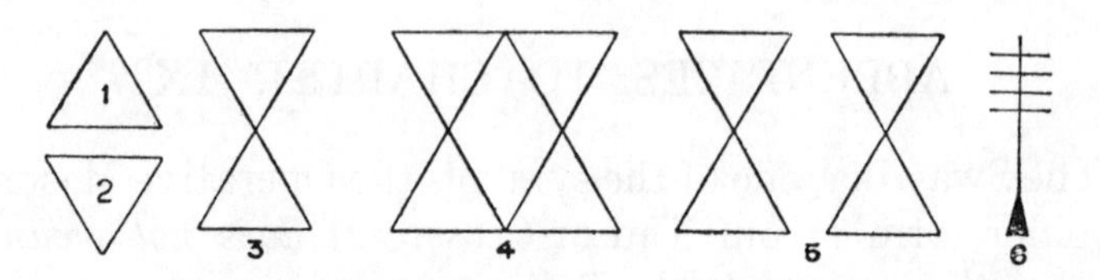

fig. 6, and that for the name of Horus was as No. 2, fig. 6. Fig. 10 was also an Ideographic Symbol for Horus, as Amsu, but was never attached to, or associated with, the God Set or El Shaddai.

The reason why the Operative Masons have gone wrong in this part of their ritual is that they have mixed up the Gods of the four quarters with the One Great God. These only represented attributes ; and they have also mixed up the God of the Pole Star South, El Shaddai, with the God of the Pole Star North, which was Horus, or Ihuh, of Israel, or Iu, or Ea, of the Chaldeans, Assyrians, and Babylonians, which is later than the Sumarian El Shaddai of the Egyptian Set. These four Gods of the four quarters were, first, the brothers, and, secondly, the Children of Horus ; in Egyptian, Amsta, Hapi, Taumutf, and Kabhsnuf ; in Mexican, Acatl, Tecpatl, Calli, and Tochtli ; the four Bacabs of the Mayas ; the Man, Lion, Ox, and Eagle of the R.A.C., and St Matthew, St Mark, St Luke, and St John of the Christians.

That the Swastika is one of the oldest forms of Crosses or Symbols for the four quarters and dates back to Totemic Sociology is proved by it being the Totem of a tribe of North American Indians. I must call *Brother Dr Carr's* attention to, and ask him to read this before he lectures again and makes such statements as he did before the Dorset Masters' Lodge (p. 84 in their Transactions for year 1911-12).

That the Operative Masons have seven so-called degrees now is because they have converted their Initiate, Apprentice, and Master's degree into seven ; but this is of quite a comparatively recent date. The *Ritual* of Ancient Egypt states distinctly what I have here written (*supra*). The Initiates and Apprentices were called " Companions," and a few of the higher class were " Masters." *Brother Dr Carr* states that the reasons for much of the Speculative Ceremonies can be seen in the Operative Rituals, while the Operative Ceremonies get no elucidation from the Speculative Ritual, and he would specially draw attention to the obligation in the First Degree. The reason for this is obvious from what I have stated above. *The Operative Masons or "Companions" were initiated in part of the old Ceremonies and Rituals* only, so that they were bound by Oath to keep the secrets of, and know the reasons for, the peculiar and distinctive construction of the old Temples, and they never violated their obligations; but the Operative Masons have no Esoteric Eschatological rites at all. These were never taught them, *yet these existed before the Operatives*—when the old Temples were formed by a simple double circle of stones, surrounded by bushes. Thus a Brother who understands and knows all the ten Greater Mysteries, knows and understands all the Operative Masons' work, whilst the latter are completely ignorant as to the former.

But the Operative Masons' origin dates back at least 300,000 years, and so I have no doubt they will be contented with their great antiquity. *Brother Dr Carr* will find proofs of all my contents in the *Ritual* of Ancient Egypt, and on the various monuments; these I shall always be pleased to identify and point out to any Brother who may feel interested in this subject. The Operative Masons, like the Speculative, have made many "innovations" since they left Old Mother Egypt, but this is not surprising considering all the vicissitudes they have passed through; the wonder is that so much remains of the original, and that so little innovation has taken place after all these years, remembering the trials and tribulations they have endured.

2. The Jews used the word Iah-Jehovah; Phœnicians, Iao; Hebrew, Iah; Assyrian, Iau; Egyptian-gnostic, Ieou; Polynesian, Iho-Iho; Dyak, Yavuah or Iaouh; Nicoban Islanders, Eewu; Mexican, Ao; Toda, Au; Hungarian, Iao; Manx, Iee; Cornish, Iau; Welsh, Iau; Chaldean, Iao-Heptaktes; Greek, Ia and Ie.

The sign and symbol was ideographically the same, and found this depicted throughout the many countries of the world, and all derived it from the original Egyptian.

3. Here we have one source of the origin of Freemasonry,

both in the Lesser Mysteries (7 Degrees) and in the 10 Greater Mysteries—so-called Higher Degrees in this country.

The Druids, in Gaul, were mostly put to the sword, others fled to this country for protection, when the Roman Christian doctrines were brought to them. In America it was the same. As soon as the Spanish Roman priests arrived there they persecuted all the Solar and Stellar people, murdered their priests, overthrew their temples, and scattered them with fire and sword. Yet there is sufficient evidence left in their Signs, Symbols, and Writings on the Wall which prove my contention that all these had the same Eschatology, signs, symbols, and rites as the Old Egyptians, from whence they came, and that all these are analogous to our own with really very little innovation, considering the many thousands of years that these have been handed down from country to country, and generation to generation, as we must acknowledge to have been the case if we study the history of the human past.

There were also many who crossed over to Europe from Egypt, and spread from Italy into France, who possessed and clung to the true doctrines, endured torture, and some even death, by the early Roman priests, who tried to usurp the temporal power by destroying the spiritual ideas ; and yet these Brothers would rather suffer death than give up their secrets and beliefs. Many of these migrations can be traced through Europe, and finally to Scotland. They were mostly traders, as Printers and Papermakers. *Mr Harold Bayley*, in his "New Light on the Renaissance," has given therein many instances of how the conversion of the Old Egyptian Signs and Symbols took place, and how they brought on a remnant of the old doctrines.

4. The "Star Sothis" was "the Star of the White Spirits"—*i.e.* it was the place where all the white spirits came forth after travelling through the underworld in the earliest Totemic times and Mythology, also during the whole of their Totemic sociological state and during the time of their Stellar Cult, before Amenta was ideographically formed, therefore pre-Solar. In fact amongst all Totemic natives at the present day it is so.

In Stellar Mythos it was the Star of Annunciation ; it heralded the birth of Horus.

It was the morning star of the Egyptian year—365¼ days—and their Great Year—25,827 years.

In Lunar Mythos it was the Star of Hathor, and her infant son Horus, and above all to these oldest observers it was the herald of the Inundation, telling them when the Nile would come down and fertilise the land, so that food would be plentiful as a good result of inundation.

Most important and sacred rites were connected with the rising of this star.

APPENDIX TO CHAPTER XIV

That is two squares end to end, one square as representing Heaven, and one Earth (the Pedestal situated in the centre at the junction in R.A.).

APPENDIX TO CHAPTER XV

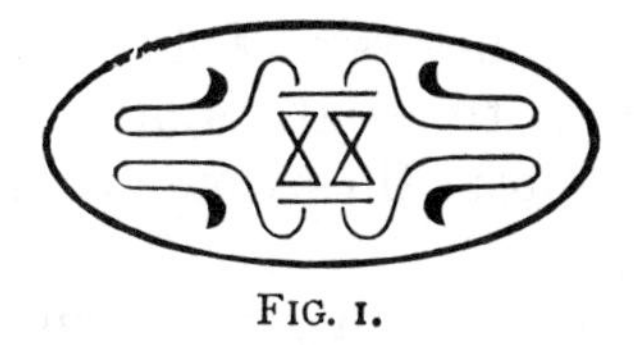

FIG. 1.

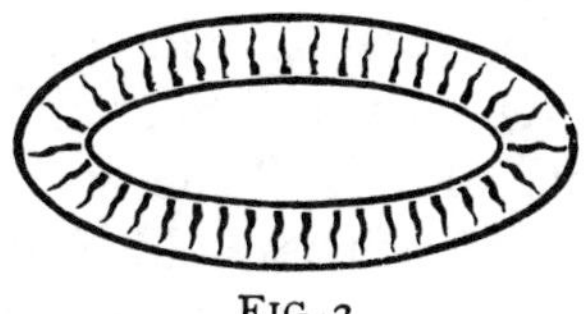

FIG. 2.

I give here the symbol of the *oldest form* for the Khui Land (Fig. 1).

It is the exact representation of one of the oldest Scarabs ever made in Egypt; the original is in my possession. It belonged to one of the old Egyptian High Priests; in fact, it was *the most sacred emblem in Egypt, and was the Jewel which was worn by the Highest or "Most Illustrious Grand Master" in the Stellar Cult. I believe that only one was ever made,* which was passed on from the one Grand Master to the other, *with the sacred word, which is also known to me.* The double triangle here represents Heaven in two divisions, and these are the two triangles of Sut and Horus as the "two brothers"; the lower one △ is the ideograph for the name of Set, and ▽ is the ideograph for the name of Horus. It thus depicts the Heavens divided into two divisions—North and South. But these are repeated, and the reason is that as they divided the Heavens into North and South so they divided Egypt into North and South. The two combined represent the "Khui Land," and this is symbolised and proven by the Urcei guarding the same. On the reverse side (Fig. 2), we have portrayed in symbolical language "an Island surrounded by water," and this again by earth—*i.e.* "an island in a lake." In sign language it represents the "Khui Land" or "Land of the Spirits of Parad[illegible] "the Celestial City" surrounded by the waters of Space. This was typically represented again by the old priests by building their most sacred temple on an island in a lake in the Land of Egypt.

This was their most sacred temple on Earth.

The Scarab here depicted is probably one of the oldest, if not the oldest, in existence, and certainly the most sacred symbol ever produced.

For reasons which my Brothers will understand I cannot give them the "Sacred Word," which, so to speak, is attached to it, and is "the word" for "the Most Illustrious Grand Master" of these old Egyptian High Priests.

I should say it had been handed down from generation to generation—*i.e.* from High Priest to High Priest for many thousand of years—how many I should not care to positively affirm, but being formed at the early part of the Stellar Cult, at least 300,000 years. It has come into my possession direct from Egypt since writing the first edition of this work, and if any "*Grand Master*" wishes to see it I shall be pleased to show this to him.

APPENDICES TO CHAPTER XVI

1. Holy House of Anup or Horus. The name "Anup" is equally applied to Set and Horus, which was ideographically depicted by two jackals in one phase, two eyes in another.

2. These Ari were styled "Companions," because they worked in Companies, and were initiated in the 1st and 2nd degrees, and *these were the originals of the "Operative Masons."* None of them were initiated beyond the 3rd degree, and were quite a distinct class from the "Old Religious Brotherhood," who employed them to build their temples and initiated them so that they should keep the secrets of the same. A body of these left Egypt at the time of the Stellar Cult and travelled throughout the world wherever the Stellar priests went; the first exodus were the Botyia, the next the Turanians.

The buildings of these old Stellar people can always be identified in whatever part of the world found. These were always *iconographic,* which the people who followed did not copy. Both the Stellar and Solar built in polygonal and monolithic forms, but the Solar was never iconographic.

3. None of our passwords are of pure Egyptian language, because these were lost for thousands of years; we use many Hebrew words which mean the same as the Egyptian. I have discovered the old secret words, some of which I have given you. The true word for the Master's chair is Maat-heru—"one whose voice must be obeyed." Thus G. is a substituted one, and means "Stone Squares."

The first worker in metals was not T.C.; the P.W. in Egyptian is Horus-Behutet, but any Brother who is interested will find all in the *Ritual* of Ancient Egypt. *Dr E. A. Wallis Budge,* in "The Gods of the Egyptians," page 485, states: "It is, of course, impossible to say who were the 'blacksmiths' that swept over Egypt from South to North, or where they came from," but believes "that they represent the invaders in predynastic times, who made their way into Egypt from a country in the East, by way of the Red Sea and by some road across the eastern desert—that is, through the Wâdi Hammâmât. They brought with them the knowledge of working in metals and of brick-making, and having conquered the indigenous people in the South—*i.e.* those round about Edfu—they made that city the centre of their civilisation, and then proceeded to conquer and occupy other sites and to establish sanctuaries for their God."

But I have proved that man originated in Africa and not Asia ("Origin and Evolution of Primitive Man"), and these came up from the South—Nilotic Negroes, the Kaverondo tribes. Remnants of these still exist in Africa. These were workers in iron and copper; and amongst these people the blacksmiths are called "Yothetth"; there is also a separate class called "Uvino," and amongst the Gemi tribe the black-smiths were founded with a religious secret society, and still possess all the secrets of Horus of Edfou. Horus was their Great Chief in their Hero Cult, and is the Chief Artificer in Metals—*i.e.* he was recognised as "the Chief Hero" of this Clan or Secret Society, in the time of the Totemic Sociology.

Many of our signs and secrets exist amongst these African people at the present day, and have been handed down from generation to generation by the old Turanians. It was these "blacksmith men" who knew how to smelt iron ore and forge the metals into weapons of offence and defence, that formed themselves into the "big clan of blacksmiths," having Horus as their Astronomical Chief. They came up from the South to the North in predynastic times, and, having conquered the Masaba Negroes and lower types of Nilotic Negroes, who were then the inhabitants of the land of Egypt, established them-selves in Egypt, making Edfu their chief city and centre.

The Egyptians called these "followers of Horus" Mesnitu, or Mesniti, which, I believe, was the original name for all their tribes, and which may now be applied to the Masai Group. As we know, Horus was their deified God, and as Edfu became their centre, he was styled "Lord of the Forge City," "The Great Master Blacksmith." It was here that they first built a sanctuary or temple, which was called Mesnet. One hiero-glyphic which they used proves that these people were those belonging to the Masai ancestors. Priests were appointed to attend to the temple. One might say that this was the first representative of our Masonic temple. Those who erected and looked after the construction of the temple were styled " Companions." Thus we see that our word T.C. is a substituted name. The original and real " Great Master in Metals " was " Horus of Edfu "—or " Horus-Behutet." I have given the above fully, as an example of the falsity of some of the secret names we have substituted for the originals. Many other words which we have adopted have no relation or meaning to the originals.

If we merely consider the tokens of recognition, the passwords, secret words, and the decorations of the Lodges, according to the degrees into which modern Masonry is divided, we find that many of them are taken from the Bible, and are symbolical of events, real or imaginary, some of which are said to have taken place in those comparatively modern times which followed the decline and destruction of the old Egyptian Empire, and marked the commencement of the Christian era ; others as having occurred before the Christian Cult commenced, others at the building of King Solomon's Temple, all of which some think, and have stated have nothing to do with the Religious Mysteries of the Egyptians that were in existence ages before the above pretended occurrences. Where do those who positively affirm that all these have not been derived from the Egyptians suppose they originated ? From whence did the above obtain them ? I candidly affirm, from personal observation and study—and it is open to all students to confirm my observations and translations, or to bring forward further evidence in which they will critically demonstrate that the photographs I have taken of these signs and symbols still existing on the walls of ancient temples and walls of ruined cities, in Africa, Asia, Central, North, and South America, as well as other parts of the world, have nothing whatever to do with those in use amongst ourselves, and yet these are identical in every form and shape, whatever may have been the esoteric meaning given to them by the initiated of these countries—that we are bound to admit that the signs, symbols and the decorations are identical. I further maintain, and here challenge all and everyone throughout the world, that the translation of their *Rituals*, which we have now discovered and can read, are analogous to our own ; at the same time I grant many innovations have naturally been made because it became necessary to replace those that were lost, and to meet a higher state of evolution, which man has now attained.

Masons at the present time are like the poor Aboriginal natives who perform the Totemic ceremonies, not knowing (having lost) the true, original meaning and substituting their own. So Masons perform their rites and ceremonies, being ignorant of the origin and gnosis, and so continue to repeat these, only thinking of the "letter-perfect oratory," the true and beautiful Eschatology being known to a few only.

APPENDICES TO CHAPTER XVII

1. That Sut or Set was the first primary god of the Egyptians, but was god of the *South Pole or Southern Hemisphere,* is amply proved and borne out by the monuments as well as the *Ritual.*

Set or Sut, according to Plutarch, is the Egyptian name of Typhon—*i.e.* Satan of the Christian Cult. On the oldest monuments, although it has been almost invariably chiselled out, we find names of kings who have taken his name, in the same manner as we afterwards find the Horus name, and although the legend of the conflict between Horus and Sut is as old as the *Ritual* at least, it is, however, likewise a proof of Set's position having once been very different. It is he whose sign is changed for that of Osiris in the letters of the father of the Great Ramesis, and two other kings of that dynasty; it is the same god, with his ordinary monumental name, Nubi (in Nubian) who is pouring out life and power over the king. Also we see Horus and Set pouring out life over Seti. *Dr Budge's* "Gods of the Egyptians," page 248, vol. ii., shows the equal divinity of these two gods at one time, as Horus and Set, as two brothers, reigning together. His hieroglyphic figure of a giraffe is the Nubian Primary God, Set or Sut, and, with Anup added, the translation is "The Lord of the Southern Hemisphere," as witnessed in the monuments of Karnak and Medinet Habu. The first figure here to remark is Horus (Amun-Khem), to whom the king is sacrificing and doing homage, and Horus is pouring out life and power upon the king. The fact that we find Sut here as one of the great gods is a proof that he was considered and looked upon at the earliest period of their mythology, as, at least, a brother to Horus, and that now Horus was primary. The myth had shifted or changed places, the domain of Paradise from the South to the North, and the great fight between Horus and Sut had not yet come into being. There can be no doubt that the primary part of the Mythos was first evolved at the lakes at the head of the Nile, where the Southern Pole Star was most predominant; how far they had worked out their Mythology here one is at present quite unable to say, but probably they had made considerable advancement, which was afterwards absorbed and blended with the Horus who became the primary god of the Pole Star North. The different names of Set or Sut taken by kings, which we find on the oldest monuments, some of which have been obliterated, and Horus or Osiris substituted, prove this ; later, on monuments we find that the great contest had been worked out in their Mythology, and his name is then found as the Great Evil King of Darkness. In the Book of the Dead or *Ritual* he is also called Baba—the Beast (chap. xc. 17, 66, 67), and the struggle of Horus and Sut is mentioned in the *Ritual*, viii. 17, 9, 25, " The day of the battle between Horus and Sut."

The apparent internal connection which we find on the monuments and in the *Ritual* can only be understood and explained critically in the manner we have set forth, and the points of resemblance in the oldest types and monuments would indicate a general amalgamation of the attributes and their order which they had first worked out in the Southern Hemisphere, to that of the Northern, in the type of Horus, Lord of the Northern Heavens. The two consorts of Sut were Septet and Khekhsit.

Further proof is found in the Pyramid Text, which also shows and proves the change from Sut to Horus and the appropriating of all Set's or Sut's previous attributes to Horus. (We give here the God Set taken from *Dr W. Budge's* " Gods of the Egyptians," whom we have to thank, and his publisher, Methuen & Co.) Observe that he wears no crown, but that of two feathers, of the South, and is supported not by Hu and Sa, but by a male and female attribute (name of Septet). He has the Ank of life in his right hand and hare-headed sceptre in his left. In the Pyramid Text and in the text of Unas we meet the change as Heru-Sept, who is mentioned in connection with Ra-Tem, Thoth, Horus of Tat and the Star Nekhekh [hieroglyphs]. In *Ritual*, chap. xxxii., the deceased drives away *the Crocodile of the South*, and says, " I am Set," and in *Ritual*, chap. cxxx., there is mentioned " the slaughtering block of the God Sept." There is, therefore, quite sufficient evidence to prove that these old people had first worked out their Paradise in the *Southern Heavens*,

THE GOD SET.

[*Facing page* 478

and given the primary position to Set or Set-Anup, and afterwards transferred this to the Northern Heavens, with Horus as Primary God, who took and appropriated all the attributes hitherto attached to Sut. *De Rouge's* "Geographie Ancienne," page 141, states "that he was called the Bull that trampleth on the Menti" and "was strengthener of Egypt and the protector of the Temples of the Gods"—*i.e.* the Bull of his Mother Apt—her first-born. The Menti were evil elementary powers, the Sebu. I have answered *Dr Budge's* question, "The Hidden of the Khas," in another part of this work.

"The Slaughtering block of the God Sept." This is a very important passage in the *Ritual*, because in the remains of the oldest temples of the Stellar Mythos people this "Slaughtering block" has been found—namely, one amongst the remains of the old temples in Tunis, in Africa, and a fine specimen now in the Museum of the City of Mexico—found in the oldest temple in that country.

It is a question if these existed for "human" sacrifices or not, as the Masai Group still offer sacrifices—but not human—at the same time from monumental evidence still extant there is a proof that some of the captives of war were sometimes offered as sacrifices in the earlier part of the Stellar Cult, and during the early part of Totemism homo was certainly Anthropophagus as regards his Tribal Mother. I do not consider, however, that much reliance can be placed on what the Spanish priests recorded on this point: 1st. They did not understand the Cult. 2nd. They would blacken the characters of the old Stellar Cult priests as much as possible to leave themselves whitewashed for all the horrors they committed in the name of Christianity.

2. That the dead were buried in the faith founded on the Mystery of the Cross over 30,000 years ago is proved by the Pyramid of Medam and other remains still extant; the so-called Tomb of Olham Fodhla, in Ireland, is an instance of this. The gnosis of the Crucifixion, however, was the same in the Stellar Cult 300,000 years before this, as is witnessed by this pictograph taken from the Central American ruins (see Fig. 1). It is over 200,000 years old, and represents the Crucifixion during the period of the Stellar Cult. He is crucified on the two Poles—North and South. The hieroglyphics state that he is the God

of the North and South. He is the Great One of the 7 Glorious Ones (attributes). A Crown of Thorns is depicted on his head. His side is pierced with a spear, from whence blood and water is falling on his Spiritual Name, which, in Egyptian, is Amsu. He is supported by his four brothers, Amsta, Hapi, Taumutf, and Kabhsenuf; representing Matthew, Mark, Luke, and John of the Christians, represented by four squares. Tears are in his eyes: "Ye are the tears made by my eye in your name of men." I give the different names by which he was known in different countries—namely, Horus, of the Stellar Cult of the Egyptians; Huitzilopochtli, of the Aztecs; Zipe, of the Zapotics; Hacaxipectli, of Guatemala; Ptah-Seker-Ausan, of the Egyptians in their Solar Cult; Tien-hwang Ta-Tici, of the Chinese; Merodach, of the Babylonians; In, or Ea, of the Chaldeans, Assyrians, and Druids of these islands; Uiracocha, of the Peruvians, and many other names in various parts of this world; yet all one and the same, as proved by the same signs and symbols always associated with him in whatever part of the world found.

FIG. 1.—Crucified Victim of the God of the Zapotics, Zipe. Ptah, Seker, Ansar, of the Egyptians. Maœ-il-Xochetle, of the Mexicans. Ilacaxipeotli, of Guatemala. Christ, of the Christians.

The signs and symbols herein portrayed read that He is the Great Lord and God of Heaven, situated at the North Pole; He is God of the Pole Stars and God of the North and South, and the Heavens and Paradise, and his age is given as 33 years in the Mexican Codices, 95 f.; it is written in the hieroglyphics of Egypt as 33 years.

Stellar Mythos

Further proof may be found in the fact that the Aztecs used to make an image of the Mexican God, Huitzilopochtli or Vitzilipuztli, in bread or dough, at two festivals in the year, and this was solemnly eaten sacramentally as representing the body and blood of the God, in fact it was identically the same as the Christians of the present day do at their " Holy Communion," the Eucharist—this was not an act of transubstantiation, as the Spanish priests and others would have you to believe, but was symbolical. The doctrine of transubstantiation, or magical conversion of bread into flesh, was left for the Christians to establish, the same as the infallibility of the Pope. *The Brahmans taught that the rice-cakes offered in sacrifice were substitutes for human beings*, and the Christians have added that they were actually converted into the real bodies of men by the manipulation of the priests ; but these latter wise men have deceived themselves. These old priests knew it was only a symbol : that originally, in the first form of Totemic Sociology, " the Mother of the Tribe " was eaten ; she was never allowed to grow old, she represented ever-living matter, and her children fell upon her when she became past child-bearing, and literally ate her alive, the whole tribe seized her, ate every part of her alive, that she might still live and never die. But as time grew on this practice died out, and instead of the Mother of the Tribe they took her Zootype as her representative symbol and solemnly ate her once or twice a year. This is the reason of the Pig in New Guinea, and the Bear of Asia, being decked out in female attire ; these are the signs and symbols of the Great Mother, and these are eaten as a sacrificial meal. There is no transubstantiation or any such belief, these people knew better ; if the symbol was the representation of the God, it could not be the symbol that was worshipped—but the God.

As for the two distinct customs of killing the animal god, it is simply this—the difference between the Tribal Mother Totem, and the Clan Mother Totem, or, in other words, the Zootype of Great Mother mythologically and the Zootype of the Mother of the Clan or Tribe; these might be and in some instances are the same—*i.e.* both are represented by the same Zootype; in other cases it is not so, they are different Zootypes.

The Egyptian initiatory ceremony was conducted with great secrecy and care. The candidates were divested of most of their clothing, and a chain or rope of some kind placed around their neck, to signify their belief in God, their dependence on Him, and their solemn obligations to submit and devote themselves to His will and service. The fact that they were neither naked nor clothed was an emblem that they were untutored men, children of nature, unregenerate, and destitute of any knowledge of the true God, as well as being destitute of the comforts of life. The chain or rope was a symbol that the candidate was being led from darkness to light, from ignorance to a knowledge of the One True and Living God, Creator, and Judge of all things in Heaven and Earth. The candidate was blindfolded, and then led by a Brother (called in Egyptian An-er-f) to the door of the temple or Lodge, which appeared as a blank wall in the form of Fig. 9. Arriving at this door he asked for admittance, and was asked by the "watcher" who he was. His answer, translated from the Egyptian, was "The Kneeler" —*i.e.* Shu. He was then given a password which, in Egyptian, is Ra-gririt. The door was an equilateral triangle, a symbol typical of Heaven. The square on which he trod as he passed through was a symbol typical of Earth; the whole entrance symbolised passing from Earth to Heaven. The candidate was then conducted through long passages, where he had to answer various questions, words of "power and might" being given him. Finally, he was conducted to the centre of the Lodge and asked what he desired mostly; his answer was: that Light might be given him. The candidate had to commence his perambulations with his left foot first, the reason for which is given in the Papyrus of Nesi-Amsu, which gives the destruction of Apap, the greatest serpent of Evil. The left foot was first placed on him, and is symbolical of commencing our journey through life by putting all evil thoughts and actions under and away from us; we should tread down the great evils which beset us through life. The destruction of Apap is given

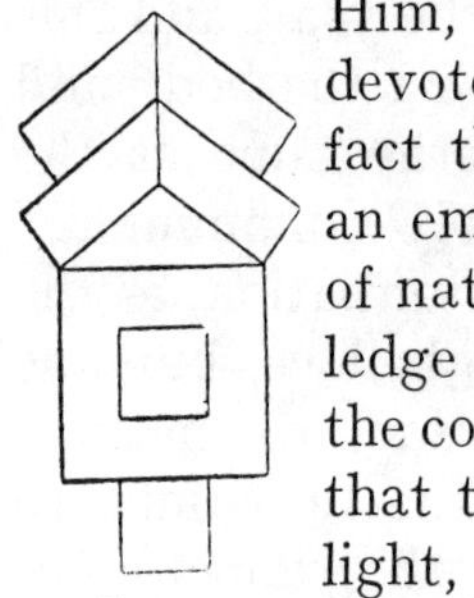

FIG. 9.

in these words: "His body shall be cut in pieces and burnt to ashes, and these ashes scattered over the face of the earth and water by the four winds of Heaven."

If the candidate turned back, or violated his obligations, his Throat was cut and Head chopped off (*Ritual*, chap. xc.) after his Heart had been torn out (*Ritual*, chaps. xxvii. and xxviii.).

Their W.M., or High Priest, was placed in his chair with the same Grip and Token as we use at the present day, as may be seen on one of the bas-reliefs of the Temple of Khnûmû, at Elephantine. Here the W.M.E. is presented to the Master in the chair, who then places him in his chair with the Grip and Token, and gives him the word of the Chair, which in Egyptian is Maat-Heru, meaning One whose voice must be obeyed.

The emblem of Power and Might which is given to the W.M.—the Gavel—took its origin from the original sacred sign still used amongst the Pygmies in Inner Africa (Fig. 10). It is their symbol for The Great One, The Chief. It is just three sticks crossed. The development of this can be traced to our present day; not as a theory, but as a fact, for the evidence and proofs are still extant. In following the evolution and history of the human race, I find that two developments have been evolved out of this original sign; yet the meaning and symbolism is the same in each.

Amongst some of the Nilotic Negroes, who followed the Pygmy all over the world, and are a higher type of man (see "Origin and Evolution of Primitive Man"), they converted the crossed stick (Fig. 10) into a double cross (Fig. 11) by placing the two sticks in a different way, and this was used amongst these people as one of their most sacred signs in their Totemic ceremonies, and has been adopted by those who followed, down to our present Christian Cult; it is also used by Brethren of the higher degrees. The symbolism and meaning are identical all through.

Amongst the Stellar Cult people (those who first reckoned time, and kept their record by observation of the procession of the 7 Pole Stars) it was used in its primary form, and is an Egyptian ideograph for Amsu, which is the first name given to the risen Horus, or as the Christians would say, the risen Christ. In a later phase it was used as a symbol to represent the Great

One, the Great Prince, in the form of a double-headed Hammer or Axe (Fig. 12), when stones took the place of these crossed sticks, when primitive man began to learn more, and acquired the knowledge of hafting (Nilotic Negroes). It became of great import amongst some tribes, and a special hut was built for it.

FIG. 10. FIG. 11. FIG. 12.

The Priest and Great Chief were the only people allowed to see it. This is extant at the present time amongst the Dinkas-Nilotic Negroes.

The old Brothers of Egypt wore leather aprons, as do Freemasons of to-day, only of a different shape. The Egyptian apron was triangular, the strings or sash being fixed at the apex. They also wore collars. One apron, which I have seen, was that of the High Priest. It was yellowish-white in colour, made of leather, with tassels of gold, bearing the name of Amsu with an emerald stone in the centre. The collars worn by the High Priests were of gold, while another suspended collar bore twelve different stones, set in gold, representing the twelve divisions of Heaven, or the Signs of the Zodiac. As there were various degrees—seven in the Lesser Mysteries and ten in the Greater Mysteries—so the aprons and collars varied in colour and ornamentation as they do with modern Masonry.

The G.W. in our 30th degree, as now given, and which we are informed is to be found in Maccabees (but that is not so), is, in Egyptian, " Montu-anhûri," the meaning of both the ancient and modern word being identical.

Let us now see what the formations of these Lodges were, and the reasons for the same; the ceremony of their initiation; and, lastly, their Signs, Symbols, Secret Words; and the explanation and meaning of these. The Brothers throughout the world can then judge if my contention is not right.

In the Old Stellar Cult, when the 7 Lesser Mysteries were taught, the formation of the temple was " a double square " end to end (Fig. 2), and the reason of this was because it represented Heaven as a square, and the Earth as a square, and the orientation was South for 52,000 years; their North for at least 250,000 years. In the centre of the temple there were three cubes, one above the other (Fig. 3), representing the Primary Trinity. In some temples these were ornamented by a double axe (Fig. 4). The temples were sometimes called the House of

GRAND MASTER'S APRON AND COLLAR

Satit presents the Pharaoh Amenothes III. to Khnûmû.

Drawn by Faucher-Gudin, from one of the bas-reliefs of the Temple of Khnûmû at Elephantine. This bas-relief is now destroyed.

THE COMPANION'S (F.C.) APRON

Stele in the form of a door, and the Statue of the tomb of Mirruka.

Drawn by Boudier, from a photograph taken by M. de Morgan.

MASTER'S APRON AND COLLAR

The Pharaoh Menkauhoru.

Drawn by Boudier, from a photograph taken by Faucher-Gudin. The original is in the Louvre, Paris.

the God of the Axe, in their language. The single Axe, in Egyptian, is termed Neter, and may be translated as The Great One—Prince or Ruler is probably the correct translation. (The late *Sir L. Page Renouf* agreed with me in this translation.) Therefore we have these symbols representing The Great One of the North (*i.e.* Horus), The Great One of the South (*i.e.* Set), and The Great One of the Equinox (*i.e.* Shu), the Primary Trinity.

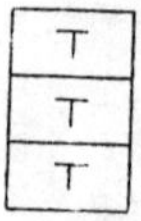

Fig. 3. 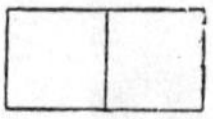 Fig. 2.  Fig. 4.

At the principal entrance of the temples there were always Two Pillars. One was the Pillar of Set and the other was the Pillar of Horus, representing the two divisions of Heaven, North and South, and their portrayal was in the form of Fig. 5. On the top of the columns were four lines, which represented the Heaven as a square and the Earth as a square ; the Egyptians could not draw perspectively, but only on the flat, at this early period. At the present day these are represented by the Celestial and Terrestrial Globes.

Now this was the form of every temple throughout the world, and at the porchway entrance these two Columns always stood ; in whatever country these ruins are found the form is the same ; it is also the correct form of a Masonic Lodge, and, as is well known, these two Columns stood at the porchway entrance of King Solomon's Temple and bore the names of J. and B.

At the entrance of their temples there were always "two watchers," each armed with a knife. The one outside the door was called the Watcher ; the one inside the door was called the Herald.

These two Pillars, in Egypt, were placed at the porchway of all temples in the Solar Cult to represent the entrance of their Amenta ; one was called Tatt, which means in their language, "In strength" ; the other Tattu, which in Egyptian is, "To establish." The word Tattu also denotes the two Tatt Pillars, and means also the Place of Establishing for ever. The Tatt is a figure of stability ; it supports the four corners, and is equal to the Square. Thus two Tatts at the entrance to Tattu is equivalent to a Double Square. Tattu is the entrance or gateway to the region where the mortal Soul is blended with the Immortal Spirit, and thereby established for ever.

According to the Egyptian wisdom all these temples were

simply representatives, so to speak, of their Heaven. Their priests were human representatives of the Divine Master in His various attributes, and bore Divine titles—the same as the Principal O's in our Lodges. Their teachings, forms, and ceremonies represented their beliefs as to the life that must be led on this earth to attain the everlasting life of happiness in the next; and the trials the Spirit would be subjected to until that end was accomplished.

Although the form of our Lodges and the ancient temples is the same, also the two Pillars or Columns at the entrance, we do not have in our M.M. Lodges the Cubes in the centre; but the R.A. does, the reason being that we have divided the "7 Ancient Mysteries" in a different manner.

APPENDIX TO CHAPTER XVIII

In all probability the "let-in stone" which *Mr Dow Covington* discovered, "clearly incised" in the dressed surface was the full tenth part of an 18-inch diameter circle. It was the only known inscribed stone ever found in the Great Pyramid. *Mr Dow Covington* is of opinion that it had been let into a south flank casing stone at a place from which another inscription had been for some reason "chiselled out." This evidently was done either at the commencement of the Lunar or Solar Mythos, and the hitherto symbol which had originally been here at the time of the erection of the building during Stellar Mythos was obliterated, and the circle of the sun or the part of a circle of the moon  took its place. The evidence of *Manetho* is most conclusive in the statement he makes as regards the ages of time that had elapsed since the Egyptian Astronomers had begun to record time —also when the Great Pyramids were built. He states "that the Pyramids were built at the end of the reign of the Gods and the Heroes, who reigned over Egypt more than 16,000 years"— that is to say, that the end of the reign of the Gods and the Heroes was at the end of their Totemic Sociology. Therefore these were built during the Stellar Cult, which was the next evolution in progressive development. This is also borne out by the *Ritual*.

Herodotus states "that Kufu (who was the supposed builder of the Pyramid) lived and reigned in Egypt during the Solar Mythos, *but that Kufu was not the builder*."

Manetho, who was a High Priest and kept the Records of Egypt, states that the Great Pyramid was built at the end of the reign of "the Gods and the Heroes"—that is, at the time their Totemic Sociology had arrived, by evolution, to the Stellar Mythos—"and that it was built by the followers of Horus." Moreover, he states that "the Gods and Heroes were not human, nor ever had been human." The followers of Horus were the Stellar Mythos people, in the same sense as Christians are the followers of Christ.

It was here, in old Egypt, that man began to develop his faculties, and then spread all over the world, taking with him, at various epochs, all the knowledge, at the time of his exodus, with which he left.

The first were the Pygmies, with no Totems and no Totemic ceremonies, but with a belief in a Great Spirit and a knowledge and propitiation of elemental powers.

The second were the Nilotic Negroes, with Totems and Totemic ceremonies only, then a later exodus of these Nilotic Negroes, with Hero Cult and the commencement of the elemental powers becoming divinised. Then the Stellar Mythos people, who had divinised the elemental powers, 7 of which had been given stars on high (Ursa Minor) termed "the 7 Glorious Ones"—"these were the Gods and the Heroes." The Stellar Mythos people, whose cult lasted 258,270 years at least, as witnessed and proved by the *Ritual*—"They covered up my eye after them with bushes (a hairy net) twice for ten periods" (a period being one Great Year of 25,827 years, or the time it takes for one revolution in precession for the revolution of the Stars of Ursa Minor)—had reached a high stage of evolution eschatologically and astronomically, which probably has never been surpassed.

It was these people who built the Great Pyramid in Egypt, the Great Pyramid and temples in Central and South America, and other parts of the world, where we now find the remains of their former greatness.

The Pyramids were built during Stellar Mythos, when the old wise men of Egypt had worked out the Astral Mythology, which was then carried all over the world, as witnessed by the ancient remains, huge and magnificent buildings once which flourished in a high state of civilisation, critically proven by the similarity of the buildings, identical signs and symbols, and fragments of ancient writings, Egyptian hieroglyphics, which can only be deciphered now by the wisdom of old Egypt. The exodus of these, which we may class under the name of early Turanians, occurred some 300,000 years ago, probably much more, because we have still the colossal wrecks of wonderful empires which stand to-day pitiful monuments to the greatness of the builders, and the everlasting shame of the men who accomplished their ruin. The Titanic monuments of a forgotten past found in Central and South America, and some parts of Asia, like the African ruins of Zambesi, the Great Pyramids, lead most men to exclaim, " Who were these old builders ? Whence came they ? By what lost art did they chisel those perfect edges and angles ? By what means did they move these ponderous masses to such perfect adjustment and a marvel of delicate and beautiful workmanship ? Overwhelming in their grandeur are those scattered remains." It is only by the origin and evolution of man that an unanswerable answer can be given. They came from Egypt. In my forthcoming book, " The Origin and Evolution of Man," critical proofs will be given.

The Pyramid is an artificial figure of the mount as a means of the ascent to heaven. The Initiate, placed at the bottom of the well, would see the tubular shaft of the Great Pyramid represented the way to heaven as it was imagined in Egyptian thought. Resting at the foot he could scan not merely the starry vast, but could fix his gaze in death upon the heaven of spirits at the summit of the mount, the Paradise of Peace, the enclosure that was finally configurated in the circle of the seven Pole Stars that crossed the passage pointing northward, one by one, in the circuit of precession, or the heaven of eternity. The Pole Star α Draconis was not the only one that would cross within range of that great tube. The Great Pyramid was founded on the Egyptian astronomy, but was not built to register the fact that α Draconis was the fixed point and polar pivot of all the Stellar motion during some 25,827 years in the vast circle of precession. The ceilings of the chambers were sprinkled with stars to resemble the sky by night (*Maspero*, " Dawn of Civilisation "). Astronomical tables gave the aspect of the heavens, tenat by tenat, throughout the year, so that the Initiates " had but to lift their eyes " and see in what part of the firmament the course lay night after night. Thus he found his future destiny depicted thereon and learned to understand the blessings of the gods. The chief course was mapped out along the river of the Milky Way, as is shown in the *Ritual* by the boat of souls ascending to the Polar Paradise. The Initiate (who has been placed in the position of a mummy) now is risen up, and he is set in motion, prays that he may go up to Sekhet-Aurru and arrive in Sekhet-

Hetep. There are three forms of the boat of souls, one in the Stellar, one in the Lunar, and one in the Solar representation, at three different stages of the Mythos. The Sun, Moon and seven Stars are frequently grouped together on the Assyrian monuments. The Chinese call the Sun, Moon, and seven Stars the nine Lights of Heaven. The same grouping is observed in the nine Pyramids of the Mexicans—one for the Sun, one for the Moon, and seven small ones for the seven Stars. The three Pyramids of Gizeh answer to those of the Sun, Moon, and seven Stars elsewhere. The Great Pyramid is in itself a sign of seven, comprising, as it does, the Square and the Triangle in one figure. Its name, Khuti, means also the Seven Glorious Ones, as well as Light. It was designed by the Har-seshu, or servants of Horus, which were the seven Khuti in the Stellar Mythology, who had been the rulers in the celestial heptanomes before they became the seven servants of the solar God. The seven periods of the Pole Stars were also imaged by seven Eyes, in consequence of an Eye being the figure of a cycle. This type is presented in Joshua, in the book of Zechariah, in the shape of seven Eyes on one stone: "Behold the stone that I have set before Joshua; upon one stone are seven Eyes." These are the seven Eyes of the Lord: also the seven Lamps: as in Revelation.

INDEX

I

J

K

L

M

N

O

T

U

V

W

X

Y

Z